AF541453

WATERS OF HOPE

Facing New Challenges in Himalaya-Ganga Corporation

B.G. Verghese

Fourth Edition, Revised and Updated

India Research Press, New Delhi

India Research Press
Flat-6, Khan Market, New Delhi – 110 003.
Ph.: 24694610; Fax : 24618637
bahrisons@vsnl.com; contact@indiaresearchpress.com
www.indiaresearchpress.com

2007

ISBN thirteen: 978-81-8794-388-4
ISBN ten: 81-8794-388-2

Cataloguing Publication Data

WATERS OF HOPE
Face New Challenges in
Himalaya-Ganga Corporation
Fourth Edition, Revised and Updated

B.G. VERGHESE
Under the auspices of the Centre for Policy Research, New Delhi

Includes references and index.
1. Water / Water Management 2. South Asia
3. Himalaya 4. Ganga 5. Development
6. Cooperation 7. Irrigation

i. Title ii. Author

Printed for India Research Press at Focus Impressions, New Delhi-110 003.

Contents

ERRATA (Waters of Hope – Revised 4th Edition 2007)
Page 141 Read CHITTAGONG in place of CHATTAGONG
Page 159 Read RANGELANDS in place of RAIGELANDS
Page 182 Read SUPER-THERMAL in place of SUPER-THEMAL
Page 193 Read NON-CONVENTIONAL in place of NON-CONENTIONAL

Preface to the 4th Edition

The world's population touched six billion in October 1999, having doubled in 40 years. Since then some 400 million more souls have been added. A large part of this huge increase has been registered in South Asia, with India alone now accounting for a sixth of the human race. World production of farm and industrial production has risen exponentially to meet growing demands. This has exerted growing pressures on humankind's finite resources of fresh water, aggravated by pollution and uncertainties of climate change.

Water and energy loom large among the many security concerns that have come to engage people as much as the chanceries of the world. There are substitutes for energy; none for water. Shrinking numbers in terms of per capita water availability across countries and regions within them have sent alarm bells ringing. Huge vulnerabilities of potable drinking water, hunger, health and insanitation and increasing disparities between North and South, rich and poor, have lent urgency to the United Nations' Millennium Development Goals.

Of the eight Millennium Development Goals, six directly pertain to water: the eradication of extreme poverty and hunger, gender equity, a reduction in child mortality, an improvement in maternal health, combating malaria and other diseases, including HIV/AIDS, and ensuring environmental sustainability. Even the two remaining goals, namely, the universalisation of primary education and developing a global partnership for development, are indirectly water-related. The former has been hindered as the Third World girl child is often committed to fetching and carrying water, fodder and fuel, walking a lifetime for mere survival. The latter is essential to regional cooperation and managing international water systems such as the Eastern Himalayan rivers.

In all of this, South Asia stands out as a region in peril, especially the vast Ganga-Brahmaputra-Barak (GBM) basin that constitutes its top-right quadrant. Despite some progress and achievement, it remains a sink of poverty, misery, out-migration and strife. Water wars have been predicted as a menacing global future. The GBM basin could be a locale for such conflict. It is visited by both flood and drought. For millions of those without the gift of regulated water supplies, impatience and despair have begun to translate into anger. Both India's federal and international relations have soured over water. The reactions to the Government of India's move to develop a long-evolving concept of inter-basin transfers from surplus to deficit regions into a series of specific, implementable projects, after close examination and wide consultations, give ample evidence of the primordial fears and emotions surrounding water. The Inter-Linking of Rivers "Project" (ILR), as it was unwisely and inaccurately christened, aroused a good deal of hysteria at home and abroad, feeding on lack of communication that served to enlarge misperceptions.

Yet, the fact is that, if well managed, the bounty of GBM waters is a huge and prized natural resource that could lift the 500 million people currently living within the basin from penury to prosperity. The potential is enormous. Water cannot be seen in isolation, but must be considered together with the land, forests and grasslands from which the populace derives sustenance. Only such a holistic approach can assure sustainable development and give real meaning to the concept of integrated water resource (and watershed) management.

It is 15 years since *Waters of Hope* was first published, with an update in 1998. Much has happened since then. The sub-title to the first edition was "Himalaya-Ganga Development and Cooperation for a Billion People". For the second edition, this was amended to "From Vision to Reality in Himalaya-Ganga Development Cooperation". There have, alas, been hiccups and delays. A new concluding chapter to this edition, looks in very broad terms at what transpired during those intervening years and what remains to be done, nationally and regionally. It is titled "Hope Remains".

India is an emerging regional and global power that is poised to become the world's fourth largest economy by 2020, leaving behind the worst of dire poverty. But this will only be possible if it can overcome the looming water and energy crises at home and within the larger South Asian neighbourhood of which the GBM basin is a part. Regional cooperation has to be an integral element in that endeavour. There is no other way.

The next 15 to 20 years will therefore be crucial. Can we do it? Hope remains.

B.G. Verghese
New Delhi 2007

Acknowledgements

It would be difficult to list in *extenso* the very large numbers of people to whom I am indebted for this work. Many scientists, experts and scholars guided me through a maze of technical intricacies. If there are any shortcomings or errors in presenting these complex issues to the lay reader, the blame is entirely mine, for they could not have been more lucid or more generous with their time.

Many officials and decision-makers were kind enough to share their wisdom and experience with me. Their confidence and anonymity has been respected but many will find their ideas and thinking reflected in the text.

I travelled widely through the Ganga-Brahmaputra-Barak Basin over the years within India and in Bangladesh, Nepal and Bhutan. The Chinese Embassy in Delhi helped fill a blank on China-Tibet. All doors were open and I received every assistance from the respective governments, embassies, and personnel at all levels. My thanks to them.

Within India, officials of the Central and as many as fifteen concerned State Governments, the Press Information Bureau, various specialised agencies, public undertakings, research establishments, project authorities at headquarters and in the field, several universities, academics, professionals and representatives of voluntary agencies are among the manifold sources on whom I have drawn. To all of them my warm thanks.

Ready assistance was always available in Delhi from the World Bank, the American Centre Library and USAID, the Ford Foundation, the U.N. Information Centre, and other Missions and agencies. The libraries of the International Commission for Irrigation and Drainage and of the Central Board of Irrigation and Power were frequently consulted. Their librarians and officials were unfailingly helpful, as were those of the Tata Energy Research Institute and INTACH.

Similar cooperation was readily forthcoming from the International Centre for Integrated Mountain Development (ICIMOD) in Kathmandu; the International Irrigation Management Institute, Kandy; and the Interim Mekong Committee and ESCAP, in Bangkok.

I must thank the Gandhi Peace Foundation, New Delhi, where I did some initial work on this subject many years ago.

It is however the Centre for Policy research that primarily enabled me to pursue and complete this study. I have greatly benefitted from the assistance and encouragement of my colleagues and especially, the President, Dr. V.A.Pai Panandikar at all times.

The CPR Librarian, Mr. Kamljit Kumar and his associates were most assiduous in assembling documents and references, and providing quick access to books and other material through the inter-library exchange network.

The draft manuscript was read in part or whole, among others by Mr. J.S. Mehta, Dr. T.N. Khoshoo and Dr. B.M. Bhatia who offered some helpful suggestions. Meticulous comments on two technical chapters and other aspects by Dr. Vinod K. Gaur and Mr. Ramaswamy Iyer enabled me to incorporate certain revisions and additions that have improved the text. I am especially grateful to them.

The maps appended to this volume, were prepared by Mr. Harikishan Narula of Cartographic Arts, New Delhi, His cartographic skill will no doubt enhance the understanding of the narrative.

Finally, my thanks to Ms. Kalpana Missar, Mr. Neelam Grover and Mr. A.K. Saxena of the CPR staff who laboured meticulously over word-processing, reading and correcting the manuscript and getting it ready for publishing.

I have again to thank innumerable experts and professionals of every description, water resource officials of the Union and State Governments in India and of Bangladesh and Nepal, various project authorities, representatives of international agencies and others for whatever additional knowledge and wisdom that may have gone into this update.

Not least, I am grateful to my colleagues at or associated with the Centre for Policy Research's eastern Himalayan rivers study group for their most helpful interactions.

Dr. Pai Panandiker, has consistently supported these continuing water studies and has been generous in looking upon the peregrinations of a somewhat footloose Fellow as hard labour in aid of arduous research.

B.G. Verghese

Note on River Names

The rivers of the Ganga-Brahmaputra-Barak Basin bear different names in different segments.

The Bhagirathi and Alaknanda rise in the Garhwal Himalaya and meet at Devprayag to form the Ganga. The Ganga in turn divides into a number of streams below Farakka in West Bengal which marks the apex of its delta. The western-most distributary, turning south, is again known as the Bhagirathi which becomes the Hooghly, on which Calcutta stands, lower down.

The main arm of the Ganga continues flowing southeast, marking the international boundary for some distance below Farakka before entering Bangladesh. On meeting the Jamuna (Brahmaputra) at Goalando Ghat, the combined stream is called the Padma which falls into the Meghna at Chandpur. A number of distributaries take off from the Ganga and Padma in Bangladesh and flow down to the sea through the Sunderbans.

The Brahmaputra rises in Tibet, just east of Kailas-Mansarover and is known as the Tsangpo or Yalu-Tsangpo until it enters India. Thereafter it takes on the name of Dihang or Siang in Arunachal. The Dibang or Sikang and the Lohit meet the Siang near Saidya below which the combined river assumes the name Brahmaputra in Assam. This is turn divides below Bahadurabad in Bangladesh. What is now the main stream continues south as the Jamuna to join the Ganga to form the Padma. The other arm, swinging east through Mymensingh, was once the main course but is now a lesser channel. This is called the Old Brahmaputra and falls into the Meghna at Bhairab Bazar.

Several streams rising in Manipur form the Barak which flows through Cacher in Assam to enter Bangladesh as the Kushiyara which, on meeting the Surma from Meghalaya, becomes the Meghna which receives the Padma at Chandpur.

The main Himalayan tributaries of the Ganga have different names in Nepal. Thus the Mahakali becomes the Sharda in India, and the Karnali the Ghaghara. Likewise, the Gandak in India is known as the Narayani in Nepal, though the different arms of the Sapt Gandaki bear different names within the Kingdom, The Kosi too has seven arms in Nepal. The major ones are the Sun Kosi, the Arun (which rises in Tibet) and the Tamur.

The rivers rising in Bhutan similarly take on different names in India before falling into the Brahmaputra. Thus the Chukha hydro-project is on the Wangchu. This becomes the Raidek. The Amo Chu is known as the Torsa in India.

Conversion Table

Water flows and volumes can be expressed in foot-pound or metric measures. Both are used in South Asia, though India has switched to the metric system.

Both measures have been used in this volume, depending on the original source. But metric equivalents have been given in all cases.

Water flow is expressed in cubic metres per second (cumecs) or cubic feet per second (cusecs), while water is volumetrically measured in cubic kilometres, cubic metres, hectare-metres or acre-feet.

The following are foot-pound equivalents of metric measures:

One hectare is 2.47 acres.

100 hectares make a square kilometre.

One million ha-m equals 6 million cukm.

One cubic metre equals 35.315 cubic feet.

10,000 cubic metres make one hectare-metre.

One hectare-metre equals 8.107 acre-feet.

One cusec-day equals two acre-feet.

One cumec equals 35.32 cusecs.

1.23 billion cum (Bcm) equals one MAF (million acre-feet).

One litre is equivalent to 0.22 gallons.

Abbreviations and Acronyms

ABE	:	Advisory Board on Energy, Government of India.
AFC	:	Agriculture Finance Corporation, India
ARTEP	:	Asian Regional Team for Employment Promotion I.L.O., Bangkok
BADC	:	Bangladesh Agriculture Development Corporation
BIWTA	:	Bangladesh Inland Water Transport Corporation
BWBD	:	Bangladesh Water Development Board
BDWAPDA	:	Bangladesh Water & Power Development Authority
CADA	:	Command Area Development Authority (in India)
CEA	:	Central Electricity Authority, India
CISNAR	:	Commission for Integrated Survey of Natural Resources, China
CGWB	:	Central Ground Water Board, India
CWC	:	Central Water Commission, India
CWPB	:	Central Water Pollution Board, India
DNCE	:	Department of Non-Conventional Energy, India
DDNER	:	Department for Development of the North-East Region
DPR	:	Detailed Project Report
DST	:	Department of Science & Technology, India
DVC	:	Damodar Valley Corporation, Calcutta
EIA	:	Environment Impact Assessment
EMP	:	Environment Management Plan
FAP	:	Flood Action Plan, Bangladesh
FSI	:	Forest Survey of India, Dehra Dun
GBM	:	Ganga-Brahmaputra-Meghna/Barak Basin/Region
GDA	:	Ganges Dependent Area, Bangladesh
GHG	:	Green House Gases
IARI	:	Indian Agriculture Research Institute, New Delhi
ICAR	:	Indian Council of Agricultural Research
ICID	:	International Commission for Irrigation and Drainage
ICIMOD	:	International Centre for Integrated Mountain Development, Kathmandu
ICOLD	:	International Commission on Large Dams
IIMI	:	International Irrigation Management Institute, Kandy, Sri Lanka
ILC	:	International Law Commission, United Nations, New York
IRD	:	Integrated Rural Development, India
ILR	:	Inter-Linking of Rivers
ISRO	:	Indian Space Research Organisation

IWAI	:	Inland Waterways Authority of India
JCE	:	Joint Committee of Experts, Indo-Bangladesh
JMJB	:	Jamuna Multipurpose Bridge across the Brahmaputra in Sirajganj, Bangladesh
JRC	:	Joint Rivers Commission, Indo-Bangladesh
JRY	:	Jawahar Rozgar Yojana, India
MCE	:	Maximum Credible Earthquake
MPFN	:	Master Plan for Forestry, Nepal
MPO	:	Master Plan Organisation, Dhaka
NABARD	:	National Bank for Agriculture & Rural Development, India
NBFGR	:	National Bureau of Fish Genetic Resources, India
NCA	:	National Commission on Agriculture, India, 1976
NEC	:	North Eastern Council, Shillong
NECC	:	National Egg Coordination Committee, Pune
NEEPCO	:	North-Eastern Electricity Power Corporation
NEWRA	:	North Eastern Water Reservation Authority
NHPC	:	National Hydro-electric Power Corporation, New Delhi
NLUCB	:	National Land Use & Conservation Board India
NMEP	:	National Malaria Eradication Programme, India
NNRMS	:	National Natural Resources Monitoring System, India
NREP	:	National Rural Employment Programme, India
NRSA	:	National Remote Sensing Agency, India
NTPC	:	National Thermal Power Corporation, India
NWDA	:	National Water Development Agency, India
NWDB	:	National Wasteland Development Board, India
NWP	:	National Water Plan,Bangladesh
PGA	:	Peak Ground Acceleration
R&R	:	Resettlement and Rehabilitation
RBA	:	Rashtriya Barh Ayog (national Flood Commission) India, 1980
RITES	:	Rail Indian Technical & Economic Service, New Delhi
RLEGP	:	Rural Labour Employment Guarantee Programme, India
RAP	:	Raw Action Plan
SCR	:	South-Central Region, Bangladesh
SEB	:	State Electricity Board(s) in India
THDC	:	Tehri Hydro Development Corporation
UGC	:	Upper Ganga Canal
UTWSRP	:	Uttar Pradesh Water Sector Restructuring Project
WALMI	:	Water & Land Management Institute(s), India
WAPCOS	:	Water & Power Consultancy Services (India) ltd., New Delhi
WARPO	:	Water Resources Planning Organisation, Bangladesh
WEC	:	Water and Energy Commission, Nepal
WGA	:	Water Gas Association

Notes

Notes

Notes

Notes

CHAPTER 1

Changing Nature Sets the Stage

The Earth is but an infant in cosmic time, its age not more than about 4600 million years. Its greatest physical feature, the Himalaya, is also the youngest of mountains that came into existence barely 20-40 million years ago. The Ganga, though now descending from that Adobe of Snow, like the Brahmaputra, is an "antecedent" river that witnessed the mighty orogenic labour that marked the Himalayan creation. This stupendous mountain barrier, the Third Pole as Dyhrenfurth called it, makes and shapes the weather and is a prime actor in the great yearly monsoon drama. The Ganga-Brahmaputra-Barak plain and the High Himalaya constitute an interactive system that has cradled an unbroken civilization from earliest history.

The story began aeons ago with the formation of the Earth out of a swirling mass of gas and dust. Evolving through various phases over time, the outer, brittle crust of a cooling Earth formed the lithosphere, about 70 to 100 km thick, which glides over a warmer, yielding asthenosphere bearing on its back a continental or oceanic crustal passenger. The lithosphere is not a monolithic layer but is broken into a number of spherical caps called plates. It is surmised that at some point of time the continental lithospheres happened to converge to form a continental mass, Pangaea, surrounding the Panthalassa Ocean. In time, this supra-continent divided into Laurasia or Angara (Eurasia and North America) to the north and Godwanaland (named after the Gonds who inhabit middle-India) to the south, separated by the Tethys Sea. Subsequent perturbations caused some of the world's oldest mountain chains to form, the Aravalli between 2500 and 2000 million years and the Vindhya around 1000 million years. The two continents further divided approximately 200 million years ago with Australia, Africa, South America, Antarctica and India variously breaking away from Gondwanaland as crustal rafts riding new tectonic plates.

The Indian Plate began moving north as the widening chasm behind was filled with molten material from below to form a new ocean. Initially it drifted at a goodly speed of 3.5 cm a year and then considerably faster at nearly 20 cm a year between 80 and 53 million years. The pace of drift decelerated thereafter, but the gulf kept narrowing and around 40 million years the continental part of the Indian Plate, having traversed over 5000 km since the commencement of its journey, collided with the Eurasian Plate, forcing the Tibetan front to buckle and its own northern apron to be fractured, sliced and stacked upon itself. Thus the Himalaya was born, dividing the river flows both north into the Tethys Sea and south into the Ganges Sea or The Indian Ocean (Hagen 1960).

The Earth's crust maintains a isostatic equilibrium, losing by subduction or downward withdrawal and transformation into a molten mass or magma what it gains by orogenic upthrusts through a complex compensatory mechanism. If this equilibrium is disturbed by any process, stresses build up within the solid rocks in the form of elastic strain till they just exceed the breaking strength of the material. At this point the accumulated strains are released by a sudden slip. Many earthquake shocks in the Himalayan region are caused in this way.

HIMALAYAN OROGENY

The inter-continental collision occurred not on the "mainland" but along the ocean floor. The line of subduction is believed to have been along the Indus-Tsangpo Suture where the two plates joined. As Gondwanaland kept pressing forward, the Tibetan plateau was heaved out of the sea to the north of the Tibetan Himalaya, damming rivers and streams into remnant tectonic lakes. The new mountain formation created a watershed, inducing aridity to the north and greater precipitation to the south, thus arming the antecedent rivers with growing erosive power as a result of an increasing gradient and a larger runoff. This enabled rivers like the Indus, Karnali, Gandak, Arun (Kosi) and Tsangpo to rupture the High and Middle Himalaya which were still forming in response to successive thrusts, carving out incredibly deep gorges and slicing the Himalaya into a series of discrete massifs. Thus the walls of the Kali Gandaki gorge soar 6500 m above the river bed between the summits of Dhaulagiri (8172 m) and Annapurna I (8078 m) just 35 km apart.

The Himalayan system comprises four belts or ranges that were formed between 40 million and 600,000 years ago. They were created in a series of upheavals or thrusts that deformed the underlying structure in faults, shear zones, nappes and synclines. The seas were lifted to the pinnacles of the Earth which is why sedimentary rocks, characteristic of ocean environments, and marine relicts like ammonites are found way up under the Himalayan ice within bands of limestone originating in seabed deposits of marine shells. Subsequent glaciation added river terraces to the Himalayan architecture. The orogenic process was prolonged and Proto Man was witness to the last convulsions that gave us the landscape we know today.

The Main Boundary Fault, running almost along the entire Himalayan axis from Kashmir to Assam, marks the northern margin of the Siwaliks. This southernmost, lowest and youngest rampart is rich in vertebrate fossils including the gigantic Stegodan Ganesa, named after the elephant god, Ganesa, now preserved in the National Museum, Kolkata (Jhingran, 1981). The Lesser or Middle Himalaya lies to the north of the Main Boundary Fault. This range is well known for its hill stations like Simla, Mussoorie and Darjeeling, relict river lakes such as around Naini Tal, and the Kathmandu and Srinagar valleys. The Kathmandu lake dried up 200,000 years ago.

The northern boundary of the Middle Himalaya is marked by the Main Central Thrust from where commences a crystalline belt that rises to the High or Great Himalaya. The High Himalaya is not the Ganga-Brahmaputra watershed, though many major influents like the Yamuna, Beas and Kameng now rise from it, while medium rivers such as the Ramganga, Rapti, Bagmati and Kamla take off from the rainfed Middle Himalaya or Mahabharat Lekh as it is known in Nepal. The antecedent rivers, namely the Mahakali (Sharda), Karnali (Ghaghara), Gandak, Arun (Kosi), Torsa, Manas, Subansiri and Tsangpo (Brahmaputra), and the Sutlej and Indus to the west, cut through this barrier even as the Himalaya was being formed. They took their origin with early precipitation on the newly formed Tibetan Plateau and rise in the somewhat lower and gentler Tethys or Tibetan Himalaya some 100 to 150 km to the north.

ANTECEDENT RIVERS

The antecedent and "consequent" Ganga basin river, therefore, drain the northern as well as the southern slopes of the Great Himalaya. It is the Tibetan Himalaya that marks the greater water divide. The Brahmaputra (Tsangpo), like the Indus (and the Sutlej), originates in the vicinity of Mount Kailas and Mansarover Lake and drains the northern face of the Tibetan Himalaya and the southern slopes of the Kailas, Aling Kangri and Nyenchenthangla ranges.

Both rivers traverse the Tibetan Plateau along the so-called Indus-Tsangpo Suture, the Tsangpo west-east and the Indus northwest, and then take a hairpin bend to round the two ends of the Great Himalaya. The Indus does this around Nanga Parbat, and the Tsangpo between the lofty Manche Barwa and Gyala Peri peaks. This phenomena is not unrelated to the creation of so-called syntaxial bends in the Himalayan axis at just these points, with the mountain swiveling south along with the river. The eminent geologist D.N. Wadia established that the Salt Range and Suleiman Range, running down the North-West Frontier into Baluchistan, exhibit identical rock formations, strata by strata, and indubitably form a north-south extension of the Himalaya. A similar hypothesis postulating a syntaxical bend to the south at the eastern end of the Great Himalaya, where the Tsangpo cascades from Tibet into Arunachal Pradesh in India, is not quite so strongly held, though there is a view that the north-south Mishmi-Patkai-Naga-Manipur Hills, drained by the Barak, and the parallel Burmese ranges represent a Himalayan continuation (Jhingran and Wadia Institute).

The rocks are gradually yielding their secrets and the orogenesis of the Himalaya is better known today than before. Contentious issues remain and not all the riddles have been solved. Tibet, particularly, is dotted with a large number of glacial lakes. These are end-products of a metamorphosis from the fluvial to a lacustrine condition of earlier rivers whose southward drainage into the Tethys Sea was dammed or blocked by recurrent Himalayan upthrusts. The existence of these water-bodies and their management and potential, whether as hazards or assets, cannot be ignored.

The more vigorous antecedent rivers, finding their passage to the south impeded, altered course east or west until able to break south again. These long transverse valleys are characteristic of the Karnali, Gandak and Kosi in Nepal (Zollinger, 1979). The resultant hairpin bends, where the rivers drop hundreds of metres, today offer splendid sites for run-of-river hydroelectric generation.

The eroding of watersheds has also led to river capture. The theory of river piracy is, however, sometimes offered as an alternative to that of antecedent drainage and suggests that headward erosion of south-flowing rivers on account of steep gradients resulted in their capturing or pirating north-flowing river basins. Landslips and glaciation may also have had the effect of forcing rivers to work their way backwards (Ganga Flood Control Commission, 1986). The Arun (Kosi), flowing between Everest and Kanchenjunga, has sculpted a stupendous 6000-m trans-Himalayan gorge. Its headwaters in Tibet – known as the Phung Chu – are just a few kilometres from the west-east course of the Tsangpo on the other side of the Tibetan Himalaya. "The Arun, with its erosive strength and steep gradient must sooner or later claw its way through the narrow watershed and thus 'capture' the Brahmaputra, reducing one of the greatest rivers of the world to a miserable trickle" (Nicolson, 1975).

AQUIFERS IN THE ALLUVIUM

If orogenic movements uplifted the Tibetan plateau, they also created a trough or foredeep to the south where the rivers deposited their sediment to build the extensive and extraordinarily thick alluvial Gangetic plain. The Aravalli Hills mark the northwestern boundary of that plain and the Vindhya-Kaimur chain its southern limit. The Shillong Plateau confines the Brahmaputra to the narrow Assam Valley until the river pivots south around the Garo Hills, as the Ganga does around the Rajmahal Hills, to enter Bangladesh and the Bengal plain where delta formation begins.

Along the Himalayan-Siwalik foothills is a narrow gravel and boulder-strewn belt or Bhabar tract which trapped the heavier detritus and Himalayan debris brought down by the rivers before filtering the finer alluvium into the downwarp or foredeep below. A massive springline runs along the entire terai and constitutes a major groundwater recharge zone. This is a tract of rich aquifers, many of them under artesian pressure, and forms part of the regionally unconfined groundwater aquifer underlying the Ganga plain and Bengal Basin. This rich multilayered water-bearing strata going down to depths of 300 m has been exploited for shallow and deep tubewells programmes since 1934 in Uttar Pradesh and later elsewhere in India as well as in Nepal and Bangladesh. The shallow tubewells draw water from no more than 30 to 50 m while the deep tubewells so-called tap lower water-bearing horizons 100 to 200 m below the ground level. The water-bearing strata are interleaved with saline aquifers and the groundwater table tends to be brackish, particularly along the Aravallis in the semi-arid regions of northwest India as in western Haryana and Rajasthan, and in the coastal approaches of the Bengal Basin in Bangladesh and West Bengal on account of tidal ingress. Heavy groundwater pumping in or near coastal areas can also invite saline intrusion.

Groundwater exploration has not gone really deep. Petroleum geologists, however, have done so, boring down to 5,000-10,000 m in search of oil and gas. Being uninterested in water and basically trained to interpret data in relation to oil or gas, they did not know that many of their "dry holes" had perhaps struck rich with water. The rapid depletion of traditional groundwater sources in many parts of the world has in recent decades led geohydrologists to peer deeper into the earth by examining the oil explorers' electro-logs and core samples. This heralded the discovery of new water sources deep within the bowels of the earth.

Studies by or on behalf of the World Bank in South Asia over the past decade suggest the existence of a series of truly deep aquifers underlying the Nepal terai and the Ganga plain and, separately, the Bengal Basin both in West Bengal and Bangladesh at depths of 1000 to 3000 m. These underground pools may constitute the largest single groundwater resource anywhere in the world. An examination of electro-logging data made available by Petro Bangla in 1985 and electric logs, completion reports, seismic data, structure maps and geological reports with the K.D. Malviya Institute for Petroleum Exploration and the Oil and Natural Gas Commission of India, at Dehradun, in 1987 have confirmed the hypothesis (P.H. Jones Hydrogeology, Inc., 1987).

The springline along the Himalayan piedmont (terai) is marked by the Bhabar zone, earlier described as a boulder gravel filter which extends downwards through "alluvial cones in obate tongues" to depths of 1000 to 1500 m (World Bank, 1985). Just as the Ganga and its northern tributaries along with a myriad other streams recharge the Bhabar springline as they traverse the terai, so they did, turning back the pages of the geological calendar, as the Ganga foredeep gradually filled with alluvium to create the present Gangetic plain. This however, was not a continuous process but followed four inter-glacial periods over hundreds of thousands of years. During each glacial epoch, the weight of ice compacted and consolidated the sediment below it to form an aquitard or impervious layer, trapping the water-bearing horizon below it. During the next inter-glacial melt period of rivers would flow once more, charging a new depositional strata until that too was confined by yet another aquitard as a result of a subsequent glacial epoch.

Thus four to six regionally confined, deep freshwater aquifers, each hydraulically separate from the other, are found to underlie the Ganga plain at depths of 1000 to 2500 m. They are also hydraulically distinct from the unconfined water table above them which is currently being exploited. The upper unconfined groundwater aquifer gains from or loses to stream flows in the rivers with which it forms a single interconnected hydrological system. The deep aquifer system is an independent and additional resource consisting of a series of vertically differentiated horizons that are likely to be free-flowing in view of the 50 to 100 m artesian head available between the Bhabar zone where they would even now be recharged, and the plains below. This is not fossil water, it is claimed. Proposals for exploratory drilling to prove the precise extent and characteristics of the deep aquifer system are discussed in a later chapter.

The Ganga-Brahmaputra foredeep in Assam was confined in its southward extension by the Shillong Plateau. The "ancestral Brahmaputra", Paul Jones elaborates, originally flowed directly south along the eastern flank of this plateau into the Bengal foredeep through the Surma-Sylhet trough. As the foredeep began to fill, subsidence of this sediment was accompanied by an uplifting and folding of the northeastern margin causing the Brahmaputra to change course. The river started flowing west, along the northern edge of the Shillong Plateau until able to find passage south again around the Garo Hills and into the Bengal Basin. The Barak now occupies that vacated drainage outlet and flows through Sylhet.

According to Paul Jones, the regionally confined artesian aquifers in the Bengal Basin in Bangladesh are recharged in the Tripura and Chittagong Hills and in the Upper Surma Valley draining the eastern flank of the Shillong Plateau into the Barak (Meghna). In West Bengal on the other hand, deep aquifers are believed to exist at depths of about 1000 m south of the Rajmahal outcrop, around which the Ganga bends south, and east of the Santhal Pargana plateau. This region is traversed by the Bhagirathi-Hooghly and Damodar and the deep aquifer is recharged at upland outcrops.

MASS WASTING

The Ganga-Brahmaputra-Meghna system carries a phenomenal load of 2.9 billion metric tonnes of sediment into the Bay of Bengal every year. It has done this over a vast period of geologic time, eroding the Himalaya to build the Ganga-Brahmaputra plain. The Indian Plate continues to creep forward at a rate of 5 cm a year which means that the Himalaya remains a geologically active locus subject to tectonic strains and slips manifested in frequent earthquakes, tremors and landslides. The implications of this for water resource engineering and other development are discussed later. But, given the fact that the mountain is young and still growing and its steep gradients experience heavy precipitation and extreme variations in temperature, there is inevitably a great deal of mass wasting and natural erosion. "In the high-relief areas of the Himalaya, weathering is mostly due to block disintegration by alternate freezing and thawing and the production of scree due to frost action. The transportation and erosion is by the glaciers and glacier rock floor, respectively. A considerable movement of scree also takes place simply through the force of gravity. (In the Outer Himalaya and Siwaliks) subaerial denudation is the major natural process contributing to the instability of the hill slopes, the silting of the river valleys and flooding because of the obstruction of the river courses…(These ranges) mainly comprise soft tertiary sediments, sandstones, siltstones, shales and clays, and are readily subject to mechanical disintegration. These ranges also face the full force of the monsoon currents and have torrential rains. Hence mass-wasting is very common in these areas and all along we see huge landslides or scars of old landslides…" (Raina, B.N. et al., 1978).

According to another source, the high solar radiation at great Himalayan altitudes occasions large fluctuations in temperature leading to a severe freeze – thaw cycle resulting in considerable erosion of soil and rock formations. "It is estimated that the rate of present erosion is 100 cm/1000 years compared to 21 cm/ 1000 years in the past 40 million years, demonstrating the seriousness of the problem for the region" (Bahadur Jagdish, 1985).

In this fragile situation, human intervention has often been an aggravating factor. This aspect too must be held over for subsequent discussion. Suffice it to say that the process of Himalayan orogeny remains incomplete and that elemental forces of nature are still at work.

DEEP SEA FANS AND LAND FORMATION

The ocean too has been influenced by the interplay of the Himalaya and Ganga-Brahmaputra as well as by plate movements and geological episodes of the kind that caused the formation and filling of the structural downwarp or foredeep. The mouth of the Ganga-Brahmaputra-Meghna, known as the Sunderbans, is by far the largest in the world. The enormous load of sediment brought down by these rivers has engendered a continuing process of land-formation. New islands, such as the disputed New Moore (South Talpatty), are surfacing even as others are being washed away in an interaction of fluvial and tidal currents.

Unlike the Pacific and Atlantic Ocean, the Indian Ocean, and more especially the Bay of Bengal, is closed to the north. Thus the upper latitudes of the bay have a markedly low saline content on account of the tremendous combined discharge of the Ganga-Brahmaputra-Meghna which has a bearing on the nature of marine life found in this part of the sea.

Exploration and mapping of the ocean floor has revealed the existence of super-Himalayan mountains and deep canyons. The broad continental shelf fronting the Sunderbans is incised by the Swatch-of-no-ground or Ganges Canyon. Beyond this is a series of fanlike formations radiating out some 30,000 km into the mid-Indian Ocean and attaining a width of almost 1000 km across at its lowest extremity a little above the Equator.

The Department of Science and Technology of the Government of India in 1984 launched a study of the Deep Sea Fans of the Bay of Bengal. Speaking at the inaugural consultation, S.N. Talukdar, then Member (Exploration), Oil and Natural Gas Commission, said that the Bay of Bengal provided the key to understanding the fragmentation of Gondwanaland. The Indian Plate had undergone the maximum translation. The sedimentary basin the ONGC has set out to explore for oil, he said, extended over 1.5 million square kilometres due to the phenomenal amounts of detritus brought down by the Ganga and the Brahmaputra river system (Science Technology and Department, 1984).

At the same consultation it was stated that the northward movement of the Indian land mass is resulting in the creation of new lands under the sea. In the mid-seventies, satellite imageries were said to show signs of a still underwater land formation extending over an estimated 50,000 to 70,000 square kilometres out in the Bay of Bengal. Was this but a romantic interpretation of a huge patch of highly turbid deltaic wash carried out to sea? The Deep Sea Fans project should in due course have a more definite explanation to offer.

According to a report on the Deep Sea Fans in the Bay of Bengal, "the fan is the uppermost four kilometres of the geosynclinical pile of sediments ... underlying (which are) the continental rise sediments up to 12 km thick which extend in (to) the Bengal and Assam Valleys..." This makes it one of the thickest sediment sections anywhere. The continental shelf, which is the offshore marine floor up to the 200 m fathom line, is widest opposite the mouths of the Ganga, extending to some 210 km. This is however sharply indented by a 150 km canyon, the Swatch-of-no-ground, believed to have been formed by turbidity currents.

RIVER MIGRATION

Tectonic movements, Himalayan erogeny, and successive phases of uplift and subsidence, as the Indian Plate advanced northwards and the foredeep began to fill, caused dramatic river migration. The story of the antecedent rivers and their transverse movement in a bid to force a passage south as the mountains rose before them has already been narrated.

One theory holds that much of the Himalayan drainage initially flowed west as the Indo-Brahm. The rise of the Potwar Plateau, where the Pakistani capital, Islamabad, now stands severed the Indo-Brahm into two. The upper system, with the Sutlej at its eastern end, joined the Indus while the lower system, the Ganga was compelled to reverse direction and flow towards the Bay of Bengal. Subsequent tectonic movements deflected the Yamuna, until then an independent river draining into the Rann of Kutch, leading it eastwards ultimately to join the Ganga at Allahabad (Uppal H.L., 1978).

Further east, we have seen how the Brahmaputra found its southward passage blocked along the Surma-Sylhet gap and had to move east along the Assam Valley until it could round the Garo Hills at the edge of the Shillong Plateau. It then swung east again in a bid to regain its earlier course south of the new Surma-Sylhet saddle and indeed flowed through Mymensingh until 1787 when it started moving west. The Teesta in turn formed the easternmost branch of the Ganga. With the rise of the Barind tract in northwestern Bangladesh, the river moved into the Jamuna, a spill of the Old Brahmaputra which thereafter started favouring this channel. The Jamuna is today the mainstream of the Brahmaputra and the Old Brahmaputra constitutes the spill channel (Hussain, Licquat, 1974).

River migration continues unabated. Perhaps because of a slight up-warping south of the Ganga, the Himalayan drainages of that river show a tendency to migrate northwards. With the filling of the foredeep and subtle changes in the hydraulic gradient, the confluences of these rivers are constantly moving upwards. This is true of the Ghaghara and other rivers. In the Gupta period, Patliputra was located at the confluences are today wide apart and have migrated upstream by about 20-30 km (Tangri, A.K. and R.P. Sharma). In more dramatic fashion, the Kosi progressively shifted 112 km westward over 130 years and was only anchored by the Hanumannagar Barrage and jacketed within embankments three decades ago.

During the past couple of centuries, the mainstream of the Ganga has departed from the Bhagirathi-Hooghly, below Farakka, the apex of its delta, to favour the most easterly branch which flows into Bangladesh and becomes the Padma on joining the Jamuna (Brahmaputra). Over time this resulted in a deterioration of the Bhagirathi-Hooghly to the detriment of Calcutta Port, a factor aggravated by the waywardness of the Damodar, which used to fall into the Hooghly at Nayasarai, 63 km north of Calcutta, and now joins it some 120 km south of the port, near Falta (Sharma, C.K., 1983).

A GREAT DIVIDE

The Himalaya is a climatological and meteorological barrier separating the cold, semi-arid Gobi-Siberian desert to the north from the monsoon lands to the south. It deflects the moisture-bearing southwest winds laterally, causing heavy precipitation along the mountain wall, the intensity decreasing from east to west and increasing up to the Middle Himalaya beyond which there is some slackening, resulting in elements of desertification in rain-shadow inner valleys in the northern most parts of the Central and Western Himalaya. The Western Himalaya receives relatively more precipitation, often in the form of snow, from currents known as western disturbances originating in the Mediterranean-Caspian region and moving east across Iran, Afghanistan and the southern part of the USSR between November and April. About 30 western disturbances may occur in an average season (Ramamoorthi, A.S. 1986). The very height and length of the mountain wall imparts great complexity to the climate and the High Himalaya also creates its own weather

(Mani, Anna, 1981). Altogether, the Western Himalaya has a longer and colder winter and the snowline is lower than in the eastern part which, however, experiences greater rainfall and is characterized by far more luxuriant and varied forest types.

The Himalaya is not merely a climatological barrier with an influence on the global climate and atmospheric circulation in the northern hemisphere, but a zoographical, cultural and hydrological boundary. There is an obvious floral and fauna divide, though migrant species such as Siberian Crane fly great distances in winter to the warmer southern latitudes. Of the 2100 bird species found in the sub-continent, some 300 are winter visitors from the north (Ali, Salim, 1981). The Eastern Himalaya, from Arunachal and Bhutan up to Sikkim or even the Kosi region in Nepal, is phytographically the meeting ground of Indo-Malaysian (Southeast Asian) and Sino-Japanese (East Asian) flora and the gateway to plant migration into India, Bangladesh and Nepal (Sahni, K.C., 1981). The Eastern Himalaya is perhaps the richest botanical repository in the world. Plant collectors like Joseph Hooker through to F. Kingdon-Ward and more recent Japanese and Indian expeditions have as yet not completely explored this priceless genetic storehouse.

Being more humid, the Eastern Himalaya has a higher treeline going up to 4570 m as against around 3500 m in the West. There are an estimated 3165 endemic plant species in the Himalaya of which the largest number is to be found in the eastern zone. These include 1200 species of orchids, and a large variety of rhododendron, fern and bamboo. Some of this rare diversity, including surviving tropical rain forests, is being sought to be preserved in biosphere reserves, wild life sanctuaries and national parks. Many faunal species have been gravely endangered not only on account of poaching and trapping but more because of increasing biotope pressure from domesticated species (Rau, M.A. 1981).

Hydrologically, the major discharges of the Ganga-Brahmaputra system come from southern Himalayan runoff. "Antecedent" rivers such as the Mahakali, Karnali, Gandak, Arun, Torsa, Manas and Subansiri, do drain quite considerable catchments between the High Himalaya and the Tibetan Himalaya. But the volume of flow is nothing comparable to the huge runoff from the southern side. The same is true of the Tsangpo, the bulk of whose basin lies in Tibet which enters India as the Dihang which in turn becomes the Siang and, finally, the Brahmaputra.

SNOW AND GLACIER MELT

Snow and glacier melt constitutes the most important part of Tibetan runoff and makes much more significant contribution to the southern Himalayan flows in the Central and Western Himalaya during summer. Precipitation in the snow accumulation period as part of total yearly precipitation progressively decreases from the western to the eastern Himalaya. Thus it is 22 per cent in Kashmir, 11 per cent in Himachal, 6 per cent in Garhwal, 4 per cent in Nepal, and 2 per cent in Assam (Dhanju, M.S., 1983).

The glacial lakes that dot Tibet feed numerous streams. Glacial deposits that block their outflow often build up temporary dams which give way sooner or later. Such glacier lake outbursts can cause sudden, torrential floods and constitutes a hazard that is now being sought to be mapped and studied as an aid to developing forecasting and warning systems wherever possible in remote and inaccessible regions. A Sino-Nepalese joint expedition has recently enumerated 229 glacier lakes at the sources of the Pumgo and Poiqu rivers in Tibet and the Arun and Bhote Kosi in Nepal. Twenty four of these lakes were classified as outburst-hazards. The data has been passed on to the Nepalese authorities, according to the Chinese Xinhua news agency, with recommendations for pipe-drainage schemes and controlled explosions to lower their water levels to safe limits.

The Himalaya constitutes the largest reservoir of snow and ice in the world outside the polar regions. Despite its low latitude, its stupendous height makes this mountain chain an area of high glaciation (Bahadur, Jagdish, 1985). Some 15,000 glaciers drain into the Himalayan-Karakoram river system. The average intensity of mountain glaciation varies from 3.4 per cent of its total mountain drainage in respect of the Indus to 3.2 per cent for the Ganga and 1.3 per cent for the Brahmaputra (Ibid). It has been estimated that some 17 per cent or 33,200 sq km of the Himalaya and about 37 per cent or 17,000 sq km in the Karakoram is under glacier ice. The volume of Himalayan ice cover is believed to be of the order of 1400 cubic kilometres (Vohra, C.P., 1981).

The Karakoram boasts the greatest glaciers, the largest being the disputed Siachen from which the Nubra river emerges. It is 75 km long and contains 12.32 million hectare-m of water which is just a little less than the total irrigation diversion in the Indus plain in Pakistan (Information and Broadcasting Ministry, Islamabad). The Himalayan glaciers are smaller, among the larger ones being the Gangotri glacier from whose mouth, Gaumukh, springs the Bhagirathi, one of the two arms of the Ganga. This has a 200 sq km spread and contains 20 cubic kilometres of ice or two-and-a-half times the Bhakra Dam storage.

Satellite imagery is now being used to map and measure Himalayan glaciers and snow cover. The Indian Bhaskara and INSAT satellites have been so employed. American NOAA imagery has been used to map and forecast seasonal snowmelt runoff in the Sutlej since 1980, to make regular predictions based on snow-cover area mapping and to develop snowmelt runoff simulation models (Ramamoorthi A.S. 1983 and 1986).

Most glaciers are in retreat, having attained their maximum size in recent times during the mid-19th century. Some glaciers in the Alps have started advancing again. The rate of retreat of the Gangotri glacier which ablated over 600 m between 1935 and 1936, has declined since 1971. The same is true of the smaller Gara glacier in Himachal which in fact became stationery in 1977 (Vohra).

Glaciers, like snow cover, constitute a vast water storage system, accumulating over the winter and undergoing depletion through the summer. The effect of their changing mass balance in annual and seasonal runoff obviously plays the most important role in water resource management. This is a still relatively little known area and, with avalanches, merits greater study. The Snow and Avalanche Study Establishment in Manali, Himachal Pradesh, is engaged in high altitude studies in the Himalaya. The India National Remote Sensing Agency has now joined these endeavours.

DESERT, PLATEAU AND DELTA

The soils of the Ganga-Brahmaputra-Barak region are varied and characterized by an unparalled stretch of rich alluvium. Rainfall ranges from 11,142 mm at Cherrapunji near Shillong, said to be the wettest place in the world, to the cold, arid wastes of Tibet and the semi-arid region bordering the Thar desert to the west of the Aravalli range (600 mm).

The Aravallis too mark a climatic divide, the lands to the east of it being fertile and well drained. The Aravalli Hills are discontinuous and gaps exist. According to one view, in the absence of adequate afforestation "these gaps are acting as windows through which the desert is drifting towards the fertile areas of Jaipur, Ajmer and Sikar districts within the Ganga basin" (Anon. 1987). The onset of aridity in the western desert area is believed to have followed the rise of the Himalaya, the lowering by erosion of the Arvallis, changes in the river system with the diversion and desiccation of the Yamuna, Saraswati and Ghaggar and the consequent lowering (and salinisation) of the water table between 4000 and 1000 B.C. Biotic interference with natural resources further accentuated arid conditions at a later stage (Mann, H.S. 1977).

The First Five Year Plan document (1952) opined that "Recent topographical surveys show that the great Indian desert of Rajasthan has been spreading outwards in a great convex are through Ferozepur, Patiala and Agra, towards Aligarh and Kasganj at a rate of about half a mile a year for the last 50 years and is encroaching upon approximately 50 square miles of fertile land every year." This claim was, however, not sustained by the Proceedings of the Symposium on the Rajputana Desert, sponsored by the National Institute of Sciences of India in 1952. Nor did the meteorological record of the previous 70 years show any significant changes in rainfall, temperature and humidity to support the theory of desert creep (Singh, Gurdip, 1977). Chambal and Yamuna irrigation has since greened some part of this northwestern arid tract while sand dune stabilization programmes in Hissar, Bhiwani and Mahendragarh districts in southwestern Haryana have begun to anchor the desert.

The Chambal, the western-most arm of the Yamuna, flows through a trough that separates the Aravallis from the Vindhya region consisting of the Vindhya

Hills and escarpment, the Malwa Plateau, and the Kaimur Range. This region is drained by the Chambal, Betwa, Sind, Parbati and Ken, all of which fall into the Chambal-Yamuna basin in this region is heavily gullied and ravine formation has resulted in massive erosion and a historical problem of dacoity. These plateaus and ridges also divide the Gangetic plain from peninsular India and its drainage system. Further east, the Chota Nagpur plateau and Rajmahal Hills mark the southern boundary of the Ganga plain which then opens out into the Bengal Basin. The Ganga is here fed by a number of smaller rivers such as the Damodar, Rupnarayan and Haldi which drain into the Hooghly estuary.

The Sunderbans, the larger part of which falls in Bangladesh, is an extraordinary network of interconnected waterways. It is the world's largest deltaic formation and hosts the greatest mangrove forest anywhere. The lower part of Bangladesh is the flat deltaic flood plain of the combined Ganga-Brahmaputra-Meghna system, which perhaps ranks only second to the Amazon in its immense discharge and exceeds the Huang Ho in China in terms of sediment load. The country exhibits the gentlest gradient and about a third of it in the lower region is below the high tide level. This poses problems of saline intrusion. An elaborate network of polders and sea-walls extending over 3000 km has been constructed for the better hydraulic management of this environment. Almost 94 per cent of Bangladesh's water resources flow into it from India, the exception being the few southeastern rivers rising in the Chittagong Hill Tract such as the Sangu.

FROM RAMAPITHECUS TO RECENT TIMES

Much has happened since proto-Man, Ramapithecus, made a home in the Siwaliks some eight million years ago. Step by step, nature set the stage for homo sapiens. It was not until 7000 years ago that Neolothic man took to agriculture and began to domesticate animals. The Harappan Civilisation of the Indus Valley dates back to 2500-2000 BC and spread to Kalibangan, on the lost Saraswati in Rajasthan, and Ropar on the Sutlej. The Puranas, Rig Veda and subsequently Upanishads were composed. The ethereal majesty of the Himalaya and the bounty of the Gana vested them with attributes of divinity. The very names of the Himalayan peaks identified them with the abode of the gods. What more beautiful allegory than the descent of the celestial Ganga through the labours of Bhagirath, or a theme for the musc than Krishna sporting with the *gopis* on the banks of the Yamuna around Mathura. Kalidasa spoke for poets and philosophers alike in describing the Himalaya as Earth's measuring rod which, "being great and free from change, sinks to the eastern and western sea."

The dawn of the first millennium BC witnessed the enactment of the Mahabharata, set in the rival Pandava and Kaurava capitals at Indraprastha (the site of modern Delhi) and Hastinapur (near Meerut), with the final reckoning on the battlefield of Kurukshetra. The epic, Ramayana, followed some centuries thereafter, with episodes set in Ayodhya and the Ganga-Ghaghara doab. Siddhartha Gautama, a Sakya prince, was born at Lumbini near Kapilavastu in Nepal, in the middle of the sixth century BC. He attained enlightenment at Bodh Gaya and preached his first sermon at Sarnath near Banaras (now Varanasi) which was already a city of great antiquity. The Asokan lion capitol, independent India's national emblem, discovered there tells of the wildlife that must have abounded in the surrounding forests.

Alexander led his Macedonian army through Persia and Afghanistan but turned home after his victory over Porus in Punjab. His Viceroy in Bactria, Seleucus Nicator sent Megasthenes as Greek ambassador to the Court of Chandragupta Maurya at Patliputra, modern Patna, the legendary capital of the mighty Magadh empire. Kautilya, also known as Chanakya, a powerful figure behind the throne, wrote his celebrated treatise on statecraft, the Arthashastra. His descriptions of various cropping patterns and modes of irrigation speak of an advanced system of farming. Tamluk, on the Rupnarayan river just before it falls into the Hooghly estuary, was a thriving port that handled a considerable international commence. Known as Tamralipti or Damalipta, it was mentioned by the Alexandrian scribe, Ptolemy, as trading with China and Java. The prosperity of the land had not diminished when the Chinese traveller, Huen Tsang, came to India in the 6th century AD in search of authentic Buddhist texts. He too visited Patliputra, then one of the greatest cities in the world, and Tamluk and wrote of the scholarship he found at the famous University of Nalanda.

The Himalaya was a marginal area for human occupance during the pre-historic period but, wedged between the rising India and Sinic civilizations became "both a new frontier and vertigial haven of refuge for diverse races. Although Neolithic people of Austro-Munda type might have roamed the foothills, the peopling of the Himalaya was basically the outcome of successive waves of migration of Mongoloids from the northeast and Caucasoids from the west ... They migrated in stages, each carrying their eco-culture to this new environment: Mongoloids with pig and root crops and the Caucasoids with cattle and grain ... Thus, both due to their source and routes of migration, the zone of Mongoloid-Caucasoid interface became tangential to the mountain crest, whereby Mongoloids are dominant east of the Gandak basin and the Caucasoids spread over the western Himalaya" (Gurung, Harka, 1982).

The Himalaya is not by any means an impassable barrier and there has been trade and intercourse across the passes over the centuries. Nevertheless, it remains an ethnic, linguistic and cultural zone of transition and, to some extent, a political buffer.

By the 7th century Buddhism had travelled to Tibet during the golden age of Srong-btsan-sgam-po. Nepal and Bhutan too absorbed Buddhist influences from both south and north. Prithvi Narayan Shah of Gorkha united a number of warring principalities into what has become modern Nepal in 1769 and established the capital in Kathmandu. In 1907 Bhutan similarly united under the Penlop of Tongsa, Ugen Wanchuk, to found a hereditary monarchy of which the present king is fourth in line of succession. Gurung notes the evolution of three economic systems in the Himalayan contact zone: tribal subsistence in the humid east, trade-astoralism in the arid north, and agro-artisanship in the central and western Himalaya.

Meanwhile, in India, empires rose and crumbled. Came the Mughals. Then the British. The face of the Ganga-Brahmaputra-Barak plain and enveloping mountains and hills began to change under the influence of axe and plough, urbanization and technology.

George Mallory, the British mountaineer, asked in the 1920s why he wanted to climb Everest, gave the classic reply: "Because it is there." The fact is that it was not always there. Nature itself has transformed the landscape. The seas have been lifted up and mountains levelled. The earth trembles as the continents continue to push against one another forcing the Himalaya to "grow". Rivers have changed course. Fauna, flora and eco-cultures have migrated and intermingled. Nature is not unchanging. And what Man has done to change this changeful Nature is what we shall now examine.

CHAPTER 2

What Happened in History

Stone Age Man was a hunter-gatherer. The extraordinary cave paintings of Bhimbetka on the northern escarpment of the Vindhyas in Raisen district near Bhopal, were discovered by V.S. Wakankar in 1975. They depict dancers, hunters, warriors armed with spears and bows and arrows, and a variety of game in vivid relief and colour. The paintings have been classified in several periods ranging from 20,000 years ago to relatively recent times. Similar cave paintings, though not quite so old, exist in the Kaimur range in Mirzapur district. Here too rhinoceros abound (Randhawa, M.S., 1980). India continues to live in many ages, and some tribal communities of Middle India and the Northeast are still hunter-gatherers or practice shifting cultivation or are nomadic pastoralists like the Gujjars and others practicing transhumance in Bhutan and Nepal.

The Harappan settlement of Kalibangan was abandoned with the migration and desiccation of the ancient Saraswati. Later Harappan settlements have been found along the Ghaggar, in Chandigarh and elsewhere, at Nagda on the Chambal, in Western Uttar Pradesh along the Yamuna and Hindon, and as far as Kausambi near Allahabad. Zebu cattle and buffaloes were domesticated well ahead of the horse. The Mohenjodaro seals show ox-drawn carts, and the swift horse-drawn chariot was in use by the time of the Mahabharata. Wheat like barley was cultivated by 2500 BC in Uttar Pradesh and Bihar, its propagation moving from west to east. Rice cultivation, however, spread west from its original home in Assam, Bengal and Bihar. Radio carbon datings of finds in Chirand, near the Ghaghara-Ganga confluence in Saran district, Bihar, reveal the cultivation of rice, wheat, barley, peas and green-gram going back to 2500-1650 BC. (Randhawa).

ARYAN ADVANCE

Randhawa, whose monumental *History of Agriculture in India* is an invaluable treasure-house of information, opines that the Aryan advance into Uttar Pradesh and Bihar brought with it an early green revolution with a changeover from the wooden to the iron ploughshare. This enabled farmers to turn the clayey soil in virgin lands and increase food production. The Yajur Veda (1000-800 BC) is also cited as evidence of a sure transition from pastoralism to agriculture.

Irrigation by river lift or simple diversion came to be practiced very early on. Engineering and hydraulic principles were mastered and elaborate works constructed. Neither water nor land was in short supply in the fertile Ganga Basin but there were problems in certain areas, sometimes on account of prior appropriation. An early water dispute was resolved thanks to the Buddha who, on a visit to Kapilavastu, interceded between the Sakyas and Kollyas, both his kinsmen, over a matter of sharing the waters of the river Rohini (Directorate of Information HMG Nepal, 1978).

Terracotta ringwells were popular in Mauryan times and Kautilya's *Arthashastra* discusses land use and inter-cropping with reference to river banks, frequently flooded lands, the moist beds of depressions, and lands around wells which were said to be best reserved for vegetable gardening. Sugar cane, pepper, vine, pumpkin, gourd and medicinal herbs are mentioned. Some streams were dammed and cascades of interconnected tanks with sluice gates were constructed. Water rates were prescribed.

In the course of directing a project that commenced in 1977 on the archaeology of the Ramayana sites, B.B. Lal excavated a massive water tank, over 250 m long, at Shringavarapura about 35 km northwest of Allahabad. The tank was fed from the Ganga by means of a canal and water was filtered through silt chambers. A series of wells dug in the tank bed provided supplementary water during the dry season. This urban water supply source, built in the manner of a step well, was also used for religious ceremonies. Believed to have been constructed by a Kosala king, the Shringavarapura tank is reckoned to be over 2000 years old (Lal, B.B., 1985).

Karl Wittfogel has theorized about the baneful centralizing effect of "hydraulic civilizations" as opposed to rainfed "hydrological civilizations". By virtue of the heavy investment and mass mobilization entailed by large irrigation and flood control works requiring close supervision and management, these inevitably had to be constructed under governmental auspices. Hydraulic government, it was argued, therefore inevitably led to "oriental despotism" (Wittfogel, Karl A., 1956).

Whether this was necessarily so is open to debate. But in the sixth century BC, India was divided into 16 *mahajanapadas* or states of which Magadha, Kosala (Ayodhya), Vatsa, Videha, Avanti (Ujjain), Panchala, Surasena, Matsya and Kuru lay within the Ganga Basin. The next millennium witnessed an efflorescence of spiritual inquiry, science and literature that climaxed in the Gupta period, AD 300-550. This was the age of the Buddha, Mahavira and Asoka; of Ajanta, the *Laws of Manu*, the *Panchatantra*; Varahamira (astronomer) and Aryabhatta (mathematician); of Kalidasa, and Vatsayana's *Kamasutra*. The concept of zero and the decimal system were expounded. In 415, Kumargupta I erected in memory of his father the Iron Pillar that still stands unblemished in what is now the great forecourt by the Qutub Minar in Delhi.

It is to Megasthenes that we owe a description of Chandragupta Maurya's capital, Patliputra. A splendid city, standing on the north bank of the Sone ... roughly nine miles by two ... The city wall was a massive timber palisade, with drawbridges, towers and gates ... The houses were two or three storeys high, and, as they were mostly wooden, elaborate precautions were taken against an outbreak of fire. In the heart of the city was the royal palace ... built of wood, exquisitely carved ... (Randhawa).

Agriculture and animal husbandry continued to develop. By the Gupta period paddy was being transplanted. Though the population had grown, there was sufficient land for all and enough pasture for livestock. Megasthenes reported in a dispatch that "The greater part of the soil is under irrigation and consequently bears two crops in the course of the year. It is accordingly affirmed that famine has never visited India and that there has never been a general scarcity of nourishing food" (Durant, Will, 1954). Forests, however, had begun to be cleared for extending agriculture, smelting iron, and construction.

Invaders and traders both brought new crops to India. Among these were certain varieties of wheat, chickpea, peas, onion, garlic, turnip, cabbage, carrot, radish, coriander, cumin seed, lucerne, flax, and poppy from West Asia. From Africa came pearl millet (bajra), sorghum (jowar), castor, sesamum, guines grass, napier grass and coffee. From China soybean, walnut, litchi, apricot, peach, plum, loquat and tea. And from Southeast Asia and the Pacific Isles there was introduced lemon, grapefruit, coconut, arecanut and betel pepper (Randhawa).

Alauddin Khilji extended his empire and defeated the Mongols. But whether to meet the cost of his campaigns or otherwise, the Sultan raised the revenue demand from the traditional one-sixth to one-half of the produce, with a grazing tax to boot. He, however, fixed the price of grain which benefitted his urban subjects but added to the hardship of the peasantry. Mohammad bin Tughlak's transfer of the capital from Delhi to Daulatabad (near Aurangabad) and his bid to substitute copper for silver currency played havoc with the administration and treasury. The Ganga doab, ever prosperous, was brought to ruin with yet more oppressive taxes. Sheikh Nuru-I-Hakk, a contemporary historian wrote that "the people in despair set fire to their barns and stacks and, carrying away their cattle, became wanderers in the wild world. Upon this, the Sultan gave orders that every such peasant who might be seized, should be put to death, and that the whole country should be ravaged and given up to indiscriminate plunder ... in this way he utterly depopulated whole tracts of his kingdom." (Randhawa).

The passing of Mohammad bin Tughlak brought relief to the people and farming began to revive under the benign rule of Feroz Shah Tughlak who expanded irrigation. The Western Yamuna Canal, constructed in 1355, was a notable achievement. The Moroccan traveller, Ibn Batuta speaks of kharif and rabi cropping and mentions the mango as the most prized fruit. Feroz Shah laid out 2000 orchards around Delhi to grow seven varieties of grape (Habi, Irfan, 1982).

THE MUGHAL ERA

By the time of the Mughal invasion, sericulture had been introduced over wide areas and the Persian wheel was known. The emperor Babar, like Jehangir after him, was a naturalist and minutely recorded the fauna and flora of Hindostan. As others before him, Babar found the country full of rhinoceros and wild elephant. Irrigated tree-farming was practiced in his time. The interloper Sher Shah Suri undertook land measurements as a basis for revenue collection, a procedure that Todar Mal was to refine under Akbar. Abul Fazl's *Ain-i-Akbari* details the evolution of a standard 60 square yard bigha and three classifications of soil fertility on the basis of which the revenue due to the government was settled and expressed in money (Randhawa, 1982). Cattle and orchards were taxed and *takkavi* loans were advanced to needy cultivators for purchase of inputs.

The population of Mughal India in 1600 was estimated at 100 million and that of the plains "from Multan to Monghyr" at between 30 and 40 million (Ibid).

The pressure of population on land was not heavy. Even in Akbar's time the peasant enjoyed the hereditary right to his land, which he could sell subject to revenue payment. But he could not leave the land uncultivated unless he found a successor to till it. There was no dearth of pasture either and both cows and buffaloes were reared extensively through the State and nobility attached higher importance to elephants and the breeding of horses for military purposes and speedy communication. There were dense forests in the Chambal and Yamuna basins, around Agra and north of Jaipur towards Jhunjhunu, along the Vindhyas and in the Terai. Several imperial hunting grounds were stocked with cheetah and wild elephant. These are well documented in Irfan Habib's *Atlas of the Mughal Empire* (1982). The *Ain-i-Akbari* and the diaries of Ralph Fitch (1583-91) and William Finch (1608-11) and others recorded forests infested with lions and tigers and other game south of the Ghaghara, between Jaunpur and Allahabad and in Bengal, especially around Sylhet, Dhaka, the Chittagong Hill Tract and Sunderbans. Bengal was particularly well stocked with bamboo (Randhawa).

Shahjahan repaired and extended Feroz Shah's Western Yamuna Canal and brought one branch to Delhi. Irfan Habib, however, notes that many other Mughal canals were not constructed on high contours and water had, therefore, to be lifted.

The Portuguese had arrived in India in the 16th century and, over the years, introduced a number of new plants into the country, many of them from the Americas. Among these were groundnut, tobacco, potato, amaranth, cashew nut, guava, sharifa or custard apple, chiku, pineapple, chillies and agave. They also introduced the technique of grafting. Within a few decades many "exotics" had spread far and wide, the amaranth giving a new touch of colour to the Himalaya from Kashmir to Bhutan and all of them adding greatly to the diversity o Indian agriculture (Randhawa). Irfan Habib adds maize and papaya to this list of New

World immigrants and notes that sericulture spread to eastern India in great profusion making Bengal, already a cotton-growing tract, one of the greatest silk-producing regions in the world. Calico, chintz, silk and tassar weaves acquired international fame and Dhaka muslins were much sought after by European traders.

Estimates of grain yield made by Irfan Habib show little improvement or even some decline between 1540-45 and 1870 in the Delhi-Agra region. The production of indigo, another significant crop, showed no great change; but sugar cane yields registered a rise. Poppy too was an important crop over much of south India.

The Ahoms from upper Burma had meanwhile conquered Assam where rice and betel were important crops. The militia was used to reclaim swamps and clear forests for cultivation around new settlements. Hundreds of miles of river embankments were similarly raised to secure the land from inundation. The population of the Ahom territories up to the Manas river was estimated at between two and three million in 1750 whereas that of the kingdom of Koch-Behar, lying further west up to the Sun-Kosh, to which the Mughals later advanced, was perhaps between 1.6 and 3.8 million in 1600 (Guha, Amalendu, 1982).

Whatever the agrarian condition during the Mughal era until the time of Shahjahan, famine, war and increasing imposts began to tell thereafter. Aurangzeb's accession to the throne was marked by severe famines followed by pestilence in northern India in 1660 and in Bihar in 1670. Thousands died, some 90,000 in Patna alone. The Maratha armies harassed the Empire. Land revenue exacted much of the peasants' surplus leading to the large-scale abandonment of farms as testified by contemporary observers such as Francois Bernier and Jean-Baptiste Tavernier. With the decline in the number of peasants, *jagirdars* were correspondingly reduced resulting in greater exactions by the latter. Land revenue, estimated by Lane Poole to have been around £18,650,000 under Akbar in 1594, had reached £30,0000,000 by the time of Shahjahan in 1655 and £43,500,000 towards the end of Aurangzeb's rule in 1697. The Jat peasantry in what is now Agra division and Haryana rose between 1669 and 1707 and the Satnamis, a peasant-artisan-trading community of Narnaul-Mewat, revolted in 1672 (Randhawa).

Such then was the condition of the country when Clive established British supremacy in Bengal after the Battle of Plassey in 1756. The decline of Surat, the Mughal's main maritime outlet, and the rise of British power in Bengal, had a profound influence not merely on trade, which the Ganga waterways funnelled into the rapidly growing port of Calcutta, but on agriculture and industry as well as in the service of British mercantile interests. The demand for indigo, cotton, sugar and later opium (for China) grew, the impulses for change radiating out of Calcutta and travelling up-country along the waterways which were the principal arteries of internal and international commerce – both ways.

TOWARDS PERMANENT SETTLEMENT

The exactions of the class of rentiers, or landed aristocracy, that had grown up over the past couple of centuries became more insistent during the transition from a declining Mughal rule to the rise of British power. The East India Company took over the *dewani* of Bengal from Shah Alam II in 1765. The old system of sub-infeudation had left the tenant at the bottom of an agrarian hierarchy but with certain minimal rights which were fairly well entrenched. The British now fostered a new landed order by sale of zamindari through auction, the high winning bids being recouped from a hapless peasantry. "The new zamindari system marked the beginning of a new feudal landlordism in total disregard of the peasant's traditional rights ... Land had become a commodity ... The new economy ruined the rural artisans, and smashed the close bond between agriculture and industry" (Sen, Bhowani, 1962).

There was a series of terrible famines between 1770 and 1790. Millions perished. The Gola Ghar in Patna is a monument to the Great Bengal Famine of 1770. Appalled by the disaster, Warren Hastings had this huge rotunda built as a granary in 1786 "for the perpetual prevention of famine in these (eastern) provinces". Alas, the entrance was constructed opening inwards and was found jammed against the weight of grain stocked inside when the need arose. So much for that pious hope. Agrarian unrest was manifest in the Fakir and Sanyasi agitations between 1772 and 1782 and the peasant risings in Rangpur and Dinajpur (in today's Bangladesh) in 1783.

With the passage of Pitt's India Bill, the Crown assumed a measure of control over the East India Company. The new Governor General, Lord Cornwallis was sent out to India with instructions to end frequent destabilizing changes in the revenue system and to introduce instead a permanent settlement, but only for 10 years in the first instance. A preliminary survey conducted to this end brought forth a minute from the new Governor General. "I may safely assert that one-third of the Company's territory in Hindustan is now a jungle inhabited only by wild beasts. Will a 10-year lease induce any proprietor to clear away that jungle and encourage the ryots to come and cultivate his lands ...?" Cornwallis, therefore, determined on announcing a permanent settlement and did so in 1793 fixing the assessment at a much higher level. The total revenue obtained from Bengal, Bihar and Orissa for the base year was 26.8 million or double that collected in the first year of the Company's *dewani* (Dutt, Romesh, 1901).

Romesh Chunder Dutt, who retired from the Indian Civil Service in 1896, believed the permanent settlement to be "the wisest and most successful measure which the British nation has ever adopted in India". Many will disagree. The *ryot* was left at the tender mercy of a usurper, an absentee landlord. In Assam, where labour service including defence of the realm and maintenance of public works was given in lieu of the right to cultivate three acres of rice land free of rent, the abolition of the so-called *paik-khel* system and its commutation into cash rents under the permanent settlement impoverished the Assamese gentry. Though it relieved others of forced labour, the peasantry were also affected by subsequent sharp increases in the rate of revenue demanded. Writing of agrarian relations in Bangladesh, Jannuzi and Peach (1980) described the permanent settlement as a system where "superior rights in the land and greater security of tenure on holdings were accorded to non-cultivators (while) actual tillers had inferior (and) less secure rights in land."

The British effort to create the equivalent of the English squire who would be loyal to the Raj was seen as a built-in "depressor" by Daniel Thorner (1981). "The result has been a layer of rights from those of the State as super-landlord (or ultimate owner) down to those of the sub-landlords (penultimate owners) to those of the several tiers of tenants. Both the State and the superior landlords exercise the right to draw income from the soil in the form of rents; whenever possible the tenants also try to subsist by collecting rents from working cultivators with rights inferior to their own." He adds: "This complex of legal, economic and social relations uniquely typical of the Indian countryside served to produce an effect which I should like to call that of a built-in 'depressor'. Through the operation of this multi-faceted 'depressor' Indian agriculture continued to be characterized by low capital intensity and antiquated methods. Few of the actual tillers were left with an efficacious interest in modernization, or the prevention of such recognized evils as fragmentation. The pattern of landholding, cultivation and produce-sharing operated to hold down agricultural production." How true. It was not until Bentinck that ryotwari settlements directly with the peasant proprietor were made the basis of the new settlements in northern India under Regulation IX of 1833, with the state demand fixed at 66 per cent of the rental over a period of 30 years.

BOTANICAL INITIATIVES

Although impelled by profit motives, the Company's labours were not devoid of benefit to India and many of its servants rendered the country great service. Wellesley, Governor General from 1798 to 1805, was a keen naturalist whose support for botanical and zoological research resulted in the establishment of the Sibpur Garden in Calcutta in 1787 and the Barrackpore Menagerie. He also encouraged the drawing by Indian artists of plants, trees, birds, insects and fishes, an activity enlarged and systematized by William Roxburgh who took charge of the Calcutta Botanical Garden. This formed the basis for the first standard works on Indian botany (Randhawa). New crops were introduced and Hastings noted in 1814 that the spread of potatoes in Bihar "will be a material security against dearth", surveys of Nepal, Sylhet and Kumaon followed. The Saharanpur Botanical Garden, founded by a lesser Mughal notable in 1750, was formally taken over in 1817 and utilized to naturalise many plants from America and to develop a herbarium. The flora of the Himalaya was studied. Hastings ordered that plants and trees of the "hill country" might be sought to be acclimatized at Saharanpur and, if successful, propagated first in Agra and later in Bengal. Among the new plants introduced were the mahogany tree, coffee and nutmeg, cinnamon, camphor, vanilla, rubber, Japanese mulberry, cardamom, tapioca, cocoa, and a whole variety of fruit and "English" vegetables. In 1820, William Carey, the missionary, founded the Royal Agri-Horticulture Society which published a journal. Improved varieties of existing species were brought into the country. Thus Sea Island, American and Egyptian cotton, Mauritian sugar cane, Australian and European wheat, and the mouldboard plough from America. Meanwhile, land had been purchased near Pusa in Bihar where William Moorcroft, a veterinary surgeon, set up a stud farm to breed horses for the Company's cavalry.

FAMINE: CANALS VERSUS RAILWAYS

Attention turned also to irrigation. The Western Yamuna Canal had been damaged by war and neglect. Hastings lamented this and noted in his diary that along its length "no tolerable water is to be procured but by sinking wells to such an enormous depth as is beyond the compass of ordinary funds. All the water found in the higher strata is brackish and is deleterious to vegetables as well as unwholesome for man. The stream of the Jamuna is running through this country becomes so tainted, that the necessity of drinking it in Delhi since the canal has been destroyed, has product great unhealthiness in the city." The task was entrusted to the Bengal engineers who completed the restoration in three years, but without permanent headworks at Hathnikund. By 1847 the project was yielding a 13 per cent return on an investment of Rs 13.81 lakhs. Bentinck took up the restoration of the Eastern Yamuna Canal (250 km), which was opened in 1830 for an outlay of Rs 4.37 lakhs.

Sir Arthur Cotton had launched on this great irrigation works in south India when famine ravaged north India in which some 800,000 people died. This triggered action on the construction of the great Upper Ganga Canal, preliminary work on which had been suspended. Hardinge sanctioned the project in 1841. Military engineers were assigned the task as they were the only organized technical resource available and Major Proby T. Cautley of the Bengal Artillery constructed the canal. Envisaged was a 412 km canal with 117 km of branches to be constructed from Haridwar for Rs 26 lakhs. The Thomason College of Engineering, later to become Roorkee University, was started in 1847 to train the necessary manpower. This was a truly pioneering project and a most challenging engineering work entailing complex aqueducts and siphons. The work was financed by the East India Irrigation Company and was completed in 1862 at a cost of Rs 36.63 lakhs. Certain construction faults, including an excessive gradient, caused some problems and the idea of navigation had to be abandoned.

Arthur Cotton published a critique of the work in 1863 at the behest of the East India Irrigation Company listing "fundamental mistakes" by Cautley. These included a choice of site too far up-river which made for an excessive gradient, many expensive cross-drainage works, a wastefully long feeder channel and the absence of a permanent diversion barrage thus necessitating the extravagant construction of temporary diversion structures every year (Whitcombe, Elizabeth, 1971). The Lower Ganga Canal followed between 1872 and 1878.

Irrigation, like the Railways, had thus far been financed through loans and equity raised in London and guaranteed by the government. The Sone canal of the Madras Irrigation Company and the Orissa canals of the East India Irrigation and Canal Company both failed and the government had to take them over. This led to a review of policy and in 1866 it was decided that future irrigation works be undertaken directly by the State irrespective of the territorial boundaries separating British and Princely India. Furthermore, productive irrigation projects would be financed through public loans (Randhawa). Pursuant to this decision, a new office of Inspector General of Irrigation was established and government works were classified into "major" and "minor" to be funded through loans or from general revenues, respectively (Whitcombe, 1982). The Agra canal was one of several projects taken up under the new dispensation. Following the famine in 1876-78 a special Famine Relief and Insurance Fund was constituted and a sum of Rs 15 lakhs was set apart every year, half of this to be committed to irrigation and railway construction if not already absorbed in famine relief (Irrigation Commission, 1972). The Betwa canal was taken up under this scheme. Lord Mayo believed that "by the construction of railways and the completion of great works of irrigation, we have it in our power, under God's blessing, to render impossible the return of those periodical famines which have disgraced our administration and cost an incredible amount of suffering, with the loss of many millions of lives" (Randhawa). The Famine Commission recommended that "among the means that may be adopted for giving India direct protection from famine arising from drought, the first place must unquestionably assigned to works of irrigation" (Famine Commission, 1880). Sir Arthur Cotton thought expenditure on railways was a waste and argued vigorously for canals both for irrigation and cheap transit.

Other than the delta irrigation works, not all the other major irrigation schemes had been paying. Sixteen million sterling had been spent on irrigation in India under British rule by 1872. The question asked in the House of Commons was whether railways or irrigation were better calculated to yield a profitable return and prevent the recurrence of famine. The railways, it was assumed, would enable grain to be moved speedily from the areas of surplus to areas of deficit. John Bright rose to say that £16 million was nothing for India when the city of Manchester alone was spending £5.5 million for its water supply. Cotton told a parliamentary select committee that whereas the railways had cost India £23,000 per mile (for

7500 miles in 1872) and had lost £3 million per annum, the Treasury had gained half a million sterling a year on irrigation works (Dutt).

Dutt concludes: "As might be expected, preference was given to railways which facilitated British trade with India and not to canals which would have benefitted Indian agriculture. So great was the influence of British traders on the Indian administration that the Indian government guaranteed a rate of interest out of Indian revenues to companies constructing railroads in India; and £ 225,000,000 were spent on railways, resulting not in a profit but in a loss of £ 40,000,000 to the Indian taxpayer up to 1900. And so little were the interests of Indian agriculture appreciated that only £ 25,000,000 were spent on irrigation works up to 1900."

IMPACT OF IRRIGATION

Canal irrigation in many areas resulted in the decline of wells but canal water was often only used for profitable cash crops or protectively in drought years. The government generally only constructed the main distributaries, leaving it to the zamindars and peasants to complete the minor and water courses, which left too much to chance. Nor did the hierarchy or irrigation and revenue functionaries miss the opportunities to take a cut.

The growth of the canals and railways had other implications: water logging and salinity in the absence of drainage which was in fact impeded by railway and canal embankments; malaria; deforestation to provide firewood for the steam engines (as Bihar-Bengal coal was more expensive) and timber for sleepers and rolling stock; and diversion of dung from the fields for use as a fuel for baking the bricks required for irrigation works. The railways and waterways influenced a change in the cropping pattern in favour of the production of "valuable" or revenue earning crops or those providing raw materials for direct export.

The common staples such as millets, pulses and fodder were primarily rainfed while wheat, sugar cane, cotton, indigo and opium were irrigated. Mixing of three to four different crops in the same field was practiced by poorer farmers as a means of crop rotation and insuring against risk while a form of shifting cultivation was prevalent in part of Bundelkhand and Oudh, again as a form of rotation to rest the soil whenever a low population density allowed (Whitcombe, 1971).

The spread of saline/alkaline *usar* or *reh* lands led to the setting up of a Reh Committee which reported in 1878. It found "flush irrigation" greatly responsible for the malady. Thirteen years later, the government's agricultural chemist found "enormous tracts in the plains of northern India" affected by *usar*, some 4000 to 5000 square miles in the North-Western Province alone (Whitcombe). The rise of sub-soil water further caused the walls of *kachha* (unlined) wells to cave in.

The substitution of the poor man's bajra and jowar by wheat and even rice under irrigated conditions and their export aggravated famine. About one-tenth of the total wheat crop was being exported along with oil seeds and cotton (Voelcker, 1891). Cash crops also tended to oust "less valuable" staple grains from canal acreage while the extension of cultivation to new lands resulted in a shrinking of pastures and other common lands at the cost of the poorer sections of the community. The effect of this trend in Bundelkhand in the second half of the 19th century was rising indebtedness, revenue default, consequence withholding of credit, migration, depopulation, and the spread of the stubborn *kans* grass, taking lands out of cultivation for 10 to 15 years or more until subsequently reclaimed (Stokes, Eric, 1982).

AGRICULTURAL INNOVATION

Concern over agricultural conditions in India came to a head with the terrible 1876-78 famine affecting an estimated sixty million people and taking a toll of more than five million lives. The resultant Famine Commission urged agricultural improvement as a task that the government must undertake. Accordingly Dr John Augustus Voelcker, Consulting Chemist to the Royal Agricultural Society of England was deputed to report on possible improvements in Indian agriculture. He toured the country extensively over 14 months and in 1891 submitted his Report on the Improvement of Indian Agriculture. This remarkably perceptive document had much praise for many aspects of farming in India – tillage practices, rotation, green manuring, well irrigation, use of silt, and sheep and cattle folding in the fields. He found little to teach the peasants in Meerut but felt he could suggest improvements in areas such as Dhaka, Kanpur and Hissar, where too it was the lack of facilities for improvement that was mainly at fault.

His key recommendation was that forestry be related to agriculture and not "excluded", and that fuel and fodder reserves and fuelwood farming be encouraged so that cowdung would not be burnt in cooking hearths but returned to the soil as manure. He estimated wheat yields at seven bushels (61 lbs) per acre in unmanured fields with irregular rainfall, 10 bushels in tracts with better rainfall and from 15 to 25 bushels on manured and irrigated land as compared with 28 bushels in England with fertilizer use. A.O. Hume, (later to found the Indian National Congress), in Agricultural Reform in India (1879) had stated 14 bushels an acre of wheat to be a high average for good fields around Aligarh and Etawah compared to 19 bushels mentioned as the contemporary wheat yield in the *Ain-i-Akbari* (PPST Bulletin, 1982).

Reporting in 1926, the Royal Commission on Agriculture in India found that no action had been taken on Voelcker's recommendation, and that the import of nitrogenous fertilizer too was no more than 4,724 tonnes.

Voelcker deplored the deforestation that had taken place under the Raj (first for timber for building ships for the British navy and later for the railways) resulting in a squeeze on village grazing lands and other common property resources. He also linked the loss of forests to a deterioration in the climate and a reduction in rainfall. He quoted an old Sanskrit saying dividing rainfall into 12 parts and assigning them as follows: six for the sea, four for the forests and mountains, and two for the land (PPST Bulletin).

Departments of Agriculture were set up both at the Central and provincial levels into which veterinary sections were incorporated. The pure Indian cattle breeds were rated highly and J. Mollison of the Bombay Agricultural Department after study found this to be a result of careful breeding. Voelcker too commented on "the old Hindu system of breeding carried on by means of sacred bulls or Brahmani bulls as they are generally termed. These bulls, dedicated to Śiva or some other deity, are let loose when still young ... They are picked cattle and, being sacred, are allowed to roam where they please and fed on the best of everything." These stud bulls rendered services. Many Brahmani bulls were imported by the United States.

An Inspector General of Agriculture was in place by the turn of the century. And another devastating famine in 1899-1900, led to the appointment of the first Irrigation Commission (1901-03).

The total irrigated area from all sources in 1900 was 13.4 million hectares, of which public works accounted for 56 per cent. The gross sown area was 82.2 million hectares of which about 16 per cent was irrigated. Source-wise, canals irrigated 45 per cent of the area, wells 35 per cent, tanks 15 per cent, and other sources 5 per cent (Irrigation Commission, 1972). The First Irrigation Commission drew up a 20-year programme estimated to cost Rs 44 crores to irrigate 2.6 million hectares (6.5 m acres) in British India. Lord Curzon accepted this recommendation. In his Budget speech in 1905 he emphasized that "as we draw towards the close of this gigantic programme we shall no longer be able to talk glibly of remunerative programmes or of lucrative interest on capital outlay, but shall find ourselves dealing with protective works, pure and simple, where no return or little return is to be expected, and where we shall have to measure the financial burden imposed on the State against the degree of protection from scarcity and famine obtained for the people" (Randhawa). That injunction continues to hold today.

In related developments, the Imperial Agricultural Research Institute was established in Pusa, Bihar, marking the beginning of what is today the Indian Council of Agricultural Research's network of research centres. The first agricultural colleges came into being. The cooperative movement was started in 1904. The very extensive Sharda canal project was taken up between 1915-26, entailing an agreement with Nepal in 1927 for construction of the headworks and constituting possibly the first international water agreement in the subcontinent in modern times. Nepal constructed its first diversion irrigation project, the Chandra Canal, on the Kosi in 1927.

INROADS INTO HILL AND FOREST

In all this while the Himalayan tracts were protected by their relative isolation which was enhanced by the "malarial moat" and impenetrable forest along the Terai. Yet they too were not immune to change.

The discovery that the tea plant was indigenous to Assam encouraged the East India Company directors to sanction its commercial cultivation. The development of the tea gardens in Assam through private enterprise dates to 1840 (Dutt). Earlier an experimental plantation had been raised near Sadiya and some others in Kumaon with seed imported from China. It was soon discovered that tea was native to Sylhet and the first garden there was opened in 1857. A year earlier the first tea garden was established in Darjeeling and within 20 years 113 estates were in operation there and up to 200 in western Assam. A steady stream of labour moved into the Darjeeling gardens from Eastern Nepal. The emigrants found they had traded "oppressive taxation, corvee, and debt bondage while resettlement promised a steady wage for all members of the family" (English, Richard, 1985). The Assam gardens drew labour from indebted and impoverished areas in north Bihar and further afield, while Mymensinghis and other Bengalis moved to cultivate the newly reclaimed lands in Assam, introducing superior techniques in farming jute, potatoes and tobacco and, later, deep-water paddy.

A retired British Captain started the first orchard in Himachal in 1870 growing apples, pears, plums and cherries. Captain A.T. Bannon followed to settle near Manaly which marks the beginning of the famous Kulu apple orchards. Elsewhere, in the western Himalaya, British commercial interests centred on harvesting rich stands of pine and deodar for the railways' insatiable demand for fuel and sleepers. Once again Nepali labour proved adept and was soon to be found wherever there were timber camps.

The first hill stations and hill cantonments began to dot the Himalaya. While this led to some forest clearance, this was nothing as compared to the policy of making new grants in forest lands adjacent to villages. "Katil is the method of cultivating hilly tracts (in Kumaon) without terracing them. Every year the population is increasing, and the need is felt for providing more and more food for this increasing population. This necessity, coupled with the policy of the authorities, which is to encourage cultivation at the expense of forest preservation, has given rise to this form of agriculture. The right of extending cultivation leads to new lands being taken in every year. The adjoining forest … is cleared and burnt … This originates fires which cause enormous destruction … The people who actually secure these (new forest land) grants are not the poor and needy, but merely a few grasping individuals who can easily satisfy the lower grades of state officials. Every new grant in a village means a certain curtailment of the common rights of the village community." However, katil lands are after a lapse of years brought under regular tillage and "contour drainage is eventually succeeded by beautiful and regular flights of terraces" (Pant S.D., 1935).

The Indian Forest Department was organized in the 1860s. The Forest Act of 1878 marked out reserved forests within which traditional community rights of collection and grazing were reduced to privileges. This restriction alienated the people from the Forest Department. Later policies of planting monocultures such as sal (for the railways) in the Siwaliks and chir pine in the mid-hills for resin, aggravated tensions as the villagers wanted other species such as oak which were more useful to them and their cattle. The First World War made additional demands on India's forests, impelling the extension of reserved forests. Many thousands of hectares of forests were set ablaze by irate villagers. The abolition of *beggar*, or forced labour, in Kumaon and Garhwal in 1920 might have offered a reprieve. But opposition to the forest regulations was fanned by the national movement and the hills remained afire. A Forest Grievance Committee was set up by the Uttar Pradesh administration. This recommended that the new reserved forests be restored to the people as "civil forests". The Kumaon Forestry Advisory Committee helped defuse tensions (Martins, Paul J., 1987).

CHANGES IN NEPAL AND TIBET

In Nepal, land brought wealth and prestige and land revenue was the principal source of income to the State. Land could not be left unproductive and, on unification of the country in 1769, King Prithvi Narayan Shah proclaimed that "land which can be converted into fields shall be reclaimed (Regmi, M.C., 1978). He had ascended the throne of Gorkha in 1743 and expanded his domain by conquest, recruiting additional numbers to his Gorkha army through the incentive of land grants for services rendered. "In important ways the limit of the army was set by the land, and the limit of the land was set by the army's activities" (Mahat, T.B.S. et al., 1986). The introduction of maize and potato as new crops well-adapted to unirrigated hill farming gave an impetus to the reclamation of new lands. This contributed to deforestation. Increased food production, by improving nutritional standards gave a fillip to population increase, thus setting off a vicious spiral. The long period of wars, including those with the British and Tibet, necessitated the production of arms which aggravated deforestation as fuel was needed to make charcoal to smelt iron and force weapons. The developing capital of Kathmandu with its places and temples also devoured timber in large quantities. In 1936, some 42,000 trees were felled for the reconstruction of the Singha Durbar (ibid).

The Himalaya, however, continued to export manpower whether for military service in the Gorkha, Kumaon and Garhwal regiments, or as labour in the plains, a situation that prevails to this day.

Despite the Anglo-Bhutanese war which was a rude intrusion into its seclusion, Bhutan remained almost hermetically sealed until 1959. Nepal too was relatively sequestered though there was trade with both India and Tibet and pastoralists all along the Himalayan border would move to grazing areas in Tibet every summer until its borders were closed in 1959.

Direct British penetration in northeast India, beyond the Assam Valley and Cachar was limited. Tribute was collected but, excluding Shillong and pockets elsewhere, vast areas in the jungle fastnesses were treated as partially or totally excluded areas" under the 1935 reforms until the Indian Constitution came into force in 1950.

Economic conditions in Tibet too were fairly unchanging. Something of the past can be gleaned from the autobiography of the 14th Dalai Lama (1962) now in exile in India. "The amount of revenue required from each district had always been fixed by the government; but from time immemorial it had been understood that the district authorities could collect as much extra as they liked, or as much as they were able, to pay their own expenses and salaries. As this was permitted by law, people had to pay up, and I was not very old when I saw what a temptation it was towards injustice. So I changed the whole system, in consultation with my Cabinet and the reforms committee." Henceforward district officials were paid a fixed salary from the treasury in Lhasa.

A more fundamental reform needed was of land tenure. "The whole of Tibet was the property of the State, and most peasant farmers held their land under a kind of leasehold directly from the State. Some of them paid their rent in kind with a proportion of their produce, and this was the main source of the government's stocks which were distributed to the monasteries, the army and officials. Some paid by labour, and some had always been required to provide free transport for government officials and in some cases for the monasteries too." The 13th Dalai Lama abolished free transport and fixed the charges for hire of horses, mules and yaks. "A peasant's land was heritable, and he could lease it to others, or mortgage it, or even sell his rights to it … He could only be dispossessed if he failed to pay his dues." Peasants were advanced loans when times were bad. But huge debts had accumulated. Many of these were scaled down or written off.

The most urgent single reform related to large private estates, granted long back to aristocratic families in lieu of one male heir in each generation being mandated to work as a government official. Peasants worked on these estates in feudal conditions. The Dalai Lama's reforms committee resolved that these estates should revert to the State on payment of compensation and the land should be distributed among the peasants working on it. A similar policy was contemplated regarding monastic lands. But before any of these proposals could be implemented, the regime changed in 1950.

An independent observer, Heinrich Harrar (1953), complements this account. Visiting some private estates in the late 1940s, he found them "completely medieval". The farmers used wooden ploughs with an iron ploughshare drawn by *dzos* (a cross between a yak and an ox). Surprisingly, despite the proximity of brooks, there was no irrigation. And the peasants were "serfs".

POPULATION AND POVERTY

India and (East) Pakistan became independent in 1947 though it was not until 1971 that Bangladesh as such came into being. The entire Ganga-Brahmaputra-Barak Basin was swept by change. Rana rule yielded to a monarchical restoration in Nepal; the Chinese revolution brought in a new order in Tibet, and Bhutan before long ended its isolation.

As of mid-1986, the population of Bhutan was estimated at 1.3 million; that of Nepal 17 million; of Bangladesh 103.2 million and of India 781.4 million of which some 43 per cent or approximately 351 million lives within the basin, and perhaps another million in Tibet. The corresponding per capita income was $ 150 each in Bhutan and Nepal, $ 160 in Bangladesh, and $ 290 in India (World Bank, 1988) though the figure for the region within the basin according to Indian national income figures could be 25 per cent less. Data for Tibet, China's poorest province, is hard to come by but according to one estimate quoting *The Poverty of Plenty*, a book by Wang Xiaoquiang and Bai Nanafeng (Macmillan), the average rural income in Tibet is only $ 93.80 per year, though many yak herdsmen are much better off (South, July 1988). A very large segment of the basin's population continues to live below the poverty line, on the margin of subsistence. It suffers from hunger and malnutrition, high infant mortality, low literacy, and significant unemployment or underemployment. Agricultural productivity and energy consumption, most of it from non-commercial sources in respect of the rural and even urban poor, is generally low. Farm production is unstable, being for many a gamble in the rains. Ecological degradation has reached crisis proportions over large areas and is worsening with the relentless pressure of population growth. Economies in the basin region are characterized by high dependence on agriculture, indebtedness, low asset formation, and gross inequalities and marked by elements of feudalism, serfdom and forms of bondage that come close to slavery.

Given current fertility levels, the poverty-population vicious spiral, and the large yet-to-marry cohorts at the base of the pyramid, national populations are not expected to stabilize before AD 2030-2040 by when the population of Bhutan might be four million, that of Nepal 63 million, that of Bangladesh 432 million and that of India 1698 million (World Bank), with the Indian basin component being around 760 million. The prospect is horrendous but can yet be mitigated by rapid and meaningful development that rolls back poverty and affords the most underprivileged a reasonable quality of life within the next two decades. A concerted action programme is called for and the huge potential of the basin can provide much of the wherewithal. There are no more colonial masters to blame. Much has been accomplished since Independence. Much more remains to be done.

CHAPTER 3

Farm Performance and Prospects

The Ganga-Brahmaputra-Barak Basin has all it takes to be a granary. Its agricultural record has however been disappointing. Despite occasional spurts and bright patches, much of the region is barely able to feed its burgeoning population if not actually deficient in grain. Even where hunger is satisfied, health is not and malnutrition continues to tell on morbidity and productivity. This is true of much or most of mid-central, eastern and northeastern India, Bangladesh, Nepal and Bhutan. Western Uttar Pradesh and Haryana are with Punjab among the green revolution success regions in India, producing the surpluses required to feed others and withstand periodic drought. But even here as much as elsewhere in the country, agricultural production plateaued over much of the 1980s, a series of bad seasons admittedly being a major adverse factor in this regard.

With the vast majority of the population of the basin being rural and dependent on farming sluggishness in agricultural growth soon manifests itself in the form of rising prices, hunger, mounting unemployment, lack of industrial demand, a fall in exports and balance of payments pressures on account of import requirements. Many regions, have witnessed a migration of population either within national boundaries, as from the mid-hills of Nepal to the Terai, from Bihar to Punjab or from Kumaon and Garhwal to the Ganga plains, or a movement of Malthusian refugees across international borders. This erosion of human resources, often of able-bodied men or the most venturesome among the populace, has further undermined agriculture in the exporting areas even as it has aroused sensitivities in the importing regions. On the other hand, Bhutan and parts of the Indian Northeast have come up against a shortage of manpower for development in some respects.

The average annual growth of agricultural production between 1980 and 1986 was (in percentage points) 1.9 in India, 2.7 in Bangladesh and 4.5 in Nepal. The Nepalese figure appears relatively good only because of the low base with a meager 1.1 per cent rate of growth between 1965 and 1980 (Work Development Report, 1988). Over the past two decades, India alone among these four countries has been able to keep food production ahead of population, though not necessarily so within its basin states. Figures are hard to come by but, according to one estimate, grain production in this region doubled to 450,000 tonnes between 1959 and 1986.

GRAIN TARGETS FOR 2000

Per capita agricultural output has declined over large parts of the basin. The targets of grain production set for 1989-90 are 5.36 million tonnes in Nepal; 205,000 tonnes in Bhutan (1987); 20.7 million tonnes in Bangladesh; and 175 million tonnes in India. Bhutan hopes to reduce its current food deficit of around 30,000 tonnes to about 10,000 tonnes by 1992. By 2000 grain requirements are placed at 7 million tonnes for Nepal, 27 million tonnes for Bangladesh, and 230-240 million tonnes for India. What these figures imply in each case is a rate of growth of agricultural production of between 4 and 5 per cent per annum. Excluding Bhutan, and maybe Tibet, there is little or no room for expanding the area under cultivation anywhere in the basin. A larger farm output must come from greater productivity. Agricultural growth rates will, therefore, have to show considerable increase. This is certainly possible, as the potential exists, but it will take sustained research and extension effort and a whole package of policies to accomplish.

Over 70 per cent of Nepal's rice and wheat output and a third of its maize comes from the Terai and a combination of increased irrigation, more extensive use of improved seed, and a larger fertilizer application is planned. Production in this tract is, however, greatly influenced by what happens across the open border with India. Market prices of both inputs and outputs are determined by prices prevailing in India and movements take place in either direction depending on these price differentials (Agricultural Price Policy in Nepal, 1987). The mid-hills region of Nepal is more autonomous in this respect, enjoying a natural protection on account of the transport cost involved in transactions with the Indian plains.

China grows more grain than India on a smaller acreage because of its superior productivity after making due adjustments for definitions and methods of calculation. Average per hectare crop yields in India and Bangladesh in recent years have been around 1.6 tonnes for rice and between 2.1 and 2.6 tonnes for wheat. This compares with Chinese yields of 5.1 for rice and 2.8 tonnes for what in 1983 (China: Agriculture 2000 Study, 1985). The Indian figures are depressed by low performance in many of the basin states in contrast to Punjab which registered an average yield of 3.2 and 3.5 tonnes per hectare in respect of these two crops with yields in districts like Ludhiana being much higher.

Reporting in 1976, the National Commission on Agriculture (India) said that India would be in a position to produce 130 million tonnes of rice and wheat (as part of an overall grain requirement of 230 million tonnes in 2000) by raising yields to a national average of 2.5 tonnes per hectare for rice and 2.9 tonnes per hectare for wheat. It said this should be done by reducing the acreage under rice by 6 million hectares and that under wheat by 2.55 million hectares while increasing the acreage under other cereals, pulses, oilseeds, sugar cane and beet, fodder, fruit and vegetables. It envisaged an overall expansion of cropped area by 19 million hectares to 200 million hectares by resort to more multiple cropping with irrigation

(NCA, Part III, 1976). The commission recommended diversification of the cropping pattern by optimizing land use on the basis of agro-climatic parameters. The idea quite clearly was not merely to feed the country's growing population but to shift the emphasis from hunger to health by providing a more balanced diet. Other objectives were greater employment through more intensive farming, and provision of greater opportunities for income-generation from subsidiary farm occupations, including agricultural processing and exports, so as to enhance the value added in the countryside and roll back rural poverty (NCA Part VI). A notable exception to the recommended acreage reduction under cereals in the basin states was, however, West Bengal which was seen to have a significant potential for expanding the area under wheat. In Bangladesh too wheat production rose from 450,000 tonnes in 1978-79 to 1.46 million tonnes in 1984-85 and is projected to reach 2.6 million tonnes by1990 (Third Plan, Bangladesh, 1985).

INADEQUATE WATER REGULATION

The problem in the eastern region of India and Bangladesh, however, is inadequate regulation of water resulting in alternating flood and drought conditions. It is by now well established that agricultural instability is greatest in these regions for this very reason in contrast to the semi-humid and semi-arid regions of northwestern India like western Uttar Pradesh, Haryana and Punjab which are able to exercise better moisture control through irrigation systems without being at the mercy of untimely or erratic precipitation. Lower climatic risk induces quicker and more willing responses to technological opportunities resulting in larger yields and a rising ability to make further and more productive investments. It is the difference between a virtuous and a vicious circle, though climatic uncertainty is not the only inhibiting factor.

Over much of eastern India and Assam as well as in Bangladesh, most peasants are marginal farmers cultivating a hectare of land or less, and this too fragmented in up to six or eight tiny parcels. Uttar Pradesh and Haryana excluded, little attention has been paid to consolidation. The land system is iniquitous and semi-feudal, an important structural weakness which will be separately discussed. The handicaps faced by Eastern Uttar Pradesh, Bihar, West Bengal and Orissa and prescriptions for ameliorative action are well documented in *Agricultural Productivity in Eastern India* – the report of an expert committee under Dr S.R. Sen set up by the Reserve Bank of India (1984).

Shigeru Ishikawa, the Japanese economist, has described irrigation as the leading input in East and South Asian farming through successive stages of output stabilization, multiple cropping and adoption of technological opportunities provided by improved seeds and fertilizers. The Sen Committee noted that "adequate and controlled supply of water" was a precondition for intensification of crop production and the prime "accelerator" of agricultural growth. It emphasized extension, access to credit, inputs, price support and marketing facilities as essential policy issues that must be addressed. In 1981 no more than 9.3 million hectares were irrigated in Eastern Uttar Pradesh, Bihar and West Bengal against an irrigation potential of 35 million hectares estimated by the committee. But such is the agricultural condition in the region that whereas Punjab produces over five million tonnes of rice from 1.5 million hectares, Bihar produces barely six million tonnes from 5.4 million hectares.

Farming in the high rainfall eastern India-Bangladesh region is rendered more difficult by luxuriant weed growth and the high incidence of pests and diseases that go with prolonged periods of high humidity. The dry summer is relatively pest free but this is precisely the period when there is little or no irrigation, groundwater extraction being inhibited by limitations of low investment and rural electrification. And then the floods. Come the monsoon and swollen, swirling rivers inundate the countryside. But then they shrink to flow lazily in braided streams along sandy stretches within their outer banks. These *diara* or *char* lands, as they are variously known, are very fertile and are cultivated as the waters recede. Their area has been estimated at 2.4 million hectares in Uttar Pradesh and Bihar alone and could be double or triple that figure were West Bengal, Assam and Bangladesh to be included. These riverbed farms are highly productive but have not received the research, extension, marketing and infrastructural support they deserve.

SPECIAL RICE PRODUCTION PROGRAMME

Following the recommendations of the Sen Committee, the Government of India launched a Special Rice Production Programme in the eastern region. This seeks to deliver a technological package based on irrigation and water management, provision of credit, fertilizer use, pest control and marketing with institutional backing for all of this. Progress has been halting on account of a basically flawed agrarian structure which will take more political will than has been evident so far, outside of West Bengal, to reform. The SRPP was repackaged after the 1987-88 drought in a larger programme to attain an overall national foodgrain target of 175 million tonnes by 1990. Of 169 districts in the country selected for the "thrust programme", 95 are in the basin region and are primarily geared to the production of rice and wheat, and to a lesser extent, of maize, gram and arhar (lentils).

Appropriate varieties of paddy have yet to be evolved for almost a third of the 64 million hectares under this crop in India. In another 9 million hectares of upland, as in the southern plateau regions of Uttar Pradesh and Bihar, the soils have poor water retention capacity and little crop life-saving irrigation is available during periodic breaks in the monsoon. Elsewhere too, rainfed paddy is grown in regions of insufficient rainfall. Yet rice continues to be cultivated in these areas as it is the traditional diet, though it would be far more rewarding to grow maize or some other crop and import rice from other regions for local consumption. This is but one example of faulty cropping patterns which, according to an informed estimate, extends to 36 million hectares of cropland or something approaching a quarter of the total net sown area in India. The flood-prone tracts in the eastern region also need special varieties of rice unless they "grow" fish during the deep-water season or switch to a new crop calendar as is beginning to happen. As the National Agricultural Commission (India) argued, higher yields in the remaining paddy area could more than compensate for diversion of average to other more suitable uses.

One consequence of the sorry state of agrarian relations is a weak cooperative structure where it has not been taken over by vested interests. The credit system is choked. In Assam only Rs 3 crores of cooperative credit is disbursed over the entire state. In Bihar around 40 per cent of the cultivating farmers alone are members of cooperatives. The rest are forced to go to moneylenders who lend at usurious rates of interest that may be as high as 10 per cent per month, sometimes payable in kind at arbitrary prices. Rural indebtedness is crippling.

A special rabi drive was mounted in the wake of the disastrous floods in north Bihar in 1987. Despite a nominal cooperative membership of 5.2 million, there were no more than 1.2 million borrowers in the previous years with loans of the order of Rs 20-30 crores. Under a new dispensation, societies in liquidation or burdened with high overdues were revived and refinance by the National Bank for Agricultural Development (NABARD) which floated a non-overdue cover fund. Farmers were made eligible for loans without reference to land ownership and loans up to Rs 5000 were given without any collateral through land mortgage. Over a million small and marginal farmers were enrolled as new members. Some Rs 161 crores were distributed as cooperative credit during the rabi and it was aimed to distribute Rs 228 crores in kharif 1988 against an assessed credit requirement of Rs 900 crores. While this was a breakthrough in some ways, poor rabi loan recoveries in 1988 was a cause for anxiety signifying a lack of political will or political compromise.

The Special Rice Production Programme (SRPP) resulted in a production of an additional 1.1 million tonnes of rice in 1985-86. But in the absence of an adequate procurement system many farmers had to make distress sales below the support price of Rs 130 per quintal. This situation was aggravated by poor roads and a lack of markets, unlike in western Uttar Pradesh and Haryana where these facilities are now reasonably well developed. The local agricultural marketing federations need strengthen in and the States are being advised to offer a bonus above the procurement price.

Motive power for agriculture is low in eastern India. Whereas it should be two horse-power equivalent per hectare, the actual figure is 0.2 horse power. There is little mechanization and traditional farm implements are inefficient.

Some other problems have however been tackled rather more successfully. As against a fertilizer use of 159 kg per hectare in Punjab, the SRPP region was earlier targeted to use 35 kg/ha. This has now been raised to 55 kg/ha under the "thrust" programme and is being retailed from a larger network of outlets within a radius of five kilometers of any village in smaller and more affordable packs of 10-20 kg which are just right for little holdings. A kilogramme of fertilizer in the eastern region gives an incremental output of up to 11-12 kg with irrigation. With higher fertilization, weeds thrive that much better. Hence weedicides are being made available in small packs at cost price. Incentives are being offered for the production of blast resistant seeds and the sale of zinc sulphate, pyrites and gypsum is being subsidized to make good micronutrient deficiencies normal in high rainfall areas.

The construction of tubewells is being encouraged for irrigation with vertical drainage. Marginal farmers are being provided shallow tubewells free on condition that four or five of them join together to purchase a mobile pump mounted on a trolley. Since power supplies are uncertain in many areas, additional diesel oil is being provided wherever there are large tubewell clusters, and custom-hiring of pumps is picking up. All this should help increase cropping intensity with greater water dependability.

Similar measures would yield dividends in Bangladesh too as the agrarian situation there is not altogether dissimilar. Water regulation in both the flood and dry season is critical. The country's estimated 633,000 tanks have largely silted, but could be restored. Surface irrigation programmes have lagged but tubewell development and river lift schemes have made better progress to sustain a changeover from traditional low-yield aman paddy, susceptible to floods, to winter boro paddy, which has doubled the yield under high-yielding varieties but requires far more irrigation, as well as wheat. The area under irrigation was planned to be expanded by a third to a little under four million hectares between 1985 and 1990 (Third Five Year Plan, Dhaka, 1985). A more optimistic forecast of Bangladesh's agricultural prospects is to be found in a World Bank study in 1972 which concluded that with rapid development of irrigation, drainage and flood control and an expanded acreage under high-yielding varieties, the country should be able to produce as much as 51 million tonnes of rice by 2003 (Boyce, James, 1987). This seems to be the long-term potential.

On account of extensive flooding year after year, farmers in significant areas in eastern Uttar Pradesh, north Bihar, parts of West Bengal and Assam grow low-yield, low-risk varieties that are often broadcast. They too are beginning to switch to boro and summer paddy which is far more productive with assured irrigation and less susceptible to pests and weed infestation. They should be provided suitable aquaculture options such as raising fish or duck with or without flood-resistant paddy varieties, or growing *singhara* or *makhana*. Composite packages will have to be devised and appropriate infrastructure provided.

The central and western parts of the basin are wheat-growing areas and have more control over water. Haryana and western Uttar Pradesh certainly, are doing well. Parts of eastern Rajasthan and northern Madhya Pradesh are also not doing too badly though the plateau areas extending into Uttar Pradesh and Bihar do have problems. The dryland areas have a considerable potential which can be realized with better land,water management to raise improved varieties of pulses, oil seeds and coarse grain and by adopting mixed farming.

ANIMAL HUSBANDRY AND DAIRYING

Animal husbandry, and dairying in particular, has immense possibilities. At present the basin is burdened with vast multitudes of low-grade and nondescript cattle which have put enormous pressure on the forests and shrinking pastures at the cost of better livestock. The region boasts of the best buffaloes in the world and some fine indigenous purebred cattle. On account of the late start in genetic improvement, milk yields are low but have been dramatically improved with crossbreeding with Jerseys, Holsteins and Brown Swiss, standardizing on an exotic blood strain of 50 per cent. These cows require proper feed and health care. Given such management, they can produce double a good buffalo milk yield of 2000 litres. The buffalo feeds on roughage but is a larger animal and has a poorer feed-to-milk conversion ratio. Hence the future of dairying rests on selecting the crossbred cow as the prime milch animal, while continuing efforts to improve local purebreds and buffaloes through selective breeding.

Fortunately, artificial insemination with progeny tested frozen semen is now well developed and under Operation Flood and other programmes an improved national milch herd is growing in numbers. There is the further promise of fast multiplication of selected superior breeds through embryo transfer technology. Normally a cow or buffalo produces a calf every 13 to 18 months. Now, by multiple ovulations and embryo transfer, a superior female donor can produce as many as 25 offsprings a year. The Department of Biotechnology is the nodal agency for this programme in India with the National Dairy Development Board as the lead implementing agency. A donor-recipient herd of over 700 animals was established in 1987-88 and over 600 embryos were collected and some 270 embryo transfers completed in cows and a few in buffaloes. Several pregnancies were confirmed and several calves had already been born (Department of Biotechnology, Delhi, 1988).

Once established, ETT could accelerate herd improvement and milk yields. This will require the development of fodder and feed resources and the diversion of oilcake and concentrate from external to domestic markets. With expanding cereal production, a lot more agricultural residues will become available for cattle. Land is a fixed asset and its distribution is skewed against the rural poor. Animal husbandry creates multiplying assets and is not necessarily land-related. This applies to dairying as much as to improved stall-fed goats, pig rearing, which is popular in tribal areas and in Bhutan, and to poultry. Together these offer great scope for non-crop farm employment and incomes to the rural poor, or as a subsidiary occupation that could add to the people's protein diet.

On one view, India's cooking oil shortage is perhaps best made good by putting more acreage under fodder than oil seeds and converting milk fats in excess of nutritionally desirable levels into butter oil (Johl, S.S., 1988). This would give the farmer a better profit, enable more dung to be returned to the fields as organic manure, and get a better national return on the country's unrequired cattle "wealth". Improved cattle productivity would soon have farmers trading quality for quantity, in reversal of the historic trend in the subcontinent over the past century.

Whatever view one takes of this proposition, the new dairy technology mission aims to organize 150,000 village milk cooperatives in 270 districts, many of them in the basin region. The objective is to increase India's milk production from 44 million tonnes to 61 million tonnes by 1995 which would raise per capita milk availability to 186 gm.

Poultry for egg and broiler production is making good progress and some hatcheries in India have attained international yields. With the upgrading of birds and an increase in maize and other feed supplies, the National Egg Coordination Committee, India, believes it is possible to enhance egg output to 180,000 million per annum so as to achieve a supply of 180 eggs per annum per capita by 2015 as against 18 eggs per annum today. This is the target it has set for itself. The employment and nutrition value of such a programme would be very considerable and could be widely adopted as a subsidiary rural and urban occupation by many (NECC, 1987). Duck farming too has a substantial potential, especially in the wetlands of West Bengal, Bihar and Assam, and certainly in Bangladesh.

MONSOON MANAGEMENT TO CROP DIVERSIFICATION

That northwest India has been fairly well drought-proofed was amply evident in 1987-88 when surface irrigation backed by storages and groundwater pumping enabled Punjab, Haryana and western Uttar Pradesh to produce a near-normal kharif crop and a good rabi harvest despite a calamitous failure of the rains in the early and mid-monsoon. Heavy groundwater pumping was criticized by some as mining water and risking a huge recession in groundwater levels. While groundwater extraction should definitely not exceed the recharge rate, the water balance should properly be seen over an appropriate cycle, say of five years of good and bad rainfall. This would then safely permit a larger than usual drawdown in a year of severe hydrological drought in the reasonable expectation that the over-draft will be made good over the succeeding years.

However, good monsoon management requires a more finely tuned agro-met service linked to improved medium-to-long range micro-weather forecasting and crop-weather extension services based on alternative cropping packages with support services. This would enable the farmer to cut his losses in a bad year and maximize his gains in a good one. It will take time to develop such sophistication.

But it will not be achieved without a more focused, multi-layered research effect and according a higher priority to a hard-pressed agro-meteorological system.

The paddy-wheat cycle in northwestern India has helped fill the nation's granary. It is profitable but is becoming increasingly high cost with ever-rising support prices which sometimes discriminate against other crops. For both long-term agronomic and environmental reasons this needs to be modified in favour of a more diversified farm package including dairying, animal husbandry, fodder cropping, vegetable gardening, horticulture, oil seeds, pulses and sugar cane along with agro-processing. There has always been a historical trend towards the cultivation of "superior" crops, the demand for which grows with rising prosperity. The success of the special rice production programme in eastern India over the next few years should pave the way for a significant change in cropping patterns, initially in northwestern India and on the lines indicated without prejudice to the national interest. Indeed, a reduction in the area under paddy, a water-intensive crop, will enable light and protective irrigation to be extended over a larger area to support the proposed diversified cropping pattern. Such irrigation, by reducing uncertainty, will make it possible to risk higher inputs in pulses, oil seeds and other crops and thereby enhance their profitability. The farmer is not so mindful of the price he gets for a single crop as much as his net return. And he will be more sensitive to his overall return through multi-cropping the year round than to his return in a single season (Dantwala M.L., 1986).

PROMISE OF BIOTECHNOLOGY

Cost-reduction, soil health and better husbandry would all be achieved by backing away from mono-cultures, which induce pathogens and disease, and by going in for a wider spectrum of crops and rotations that would include green manures and legumes that fertilise the soil. Avoidance of excessive dependence on chemical fertilizers and pesticides would also be desirable in itself apart from reducing some of the current heavy fertilizer subsidy.

A cereal production of about 150 million tonnes in India removes some 14 million tonnes of nitrogenous, phosphatic and potash nutrients from the soil. Nearly 9 million tonnes of fertilizer was targeted to be used in 1987-88. Yet faster than the plant's absorptive capacity and there are other losses on account of leaching and volatilization. Denitrification can be retarded by the application of neem cake powder. But this is only being done on a limited scale. As a result, the soil is depleted of plant nutrients.

The alternative is to sustain and augment microbial activity in the soil. Biotechnology now offers increasing possibilities of using bacteria to fix nitrogen by symbiosis through rhizobial or leguminous species or through azotobacters which are free-living microorganisms. Blue-green algae and azolla are also free-living microorganisms which thrive if submerged in water and are, therefore, suited to paddy. Blue-green algae multiplies very rapidly and 10 kg applied to a hectare of paddy will produce two to three times as much nitrogen. There are other phosphorus-solubilising bacteria which make phosphates more assimilable and hence improve their intake. New microorganisms producing stem or aerial nodules that fix nitrogen have been identified. Treated with these, sesbania (of the hemp family) gives as much as 50 to 60 kg of nitrogen if ploughed into the soil with the succeeding crop.

Likewise, pesticides – apart from being expensive, some of these pass on residual effects down the food chain through plant uptake and leaching to groundwater or streamflows. Although certain more toxic varieties have been replaced by others that are as effective. Biocontrol of pests is now becoming increasingly possible and offers a better alternative. Pests of pests or scavenging predators can be released. Sterile males can be introduced to dislocate the reproductive cycle of certain pests. Chromosome translocation can cause malfunctioning of gametes or the reproductive cell. And plant genes lethal to the pest have been successfully introduced in the case of cotton and tobacco. All these biocontrol measures can be made part of integrated pest control systems calculated to retard the build-up of pathogens along with appropriate agricultural practices. Thus, proper weeding will control pests that find a host in weeds.

The use of biofertilisers and integrated pest control measures can quite clearly reduce costs on chemical fertilizers and pesticides with an ecological benefit as well. Indeed, algae can also be used as a protein food and animal feed and as a fuel in bio-gas plants. Blue-green algal collections have been made in various agro-climatic regions and an Indian algal map is under preparation as an aid to selection, propagation and extension. A microbial type culture collection and gene bank is also being built up. Work is in progress on developing genotypes which are tolerant of salt or adverse moisture or temperature conditions. This has been done for rice and wheat and is being extended to forest species. Once fast-growing genotypes of trees like teak or eucalyptus or bamboo are identified and isolated, they can be propagated by tissue culture. New avenues are opening up. Experiments in natural farming in different agro-climatic conditions would also be worth undertaking on the lines pioneered by Masanobu Fukuoka in Japan.

Poor water management and, particularly, inadequate drainage in irrigated tracts has resulted in waterlogging, salinity and alkalinity. The Central Soil Salinity Research Institute, Karnal, estimates that some 7 million hectares of otherwise productive land have gone out of cultivation, almost half of this in the semi-arid and semi-humid Indo-Gangetic plains, including Haryana, and in coastal and deltaic West Bengal. The Ramganga, Sharda Sahayak and Gandak irrigation commands have been affected in Uttar Pradesh and the Chambal command in Rajasthan and Madhya Pradesh. These "usar" lands can be reclaimed through improved drainage and by amending the soil with the application of gypsum. Biomass such as water hyacinth and weeds and green manures have been successfully used and algal trials are under way. Given a modest annual yield of three tonnes per hectare, the salt-affected region within the Indian Ganga Basin could itself produce about 10 million tonnes of additional crop.

FARM MODERNISATION WITH AGRO-CLIMATIC ZONING

Sugar cane is an important commercial crop, though again water-intensive. The Rajendra Agricultural University in Pusa, North Bihar, has developed early, middle and late maturing cane varieties that would give higher yields and extend the crushing period to 120-180 days. Some of these varieties can also be profitably intercropped with potatoes, garlic, lentils, maize and vegetables. Much of the cane grown in Uttar Pradesh and Bihar has a higher bagasse content than that in peninsular India. This is now fed into sugar factory boilers as an inefficient wet fuel. Were alternative supplies of low grade coal, agro-waste briquettes or electricity made available, a good deal of the bagasse could be pulped to sustain a number of paper and newsprint plants in the region as once envisaged when the Indian Paper and Pulp Corporation was conceived in the mid-1960s. Many of the eastern Uttar Pradesh and Bihar sugar mills are old and of uneconomic size and are urgently in need of modernization or replacement. The possibility of growing sugar beet is also emerging in a number of regions, the Sunderbans for one, and this too could help extend the now-limited cane-crushing season and improve the economics of sugar factories with plant modifications to accept the beet. These options are worth exploring and constitute part of the new opportunities for agro-processing, by-product utilization and off-farm employment that are opening up in a large number of sectors, not excluding traditional rice and flour milling.

In many areas, especially around cities, vegetable gardening, already a thriving business, could be greatly expanded. This is typically suited to small and marginal farmers or even to those with no more than homestead plots but with some irrigation facility. Sewage farming around cities was advocated by the National Commission on Agriculture (India), while the Sen Committee saw relay vegetable cropping with sound water management as an excellent possibility in eastern India, as it could be in Bangladesh, with due attention to input supplies, credit, development of improved garden tools, marketing, and cold storage. Vegetable producer cooperatives could be networked into the new National Dairy Development Board vegetable and fruit marketing outlets programmed in major Indian cities. Under the tribal sub-plan in Chota Nagpur, Bihar, farmers are being persuaded to give up largely rainfed broadcast paddy for irrigated farming of pulses, groundnut and vegetables around clusters of water harvesting tanks. These are being built on a subsidized basis, with pumps, within micro-watersheds through collective labour. In another experiment, an apex vegetable growers cooperative society has been formed with cold storage to eliminate the middleman and serve a growing market in the coal-steel belt.

When overall agricultural production was acutely short of national requirements, regional and even local food self-sufficiency was a compulsive tendency in the interests of food security. This is less pervasive but still persists and is the cause of much inappropriate land use and crop planning to the detriment the individual farmer as well as the nation. It has now been decided more consciously to change this situation. India has been delineated into 15 broad agro-climatic zones, as distinct from the 35 regions under which rainfall and other meteorological data are classified. Soil type, climate and water resources are among the parameters taken into account. Appropriate cropping patterns are being evolved for each of these 15 zones together with other activities relating to forests, animal husbandry, fisheries and relevant infrastructure such as storage and processing facilities (Planning Commission, Delhi 1988). Eight of the 15 agro-climatic zones fall within the basin area. These are the west Himalayan region, the eastern Himalayan region, the lower Gangetic plain, the middle Gangetic plain, the upper Gangetic plain, the trans-Gangetic plain, the eastern plateau and hills, and the central plateau and hills. Though this effort might appear obvious or redundant to some, it will make for a more scientific basis for Indian agriculture as it moves from deficit to surplus, from subsistence to commercial farming, from hunger to health, and from a narrowly self-sufficient, high cost, subsidized system to a more competitive and international-market oriented one. India must be able to exploit the many and growing opportunities for exporting grain, vegetables, fruit, milk products, meat and flowers, and processed foods, apart from traditional goods such as jute and cotton textiles, tea and spices.

The modernization of agriculture with irrigation, fertilizers and improved seeds responsive to a variety of agro-climatic situations has freed it from absolute dependence on the monsoon-weather cycle. Yet even today much of the farming practices in the basin are traditional. This includes the crop calendar which awaits the onset of the monsoon for sowing. This is not the most efficient cycle to follow and an earlier and more timely sowing of crops, or transplantation of seedlings raised in nurseries, could avoid or mitigate the effects of floods, pests and diseases brought on by humidity, cloud cover temperature, wind, hail and the rest. Many crop varieties widely grown preclude any or a more productive second or third crop, and are low-yielders besides. Advancing the crop calendar by manipulating sowing and harvest dates, and inter-cropping can not only increase overall yields and productivity, but farm incomes and agricultural employment. There is considerable scope for such innovation throughout the basin based on careful studies on optimal crop calendars for different agro-climatic regions and cropping patterns

All this calls for better "conjunctive use" of irrigation with rainfall in order to fill in critical breaks or make good modest but vital shortfalls in precipitation. More than that, it needs requisite research backing as well as a new approach to extension. The training-and-visit system of extension through progressive contact farmers is widespread in the basin. This focuses on individuals whereas there is also need to catalyze group action at the village or micro-watershed level. There are many useful improvements a single farmer cannot realize without community consent and group effort (Swaminathan, M.S. 1988). Decentralized planning and development administration through the *thana* as in Bangladesh, the panchayats in Nepal, and panchayati raj institutions in India, are steps in the right direction. This alone can ensure genuine people's participation and meaningful responses to local needs and circumstances.

SHIFTING CULTIVATION

The foregoing discussion has centred mainly on farming in the plains and plateau regions in the basin. Hill farming poses different problems and holds out other opportunities which need consideration. Nearly 40 million people live in the Himalayan zone including the horseshoe around the Assam Valley and the Chittagong Hill Tract in Bangladesh.

Early settlers in the basin were, like Neolithic man everywhere, primitive farmers, hunters and gatherers. In time communities graduated to slash-and-burn (*jhum*) shifting cultivation before moving on to settled cultivation in the valleys and plains, on terraced fields and with irrigation. It speaks of the level of development still obtaining over considerable areas that *jhumming* continues to be practiced in most of Northeast India and Chittagong Hill Tract, as well as in parts of eastern Bhutan and eastern Nepal. Some 492,000 tribal families are estimated to *jhum* 2.69 million hectares in Arunachal, Nagaland, Manipur, Mizoram, Tripura, Meghalaya and the Assam Hills with about 455,000 hectares under cultivation at any one time (ICAR Shillong, 1983). The number of tribal *jhum* families in the Chittagong Hill Tract was estimated at 350,000 some years ago.

In a bygone age when populations were much smaller and little land had been taken out for "development", the *jhumming* cycle would extend to 20 to 30 years, even more, giving the forest sufficient time to regenerate. The practice was also compatible with community land ownership which still prevails. Today, the *jhum* cycle has been reduced to three to six years and even less in some pockets. This has prevented regeneration except to a limited degree, leading to regression at every further round with early colonizing weeds, shrubs and inferior species taking over or baring the ridges to the fury of torrential rains. There was some merit in the earlier system as the ash fertilized the soil while the pattern of mixed cropping followed by movement to a new site kept away pests and minimized risk. Yields were not high but were sufficient for the community. Today it is estimated that 19 million tonnes of soil is eroded annually in the Northeast causing alarming nutrient losses. *Jhumming* destroys edible vegetables, roots and fruit; causing grave harm to domesticated animals and wild life, and resulting in the loss of valuable genetic resources and rare orchids. Yields vary, being low on steeper slopes but more in the lower slopes to which soil nutrients from the higher reaches wash down.

The tools employed in *jhumming* are of an elementary kind, and the labour expended after the initial operations and sowing is minimal. Weeding is not rigorous. But it is said that weeds reduce erosion and protect the soil from intense radiation, are recycled as organic manure and are, in some cases, eaten. There are two options available in dealing with *jhumming* which in its present form can no longer be regarded as an acceptable "way of life". It can either be ended, or improved, using a variety of combinations to fit local circumstances. The ICAR has after considerable study recommended a three-tier farming system with the upper ridges under forest or trees, the middle slopes under horticulture and pasture, and the lower portion under crops and fodder with terracing and irrigation leading to intensive multiple cropping along valley floors. Subsidiary occupations such as piggeries and poultry are also envisaged. This would be ecologically sound and economically viable (ICAR, Shillong, 1983).

Others admit that while this model appears scientifically sound, it is divorced from the social organization of tribal society and may not be immediately acceptable (Ramakrishnan, P.S. 1984). The alternative suggested is that the *jhum* cycle be sought to be extended to a minimum of 10 years which would make for an ecologically viable system. This could be done by developing valley cultivation and diverting the land saved from *jhum* to cooperatively owned horticultural plantations and fuelwood forests for community use. Simultaneously, innovations could be introduced in *jhum* by adopting superior varieties, using manures and fertilizers, timely sowing, introducing better farm implements and planting legumes in *jhum* fallows which would also need to be better managed.

Indeed some traditional farm practices in the Northeast show great sophistication. Excellent terracing in parts of Nagaland and Manipur, the meticulous management of valley lands with irrigation and farm forestry in the Apa Tani Valley in Arunachal, and an intricate bamboo drip irrigation system for betel leaf planted with arecanut along hills slopes in the Jaintia Hills of Meghalaya are examples (ICAR, Shillong, 1981).

The North Eastern Council in Shillong plans to resettle 16,500 *jhumia* families in the seven northeastern units during the period 1987-92. land use and soil surveys have been undertaken using satellite imagery on the basis of which watershed management projects have been prepared. An area of two hectares is being allotted per family in clusters of 25 families, with a hectare each under agriculture and horticulture. The investment cost is estimated at Rs 30,000 per family over five years plus another Rs 20,000 to provide education, health facilities and other social overheads in each cluster. Credit, progeny planting material, extension services and marketing support are being provided. Rubber, tea, coffee, cardamom, ginger, aromatic grasses, and tropical as well as temperate fruit, depending on elevation and aspect, are in various stages of introduction and development with plans for agroprocessing facilities to match. Off-season vegetables and potato and cauliflower seed cultivation is catching on. Manpower shortages are inhibiting the pace of change. The remoteness of this "landlocked" region, inaccessibility – with 30 out of 101 of Arunachal's administrative circles still maintained by air supply – a yet tiny regional market, and expensive transport leads to the Indian heartland up-hill and down-dale and through the distant Siliguri corridor, are handicaps, despite a transport subsidy. But once the transformation gets underway, success will propel change to tap the enormous potential of what is one of the most resource-rich regions in India.

HUMAN EROSION: HILL TO TERAI

The position in the Himalayan region proper, in Nepal and Garhwal and Kumaon in Uttar Pradesh is different. Here, the mounting pressure of population superimposed on past land policies encouraged indiscriminate conversion of forests to farmland on revenue and political considerations. The accompanying multiplication of livestock accelerated environmental degradation. Aggravated by more recent road-building, mining and other activities undertaken without due care, erosion has greatly increased and the loss of soil has resulted in a steady decline in agricultural productivity in the once fertile and still most heavily populated middle-Himalayan belt. To the traditional migration of able-bodied men to the armed forces has been added another and larger dimension of distress migration. The eradication of malaria in the Nepal and Indian Terai in the early fifties followed by massive jungle clearance in this tract. Swamps were drained and a steady stream of migrants settled in new farmlands. This provided respite for a while and certainly augmented food production and employment, but with damaging consequences for the Hills. In any event, this check dam is about to burst and unless remedial measures are taken, both Hills and Terai will be in greater crisis.

The Nepalese Terai, accounting for 23 per cent of the land and some 42 per cent of the population, produces about 80 per cent of the national output of rice and over 60 per cent of the wheat. Yields in the Hills have been declining in the case of rice and maize and have been stagnant for wheat. Overall, Nepal's food surplus has disappeared and the country has become a net importer. In the hills, "the food crisis is now so frequent that it has almost become an annual feature and the food deficit districts have been increasing in number" (Seventh Plan, Kathmandu, 1985).

A number of "push factors" are contributing to outmigration from the hills; low agricultural productivity, population pressure, a declining man-land farm ratio, natural calamities and limited alternative economic opportunities. The "push" carries people to the Terai (and beyond to India where "pull" factors operate). These are the availability of land, a food surplus, resettlement programmes and opportunities for forest encroachment. Urbanization and higher development investments make for a growing economic and social infrastructure and industrialization and hence greater opportunities for non-farm employment (Internal and International Migration in

Nepal, 1983). The consequences of such migration have been two-fold. It has aggravated deforestation in the Terai. In the hills out-migration has caused a shortage of agricultural labour leading to less intensive farming, poor land management (such as maintenance of terraces) and falling productivity (Ibid) as in Garhwal and Kumaon, the departure of the men has left the hills to the women whose burdens have increased enormously with environmental degradation adding to their labour in gathering fuel and fodder and fetching water, in addition to farming. This has in turn affected the health and strength of the women and diverted their creative energies to drudgery. The cost of this human "erosion" is incalculable.

It has been estimated that some 686,178 persons migrated from the Nepalese hills and mountains to the Terai between 1971 to 1981 (Central Bureau of Statistics, Kathmandu). At the same time the farmed area in the hills increased from 479,000 hectares in 1962 to nearly 1.28 million hectares in 1985 (Land Resources Mapping Project, Kathmandu, 1985).

Holdings are small, the overwhelming number being well below one hectare, and are parceled out and scattered in as many as five or eight fragments. This impedes terracing, maintenance and improvement, irrigation and drainage. Ecologically, steeper slopes beyond 30-40 degrees should be under trees rather than crops. But such is the pressure on land that these slopes are cultivated. Rainfed terraces are outward sloping and, unless carefully maintained and improved, deteriorate with erosion and are abandoned in due course. Irrigated slopes, especially nearer the valley floor, are however level or inward sloping. Beautifully engineered terraces rising in flights of up to 500 steps can be counted in certain parts of Nepal and Kumaon-Garhwal. Bench terracing is a very patient, labour-intensive process and expensive both in terms of construction and maintenance of the stone risers. There is no firm estimate of abandoned terraces but terraced lands left "fallow" for some years may well be assumed to be as good as abandoned.

THREE-TIER MOUNTAIN FARMING

There is a further problem. Hill farming has hitherto been largely sustained by organic manuring. It is principally for this purpose that cattle are kept. In addition to dung, leaf manure and litter from the forest provide valuable plant nutrients and animal bedding. The forests also supply fuel and fodder. The total leafy biomass taken from the forest requires 1.33 hectares of forest land, including forest shrubs and grass, to sustain one hectare of agricultural land (Applegate and Gilmour, 1987). With the extension of hill cultivation on marginal lands with low productivity at the cost of forests, a vicious circle sets in. Newer lands are brought into cultivation, more cattle are kept to provide organic manure, and the forests and available pastures are overgrazed causing forest degradation. The receding forest inevitably leads to replacement of fire-wood by dung at the margin, making further inroads into farm productivity and resulting in another twist to the vicious cycle. The depredations of multiplying livestock is very considerable. More and more impoverished hill people migrate to the plains and have brought the Terai under ecological stress.

The answer lies in a radically different land-use and cropping pattern in the hills and giving full recognition to the supremely important forest-farm relationship so often ignored, even if involuntarily, in mountain farming. Here too, a three-tier farming system is better suited to the agro-climatic conditions prevailing in the hills. This would place the upper slopes under forest, and middle slopes under pasture and tree crops (horticulture and fodder trees), and leave the lower slopes and valley floors to be cultivated under varying systems of irrigated terraced farming. The hills can also support dairying in selected areas with improved breeds of stall-fed animals.

As argued earlier, with the possibility of considerably improved and productive agriculture there is no reason for every region and valley to aim at food self-sufficiency. Hill and plain constitute a single interactive system and they must be seen as such. The fertile Gangetic plain and Terai, watered by Himalayan snowmelt and irrigated from Himalayan storages, should feed the hills. This does not imply a dependency relationship even if different sovereignties are involved. The restoration of forest cover in the hills can only be to their mutual benefit while their horticultural and vegetable produce, off-season or for seed, will find a ready market in the plains or internationally. Himalayan storages too will produce abundant energy for groundwater lift and industry in the plains and provide a most valuable and inexhaustible export for Nepal as much as for the Indian hills.

HIMACHAL SHOWS THE WAY

The agricultural potential inherent in refashioning land-use and cropping patterns in this direction can be seen in the emerging model of hill farming in Himachal Pradesh. This State has found a path to prosperity in horticulture and vegetable farming. However, it has to go a long way before it can claim to have a truly well-adjusted three tier system with high productivity.

Though apple orchards were started in the Manali region in the last century and "English" vegetables were cultivated around Simla for British residents, it is only over the past two decades that Himachal has moved towards becoming the fruit and vegetable bowl of India. Today 25 per cent of its 600,000 hectare sown area is under fruit and vegetable (about 10 per cent in Nepal) and this is growing. Fruit production totaled 341,000 tonnes in 1985-86, despite considerable hail and gale damage. The production of fresh vegetables that year was about 312,000 tonnes and that of potatoes 112,000 tonnes. Ginger production is fast growing and some new crops like hops, mushroom, olives, walnut, almonds and pistachio nuts are being encouraged. Himachal's agricultural university has been especially designated to specialize in forestry and horticulture. Some 200,000 small and marginal farmers are engaged in vegetable cultivation. Research extension, input, irrigation, storage, marketing and processing support is being developed to back the new thrust (Agricultural Research Development in Himachal Pradesh, 1986).

Like all other Himalayan regions, Himachal has two advantages. Agro-climatic conditions in the mid-hills are well adapted to the production of off-season vegetables. Winter vegetables in the plains can be produced in the hills in summer. This complementarity offers tremendous market opportunities. Furthermore, in the higher mountain altitudes, the alpine regions are free of pests and can produce virus-free potato and vegetable seeds which fetch premium prices and are in great demand all over the plains and have an export market as well. The cold, dry Lahaul-Spiti Valley and Kinnaur district, bordering Tibet, have turned to high value, low bulk vegetable and potato seed production and remain competitive despite long transport leads.

Fruit yields are still but 25 per cent of the best international standards. This indicates the leeway that must be made up and the large potential that awaits exploitation. Apple scab and other diseases have to be overcome. Green manuring with white clover is being popularized and more than 3.5 million tonnes of compost is being used. Potato production would get an impetus given price support. Cold storages and refrigerated transport have to keep pace with production. Meanwhile, "cool storages" for potatoes have proved efficacious and economical in prolonging their shelf life. Middlemen still skim the cream though fruit and vegetable storage, transport, marketing and processing are eminently suited to cooperative organisation. Hydrams have been tried in some areas and suggest an inexpensive means of lifting water, provided little storages are constructed to hold it for gravity irrigation. Existing check dams and water harvesting structures could also be replenished by hydram lift wherever conditions permit. The rather cumbersome cylindrical water turbine is being replaced by perpendicular water turbines to operate threshers, maize cob shellers and grain mills. Floriculture holds out good prospects and merino sheep and crossbred cattle are gaining popularity. These improved animals are being stall-fed and scrub animals are being castrated.

Himachal, however, has an animal population of five million head and the grazing incidence is estimated to be two to three times the bearing capacity of available grazing land. What has caused the greatest damage to the State's forests has been the ever-growing demand for wooden crates in which to pack applies and other stone fruit. Some 200,000 cubic metres of standing forest is converted into crate wood every year. A government subsidy on fruit boxes, which are not recycled, fuelled demand. Pressed pine needle board has not proved satisfactory but corrugated cardboard crates modeled on egg trays have been introduced and plastic boxes are also being tried in a bid to eliminate the use of wooden cases.

BHUTAN AND TIBET

Horticulture, vegetable farming and potato cultivation is catching on in Garhwal and Kumaon as well as in the North Bengal Darjeeling hills and in Sikkim. Bhutan and Nepal are also doing what they can in this direction and production is bound to grow with the development of a marketing and transport infrastructure in the mid-hills and remoter valleys.

Bhutan is at an earlier stage of agricultural modernization. *Tseri* or *jhum* cultivation was extensive in the eastern part of the country but is now officially banned though it will take time to eliminate in practice. A satellite land-use survey is nearing completion. About 64 per cent of the land is presently under forest and it is planned to maintain this level and not to permit it to fall below 60 per cent in any event. The government would like to limit cereal production in lands with a slope of less than 35 per cent to the extent possible and put the higher slopes under agro-horticultural or agro-silvicultural systems. Terracing is subsidized. The real problem, however, is a shortage of manpower which is going to preclude more intensive farming or forest management or innovation such as the introduction of rubber which would thrive in the south there are political sensitivities about labour migration to the mid-hills and, certainly the import of foreign labour. Mechanisation can help up to a point. But unless labour policy is revised, with whatever safeguards maybe appropriate, Bhutan may find that it has to forego many favourable options. The Indian northeast faces a similar dilemma about "outside" labour.the agricultural situation in Tibet underwent drastic change after 1951 with land reforms. Mutual aid teams were formed and these gave way to communes which were disbanded under the Deng Xiaoping reforms with the introduction of the responsibility system. However, the Chinese claim that Tibet's grain output has increased with reclamation, terracing and irrigation and that yields have doubled. Livestock farming has registered progress and horticulture has made headway.

The Tibet Agricultural Scientific Research Institute is said to have successfully introduced winter wheat at altitudes up to 4300 metres, in addition to traditional barley and pea. The acreage under winter wheat is said to have touched 600,000 mu (one mu is one-fifteenth of a hectare) in 1975, much of this along the Tsangpo river. But the yields of 200 to 700 kg per mu mentioned in "Tibet Leaps Forward" (Beijing, 1977) lack credibility and would appear to be propagandist. Other crops said to have been introduced, include rice (which grows at 2800 metres in Nepal's Jumla valley), sugar beet, tea and tobacco. In Tsayul county in southeastern Tibet, Tenpa tribesmen are said to have been weaned away from *jhum* cultivation and settled on valley floors.

Overall, agriculture within the basin, though stagnant latterly, has a large unexploited genetic and irrigation potential. The new technology has yet to spread outside the irrigated areas and water regulation in the flood-prone eastern region remains a serious problem. New technological opportunities are opening up and diversification could give a further stimulus to agricultural production, especially in the more advanced areas. With a regional food surplus, now underpinned by a modest SAARC food security system, it should be possible to reorganize hill farming on more productive and ecologically sound lines. The new technologies are neutral to scale and small and marginal farmers can be enabled to rise above the poverty line. Over large areas, however, agrarian relations constitute a major constraint. It is to this that we now turn.

CHAPTER 4

Agrarian Reform and Rural Mobilisation

Land has traditionally symbolized status and security. It still does in backward societies emerging out of feudalism. Agriculture is the principal provider throughout the Ganga-Brahmaputra-Barak Basin. It makes the biggest contribution to the GNP and is the largest employer of any. Between 80 and 90 per cent of the population within the basin lives in the countryside though rural migrants are increasingly being driven out by landlessness and penury to inadvertent cities as Malthusian refugees. The size of agricultural holdings has been continuously shrinking and vast millions barely survive below the poverty line. Agrarian prosperity has indeed grown. Yet indebtedness and bondage are widespread, and conditions bordering on slavery have not altogether disappeared in pockets, as in Bihar, despite all manner of obfuscating nomenclatures and subtle definitions. In industrializing India, agriculture remains the largest industry. Where and when it does not thrive, demand declines, causing industrial distress and stagnation.

Much of eastern Uttar Pradesh, Bihar, West Bengal, Bangladesh and a part of western Assam were brought under Cornwallis's permanent settlement which Daniel Thorner aptly described as a "depressor". The Bakasht movement in Bihar and Tebhaga movement in Bengal in 1946 provided early warnings of peasant unrest. The Indian National Congress had placed land to the tiller at the centre of agrarian reform and in the early years of Indian Independence held out the ideal of a cooperative commonwealth. There was a psychological moment when a thoroughgoing agrarian reform including land redistribution could have been carried out. The Government fumbled, then moved hesitantly, and the opportunity was lost. Jammu and Kashmir alone carried through a swift, neat and effective land redistribution programme in 1951 under Sheikh Abdullah.

ZAMINDARI ABOLITION

The area under zamindari and other statutory intermediary titles such as *talukdari*, *mahalwari*, *jagirdari* and *inams*, extended to 57 per cent of all privately owned land in British India in 1948, and more if the princely states were included. Legislation abolishing these intermediaries was enacted by Uttar Pradesh, Bihar,

West Bengal and other states between 1950 and 1960. Litigation followed and the Constitution was amended to protect all such enactments against legal challenge by placing them in Schedule 9, though it was not until 1979 that the Parliament repealed the fundamental right to property which is today no more than an ordinary legal right.

The zamindari abolition laws can be faulted for treating a whole hierarchy of parasitic rentiers as land owners It exempted their "khudkasht", "khas", and "sir" estates, or so-called self-cultivated lands from tenancy reform, the exempted area being 2.88 million hectares in Uttar Pradesh alone. In this state, bigger zamindars who were assessed to more than Rs 250 as revenue held 58 per cent of the total land. On the eve of Independence, the rental demand of all zamindars in Uttar Pradesh was Rs 17.53 crores whereas the land revenue they paid the government was no more than Rs 6.82 crores. It was this class of intermediaries that zamindari abolition generously compensated to the extent of Rs 670 crores countrywide, partly in cash and partly in bonds. Interest and maturity payments on zamindari bonds are still being made today (NA Part XV, 1976). The annual interest payment is Rs 40 lakhs in Bihar.

Tenancy laws followed, and ceilings legislation came in the sixties. Once the intention was known, and with due allowance for self-cultivation and a standing right to resume lands at any time for "personal cultivation", which could be done through hired servants and even in absentia, evictions and "voluntary" surrenders through violence, intimidation and fraud became the order of the day. The records were falsified through benami transactions. Over large areas land records, previously maintained by the zamindars, were found to be inaccurate and incomplete, the last settlement operations recorded being decades old. Zamindari is dead; long live the zamindar, the peasant might have exclaimed. The whole approach to reform kept anachronistic feudal institutions alive. With crores in compensation to jingle in their pockets, the social and economic influence the zamindars traditionally wielded did not stand "abolished". In the process of eviction and resumption, the landlords kept the best lands or those that the peasants had most diligently reclaimed. Many, being non-cultivating castes or classes and too genteel to touch a plough, fell back on share-cropping which took on the form of oral leases on shifting plots so as to prevent continuous occupancy over a period legitimizing a claim to tenurial security. Share-croppers were not recognized as tenants and consequently denied access to cooperative credit. The landlord doubled as moneylender, binding the peasant to a pitiable wage, often in kind, and extortionate interest, thereby condemning him and his family to serfdom for generations. Even deities were officially regarded as minors and so recorded, entitling landowners to hold their lands in trust. Lands might even be recorded in the names of the cows and buffaloes of unscrupulous landlords willing to bend the law.

INADEQUATE TENANCY LAWS

Admittedly some 20 million farmers were brought into direct relationship with the state with the abolition of various classes of intermediaries. But in the basin region of India, and especially in the permanently settled areas, land reform for the actual tiller was a case of darkness at noon with the ex-zamindar reincarnated as a preference shareholder in the land. Many irrigation and drainage works, embankments and tanks that the zamindar or landlord would maintain, even if by forced labour, went into disuse for lack of maintenance following zamindari abolition. The existing rural infrastructure deteriorated as a consequence and new social institutions did not arise in many areas so completely had the peasantry been ground down. Thus the seeds of the cooperative and community development movements fell on inhospitable soil.

The tenancy and ceiling laws as enacted had obvious loopholes and were grudgingly implemented in leisurely stages. Bhoodan, Vinoba Bhave's land gift movement, created a moral climate and a distributable pool of land. But this again was dissipated by the unresponsiveness of the official machinery and the inability of the Gandhians to conceive an alternative strategy and organize themselves or the potential beneficiaries to implement this, except latterly in some small degree through sarva seva farms. In Bihar, fresh settlement operations were inordinately delayed by vested interests and were no sooner completed in a few districts when drowned in litigation. As the National Agriculture Commission laments, the laws were defective, political will was lacking, officials were not trained, records of rights were not updated, and the beneficiaries were not involved in any manner. While the programme was starved of funds, smaller intermediaries in Uttar Pradesh and some other states were entitled to rehabilitation grants in addition to compensation.

In the tribal areas legislation bars land alienation. But this has been widely circumvented and forest and other lands have been invaded. Meanwhile, the common property resources of the rural community such as pastures and grazing land, tanks, forests, woodlots and culturable wastes have been encroached upon or developed or distributed to the landless, thus adding to the burdens of the poor.

Minimum wages were legislated in 1948 and have been revised periodically. These have been widely evaded with little redress for the labourers. Indeed in Bihar it was argued that zealous enforcement of minimum wages could aggravate rural tensions. Homestead plots have been allotted from time to time to eligible categories. Here again implementation has sometimes been patchy and evictions have taken place.

Earlier rounds of zamindari abolition and tenancy reform, despite drawbacks, had created a class of small landlords or secure tenants. These middle castes, taking advantage of the fruits of development and newer opportunities, gained economic ascendancy in the rural areas which was soon translated into political power which they began to assert in defence and advancement of their interests. On the other hand, pressures of population and the backlash of agrarian legislation imperfectly implemented, had resulted in eviction and oppression of lower-order tenants, sharecroppers and agricultural labourers. Even as the ever-growing pressure of population on the land caused the size of holdings to shrink the new technology, neutral to scale, irrigation and the opening up of communications resulted in an appreciation in land prices, adding to the power and influence of this class of landowners and engendering speculative land transactions.

NAXALBARI REVOLT SPURS REFORMIST DEMANDS

In 1969 the peasants rose in Naxalbari, a relatively small paddy-jute area fringed with tea gardens in the narrow Siliguri corridor between Nepal and Bangladesh in north Bengal. The community, numbering some 150,000, comprised a substantial element of tribal sharecroppers or *adhiars*. A nominal 50 : 50 split in the crop share was eroded by deductions in favour of the *jotedar* or landlord as weighment charges, cost of inputs if provided, repayment of consumption loans with interest, "contributions" towards construction of grain *golas* or storages, and maintenance of the *jotedar's* stable, if any. In addition, the *adhiar* was bound to provide the *jotedar beggar* or free labour for a variety of purposes. The peasants were organized by the Communist Party of India (Marxist-Leninist). In the tradition of the earlier Tebhaga agitation they demanded the ending of landlordism, land to the tiller, stoppage of evictions, and a reduction in the 25 per cent interest charged on borrowed paddy. There was forcible harvesting and seizure of crops; people's courts were set up, and a "liberated area" was proclaimed under a parallel government (Mukherji, Partha, 1978). The West Bengal government responded with police measures and the institution of a sub-divisional land reforms committee to redress the grievances of the *adhiars* as police gained control of the rural situation, the Naxal movement moved into urban areas.

The authorities were jolted. The Ministry of Home Affairs in Delhi brought out a monograph in 1969 on *The Causes and Nature of Current Agrarian Tensions*. It noted that 82 per cent of the farmers in Assam, West Bengal, Bihar and Punjab were tenants-at-will or subject to the landlords' right of resumption. It found that the administration of tenancy laws, little known and less understood by illiterate peasants, had been left to civil servants "who often lack both the qualifications and the integrity necessary for the job and are overburdened with (other) responsibilities". The dual role of landowners both as landlords and moneylenders and weak budgetary support to land reform measures were noticed. And it quoted Gunnar Myrdal as commenting on the status differential between the tenant and the landlord and the tendency for courts and civil servants in Asia to favour the respected man of property.

Followed an indictment of tenancy reform in India by the government's land Reforms Commission, P.S. Appu (1975), and the report of yet another Committee chaired by Raj Krishna in 1978. These recommended an end to absentee landlordism, fixity of tenure with fair rents for sharecroppers particularly in eastern India, the association of committees of beneficiaries with the implementation of agrarian reforms and the updating of records of rights. They favoured a time-bound programme for the disposal of land reform cases with limited rights of appeal, and the appointment of additional judges to ensure expeditious disposal. The Planning Commission's Task Force on "Two Decades of Land Reform" (1973) had these suggestions for incorporation in the Fifth Plan, 1976-80: the constitution of a land commission with powers to acquire, develop and resell land; the creation of a land reform organization parallel to the district revenue administration with hand-picked officials under a district land reforms officer ranking with the District Collector, supported by a well paid and closely supervised staff.

Until the end of December 1986 some 3 million hectares had been declared surplus in India under all ceiling laws. Of this only 1.8 million hectares have been distributed among little over four million beneficiaries. Nearly 1.1 million hectares could not be distributed, much of it on account of litigation. If one takes just 5 of the 15 Indian basin states, Assam, Bihar, Haryana, Uttar Pradesh and West Bengal, 1.2 million hectares had been declared surplus, as much as a third of this in West Bengal and least of all in Bihar; possession had been taken of nearly a million hectares; some 0.72 million hectares had been distributed, almost half of this in West Bengal; and just about 158,000 hectares were under litigation (Department of Rural Development, 1987 and 1988).

UNEVEN PROGRESS OF CONSOLIDATION

Another major problem is fragmentation. Until 1987-88, some 22 million hectares had been consolidated. Consolidation had been completed in Haryana and nearly so in Uttar Pradesh (second round) but was limited to pockets in Bihar and Himachal. West Bengal and Madhya Pradesh only provide for voluntary consolidation. Consolidation is land saving and permits better water conservation and more intensive cultivation with improved farm management. Uttar Pradesh started consolidation in 1954 and after 1959 adopted the Punjab-Haryana scheme of rectangularisation in 10 hectare plots or *murabbas*, further sub-divided into 25 units or *qilas* within which the new allotments were made. If contour surveys are undertaken simultaneously then water and drainage channels can be appropriately aligned. In Uttar Pradesh, whereas prior to consolidation only 21 per cent of all farms were in one unit and 35 per cent in six or more parcels, after consolidation the one unit farms rose to 59 per cent and the six and more parcel farms declined to two per cent. As a result, the number of tubewells has multiplied dramatically and productivity has risen. Small holdings are generally clustered so that marginal farmers can share common facilities which they otherwise cannot individually afford (Zaheer M., 1975).

In a second round of consolidation in Uttar Pradesh under the revised 1963 Consolidation Act, 328,000 hectares of land saved from field boundaries and pathways, which it was possible to estimate, have been returned to the community in the form of field channels, *chak* (irrigation block) roads, community lands for public utility use, extension of *abadi* (habitation) sites, threshing floors, and manure pits. One negative aspect of consolidation is that it has sometimes been done without ensuring security of tenure, especially to sharecroppers, resulting in large-scale ejectments. This clearly suggests that consolidation must be taken up as part of an overall agrarian reforms package if benefits are to be maximized.

STATUS OF REFORM IN BANGLADESH, NEPAL, BHUTAN AND TIBET

In Bangladesh, zamindari stood abolished with the passage of the East Bengal State Acquisition and Tenancy Act, 1950. This proved effective as the predominantly Hindu landlords had migrated to India in the wake of the post-Partition riots. For the rest, it left the agrarian structure largely intact. Here too landlords (and in effect the intermediaries under them) were entitled to retain their *khas* (self-cultivated) lands, homestead plots, ponds, orchards and other reclaimable land. On the other hand, sharecroppers (*bargadars*) were denied the limited protection they enjoyed under the Bengal Tenancy Act of 1885 which was simultaneously repealed, losing the right to acquire permanent occupancy title to lands tilled by them for a specified period. The ceiling prescribed was evaded on the basis of exemptions granted for cooperative and dairy farming, mechanization and so on or was not effectively enforced (Jannuzi and Peach, 1980).

There are 6.26 million farm holdings in Bangladesh. The land occupancy survey of 1978 showed that 29 per cent of rural households were landless and 33 per cent owned under 0.40 hectares. Nearly 23 per cent of the land under cultivation is share-cropped (Agriculture Ministry, Bangladesh, 1981). Agrarian reforms were not seriously pressed after the birth of Bangladesh in 1971 and the "Third Plan, 1985-90", (Planning Commission, Dhaka) does not even have a section under this heading at all, an astonishing omission. A large number of tiny landowners lease land on a crop-sharing basis in order to make up a minimally viable holding.

In Nepal, land was traditionally vested in the State but tenancies existed under a variety of intermediaries. With the change of regime in 1951 the government enacted the Nepal Tenancy Rights and Security Act. This as much as the subsequent Land Act of 1957 made little impact partly on account of inadequate land records. Intermediary titles were abolished in stages but the main push to agrarian reform came in 1964 with the passage of a comprehensive Land Act and rules thereunder. This finally did away with remnants of zamindari and imposed ceilings on the basis of 17 hectares in the Terai, 4 hectares in the Hills and 2.5 hectares in

Kathmandu Valley, in addition to homestead plots, with compensation varying between 10 and 30 times the land revenue for land held in excess of these limits. A separate set of tenancy ceilings were imposed a the level of operational holdings at the rate of 2.5 hectares, 1 hectare and 0.5 a hectare in the Terai, Hills and Kathmandu Valley, respectively. Security of tenure, a maximum rental, scaling down of debts and compulsory savings from which credit would be advanced were other features of the new law. Loopholes, inadequate records and lack of will stalled anything more than limited progress. Indeed the Agricultural Sample Census shows a sharply declining trend in the number of tenant households and the acreage operated by them between 1961 and 1981 which only suggests the growth of informal tenancies as agrarian decline and pressure of numbers compelled numerous smallholders to sell and migrate. Fragmentation has multiplied and has proved a great handicap in the absence of any effort at consolidation (Sharma, Kulshekhar et al., IDS, May 1986)

Nepal's Seventh Plan, 1985-90, (National Planning Commission Nepal) has as its land reform objectives updating the list of tenants, expanding the rent fixation system, terminating dual ownership, acquisition of ceiling surplus lands for distribution, controlling fragmentation, granting credit against tenancy certificates, encouraging commercial agriculture, and promoting cooperatives to assist small and marginal farmers

In Bhutan too, land is owned by the State and individuals merely enjoy farming, grazing and water rights. Land ceilings have been fixed at 10 hectares per family, excluding orchards. A cadastral survey has been completed in 4 out of 18 districts and land records are being compiled.

In Tibet, manorial estates and monastry lands were largely confiscated and distributed in implementation of polices of "harvest to the tiller", rent reduction and abolition of *usury* and *ula* or forced labour (His and Kao, 1977). Communes were formed, but, the position after their disbandment in the eighties, the introduction of the new responsibility system, and a more recent admission of "Left mistakes" is not very clear.

COSMETIC CHANGES PROVOKE VIOLENCE

This quick survey of agrarian relations in the region indicates, overall, a failure to get to grips with the problem. Cosmetic changes were introduced while more effective legislation has not been implemented. No wonder that agriculture growth has been handicapped. In Eastern India, certainly, rural tensions continue to mount with incidents of violence, atrocities and rape, the formation of various *senas* or private armies and so-called naxalism. If conditions in parts of Uttar Pradesh are disturbing, the situation over large parts of Bihar is alarming. In the stretch of ravine lands along the Chambal and Yamuna, especially in Madhya Pradesh, dacoity has long been a socio-economic problem of some magnitude.

Landlords in conjunction with caste and class allies in politics and the administration have armed themselves to resist the growing militancy of agricultural labourers, tribals, and small peasants who have begun to organize themselves as fear and despair have turned to anger. Here is a calendar of horror from Bihar, In Belchi, 11 Harijans were burnt alive in 1971 by Kurmi landlords on an issue of payment of minimum wages and forced labour. In February 1980, some 200 armed Kurmis avenged the alleged murder of one of their clan by Naxalites by raiding Pipra village in Patna district, killing 14 Harijans, setting on fire 27 dwellings and burning cattle. That same month, Bhumihar landlords massacred 12 Harijans at Parashiga in Jehanabad sub-division of Gaya district in revenge for an alleged killing of one of their own. In August 1984 a Bhumihar mob burnt down the huts of 100 Harijans built on government land in Ambari village, Monghyr district. In a running dispute over diara (riverbed) land, about 1000 armed Yadavs are said to have raided Lakshmipur village, Monghyr district in November 1985, killing 12 Binds, gang-raping their women and setting fire to 200 dwelling places. In December 1984, 10 sleeping Kurmis were massacred by a Scheduled Caste gang in a revenge killing in village Dhulrapur, Patna district. In April 1986, police opened fire on a crowd of alleged Naxalites who are said to have attacked them at Arwal, Jehanabad, killing 23. More than 40 Rajputs were massacred by armed Yadavs in May 1987, climaxing a vendetta over land (Rajgopal P.R., 1987). Yet another massacre of 11 Harijans occurred in two villages in Jehanabad in August, 1988.

Rajgopal also comments on the nexus between big cultivators, rich traders and musclemen and the rise of private armies. These include the Bhumi Sena of the Kurmis in Gaya, Nalanda and Patna districts; the Kuwar Sena representing Thakurs; the Brahma Rishi Sena of the Yadavs; the Lal Sena or the Red Army which has (leftist) ideological inclinations; and the Lohrik Sena, a Yadav formation set up to confront the Lal Sena. Opposing the landowners is the Mazdoor Kisan Sangram Samiti, organized by a CPI (ML) faction, which was prescribed after the Arwal massacre. According to the police, Naxalites have snatched arms and committed 147 murders from 1982 until September 1985. There are counter-allegations of willful killing of so-called Naxalites in false encounters. The government has been content to treat the matter as a law and order question. The basic issue of inequitable agrarian relations against a background of cruel poverty, age-old exploitation and exploding population has been ignored for far too long.

The situation is so bad in some parts of Bihar that the Central Government dispatched a high-level team to report on conditions in the seven districts of Patna, Nalanda, Bhojpur, Rohtas, Gaya, Aurangabad and Jehanabad early in 1988. The team recommended land reform, payment of minimum wages, prevention of forced labour, curbs on social oppression, distribution of bhoodan lands, settlement of government land, identification of (ceiling) surplus lands, and updating of land records. In pursuance of this the Centre and State governments jointly launched "Operation Siddhartha" on October 17 in 25 of the worst affected blocks in

Jehanabad, Gaya and Aurangabad districts. About 670 acres of bhoodan and government lands were distributed to 464 landless labourers as part of a Rs 31-crore programme aimed at easing tensions and restoring rural peace through land distribution and for the enforcement of minimum wages which, on official admission was hitherto only enforced in 140 out of 847 villages in Jehanabad district for lack of labour inspectors!

AGRICULTURAL DYNAMISM IMPEDED

It is against this background that one has to view the prospects of agricultural growth in eastern India where there is a very considerable agro-climatic and technological potential and an abundance of water awaiting exploitation. The National Agricultural Commission (NCA) concluded in as far back as 1976 that "the question is not merely that of meting out social justice to the rural poor. The question is essentially one having a bearing on our national life as a whole. Unless the agrarian society is regenerated and converted into a dynamic and rapidly growing system, both the base and the superstructure of the economy will remain weak and unstable". The position in Bangladesh is no different. Jannuzi and Peace observed in 1981 that "change in the traditional agrarian structure of Bangladesh is the sine qua non for sustained agricultural production increase in this region within a social and economic framework that encourages broad participation in economic progress ... The barriers to the diffusion of the new technology in agriculture in Bangladesh are subsumed within the agrarian structure."

The NCA in yet another comment described the present agrarian structure in India is outmoded and inefficient as a basis for increased production. It noted that a recent study in the Kosi command (in North Bihar) had clearly shown that whereas small landowners had fully utilized available irrigation, the bigger landholders who cultivated through sharecroppers, had not taken similar advantage "leaving a large land area unutilized" (NCA, Part II, 1976).

This writer, visiting the Kosi region in 1978 and 1979, observed that 20 per cent of the annals had silted up and about one-third of the command area was waterlogged.

An analysis of only officially recorded land sales in Uttar Pradesh between zamindari abolition and 1982-83 clearly reveals a process of proletarianisation at work in the rural areas. The major reason for land alienation was found to be "left to village" (31 per cent for State but 42 per cent in eastern Uttar Pradesh) followed by "repayment of debts" (20 per cent), with "domestic consumption" accounting for 4 per cent (Shankar, Kripa July 1988). The debt-bondage nexus has kept the peasant in thrall. The Bihar agrarian scene is semi-fuedal, its characteristic feature being "an indissoluble bond between the semi-proletariat and his overlord (which) is maintained by resort to usury" (Prasad, Pradhan H., 1974). Prasad has hypothesized that the "rural oligarchy consisting of landlords and the big landowning class being inimical to rapid overall prosperity, operates as a drag on land productivity" (1987). He found that with an increase in the area under sharecropping, the value of gross output per acre declines while crop sharing declines with an increase in irrigation. His conclusion: "The upper stratum of cultivators (mostly big peasants and landlords) are not taking advantage of the available technology because of feudal traditions."

In short, as pithily stated by Praveen K. Chaudhry (January 1988), zamindari abolition was essentially an administrative change rather than land reform. Regrettably, the political parties, almost across the board, have been guilty of a "total conspiracy of silence". They indulge in radical talk but "allow a vast gap between words and deeds, to preserve the support of the rural rich" (Joshi, PC August 1978). The same author perceptively added that "land reform is both the demolition of an old socio-economic order and the reconstruction of a new order."

James Boyce (1987) adopts Ishikawa's thesis that irrigation or "water control" is both the "leading input" and "technological constraint" in the stage of agricultural transition in which Bangladesh and West Bengal find themselves. He sees water control in the two Bengals as "a public good, in that it cannot be undertaken by individual cultivators acting alone, but rather requires institutional mechanism for collective action. In this respect, water control is fundamentally different from fertilizer or seeds, which can be purchased and used by individuals regardless of what their neighbours do." His analysis shows that as a consequence, "as compared with owner-cultivation, both wage labour and sharecropping are associated with lower use of labour and related inputs, and hence with lower land productivity." Labour mobilization in the off-season to undertake water control works are defeated by a total lack of incentive or self-interest on the part of tiny landholders and landless labourers who see no reason to contribute free labour for such asset creation within the existing agrarian structure. And when the government intervenes, rural works and benefits from irrigation projects such as deep tubewells and canals are largely captured by the big and influential landlords or are underutilized. Boyce further notes that smaller works like shallow tubewells are sited to maximize gains to powerful individuals rather than to serve the common good and maximize total returns. In Bihar, it has been found that rural electrification sometimes goes where influential people desire rather than where tubewells await energisation.

OPERATION BARGA IN WEST BENGAL

One further comment by Boyce merits attention. It is that the parties of the Left in the subcontinent that have traditionally championed the interests of the poor "have focused on distributional questions rather than production; this helps to explain why there is so little difference in terms of agricultural performance between West Bengal and Bangladesh, despite the fact that one is ruled by an elected communist government and the other by a rightist military dictatorship." The West Bengal government which has conferred tenurial security on share-croppers or *bargadars* to a large degree, surrendered Rs 20 crores to the Central Government in 1987-88 from funds allocated for constructing tubewells.

With the introduction of the three-tier district, block and village level panchayati raj system in West Bengal in 1978, the Left Front administration launched Operation Barga. As an antidote to Naxalism the State Government had earlier introduced a comprehensive agricultural development programme in 20 blocks which had to some extent reinforced the middle peasants as part of its anti-insurgency strategy. With Operation Barga a drive was launched to record and confer permanent and hereditary rights to between two and three million sharecroppers By January 1987 some 1.36 million *bargadars* had been recorded through beneficiary committees, field visits and the participation of peasant organizations. The onus of proving that a claimant is not a *bargadar* was cast on the landowner. Some 565,000 of those recorded are scheduled castes and scheduled tribes. The *bargadar's* share is fixed at 75 per cent of the crop if he provides his own inputs, or 50 per cent in the event of the owner providing the plough, seed, fertilizer and water. The *bargadar* has the right to purchase ownership provided the owner is prepared to sell at the market price. There is a proposal to set up a State land corporation to make the purchase and hand over the title to the *bargadar* after collecting a crop-rent from him for a period of years. *Bargadars* are eligible for loans from government financial institutions and *bargadar* service cooperatives are to be promoted.

Under amended ceiling legislation, some 500,000 hectares have been vested in the State and by the end of 1985 just over 320,000 hectares had been distributed to 1.64 million peasants. In addition, homestead lots of up to 0.32 hectares have been given to 2.2 million agricultural labourers, fishermen and rural artisans.

Over 32,000 cases were pending in various courts as of 1987. *Bargadars* have meanwhile been provided access to consumption credit and food-for-work opportunities for off-season or supplementary employment. Under a new Land Holding Revenue Act, holdings valued at less than Rs 50,000 have been exempted from revenue assessment while those above that valuation are assessed at progressive rates. Consolidation is voluntary unless more than 50 per cent of the landholders favour it. This has happened only to a limited degree because tiny fragments, especially near Calcutta, are intensively cultivated under banana and potatoes. However, the effect of land reform and panchayati raj has been to reduce rural migration into the Calcutta metropolitan area according to official sources.

One revealing feature of the new situation is that there are instances of farmers letting out their fields to sharecroppers in the kharif season, when water control is difficult and the attendant risks are greater, and turning capitalist farmers on the very same plots in the rabi season to grow wheat, potatoes and boro paddy wherever water management is relatively assured as in the Mayurakshi, Kangsabati and Damodar Valley commands in lower and central West Bengal.

DECLINE IN REVENUE ADMINISTRATION

It is now being argued by experienced administrators and others that water control and the new agricultural technology has exposed a new facet of agrarian relations. Accordingly, irrigation command area development should be regarded as a sociological as much as a technological concept and used for connecting and updating land records and propelling other agrarian reforms. The special rice production programme in the eastern region and even the new "thrust programme", 1988-90, offers similar leverage.

Land revenue was once the most important source of revenue and the revenue administration was the heart of the administrative structure. No longer. With the emphasis on development, the development administration has acquired preeminence. The BDO is a key figure and the district collector is now primarily charged with development functions. Small farms of 1.25 hectares in Uttar Pradesh and 2 hectares in Bihar have been exempted from assessment to land revenue. Rates have remained unrevised in Bihar since zamindari abolition and though raised elsewhere (Rs 5 per 0.40 hectares in Uttar Pradesh if unirrigated and Rs 10 if irrigated), there are shortfalls in realization while collection costs have risen. In Bihar the collection is Rs 30 crores and the cost of the revenue administration Rs 29 crores, though the department is involved in more than collecting land revenue.

According to one study, the share of land revenue in total state revenue incomes in India declined from 11 to 4 per cent between the Third and Fifth Plans. But while land revenue per hectare of cropped area rose from Rs 5.06 to Rs 8.90 during this same period, the cost of collection as a percentage of land revenue rose from 22 to 55, being as much as 118 in Assam, 421 in Himachal, 116 in West Bengal, 105 in Rajasthan, 66 in Madhya Pradesh and 55 in Uttar Pradesh (Chokkalingam G., April 1988). Betterment levies related to land value appreciation as a result of irrigation and general development were much written about in the earlier Plan documents. Legislation was also enacted in many States. Not a paisa has been collected anywhere.

The revenue administration is in decline and must be remodeled if it is to be an effective instrument of land reform and able to maintain land records. Such is the situation that even in West Bengal, Operation Barga has no system for updating the records of rights. There are no grassroots revenue officials in situ as before. The land reform administration is weak, understaffed, under-funded and untrained. Irrigation departments are required to collect water charges, but their record in this regard has been pitiable. Could there be a marriage of the revenue collection machinery as well as the land and water management functions of the revenue and irrigation departments as they are closely related? Thought needs to be given to such issues.

In Madhya Pradesh, land revenue was delinked from land settlement and updating of records in 1985. Aerial photography is being used to expedite cadastral surveys in six districts. These show trees and field boundaries and are being translated into maps. As in some other states, passbooks are being issued as a single, comprehensive document containing details of the farmer's land, survey members, revenue entries, credit status and so on. Madhya Pradesh also did well to institute a mobile revenue court in each *patwari* circle in 1985. The team moves in a given circuit, announced in advance. Over 400,000 revenue cases of mutations, land demarcation, partition disputes and so on have been settled by this means. In mid-1987 a detailed land reform proforma was being drawn up for compilation and continuous updating of records. This is being computerized. A larger national pilot project for computerization of land records is also being planned by the Central Government.

ABSENCE OF POLITICAL WILL

Is there the political will? There is no more evidence of this today than there was 10 years ago when the Bihar Chief Minister was persuaded to adopt agrarian reform, through implementation of existing legislation, employment generation and agricultural development as a single package in the Kosi command. Operation Kosi Kranti was operationalized in five blocks in Purnia district as a spearhead effort over a two-year period. It received full support from a section of dedicated senior officials and others but met with expected hostility from vested interests at all levels within the government and outside. What was surprising was the total indifference of so-called radicals and reformers alike in Bihar and Delhi (Verghese, B.G. June 1981).

Rhetoric is no substitute for action. Yet circumstances inexorably dictate a measure of reform on the ground as an economic imperative as well as for reasons of system stability and political prudence with the increasing operation of the rural poor. Implementation of a similar minimum reform package, without foolishly attempting the impossible of trying to distribute a patch of farmland to every one of the growing landless through application of lower ceilings, is advocated as absolutely essential for Bangladesh by Jannuzi and Peach. But not many will subscribe to their desperate proposition that the only way to accomplish this would be by a firm show of political will "by the establishment of martial law and the stationing of troops at key points in every district of the nation."

While zamindari abolition was no doubt important, the subsequent intellectual fascination with ceilings, to the gross neglect of far more meaningful tenancy and institution reform was quite misplaced. A recent state ministers conference in Delhi favoured a further reduction in ceilings. This would be undesirable and unsettling. Legislating a floor below which holdings should not shrink, consolidation, and a progressive land tax would be more to the point.

No effort has been made, Operation Barga only partially excluded, to create the necessary political climate for tenancy reform, carry the message into the countryside, as Gandhi did in Champaran in 1917, involve and organize the potential beneficiaries, train and concentrate adequate staff, plug legislative loopholes, bring mobile courts to the people, as Madhya Pradesh is now doing, and undertake mass mobilization of idle labour with food-for-work (that would have been the best use of PL 480 grain) to provide alternative sources of income and employment in land and water development and conservation, converting labour into farm capital assets as the Chinese have done. This is still possible, taking advantage also of irrigation and technological opportunities.

Tribal land issues are of a different kind. Apart from *jhum* resettlement, it should be the endeavour to harness the tradition of community and collective effort to promote cooperative action and institution-building for future tasks. On the contrary, signs of absentee landlordism are emerging in Meghalaya with the ruling gentry enclosing lands and illicitly leaving cultivation to others. In parts of Arunachal, as in some areas of Bhutan, scattered hamlets are being voluntarily regrouped in viable units, so as to be able to provide these communities with reclaimed valley lands or terraces and social amenities like education, health facilities, water supply and communications. The development of plantation crops – rubber in Tripura for example – and horticulture could be entry points for long range social planning to put 44,000 hectares and 150,000 hectares under coffee and rubber, respectively, by 200 in family-sized plantations in the Northeast.

INHIBITING LABOUR ABSORPTION

All the countries in the basin face an acute problem of employment. Bangladesh was expected to add four million to is labour force between 1985 and 1990, taking the figure of unemployment at the end of the Third Plan to 11 million. Nepal's last census shows that the labour force grow at the rate of 200,000 per annum between 1971 and 1981, a figure that must progressively rise in the foreseeable future. India is adding some nine million net to its labour force annually which means that it must create something of the order of 120 million new jobs, inclusive of the current employment backlog, by the year 2000. The bulk of these jobs must and can only be immediately created in the countryside, in agriculture and forestry, and in the non-crop and off-farm sectors.

Irrigation has witnessed tremendous expansion, especially in India where it now extends over nearly 70 million hectares and is expanding at a rate of over two million hectares per annum. It can "stretch" land by permitting multiple cropping. The record, however, is disappointing. Irrigated yields in the basin are, with some exceptions, low; nor has irrigation intensity increased to the extent that one would expect. We have examined one of the principal reasons, which is the singular inadequacy of agrarian reforms. Labour absorption in agriculture is consequently low. Absentee landlords, large farmers in semi-fuedal conditions, and sharecroppers who do not get a fair return on their labour or investment are, each for their own reasons, unwilling to invest more labour in farming operations. The new technology is largely neutral to scale and tiny plots have been shown to maximize both family labour and agricultural productivity. But this only follows in favourable agrarian conditions which there has been a singular failure to create over most of the basin.

Shigeru Ishikawa discusses the issues in Labour Absorption in Asian Agriculture (1978). He found 525 mandays per hectare applied to agriculture in Japan in 1956 and a similar or higher rate in China, compared to no more than a third of that figure in India, including irrigated areas, during the same period. The Indian experience and constraints are discussed in two further volumes published by the Asian Regional Programme for Employment Promotion (ARTEP ILO, 1978 and 1979). Agrarian reforms in its broadcast sense still holds the key to large-scale absorption of labour in the countryside for the next 5 to 10 years and more in creating farm capital assets. The resultant increase in production and productivity would stimulate a whole chain of supporting activity in the service sector, in processing and by-product utilization and in the mass production of wage goods. Such a development would lift the economy of India and that of Bangladesh to a new threshold.

CONCEPT OF A LABOUR BANK

Prembhai, a Gandhian sarvodaya worker, runs the Banwasi Seva Ashram in Govindpur in an area covering about 400 predominantly tribal villages in the Kaimur Range in Mirzapur district, Uttar Pradesh, south of the Sone river. He took up five "whole village plans" in 1974 and expanded this to 100 villages a year later, beginning with watershed management and water harvesting with small check dams and *bandhs* to drought-proof the region. His logic was that with 900 to 2300 mm of rainfall there should be no cause for drought if only the rain were stored. He adopted the three-tier system, growing paddy and other crops along the valley floors and on low terraces, fruit and vegetables on the middle slopes and encouraging forestry above that in a rough 40:30:30 ratio. Eight earthen *bandhs* with lift arrangements provided an initial irrigation grid which has since expanded to a network of more than 1000 *bandhs* built by the ashram plus more than 2000 other water-harvesting works constructed by the block authorities and the community on hill slopes at elevation between 200 and 500 m. These serve 340 villages in four blocks.

A dug-well in this hard rock region going down to around 15 m costs about Rs 20,000 under a contract awarded by the BDO through tenders. It is Prembhai's estimate that the actual cost of labour and materials is not more than Rs 10,000, the rest being accounted for by overheads, profits and leakages. If, however, Rs 5,000 worth of idle labour were employed, then only another Rs 5,000 would be needed to complete the investment and create a productive asset. This costing would render a well an affordable proposition for the community. If wages were fixed at Rs 10 per day of which 75 per cent was paid and the balance deposited in a labour bank, the accumulation could be utilized as a revolving fund to finance further projects, thus converting labour into capital and farm capital assets.

Having conceived the idea of a labour bank, Prembhai applied it in practice to develop wells and undertake land leveling, ravine reclamation and the digging of pits and trenches for afforestation and horticulture. The total turnover of the ashram's labour bank scheme (1986) is said to have been Rs 20 lakhs of which half was contributed by the beneficiaries. Therefore, Prembhai asks, if there is in the country idle land, untapped water, unutilized animal power and unemployed manpower, why cannot these be collectively harnessed for productive purposes? The initial seed money can come from existing government schemes such as the Integrated Rural Development Programme, the Rural Labour and Employment Guarantee Programme (now telescoped into the Jawahar Rozgar Yojana), and a number of other area development and beneficiary oriented programmes which dispose of hundreds of crores of rupees annually, often with little result but with significant leakages.

In the ashram project area, paddy and wheat are now commonplace. Each household has a vegetable plot and a few fruit trees. Some families are raising forest nurseries. Compost pits have been dug. Most boys and many girls are in school. There is little landlessness as wastelands and ravine lands have been reclaimed and distributed, though titles to ownership remain to be awarded. The ashram is insisting that the local tribals be given tenurial rights on lands they have traditionally occupied and not be evicted under the Forest Act from deemed forest land. Some 60,000 families were so affected in 433 villages. The ashram organized them in a Bhoomi Haqdari Morcha (Land Rights Association) and went to the Supreme Court which granted an interim stay order in 1986. In its final order, the court called for a fresh survey and settlement of the forest area within two years and appointed Prembhai as one among the court's commissioners to oversee the task.

The ashram has undertaken surveys on bonded labour and non-fulfilment of entitlements to the poor under the laws of the land or official programmes such as distribution of rations through fair price shops. There are primary schools without teachers and teaches without schools, buildings or blackboards. The ashram proposes to plant 10 million seedlings over the next five years which ten years thereafter are expected to provide the community an invaluable forest capital base. Community building is going on apace with development. *Lok adalats* are settling petty disputes and averting litigation. Panchayats are being strengthened.

LAND AND WATER CONSERVATION

The environment is a major new concern. Because of the close proximity of the huge reservoir behind the Rihand Dam and the vast Singrauli coal deposits just across the Uttar Pradesh border in Madhya Pradesh, six mega-thermal stations have come up or are under various stages of completion around the lake at Obra, Bijapur, Anpara, Singrauli, Vindhyachal and Renusagar with a planned capacity of 10,000 MW. This is India's energy centre. Some tribal villagers displaced by the Rihand project 30 years ago have recently been ousted once more by one or other of these giant thermal schemes. Here are two worlds, totally apart, with no larger area and human development plan to knit them into a harmonious whole.

Go to Sukhomajri village between Chandigarh and the famous Pinjore Garden at the foot of the Simla hills. Here, marginal farmers have transformed their totally degraded environment and miserable lives by acting collectively on a principle of equal sharing. Seasonal hill torrents cutting backwards on grossly abused forest land had made precipitous gullies, eroded the catchment and silted up Chandigarh's Sukhna Lake. Uncontrolled, grazing in the fragile catchment had aggravated the problem. In 1983, the annual auctions for the seasonal lease of fodder grass from the forest area was stopped and the Haryana Forest Department handed the lease to the Sukhomajri hill resource management society which in turn undertook to protect the catchment from grazing. Within a year of closure through voluntary social fencing the forest regenerated luxuriantly and the villagers have an abundance of fodder grass to cut for their stall-fed cattle which has enabled the increased dung collection to be used as farm manure. The forests also now yield plenty of bhabar grass which the women, relieved of the time spent in foraging for sufficient fodder, can now devote to rope-making, which fetches them a lucrative side-income. Rabi crop yields have increased significantly through two supplemental rabi irrigations from water harvesting storages, and larger crop residues are now available for feed. The villagers have begun to keep superior crossbreds, raising milk yields with a smaller herd. Fish is being cultured in the storage lakes. Treatment of 1,008 hectares of the Sukhna catchment reduced the sediment rate from 150 metric tonnes per annum per hectare to 7.8 m.t./ha p.a between 1979 and 1986. The department is now conducting social forestry training camps for farmers and hopes within some years to purchase all its sapling requirements from village nurseries. The message has spread. Villagers realizing that they have been robbing themselves have turned cops en masse (Bansal and Grewal, 1986). A detailed social cost-benefit analysis of Sukhomajri and two other villages shows that people's participation in the preservation of forest resources contributes significantly to increased income and its fair distribution in the village economies" (Chopra, Kanchan, Kadekodi Gopal and Murty M.N. 1988).

Filled with new hope and prosperity, Sukhomajri built a primary school for Rs 10,000 in 1986. Today all the village children are in school. The inspiration behind Sukhomajri was R.P. Mishra of the Central Soil and Water Conservation Reserch and Traning Institute in Chandigarh. He is today in Palamau in Bihar working on larger models for employment generation among the rural poor.

Examples can be multiplied. Thus the remarkable bamboo tubewell programme mounted by the Deen Dayal Research Institute in Gonda district in eastern Uttar Pradesh in 1978-79 resulting in the drilling of 28,000 shallow wells in 18 months with beneficiary participation (Verghese B.G., November 1981). In response to an acute problem of unemployment and limited land for cultivation in Imphal Valley, the Manipur Development Society has organized beneficiary committees with extension, agro-service and marketing support to develop small irrigation systems and expand multiple-cropping and horticulture. Seeds are supplied free for the second crop for some years. And handloom weaving, a traditional occupation, has been underpinned through assured yarn supplies and marketing support.

CONVERTING LABOUR INTO FARM CAPITAL ASSETS

In Purnia and Saharsa districts, mass labour, rising to 45,000 men and women at the peak, were employed from neighbouring villages through labour cooperatives alongside contract labour to construct the massive twin 115 km long Kosi flood embankments in 1957 and 1958. Local participation enabled work to proceed without completion of normal, time-consuming land acquisition and compensation formalities, and provided local employment to idle and off-season labour. More than that, it compelled labour contractors to lower their rates. In the result, this huge project was completed at less than the projected cost and a whole season ahead of schedule, a feat that has possibly not been equaled since then on any project of any description in India (Verghese, B.G. 1959).

In recent years various rural employment programmes have been mounted to utilize surplus labour. These have been limited. In Bihar, for example, the total employment annually generated by the National Rural Employment Programme, the National Rural Labour Employment Guarantee Programme and the Integrated Rural Development Programme during the period 1985-87 was able to absorb only 15.57 per cent of an estimated rural labour surplus of just under 1,721 million mandays in the State (Verma P.C. February 1988). It is now proposed to make land shaping and similar land and water conservation works by Scheduled Castes and Tribes eligible for assistance under various employment programmes even if done in their own fields.

In Nepal, the reforestation programme is Sindhupalchok and Kabre districts northeast of Kathmandu, under what is now the Nepal-Australian Forestry Project, has met with remarkable success, again on account of community participation and social fencing.

In Bangladesh, the Grameen Bank was started in 1979 as a non-governmental effort to reach out to the rural poor by advancing credit for quick income-generating activities on the basis of group security without collateral but under close supervision. Landless farmers and women were brought within its scope. In striking contrast to the normal credit and cooperative structure, loans have been advanced to the poorest with practically no default whatsoever (Ahmad, Razia S. 1983). Though basically a credit programme, the Grameen Bank has become a human development programme stimulating action in such areas as removing illiteracy, fighting superstition, sanitation, family planning, combating early marriage and dowry, vegetable gardening, and building self-reliance through group action. It has made a dent in the rural power structure dominated by the larger landlords and money lenders by helping raise agricultural wages and altering landlord-tenant, employer-employee and debtor-creditor relations (Rahman, Atiur 1986).

The Bangladesh canal digging programme during 1979-80 entailed mobilization of idle manpower voluntarily to desilt and dig canals and drains. It is estimated that over 1,200 km of ditches were dug in 250 projects which provided irrigation to 160,000 hectares of land, giving a fillip to boro rice production. About 667 million cubic feet of earthwork was completed within 40.5 million mandays of free labour excepting the distribution of 5,000 tonnes of wheat to landless and poor peasants (Films & Publications Department, Dhaka, September 1980).

The poor purchasing power to feed themselves and droughts rob them of such employment and income. Small and marginal farmers are particularly vulnerable and typically resource-poor, except for family labour. Harnessing this idle labour is therefore crucial. Food-for-work programmes and a more widespread public distribution system (PDS) have provided compensatory purchasing power and subsidized nutrition and could be self-financing if imaginatively linked to productive farm-asset creation that insures against further rounds of drought and unrequited relief expenditure. Analysing the droughts of 1986 and 1987 in India, C.G. Hanumantha Rao et al. have shown (1988) that employment created through national public works comes to no more than a third of the quantum required in a severe drought year. In 1986, ten million tonnes of grain were distributed; and in 1987 some 11.6 million tonnes through food-for-work-cum-PDS programmes, reaching 58 million poor households at a cost of Rs 870 crores in subsidies. The authors calculated that an expanded PDS and works programme in a year of severe drought would require an additional compensatory income-cum-food-for-work programme of 250,000 tonnes, adding another Rs 38 crores to the subsidy burden. The food reserve required worked out to 11.85 million tonnes in a truly bad year, over and above the normal buffer stock of 10 million tonnes that should be maintained as a hedge against production fluctuations.

Agriculture is the foundation of the economy throughout the basin, with irrigation as the leading input. However, feudal and iniquitous agrarian relations constitute key constraints in the development, utilization and sound management of water and technologies that have opened up new agricultural opportunities. A growing labour force demands gainful employment which is necessary to avert hunger. In the fifties there was hunger because there was insufficient food production. Now million remain hungry in India despite huge buffer stocks and nutrition programmes, for lack of purchasing power. The basin is capital-short, but labour-abundant. This idle labour can be productively absorbed in agriculture and converted into capital through land and water development works that are crying to be taken up. This is unlikely to happen unless there are structural changes and the poor have reasonable certainty of tangible gain and institutional support to achieve what has been amply demonstrated to be possible.

CHAPTER 5

The Irrigation Factor

Irrigation is by far the largest consumptive use of water anywhere and amounts to 85 per cent or more of all uses in developing societies that are largely dependent on agriculture. So it is in the Ganga-Brahmaputra-Barak basin. Though much of the basin enjoys good to heavy rainfall, the monsoon is seasonal and around 80 per cent of annual precipitation occurs between June and September. The rains could commence late and are often erratic, with long dry spells during critical periods of plant growth, or may end early. Thereafter, there may be insufficient soil moisture even with intermittent rains to grow a second or third crop during the ensuing winter and summer season without some irrigation. Population growth and hunger make it essential to increase food production and agricultural productivity in the basin. And for this water is the leading input. A look at the hydrological cycle would be instructive. The Indian example is cited illustratively.

INDIA'S WATER BALANCE

Nature annually carries some 1110 million hectare metres (m ha m) of moisture in the atmospheric currents that circulate over the Indian subcontinent. Of this, only 25 to 30 per cent or some 400 m ha m precipitates in about 113 days in the form of rain and snow. Of this again, 35 per cent evaporates while another 30 per cent transpires through forests and vegetation, including crops. No more than 50 m ha m or 12.5 per cent of the year's rainfall infiltrates underground. This groundwater table feeds stream flows and is in turn recharged by rivers, canals and other water bodies, depending on their relative levels at any time. Groundwater is not static as if an underground lake, but flows slowly, the rate of flow depending on the hydraulic gradient and the transmissivity of the soil and rock strata. Surface, and ground waters are part of a single, conjunctive hydrological system. Most often, surface and ground water basins are coincidental and groundwater too may, at the land terminus, flow into the sea or suffer saline intrusion as happens when there is excessive pumping of aquifers near the coast. In this broad sense therefore, surface and groundwaters can be said to share a common drainage basin. An understanding of this at once elementary and yet complex fact is essential for any policy of sound water management.

To the precipitation over India must be added the 20 m ha m of river flows it receives from catchments across its borders in Nepal, Bhutan and Tibet. Likewise, it losses water in stream flows continuing into Bangladesh and Pakistan, or running into the sea. This quantification of India's hydrological cycle is elaborately detailed by Na and Kathpalia (1975).

Measuring water resources is a complex task. Rainfall is variable from one year to the next, though conforming to certain secular trends. Rainfall, so averaged, must be superimposed on a quantum of groundwater which is affected by several natural factors apart from being subject to artificial manipulation. Normally, groundwater should not be mined but harvested. This implies a rate of extraction equivalent to annual or periodic recharge. But recharge itself can increase with pumping to accommodate the maximum possible rejected recharge which is what the aquifer does not absorb when it is saturated. A crude analogy would be a sponge which absorbs more water (up to a point) the harder it is squeezed. There are, however, limits to which this can be done without ecological hazards.

Taking this as a working hypothesis, certain scholars in the seventies proposed heavy summer pumping of groundwater along selected streams deliberately in order to lower the groundwater level, creating pore space in 'cones of depression' within the aquifer that would be available for recharge with the onset of the monsoon. The argument presupposed adequate energy for the required pumping and irrigation or other beneficial uses for the water so extracted. The enhanced underground storage was calculated to moderate floods, by inducing greater recharge, and augment utilizable water resources. Revelle, first with Herman (1972) and subsequently with Lakshminarayana in "Ganges Water Machine" (1975) envisaged underground storage of Ganga flood waters equivalent to several world class dam reservoirs through batteries of thousands of tubewells with an average pumping head of 30 m. Others expressed doubts. The cones of depression would leave existing wells high and dry; there could be danger of subsidence; the pores and bores would get clogged with dust thus effectively choking the expected infiltration; and, most important, the cones would refill with inflows along the underground hydraulic gradient or, alternatively, could require a degree of pumping that would defy any rational or economic use of the water so extracted at great energy cost. A more limited but substantially similar concept is, however, being tested along the Hindon river not too far from Delhi.

Groundwater recharge can, therefore, be induced and enhanced by land and water management strategies. Annual recharge includes infiltration from rain and flooding, reservoir and canal seepage, return flows from irrigation, and influents from rivers and water-bodies of all kinds. It grows with canal irrigation which redistributes rainfall over space and time. Detailed and repetitive hydro-geological surveys and measurements have enabled the Central Ground Water Board (CGWB) to make a continuous reappraisal of India's groundwater resources.

The total average runoff of India's river system was assessed at 167.3 m ha m by Dr A.N. Khosla in 1946 and at 164.5 m ha m by Dr K.L. Rao in 1973. It has now been more definitively placed at 188 m ha m by the Central Water Commission (CWC) in confirmation of some of its own earlier studies (April 1988). The utilizable water resources were estimated by the Irrigation Commission (1972) at 87 m ha m including 20.4 m ha m of groundwater. Four years later, the National Commission on Agriculture put the figure at 105 m ha m inclusive of 35 m ha m of groundwater. The Irrigation Commission estimated the country's ultimate irrigation potential at 81 million hectares by assuming a depth of irrigation (averaged for surface and groundwater) of 0.76 metres per hectare cultivated, based on the prevailing cropping pattern.

The NCA, however, placed the ultimate irrigation potential at 110 million hectares on the ground that India's agricultural water use was extravagant and that the average water depth for maturing a hectare of crop should improve to 0.70 m. The government has now assumed an ultimate irrigation potential of 113 million hectares based on the CWC's somewhat higher estimate of utilizable water and a yet lower water depth of 0.65 m per hectare. The Ministry of Water Resources has also adopted the CGWB's revised provisional utilizable groundwater estimate of 42 m ha m against the NCA's earlier figure of 35 m ha m (CGWB, 1986). The area that could be irrigated from groundwater is, however, being left at 40 million hectares for the moment. It could undergo upward revision in due course.

It is the object of official Indian policy to realize the estimated "ultimate" irrigation potential of 113 million hectares by 2010. However, the government's National Water Perspective envisages augmenting the utilizable water budget through additional storage and inter-basin links to irrigate an additional 35 million hectares and generate an additional 40,000 MV of hydro-electric power against the currently assessed national hydel potential of 85,560 MW at 60 per cent load factor. Implementation of the National Water Perspective, if approved, would take at least half a century to accomplish and would undoubtedly be "one of the greatest water development projects in the world" (Irrigation Ministry, 1980).

WATER RESOURCES OF THE BASIN

The estimated water resources of the Ganga-Brahmaputra-Barak Basin within India are given in Table 1 and show that where the basin accounts for over 61 per cent of the country's surface flows, over a third is locked in the Northeast which is inhabited by less than 4 per cent of its total population and accounts for an even smaller fraction of its net sown area. Not all surface flows can be utilized, the utilizable quantum being determined by the cultivable area (itself a function of land availability and topography) and storage or diversion possibilities. In this respect, although the Brahmaputra-Barak system carries a lot more water, utilizable flows and ground water recharge within the Ganga basin are far larger. The net sown area in India within the Ganga basin is over 60 million hectares compared with 6.5 million hectares in the Brahmaputra and Barak basins.

Table 1
Water Resources of the Ganga-Brahmaputra-Barak Basin in India
(in million hectare-metres)

Basin	Total surface flow	Utilizable flow potential	Ground water utilizable water	Total (col. 3 + 4)
1	2	3	4	5
Ganga	52.50	25.00	17.20	42.20
Brahmaputra	53.74	2.40	2.10	4.50
Barak	5.98		0.13	0.13
Total	112.22	27.40	19.43	46.83
Others*	3.10	(0.30)	0.03	(0.33)
Grand Total	115.32	-	19.46	(47.16)

* Minor rivers flowing into Bangladesh and Burma.
(Source: Central Water Commission, April 1988)

A further set of numbers may be usefully set out here. Some 21 per cent of all Ganga basin flows in India come from the non-Himalayan rivers and nearly two-thirds from rivers with catchments in Nepal. Further, the yield of the Ganga is about 9.6 m ha m at Allahabad and two-and-a-half and four times than at Patna and Farakka, respectively. India has so far constructed or is constructing storages with a gross capacity of 5.72 m ha m on the Ganga system and 0.16 m ha m in the Brahmaputra-Barak basin and has proposals for additional projects with a gross storage of approximately 0.89 m ha m and 6.15 m ha m in the two basins (CWC, April 1988).

Bangladesh receives an annual average inflow of 107 m ha m of surface water (virtually all of it from India) and an annual rainfall of 25 m ha m. Allowing for evaporation, this gives a runoff of 115.3 m ha m, only part of which is utilizable. Additionally, it has a groundwater potential of 1.81 m ha m as assessed by the UN (UNDP 1982) a working estimate more recently confirmed by the Master Plan Organisation after its Third Interim Report (December, 1984) had cited a higher figure. The net area sown in Bangladesh is 8.6 million hectares of which 3.75 million hectares are in the Ganga basin.

Nepal and Bhutan have abundant surface water resources but the amount that can be drafted for irrigation is limited by the mountainous terrain. The arable area in Nepal is 2.8 million hectares. The groundwater resources of these two kingdoms have not yet been scientifically assessed though Nepal has a rich aquifer along the sub-Himalayan springline that runs laterally along the Terai. A Canadian-assisted water-energy study of Nepal has been completed. More recently a Gandak basin study was done by the Australian Snowy River Authority and a Kosi basin study by the Japanese. A current feasibility study by a Canadian-US consortium of the energy potential of the Karnali, along with earlier reports, has developed considerable data on that basin. The focus in each case has primarily been on energy, unlike the Bangladesh National Water Plan prepared for the Master Plan Organisation by an American firm, Harza Engineering Co. International, and the Ganga-Brahmaputra Basin water study done by the Central Water Commission in India. Both these project long-term water requirements for all consumptive and non-consumptive uses up to 2005 and 2025 respectively, with the Indian study broken down into a series of sub-basin reports.

DEEP AQUIFER HYPOTHESIS

To these conventional water resources must be added the possibility of augmentation from deep confined aquifers formed by the interaction of tectonic episodes, the filling of the Ganga foredeep and intermittent glacial epochs. Where such deep aquifers are completely trapped or sealed without any possibility of recharge there is only a stock of fossil water which might be substantial and could be mined in the manner of a depleting asset like oil. On the other hand, the thesis advanced by Paul Jones envisages up to five very deep aquifers at depths of 400 to 2,500 m which are still being recharged in the Bhabar zone along the Himalaya in Nepal as well as in Uttar Pradesh and Bihar and on the plateau rising above the Bengal Basin in both eastern Bangladesh and western West Bengal. In the studies made on behalf of the World Bank, Paul Jones has put forward specific proposals for exploratory drilling to establish the facts (1985 and 1986). He has tentatively cited some theoretical estimates of staggering finds of up to 282.9 m ha m of water in Bihar-Uttar Pradesh and 130 m ha m in Bangladesh. The exploratory bores would provide the essential parameters relating to the depth of different horizons, water quality, confirmation of artesian pressure as surmised, and recharge values.

Though groundwater development in India on any scale goes back to 1935 when the Uttar Pradesh Government constructed a number of tubewells, with hydel power generated on the Ganga canal falls providing cheap energy, development of this resource and geohydrological data on it were limited. In a sense groundwater was "discovered" during the severe drought and famine of 1966-67 in eastern India. The government sought American assistance in formulating a water resources investigation programme and Paul H. Jones and Walter Hofmann of the Water Resources Division of the US Geological Survey were assigned this task. The mission reported in 1967 recommending the establishment of a separate agency to pursue groundwater investigations along the lines indicated. Hydrogeology came to be established as an important tool early after the Second World War and was powerfully aided by the electrical logging method of exploration mainly developed by the rapidly growing oil and gas industry. Paul Jones, who straddled the worlds of hydro – and petroleum geology, wrote a paper on Water Resource Development in the Ganges Basin in October 1983 where he posited the existence of a huge groundwater reservoir underlying the upper Gangetic Plain at great depth.

The Sen Committee on Agricultural productivity in Eastern India, reporting in 1984, had this to say: "Before undertaking construction of very costly high storage dams in the Himalayan region, the technical feasibility and economic viability of tapping the very deep aquifers (1500 m or deeper) that are supposed to exist in East U.P., Bihar and West Bengal, through artesian wells or very deep tubewells, may be explored. Pilot projects may be taken up by the Central Government in these States during the Seventh Plan. Based on the results of such pilot projects, a number of such wells with suitable canal systems may be constructed in the Eighth Plan in East U.P., Bihar and West Bengal."

The World Bank pursued the idea and its irrigation division and Paul Jones between them produced a series of papers over the next two years further detailing the geological basis for and groundwater prospects under artesian conditions in Eastern Uttar Pradesh and Bihar, the Nepal Terai, West Bengal and Bangladesh. The World Bank went public at a seminar especially called for the purpose in Washington in May 1986 at which a number of experts assembled to hear and discussion the proposition with the banks' Vice President for South Asia Dr. David Hopper in the Chair (World Bank, 1986). There was further reference to this at the 13th session of ESCAP's Committee on Natural Resources held in Bangkok (Shibusawa A.H. October 1986). The Government of India remained stoically silent while academic and official responses in Bangladesh were skeptical or hostile.

In February 1987 however, the Indian Government approved a joint mission by World Bank experts and hydrogeologists of the CGWB that visited Dehra Dun and studied the electric logs, completion reports, seismic data, structure maps and geologic reports made available by the Oil and Natural Gas Commission. A summary of the findings was prepared. Based on this, Paul Jones submitted a proposal to the World Bank confirming the existence of a "gigantic fresh water reservoir" underlying the Gangetic Plain and surmising that there could be water "enough to fill a fresh-water lake the size of the Ganges Plain to a depth of 122 m (400 feet). This amount of water would irrigate the 70 million acre cropland area of the plain for 100 years" (Jones P.H. Hydrogeology, Inc., June 1987). He proposed a twin project to drill six exploratory wells in the Ganges Basin between Kasganj (Near Aligarh) and Purnea and two wells in the Bengal Basin along the Bolpur-Kharagpur axis at a cost of $ 7.47 million, the entire project including a technical report on the findings being completed within two years. A separate proposal had earlier been outlined for drilling 20 exploratory test-wells in Bangladesh at depths ranging from 1,000 to 1,800 m, based on geohydrological data derived from use of Petrobangla's electric logs (Jones, P.H., Hydrogeology Inc., November 1985).

Likewise, a proposal for a deep aquifer exploration project in Nepal was outlined by the World Bank in April 1985. This envisaged screening of three or more aquifers through the completion of six test wells in the Terai over a 15-month period at a cost of $ 8.22 million inclusive of a training and technical assistance package.

SCEPTICISM INHIBITS EXPLORATORY PROGRAMME

Both technical and administrative opinion in India have been skeptical or even dismissive of the Paul Jones thesis. The grounds are many. It is said to rest on a whole series of surmises; that artesian conditions are unlikely to be sustained, even if found, as witnessed by the experience of so-called artesian wells drilled along the Bhabar springline which soon show a diminishing yield; that if the artesian condition is not satisfied then the pumping costs from great depths would be prohibitive; that drilling large numbers of large bore, high-yield wells to depths of 1,000 and 2,000m would be technically complex and very expensive, apart from the problem of keeping them in good condition; that the idea of a totally confined regional aquifer may not hold and that otherwise too, any deep aquifer under the Ganga must discharge at some point above Farakka in which case it must form part of the existing Ganga water balance; that recharge values, if any, and water quality are unknown; and that there could be subsidence. Besides, India's immediate groundwater priorities dictate urgent exploratory and development effort in the semi-arid and hard rock areas as the Ganga and Bengal basins have rich aquifers which still have a very considerable unexploited potential, especially in the eastern region.

All these are wise cautions. But none of them answers why there has been such a marked reluctance even to discuss the proposition in the open or to turn it over to scholars and expert bodies for technical examination, India and Bangladesh are both seasonally short of water. Existing groundwater and surface flow potentials are finite and likely to be exhausted in the near future, some sub-basins sooner than others. Large storages have evoked much controversy or been delayed by resource constraints. Major modernization programmes of existing surface systems are underway, and the huge investments proposed entail long-term commitments. All this is true. But it still does not explain the unwillingness to give adequate and early consideration at both technical and policy levels to what might be an immensely rewarding option, if proven.

The wiser course would seem to be to invest a relatively modest sum in an exploratory programme that would test the deep aquifer hypothesis and define its potential as a basis for longer term investment decisions, regional water allocation, conjunctive uses and optimized systems planning. Exploration might well prove the proposition dud. So be it. But this risk is taken every day in oil and gas exploration. So why baulk when it comes to testing what could be a vast reserve of fresh water? Bangladesh experts have their own reservations, but the fear that this proposal might put a freeze on all other water resource development in the country seems mistaken. And any notion that deep aquifers can preempt all future dams is equally fanciful. None of this need happen.

The World Bank posed the Paul Jones proposal to the Ministry of Water Resources in October 1987 and the Government of India is said to be thinking of mounting a deep aquifer exploratory programme on its own. The necessary equipment is to be obtained for a pilot project which may be expanded on the basis of the initial findings. If proven, the deep aquifer will add to the stock and quantum of utilizable water resources in India, Nepal and Bangladesh.

EVOLVING BANGLADESH STRATEGIES

Any water potential is only as good as its use. East Bengal was always an irrigation-poor part of undivided India and of Pakistan when it was a wing of that country. Floods and drainage were regarded as its principal problems, which they are – for half the year. During the dry months, however, irrigation is obviously necessary as much as supplementary irrigation during the monsoon. The very destructive floods of 1954, 1955 and 1956 first turned attention towards water conservation. The UN Technical Mission led by J.A. Krug looked at the problem in 1957 and made a series of recommendations primarily aimed at flood control. At its instance however, a Water and Power Development Authority was established in 1959 with an American firm, International Engineering Company (IECO) as consultants to prepare a master plan. This was completed in 1964 with a 20-year perspective. It identified a number of projects, including barrages on the Ganga, Brahmaputra and Meghna in order to provide flood protection and irrigation calculated to ensure self-sufficiency in foodgrain by 1985. the World Bank was invited to review the master plan in 1966. It favoured smaller, quick-yielding projects and improved agricultural practices in the flood-free areas. Further more, it had reservations about taking up large schemes on the major rivers without some international understanding with India which controls the headwaters. An elaborate World Bank-Harvard Action Plan was next prepared and this report, submitted in 1972, set the framework for water resource development under Bangladesh's First Five Year Plan. The emphasis was on low-lift pumps and tubewells (Khan, Amjad Hossain, and Khan, Akbar Ali 1985).

Only one out of 57 rivers flowing through Bangladesh has its headwaters within the country. The rest are in India. This has been an inhibiting factor. Bangladesh is short of resources and all donor nations and agencies more or less insist on international agreements on water sharing before they are willing to commit themselves to substantial investments. The Ganges-Kobadak and Karnaphuli projects are two large irrigation schemes that went ahead, the former indigenously financed. Others have been long delayed or shelved, although the Teesta Barrage Project too is now going forward.

The UNDP undertook a groundwater study (1982) which identified three aquifers, an upper and a large main aquifer, both interconnected at depths varying from 5 to 75 m, and lower aquifer. The direction of the regional groundwater flow was found to be from northwest to southeast. The upper-main groundwater reservoir, being hydraulically connected to the river system, is recharged by stream flows during the high stages and discharges into them during the dry season.

The country was divided into 15 potential groundwater development zones, and two cautions were underlined. Because of the interconnection between the upper and main aquifers, drawdown from the later should be limited to 6 m or else tens of thousands of dugwells and standpipes catering to the drinking water requirements of a vast section of the population might be left high and dry. It was also stated that drawdown should be so regulated as to preclude salt water contamination of the aquifer wherever the coastal streams are affected by saline intrusion from the sea. Accordingly, a coordinating and monitoring agency was suggested. A groundwater management ordinance imposes siting and spacing restrictions with regard to new tubewells.

By 1984-85 irrigation in Bangladesh extended over 2.44 million hectares, almost equally divided between ground and surface systems, with low river-lift pumps accounting for the largest part of surface irrigation. Liberal subsidies for shallow tubewells led to their rapid expansion and, subsequently, of deep tubewells as well, supposedly under group management on account of donor pressures to import more equipment. This somewhat unregulated expansion left much to be desired in terms of equity and efficiency in the eyes of many observers (Ali, A.A.M. Shawkat; 1985). The Planning Commission too found that irrigation efficiency had suffered and that the physical facilities created remained under-utilised. The Third Plan emphasized timely and dependent supplies of water and proposed rationalization of subsidies, standardization of equipment, better coordination and a review of water legislation. One interesting idea mooted was that large capacity pumps mounted on barges might be used to augment flows in smaller rivers such as the Old Brahmaputra, Dhaleshwari, and Bengali from the Ganga, Brahmaputra and Meghna.

By the year 2000 Bangladesh will need to increase food production to 25 million tonnes in order to remain self-sufficient. And to achieve this it will have to bring at least 3.75 million hectares under irrigation by that date as against an ultimate potential of 4.45 million hectares. The object of the National Water Plan (1985-2005) is to develop Bangladeshi water resources so as to maximize both agricultural and fisheries production, apart from providing adequate water supplies for domestic and industrial use, navigation, salinity control and environmental management. On one estimate, the cropping intensity will require to be raised from 150 at present to 200 and, later, even to 250.

An earlier estimate made by the Master Plan Organisation indicated that the groundwater and surface water potential might be exhausted by 1995 and 1998, respectively (Ali, Shawka). Drawing up a list of "National imperatives" for water resource development, some analysts conclude that the National Water Plan must ensure that all regional water development programmes within Bangladesh are implemented before 2000 and that benefits from the proposed construction of diversion barrages across the Ganges and Brahmaputra for irrigation must begin to accrue between 2000 and 2005 (Chaudhury, M and Siddiqui M.H. 1985). The idea of barrages within Bangladesh across these great rivers, possibly with some pondage, has been mooted off and on over the past 30 years. Technical and resource considerations apart, the absence of an agreement with India on the sharing of lean season flows not only on these but on other common rivers as well has stalled progress. This is the nub of the dispute between the two countries. Indeed, in the case of India also the World Bank insists that no project should adversely affect Bangladesh.

EARLIER PROTECTIVE WORK

Unlike Bangladesh, India was well advanced in irrigation and had a large pool of experienced engineers and Central and State organisations at the time of Independence. There were of course regional variations. Irrigation had made little headway in the entire Northeast, or in north Bihar; even those parts of Rajasthan and Madhya Pradesh falling within the basin had little to show by way of large or even medium works; likewise much of Haryana. The great irrigation works covered Uttar Pradesh and south Bihar on the Ganga, Yamuna, Sharda, Betwa and Sone rivers among others. These were all diversion or river-lift schemes without storage, which basically only existed in south India, coupled with some tubewell development and a large number of traditional *bandhs*, tanks and wells.

Canals were unlined and the essential feature of the irrigation system was that it was protective rather than productive. Many canals had been built or extended in response to political pressures and were quite unable to deliver even minimal flows. The huge Sharda system was a good example of a "political canal", and so it remained until the more recent Sharda Sahayak project which diverted Ghaghara (Karnali) flows into it in the 1970s. Being protective irrigation works, drainage had not been given much importance, despite warnings, in the belief that the irrigation duties were low. Consequently, considerable tracts in the upper reaches of the canal system and adjacent to the main canals or major distributaries were affected by waterlogging, alkalinity and salinity which have had to be treated or even now await attention. The idea of drainage through tubewells or laterally dawned late and remains a challenge.

In Nepal, public irrigation works were limited to the Chandra Canal (1927), a small diversion scheme, and the Juddha Canal prior to 1950, though an estimated 120,000 hectares were commanded by small works undertaken by farmers. While there were dug-wells in the Terai, systematic groundwater investigations only commenced in 1969 under USAID. Likewise in Bhutan and Tibet, irrigation in earlier periods was limited to traditional works.

NEW STARTS AND MODERNISATION SCHEMES

With food self-sufficiency being one of the primary objectives of Independent India, it was no surprise that the grow-more-food campaign and post-war reconstruction programmes included major irrigation and flood protection works. The Bhakra project, which serves Haryana and Delhi apart from the Punjab, and the Damodar Valley Corporation (DVC) multipurpose water resource development programme in Bihar and West Bengal, modeled on the TVA, were taken up. Then in swift stages storage and diversion schemes followed on the Chambal (Madhya Pradesh and Rajasthan), Kosi (Bihar and Nepal), Gandak (Uttar Pradesh, Bihar and Nepal), Rihand (hydel generation and Sone canal stabilization), Ramganga (Uttar Pradesh – the first major Himalayan storage in the Ganga basin), Ghaghara (Sharda Sahayak to benefit Uttar Pradesh), Mayurakshi and Kangsabati (West Bengal), Chandan and Badua (Bihar), to name only the more important ones. Currently under construction or on the drawing board are a series of irrigation or multipurpose storages and barrages on the Yamuna system, Betwa, Sone and Teesta. The Tehri Dam will be the first of a series of storages on the upper Ganga in Garhwal (Uttar Pradesh). A Teesta Dam is projected in supplies for the Teesta barrage project which is nearing completion in West Bengal. Some hydroelectric projects have come up or are under construction in the Brahmaputra-Barak Basin in Assam, Meghalaya, Arunachal, Manipur and Tripura while giant projects are contemplated on the Brahmaputra (Dihang dam), Subansiri and Barak (Tipaimukh dam). There are also a number of projects under discussion with Nepal on the Karnali, Mahakali (Sharda), Kosi and other rivers.

The Upper Ganga Canal is among the oldest and biggest in India and irrigates almost a million hectares in Uttar Pradesh. Constructed almost 150 years ago and remodeled over the years, this system is crumbling in parts and in urgent need of rehabilitation and modernization to enable it to serve the needs of the new high-yielding agriculture and provide assured supplies to tail-enders along its manifold reaches. Accordingly, a huge 40-year, Rs 1,437 crore (1984 prices) modernization project has been undertaken of which Phase I (18 years) is under way, a first six year component (1984-90) being currently under execution with World Bank Assistance. The objectives include risk aversion, rehabilitation and modernization of the system, using the water saving from lining and operational improvements to increase the command area, augmenting water supply through the conjunctive use of groundwater; bolstering the Madhya Ganga Canal-I which interconnects with the UC, modernizing watercourse and field structures, putting down 33 augmentation tubewells, installing a modern two-way radio and teleprinter canal communication system, drainage improvements, replacement of two old hydel stations on canal falls within the system, the establishment of a water and land management training institute (WALMI), and other training inputs (World Bank, April 1984).

The earlier barrage and canal headworks at Bhimgoda, near Haridwar, have been replaced and redesigned to augment the capacity of the canal to sustain the requirements of the modernized system. A number of cross drainage works, escapes and bridges which are in distress are being replaced. A lined parallel Ganga Canal is being constructed between kilometres 238 and 291 and three distributary commands serving some 43,000 hectares are to be completely modernized. The old UGC could no longer run to capacity. Farmers in the middle and lower reaches had been compelled to adopt less profitable cropping patterns on account of inadequate and unreliable supplies, thus creating equity as much as efficiency problems which will now be corrected.

Remodeling of the Eastern Yamuna Canal was completed some years ago and modernization of the Western Yamuna Canal system, originally built over 500 years ago but remodeled from time to time, is being undertaken. The Sone barrage and canals in Bihar (constructed in 1876) have also deteriorated resulting in siltation and loss of efficiency. Here again a modernization programme (Rs 1,300 crores) is under consideration.

UTTAR PRADESH PERSPECTIVE PLAN

To return to Uttar Pradesh, over 10 of the 17.5 million hectares of net cropped area in the State were under irrigation in 1985-86, about a third of this from groundwater and utilizing some 30 per cent of the available groundwater potential. Uttar Pradesh has drawn up a perspective plan for developing its water resources to the fullest extent by 202, by when its population might be of the order of 275 million (UP Department of Irrigation, Lucknow, 1985). The Uttar Pradesh Planning Department had estimated the State's ultimate gross irrigation potential from all sources at 25.7 million hectares of which 12.5 million hectares is likely to be served by major and medium projects based on available surface flows. Projects that will irrigate all but 0.7 million hectares of this total are already in operation or under construction or were posed for inclusion in the Seventh Plan (1985-90). With conjunctive use of water, the intensity of irrigation by 2020 is likely to be 164 per cent.

The Uttar Pradesh perspective plan sought an investment of Rs 8,200 crores at 1984-85 prices to realise the assessed ultimate 12.5 million hectare potential from major to medium schemes by the end of the 13th Plan in 2020 at an estimated cost of Rs.18,000 per hectare as against a national average cost of Rs.32,700 per hectare however, the use-efficiency of water is low with a potential of 1.295 million hectares unutilized in the Sharda Sahayak, Gandak and Ramganga commands, the largest gap by far being in the first. The perspective plan states it takes about seven years for utilisation of 90 per cent of the potential created in a particular scheme which seems more a historical estimate than a prescription for the future. With low productivity gains from growing irrigation the incremental capital-output ratio has shown a significant rise. Another point worth noting relates to the spatial imbalance in the availability of surface flows. Thus there is an estimated monsoon surplus of 3.8 m ha m of water in the Ghaghara basin whereas the Buldekhand plateau region south of the Ganga is water short. Therefore the perspective plan calls for efforts to see whether some of the Ghaghara surplus could be diverted south. Alternatively, with reverse pumping it might be possible to have the Ghaghara's surplus "brought up to the Banbassa Barrage" in the Himalayan foothills and 1thereafter diverted though the Sharda canal system to Central Uttar Pradesh or into the Yamuna Basin. A third possibility envisaged is a negotiated exchange of Ghaghara for Sone waters with Bihar to augment available supplies in the water-short Baghelkhand region which marks an extension of the Bundelkhand plateau further east along the Kaimur Range.

LIMITED PROGRESS IN BIHAR

Bihar is another water rich State with a low rate of irrigation development. Unlike Uttar Pradesh it has no long-term master plan although the Sen Committee (1984) stated that it had an "identified irrigation potential: of 12.4 million hectares, more than two-thirds of this from surface water schemes. The groundwater potential of the State has been estimated at 2.86 m ha m of which no more than 21 per cent had been utilized at the commencement of the Seventh Plan (1985). North Bihar and Nepal constitute a single hydraulic entity but there is no joint water planning. Failure to plan for the conjunctive development of water and to provide for lateral drainage, as in the Kosi region, has resulted in waterlogging. Bamboo tubewells have proved popular in certain deep alluvial tracts in the Kosi and even the Gandak basin, but high fragmentation of smallholdings (with provision only for voluntary consolidation) and inadequate and uncertain power (or even diesel) supplies has impeded tubewell development. As in much of the region, agrarian relations are not conducive to investment and risk-taking on the basis of technological improvements that could yield considerable productivity gains.

Floods are an annual hazard and, unless moderated, will remain an impediment to agricultural improvement in North Bihar. Paucity of funding has also slowed down programmes. The Gandak project was started in 1961 with a sanctioned estimate of Rs 47 crores. It has yet to be completed though a sum of Rs. 470 crores has already been spent. In the case of the Kosi project, the eastern Kosi Canal started in 1959 was opened for partial irrigation five years later. By 1986 a potential of no more than 374,000 hectares had been created against the projected potential of 434,000 hectares. More dismaying was the fact that utilisation in the preceding year was limited to 190,000 hectares while 182,000 hectares were waterlogged though some argue that about 120,000 hectares were always waterlogged even before the canal was built. Delays and consequent cost escalation have been attributed to problems of land acquisition and shortage of cement. Additions have been made, such as lining of certain canal reaches, which basically go back to inherent defects in the original concept and design which were hurriedly put together in the wake of the devastating 1954 flood. The very sandy soil in the eastern Kosi Canal command requires heavy watering of between 2,200 and 2,500 mm to grow paddy. This degree of irrigation, often done by field to field flooding in the absence of water courses, invites trouble without proper drainage. Another cropping pattern might have helped, though the soil no doubt has become less pervious with some years of cultivation.

The performance of the Water Development Corporation that manages the State-owned deep tubewells has not been found very satisfactory by the Bihar Planning Department on account of "poor maintenance, idle capacity due to breakdown of power supply, high overheads, and high cost of operation, etc" (Bihar Planning Department, 1985). The efficiency of the Bihar Hill List Irrigation Corporation, catering to the predominantly tribal areas of Chota Nagpur and Santhal Parganas, both plateau regions, was also found wanting. The Sone system in South Bihar, on the other hand, is in urgent need of modernization, which has been taken up tentatively pending commitment of funds. The Bansagar Dam in Madhya Pradesh will however provide it with larger supplies of Sone water when completed in 1990.

WEST BENGAL'S OPTIONS

West Bengal has a net sown area of 2.25 million hectares and an ultimate irrigation potential of 6.1 million hectares. It had by 1985 utilised less than one third of its groundwater potential of 1.6 m ha m. Phase I of the Teesta Barrage project, nearing completion, will add some 0.3 million hectares to irrigation in North Bengal and this will be extended to a million hectares in all when the Teesta project is completed with high dam storage in Sikkim. The State suffers from many of the problems experienced by Bihar and eastern Uttar Pradesh with 0.8 million hectares waterlogged in 1984, but its utilization ratio is far better.

Though West Bengal draws up to 1,132 cumecs through the Jangipur canal from the Farakka Barrage to flush the Bhagirathi-Hooghly and control salinity, it receives no irrigation supplies from the Ganga. It has, however, sought an allocation of at least 425 cumecs during the dry season from January to May though it claims that it could beneficially use even three times that amount. If it gets any part of the minimum allocation it seeks it has prepared a Rs.2000-2500 crore outline plan spread over several Plan periods to pump this water from the Ganga into existing dam storages on the Mayurakshi, Kangsabati and Ajoy and in the DVC which could entail manageable lifts of 6 to 16 m. Such a programme would stabilize rabi and summer irrigation.

Like Bangladesh, West Bengal faces a unique problem in the Sunderbans. In the Indian segment of this vast dynamic delta with tidal and cyclonic influences, the Sunderbans consists of 54 deltaic islands spread over 9000 square kilometers with a population of about three million. Drainage must precede irrigation and agricultural development and communications are necessary for any of this or fishery (basically shrimp) development. Under a World Bank assisted programme (Phase I, 1982-88), 10 river closure schemes have been taken up on derelict creeks with heavy siltation. Once the mouth is closed with sluiced earthen embankments or polders, the inner channel is excavated to a depth of maybe two-and-a-half metres which stores rainwater for winter irrigation. Though there is saline intrusion through bottom seepage, salinity is maintained within tolerable limits and, with leaching, sweet water can be ensured within four to five years. Water-intensive crops such as winter paddy are disallowed. But kharif (aman) paddy is permitted followed by vegetables and chillies. Beneficiary groups of 30 to 40 small farmers, each generally owning less than 0.4 hectares, group management and maintenance is required. Solar pumps are to be tried out as a possible low cost mechanism.

Brackish water shrimp fishery is more profitable than paddy and there is a temptation, as Bangladesh too has discovered, for people to break polders in order to secure transference from paddy to shrimp. This has to be policed through community effort. It is the West Bengal government's policy to apportion shallower stretches of the Sunderbans for polderised cropping and to confine shrimp farming to deeper channels which cannot be easily reclaimed. Sugar beet grows well and is being encouraged though there is a marketing problem that must be overcome. In the next phase of the programme, integrated crop-cum-fish/duck/piggery systems are to be developed.

In the vast northeastern region of India, the net sown area is limited to 3.30 million hectares of which 2.56 million hectares, or an area equivalent to that in the Nile Valley in Egypt, lies in Assam. The ultimate gross irrigation potential of all the seven Northeast States put together is estimated at 3.61 million hectares. Irrigation development started late in the region but Assam, which has brought a million hectares under irrigation so far, is endeavouring to develop its full potential by 2005. Under three per cent of Assam's groundwater resources have been tapped as yet and considerable emphasis is now being given to encouraging tubewells. With floods sweeping the valley during the monsoon, winter irrigation is essential for agricultural stability and to augment production.

Other parts of the region are predominantly mountainous except for Imphal Valley in Manipur and the Tripura plains fringing Bangladesh. Arunachal, Nagaland, Meghalaya and Mizoram are limited to modest valley schemes and hill channels with hydram lifts to small storages on upper ridges wherever conditions permit. Manipur however has a significant potential, much of this in the fertile Imphal Valley where the Loktak hydel project has energized a lift programme. With six other projects under construction, 108,000 hectares will be brought under irrigation and more under minor schemes. Tripura has planned some projects on rivers that flow into Bangladesh. This has raised issues of international water-sharing that have yet to be finally resolved.

SALINITY IN THE SEMI-ARID TRACTS

Moving from eastern to central and northwestern India entails a transition from a wet and humid region with drainage congestion to semi-arid regions that are water short or face salinity. Yet even within large basins there are sub-basins that have more or less water than they require. After decades of disputation, the flows of the Narmada have been allocated under a tribunal award that gives 2.25 m ha m to Madhya Pradesh. Of this amount, the State plans to reserve 0.3 m ha m for domestic, municipal and industrial uses in the future. The remaining water, however, would appear to exceed reasonable irrigation requirements in the Narmada Valley which has limited arable land. It is therefore proposed in the long term to transfer some 167,000 ha m to the Tons and Sone Valley by a high level gravity canal for utilization through the Bansagar Dam and another 61,000 to 85,000 ha m by the Bargi-Mandu lift scheme to the Malwa plateau and thence to the Chambal system with a 200 to 230 metre lift. These inter-basin transfers will redistribute available water more equitably within Madhya Pradesh.

The groundwater salinity belt starts in the Mathura and Agra districts of Uttar Pradesh and extends west into Haryana and Rajasthan. Not all the aquifers are brackish by any means and it has been possible to utilize some brackish sources for irrigation with suitable blending and the evolution of salt-tolerant crop species. However, the region has attained a higher degree of agricultural stability despite limited rainfall with irrigation from surface storages coupled with larger groundwater utilization. It has also been aided by a longer tradition of modern irrigation and requisite organizational backing. Though there are tenancy and other land problems here too, they are nothing as acute as in the eastern zone and farmers are more enterprising and willing and able to take risks.

Not that there is no waterlogging. Long years of surface irrigation has resulted in a steady rise in the water table. Some 167,000 hectares were waterlogged in the Chambal command in Rajasthan in 1986 and more than that in Haryana. Conjunctive uses are now being planed and tubewell development is likely to bring down or control waterlogging, the battery of augmentation tubewells put down by Haryana on its side of the Western Yamuna Canal nearly 20 years ago being an early example of forethought in this regard. But there is a long way to go. Haryana in particular has also gone in for lining canals to limit seepage. Limited availability of water is also encouraging use of water conserving irrigation methods such as sprinklers for high-value crops under sound management, and even drip irrigation, an indigenous variant of which is to plant a pitcher of water next to a tiny crop cluster and let the moisture ooze out to match plant-water requirements. These are expensive systems, no doubt, but they are highly efficient and, with underground pipes, land saving.

Large tracts in Haryana are affected by alkalinity and salinity as a result of earlier ill-drained irrigation. These lands have been treated with gypsum and considerable areas have been reclaimed. Saline-affected return irrigation flows are stored in sumps and then lifted and drained into the Yamuna when the river is in flood and has sufficient water to dilute these waste flows. Central Haryana is a tough and hence the necessity for drainage lift. In southwestern Haryana, as in the adjacent areas of Punjab, it has been suggested that brackish water from salt-affected fields should be drained into lined canals and led into the sand dunes in Rajasthan where inter-dunal culture is possible at salt levels of 5,000 to 10,000 parts per million. The terrain being sandy, even one good rain will leach the salt. The Central Arid Zone Research Institute at Jodhpur is reportedly working on inter-dunal culture which is well established in Israel. Two other options suggested are to drain brackish waters into ponds and raise salt water fish or to pump these waters into solar pans and extract salt and other chemicals at a potential extraction rate of 10 tonnes per hectare per annum. Such ideas may not be entirely fanciful and call for experimentation and techno-economic analysis.

LIFTS AND SPRINKLERS

Irrigation is not possible in undulating terrain except through sprinklers. The alternative is land leveling and shaping, preferably in rectangles after consolidation, which is not mandatory under the Rajasthan Land Development Act. Bhiwani, Laharu and Hissar districts in Haryana have taken a lead in sprinkler irrigation which is also being increasingly used under some of Haryana's lift irrigation schemes to avoid land leveling costs or to reach high points within the command area especially during the rabi season.

The Yamuna, Ghaggar, Markanda, Sahibi and other flood waters coursing through Haryana have been diverted into four or five depressions to hold some 15,160 ha m of water, some of which has been available for irrigation or has facilitated cultivation on the moist bed after the waters have withdrawn. South-eastern Haryana rising up to the Aravalli watershed marks the western edge of the Ganga Basin. The land is fertile but is short of water. With periodic droughts, some branches at the tail end of the Western Yamuna Canal system would be extended with low lifts as a relief measure. After Haryana came into being in 1967, the new administration decided to try and irrigate the entire upland belt from Hissar to Mahendragarh with a series of lift schemes. Four systems have since been developed with lifts ranging from 35 to 120 m. These will ultimately command a culturable area of over 450,000 hectares, the area actually irrigated being, of course, smaller. Currently about 42 cumecs of water is being provided, with a low ration for critical waterings, as against a full requirement of 128 cumecs. Likewise, no more than 75 MW of power is being used against a total requirement on completion of 175 MW. The four schemes combined are expected to attain an irrigation intensity of 62 per cent, 22 in kharif and 40 in rabi.

Water for this ambitious lift scheme comes from Bhakra and is fed into the Western Yamuna Canal system. Fuller development awaits realization of Haryana's share in the disputed Ravi-Beas surplus over which it has yet to reach a final accord with Punjab despite the (Eradi) Ravi-Beas Tribunal Award (1987). The Sutlej-Yamuna Link Canal also remains incomplete.

Fortunately, inter-state water disputes have not been so acute in the Indo-Gangetic basin as in Peninsular India where water resource development has long been held up as on the Narmada and even today on the Cauvery. A series of agreements were arrived at prior to Independence and many more thereafter pertaining to the distribution of the waters of the Yamuna, including remodeling of certain headworks between Uttar Pradesh, Haryana, Rajasthan, Delhi and Himachal (1954, 1955, 1963); the Betwa (Matatila and Rajghat dams and canals) between Madhya Pradesh and Uttar Pradesh (1965 and 1972); the Rihand, between Bihar and Uttar Pradesh (1973); the Sone, relating to the Bansagar dam and water-sharing between Madhya Pradesh, Uttar Pradesh and Bihar (1973); and on the Damodar, Barakar, Ajoy, Mayurakshi and Mahananda basins between Bihar and West Bengal (1978) (CWC, 1979).

As a hill State, Himachal has limited irrigation potential. Farmers have traditionally taken small contour channels or kuls from springs or streams over considerable distances, all the farmers in the command joining to construct and maintain these works. Over the decades springs have run short or the water line has receded necessitating going higher up the mountain or further upstream, thus increasing *kul* leads from 2 to 18 kilometres. This requires governmental assistance. Now small water harvesting storages are being created with earthen check dams and structures to command some 15-20 hectares and supply water to small and marginal farmers for vegetable and other cultivation.

Nepal too is constructing small water harvesting storages for hill irrigation. The government has had to step in to construct larger schemes with longer leads, some of them with staged pumping or hydram lift. But storage-cum-kul schemes that command anything much in excess of five hectares tend to destabilize the hillside and cause slides and are moreover expensive to maintain. India has recently handed over the completed Nepal segment of the Western Kosi Canal in the Terai to the Nepalese administration. Elsewhere, hill torrents are of little use for irrigation as they only discharge silt-laden flash floods. There is, however, scope for irrigation in the basins of the medium rivers that come down from the Mahabharat Range such as the Kamla, Bagmati, Rapti and Kankai, and on some of the small boundary streams. But progress has been held up by the Indo-Nepal disputes, with India claiming protection for older schemes locally undertaken on its side and Nepal desirous of expanding Terai irrigation. The Nepalese argue that some of the works India has objected to are essentially no more than remodeling or modernization of old projects rather than new schemes and that any reduction of low flows is probably due to deforestation rather than additional abstraction. A solution of this problem is necessary but has got enmeshed in the larger issue of water-sharing and cooperation in water-resource development between the two countries.

DEVELOPING AGRO-MET SYSTEMS

This thumbnail sketch of irrigation development within the basin throws up a number of policy issues. The focus has so far been on irrigation projects, on measurements of potential and building engineering structures, rather than on irrigation policy which must henceforward be accorded the importance it deserves (Ramaswamy Iyer 1987). There must be a shift from the quantitative to the qualitative aspects of irrigation. As mentioned earlier, the older irrigation systems were intended to be protective, not productive, as a hedge against famine. This is no longer good enough. These systems have to be remodeled and modernized, structurally perhaps in some cases, but certainly conceptually, in order to ensure reliability, equity, efficiency and accountability both to the farmers whom they are intended to serve and to the taxpayers who pay for them and are entitled to a reasonable overall return. Where water is scarce the effort must be to maximize productivity per unit of water; but where there is sufficient water but limited land, the object should be to maximize production per unit of land. In either case, is more important to maximize farm income year-round rather than just the yield of a single given crop. Cropping patterns in relation to soil and water characteristics must, therefore, be planned with care. If the conjunction use of water is a basic principle of irrigation, its first application must rest on the conjunctive use of irrigation with rainfall. This calls for devising careful systems of project design and operation, water rates and extension services.

With better and more long-range weather forecasts, crop and irrigation planning must be conceived of in larger terms of drought or monsoon management, insuring against too much or too little rainfall, and with contingency plans to maximize gains that go with favourable opportunity. The Indian Irrigation Commission had recommended water budgeting for projects or rivers basins and this was in some sense attempted during the 1987 drought with a measure of success. The Indian Meteorological Department has evolved a multiple regression model for long-range weather forecasting on the basis of 15 broad parameters. Based on this, the IMD predicted in May 1988 that the ensuing monsoon rainfall would be well above normal countrywide – a prediction that proved to be remarkably accurate. It would be premature to draw any firm conclusions from this without further experience of such modeling aided by the more powerful computational facilities recently acquired.

Instead of limiting its readings to 35 meteorological sub-divisions in India the IMD collects data for 385 meteorological districts and an agro-met advisory service started in 1977 now serves farmers in nine States. While this is only a monitoring service with a weekly aridity or moisture index, and makes no predictions, longer term forecasts based on stochastic methods need to be developed and refined. Reservoir and groundwater modeling too might receive useful support were such meteorological data and forecasts prepared not just for the newly defined agroclimatic regions but for specific river basins or even sub-catchments. Attachment of small meteorological units to the Bhakra-Beas Management Board and the Brahmaputra Board mark a beginning. Irrigation cannot be considered in isolation from meteorological, input and crop planning on which, taken together, the season's agricultural output depends. Some 127 agro-met advisory service centres are in the process of being set up to link farmers to the 47 agricultural universities in India through the National Informatics Centre and All-India Radio via satellite. Irrigation has to move on to a new level of sophistication.

Even dew can make a useful moisture contribution to winter crops with increased vegetation inducing greater dew accumulation. Data collected since 1968 indicates that dew accumulation ranges from 15 to 30 mm during the period October to March over the plains of north and northwest India, being largest over Assam (Raman C.R.V. et al., 1973). This same study concludes that dew catch in winter may eventually provide an additional moisture source for crops along the sub-Himalayan plain though it could bring on pests as well. Israel has shown that dew cultivation is possible.

DISMANTLING SOME FALLACIES

A barren argument rehearsed from time to time is that small projects are not merely better than, but can be a substitute for, big projects and large dams. This is a fallacy, and the very notion that "big" projects are necessarily divisible into smaller component projects is mistaken. If projects have been divided into large/major, medium, and small/minor on the basis of investment or, as in India nowadays, of command area (above 10,000 hectares, between 2000 and 10,000 hectares, and below 2000 hectares), this has essentially been done on considerations of financial and administrative convenience rather than on account of any hydrological imperatives. Neither is better or worse per se; each has its place. Nor are the two competitive as such and should be regarded and, ideally, operated as integrated and conjunctive systems. Larger projects often sustain smaller ones, such as so-called percolation tanks that maintain water levels in wells and ponds in farmers' fields. Minor schemes often have a shorter life and fail more easily as they are fed by rain over small catchments. In such situations, as the 1987 drought in India amply demonstrated, it is the large storage dams regulating large catchments, some of them snowfed, that are far more dependable.

Since surface and ground water are by and large part of a single hydrological system, they too should not be regarded as competitive but as complementary resources to be conjunctively used. Seepage losses from surface systems together with normal percolation into the soil in the farmer's field recharge groundwater. Therefore groundwater recharge is augmented by surface irrigation. Suggestions made from time to time that India should opt for groundwater instead of surface irrigation are based on a lack of understanding of the hydrological system. It is now a declared Indian policy that all projects must be designed for conjunctive use of surface flows and groundwater from the very inception. But this has yet to be fully translated into practice. Available groundwater estimates and overall water balance studies have been excluded from the terms of reference given to tribunals appointed to adjudicate Inter-State water disputes.

Another cardinal principle is that drainage and irrigation must go hand in hand as irrigation in the semi-humid, semi-arid tropics will invariably raise the water table and bring harmful salts up to the root zone or even to the surface, causing waterlogging, salinity and alkalinity of which there is a good deal of evidence in the upper Gangetic basin. The time this takes is a factor of irrigation intensity, soil, temperature, rainfall, and flooding and natural drainage conditions. Drainage can be both vertical, through tubewells, as well as lateral, through drains. Protective schemes with light irrigation did not earlier appear to require drainage. Hence the original neglect which can no more be condoned. Lining of canals and watercourses is important not only to save water losses on expensive systems but, in some cases, to prevent waterlogging, salinity and groundwater pollution with agro-chemical down-wash. It has been well said that maintaining a proper salt balance within a river basin is as important an element of conjunctive use as reservoir scheduling and well-field development (Hal, Warren A. 1986). The Irrigation Commission reported (1972) that unlined canals in India, estimated to be carrying 11,300 cumecs, could if lined save enough water to irrigate an additional six million hectares.

Ground water should not be mined but an overdraft in a drought year may be permissible so long as, say, a five year hydrological balance is maintained. Rapid development of groundwater resources in certain areas has resulted in a total disregard for adequate spacing. Excessive pumping has consequently led to shortages or has left shallow tubewells, standpipes and dug-wells high and dry. This basically affects the traditional small user and marginal farmer who cannot afford to see his investment literally dry up. It is, therefore, necessary to protect the prior appropriation of small users and to regulate groundwater. This is possible through legislation. Under the Indian Easement Act, 1982, all groundwater vests in the Government and restrictions imposed in the public interest on the use of groundwater by existing users do not entail payment of compensation, (NCA Part V 1976). The Government has circulated model groundwater rules regarding spacing and other matters. But most states have yet to adopt and implement them.

Since ground water recharge can be augmented by increased pumping up to a point, thereby adding to net water utilization, long-term policy dictates strategies that would achieve this end. An experiment is under way on a five kilometers stretch along the ephemeral Hindon, a tiny tributary of the Yamuna, near Saharanpur, to test the Ganga water-machine principle of high summer pumping to create additional pore space underground to augment monsoon recharge. The great 1987 drought provided a natural lowering of the water table by 5.5 m. Recharge was measured during the 1988 monsoon through a number of observation wells in a 10-square kilometer zone and was found to be very satisfactory. It is now proposed as far as possible to give every small farmer a virtually free low-capacity tubewell to encourage heavy pumping and lower the groundwater table by up to four m before the monsoon as part of a pilot project being under-taken by the Uttar Pradesh government under the guidance of Prof. Rama of the Tata Institute of Fundamental Research, Bombay. If the hypothesis is borne out by the test, larger programmes could follow.

A new aspect of groundwater remodeling and modernization is emerging which must, however, be implemented in stages that include assistance to small and traditional well-users to go deeper down to extract more water. Matching energy supplies and cropping patterns with related credit and inputs will be necessary. In Bangladesh the government may divert water for irrigation or public purposes but only after a three-month notice under the Bengal Irrigation Act. This gives affected landowners time to make alternative arrangements and claim compensation for the stoppage or dimunition of water in any natural or artificial channel or underground if these sources were in use (Khan Amjad Hussain and Khan Akbar Ali 1985). Bangladesh is also propagating deep-set shallow tubewells as a technique to save on equipment costs by re-setting old pumps in pits at the same site. Here are principles on which to build:

NEGLECTED POLICY ISSUES

There have been distressing cost and time overruns in Indian irrigation projects. As many as 181 schemes with an outstanding expenditure of Rs 26,400 crores spilt over into the Seventh Plan which itself provided no more than Rs 11,500 crores for major and medium projects in the irrigation sector. Excessive new starts for political reasons, consequent under-funding, poor or incomplete project formulation and investigations, and changes in scope have contributed to this state of affairs. The actual spillover on committed projects (excluding new phases of old projects) is probably far less. Yet, for lack of resources, distributaries were only being taken up to large outlets, leaving it to a medley of small farmers to build watercourses and field drains which consequently remained long undone. Even otherwise, lower order canals are not always fitted with appropriate control structures. This in turn could result in wasteful use of limited headwater supplies which may be inadequate in the first place. How this happens and what is being done about it through command area development is discussed in the next chapter. However, a fresh prioritization of all projects through periodic review is necessary so that frills are shed and essential tasks to ensure completion and use-efficiency are allowed to progress unhindered.

Likewise, engineers too often believe that the design and construction of the dam and maybe the main canal is paramount. Less attention is, therefore, paid in descending order to the hierarchy of distributary canals and crucial management systems. Less time and thought go into operational details of reservoir and main canal management, with uncertain and slow lines of communication that preclude optimal regulations or responses to changing crop-weather requirements. There are a few if any intermediate or buffer storage, especially at the lower end of the system, in the form of tanks and even farm ponds and depressions. If constructed or made available to the extent they exist, they could be filled by the canal and impart greater operational flexibility with fine-tuning of deliveries. Indeed, prior development of these facilities and groundwater use through tubewells could prepare farmers for the release of canal supplies from dams still under construction thereby minimizing delays in the full utilization of expensive storage. The existing tubewell grid and intermediate mini-storages and ponds could later be conjunctively integrated as part of a single larger system.

As it is, irrigation efficiency is low. Of every 100 units of water let down the main canal from a reservoir only about 40 units reach the farmers' fields after allowing for seepage and evaporation losses at various stages. Crop water requirements may be met inadequately, or in an untimely manner or exceeded. Whichever the case, valuable water is lost and plant growth impeded. Revealing data on irrigation deliveries far in excess of actual crop water requirements in different places and conditions has been published by the Indian Agricultural Research Institute, Delhi (Water Technology Centre, 1977). The NCA recommended a lower national average water allowance of 0.7 m per crop-hectares in 1976 than the 0.76 m stipulated in 1972. If average irrigation efficiency, now 40 per cent in India and no higher elsewhere in the Basin, were to be increased to 60 per cent, a figure that the CWC believes to be attainable, the country's "ultimate" irrigation potential now placed at 113 million hectares (without implementing the National Water Perspective proposal) could be greatly increased. In Sri Lanka, the Mahaweli project started by calculating on a water depth of 1.47 metres per hectare per annum in 1977. This has now come down to between 0.74 and 0.86 m per hectare through improved water management and changes in the cropping pattern.

The question that must be addressed then is whether India should rush pell mell to attain its "ultimate" irrigation potential of 113 million hectares by 2010 (with current costs of surface water irrigation running at over Rs 30,000 per hectare in the Seventh Plan). Or should it be devoting more funds and care to completing on-going schemes together with higher priority for on-farm development and operational, maintenance and management improvements that would significantly enhance the use-efficiency of water?

It would certainly appear desirable and sensible to complete the essential operational components of on-going schemes, whether new or modernization projects. Yet, with economies through better design and investigation, and quicker commissioning, new starts might still be made selectively. This is important as environmental costs are steadily rising with population increase and development and a project delayed may later be a project denied on account of unacceptable displacement costs. The storage of funds or even material is in some ways more apparent that real, with large sums being squandered in populist give-away programmes. A larger and stricter ordering of priorities could enable substantial funds dedicated to relief and employment, for example, to be used for these very purposes while creating significant water resource assets with matching land development. Like other basin states, the challenge India faces demands expedition. The problem, in essence, is one of political management. That is where the answer lies.

CHAPTER 6

Water Management

India has the largest irrigation system in the world with over 70 million hectares under irrigation from all sources as against 45 million hectares in China, which plans to increase it to 55 million hectares by 2000 (World Bank, 1985). But water efficiency averages no more than 40 per cent. Though heavily subsidized, irrigation losses have been steadily mounting and touched by Rs 898.78 crores in 1984-85 of which Rs 772.36 crores were on major and medium projects and the balance on minor irrigation works, including groundwater exploitation. About 36 per cent of the total loss was sustained in irrigation schemes within the Ganga-Brahmaputra-Barak Basin. No comparable figures are available for Bangladesh or Nepal but available information would suggest that the position is no better and may well be worse.

Any judgement based exclusively on financial returns can be misleading as indirect returns and social and even political benefits cannot be altogether discounted. Nonetheless they do provide an indicator that simply cannot be ignored especially as irrigation systems within the basin are rapidly expanding and at an increasing cost per hectare. Equally worrying is the fact that gestation periods of irrigation projects have been unduly prolonged, utilization has been slow and, most important, neither cropping intensity nor productivity gains have matched expectations. All these factors call for careful examination and correction.-

Farmers demand water both to protect their crop and to augment production, two somewhat different functions. Many of the earlier irrigation projects commissioned within the basin in India prior to Independence and until the introduction of the high-yielding, water intensive "green revolution" technology were protective rather than productive schemes. Barrages, without storage backing, diverted water into extensive canal systems running hundreds of kilometres with relatively simple communication and control systems. These were intended to provide insurance against monsoon failure during the kharif season when river supplies were plentiful. If the rains were adequate kharif irrigation demand would be low to save on fixed crop changes. But during the rabi season there would be inadequate canal water to meet demand, especially in the lower reaches. In such a situation irrigation systems have not been able to respond adequately to demand-supply related crop-water requirements. In many old and new systems, unlined canals have resulted in heavy seepage and waterlogging in the upper reaches, aggravating supply shortages at the tail-ends. Inadequate control structures and regulators at outlets commanding 40 hectares or more, below which farmers may not have constructed water courses, often results in field-to-field irrigation causing wastage and waterlogging in the absence of proper drainage. In any case, the assumed or designed cropping pattern has invariably been upset by the failure to synchronize the construction of the distributary system with the storage dam or barrage. In consequence, an abundance of supplies in the head reaches during the early years has encouraged farmers to grow paddy, sugar cane and other water-intensive crops and establish user rights by prior appropriation, leaving insufficient water for farmers in the lower portion of the command area by the time the canals get to them.

COMMAND AREA DEVELOPMENT

The slow pace of utilization of potential created in India with the general lack of preparedness on the part of farmers and official agencies to ensure optimal use of available supplies, led the Irrigation Commission (1972) to recommend the establishment of command area development authorities to bridge the gap. Commencing in 1974-75, the CAD programme is currently operational in 132 commands with an ultimate irrigation potential of 16.5 million hectares under 50 CAD authorities. CADAs are charged with operation and maintenance below the last 0.028 cumec (one cusec) outlet commanding 40 hectares; on-farm development works such as construction and maintenance of field channels, field drains and farm roads; land shaping and consolidation; organizing *warabandi* or fair rotational water releases to individual farmers; devising suitable cropping patterns with adaptive trials; developing groundwater, marketing and processing facilities; soil conservation; and planning market centres. Indeed their charter is all-round farm development built around irrigation. Funding is provided through Central and State contributions and institutional finance. Rs 1,158 crores had been spent until 1985 and a sum of Rs 1,600 crores was allocated under the Seventh Plan (1985-90). Until April 1988 field channels had been constructed on an estimated 10.76 million hectares, land leveled over 2.94 million hectares, and *warabandi* introduced in 4.95 million hectares. All CADAs have more recently been asked to undertake crop-cutting experiments to measure productivity gains; take water courses from the project outlet to five to eight hectare blocks on a wholly grant basis so as to enhance the use-efficiency of water; initiate pilot schemes to foster farmer-participation in water distribution and management; experiment with farmer associations which may be willing to take water on a volumetric basis below the minor (which might command several hundred hectares); and improve canal communication.

In the Chambal command in Rajasthan, a non-statutory CADA unlike in Bihar, 45,000 out of 229,000 hectares had been serviced with field channels, land leveling, consolidation and field drains by 1986 at an average cost of Rs 4000 per hectare. This amount is to be recovered from cultivators within 10 years of completion at 10 per cent interest. There has been farmer resistance on account of crop loss during the implementation period. The OFD is generally carried out between March and June when the fields are normally vacant or during October-December when farmers are compensated for leaving their fields uncropped. Participation by panchayat leaders would help, but has not been greatly forthcoming. In West Bengal, the panchayats are assisting in the execution of OFD works. Even so the programme there has been lagging behind schedule.

The Sharda Sahayak project in Uttar Pradesh has established a potential of 1.4 million hectares in a command area of 2 million hectares. Irrigation commenced in 1967 through an unlined feeder canal, resulting in seepage losses and waterlogging and a reduction in its actual operational capacity to 396 cumecs against a design capacity of 650 cumecs. Water availability has therefore been low. Lining of the feeder was taken up in 1987 and is to be completed in five years at a cost of Rs 100 crores. It is also planned to stabilize the system by building regulators, gates, embankments and headwalls at outlet openings and by completing other works which were left undone earlier in response to down-reach farmer pressure to extend the canal. Surface drain construction has also been taken up along side a plan for conjunctive use of water by reboring wells and fitting them with subsidized pumping sets. Tubewells are being encouraged at the tail-end of all minors, *kulabas* (field outlets) and at the lower end of the system as a whole.

As a result of all these measures the waterlogged and salinity-affected area has been reduced to 25,000 hectares or a quarter of what it was five years ago. A rising water table had touched the danger level in some 300,000 hectares. This has now been lowered to safer levels in all but 18,000 hectares. Rabi utilization touched 510,000 hectares in 1987. Kharif irrigation demand is low during years of normal rainfall. But come a drought and farmers think nothing of cutting canals to flood their paddy fields. The canals are closed in summer for lining. Other than the main canal, lining is being limited to critical portions such as through *usar* (sodic) patches, on curves, and near cisterns to the extent of 10 per cent of the total length of channel, this cost being recovered from farmers. Consolidation is being done by the Consolidation Department and construction of *chak* (irrigation block) roads has been transferred by the National Rural Employment Programme, *Warabandi* (locally known as *osrabandi*) is taken up after OFD is completed. Awareness is still to grow and tail-enders continue to suffer from inadequate supplies.

As elsewhere in Uttar Pradesh water rates are calculated on the basis of area irrigated. However, an experiment was initiated in five *kulabas* totaling 220 hectares with about 320 farmers to make available water to a cooperative on a volumetric basis from kharif 1988. Supplies were to be guaranteed by the Irrigation Department in relation to an optimal rotation linked to crop-water requirements as determined by the members. The Irrigation Department had been recovering only about Rs 200-250 or 60-65 per cent of its demand per *kulaba* (40 hectares). The cooperative has agreed to pay Rs 500 per *kulaba* for the guaranteed supply at 16 paise per 1,000 litres, a rate that would entail no loss to the department. The experiment remains to be evaluated but could provide a model for the future, combining as it does elements of improved water management with farmer responsibility.

Nevertheless, problems remain. Experience in the Sharda Sahayak command shows that the broad CADA mandate has been lost and emphasis is being given almost exclusively to construction of water courses and lining of channels. Integrated development of the command area with single-window clearance has not been achieved. Cropping intensity has indeed gone up but remains below the target figure. The CAD authority's intended coordinating role has been greatly diluted as the ego of other departments has been hurt. Extension support has been transferred out of CADA under the training-and-visit extension system. As elsewhere, CADA administrators have not been left undisturbed to get on with the job. Quick transfers have become the norm.

EXPERIENCE IN RAMGANGA AND GANDAK COMMANDS

The adjacent Ramganga command was established in 1973 and covers 11 districts lying between the Ganga and Yamuna. It is irrigated by the Upper and Lower Ganga canals whose supplies are supplemented from the Ramganga dam through a feeder channel which falls into the Ganga. These waters are picked up some 100 kilometres down-river at the Narora headworks (now the site of a nuclear power plant). Here again, the concept of integrated development has given way primarily to construction of water courses, a task that will be completed in 1990. Only 10 per cent of the siphons, culverts and retaining walls are cemented, the balance being of simple earthwork. This creates a problem. The brief given to the Consolidation Department, working in parallel with OFD, is to avoid damage to pucca structures, which means that earthen structures are not protected. Although CADA is staffed by Agriculture Department personnel on secondment, soil conservation works including land leveling and shaping is done directly by the parent Department. CADA is building field drains, but the main as well as feeder drains are being constructed by the Irrigation Department and were still to be completed in 1988.

A potential of 1.3 million hectares has been created by area though this is yet to be backed by water availability in relation to crops and specific locations. Warabandi follows OFD and tailenders were still in distress in the lower districts in 1988 resulting in unauthorized tapping of water. Each *kulaba* has a *samiti* or informal society of about 50 farmers An experiment is under way along one distributary whose *kulaba samiti* have been handed the responsibility of managing supplies and rotations below the outlet. The samitis do their own policing but can only apply moral sanctions as they enjoy no legal power. Volumetric rates would engender better water use but would also entail closer supervision. Some 386,000 tubewells had been put down in the command by 1985-86, only 4442 of them state-owned. About a quarter were electrically operated and the rest used diesel. *Usar* (saline-affected) lands have been reclaimed. According to CADA figures, productivity in the Ramganga command rose from 9.46 quintals per hectare for all foodgrain crops in 1973-74 to16.18 q ha in 1985-86. Similar gains were recorded for potatoes and sugarcane. Eight growth centres or *kisan nagars* have already been established. These provide a variety of services relating to custom-hiring and implement repair; credit and banking; sale of diesel and inputs; animal husbandry, health, and provision of seeds and plant material. In them is also located a community training centre, a women's centre, a milk collection point, a fishery tank, the post office and market yard.

The CADA Administrator has all the additional or joint heads of development departments under him. Despite this, coordination is loose. The suggestion that Irrigation engineers within the command be brought under CADA has been resisted. Relations with the neighbouring Chandrashekhar Azad Agricultural University, Kanpur, are close. The University is responsible for extension education and training in Central Uttar Pradesh and Bundelkhand. It is trying to propagate new varieties such as spring cotton and summer sunflower, groundnut and green gram. But water availability and water management must improve if there are to be significant results. Advancing the crop calendar with earlier kharif sowings is advocated from the point of view of establishing a sturdier crop better able to withstand the vagaries of either drought or flood, reducing pest attacks and plant diseases, and permitting timely rabi sowing. A good irrigation system should enable farmers to switch to a more optimal crop calendar.

The story is very similar in Bihar. The Gandak project straddles Nepal, Uttar Pradesh and Bihar. It covers a culturable command area of 0.96 million hectares in nine districts of Bihar which are supplied by the Tirhut Main Canal and the Saran Main Canal. The project was commissioned in 1971 and was declared complete in 1984-85. But 20 to 25 per cent of the main canal and distributaries were yet to be constructed in 1988 because of land acquisition problems, while several structure and outlets remained unfinished. There is however a proposal to extend the Tirhut Main by another 80 kilometres as there is said to be sufficient water. The upper reaches of the Saran Canal have suffered heavy siltation and de-siltation is carried out subject to the availability of funds. In the result, the canal is operating at only 60 to 70 per cent of its capacity and has on occasion breached its embankments. It is said that the canal cannot be closed for desilting as India is committed to provide constant supplies to operate the Surajpura power house (on a canal fall) which feeds the Nepal grid. Yet the Indo-Nepal Gandak Coordination Committee had apparently not met after 1984-85. In the absence of consolidation, CADA is aligning field channels on the "best release line" as consolidation is to follow. Leveling is taken along with consolidation and is financed by farmers through institutional loans. So this too has been relegated to the future. The trunk drains were to be constructed by the Project authorities under Phase II commencing in 1988-89. Hence CADA too will take up construction of field drains at a later stage.

By early 1988 soil surveys had been completed over 0.57 million hectares and field channels laid to serve 0.43 million hectares, the rest of the command area being under flood irrigation. *Warabandi* had been introduced in no more than 24,000 hectares, with releases being made from the tail-end backwards. Water rates cover only 40 per cent of operational and maintenance costs and collections average half the demand. Under the Bihar CAD Act, the Chairman was to have all development departments under him. The Gandak CADA Chairman has traditionally been an engineer who has been unable to exercise that coordinating role. In 1988 the Divisional Commissioner, Muzaffarpur, was concurrently CADA chairman and had both line and CAA powers. This was working better. The CADA budget of Rs5.50 crores in 1987-88 as limited to OFD. But on amount of a paucity of cement almost half this amount was unutilized. The water table has risen to danger levels in West Champaran and Gopalganj districts and salinity patches have appeared. CADA is to put down 46 large-diameter/diesel operated tubewells to arrest this problem.

Research scientists at the Rajendra Prasad Agricultural University at Pusa say that farmers will move from mono-culture to multi-cropping given agrarian reforms that assure them security of tenure, and provided also that there is adequate water control and sound water management. Advancing the crop calendar to ensure earlier rabi sowings is strongly advocated as this will ensure higher yields and higher incomes.

Like many other large canal systems, the Gandak project is poorly equipped with communication facilities. Being a high rainfall area, farmers are reluctant to take water. But if the rains fail there is a hue and cry. The headworks are 300 kilometres away and indents for additional releases sometimes have to be sent by jeep. This entails a lead time of 48 hours Meanwhile, if there are heavy rains, water must be allowed to escape into the fields causing local flooding. There are no intermediate storages on which to draw, or for conservation.

EVALUATION STUDIES

The Indian Institute of Management Ahmedabad, was asked to evaluate the CAD programme in 1987 in response to a recommendation made in the 141st Report of the Public Accounts Committee of the Lok Sabha. It found that while OFD had made progress, coverage was less than scheduled and maintenance was poor. Uncertainty remained the main problem due to design constraints, lack of control structures and measuring devices, unauthorized uses, faulty demand estimation, limited *warabandi* and a lack of responsibility centres. Water losses were heavy and drainage poor; targeted productivity and cropping patterns were often unrealistic and irrigation supplies not conducive to the growth of high-yielding varieties. Furthermore, extension services were not effective and not at all oriented to water management. The organizational structure was found top-heavy, bottom-thin and lacking in adequate linkages or professional management, with poor integration between irrigation and agriculture. Beneficiary participation was still limited with no incentives for users to assume responsibility. Finally, the study found that irrigation charges bore no relationship to the incremental income earned under irrigated agriculture. Despite that, recovery of dues was poor and arrears large (National Workshop on CAD Programme, February 1988).

A workshop held on the basis of the IIM Study listed reliability of supplies as the core function around which command area development must be built. To remove uncertainty it proposed unified control of irrigation and water management from the headworks t the farm gate under CADA. It advocated modernization to overcome system inadequacies, active participation of farmers in CAD programmes, promotion of conjuntive use and drainage works as integral aspects of irrigation, lining of channels and land shaping only where cost-effective, management through multi-disciplinary teams, and training of both CAD personnel and farmers As groundwater charges are considerably more than those for canal supplies, the workshop favoured rate rationalization in order to render conjunctive use more attractive and cover annual maintenance and operational charges as part of the fixed cost. The rates must convey the scarcity value of water.

Other studies on CADA performance in Bihar give high importance to consolidation. Without this the construction of field channels and field drains is impeded, flood irrigation from plot to plot prevails, land leveling is discouraged and *warabandi* is not possible. As field channels are at present constructed along the boundary ridges and no land compensation is paid, no legal rights govern the passage of water. This is found to have resulted in large scale destruction and obliteration of both lined and unlined channels with neither CADA not the State Government having any legal remedy (Water and Land Management Institute, Patna August 1987).

In order to promote better water management, the Government of India with USAID assistance has set up Water and Land Management Institutes (WALMIs) in 10 states including Uttar Pradesh, Bihar and Madhya Pradesh. These institutions have been placed under CAD departments and are intended to train irrigation functionaries from chief engineer downwards.

WARABANDI AND OTHER ALLOCATIVE SYSTEMS

Because of water constraints most Indian irrigation systems follow a supply approach whereas American systems respond to demand which ensures the indenting farmer the water he requires, as and where needed. In India canal supplies are highly subsidized, ostensibly on grounds of equity. But inadequate supplies together with uncertainty about timing result in an inefficient, inequitable and high cost system. *Warabandi* is a supply-constraint or rationing system related not to crop requirements but to the size of land owned within the irrigation block or *chak*. It is not related to cropping patterns as in Maharashtra which follows the Shejpali system, a crop-related water sanction, or the Phad system in parts of the Deccan which is based on equal sharing. These systems are in turn different from the practice in South India where the command area or *ayacut* is put under a scheme of localization. This is an optimal land use crop plan supposedly backed with matching irrigation. But in the semi-arid northwest of the country, *warabandi* traditionally developed as a simple means of affording reasonable assurance of regular supplies to large numbers of small holdings.

Under *warabandi*, the cultivator determines his crop pattern on the basis of his water allocation, the water being distributed by turns according to a predetermined schedule specifying the day, time and duration of supply to each irrigator in proportion to his holding in the outlet command (Malhotra, S.P., April 1982). Each farmer is entitled to equal running time, but this does not ensure equal water supplies as tail-enders suffer losses from seepages in the water courses. As seepage losses by absorption are a direct function of the wetted perimeter, water courses should be kept as short as possible from the outlet head, unless lined. Since many canal systems are short of water, and irrigation turns are fixed, farmers under *warabandi* are inclined to take their full share whether this is a crop requirement or not at the time, since they are not sure how much water will be available when their next turn comes around. This too leads to wasteful use of water, drainage problems and tail-end shortages. Volumetric charges have often been suggested and would certainly encourage economy. But this would need a more reliable system and there would be the problem of metering a large number of small fields which could end in much disputation, fiddling and wrong billing.

Volumetric systems are easier to adopt when groups of farmers or water user associations purchase water in bulk and retail it among their members. A widely-quoted model is the Mohini cooperative irrigation society in Surat District, Gujarat, irrigating 280 hectares in three villages in the Mahi canal command. The society was established in 1979 with 181 members each holding a Rs 50 share. It has three sub-minors under its jurisdiction and purchases water wholesale from the department and retails it on a volumetric basis at a rate of 25 paise per 10,000 litres. A rebate of 10 per cent is given on advance payments before the cropping season or of 5 per cent if paid during the season. Water management improved and the area irrigated doubled as a result of farmer cooperation and the adoption of more efficient distribution systems. The society gives a 50 per cent subsidy for the construction of field channels, offers credit, and has a tractor with tools which is available for custom-hiring (Water Technology Centre, New Delhi, 1983).

Bihar followed yet another pattern. In the Sone command the 'satta' system was in vogue for almost a century. Under this, if 85 per cent of the farmers in a block applied for a long-term irrigation lease, water would be released according to a pre-planned roster called *tatil*. These releases were made from the distributary for a significantly large command in contrast with *warabandi* where the rotation is worked out below the last 0.028 cumec/40 hectare outlet. The *satta* applications would be collected and coordinated by an elected *lambardar* through an informal committee of management set up by villagers in the *tatil* command. Having virtually leased the channel the *lambardar* would organise its maintenance and collect the water dues for which he was paid by the Irrigation Department at the rate of 1.5 paise per rupee collected in addition to an honorarium. Over time, the system proved cumbersome and was abolished in 1974 on the recommendation of the Bihar Irrigation Commission.

DEFECTIVE MACRO AND MICRO CANAL MANAGEMENT

Centralized management and maintenance of huge command areas has caused innumerable problems with various inadequacies. There has been indiscipline and resort to political influence, muscle and money power. Farmers at the upper end of systems do not hesitate to make inroads into tail-end rights or to cut canals. Canal roads rutted by farm carts render inspection and maintenance that much more difficult. Water user associations that can manage the system below given outlets offer the best solution. But even if introduced, success will depend on farmers' education, greater egalitarianism in the matter of land rights, and greater reliability and efficiency in overall operation and maintenance of irrigation systems.

Most discussion of water management in India relates to problems at the level of the *chak* or irrigation block commanded by the last project outlet which is generally some 40 hectares but could be smaller or larger. It is here that the farmer was left to construct water courses and farm drains until this was brought under the CAD programme of on-farm development. While CADAs are certainly a most useful innovation they still divide projects at the last outlet into two department or project authority such as a control board, while responsibility below this vests in the farmers and CADAs. These macro and micro jurisdictions have not always been harmonized and coordination has been wanted in actual practice.

There is however an even more basic problem. Unless reservoir and main-canal management is well tuned to crop-water requirements and farmer needs at the *chak* level there will more likely than not be a mismatch between macro and micro operations. Uncertainties below the farm outlet are often a product of inadequacies in managing the main system. There is much merit in Robert Chambers' comment (1986) that bad water management below the outlet, poor maintenance of water courses and conflicts between farmers are not independent maladies which farmers inflict on themselves, but rather symptoms of deficiencies in the main system and its management. Systems and practices inherited from the 19th century must now be discarded in favour of designs and performance standards for the 21st century (Leslie Abbie et al., 1982).

Inadequate reservoir storage can be supplemented by conjunctive use which is also necessary to maintain the water balance through vertical drainage. But conjunctive use does not come about with piecemeal drilling of tubewells or augmentation wells after the design and completion of the surface system. Knowledge of groundwater conditions and the likely recharge on account of seepage and infiltration from canal irrigation over a period of time should enable the project engineers to design the entire system for conjunctive use from the very start, with mandatory consolidation and rectangularisation. This is now conceded, but groundwater development continues to be executed as a supplementary irrigation and drainage system. Earlier water releases from reservoirs could facilitate early kharif sowings which, as many experts have testified, would enhance productivity both in regard to this crop and the ensuing rabi. In some circumstances this could be done by groundwater pumping. But if reservoir releases are possible, especially in high rainfall and snowmelt catchments, this would leave a larger flood cushion and permit greater compensatory pumping during the monsoon when secondary energy might be available from hydel stations and farmers would essentially want to make good rainfall deficiencies and no more except in the case of water-intensive crops.

Optimal crop-weather reservoir schedules would need to be worked out with different configurations depending on medium to long range monsoon forecasts. Carryover storages could be planned from one season to the next, where conditions permit. Creation of buffer storages and a string of ponds and tanks in the middle and lower ends of the canal system would also permit a degree of flexibility in canal operations that is currently lacking. Whether canal supplies in the lower reaches could be ponded up in natural depressions with gated weirs, or the dry beds of nullahs, natural floodways and streams could be similarly used for small downstream or intermediate storages, merits examination system by system. In all such cases, evaporation losses less savings through use of evaporation retardants would need to be calculated and a balance struck. The Chinese have adopted such systems, known as melons on a vine which integrate small facilities owned by terminal users with that of the larger core project (James, Nuckum, B 1982). This has certainly entailed extra burdens in time and effort, with expert advice to peasants on how to redesign their ponds, and the promotion of fisheries and other economic uses in such user ponds as an added inducement to construct and maintain them.

IMPROVED INFORMATION SYSTEMS

Canal systems are now being equipped with better communication systems under modernization programmes. But it is possible to go beyond that too. A quick information system could facilitate rapid adjustment of reservoir releases conjunctively with rainfall within the command area thus avoiding waste of stored waters. In Haryana some years ago a system was developed for the communication of discharge from a variety of measurement points on different canals to a regulatory control centre in Chandigarh by the canal telegraph system maintained by the Telegraph Department. Since water supplies were short, the purpose was to establish which sectors needed water and when. Based on this a rotational programme of canal operation was worked out with priorities established for first, second, third and fourth preference channels. The next step was to upgrade the system by studying crop water requirements in relation to temperature, soil, wind velocities and other parameters. An experimental project was started on four small channels of the Bhakra system near Hissar with World Bank assistance (Narayana Murthy, S.G. December 1985). A more advanced pilot project with microwave transmission is now proposed to operate a computer-controlled automated dynamic canal regulatory system. WAPCOS, an Indian consultancy firm in the field of water resources, introduced an advanced telemetry system for automatic canal regulation in Iraq and similar systems are to be installed in the Sone and Narmada projects.

If the main canal system is better regulated and responsively operated, then availability of assured and reliable supplies when needed will correspondingly reduce uncertainty, conflict, indifference, waste and defiance below the outlet as the farmer will have a great deal to lose by not adhering to prescribed norms. Apart from rotational systems like *warabandi*, that are intended to ensure equity and regularity in farm gate deliveries, proper regulators and structures at the last outlet can also improve system efficiency. In the Chambal command in Rajasthan, adjustable proportionate modules were introduced which permitted only calibrated amounts of water to pass through the discharge outlet into the water courses. The farmers were not ready for this innovation and dislodged these devices in order to secure a free flow of water as before. The experience only underlines the importance of farmer education and consultation through recognized associations such as *chak samitis* or water user associations.

An alternative system is being tried in the Indira Gandhi Nahar (Rajasthan Canal) command. So-called improved water management zones have been marked out in an area of some 80,000 hectares within which agreed cropping patterns have been worked out through tripartite consultations between the farmers and the Departments of Irrigation and Agriculture. Handbills are distributed indicating when participating farmers will be supplied water during a crop cycle of, say, 18 weeks. Since each crop has certain critical stages of plant growth when irrigation is vital for higher productivity or even survival, a full allowance is guaranteed in each of those periods while reduced supplies, tailored to the overall water budget, are made available during the other weeks. The system is said to have enabled the irrigation intensity to be raised and has promoted a shift towards higher value crops (World Bank, October, 1984).

POOR MAINTENANCE AFFECTS OPERATIONS

In many irrigation systems, poor maintenance has affected operations, magnifying design defects or inherent limitations such as inadequate storage. These defects could further reduce reliability or enhance waste. Farmers are unwilling to pay higher water rates and even decline to pay existing rates, that more often than not do not even cover bare operation and maintenance costs, because of unreliable and inadequate supplies. The canal authorities in turn are handicapped in providing a reasonable service even within design limitations because of lack of funds for proper maintenance. The Irrigation Commission (1972) expressed dismay at mounting losses on public irrigation works since the commencement of planning. The cumulative loss in the First Plan (1951-56) was Rs 4.84 crores and this had risen to Rs 53.60 crores (1961-66). It recommended that irrigation works as a whole should yield an annual income at least equal to their annual cost of operation and that no burden should fall on the general exchequer.

The Sixth Finance Commission (1973) estimated that the aggregate loss on irrigation projects, including interest charges, might be as much as Rs1000 crores during the Fifth Plan (1971-76) and stated that the immediate objective should be to ensure the maintenance charges on major and medium projects are fully covered. This did not happen and in a note to the Seventh Finance Commission (1978) the Irrigation Department said "Many of the older irrigation systems are still getting the same grants for operation and maintenance which they were getting several decades before and thus their efficiencies are getting continuously reduced." It referred in particular to the Upper and Lower Ganga canals and the Sone Canal. Against the Sixth Finance Commission's recommendations of an O&M rate of Rs 25 per hectare, the Seventh Finance Commission suggested a rate of Rs 50 per hectare with an additional 20 per cent thereof for special repairs. It was hoped this would cover O&M costs and also provide for 1 per cent return on the total capital invested as of 1978-79. Reporting in 1984, the Eighth Finance Commission was confronted with a further deterioration in the position. It accordingly recommended a consolidated fee of Rs 100 per hectare in the plains thus another Rs 30 per hectare for maintenance of the unutilized potential. A 30 per cent increase was recommended for hill areas. The finance commissions have found that the situation pertaining to minor irrigation schemes is no better. The Irrigation Commission favoured a revision of water rates every five years. In effect such a review has been undertaken by the Finance Commissions. Whether this is a good enough mechanism or whether some other machinery might be set up with provision for indexation to cover cost escalations is a matter for consideration.

MERITS OF WATER USERS ASSOCIATIONS

The best course in any circumstances would be to associate farmers with the planning, design, operation and maintenance of irrigation projects as the ultimate beneficiaries must have a stake in the systems. As in all technologies, software planning should inform hardware choices. Water user associations in some form are clearly indicated and have been experimented with, howsoever tentatively, in one form or another. These might be informal bodies but should grow into formal associations or cooperatives with a micro command rather than village-wise as functional responsibilities must be assumed. The experiments being carried out in Uttar Pradesh, the Mohini irrigation cooperative in Gujarat, the *chak samitis* in Bihar, the 'pipe' (outlet) committees established in the Pochampad command in Andhra, the Pani Panchayat at Maharashtra and the Dusi-Mamandur tank in North Arcot, Tamil Nadu (which serves 18 villages through a representative board) are possible models that could be developed. There is no reason to adopt a single pattern everywhere. Indeed, adapting traditional systems to modern needs would be best.

It has been truly said that low supervision with low delegation characterizes the pattern of official-farmer relationships in the Indian subcontinent (Anthony Bottrall, 1981). The degree of responsibility delegated within a large command must necessarily depend on the ability of farmer associations to manage different levels of responsibility which will undoubtedly grow with experience in running an "irrigation democracy". The smallest cooperative or association would be that managing water courses below the last outlet, generally a block of about 40 hectares. But I should be possible to federate a number of such units within the command of a sub-minor and again at the higher level of a minor in a series of upwards tiers that could be built over time with growing confidence, training and experience. The Bihar tatil, for instance, was organized at a higher level than the water course. A greater degree of beneficiary participation at upward levels of organization would facilitate closer liaison between farmers, irrigation engineers and agronomists and other agricultural extension specialists. This might be for close-growing and row crops respectively, as well as for superior cropping patterns and improved reservoir release schedules with conjunctive pumping.

Existing water rates are generally pegged at unduly modest levels and collections are most often only a fraction of the total demand. In part this reflects the farmer's own estimation of the indifferent and uncertain service he receives, though an element of straight subsidy is obviously there. Given responsibility, water user associations would probably be willing to raise the charges to more realistic levels in return for an improved and more reliable service with better maintenance, less waste, lower overheads without a bloated irrigation-revenue bureaucracy, and less corruption. At present, the Irrigation Department or project authority makes the levy which is collected by the Revenue Department and credited to general revenues. Since collections are not returned to the Irrigation Department or *chak sabha* there is no incentive to improve collections since the O&M budget (or subsidy) comes from the exchequer. Hence, were collections to be retained by water user associations out of which they paid a fee to the management tier or department above them, they would soon discover that better collections ploughed back ensure a better service and enhance productivity gains, leaving them financially better off at the end of the exercise.

The corresponding reduction of the irrigation bureaucracy, or its selective re-employment under the water user association, would also make for a more responsive system less prone to corrupt practice to lubricate its operations. That corruption is widespread in irrigation systems, and not necessarily only at the lowest levels, has been well documented by the Santhanam Committee (1964), Niranjan Pant (1981) and Robert Wade (April 1982). The UP Irrigation Commission (December 1984) reported that "a determined effort is required at the political level to minimize the corruption rampant in all walks of life and to enforce discipline with an iron hand so that a fear (sic) might be generated in the minds of anti-social elements and corrupt officials." Getting water releases or favourable turns, the award of contracts, passing of bills, and postings and transfers have been up for sale in more than a few instances. A more open system under democratic supervision would provide a powerful countervailing influence.

It might act as an incentive were water user associations permitted to retain part of the charges collected for on-farm development or other approved purposes. In China farmers management organizations have been permitted and even encouraged to undertake "sideline" activities such as wasteland reclamation which might be used for cultivation of crops, raising orchards or vegetable gardening, or for rearing pigs and poultry, or even operating mini-hydel plants on canal falls in order to augment their income in the interests of viability.

CASE FOR VOLUMETRIC CHARGES

The present system of charging rates by crop or area does not encourage economy in the use of water. There is no penalty for waste, except that others are deprived of the limited supplies available. The case for volumetric rates has been made time and again. This will foster an attitude of conservation as excessive use will entail correspondingly higher fees without any increase in marginal returns. The water saved would ensure greater adequacy in supplies for all and greater equity, especially to tail-enders higher rates could also be levied reflecting the scarcity value of water. Canal charges should be raised and groundwater or lift charges reduced to narrow the existing differentials which inhibit conjunctive use within a single integrated system. Indeed, there is a good deal of evidence to show that marginal and small farmers are far more meticulous in paying their dues than bigger farmers and waterlords who depend on money, muscle-power, or political clout to get away with a great deal. Even otherwise, dependability and equity are worth a price and it is for this reason that all classes of farmers pay considerably more to operate their own tubewells. The deep State tubewells in Uttar Pradesh do in fact charge higher volumetric rates.

The real objection to volumetric rates has been the problem of metering a large number of small outlets, ensuring accurate measurements, preventing tampering, policing the system, and avoiding disputes about wrong billing which are common enough in the electricity and telephone departments. The solution would seem to lie in the Irrigation Department or project authority selling water wholesale on a volumetric basis at the sub-minor, minor or sub-distributary levels where discharges could be more easily metered and monitored. It would then be for water user associations or their federations at higher levels to retail the water thus purchased in bulk among their members through self-regulated procedures. The Royal Commission on Agriculture in India (1928) had in fact recommended both volumetric charges and the formation of irrigation panchayats. That such a system would be ideal is not in doubt. Whether it is practical is to be tested. The only way to proceed would be to move in that direction in stages after due experimentation, feedback and adjustment combined with farmer education and training. Such a reform would also bridge the gulf between the Irrigation Department, traditionally staffed with civil engineers, and water managers who need a different set of skills. The precise point at which farmer management must give way to departmental or project control will be determined by several factors B. Pasternak has sensibly referred to "a threshold of complexity in irrigation systems at which cooperation must give way to co-ordination; at which those served by the system relinquish their decision-making power and their direct role in settling disputes" (Bottrall, 1981).

Much of what has been said and quoted is well known and well understood and was put together in an admirable *Manual on Irrigation Water Management* published by the Department of Agriculture (Delhi, 1979). This offers guidelines on the entire range of issues including such neglected areas as agro-meteorological requirements and the importance of drainage and leaching of the land in relation to the crop grown in order to maintain the right salt balance. Unfortunately, institutional mechanisms for implementing and monitoring such guidelines and providing the necessary coordination have yet to take root. More recently, the ICAR'S Water Technology Centre has commenced publication of a series of district studies on "Resource Analysis for Integrated Development" such as for Sultanpur District in Uttar Pradesh (IARI, Delhi 1986). Though CADAs have been placed under the Irrigation Departments of States, inter-departmental pulls and pressures remain. May be it is time that larger irrigation projects at any rate were restructured as independent utilities able to engage and deploy their own staff and interact with water user associations and farmers directly without the mediation of any department of government. It would perhaps be more purposeful to forge closer links between CADAs and panchayati raj institutions wherever democratic decentralization genuinely takes place. This would render it possible for land and water conservation and management to be planned and developed together with popular participation.

PROBLEMS OF GROUNDWATER MANAGEMENT

Groundwater use has grown rapidly in some areas but not adequately in eastern India which has a large unexploited potential. Absence of consolidation has been an inhibiting factor along with a lack of title to land and consequent high risk. Subsidized credit is, however, being made available to small and marginal farmers. Most tubewell development has taken place through private enterprise. Power connections are not easily available except where there are clusters of pumps. But electricity supplies are uncertain and erratic in many areas although State administrations have stepped in during drought years to divert as much energy as possible for the agricultural sector. Mismatching of pumps has been a problem but this is being corrected through assisted rectification programmes.

State tubewells have been established to serve groups of small and marginal farmers or to draw on deeper aquifers which farmers might find expensive to tap. In Uttar Pradesh the are commanded by State tubewells declined from 153 hectares in 1966-67 to 35 hectares in 1983-84 on account of a sharp decline in power availability from an average of 3,432 hours to 780 hours per tubewell per annum during that period (UP Irrigation Commission). The siting of tubewells too has tended to follow the dictates of local influentials, including legislators, and not prescribed criteria. The net loss on operation and maintenance on State tubewells in Uttar Pradesh in 1982-83, including power charges and interest on capital was estimated at Rs 7,000 per tubewell or Rs 200 per hectare. A more detailed analysis ascribes this trend to operator absence, construction of private tubewells in State tubewell commands, low voltage supplies to State tubewells because of private connections from the feeder line, absence of hour-meters resulting in revenue leakage, and poor management and maintenance in addition to inadequate power availability (M.K. Singhal, March 1984). Here again it has been suggested that State tubewells might perhaps be sited only where cultivators in the command agree to set up a cooperative or water user's association to operate and manage the facility efficiently.

State tubewells in Uttar Pradesh are not allowed in canal commands. This is because differential water rates apply, with canal and tubewell supplies being charged on an area and volumetric basis, respectively. Private tubewells on the other hand are permitted in canal commands. But management problems arise if tubewell waters are conveyed through the canal network or water courses for in that case tubewell supplies are also charged as if they are canal water. In order to avoid such additional payment, farmers have been known to stop canal flows below the point where they use the water course for tubewell supplies thus causing both operational and law and order problems (Ibid, 1986). Such developments reinforce the view that surface and canal water charges should be rationalized and the gap narrowed. This could best be done through water user associations which would be in a position to assess local circumstances and negotiate appropriate norms and terms and monitor them. As Singhal remarks, "like any government department, the Irrigation Department too is not result-oriented but rule-bound."

Obsolete laws too are an impediment to better management. Uttar Pradesh is governed by the Northern India Canal and Drainage Act, 1873, the UP Tubewell Act, 1936, and the UP (Command) Area Development Act, 1976. The purpose and practice of irrigation has undergone considerable change with the objective of protective irrigation giving way to optimization of production and equity. These laws need revision as do those in Bihar which is governed by the Bengal Irrigation Act, 1897, and the Bihar Public Works and Drainage Act, 1947.

The Government of India did circulate a model Irrigation Bill in 1976 with the object of improving operation and maintenance and ensuring better service. Among other things this provided that all (irrigation) offences be made cognizable and attract heavier punishments; conferred immunity on canal officers against legal action for acts committed in the discharge of their duties; made provision for water user associations; empowered canal authorities to control groundwater extraction and discharge of effluents within the command; penalized damage to watercourses and irrigation works and theft of power; and enabled canal authorities to control cultivation and obstructions on river beds and drains. Other suggestions have been made to expedite land acquisition proceedings and payment of compensation and enhance penalties under the Cattle Trespass Act, 1871. At present, one of the difficulties coming in the way of the construction of watercourses is that this is not covered by the Land Acquisition Act and therefore no compensation is payable to those farmers who are compelled to give away some land for this purpose. The States have also been advised to create a separate cadre of water managers for the operation and maintenance of canal systems and to establish separate water management and land development wings under their irrigation departments in accordance with a recommendation made by a Committee set up by the State Irrigation Ministers' Conference in 1981.

Better management of irrigation as of any other service will obviously give better returns. This is manifest in the higher gains to productivity from wells, tubewells and canals in that order. Examining the position in Punjab and Haryana in the late seventies, B.D. Dhawan (December, 1985) found that the productivity of private tubewells was between 5.5 and 5.7 tonnes per hectare as against between 2.4 tonnes to 3.2 tonnes in the case of canal irrigation. Assuming a production of no more than 0.5 tonnes per hectare from dryland farming, he concluded that irrigation had a key role to play in India's agricultural growth, a point differently emphasized by Y.K. Alagh (November, 1987) in postulating that a one per cent increase in irrigation leads to a 0.31 per cent increase in the gross cropped area, such increases in irrigation intensity being a critical part of the Seventh Plan agricultural strategy. But to argue, as some do, that canal irrigation must yield to groundwater as a general principle is misconceived as surface irrigation has a significant part to play in augmenting groundwater resources. Furthermore, electrical energy for pumping is heavily subsidized (Arokiaswamy, N.S.S., November 1986). Relating the tariff to the horse-power of the motor rather than to actual consumption in many States makes well-owners behave "as if the marginal cost of pumping water is zero" (Dhawan, September 1987). Part of the reason clearly lies in the far lower cost to the cultivator of canal supplies which are similarly subsidized.

Low water rates confer a proportionately larger subsidy on bigger farms with more land. The difference between the marginal value of additional water to the farmer and the amount charged is an economic rent which "accrues to the user not by virtue of superior efficiency and foresight in farming, but through the water allocation his land receives" often charged per unit of land irrigated (Robert Repetto, December 1986). But both canal and power subsidies are sometimes defended on the ground that procurement prices lend to be pegged at artificially low levels and that the only justification for this, with the industrial-farm terms of trade turning against the cultivator, can be the various subsidies available to the agriculturist. This does not appear to be a sound argument either on grounds of equity or of economy. Underpricing of scarce assets entails waste and an opportunity cost which cannot be ignored. The United States too pays out huge irrigation subsidies. But there the farming population is tiny and the impact on general revenues correspondingly small. Indian practice is also faulty to the extent that water supply charges do not generally take account of the related and necessary water disposal liability through an effective drainage system.

TOWARDS IRRIGATION UTILITIES

The World Bank has imposed certain lending conditionalities which in the case of irrigation stipulate that operation and maintenance costs must at least be recovered (June, 1986). Other objectives set out are economic efficiency, income distribution and public savings. However, as a result of poor operation and maintenance farmers have not been willing to pay the low rates being charged, let alone any more economic rate.

Reliable irrigation, the assessment goes, is a precondition though not a sole condition for profitable farming which alone can ensure cost recovery of irrigation investments. In India, operation and maintenance costs are not being met in most States and the official view has been that this is not necessary as provision of irrigation to large numbers of poor farmers must be seen as a developmental or even a welfare activity and not a self-sustaining programme. Water charges must, therefore, be related to the farmer's capacity to pay and to view water charges as a service fee rather than as a tax is unlikely to make any real difference. This does not appear to be a very sound view and attitudinal changes are necessary all round if the viability and dynamism of the economy is to be ensured. In fact the transition must be from public service departments to public utilities which each project mandated to earn its own keep. Since a good part of irrigation maintenance such as weeding, de-silting, repair of canal roads and embankments and so on entails earthwork, there is no reason why farmers cannot pay part of their dues in kind, through off-season labour. Where farmer-manager systems develop there would be a vested interest on the part of beneficiaries to maintain the asset in good order.

Water rates vary a good deal from one State to another in India. As of August 1987 the rates had last been revised as far back as 1975 in Haryana and as recently as 1984 in Madhya Pradesh. In relation to the amount assessed on major and medium schemes, actual realizations in 1981-82 ranged from nearly 89 per cent in Haryana to 41 per cent in Madhya Pradesh and 16 per cent in West Bengal. Bihar boasts better figures but even with a 73 per cent collection in 1986-87, the cumulative arrears that year showed a steadily rising trend and stood at Rs 32 crores (WALMI, Patna August 1987). The performance of State irrigation works in Uttar Pradesh during 1984-85 tell their own story. Just over half the irrigation potential created at a capital outlay of Rs 2493 crores actually utilized that year. Establishment costs accounted for over 71 per cent of the revenue receipt of Rs 67.67 crores. Adding all costs, inclusive of maintenance, energy, interest and depreciation, there was a net loss of Rs 171 crores. Calculated in per hectare terms for the same year, the total costs came to Rs 374 for canals and Rs 1,979 for State tubewells which showed far higher energy and establishment costs. The overall losses came to Rs 162 for canals and Rs 1,123 for State tubewells (Irrigation Department, Lucknow).

There could be ways to augment revenues other than through raising water rates. Betterment levies have been legislated but not collected by any State in India. Land revenue too has been stagnant and will in most cases have declined in real terms. It used to average 25 per cent of crop value prior to Independence but has come down to barely 6 per cent now. At least those owning more than two hectares of land in irrigation commands can be assessed at a higher rate (Singhal, M.K. December 1986). Suggestions for a progressive agricultural land tax have also not been found acceptable. The Irrigation Commission (1972) recommended that water rates should be related to irrigation benefits rather than to the cost of projects and might range from 5 to 12 per cent of the gross income from the crops grown, the upper limit being applicable to cash crops. The object was to ensure that taken as a whole irrigation schemes do not impose a burden on the general revenues of any State. This remains a desirable norm. So also the recommendation that betterment levies should be enforced so that half the capital cost of irrigation projects is recovered from the beneficiaries, the levy being applied three years after the commencement of irrigation and spread over a period not exceeding 30 years. All this, however, must presuppose implementation of a whole package of related measures ranging from agrarian reform and consolidation to reliability in irrigation supplies with rationalized conjunctive rates and the fostering of water user associations to attain a far higher use-efficiency of water that should reach 70 per cent by 2010.

BENEFIT-COST CALCULATIONS

What should be the return on irrigation? Initially under the Raj, it was seen as a commercial proposition. Irrigation companies were floated. In 1879 a financial test was laid down as a criterion for investment in irrigation. This was fixed at a rate of return that varied from 4 to 6 per cent, the actual average return being 8 per cent at the time of Indian Independence after meeting the cost of maintenance and interest charges. Calculating a direct rate of return was all right at a time when simple diversion schemes were in vogue, but was otherwise restrictive. In 1936 the Central Board of Irrigation advocated a benefit-cost ratio by including indirect returns fro irrigation. The (Niten Desai) B-C Ratio Review Committee (1983) traces the subsequent evolution. In 1949 the financial return was reduced to 3.75 per cent but indirect benefits were excluded. A review of certain established irrigation projects by the Gadgil Committee in 1958 attested to a number of indirect benefits on account of employment, double-cropping, and processing industries and the stimulus generally given to trade and transport. The return was therefore taken as the difference between the value of agricultural production (less cost of cultivation) minus interest on capital, depreciation and O&M costs.

In 1964 the Gadgil Committee recommended adoption of an economic benefit criterion since the financial benefits could be manipulated by changing water rates. The benefit was to be calculated on the basis of the net value of agricultural production before and after irrigation while cost was to include interest on capital at 10 per cent, depreciation at 10 per cent (assuming a project life of 100 years) plus O&M expenses. If on this calculus the B-C ratio was 1.5:1 a project would be approved, though projects in tribal area may be accepted even on a 1:1 ratio.

The Desai Committee found that the real problem was to value agricultural production, without reliable data before and after irrigation. Moreover, of 921 major and medium projects taken up between 1951 and 1980, only 476 were "complete". Hence a lack of ex-post evaluation studies. Project costs were found to have escalated on account of delays covered by changes in scope, difficulties in land acquisition, inadequate investigation and so on. Project costs tended to be under-estimated while the area actually irrigated and yields from there were being over-estimated in certain instances. The Committee, therefore, concluded that the main purpose of cost-benefit analysis of irrigation projects must be to establish an order of ranking in terms of increasing agricultural production, promoting rural development and improving income distribution. There must however, be a floor to expected returns below which a project should be rejected. The discounted cash flow method was advocated as this would appropriately reflect the value of the time taken to realize the full benefit. Credible crop-cutting experiments would be nec ssary for a true comparison of agricultural production, not before and after irrigation as much as with and without irrigation. The Committee recommended expanded programmes of agro-economic and statistical research in the field of irrigation and a strengthening of the techno-economic capability of the Central Water Commission and State Irrigation Departments to conduct rigorous benefit-cost analyses. It also emphasized the need for ex-post evaluation of irrigation projects on the same lines as ex-ante appraisals. These should be done three to five years after project completion and before taking up any modernization proposal.

This is generally the approach now being adopted. Irrigation planning and development require a closer interface between the Irrigation and Agricultural departments as well as several other disciplines. Local involvement in decision-making and management and in determining canal alignments, cropping patterns and the rest is no less important.

Latterly a new element, that of environmental costs and benefits has been introduced into the debate. This is considered in a later chapter. However, a basin approach rather than an individual project approach would be more appropriate here and is indeed a recommendation of the National Water Policy (Ministry of Water Resources, Delhi 1987). The Conference of Irrigation and Water Resource Ministers is also on record as stating that catchment area treatment "should be dealt with as a separate aspect without making it an integral component of river valley projects, since this work is even otherwise necessary whether or not there is a river valley project" (July 1986).

VIABILITY OF LARGE PROJECTS

At the same Irrigation Ministers' Conference, the Prime Minister made some strongly critical remarks about time and cost overruns. He said: "The situation today is that since 1951, some 246 big surface irrigation projects have been initiated. Only 65 of these have been completed; 181 are still under construction. We need some definite thrust from these projects that we started after 1970. Perhaps we can safely say that almost no benefit has come to the people from these projects. For 16 years we have poured money out. The people have got nothing back; no irrigation, no water, no increase in production, no help in their daily life. By pouring out money to a few contractors or a few "*thekedars*" and labourers to build canals and may be to Public Works Department to construct the dam, we are not really doing our people a favour. The favour comes when the project is completed, when the benefits of the project start flowing." While the Prime Minister's anguish over time and cost overruns will be widely shared, the statement, taken at face value, could be misleading. The word "completion" is loosely used in Indian irrigation jargon. Many schemes are not declared "complete" as it is sometimes easier to get sanctions for enlargements in the scope of works which are officially on-going, than to make fresh starts on "new" projects. New phases are added on to "incomplete" projects which also manage to avoid scrutiny and ex-post appraisal for that reason.

Projects starts in a true sense, after notional approvals, can be delayed as there is no single-window sanction and elements such as environmental clearance may come much later this is true of the Tehri and Sardar Sarovar projects while the Indira Gandhi (Rajasthan) Canal is a classic case of willful under-funding. In the initial stages projects like Bhakra and the DVC were Centrally funded, the amounts extended being transferred to the States as loans at a later stage. These projects were seldom if ever starved of funds. After the Third Plan the pattern of Central assistance changed to a block loan under the Gadgil formula and States were entitled to use these resources in any sector of their choice. This led to under-funding as well as proliferation of new starts for political purposes. The Planning Commission is now seeking to prevent this tendency by earmarking funds and is considering extending this principle to drainage schemes as well. No new major starts were by and large permitted in the Seventh Plan. In view of cost escalations and the parlous state of their finances, many states have sought to have some of their major schemes declared "national projects".

To conclude from this recitation that major and medium projects have become "non-viable" on account of excessive costs and that there should therefore be an "orderly retreat" on this front in favour of groundwater programmes and minor irrigation schemes (Vohra, B.B. January 1987) is wholly mistaken and a counsel of despair. The other notion, that large projects are divisible into a number of equivalent medium or small projects is again quite misleading. Smaller projects have a far shorter life, take up far more land and often exhibit considerably higher unit costs. Moreover they fail in critical periods. Groundwater is recharged by canal irrigation and, while efficient, tubewells entail far higher operation a maintenance costs even excluding the capital cost of rural electrification. Figures about the sharply rising cost of major and medium irrigation projects per hectare also usually fail to make the comparison in terms of constant prices thus resulting in an exaggerated view about cost escalation.

The truth is that no question of competition is involved. Large, medium and small projects just as much as surface and groundwater schemes each have their own place. They complement and supplement one another and need to be considered and operated as part of integrated systems. Costs of irrigation will rise as the country moves from simpler projects at the most favourable sites to more complex and difficult projects with higher design standards. In constant 1970-71 prices, the expenditure per hectare of potential created rose from Rs 2,770 in the First Plan to Rs 6,696 (targeted) in the Sixth Plan (Abbie et al, 1982). All things considered, irrigation investment in India remains highly advantageous and central to underpinning agricultural productivity, employment and economic growth.

CASE STUDIES IN NEPAL

This discussion about project planning, water management and command area development in India is relevant in large measure to the other countries in the basin, though local factors must be taken into account.

Hill irrigation, of course, has its own parameters. In Nepal, a number of irrigation systems are farmer managed. The Chattis Mauja system built 150 years ago serves 3,000 hectare. The project is managed by a three-tiered structure of 54 village committees, nine area committees and a central committee. Some 4000 farmer members elect their own officials and contribute 60,000 man days of labour for main canal maintenance and additional man-hours for operation and maintenance of branch canals and field channels. All costs, inclusive of salaries, are met by the farmers (Norman Uphoff et al. December 1985). In another project, farmers have built three diversions from the western arm of the Karnali to irrigate about 15,000 hectares in the Terai. Approximately 100,000 man-days are mobilized by the beneficiaries annually for diverting the water and desilting the canal (IIMI, 1986). In the Hills, farmers organize patrols to watch for landslides that might block water channels so that these can be cleared and repaired without delay. The public irrigation systems are however subsidized. The revenue realised from farmers in 1984 is estimated (in US dollars) at 9.10 against an O&M cost of 16 and a capital and recurrent cost (on a moderate calculation) of 126. The corresponding figures for major surface systems in Bangladesh in 1985 are estimated at 3.75, 21 and 375 (Repetto, December 1986).

A study by Leslie Small et al. (IIMI, December 1986) notes that low service fees and low collections made for high collection costs in Nepal, rising to as much as 78 per cent in one project in 1984-85 and 43 per cent in the case of even the tubewell portion of the scheme where collections were better. The conclusion drawn is that little importance is attached to collection of irrigation dues. "Difficulties are encountered in determining the land actually irrigated; ambiguities arise with respect to responsibility for payment in cases where the land is not operated by the landowner; farmers are expected to come to the project office to pay the service charges, even though no bills are sent directly to them; and no effective system of penalties for non-payment has been implemented, at least in areas served by surface water." That there is no scope for levying higher water charges and securing better collections is, however, evident from studies that show that the incremental net income from irrigation in the Chandra and Mohana commands was about 75 to 100 per cent greater and that this could rise to 400 per cent after command area development.

While farmer participation is low in the operation and maintenance of state-controlled schemes in Nepal, there are examples of successful communal irrigation projects in which farmers hold shares. "Originally issued in proportion to participation in the investment to construct the system, the shares may be sold separately from the land, and command a high price. As a result, farmers have an incentive to economise on their use of water in order to be able to sell a portion of their shares for cash," resulting, in one case, to a doubling of the area irrigated over time (Ibid).

LESSONS FROM BANGLADESH

Bangladesh is attempting to confront a number of policy issues such as rationalization of irrigation subsidies and enforcement of recently enacted legislation for collection of water rates in gravity projects; standardization of irrigation equipment, especially engines; effecting better coordination among various agencies; and enacting suitable water legislation (Third Plan, Dhaka 1985). There is provision for betterment levies but, as in India, these have not been collected so far. There is a similar problem with shortfalls in utilization of the potential created. This has been attributed to inadequate delivery systems, especially to tail-enders; inadequate operation and maintenance provisions; lack of training in on-farm water management; lack of coordination between the irrigation and extension agencies; and the high cost of operating low-lift pumps, shallow tubewells and other equipment or diesel (Kamaluddin Choudhury, A.K.M.). Low utilization of created potential is said to stem from a combination of organizational and technical problems some of which might, hopefully, be resolved by setting up water-user groups and the development of an irrigation management programme within the cooperative structure. Farmers education is necessary especially where modern schemes are introduced to replace traditional irrigation practices. Failure to understand farmer cropping and investment preferences is said to have resulted in the poor success of the Barisal Irrigation Project (Khan, Akbar Ali, August 1985). Minor irrigation through low-lift pumps proved popular as it is inexpensive and has a quick pay-off. However, there are limits to exploitation of this resource at current levels of water conservation.

The shallow tubewell project was proceeding cautiously with the state-renting equipment to irrigation groups. Partly out of an anxiety to hasten the pace and partly in response to donor pressure, the STW programme was dramatically expanded in preference to deep tubewells and, on the plea of a looming resources crunch, was privatized. This, however, led to an unplanned expansion strongly criticized by some observers, with tubewells in certain areas running dry as spacing requirements were ignored. Equipment was mismatched in some cases resulting in unproductive investments. After-sales services were lacking and loan recoveries by banks began to fall. More important, the programme gave rise to "rural brokers", who expedited loan sanctions for a fee, and to "water lords". As small and marginal farmers, many of them share-croppers, were unable to meet institutional finance conditionalities such as proof of title to land free of all encumbrances, bigger farmers stepped in to offer their land for the siting of tubewells, thereby gaining control over both ownership and operation of these assets (Ali, Shawkat, August 1985). There was also donor pressure to privatize the deep tubewells by stopping the rental programme. This, too, is said to have increased their cost paving the way for water-lords to step in, as a the result there was a decrease in actual irrigation coverage by DTWs.

As far as surface schemes are concerned Bangladesh ran into difficulties in designing and operating large lift scheme such as the Ganges-Kobadak Project in the southwest with three very large 36 cumec pumps. According to one observer, the project has not been able to meet its objectives as a result of a mistaken technological choice (Khan Hamidur Rahman, August 1985).

Nevertheless, despite a cost in learning experience, there has been an expansion in irrigation. All over the basin there has to be more emphasis on better planning and design of projects and more careful attention to irrigation policy in partnership with farmers. But which farmers? Unless a minimal programme of agrarian reform is implemented, the benefits will in large areas go to the bigger and more affluent farmers and the objective of stabilizing agricultural yields at ever higher levels may be long delayed or never fully realized.

CHAPTER 7

Floods and Conservation

Rivers flood. None more so than in Asia. And none in Asia as much as the Ganga-Brahmaputra-Barak system which drains a more populous basin than the Yangtze and carries a larger flood discharge (150,000 cumecs and more) than any other river, barring the Amazon, and immeasurably more silt (2.4 billion tonnes) than China's notorious Huang-Ho. Hence the annual havoc as these rivers spill over their banks and ravage the countryside.

Rivers of this magnitude cannot be controlled in an absolute absence. Their floods can at best be moderated. The "flood control" wing of India's Central Water Commission has sensibly been redesignated as the River Management, Hydrological Observation and Forecasting Division. This more accurately describes its proper scope and function. To the extent that floods cannot be altogether eliminated, they have to be endured and nations and people must learn to live with them and follow the rhythm of the rivers as they rise and fall. Indeed this is what has happened in all riverine civilizations throughout history. It is man-made interventions in the regime of these rivers, obstruction of the natural drainage, and invasion of the flood plain as a result of development and runaway population growth that has turned an otherwise often benign phenomenon into a dreadful visitation.

BANGLADESH'S UNIQUE DRAINAGE PROBLEM

About 2.6 to three million hectares of Bangladesh are flooded annually. In an abnormal year, when there is a synchronization of very heavy rainfall with peak discharges simultaneously in the Ganga and Brahmaputra, this figure may touch 6.5 million hectares or some 45 per cent of the total area has happened in 1955 and 1974 (Khan, Tauhidul Anwar, August 1985). Two-thirds of the country was inundated in the unprecedented 100-year flood of 1988. According to official figures, the total area vulnerable to floods in Bangladesh is 8.28 million hectares of which 32 per cent had been protected by 1984-85 leaving 5.7 million hectares still at risk (Bangladesh Third Plan, December 1985). The overall area under protection was targeted to increase to 41 per cent by 1990. the corresponding area vulnerable to floods in India is about 24 million hectares in the Ganga basin and

3.5 million hectares in the Brahmaputra-Barak basin of which some 4.4 million hectares and 1.4 million hectares respectively had been protected by 1978 (Rashtriya Barh Ayog Report, 1980). Some further areas will have been brought under protected since then.

Bangladesh is prone to severe flooding because 80 per cent of its total land surface falls within the flood plain of the Ganga-Brahmaputra-Barak which has been built up over the millennia through the flood deposits of this enormous river system. Much of Bangladesh is a dynamic delta region. A huge monsoon flood discharge, draining over 1.5 million square kilometers in five countries straddling both sides of the Himalaya and containing far and away the highest rainfall density zones in the world, funnels into the sea through the Bangladesh nozzle faces a flood problem of the nature and magnitude that Bangladesh does. The best that the co-riparians can do, can only partially mitigate the flood of which Bangladesh is a child. Any solution or strategy envisaged, nationally or regionally, must comprehend this unalterable fact. This is not a sentence of doom but a call to reality with which an accommodation can be found.

The very year that Bangladesh was born, the Chairman of its Water and Power Development Authority wrote: "So far as flood is concerned, since control of the upper catchments is not within our means, we have taken up the protection of lands from flood inundation by embankments and empoldering as the only practical remedy. The overall long-term flood protection plan will include three basic elements; first, a system of embankments to protect the flood plains from overflow; second, a channel rectification programme to arrest the meandering of rivers, to increase their hydraulic efficiency and to help ensure the integrity of the embankments; and third, diversion of flood flows from the main rivers into the other channels where feasible" (Abbas B.M., Bangladesh WAPDA, 1971).

The Brahmaputra (or Jamuna in Bangladesh) rises earlier than the Ganga with earlier snowmelt and rains. Once these rivers (known as the Padma below their confluence) are bank-full in an almost zero-gradient lower delta, much of which is below high tide level, any further discharge must spill. Even the other tributary streams which may not be in spate back up as their flows do not gain admittance at the confluence, thus causing floods upstream. The Meghna, no small river itself, backs up into the Sylhet depression which acts as a flood detention reservoir until the congestion in the Padma is sufficiently relieved to enable it to drain out to sea. Even heavy precipitation may be impounded in situ by the high stages of the rivers, causing local rain floods for lack of drainage. Another factor that Bangladesh must contend with is cyclonic tidal bores or storm surges along the southern coast between April and December. These may rise up to seven m and sweep over the polders and sea walls that have been constructed over many thousands of kilometers (Hossain, Mosharaff, et al. August 1987).

INITIAL STRATEGIES UNTIL 1971

The floods of 1954, 1955 and 1956 that devastated East Pakistan (as it then was) and eastern India resulted in the dispatch of a United Nations Technical Assistance Mission to Pakistan under the leadership of J.A. Krug. The mission reported in 1957, spelling out the need for a comprehensive integrated plan combining a measure of flood protection with improved drainage, irrigation and some hydel generation. It stressed the need for improving the adequacy and efficiency of channels and river embankments for both water and land transportation. It suggested the preparation of a comprehensive water and power development plan, the creation of an agency for this task and joint action with India "considering the river system as a whole". It stated that the contribution of the Brahmaputra, Ganga and Meghna (Barak) to the flood discharge between June and October was in the ratio of 5:4:1 as a rule. It found that floods may be caused by a combination of factors and any excess above the normal volume of flow must create problems. Thus, "each increase of one foot above normal flood level of the Ganges at Hardinge Bridge over a period of 12 days represents about seven million acre-feet (0.862 m ha m) of water. A similar increase in the Brahmaputra represents nearly two million acre-feet (0.246 m ha m). Thus six inches of additional rainfall…is equivalent in volume of flow to a one foot (0.3 metre) rise in level of the two big rivers over a period of 12 days. These figures, though rough, indicate some measure of the relative effects of river flows and rainfall". The mission recommended confining the major rivers "within a reasonable range of their respective channels by embankments". This, with dredging, would reduce flood damage and permit a different and better system of cropping. The raising of habitations on mounds or relocating them on or behind embankments was seen as a useful and practical measure, but the idea of trying to build flood storages on the Ganga and Brahmaputra within Bangladesh was strongly discounted. More practical would be "the clearing and straightening of the smaller rivers".

As far as cooperation with India was concerned agreement was reached about supplying river discharge data on the Ganga, Brahmaputra and Teesta to facilitate better flood forecasting in East Pakistan. These arrangements are now being further strengthened again.

A Water and Power Development Authority was established in 1959 and set about preparing a master plan for coordinated water resource development, including flood control, with international consultancy. Meanwhile two other experts were called in. General John R. Hardin, ex-chairman of the Mississippi River Commission (1963) endorsed the concept of channel improvements and sluice and fuse plug sections in embankments to release flood waters into protected areas whenever embankments came under undue pressure. A year later Prof. J. Thijsee of the Netherland reiterated these recommendations but once again ruled out flood storages within the territory (Bangladesh Water Development Board, 1979).

In 1964 WAPDA's consultants, the International Engineering Co., USA, presented a master plan comprising 51 major projects to provide flood protection and drainage to 3.2 million hectares by 1985. There were to be three types of flood embankments and polders with gravity drainage, tidal drainage sluices, and pump drainage with related irrigation. Implementation was taken up over the next three plan periods and a selected group of schemes was completed or on-going when Bangladesh came into being in 1971. With liberation, emphasis shifted from flood control to irrigation for food self-sufficiency. An agricultural strategy was developed on the basis o depth of flooding, surveys having established that about 36 per cent of the area inundated is liable to flood up to a depth of 0.3 m, 35 per cent between 0.3 and 0.9 m, 16 per cent between 0.9 and 1.8 m, and 13 per cent over 1.8 m (Chaudhury, M. and Siddiqi, M.H. August 1985).

SEARCH FOR A REGIONAL APPROACH

A fresh effort to evolve an overall long range water resource development programme was made with the creation of a Master Plan Organisation. This in turn selected Harza Engineering Co. International, USA as a consultant for the preparation of the National Water Plan 1985-2005, which was submitted to the government in 1986.

The 1988 floods were particularly devastating and possibly unprecedented in intensity and extent. Over 46 millions were affected. There was a toll of 1,624 lives from the floods and 459 subsequently as a result of diarrhea caused by contaminated water supplies. Over 7.5 million hectares of cropped area were affected; some 115,000 head of cattle perished. Over 1.2 million houses were estimated to have been completely destroyed and double that number partially damaged. Large numbers of schools, bridges and culverts were damaged as were many hundreds of kilometers of rail track and roads. The charge that the floods were caused by releases from or siltation as a result of the Farakka Barrage are quite fanciful as a barrage does not store water whereas it does trap silt. Moreover the Ganga flows within India and then as a border river for 100 kilometres below Farakka before it enters Bangladesh exclusively, and no such effects were noticed in that stretch as these would have affected both countries. The fact is that the Ganga that year did not touch the peak it did in 1987 and the real fury of the 1988 flood was unleashed by the Brahmaputra which wreaked terrible havoc in the Assam Valley as well.

The SAARC summit in Kathmandu in December 1987 decided on a joint study of natural disasters including flood and drought in South Asia following the very severe drought followed by floods that year. The work has been taken in hand through the SAARC Secretariat and is to be completed by 1992, a schedule that could well be expedited. Meanwhile, President Ershad met with Rajiv Gandhi in Delhi on September 30, 1988 and it was agreed to set up a joint task force to report on short-term and long-term proposals for flood and water management in the Ganga-Brahmaputra basin within six months. Bangladesh also held high-level consultations with Nepal, Bhutan and China and appealed for international assistance through the United Nations, UNEP and the World Bank in tackling the flood problem regionally.

Soil conservation and afforestation throughout the upper catchments in the Himalaya and Northeast India, as well as in Bangladesh itself, is of great importance as this could reduce sedimentation over time. But any notion that the 2.4 billion tonnes and more of silt carried by the Ganga, Brahmaputra and Barak can be reduced by any large order of magnitude would be fallacious as much of this is a product of natural geological processes of mass wastage, bank erosion and bed transportation. Other non-structural steps such as improved meteorological forecasting, rain and discharge gauging, and flood warnings through reliable and instant communications are required. Given this, various precautionary measures can be taken or the more vulnerable areas within the flood plain evacuated. A rigorous disaster preparedness drill, suitable cropping patterns and prompt relief and prophylactic measures would complete the package. Dredging and desilting of waterways or emergency floodways can be expensive but these efforts could be turned to good account with food-for-work to raise the level of habitations, strengthen and repair embankments and build flood-proof infrastructure such as roads, telecommunication lines and concrete warehouses-cm-shelters on such high ground. Some infrastructure and shelters could also be built on floating jetties or tethered barges that would ride the flood. Such devices exist and are by no means unknown. The object should be to network them into total systems.

Floods have not merely an economic cost but a heavy social cost as well. A survey undertaken by Mosharaff Hossain et al reveals a greater degree of pauperization with low asset formation among flood prone families. These families suffer longer periods of semi-starvation or malnutrition. The economy of flooded areas is permanently depressed and there is little incentive to depart from traditional agricultural practices as the farmer's objective is to avoid risk rather than maximize production. Development investment in these regions also tends to be low.

TAMING THE BRAHMAPUTRA IN ASSAM

A considerable part of the answer to affording a larger degree of flood protection to Bangladesh lies in India and Nepal. Both in terms of area and intensity, the gravest flood threat to Bangladesh comes from the Brahmaputra which also backs up the Meghna. India's efforts to moderate floods in Assam and the Northeast generally will, therefore, have a significant bearing on the fortunes of Bangladesh as well. The problem of erosion control in the Northeast has been discussed in the context of *jhum* reclamation. Whatever its earlier merits when population was small and the return cycle long, *jhumming* can no longer be justified and is today a major engine of erosion, ecological degradation and flooding. Jhum erosion is estimated at 40 tonnes per hectare, resulting in an annual loss of 2.5 million tonnes of topsoil per annum. Various programme are under way for jhumia resettlement and it is hoped that by 2000 practically all the 2.6 million hectares under jhum, only a sixth of which is actually cultivated in any year, will be brought under plantations and field crops, horticulture, grass and forest. This will do much for soil conservation and control of erosion which is choking the rivers with additional sediment.

The Himalaya lies in an active seismic zone. The great Assam earthquake of 1950 caused whole hillsides to crumble and slide into the Brahmaputra whose bed level rose by over 3 m. Sadiya town simply disappeared in the river and Dibrugarh was almost chewed up by an angry Brahmaputra over the next few years. The vast amount of debris and sediment poured into it altered the regime has been transported slowly, ground and crushed in the process, causing floods. How many years it will take for the remnants of this catacyclsmic earthquake to find a stable resting place or be carried out to sea is not known. Measurements at Bahadurabad in Bangladesh show that the "dominant low water level in the Brahmaputra of 11.9 m in the early fifties had gradually gone up to 13.4 m, a rise of 1.5 m, in the sixties. However, since then a lowering trend can be observed" (Mosharaff et al).

The Brahmaputra in Assam is a braided river, 6 to 10 kilometres wide between a number of nodal points, and courses through a valley itself no more than 80-90 kilometres in width. All the northeast rivers drain steep hills and mountains that experience very high rainfall and deposit a lot of sediment as they debouch into the plains. Coupled with the backwater effect of the Brahmaputra when it is in spate, this causes many of its tributaries to flood above their confluence.

The Brahmaputra and Barak are jacketed within embankments extending over 3400 kilometres and 700 kilometres in India, respectively. Some of the embankments in the Assam Valley date back to Ahom times. As the river has silted between the embankments and threatened to top them, retirements or new embankments have been built further back. Three to four hundred kilometers of retirements have been built in Assam and in some bad stretches several retirements, going up to a record ten, have been constructed. Endangered habitations and towns have been protected by spurs, anti-erosion works and ring bunds.

Generally embankments are built to contain a 25-year return flood and town protection bunds to withstand a 100-year return flood as an all-India norm. not all embankments have been provided with the sluices and other regulatory devices or are well maintained. Despite the Assam Embankment and Drainage Act 1962 there has been much encroachment and cultivation of drainage channels. Water hyacinth growth also reduces drainage efficiency.

Until 1970, flood control was being handled by the Assam administration. In that year a three-tiered Brahmaputra flood control agency was set up only to be replaced by a statutory Brahmaputra Board in 1981. The board's membership and mandate encompass the entire Northeastern region. It is charged with preparing a master plan for flood control and bank erosion and improving drainage in the Brahmaputra and Barak valleys together with project reports and estimates for engineering works and dams for irrigation, hydel generation and navigation. The board submitted two master plans in 1986 and 1988. These relate to the main stem of the Brahmaputra and the Barak. This is to be followed by another report on the tributary streams.

Of a culturable area of 3.4 million hectares in Assam some 3.1 million hectares are flood prone. Only 270,000 hectares are protected. There have been extensive floods periodically, most recently in 1987, 1988 and 1989.

PROPOSED DIHANG AND SUBANSIRI DAMS

The Brahmaputra Board has recommended a series of measures including jhum control for flood moderation. Pride of place has been given to the construction of two giant multipurpose dams on the Dihang (Brahmaputra) and the Subansiri, its principal tributary, both in Arunachal. These are estimated to store 4.70 m ha m and 1.34 m ha m (gross), respectively and reduce the flood peak by well over a metre below Pandu (Guwahati) and to a far larger degree in Upper Assam. With this degree of moderation, lower embankments that are land-saving and easier to maintain would afford greater protection. Flood moderation would extend further into Bangladesh and protect significant areas now subject to shallow-to-medium inundation. The Tipaimukh dam, proposed to be built on the Barak on the Manipur-Mizoram border, will similarly protect the Cachar plain and greatly benefit the Meghna basin and Sylhet in Bangladesh.

The report of the Brahmaputra Board Phases I and II are under examination by the member States and the Centre. While the proposed Dihang and Subansiri dams are particularly attractive for the huge 8170 MW of very cheap firm power and considerable secondary power that they will together generate, there is a view that the initial benefit-cost ratio purely in terms of flood control might be higher if an alternative strategy were adopted. Keeping in mind that the Dihang has a high base flow and a relatively low ratio of peak flow to this base discharge, a series of check dams on a number of smaller but destructive tributaries like the Pagladiya is advocated before embarking on major mainstream dams. These would give fairly early cost-effective flood cushioning with 200/400 MW of power at each storage which the Northeast would be in a position more easily to absorb. Simultaneously, in order to ease the problem of poor drainage behind existing embankments, it would be desirable to provide gated embankments which could give relief to almost half the flooded area within five years with a manageable investment of Rs.300-500 crores. Of the 2.6 million hectares of sown area in Assam, 0.8 million hectares is within the ambit of the Brahmaputra's swing reach. Provision of rabi irrigation for this area would yield an output that could compensate for the kharif loss. The

Tipaimukh dam, however, will effectively regulate the Barak and should, therefore, not be delayed. The skepticism about the flood – moderating effect of the Dihang and Subansiri dams is not shared by other experts who advocate their early execution. Assam is keen that the two high dams be taken up. Arunachal is as yet diffident.

There is no real conflict between the Brahmaputra Board's high dam proposal and the alternative suggested, with some prioritization in view of the resource constraint. As the Brahmaputra is by far the greatest storehouse of unutilized water and energy in the entire subcontinent, not to harness its vast potential is unthinkable unless there are clear and convincing technical, economic, environmental or other considerations that dictate otherwise. This is by no means so. Priorities can be established and meaningful starts made in the Eighth and Ninth Plans (1990-2000). The remaining part of the Brahmaputra Board's master plan also needs to be expedited with more staff and budgetary support so that an overall assessment can be made.

GANGA FLOOD PROTECTION PLAN

The Ganga and its Himalaya tributaries are also responsible for considerable flooding. As in Assam, embankments have been built on a number of major rivers from Mughal times onwards, whether by the State or by zamindars. Many of these have been strengthened, extended or newly constructed in the past decades. While affording a measure of protection to the surrounding countryside they have not always been well maintained and have in any case built up the beds of the silt-laden rivers. There is currently very little flood storage in the Himalayan tributaries as there are no storage dams in Nepal at all and only a few in India such as on the Ramganga and the Yamuna. The Tehri dam and some others are being built in the Ganga-Yamuna basin and the Chisapani (Karnali) and Pancheshwar dams are under discussion with Nepal. The latter two would regulate the Ghaghara (Karnali) and Sharda (Mahakali) rivers.

The Ganga Flood Control Commission was set up in 1972 with a charter to prepare a basin master plan. A comprehensive outline plan was completed in 1973 and filled out in more detail in 1980. The final plan was submitted in 1986. The Ganga basin has been divided into 23 sub-basins. Fifteen sub-basin plans have been completed and the rest were to be ready by 1989-90. These have been sent to the concerned States which are expected to develop investment proposals for specific projects and programmes. At 1979 prices, the cost of schemes proposed came to Rs. 743 crores for UP, Rs. 567 crores for Bihar and Rs. 254 crores for West Bengal. By now the costs will have doubled on account of inflation.

The problem is that floods are forgotten once the waters recede and flood programmes are grossly under-funded through large sums are paid out for relief and rehabilitation as well as restoration of damaged housing and infrastructure every year. Such expenditure yields some political dividends though it is not otherwise very productive. The average annual loss on account of floods during 1953-86 is estimated to have been Rs 224 crores in UP, Rs 71 crores in Bihar and Rs 53 crores in West Bengal. But in a bad year the loss has gone up to Rs 300-400 and more. Yet Bihar budgets no more than around Rs 30 crores per annum on flood programmes. This rate of expenditure is self-defeating as incomplete works are washed away or rendered obsolete as the river regime undergoes change before the project can influence it in the manner intended. The Bagmati embankment for instance was started in 1974 at a sanctioned cost of Rs 8 crores. It had yet to be completed in 1988 by which time its cost had spiraled to over Rs 100 crores. Bihar was estimated to require Rs 175 crores for anti-erosion works during 1987-89. Only Rs 50 crores was sanctioned in 1988-89 of which no more than Rs 20 crores was in sight. Under-funding also means that no maintenance is possible. Such penny-pinching is grossly wasteful.

North Bihar is ravaged by severe floods and suffered heavily in 1987. The rivers coming down from Nepal carry a great deal of sediment, especially the Kosi. Old spill channels and drains in the Gandka basin were found to be choked with silt or hyacinth and often occupied or cultivated. The Buhri Gandak embankment was breached. The main cause of the disaster was a cloudburst that sent down 676 mm of rainfall in just five days over Nepal and North Bihar. The rivers simply had to flood, though better structural and non-structural management could have mitigated the loss to life and property.

BATTLING THE KOSI

The Sone carries the highest flood discharge of Bihar's rivers (40,000 cumecs) because of its large catchment, followed by the Gandak and the Kosi. But the Kosi is the most destructive on account of its extremely high silt content, like the Huang-Ho, a river of almost equal size in terms of flow. The Kosi is aggrading not only because it is confined within embankments but on account of its steep gradient which falls from 0.76 m to 0.08 per mile (1.6 kilometres) 60 kilometres from its confluence with the Ganga. In the 30 years since the Kosi was jacketed, the berm within the embankments has risen, resulting in higher flood levels with the same discharge. The rise in the berm level has also rendered many old drainage sluices ineffective. The deepest bed of the river's main flow channel, however, remains at the same level as before.

National concern over floods in India has been spasmodic following the episodic disasters that seem to come in cycles. One of the earliest after Independence was in 1954 and centred in large part on Bihar's River of Sorrow. The wayward Kosi which had swung 112 kilometres west in an arc from Purnea to Saharsa over 130 years, destroying huge agricultural tracts, was put on the agenda of the then Central Water, Irrigation and Navigation Commission when it was first set up in

1945. Kanwar Sain recounts the story (1978). A multi-purpose project was prepared in 1950 comprising a 239 m high dam at Barakshetra in Nepal which would store a gross 0.85 m ha m and moderate the Kosi flood from 25,000 cumecs to 5660 cumecs, generate 1800 MW, irrigate over 1.5 million hectares in Nepal and Bihar from a diversion barrage lower down at Chhatra (in Nepal), and provide a measure of navigation and silt control. The cost was placed at Rs. 177 crores. It was, however, felt that there was no demand for the magnitude of power generation and irrigation proposed and that the high dam should, therefore, be postponed for the time being. The alternative of a lower dam below Chhatra at Belka was considered but dropped as it appeared unlikely that this would ensure adequate river control. Thereupon the present project of a barrage 37 kilometres below Chhatra, straddling the Indo-Nepal border, was conceived and finalized after a team of Indian engineers led by Kanwar Sain, then Chairman of the Central Water (and Power) Commission, visited China to study flood control works on the Huang-Ho.

Embankments were to be constructed to hold the Kosi to a fixed course. Work on these started in 1955 amidst controversy that any barrage which might be built would silt very soon. Nevertheless the barrage was taken up in 1959 and the canals were opened for irrigation in 1964 by when flood protection over an area of 210,000 hectares had already created a sense of security and triggered a process of asset-formation. The river stood anchored and its westward migration arrested. Embankments also afforded protection from moderate flooding to over 51,000 hectares in Nepal, which further benefited from reduced erosion, an all-weather east-west bridge over the barrage, some irrigation, and power generation from a small canal-hydel station. Yet there was a feeling among Nepalese, that remains to this day (and with regard to the Gandak barrage too), that had the Kosi barrage been located further upstream and the canals differently aligned, the benefits to Nepal from irrigation and flood and erosion control would have been greater.

Owing to continuing problems of siltation and erosion, subsequent committees toyed with the idea of a second barrage lower down to flatten the gradient. Soil conservation works in the Kosi catchment in Nepal were also urged. The first suggested was never pursued and the second, though adopted, was not seriously followed through. In 1974 a board of consultants revived the idea of a high dam at Barakshetra to save the barrage and embankments after an alternative site was found wanting. Nothing followed for more than a decade until the severe 1987 flood brought the Kosi high dam back on the agenda. India has now again offered to fund a substantial watershed management and soil conservation programme in the Kosi catchment in Nepal. While this is certainly desirable, the engineering view is that a high dam would additionally moderate a 100-year Kosi flood to a quarter of its value and that the region could now beneficially use both the energy and the water stored.

DVC AND YAMUNA AUTOMATED FLOOD FORECASTING SYSTEMS

Perhaps one of the most successful flood control programmes has been that of the Damodar Valley Corporation though even this is often mistakenly criticized. The Damodar Valley is a small river draining a part of the Chota Nagpur plateau in Bihar and the lower part of West Bengal. This highly industrialized area in the heart of the coal-steel belt was periodically subject to damaging floods, as in 1943, which turned attention towards seeking a permanent solution to the problem. The Tennessee Valley Authority model was adopted for integrated river valley development and with TVA expertise a plan was drawn up and the DVC set up under an Act of Parliament in 1948. The project envisaged catchment area treatment in Bihar and a family of eight dams to moderate a 100-year return flood of 28,000 cumecs to 7100 cumecs, which is the rivers' bank-full capacity. The 1943 flood had a peak discharge of 9,910 cumecs. In point of fact only four dams have been built with a capacity of moderating a flood of 18,400 cumecs. However, owing to incomplete land acquisition for the Panchet Hill and Maithon reservoirs, submergence has had to be limited, reducing the flood moderation by a third of the design values. Even so, the DVC has successfully regulated eight floods in excess of the 1943 flow and was able to moderate the unprecedented 1978 flood of 24,100 cumecs to 4,500 cumecs (DVC, December 1986). The reason for not acquiring the lands falling within the maximum reservoir spread of the Maithon and Panchet Hill dams was to avoid the loss of some valuable coal seams. Sanction has now been accorded to acquisition of the full area which, once accomplished, will add significantly to the flood cushion. There has, however, been deterioration of the lower Damodar channel on account of siltation which causes spilling. River training works or dredging is required for channel improvement.

The DVC operates a wireless-based, manual system of dynamic reservoir management for flood regulation. This was designed some years ago in collaboration with the CWC which has operationalised an automated system for flood forecasting in the upper Yamuna basin up to Delhi. The CWC initiated its flood forecasting and warning system in 1958 with one forecasting site at Delhi to monitor the Yamuna. This has since grown to a national network of 145 CWC stations.

More advanced techniques were introduced in the upper Yamuna catchment in 1980 and a second phase has just been completed. Under this, a computer at the CWC control room in Delhi receives water level, precipitation and temperature readings from 27 unmanned sensors located all along the Yamuna and its main influents over 10,000 square kilometres of catchment in real time through a VHF telemetry link powered by batteries automatically charged by solar cells whenever mainline energy is not available. Each sensor is equipped with automatic radio repeaters in the VHF radio band and a micro-processor. At the control room in Delhi, the master teleprocessor issues programmed commands to its slave stations directing them to transmit data in a specified sequence and at stated intervals. The data is stored in a floppy disc and can be processed through a computer print-out as required (CWC, 1986). The system was first tested in 1985 and various improvements including snow hydrology and snow-melt runoff observations have been added on since. The system is proposed to be satellite-linked in due course. Various mathematical models have been adapted or developed for the upper Yamuna on the basis of the real-time data obtained from hitherto remote and inaccessible stations in order to permit predictions leading to more sophisticated forecasting and warning systems and flood routing techniques which will gain flexibility with the development of storages and regulatory devices within the upper Yamuna basin. The system cost Rs. 3 crores and is a pilot project and training model for replication in other critical flood prone basins.

Unfortunately flood forecasting is a non-plan item of expenditure and has, therefore, been subject to capricious cuts whereas it could save crores in damage prevention or mitigation. The 1953 Godavari flood took a toll of 2,000 lives. The CWC was however able to make a 48-hour worst-flood-of-the-century forecast in 1986 enabling a million persons to be evacuated from the danger zone, thereby saving countless lives.

REASONS FOR RISING FLOOD INTENSITY

The widespread floods of 1954 evoked a first catchment of national policy which offered hope-of programmes that would ensure that "the country may be rid of the menace of floods". Subsequent statements were more realistic and, referred total flood control as an "illusion", promised "a reasonable degree of protection" instead. Apart from some initial flood storage programmes, primary emphasis for wide, low-cost protection was placed on embankments to be followed by storages together with channel improvements, drainage works, and continued to rise, especially in the Ganga-Brahmaputra-Barak basin, impelling the government to appoint a National Flood Commission or the Rashtriya Barh Ayog in 1976. Its report, submitted nearly four years later, made an exhaustive analysis of the problem but has not been treated with the urgency and respect it deserves. More money is still spent on relief and rehabilitation than on flood protection works, a totally false priority and extremely wasteful of national resources. Counting any area over flooded, the RBA reported that the flood prone area in the country has risen from 25 million hectares in 1953 to 34 million hectares in 1978 which, together with six million hectares fully protected, would render a gross 40 million hectares "liable to flood", the largest area and greatest intensity being by far in he Ganga-Brahmaputra-Barak basin.

To deduce from this figure that floods have increased really would be misleading. More accurately, the effects of flooding are greater as is the trend in the U.S., Japan and elsewhere. With development and population increase and the sense of security that goes with flood protection, drainage has deteriorated and the flood plain has been increasingly invaded for agriculture, settlement and other development purposes. Even *diara* or *char* lands, which belong to the river or the floodways between embankments and the beds of drains have been cultivated. Wetlands and spill channels have been reclaimed or allowed to choke with silt and hyacinth. A population of two million has been settled in the trans-Yamuna area of Delhi within the active flood plain of the river. Salt Lake in Calcutta has been reclaimed. Yet the same volume of rainfall and discharge, sometimes with extraordinary cloudbursts, must pass through even more restricted channels without the benefit of "bank storage". It is something like traffic jams on the roads with pavement dwellers and stalls crowding the sidewalks, forcing pedestrians on to the highway along which cars are parked with abandon.

Embankments can enhance sediment build-up resulting in rising bed-levels in many aggrading waterways and thereby accentuating drainage congestion in the protected area. Embankments also cause a rise in water levels and a greater velocity of flow as the river is squeezed between narrower confines, which can result in flooding both up and down stream and increase erosion. Low budgets and incomplete works as a consequence, coupled with poor maintenance, invite trouble. After 1978 floods, U.P. Haryana and Delhi strengthened and raised many embankments along the Yamuna and closed existing gaps. "Thus the flood plain storae which helped in attenuating the flood peak at Delhi during 1978 will not be available now and in case such a high flood recurs in the river Yamuna, Delhi is likely to experience higher peaks … than … in 1978" (Rangachari, R and Mathur P.C. November 1986). And this is presumably what happened in 1988 when Yamuna waters entered Delhi. Vacant, wilderness or lightly developed areas that once provided emergency floodways are no longer available to hold or pass high flood stages that will periodically occur. With intensive development, more valuable investments and inflation, the value of flood losses has escalated.

FLOOD PLAIN ZONING AND CROPPING PATTERNS

The RBA has recommended rigorous flood contour mapping and flood plain zoning as a basis for regulating settlement and development which is a world-wide practice and is one of the most practical and effective non-structural means of avoiding or mitigating flood damage. It suggested that the Government of India circulate a comprehensive model bill on flood control for adoption by the States. This should deal with preparation of flood control schemes, acquisition of land and property, land-use regulations in flood plains, prohibition and removal of obstructions on rivers and drains, disaster prevention and preparedness, compulsory evacuation of people from endangered areas, requisition of labour in times of emergency, and contributions from beneficiaries. The proposals took account of existing legislation and experience both in the country and abroad. The Centre did prepare and circulate such a bill. But barring Manipur no State has cared to do anything to adopt or enforce such legislation despite the lapse of more than a decade.

There is also the problem that floods vary and different areas are differently affected in different areas. A high return flood may not recur in a given area for some years after some partial protection measures may have been taken thus encouraging the belief that the problem has been permanently solved and there is no danger in further occupation of the flood plain or in enhancing the density or value of investments made in what are still vulnerable areas. The authorities connive at this as it is politically expedient to do so. Comes a high return flood and there is obviously far greater damage and even loss of life than before resulting in a hue and cry, a search for scapegoats and extravagant crash programmes to protect vulnerable investments and settlements that should never have been sited there in the first instance and can scarcely ever be permanently protected. The worst of these programmes merely steal money, time and attention from other more worthwhile and important works or maintenance and must be deplored. The flood plains of India occupy some 20 per cent of its total area but are home to 30-40 per cent of the population. This proportion has grown over the years.

Closely allied to occupation of the flood plain is the adoption of appropriate cropping strategies. Just as much local "drought" is caused by rashly planting "wet" crops in "dry" areas, correspondingly growing certain crops or particular varieties insuited to lands that will invariably be flooded to a certain depth for a certain duration of time must be discouraged. The crop calendar may need to be modified to avoid the flood or to enable the crop to withstand it; or some form of fish or duck farming or aquaculture during the flood season may be the better and possibly the more profitable alternative. This would certainly be true of natural depressions and old or derelict river beds, cut-offs and ox-bows, including *jheels*, *tals*, *beels* and *chaurs*. Some *diara* lands can be developed into good *diara*-pastures to sustain a viable dairy herd, the RBA opined. This again may be a useful alternative "crop" to explore.

Providing for drainage and proper maintenance is important and all new development programmes, whether of urban expansion, laying of roads, rail tracks, canals, other structures and hard surfaces must be examined from the point of view of their impact on drainage and changing the direction of drainage flows. This is not being sufficiently done or coordinated. Culverts are often inadequate and the design of bridges must also be such as to avoid any afflux in water levels.

Storage reservoirs and check dams are certainly among the engineering measures that can be taken up. Multipurpose dams make competing demands on reservoir management. But in any project in which there is a defined flood component, a certain proportion of storage, say 15 per cent, is kept in reserve up to a given date, usually October 1, in order to absorb a late monsoon flood. Thereafter, flood storage yields to irrigation or energy uses. During the monsoon itself, reservoirs may be allowed to fill while the river is at a high stage and then be emptied in a controlled fashion to restore the necessary cushion to absorb further floods later in the season. Good meteorological data and feedback on rainfall and discharge in various sub-catchments and tributaries is necessary so that flood releases from a dam do not coincide with heavy precipitation or releases from other storages or detention reservoirs within the same basin to create a flood. Mistiming of flood releases can cause problems. This apart, dams must have sufficient spillway capacity to manage releases appropriately.

Reference has been made to proposals for underground monsoon storage in certain regions by summer groundwater pumping to create additional "pore space" within the aquifer which might thereby be enabled to sponge up more water through greater recharge values with the onset of the rains. This cannot be done in an ad hoc fashion but, if at all, as part of a large system into which irrigation, cropping patterns, energy inputs and flood management are integrated. Initial experiments are now under way in the upper Hindon catchment within the Yamuna basin near Saharanpur. The cost-effectiveness of such systems will also need to be measured.

COST-BENEFIT AND RELIEF NORMS

Cost-benefit criteria for flood works were sought to be spelt out in 1955. Annual cost was to be calculated at 16 per cent of the cost of an embankment or drainage scheme and the flood storage allocable to a dam. Benefits on the other hand were to be assessed on the basis of the value of flood damage previously caused and now prevented, minus the loss entailed to agriculture from deprivation of the assumed fertility of flood silt formerly deposited on crop lands. Wider social costs and benefits going beyond purely financial costs and benefits to project authorities were proposed to be taken into account but the RBA felt that these would be difficult to evaluate without further research. The expert committee on Rise in Cost of Irrigation and Multipurpose Projects (1973) pointed out that costs were often underestimated and benefits exaggerated in order to secure project sanctions. But, as with irrigation projects, poor maintenance for whatever reason, including under-funding results in qualitative deterioration and less benefit.

The Sixth Finance Commission (1973) recommended 4 per cent of the capital cost as an adequate provision for maintenance of flood works. The Seventh Finance Commission (1978) set certain norms which worked out to 3 per cent of the capital cost initially and 2 per cent thereafter for earthen embankments. The Eighth Finance Commission (1984) was urged to adopt the norms laid down by an expert committee set up by the Government in 1982. This recommended various rates per kilometer for the first three and subsequent years depending on whether it was an earthen embankment or armoured with stone, the height of the structure, and the volume of discharge (also applicable to drains) with an additional amount for tidal channels. It was felt that lack of accurate data would pose problems and so the Finance Commission took the actual maintenance expenditure incurred in 1981-82 as the base and, allowing for some escalation, set that as the next five year norm. This again suggests a very ad hoc approach and the whole issue merits careful reconsideration.

Flood damage, like drought damage, has become politically inflatable to a considerable degree as a springboard for demanding correspondingly large disaster relief which is doled out on the basis of very variable political arithmetic. Poor maintenance resulting in willful damage might, therefore, actually be rewarded and financially lagged administrations find relief bounty an expedient way of balance their mismanaged finances. The beneficiaries have not been asked to pay betterment or otherwise contribute while generous ad hoc "relief" has really become a form of crude flood insurance, the premium being paid by the general taxpayer.

Crop insurance has not worked for a number of reasons but has once again been revived. Under the 1988 proposal the Centre will contribute two-thirds of the claim amount due to farmers and the States one-third. The scheme is to cover drought, flood and other disasters with farmers being entitled to claim up to 100 per cent of the value of loans taken for inputs or improvements. This has been criticised as being no more than a loan insurance programme which might leave out tiny peasants and others who may be affected by floods but not be loanees.

Following the severe floods in northwest India in October 1988, the Prime Minister made a whirlwind tour of some areas and announced Rs. 176 crores by way of relief to Punjab, Himachal and Haryana. Assam for some reason had been awarded a more modest quantum of relief. The Prime Minister described the existing norms laid down for flood relief as "old" and said he was directing the Planning Commission to revise them, relating payments to real damage and working out average disaster relief rates. He declared that Punjab had been the mainstay of the green revolution and was the nation's bread basket. It therefore merited special treatment. While due relief to Punjab or any other State must not be denied, a proper systematization of flood relief is overdue if disaster management is to rise above political gestures. Apart from rationalizing crop or flood insurance, there is considerable merit in the RBA's recommendation of a general flood cess recoverable from regions or sections of the population benefiting from flood protection which will have resulted in appreciation in land values, higher investments and greater productivity, income and employment.

CLOUDBURSTS AND GLACIAL LAKE HAZARDS

Cloudbursts, cyclones and depressions can bring down torrential rain that will cause flooding. This happens off and on and can have devastating effects. The Teesta Valley experienced 40 occasions between 1891 and 1965 when there was more than 250 mm of rain within 24 hours, with precipitation exceeding 403 mm on one occasion. Three days in October 1968 experienced 1500 mm of rainfall causing landslides that blocked the Teesta and caused heavy floods. In July 1970 a cloudburst in the Patalganga Valley in Garhwal brought a deluge of 275 mm overnight. Landslide debris and boulders created a 60-metre high dam which burst, flooding the Alaknanda and sending a surge of wate and coarse sand 200 kilometres to Haridwar and filling the Upper Ganga Canal with mud over a 10-kilometre stretch. Immense damage was caused (Anil Agarwal et al, April 1987). Another landslide in August 1978, following incessant rain, choked the Bhagirathi until the dam gave way sending down a furious flood.

Nepal and Tibet are prone to glacial lake outbursts. Slides block the outlets, building up a column of water under the pressure of which the dam finally gives way causing havoc as the flood cascades downstream. On August 4, 1985 such a glacial lake outburst sent a 10-15 metre wave of water crashing down the Bhote and Dudh Kosi rivers in Nepal over a distance of 90 kilometres. The initial release of water had a discharge greater than the river's monsoon maximum. The flood all but wiped out the micro-hydel project under construction at Namche Bazar (3300 m), below Everest, and several bridges lower down.

Earlier, in 1981, a larger episode of this kind in Tibet on a tributary of the Boqu river (Sun Kosi) sent down an initial discharge of 16,000 cumecs, ripping up the Kathmandu-Lhasa highway over 30 kilometres, destroying the Friendship Bridge near Kodari and modifying the river channel for 30 kilometres further downstream (Ives, Jack D, November 1986). Similar occurrences have been reported from Bhutan. Such events are not merely dangerous and destructive in themselves but pour an enormous quantity of debris into streams which is gradually ground down into silt and transported down river over the years. Glacialogical hazards risk mapping is now being attempted, aided by remote sensing. This could provide base data regarding the estimated volume of water in different lakes and enable classification by size, shape and risk factors. Thereafter, changes could be monitored where possible so as to facilitate artificial drainage, forecasting and warning in good time. The Chinese are contemplating similar programmes in Tibet, and India would be advised to follow suit. Glacial lakes occur above 4,250 m. According to Nepal's Remote Sensing Centre there are over 200 glacial lakes in the Kosi, Trisuli, Karnali, Mahakali and Tsangpo catchments, mostly in Tibet.

Apart from episodic hazards of this kind, Nepal also has a flood problem in parts of the Terai. A good part of this can be mitigated by the regulation of medium rivers like the Rapti, Bagmati and Kankai which would also yield irrigation and power benefits. Rising river bed levels as a result of sedimentation has been reported. According to one study, the bed level of some Terai rivers is rising by 15 to 30 centimetres every year causing increased flooding (Eckholm, Eric 1976).

Nepal's hydro-meteoroloical network is still in its infancy with only seven stations feeding data into Kathmandu. This was being relayed to Delhi on a monthly basis which was inadequate as a forecasting input, though useful for purposes of record. The collection system being rudimentary and slow is prone to a significant margin of error. Following the 1987 floods in eastern Uttar Pradesh and North

Bihar a new agreement was negotiated under which India is assisting in strengthening and upgrading Nepal's data collection and forecasting infrastructure with special wireless equipment and a training input. This system should be operational in 1990.

SOIL CONSERVATION FOR SEDIMENT CONTROL

The surest answer to sediment control is soil conservation. This is a programme that relates both to flood and drought and to a considerable degree represents two sides of the same coin. The two phenomena must be treated in an integrated manner and preventive measures, including flood storage and soil conservation, taken together. Mr. Rajiv Gandhi estimated the 1987 drought and flood damage at about Rs.3,000 crores – the cost in part of environmental degradation. This suggests the priority and the kind of budgetary support that it would be worth according to programmes of land and water conservation.

India's Sixth Plan (1980) categorized 175 million hectares of the total land mass of 329 million hectares as "degraded". Of this, by far the largest chunk of 150 m ha was classified as suffering from wind and water erosion, seven m ha from alkalinity and salinity and nine m ha from river erosion and other factors. An experienced civil servant, B.B. Vohra, collated available data to argue the case for a Land Charter (1974) and an integrated plan for conservation. In subsequent writings he cited an annual loss of six billion tonnes of topsoil from some 85 m ha of degraded agricultural lands through erosion as leading to an enormous loss of plant nutrients and corresponding crop production annually (Ibid, 1985). An official estimate more recently placed the national crop loss on this account annually at between 30 and 50 million tonnes of foodgrain (National Land Use and Conservation Board, 1988). Separate figures for the basin area are not available but a large part of the affected lands are located within it. An over-arching policy-making National Land Use and Wasteland Development Council is now coordinating a national effort to arrest and reverse past trends. As of 1986-87, about 31.22 m ha had been treated under various headings at a cost of Rs. 1,524 crores, some five to six million hectares of this within the basin region.

Work has been taken up on a watershed basis with 3,200 watershed delineated in a national watershed atlas. Twenty seven river valley and eight flood prone catchments covering 85 m ha have been progressively brought under treatment. Priority watersheds extending over 32 m ha within these catchments were selected by the All-India Land Use and Soil Survey through aerial and ground reconnaissance, and critical areas covering 20 m ha identified within these for treatment on the basis of a weighted erosion intensity index. Actual treatment thus far extends to no more than three million hectares at an average cost of Rs 4000-5000 per hectare or somewhat more if bench terracing is taken up with stone risers. Some cost reduction has been possible by using local utility vegetation and shrubs. An integrated approach has been adopted with afforestation, agro-forestry, plantations, gully plugging, small water harvesting structures and land reclamation being taken up with local participation and extension support.

The World Bank has been experimenting with the use of vetiver grass or khas in the Himalayan Watershed Management Project spread over 315,000 hectares in Garhwal and Kumaon. This propagates by vegetative growth (which means it cannot multiply like a weed). A strong root network binds the soil and it keeps growing above the sediment it traps to form natural contour terraces that are not washed away or in need of constant and expensive repair like earthen contour bunds. The belief that cattle do not eat vetiver grass was said to be a further encouraging factor, eliminating the need for protection against grazing and browsing. But local experience suggests otherwise, though vetiver may not be a favoured grazing species. Khas has been planted on abandoned terraces between 700- and 3000-metre altitudes. Experiments have also been conducted with rhus cotinus, carissa and other wild Himalayan shrubs. These have been planted as stabilizing hedges along the contours of barren slopes. Rhus is propagated by cuttings and is a good fuel wood which can be harvested by coppicing. Clover seeds from New Zealand are being pelletised for aerial seeding of these slopes. Pelletisation prevents the seed from being eaten by birds. The introduction of a leguminous fodder plant like clover is expected to induce a better growth of grass and provide forage and silage for stall-feeding hill cattle. It is too early to judge the result of this experiment. If successful, it could open up low cost opportunities for land reclamation and erosion control in the hills as well as in other eroded watersheds.

CATCHMENT AREA PROGRAMMES

Some 351 hydrologic and sediment monitoring sites have been established in 24 catchments and readings over a period of time have shown a progressive decrease in the silt load in the Damodar-Barakar, Chambal and Mayurakshi catchments as a result of soil conservation measures. In the Damodar-Barakar catchment, the yield of crops increased by 1.9 quintals per hectare and the yield of lowland paddy rose by over 28 per cent in the treated area. Over 11 million man-days of casual employment had been generated until 1981-82 under the conservation programme (Das, D.C. et al., 1985).

Alarm over the observed rate of reservoir sedimentation exceeding the assumed rate, thus threatening the storage life of dams, gave an impetus to the catchment area conservation programme. Studies show that these have paid off in some measure at least. In an evaluation of the Matatila Project (on the Betwa in Uttar Pradesh), the Agricultural Finance Corporation found that the sediment inflow rate (defined as hectare-metres of sediment per 100 square kilometres of catchment per million hectare-metres of inflow into the reservoir per annum) declined from 3.96 to 0.23 or by 94 per cent between 1962 and 1985. With treatment, the sediment production rate in mini-watersheds within the Matatila catchment showed reductions ranging from 44 to 94 per cent. Cropping intensities rose from 85.6 per cent to 115.4 per cent; crop yield increases ranged from 10 to 76 per cent; and the benefit-cost ratio was very favourable. The report stated that programme efficiency could be further improved if field plans provided for hundreds of thousand of small storage structures through the creation of a pond conservation crops. It also recommended land leveling in preference to contour bunding wherever soil depths permit. It urged the creation of a soil conservation commission as a counterpart to the Central Water Commission to undertake sound watershed management programmes for all river valley projects and other strategic catchments (Bali J.S. et al., AFC, 1988).

A similar evaluation of the Machkund, Sileru and Pochampad projects in Andhra-Orissa and Maharashtra respectively showed varied benefits in terms of reduction of the sediment projection rate, increase in crop yields and land values, and employment generation. The report also cited evidence of a declining trend in sediment production with treatment of the Bhakra, Chambal and DVC catchments (Rao C. Sitapathi, et al., Administrative Staff College, May 1987). The sediment production rate (measured in ha-m/100 sq km/yr) in the Ramganga catchment was assumed to be 4.29. It was observed to be 18.20 in 1958 but fell to 17.30 in 1974. For Bhakra the assumed rate was also 4.29 but was observed to be 8.14 in 1964 and declined to 6.22 by 1979 (NLUCB, 1988).

The AFC Evaluation Study makes the point that "Soil conservation is the infrastructure of agriculture and forestry, just as a road is necessary for area development. When the government does not recover the infrastructural cost of roads (and irrigation) from people directly, why (should it) recover costs of soil conservation which ensures the health the land security to food supplies and the environment". With only loan funds available for soil conservation, programmes are limited and community ponds, sediment basins and erosion control structures cannot always be constructed. It adds: "Soil conservation is a poverty removal programme and is one of the major items of work for rual employment guarantee schemes. Like other such programmes, it should also be treated as a relief measure in the short run and a drought-proofing measure in the long run. The programme creates productive rural assets for the nation". The point is not without substance as larger, accelerated programmes will bring an additional return in the form of savings in disaster-relief and in direct and indirect revenues to the exchequer.

Soil conservation in upper catchments tends to follow initiation of major water resource development programmes. The sequence could well be reversed and need not await any river valley project at all. It has been argued that if soil conservation and watershed management practices are included in river valley projects from their very inception and a 25 per cent silt charge reduction is planned, the percentage increase in water utilization can range between 1.48 to 1.79 and 3.02 to 3.81 over a design period of 50 and 100 years respectively. Another case study indicates that a preplanned 25 per cent reduction in sediment would allow a reduction in the height of the dam from 32.6 m to 32 m thereby reducing construction costs by 5 to 6 per cent and saving on submergence, rehabilitation and loss of forests (Tejwani K.G., October 1985).

Reference has been made to jhum control in the Northeast. Ravine lands constitute another problem. About 1.6 million hectares of land have been affected by ravines in the basin, a large part of this along the Chambal and Yamuna in Madhya Pradesh, Rajasthan and Uttar Pradesh. Both agronomic and mechanical measures have been tried and an EEC-assisted integrated watershed management programme in ravine lands has been taken up in Uttar Pradesh. Wiser for the 1988 floods and mindful of the success of the Sukhomajri project near Chandigarh, Haryana has resolved to construct a chain of 100 small water harvesting dams along the Siwalik foothills at a cost of Rs. 16 crores as a soil and water conservation measure. The sand dune stabilization programme in south-west Haryana has made some headway though further steps are necessary to hold and reclaim the desert.

Initial survey, classification of land capability and monitoring has been greatly simplified by aerial photography and satellite imagery. The National Remote Sensing Agency has in hand or plans to take up programmes of snow, flood, drought, erosion and sediment transport, salinity and crop mapping. A National Natural Resources Management System (NNRMS) network has been established and will increasingly be in a position to support soil and water conservation programmes.

Concern for Himalayan watersheds should not obscure the importance of Aravalli, Vindhya-Kaimur-Satpura and Northeastern catchments as these too are fragile and under critical pressure. Specific inter-State authorities charged with developing master plans for their integrated conservation and development would be desirable as ad hoc projects are hardly adequate. Catchment area authorities are as necessary as command area and basin authorities.

INTEGRATED WATERSHED MANAGEMENT IN NEPAL

Nepal, much more than Bhutan, faces an equally acute problem of soil and water conservation. A number of integrated watershed management programmes have been taken up but soil conservation is often treated as an incidental part of integrated rural development and has, therefore, had little impact. As degradation is far advanced in man areas, soil conservation programmes tend to be rehabilitative rather than preventive. There has also been a resource problem with administrative decentralization. Conservation plan have to fit into the IRD programmes drawn up by local authorities for adoption by the district panchayat. Technical evaluation has to compete with political pressure. As of now district plans lack adequate management support, monitoring and evaluation. Because of economic opportunities in the Terai and the spread of trekking and tourism in the hills, able-bodied hill men are migrating to the Terai while tourism is generating new demands for fuelwood, roads and trails. Eric Eckholm's estimate of 240 million tonnes of soil being washed down from Nepal as an unrequited export to India and Bangladesh and out to sea may be exaggerated but could become a self-fulfilling prophecy. The sediment load in rivers is rising as farmland productivity declines with increasing soil wash in the Middle Hills.

Sixteen integrated watershed management programmes are under implementation in Nepal of which four are Central schemes (Bagmati, Kulekhani and Phewa Tal among them) and the rest district-level programmes. Channel repair, terrace improvement and grass plantation (citronella, lemon grass, napier grass), poultry and drinking water schemes have been taken up as immediate programmes. Longer term strategies must rest on changes in land-use patterns, afforestation, gully plugging, reducing the pressure of livestock, and stall feeding. The Soil and Water Conservation Act, 1962, was brought into force in 1984. But for the Act to apply, a watershed boundary must first be identified and gazetted. As of 1988, the Act was in actual operation only in the Kulekhani and Phewa Tal watersheds. The programme has, however, received a measure of support with World Food Programme backing for food-for-work schemes. Payment in food cannot exceed 50 per cent of wages. The rest must be paid in cash.

A modest Indo-Nepal soil conservation programme was taken up in the Kosi catchment in the mid-1950s as a follow up to the Kosi project. A soil conservation research, demonstration and training centre was established at Chatra under the aegis of the Kosi Coordination Committee. The Kosi catchment is the most densely populated in Nepal and a combination of high intensity rainfall and improper land use, including shifting cultivation in friable hills subject to tectonic shocks, has rendered it highly erodible. The progress of the project has been fitful. Negotiations are now afoot for a larger Indo-Nepal soil conservation and watershed management programme in the Kosi catchment. Such programmes should indeed be replicated in other catchments as there is a strong mutuality of interest in watershed management, erosion control and employment generation for the common good.

LHASA RIVER TO CHATTAGONG HILL TRACT

The Chinese have taken up a Kyi Chu (Lhava River) area development programme in Tibet. The catchment covers 30,000 square kilometres and holds a population of 200,000 three-fifths of this being resident in Lhasa itself. The altitudes range from 3,600 m at the confluence with the Tsangpo to 5,000 m, and planning data for the project has been provided by the Commission for Integrated Survey of Natural Resources (CISNAR), Beijing. The project commenced in 1958 when work was organized through state and collective farms and with reliance on military and unpaid labour. But after 1980, much of the activity has been privatized under the responsibility system. Achievements include agriculture and livestock improvement, improved pasture and rangeland management, 2,700 hectares of irrigation, poplar plantations and the construction of a 7,000 kw hydro-electric station. Agricultural taxes and irrigation charges have been suspended to encourage investments and asset formation (Dani, Anis A and Campbell J Gabriel, July 1986).

Bangladesh faces problems of bank and tidal erosion as well as surface erosion with tremendous pressure on vegetation and biomass as a prime source of non-commercial energy and feedstock. Shifting cultivation is practiced by tribal communities in Chittagong Hill Tract where a jhumia rehabilitation project has been taken up in the Sangu watershed. The jhum cycle had been reduced to five years and was laying the hills bare as very limited regeneration was possible. Jhum families are being given two hectares of government land, inclusive of a homestead plot, for settled cultivation on the basis of scientific cropping systems with horticulture and multi-storey agro-forestry. Health, education, communication and off-arm income-generating facilities are also being developed. A similar programme has been taken up in three watersheds of the Karnaphuli catchment above above the Kaptai lake and hydro-election station. Each jhumia family is being allotted 2.5 hectares of land, the larger part of this to raise rubber and the rest for horticulture, together with a homestead plot. Some 7,300 hectares of steeper slopes are being afforested. Other programmes to resettle plains people in the denuded and degraded Chittagong Hill Tract have, however, run into strong Chakma opposition. The Government is reviewing such colonization programmes and has sought to win over tribal opinion by legislation for local autonomy (corresponding to that developed on the tribal people in the adjacent Indian state of Tripura) so as to end insurgency and induce Chakma refugees in India to return home.

The real lesson to be learnt is that flood and drought, land and water management, go hand in hand. Soil and water conservation is best taken up as an integrated watershed management programme with peoples' participation. While technical support and some funding might necessarily have to come from above, these have to become panchayat/thana/district level programmes adopted and monitored by local communities. Contrary to widely held belief, these programmes do not merely entail expenditure but are revenue earning and employment generating. People do no despoil the good earth out of choice but from ignorance and, most often, from necessity, for survival. They must, therefore, be assisted to develop alternative strategies for sustainable growth at higher levels, which is demonstrably possible, so that they do not eat away their remaining resource-capital base.

Floods cannot be banished but can be moderated. For the rest, one has to live with them through sensible flood plain management, good forecasting mechanisms and preparedness. If the large and rising sums spent on disaster relief could be partly diverted to land and water conservation and management programmes the results would be greatly rewarding.

CHAPTER 8

Green Mantle

Forests precede agriculture and are with land water, air and energy a basic element of the ecosystem. Their contribution to the quality and efficiency of nature's life support systems is critical and civilizations that failed to devote sufficient care to them have been lost to the desert. Forests therefore are friends to man and need to be nurtured and sustained. Yet forests will be cleared or otherwise exploited for beneficial use and little may be lost and much is to be gained provided this is kept within reasonable limits. Attributing too much to forests however is mistaken, for far from serving any cause it could well confuse issues and inhibit progress.

Much of the Ganga-Brahmaputra plain was in large part densely forested even in fairly recent historical times. Much of the world's prairies and steppes too were forested at one time as pollen analysis has established. Hunter-gatherers first took to slash and burn shifting cultivation, remnants of which are extants in the Ganga-Brahmaputra-Barak Basin, and then to settled agriculture which entailed forest clearance. Forests were used for construction and firewood, for smelting metal and ship-building. Much of this is detailed in "Man's Role in Changing the Face of the Earth" (Thomas L. William, 1956). England's forests had so depleted by the 13th century that Henry III consented to the mining of coal in Newcastle. In 1669 a forest ordinance in France decreed that no wood should be cleared without authority. As the Anglo-French wars exhausted stocks of build and replenish its fleet. The new steel works and the railways devoured more forests. By 1890, large European forests had disappeared. Mixed natural forests increasingly gave way to conifer stands and new plantations gave preference to softwoods as demand moved from fuelwood to pulpwood. The same cycle repeated itself many times over, in Russia, the United States, and in Japan. The great dustbowl years of the 1930s in America saw Roosevelt launch the Shelterbelt Project in 1934 for tree planting in the great plains. Switzerland was losing forests until 1876 when in the first federal regulations were introduced. The situation was not retrieved until 1902 (Guller, Peter, 1986).

REPEATING A HISTORICAL CYCLE

The Indian experience, as elsewhere in the Third World, has not been dissimilar. The Himalaya is going through a phase that the Alps faced a century and more ago with one difference. The population and grazing pressure in the Himalaya and Third World generally is today far greater than anything that confronted Europe or the Untied States, even Japan. Tropical climates and rainfall are also more exacting.

In ancient India, forests were places of meditation and hunting. Sacred groves were maintained around temples and by tribes. The great prize was not timber as much as war elephants. T.B. Mahat et al. have described how decades of warfare encouraged forest clearance in some districts around Kathmandu 150-200 years ago as timber was needed to smelt iron with which to fashion weapons. Military retainers were noticed with forest land grants and tax reliefs thereon. In India too, smelting, expanding cultivation, ship-building, the railway and telegraph expansion, and new industries (like steam locomotives) that used wood-fuel in their boilers, all made heavy demands on the forest. The Bhadravati Iron Works in Mysore State operated its blast furnaces on wood well until after Indian Independence. Nepal's Terai forests were long protected by the malaria mosquito. The axe followed DDT in the 1950s. Shifting cultivation continues to take its toll alongside uncontrolled firewood collection and grazing. The idea that large tracts of primeval or "natural" forests still remain to be protected against all comers is for the most part no more than a romantic myth. Today's forests are largely products of regeneration or are man-made.

In Garhwal and Kumaon, the classification by government of large areas as "reserved forest", where traditional rights were extinguished or regulated, caused resentment to telescope into resistance during the freedom struggle resulting in large scale incendiarism in the 1920s and 1930s. Ten of thousands of hectares of forest were burnt down. Forests had largely come to be regarded as an inexhaustible common property resource to be freely used by whomsoever and whensoever required. Uncontrolled and increasingly excessive fuelwood gathering and grazing has devastated forests other than the reserved forests which have survived by virtue of the restrictions imposed on their use. The scientific working plans introduced were intended to limit commercial exploitation of timber to an annual cut no more than the incremental growth to ensure a sustained yield.

There has indubitably been misuse and illicit felling or excessive extraction of resin in order to maximize revenue as part of State policy and on account of corrupt practice at lower levels. Yet, listen to a scholarly assessment: "It is often claimed that the locals have an inherent long-run interest in the forests which ensures their sustainability and conservation, while the State (the Forest Department included) acts under the pressure of commercial interests ... The findings of this study (in Uttar Kannada and Shimoga in Karnataka) go counter to such a claim. The locals have hardly shown any more concern for the environment than private commercial interests, and the lion's share of local access to forests has been cornered by the local elite rather than by the local poor. At this stage of economic development, going back to an earlier and supposedly idyllic stage of exclusive local use, and denying any right to the larger economy even to protect the forests against extravagance, is just not practical, just as purely policing and bureaucratic and oppressive regulation of local use is equally impractical". (Nadkarni, M.V. et al., September 1987).

Concerned over the loss of forests, to which its own policies had contributed, the British Indian Government began to evolve a forest policy. Interestingly, the ecological value of forests received early emphasis. A statement made by the Secretary of State in 1863 said that "the poor growth and preservation of the forestry is as important to government as the cultivation of any other crop which the soil produces and, in some instances, more important, since the destruction of forests would affect most injuriously the climate and perhaps the fertility of the soil". There followed the creation of a Forest Department in 1864 though the first Forest Policy of 1894 acknowledged that forests would have to give way to agriculture wherever necessary. The new departure lay in a classification of forests into reserved and protected categories under the Forest Department with a diminishing, order of local rights. At the bottom of the scale, a class of village, panchayat or civil forests was created for local use. Accepted or intended policies were however rudely disregarded owing to the exigencies of the two World Wars. Despite these setbacks forests, which were provincialised under the 1921 and 1935 constitutional reforms, were by and large brought under sound forest management, though commercially exploited. The approach, however, was paternalistic and popular involvement not invited.

EVOLVING POLICY PARAMETERS

With India's Independence, a new national forest policy was enunciated in 1952. This clearly recognized the protective or ecological role of forests which were no longer to be treated as a residual category after the demands of agriculture had been met. It was provided that a third of the total land mass should ideally be under forest, the proportion ranging from 20 per cent in the plains to 60 per cent in the hills and catchments. Forests were to be functionally classified as protection, national and village forests, in addition to scattered treelands for community use. The protection forests were intended to prevent erosion, conserve water and maintain the climate while the so-called national forests were to be available for economic exploitation. Efforts were to be made to meet the increasing demand for grazing and firewood and to wean away the tribal population from shifting cultivation. As before, grasslands and rangelands received scarce attention and were left unprotected without any central supervision or direction, a weakness that persists to this day. Nor was there much budgetary or Plan support for forestry which continued to be regarded as a revenue earning activity, earning a surplus over expenditure until the end of the Fifth Plan (1981). As a result, India's forests have been characterized by little investment and low yields. The new 1988 Forest Policy emphasizes the role of forests in maintaining environmental stability, promoting soil and water conservation and preserving biological diversity. But it also talks of enhancing forest productivity and recognizes the need for substantial investments (Environment & Forests Ministry, 1988).

The National Agriculture Commission had advocated a new categorization into protection, production and social forestry. It favoured "strictly regulated and controlled grazing" in the forest, subject to nominal grazing fees, the replacement of forest contractors by tribal or other forest labour cooperatives, and State forest corporations. It attached high importance to production forestry, especially the production of industrial wood with a pricing policy that would give a commercial rate of return and advocated the development of man-made forests with institutional finance (NCA Part IX, 1976).

Ecological concerns had been growing since the World Environment Conference in Stockholm in 1972 and thinking about forests began to undergo radical change propelled by a new grassroots awareness manifested by such movements as Chipko in Garhwal. Forests were placed in the Concurrent List of the Indian Constitution, vesting the Central Government with legislative power which it exercised to enact the Forest Conservation Act, 1980. This was a reflection of mounting alarm over loss of forests and the possible effect of this on their ecological role in conserving land and water at one level and equal concern for the well being of tribal and other local communities living in or in association with the forests. The preservation of biological diversity came to be seen as a major goal and Project Tiger, biosphere reserves and national parks and sanctuaries got a fillip as means of protecting endangered species of flora and fauna.

EXTENT OF FOREST IN INDIA

Concern over deforestation found specific quantification in the publication by the National Remote Sensing Agency of two comparative surveys of the extent of India's forests for the period 1972-75 and 1980-82 (NRSA, December 1983). NRSA interpreted Landsat data to conclude that the aerial extent of forest had declined from 55.51 million hectares in 1972-75 to 46.34 million hectares in 1980-82. In other words, 9.17 million hectares of forest had been removed over a period of nine years, implying the loss of roughly a million hectares per annum. Another set of official figures placed the amount of forest diverted to other uses between 1951 and 1980 at 4.33 million hectares or a little under 150,000 hectares per annum. Reading these figures together it appeared that the rate of forest loss or diversion was obviously accelerating over time. Seen alongside the officially recorded forest area of 75.18 million hectares compiled between 1952 and 1986, the decline in forest cover assumed catastrophic proportions.

The mystery of the missing forests and many other facets have been admirably explained and analysed by the Director, Forest Survey of India, J.B. Lal, (1988). In the years immediately following Independence, the extent of forests in the country on the accession of princely states and the abolition of zamindari and other intermediary tenures was first estimated at 68.02 million hectares. As the application of the Indian Forest Act was extended, the final figure steadily rose to 75.18 million hectares by 1986-87. These lands were under forest jurisdiction but did not necessarily have any forest or even trees growing on them. The legal status of some of these lands was doubtful while 0.7 million hectares had been encroached upon over the years. The Central Forestry Commission and the Central Statistical Organisation put out different figures. Nobody really knew.

It in this context that NRSA's forest mapping exercise was useful. But the interpretation of the satellite imagery data was challenged by the Forest Survey of India which places the 1980-82 estimate at 64.87 million hectares as against the NRSA's 46.35 million hectares. The two agencies thereupon sat together and after a close examination reconciled their interpretations and published an agreed figure of 64.20 million hectares. It was discovered that the NRSA lacked sufficient ground that, that satellite imagery recorded in the winter months failed to "identify" deciduous forests whose trees had shed their leaves, that young regeneration, eucalyptus plantations, khair, babul and small forest patches were either omitted or not "recognised". Coffee plantations had also been excluded. Corrections under these headings made up the difference of 18.52 million hectares between the two estimates and resulted in an agreed finding that forests in India extended over 64.87 million hectares. The notion that India has been losing a million hectares of forest annually in recent years is therefore quite unfounded. Much of the increment in the agreed estimate did indeed come in the category of open forest. But definitely, the FSI had taken open forests and closed forests to be those with a crown cover of over 10 per cent and 40 per cent respectively, while the NRSA had adopted a lower standard of 30 per cent crown cover and more for closed forests. Thus by the FSI's yardstick, which follows international practice, the quality of both closed and open forest is higher than what the NRSA's initial figures suggested.

The officially accepted position, therefore, is that India has only 19.7 per cent of its land mass under forest as against a desired proportion of 33 per cent. Of the area under forest in 1982, 35.77 m ha was closed, 27.66 m ha open, 0.40 n ha under mangroves, and 0.37 m ha under coffee plantations. Much of the open forest is patchy and degraded and needs to be improver with denser stands. About 30 million hectares of India's forests like within the Ganga-Brahmaputra-Barak Basin.

DISPOSING OF SOME MYTHS

It would be as well to dispose of some other myths here. It is widely believed that deforestation causes floods by reducing infiltration and augmenting runoff. Hence statements that floods are becoming more extensive because of deforestation and that this casual connection applies to the Basin as well. Rising flood damage owing to increased occupancy of flood plains and other factors has been discussed in the previous chapter. Infiltration is a slow process and vegetation, bunding and pondage do augment percolation by extending the residence time of each raindrop that falls to the ground. But only up to a point. Infiltration depends on a number of factors including the intensity of rainfall over a given period of time, the nature of soil and rock strata as well as of vegetation, temperature and wind conditions, and topography. Even in optimal conditions average infiltration in India has seldom been found to exceed 10 to 20 per cent of overall precipitation. Once the soil is saturated, all excess water must runoff as rejected recharge or be lost to evaporation. If infiltration were infinite, there would be no reason to see burrow pits and depressions filled with stagnant water for months on end. Forests do increase residence time by intercepting rainfall and letting it down gradually, by absorbing it in humus and leaf litter and in facilitating infiltration through the root structure which too acts both as a passage and sponge. But once the sponge is full is retention capacity is exhausted.

This is worldwide experience. Gauging over 20 years in a 200,000 square kilometre catchment in the Mekong basin, all of it under dense tropical forest at the trijunction of Thailand, Burma and Laos, shows a peak discharge 46 times the average low water flow, resulting in regular flooding of the lowlands below (Prereira, H. Charles, 1986). Therefore, after the first monsoon rains, forests have a diminishing capacity to "hold" water unless there are long dry spells in between. A cloudburst produces torrential rain of an order that no forest can absorb, resulting in severe flash floods such as many parts of the Basin experience every year with regular frequency. This was true of North Bihar in 1987 and northwester India in 1988. To blame these floods on deforestation is mistaken. There is, however, a contrary view (Das D.C. December 1981).

What forests do is to reduce erosion and consequent sedimentation. But this is best done by leaf litter and undergrowth covering the forest floor. Even on bare plains and hillsides, pre-monsoon showers can cause grass and shrubs to sprout within days to provide a measure of protective cover by the time the rains break in all their fury. Sadly, measurements of such factors and the hydrological effects of different types of vegetation, land use and cropping practices have not been as adequately, widely or consistently undertaken and analysed as would be desirable.

Then again it is believed that forests mitigate drought by storing water and releasing it over time through more even streamflows. This is only related to the point of saturation storage. But against this additionality must be set off the loss due to evapotranspiration by the forest which drinks up water for its sustenance, thus acting both as a sink and a pump. Forest interception of rain can also enhance evaporation loss from leaves. The net water balance will vary in accordance with conditions and circumstances. Indian forest meteorology should establish the facts.

Forests are also believed to create or induce rain. There is no conclusive evidence of this other than, maybe, in the Amazon basin to a limited extent but not in the Congo basin where this aspect has been studied. V.M.Mehr-Homji's study of rainfall in relation to forest cover in Western Karnataka and Kerala between 1906 and 1975 is however cited as indicating that forest clearance seems to reduce the number of rainy days (Agarwal, Anil et al., April 1987) and diminish convection rain (Mehr-Homji, V.M. 1989).

LARGE GENERALISATIONS ON LIMITED DATA

A study of erosion in Nepal has led to the conclusion that "deforestation likely plays a minor, if any role in the major monsoon flood events in the lower Ganges. Better management of existing forest lands and marginal agricultural lands in mandatory however, to ensure the continued livelihood of the Himalayan hill farmer" (Carson, Brian, August 1985). Soil conservation, sound logging and cropping practices, and careful watershed management are eminently desirable and must be pursued. But absolute correlations between forests and floods must be questioned other than the fact that sediment carriage by rivers from eroded catchments do choke waterways and uplift their beds over time thereby aggravating floods. A caustic comment by Lawrence S. Hamilton (1986) sums up the debate: "...Beautiful correlations between the reduction in forest cover in a basin over time ... and the increasing frequency and extent of flooding in the lower basin are not proof of cause and effect. They are simply correlations, and similar significant correlations could be found associated with the increased mileage of roads, the increased number of children in the basin or the decrease in the number of tigers."

A prime source of confusion stems from large generalizations based on data confined to small and possibly atypical areas. The 1987 drought and floods in India were widely attributed to "deforestation", a palpable absurdity in view of the fact that the monsoon is part of a global system of atmospheric circulation and is not even a regional let alone a local phenomenon. Further, while forests can and do affect the micro-climate they do not control global weather though the huge Amazon forest may influence it to some degree. Likewise, the Ganga-Brahmaputra-Barak floods are a product of rainfall and discharge over enormous catchments which do not in sum replicate the watershed management measurements of mini-watersheds which is generally all that is cited. This is not to denigrate soil conservation, watershed management and forests for afforestation in the slightest but to caution against being diverted too far along what could be false trails. Arunachal and Bhutan are heavily forested (over 60 per cent) and were even more so 50 years ago, as was Assam. Why then has the Brahmaputra never exceeded the peak flood discharge of that time. The Godavari barrage and the Mettur dam on the Cauvery were built 100 and 60 years ago for flood levels and discharges that have not been exceeded to this day.

FUELWOOD AND GRAZING PRESSURES

There is no doubt that India needs to bring a larger area under actual forest cover and that the dimunition and degradation of the country's forests is to be deplored. What caused the regression? Population pressure and the extension of agriculture rank high. In the decades after Independence the available common property resources, community assets on which the poor most especially could draw upon were steadily privatized (Jodha, N.S., July 1986). Land was distributed to the landless (as unstated compensation for the lack of will to implement land reforms), and the commons were settled, built on, encroached and totally degraded over large areas in the absence of either a policy or organized management. Consequently the poor, in a situation of burgeoning numbers, began increasingly to press on and invade the forest for fodder, fuel, small timber and anything else. Forest regulations, considered legacies of the Raj, were removed or relaxed and what had been concessions or privileges hardened into "rights". Individual needs may have been immediately satisfied in some measure, but longer-term community and social interests were thoughtlessly disregarded. Populism and absent-mindedness combined to rob the future.

Perhaps more than fuelwood demands on the forests, grazing pressure has been the greatest source of damage. The 12 million hectares of recorded grazing and pasture land having all but disappeared, the forests have been subject to that much greater pasture from the growth in livestock numbers from 292 million in 1951 to 420 million in 1982. a large part of this population is resident in the Basin or migrates into it from Western Rajasthan and Madhya Pradesh. J.B. Lal estimates that the number of animals grazing in the forest was 35 million in 1957-58 and is over 90 million today.

The Committee for Review of Rights and Concessions in Forest Areas, 1981, lamented that the States had freely granted grazing rights and concessions in utter violation of the 1952 Forest Policy disregarding any criteria of carrying capacity. "As an average for the country, the grazing incidence in forests in sought to be regulated at 1.6 hectares per cow-unit. (A buffalo rates as two cow-units and sheep and goat as half a cow unit in terms of feed). However, it is seen that in most States, the grazing incidence is far more … For example in Bihar … (it) is more than three times. This over-grazing obviously has threatened the existence of forests … Over-grazing impedes regeneration, both natural and artificial. In addition, it retards the growth of grass and at many places leads to extinction of good palatable grasses … The damage to regeneration of bamboo an conifer species is rapid and of a magnitude beyond imagination. Trampling by livestock affects the soil. Excessive trampling makes the soil compact and impervious and prevents the circulation of air and water needed for its organic life. Herbaceous plants disappear increasingly and the denuded soil is exposed to erosion by wind and water. In the wooded areas, the trees wither, their roots are exposed, injured by hoofs, and ro sets in." Regeneration, erosion control and infiltration are all affected. In Bihar, grazing rules were set aside and free grazing permitted to any number of cattle. In Himachal, the Committee found almost all forests open to grazing with no increase in grazing fees since 1950. In West Bengal grazing fees had not been enhanced for 30 years. In Madhya Pradesh, grazing fees were abolished in 1973 and norms of grazing units abandoned. "This has resulted in grazing by lakhs of sheep, oats, camel and cattle from other States (sic) wandering through and destroying valuable forests." Even reserve forests were not spared and concessions were extended to them.

According to Forest Survey of India figures, grazing in forests extends to 83 per cent of forest lands in U.P. 75 per cent in Sikkim, 70 per cent in West Bengal, 53 per cent in Nagaland. In Rajasthan it is 100 per cent. If the prescribed norms were observed India's forests today could provide grazing for 31 million cow-units whereas the 90 million cow-units that in fact graze the forests would require a forested area of 165 million hectares (Lal, J.B.).

The energy demand on forests is equally burdensome. Whereas firewood accounts for 30 per cent of national energy consumption, it rises to over 68 and 45 per cent of per capita household energy consumption in rural and urban India, respectively. Like cowdung, it has been regarded as a free commodity entailing no more than the cost of family labour for collection. The FSI figures of recorded fuelwood production from forests (19 m.t.) together with dead, dry and fallen wood collected in headloads (9 m.t.) and fuelwood obtained from private and non-government forest land (30 m.t.) add up to around 58 million tonnes as against an estimated fuelwood consumption in 1987 of 157 million tonnes. The difference of 99 million tonnes between the two figures of official supplies and estimated demand is believed to be the quantum of firewood pilfered from the forest, "a cut in excess of the silviculturally permissible limit" resulting in forest depletion and degradation. Calculating the excess cut pilfered from forests between 1953 and 1987, J.B. Lal concludes that the net removal of 1645 million cubic metres of wood implies the total destruction of 3 million hectares of forest and reduced stocking over 27 million hectares. The answer lies not merely in seeking alternative sources of household fuel but in increasing the thermal efficiency of firewood by drying it and by using improved fuel-efficient chulahs (hearths) and stoves and, if they can be designed, cheap janata pressure-cookers.

JHUM, FIRE AND DIVERSION

As much as 2.70 million hectares of forest within the basin is under shifting cultivation in India, with additional areas being jhummed in Tibet, Bhutan, Nepal and Bangladesh. Upwards of 250,000 hectares have been encroached upon. The largest part of the forest in the Indian Northeast is under private or commercial ownership and categorized as "unclassed". The unclassed forests extend over 90 per cent of the forest area in Meghalaya, 75 per cent in Arunachal and 63 per cent in Manipur. In Nagaland over 88 per cent of the forest is privately owned (Lal J.B.). scientific management in these areas is obviously problematic. Excluding Jammu and Kashmir, 16.62 million hectares of the Indian Himalaya is forested which gives a 58 per cent forest cover overall. But more than 41 per cent of the forest is inadequately stocked (Forest Survey of India, 1987).

A major cause for the destruction and degradation of forests is fire. Some fires may be natural or incidental. Many are deliberately caused as in the Western Himalaya to get a new flush of grass for grazing or, as in Madhya Pradesh, Bihar and elsewhere, to clear the forest floor in order to facilitate the collection of mahua, sal and other seeds or produce. In the Northeast, jhum fires can spread and burn or damage adjacent forests. According to official estimates, 17,852 forest fires were reported from all over India during the Sixth Plan (1980-85) burning an area of 572,417 hectares. FSI inventories establish that the percentage of State forest annually liable to ground fires range from over 90 per cent in several parts of the Northeast, to 76 in Madhya Pradesh, 69 in Himachal, 67 in Bihar, 58 in U.P. 37 in Sikkim and 33 in West Bengal (FSI). A tribal population of 65 million depends on or lives in the forest, a considerable proportion of this within the basin. Until very recently, forest policy and development policy generally have been rather uncaring for this segment of the population despite lip-service to the cause of tribal upliftment. However, the claim that tribal communities have lived in harmony with nature for centuries and that this symbiosis has been broken by forestry, commercial logging and development generally is exaggerated. The growth of tribal populations within shrinking forests as a result of the general expansion of population and agriculture over many decades has shaken if not shattered the symbiosis. Witness the rapid shortening of the jhum cycle in the Indian Northeast.

Between1 951 and 1980, 4,238 million hectares were diverted from forests to other uses: 2,623 million hectares in agriculture, half a million hectares on account of river valley projects, 134,000 hectares for industry and townships 61,000 hectares for roads and transmission lines and the remaining area for miscellaneous reasons. This must include refugee resettlement as in the U.P. Terai and Dandakaranya. After the promulgation of the Forest Conservation Act of 1980, no more than 46,582 hectares of forest land had been diverted until early 1987 (FSI).

Even if commercial forestry or the population of forest goods is isolated, of the 52 million cubic metres of wood produced in India annually, nearly 40 m cu m is used for firewood, eight m cu m for the manufacture of arts and rural implements, etc and only four m cu m goes to industry (paper and board, newsprint, pulp, plywood, safety matches, sports goods, and saw mills). India's per capita consumption of paper is only two kilograms per annum compared to over 10 kg in Thailand and Egypt and 122 kg in the U.K. Millions of so-called headloaders, many of them tribal women, pilfer wood from the forest to supply Calcutta and the adjacent industrial area from around Ranchi (Agarwal, Anil 1986), and Delhi and other urban centres from Madhya Pradesh. As against the 12 m cu m of wood supplied to industry from the authorized forest cut, the industrial demand is currently 25.58 m cu m, the requirements of packaging material, pulp and paper and agricultural implements being around six m cu m each. Substitutes are being found, such as corrugated cardboard cartons for applies and other fruit.

Those diverting forests to other uses are now required to undertake or finance compensatory afforestation, sometimes in a ratio of 2:1. The availability of land, especially in compact blocks, is an inhibiting factor. As a conservation measure, felling of trees above 1000 metre altitudes has been banned in many regions to protect vulnerable catchments. Blanket prohibitions are however unwise. Scientific logging under revised working plans should be permitted in the interests of efficient forest management. Felling may be precluded from very fragile or vulnerable areas prone to landslides or where regeneration may be difficult, as demarcated in parts of the Alaknanda catchment by Chandi Prasad Bhatt and his Chipko associates.

What should cause concern is the low productivity of India's forests. The growing stock per hectare is about 65 cubic metres per annum as against a world average of 110 cubic metres and far higher yields in many countries.

PRESERVING BIO-DIVERSITY

In order to preserve endangered species and valuable gene pools, over 60 national parks and 257 game sanctuaries covering 13 million hectares have been established in India. This includes 25,545 square kilometres of tiger reserves. Many of these parks and reserves are within the basin. Nepal and Bhutan have developed similar sanctuaries, but many more biosphere reserves need to be set apart.

Much criticism has been leveled at foresters for allegedly converting rich mixed forests into monocultures for commercial exploitation without reference to the needs of the people or ecological prudence. Once again there is an element of exaggeration. The ravaging of the forests by fire and livestock and intense lopping and cutting for fodder, cattle bedding and firewood has impeded healthy regeneration and promoted secondary succession of hardy pioneers and early colonizers such as chir pine and rhododendron. In parts of the Northeast that have been heavily jhummed, there are clear signs of regression. Whole forests of bamboo have been wiped out. Many of the fine "natural" forests that are so acclaimed are in fact products of healthy regeneration. And given time, forests affirm that even predominantly single-species forests will grow into mixed forests. Of course where plantations are put down to serve a given purpose, monoculture must prevail as that is the objective.

Forests produce both good sand services. The goods range from timber and firewood, to grass, cane, minor forest produce or whatever. The services are ecological: erosion control, building the soil, water regulation, provision of shelterbelts, filtering dust, absorption of carbon dioxide, the release of oxygen, and the maintenance of biological diversity. These functions are undoubtedly of the highest importance as rightly stressed by the Chipko leader, Sunderlal Bahuguna. But manmade forests and production forestry do not militate against provision of these services either. "In essence the naturalness or otherwise of a forest is of only theoretical interest. All services rendered by forests, other than their serving as a genetic pool, depend on their leaf area index, and a semi-natural forest is as good as a natural forest" (Lal, J.B.).

The preservation of India's extraordinarily rich genetic diversity must remain a paramount national interest as indeed it must in Nepal and Bhutan as these are global repositories of rare biological wealth. Gene erosion is as important as soil erosion (Khoshoo, T.N., January 1986). Conservation can be done ex situ in gene banks and in situ in biosphere reserves as recommended by UNESCO as part of its Man and Biosphere Programme. Pursuant to this the Government of India has identified 12 potential biosphere reserves embracing 9 of the 12 bio-geographic regions of the subcontinent. These include eight sites in the basin, the Nanda Devi sanctuary, the Valley of Flowers (Garhwal), the Sunderbans, Manas, Nokrek (Garo Hills, Meghalaya) and Namdapha (Arunachal) among them (Environment & Forests Ministry, June 1989).

Population agitation in the 1970s led to the abandonment of the Silent Valley hydro-electric project in Palghat District, Kerala, on the ground that this perhaps came closest to a pristine tropical rain forest in the entire country and contained a number of endemic and unique species of flora and fauna, many of which had not even been scientifically studied. The Silent Valley forest was therefore sought to be preserved as a total closed eco-system that had climaxed, a scientific treasure-house worthy of preservation as part of the heritage of mankind (Swaminathan, M.S., 1979). Since the, pretentious claims have been made to preserving sundry other "rain" forests, possibly with fine stands, more by contrived than real analogy. If there are any remaining patches of rain forest in India they must exist if at all only in some remote parts of the Northeast.

DEBATE ON HIMALAYAN UNCERTAINTY

Great concern has been expressed over environmental degradation in the Nepal Himalaya with pressures of population, livestock and reclamation of marginal slopes for cultivation setting off a vicious spiral of deforestation, erosion, loss of productivity and increased sedimentation and flooding in the plains below. The concern is entirely appropriate but several scholars have more recently questioned the assumed causal linkages in the hypothesis. A number of authors (Ives and Messerli, June 1986; Thompson and Warburton, 1985; Hamilton, 1987) have begun to question these assertions which they discount as broad regional generalizations on the basis of limited or highly localized data, much of it tentative and uncertain. The degree of uncertainty in the data, they plead, should be reason for wider and more sustained and coordinated research rather than for instant and over-dramatised conclusions either way.

The Himalayan-Ganges floods ending up with Nepal sliding into the sea to from huge islands in the middle of the Bay of Bengal is a misperception, says Ives. "Once more, effect is taken for cause, and corrective measures run the risk of being misdirected" (1987). He adds: "Nepalese interests are served well – by this perceived image of helpless drift into environmental and socio-economic chaos, since it may account for its disproportionate amount of international and bilateral development aid in relation to is total size and population". Certainly poorly designed roads and greedy mining and quarrying of delicate hillsides can cause or aggravate landslides as experienced all over the Himalaya. Limestone mining in the Mussoorie Hills is a widely noticed case wherein the Supreme Court of India passed a trend-sitting order stressing the need for conservation in the broader interests of social and economic development, tacitly accepting environmental safeguards as a human right (Ramamurthy, M.K. 1985).

Empirically there is no question that Nepal, like India, has lost a lot of forest, but over long periods and in various circumstances. Forest settlements were officially encouraged in some areas whether to produce more food or augment revenues or in lieu of agreement to bear arms for feudatory princes. In Kumaon, "katil" (unterraced cultivation) was similarly fostered by the authorities at the cost of forest conservation in order to promote more extensive cultivation. Bu scientific management came late to Nepal and is still limited.

FOREST STATUS IN NEPAL

About 93 per cent of Nepal's forest production or use is related to domestic and farming needs. Assessing farm-forestry linkages, one study concluded that every hectare of farmland requires 2.80 hectares of unmanaged forest to provide fodder, 0.36 hectares for fuelwood and 0.32 hectares for timber, or 3.48 hectares annually (Wyatt-Smith J. 1982). The extent of forest from which these supplies are drawn was a matter of some confusion as in strictly legal terms in Nepal, all land that is not privately owned is under the Ministry of Forests and Soil Conservation and therefore technically "forest land". Aerial photography by the Land Resources Mapping Project in 1978-79 provided nation-wide data which, after corrections and updating, show that Nepal has 5.5 million hectares or 37 per cent of its total land surface under forest, plus 0.71 m ha under shrubland and 1.75 m ha under grassland. Of the forested area, 4.1 m ha had a crown density of between 40 and 100 per cent and the balance a density of 10 to 40 per cent. If the High Himal is excluded, than about 48 per cent of the country is under forest. Official sources believe that while significant forest areas have been protected on account of their inaccessibility, with increasing population pressure and decline in the growing stock, the rate of degradation may exceed the currently estimated loss of 50,000 hectares of crown cover per annum (Water and Energy Commission, 1985).

There is considerable regional disparity in the distribution of Nepal's forests. The area under forest was reduced by 570,000 hectares between 1964 and 1985 and only 11 per cent of the forests are now in the Terai and High Himal region and as much as 30 per cent of the forest is in the mid-western region. Fires are a major problem along with overgrazing and fuelwood felling. Yet only between 40 and 70 per cent of sustainable fuelwood supply is being used as many forests are too remote and inaccessible and firewood cannot be easily transported to demand centres.

Forest nationalization in 1957 destabilised traditional panchayat and community forest management systems in Nepal and undermined local accountability. With the legal status of the land in doubt in many areas, there was resort to clear felling. An amendment in 1975 restored the concept of community forestry. New categories of forests were recognized: panchayat forests (degraded forest land on which panchayat plantations were to be encouraged); panchayat protected forests (scattered forests placed under community protection in lieu of revenue sharing, with the panchayat keeping 75 per cent for maintenance, management and local investment); and leased forests (bare government lands made available to institutions and industry such as for plywood factories). Some 20,000 hectares had been declared panchayat forests and 30,000 as panchayat protected forest until 1987.

MASTER PLAN SPELLS LONG TERM STRATEGY

On a recommendation made by the Nepal Aid Group and consistent with the International Tropical Forestry Action Plan, the Government of Nepal commissioned the preparation of a long term plan and strategy with ADB and FINNIDA assistance and Finnish and Filipino consultancy. This 25 year Master Plan for the Forestry Sector in Nepal, 1986-2011 (Forests & Conservation Ministry, May 1988), has been posed to the Nepal donor consortium for technical and financial support. The Master Plan (MPF) assesses that the fuelwood deficit will grow from 2.1 million tonnes to 3.2 m t by 2000 and then decline to 2.1 m t as managed forests and tree farms attain full production. The timber deficit is likewise expected to grow from 0.25 million cubic metres to 1.1 m cu m and fluctuate around that until 2010. Both deficits will be concentrated in the Terai and Middle Mountains where 85 per cent of the people live. While there will be a national surplus of fodder in the Siwaliks and high alpine pastures, there will again be regional shortages in the Terai Mid-Hills zone. On present trends another 0.5 million hectares of forest could be lost over the next 25 years with corresponding declines in the availability of medicinal and aromatic plants, industrial raw material and minor forest produce, accelerated erosion, and increased pressure on wildlife reserves.

In response to this challenge, the MPF advocates that the forest area under proper management be increased from 69,000 hectares in 1985 to 1.56 million hectares through the Seventh to Eleventh Five Year Plans at the rate of around 60,000 hectares per annum on average over the next 25 years. This must include 0.33 m ha of enrichment plantings, 0.25 m ha of new plantations, and the establishment of 0.33 m ha of private tree farms. A special effort will have to be made in the eastern Terai where the forests are under the greatest pressure. This will have to be coupled with population control and the development of alternative energy sources, mobilization of rural communities, appropriate policy and legal reforms, training and R&D.

The MPF has set as its objectives the meeting of the people's basic needs, environmental protection, the conservation of eco-systems and genetic resources, the fostering of forest management and forest-based industries, and employment generation. This is to be achieved through decentralization and people's participation. Twelve programmes formulated to fulfill these medium and long term goals include community and private forestry, national and leasehold forestry, medicinal and aromatic plan propagation and utilization, forest-based industrial development, social conservation and watershed management, conservation of genetic resources, development of a forest resources information system and management planning, forestry research and extension, human resource development, monitoring and evaluation, institutional reform, and policy and legal reform.

With the liberalization of forest policy as realization grew that nationalization had failed to wok, community forestry projects were initiated after 1978 in 29 hill districts and 14 Terai districts with World Bank assistance. Fuel-efficient stoves, bio-gas plants, micro-hydel energy and stall feeding of upgraded cattle are being promoted. Rehabilitative and protective watershed management programmes have been undertaken in several catchments with donor aid. With growth in population, farmland per capita is expected to decrease from 0.18 hectares to 0.12 hectares by 2010. However, the forestry programme is likely to generate 800,000 additional jobs over the next quarter-century. The MPF is estimated to cost $ 1.5 billion of which $ 450 million will be required by way of external assistance over the 25 years period.

As in India, it is accepted in Nepal that significant forest areas can be regenerated by ensuring that while grass may be cut, grazing is forbidden. Chir pine especially has good regeneration properties in degraded soils and once these come up, given time, other broadleaved species will follow. Fencing is being done, but is expensive. Social fencing by popular consent and with community sanction is far more effective. People's participation through local institutions of self-management is best. Chipko has demonstrated this in Chamoli district, Garhwal. This again has been the key to the success of the Nepal-Australia Forestry Project in the Sindhu Palchok and Kabhre Palanchok districts east of Kathmandu initiated by a local forester T.B.S. Mahat while in service as a divisional forest officer.

SITUATION IN BHUTAN, TIBET AND BANGLADESH

Nepal was once an exporter of wood, mainly to India, but banned this trade some years ago Bhutan is more favourably placed in regard to its forests and exports 40,000 cubic metres annually. Approximately 64 per cent of Bhutan's total land area is under forest. In view of its relatively small population, the pressure on forests has been limited to certain pockets. There was no scientific management until some years after the country opened its doors to the world when working plans were prepared for certain forests in southern Bhutan. The Royal Government has now adopted a national forest policy and carried out a national inventory of land use and vegetation. The total forest area is 3.14 million hectares of which 0.9 million hectares have been set aside as parks, sanctuaries and wildlife reserves. Fuelwood consumption is estimated at 2.2 cubic metres per capita per annum and that of timber at 0.047 cubic metres. Blanks in the forest, such as that caused by fellings for the reconstruction of Thimphu Dzong, are being reforested and an afforestation programme with World Bank assistance is under way to restore degraded areas. The problems faced are familiar; shifting cultivation in the east, unregulated and migratory grazing, forest fires, lack of awareness and an inadequacy of trained manpower. However, land use is now being sought to be regulated and fuel-efficient wood-stoves and bio-gas plants are being introduced.

Bhutan legislated a Forest Act in 1969 and adopted a national forest policy five years later. In order to maintain "soil and climatic equilibrium", a minimum of 60 per cent of the total land area under forest was stipulated and conditions laid down to regulate grazing and shifting cultivation. The first step towards implementation of the policy was to demarcate the forest area (Joshi, S.C., 1986). By 1988 working plans had been prepared for half the total forest area and it is expected that the remaining area will be brought under working plans by 1995. On account of shortage of trained personnel and inaccessibility, only 4 per cent of the sustained yield is being harvested. Forest roads are being developed to facilitate better management, but on current estimates the forest yield may not exceed 10 per cent of the potential for quite some time. Fast growing species are being sought to be grown in the south for charcoal making and micro-hydel stations are being established in isolated valleys in addition to the Chukha hydel transmission system. Bio-gas plants and improved cookstoves are being distributed to provide alternative sources of fuel and more fuel-efficient systems.

Such data on Tibet as is available suggests that there has been a deterioration in the quality of grasslands while the livestock population has increased. Some efforts at wasteland reclamation have been made but there has been deforestation and increased erosion in certain areas. A study of Lhasa district, which extends over 29,000 kilometres of the Lhasa River sub-basin of the Tsang-po, indicates that livestock population increased from 0.86 million head to 1.46 million head between 1958 and 1984. During that same period, grassland per "sheep-unit" (cattle, yak, sheep, goats, horses and donkeys) declined from 1.21 hectares to 0.73 hectares. According to available evidence, much of the grazing areas are "already overgrazed and in danger of progressive and perhaps irreversible degradation" (liu Yanhua, August 1988).

Bangladesh is less favourably placed than any other country in the Basin with just 1.57 million hectares or 11 per cent of its land area under forest of this, 0.57 million hectares is tidal forest in the Sunderbans. There are 0.60 hectares of hill forest, mostly in the Chittagong Hill Tract in which there is another 0.97 million hectares of unclassed forest which is total degraded. Part of the hill forests are under jhum. The rest of the plains area has no more than 125,000 hectares of sal forest. Energy-wise, the country's gas and limited hydro-electric resources are located east of the Brahmaputra. This has placed a particularly heavy stain on non-commercial sources of fuel and lighting in the western region. As much as 83 per cent of national energy consumption is dependent on biomass which is extremely short. Some anticipate an even more serious second energy crisis than the earlier oil crisis. Shortage of firewood is leading to increasing diversions of cow dung from farms to hearths, aggravating the shortage of organic manure. In response to this problem, a community forest programme was taken up in 1981 with ADB assistance and a number of jack and mango trees have been planted. Strip plantations along roads, canals and embankments are also being encouraged.

The mangrove forests of the Sunderbans, like their counterpart in West Bengal, are a unique eco-system that nurtures a variety of aquatic life. Mangroves consolidate new land and are favourable for shrimp farming. They are also the principal source of timber in the estuarine region. Since 1950 however two of the main species of mangrove, including *sundari*, have been considerably depleted. Increased salinity and top drying is inhibiting regeneration.

NEGLECT OF RAIGELANDS

If the condition of forests in the basin is sad, that of the grasslands and rangelands is worse. There is no agency to protect or care for these areas. Within India, degradation has been very extensive with frank signs of desertification in some regions as part of a long process of regression from savanna to steppe to desert. The prime cause of this has been the huge increase in livestock numbers from 292 million in 1951 to 416 million in 1982, a figure that is likely to touch 505 million by 2000. Over-grazing has affected regeneration and resulted in secondary succession of inferior species while hardy weeds like lantana and parthenium have made inroads into the rangelands. With the shrinking of the commons, the forest fringes have been overwhelmed and the forests invaded. The policy of creating national parks, sanctuaries and wildlife reserves by excluding cattle, without providing for a buffer zone or alternative sources of feed, has triggered conflict and vandalism especially in times of drought and distress as witnessed by incidents in the Bharatpur Bird Sanctuary and the Ranthambore Tiger Sanctuary in 1987. Firing of grasslands to produce a fresh flush of tender shoots is widely practiced and not damaging in itself. But burning followed by immediate grazing can be destructive. Rotational grazing is seldom practised and stall-feeding is still limited except in Haryana and Punjab which have the least rangeland but relatively high milch yields. Grazing fees are nominal or have been abolished, leading to uncontrolled pressure on grasslands and forest and, worse, the promiscuous and prolific breeding of scrub animals thus giving a further twist to a downward spiral. The creation of separate working circles for forest grazing lands and the introduction of rotational lopping on a three-year cycle have been suggested as means of ensuring regulated grazing to the extent that it is permitted (Shrivastava, M.B. et al., 1988).

The Indian Himalaya is perhaps under even greater stress. Grazing in 17.8 million hectares of forest and 1.7 million hectares of alpine pasture in this region supports over 20 million cattle, 10 million buffaloes, 6 million goat and 3 million sheep. Says Panjab Singh (1988), "in most parts of Himalaya, the grass species found at present represent the third or fourth species of degradation. Thus ... the productive potential of the Himalayan rangelands is only 25 per cent of the optimum and quality-wise only 10-15 per cent of the possible output of nutrients per unit area per unit time. So is the case of the availability of leaf fodder .." The situation has been aggravated by the closure of traditional trans-Himalayan alpine pastures in Tibet for transhumance since 1959 on account of political factors. Further, to local pressure is added that of nomadic pastoralists like the Gujars who drip up huge herds and flocks into Himachal, Garhwal and Kumaon. Migrant herds also move from Western Rajasthan and Gujarat into the Malwa plateau in Madhya Pradesh and Mewar in eastern Rajasthan in search of greener pastures.

The area under rangelands in India is variously estimated. In accordance with official land use classification, 12 million hectares are permanent pasture and grazing lands. But to this could be added part or all of areas categorized as barren and unculturable, culturable wastelands, fallows and 8.32 million hectares reported under fodder crops in 1983-84. Computing all these on different premises, varying estimates of 67 to 85 million hectares of rangeland other than forest are cited by different authorities. Whatever the calculation, the rangelands are heavily overburdened and the position within the Basin region in India is clearly most unsatisfactory. The Report of the Committee on Fodder and Grasses estimates production in 1985 to have been 441 million tonnes of dry fodder (grass and agricultural residues) and 250 million tonnes of green fodder as against a requirement of 780 million tones of dry fodder and 932 million tonnes of green fodder (Fodder and Grasses Committee, 1987). The National Commission on Agriculture (Part VII, 1976) estimated the forage equipment of India's projected livestock population by 2000 and made an equally dismal forecast.

Rangeland management studies at the Indian Grassland and Fodder Research Institute, Jhansi, have established that production can easily be doubled by various cultural practices (Singh, Panjab 1988). Fertiliser application, irrigation where possible, intercropping of range legumes, agro-forestry and silvipastoral management have been variously suggested. Grasses and fodders can be introduced in the reclamation of soils affected by salinity and alkalinity and of ravines, desert and sand dunes, and riverine lands. This would, however, require stratification of rangelands in ecologically distinctive management units and the establishment of a central agency to plan, coordinate, and monitor this effort (Ibid). Inadequacy of quality seed will have to be overcome through registered growers and R&D based on grassland survey and germplasm collection from which new varieties can be evolved (Range Management Society of India, 1987). Other suggestions include the introduction of compulsory stall feeding in stages and the having of India's bovine population (Pandeya, S.C. 1988). This can be done by better breeding (for it is deteriorating quality that has resulted in increased numbers), the castration of scrub bulls, and culling of surplus animals, a theme cogently, developed by V.M. Dandekar in his "Cattle Economy of India". Before Independence about 50 per cent of all cows were slaughtered and 50 per cent died as a matter of course. The present cow-slaughter rate is around five per cent "indicating a huge waste of our cattle wealth" (Agarwal V.P. and Tyagi, Pramod November 1988).

TOWARDS WASTELAND DEVELOPMENT

Concerned over the deterioration and neglect of large areas in the "uncultivated half of India", whose productive potential could well be harnessed, and the loss of woodlots and trees, the Government in the early 1950s launched an annual *vana* mahotsava or tree planting festival with the onset of the monsoon. This however was no more than a ritual and the survival rate was low. Despite advocacy of a Land Charter in the 1970s and the National Commission on Agriculture's pleas to encourage social and farm forestry to help meet some of the demand for fodder, fuel, small timber and other needs, progress was modest. With ecological awareness, national concern crystallized in Mr. Rajiv Gandhi's bold declaration in January 1985, that he proposed "immediately to set up a national wastelands development board with the object of bringing five million hectares of land every year under fuelwood and fodder plantations." He called for "a people's movement for afforestation" to usher in a second green revolution (National Land Use and Wasteland Development Council, February 1986). Estimates of wastelands and rangelands overlap. The new Board defined the term wasteland "as that land which is degraded and is presently lying unutilized except as current fallows due to different constraints". An expert group identified this area as covering 93.69 million hectares (Bhumbla D.R and Khare, Arvind 1966).

It was estimated that to afforest five million hectares per annum would require a yearly supply of 10 billion saplings at a standard rate of 2000 plants per hectare. The target called for widespread decentralization to local groups with a buy-back assurance from the forest department. Women were to be given a special role as the increasingly difficult task of collecting fodder, fuel and water falls to their lot. Women have to walk further to forage for fuel and fodder, distances of 10 to 12 kilometres being not uncommon in Garhwal (Krishna, Sumi 1987), a factor that has told on their education, health and creativity. The NWDB set to work to strengthen its data base, determine the appropriate planting species in relation to soil and climatic factors, keeping in mind local preferences, pulling together various existing programmes and departmental efforts at different levels, producing and distributing high quality seeds, undertaking research and extension and organizing credit facilities. It sought to create a conducive legal framework for action and to draw in marginal farmers and women's groups through tree growers cooperatives and tree patta schemes that vest the right of usufruct on individuals who plant and tend them, without transferring land titles. It was hoped by these means to mobilize the poor and lay the basis for a national movement with the assistance of voluntary agencies. Fuelwood plantations were also to be developed on waste lands around towns and cities.

PROGRESS AND FRUSTRATIONS

As against some 7.8 million hectares reportedly planted between 1950 and 1985, a little over five million hectares were planted in the first three years of the NWDB programme against the target of five million hectares per annum. This is by no means a bad start as a programme of this magnitude will take time to build up. There have been teething troubles and smooth coordination is still to be achieved. The Forest Conservation Act, 1980, stipulated that no forest land may be cut or used for any non-forest purpose except with the prior approval of the Central Government. Even the State governments have been left with no discretion. The guidelines issued under the Act have been very restrictive. Prohibitions include diversion of forest land for lease to private parties, developing plantations, afforestation by individuals or institutions, raising horticultural crops on jhum lands, or virtually doing anything anywhere without express approval from Delhi. No powers appear to have been delegated (Environment and Forests Ministry, July 1986). In consequence, the first chairperson of the NWDB protested that the guidelines "have made even genuine afforestration on barren forest areas a counter-productive exercise". Further, "when it comes to leasing forest land on a usufruct basis to the rural poor, the cooperatives, the voluntary agencies, etc. for afforestation activities, there is hesitancy misgivings and mistrust...People's participation, we are told, should be confined to revenue and community lands only". There are other problems too. The Tree Cutting and Transit Rules, intended to check illegal forest fellings and removal of timber, comes in the way of a farmer cutting a tree that he has grown when he needs to do so whether to secure a cash income or to meet an emergency. "It is like having a savings account but not being able to use it when needed". Getting the necessary permission to cut a tree is cumbersome, entails several visits to concerned offices and maybe a bribe (Chowdhry, Kamla June 1988). An evaluation of village-level experience in wasteland development in Himachal, Uttar Pradesh, Madhya Pradesh and Tamil Nadu also found that "uncertainty of benefits is one of the important factors which explains the poor response from the people". The transit and transport rules in Himachal and Uttar Pradesh proved formidable, causing considerable delay and loss. "I manage, you participate" appears to be the attitude of bureaucrats. This raises questions: participation for whose benefit, under whose management, and under what terms? (Saxena, N.C. New Delhi, 1988).

Aerial seeding has been tried with varying success. The Arunachal Forest Department claims that aerial seeding experiments in West Kameng and Lohia districts since 1982 have given encouraging results. The results in the Chambal ravines in Rajasthan, Madhya Pradesh and Uttar Pradesh since 1980 have not been so successful but this is said to be partly on account of poor seed. Pelletised seeds are being tried out and there is one view that if seeds are covered with moisture-retaining mulches and slow release fertilizers and insecticide and directly seeded, survival rates may go up significantly.

It is pity that no concerted programme to green the Aravalli hills has been consistently pursued. Haryana's Aravalli Hills Afforestation Project awaits funding; in Rajasthan, NGO efforts to green the Aravalli have inched along for similar reasons though the Society for the Promotion for Wasteland Development is now aiding some groups. The desert and sand dune stabilization programme is however moving forward and has met with a measure of success with intercropping of castor and kana tussock with *Acacia tortilla*, *Prosopis cineraria* and other tree varieties that yield farmers a good income while the trees mature.

TIMBER PLANTATIONS AND PULPWOOD DEMAND

There has been a good deal of strip forestry along roadsides, canal banks and even railway tracks as well as farm forestry in Haryana and Western Uttar Pradesh. Eucalyptus is the favoured species as a fast growing pulpwood with a good market demand. Eucalyptus has however been repeatedly denigrated as a damaging choice on the ground that it is a purely commercial species that cannot be browsed, soaks up all moisture and nutrients and allows nothing to grow under it (Ripley, s. Dillon 1987). The evidence is not conclusive. Some studies have shown eucalyptus to consume less water than five other species to produce a gramme of biomass. Another study indicated that the annual release of nutrients especially nitrogen, to the soil through litter fall compared favourably with teak and sal in Dehra Dun and with Palas and Laural in Varanasi (Lal, J.B.). An FAO study on the ecological effects of eucalyptus in 1985 found critical evidence lacking either to prove or disprove that eucalyptus uses more water than other species. It did however state that eucalyptus

is not good for erosion control but does well as a shelter belt. It also found eucalyptus plantations on degraded soils beneficial, though probably not when replacing indigenous forests. The Haryana Forest Department which has encouraged eucalyptus on a large scale is of the view that all the adverse findings against the species are based on misconceptions or are propagandist. On the other hand eucalyptus has put considerable sums of money into the farmers' pockets.

Raising timber plantations for industrial requirements has led to considerable monocultures of eucalyptus and tropical pine. This is said to have upset the ecological equilibrium leading to outbreaks of pests and disease, loss of plant diversity and a decline in the availability of minor forest produce and medicinal plants (Nair, C.T.S. 1985). While pest attacks on monocultures calls for care in management, diversity and supply of other forest produce must obviously come from other types of forest. There is no surplus of cellulose woods for pulp paper, and other uses and supply will need to be fast augmented to keep pace with demand. It is certainly true that forest raw materials such as bamboo and other timber have been supplied to industry at throw-away prices with little compulsion on user-industries to raise their own plantations. Some captive plantations have indeed been raised, directly or through buy-back incentives to farmers, but much more needs to be done. By 2000 the paper industry alone is expected to need 2.1 million hectares of plantations.

The Development Council for Paper, Pulp and Allied Industries had in 1983 suggested that these industries should be encouraged to produce their own wood requirements entirely by 2000. To this end it recommended that Indian industry be permitted to plant 1.6 million hectares of degraded forest land. The National Land Use and Wastelands Development Council in 1986 was of the view that forest based industries "must be encouraged to utilize wastelands for their captive plantations." However, this policy has received a setback on account of population agitation on the ground that people's rights and interests in the commons will be negated by such a development.

HAS INDUSTRY A ROLE?

The government too announced in August 1987 that it would not permit industrial plantations whether captive or in the joint sector, on forest lands. This appears to be a most unwise prohibition when there are large areas of degraded forest land. Safeguards can be built into all large programmes of captive plantations by insisting on local participation in any suitable form and a commitment by the lessee industry that a certain percentage of the land will be reserved for planting preferred species in consultation with local people for local use. Corporate plantations could also be committed to employing and training local men and women and to observing appropriate ecological safeguards. Conditionalities might vary from place to place in accordance with circumstances and the sponsors warned that infringement could result in cancellation of the lease which should in any case be for fixed but renewable periods. By such means the interests of local communities and industry could be married and made to serve the national objective of greening the country. The organizational, technological and investment capabilities of industry should not be spurned.

The same approach should inform captive plantations on non-forest wastelands. It has been estimated that Rs.15,000-20,000 might need to be invested per hectare of plantations on degraded land. Therefore were 0.6 million hectares to be brought under plantations, the investment cost would be of the order of Rs. 1050 crores over an eight year period at a rate of just under Rs. 132 crores per annum (Chugh K.L. August 1988). This effort by industry would exhaust neither the possibility nor the need for parallel community based efforts and so there would be no question of precluding local tree-cooperatives or village associations from developing their own woodlots or plantations quite apart from the activities of the forest department and individual farmers. The task is large enough to accommodate all comers. Any restrictive policy would therefore be totally unwarranted. Moreover, current productivity levels in India at 40 tonnes per hectare compare most unfavourably with yields of 400-500 tonnes per hectare on a seven year rotation in Brazil. In its own interest, industry would invest in R&D to achieve comparable results. This might call for relaxation of land ceiling laws, which would be justified, and fiscal incentives such as rebates on tax for approved plough-back or otherwise as appropriate.

Indian industry is willing to establish and has in fact proved the possibility of valuable backward linkages into farm and industrial forestry. South Indian Viscose Ltd. Consumed just under a million tonnes of pulpwood during 1978-88, mostly obtained from government forests, but distributed 4.47 million seedings free to farmers to plant, mostly in the hills. This should notionally yield 660,000 tonnes of pulpwood in eight years. Noting that wattle, rosegum and bluegum yields are only a fraction of those obtained in the Congo and Brazil, S.I. Viscose has entered into an R&D agreement with Wimco, the match company, which has a seedling subsidiary, to improve yields two or three-fold, reduce the crop cycle from 10 to 6 years, develop alternative species for the plains, and enhance pulpwood quality. Simultaneously small and marginal farmers are to be encouraged with extension support and institutional finance to inter-crop pulpwood with cash crops with a buy-back arrangement (Kesavamurthy, G.S. August 1988). Wimco Seedlings Ltd. In Bareilly, Uttar Pradesh has encouraged farmers to grow fast-growing poplars to meet its requirements for match splints. This agro-forestry project envisages planting over 10 million poplars on farmers' fields during 1984-91 in 39 districts in Uttar Pradesh, Haryana and Punjab. Some 2.3 million poplars were planted under this programme in 1988 with 85 per cent of the cost of raising and maintaining the plantations being financed by banks. Inter-cropping is possible and the poplars are ready for harvest in eight years for use in the match, plywood, packing case, artificial limb, sports goods and other industries. All inputs, suitable disease resistant clones, and technical assistance are provided by Wimco which also provides insurance cover at its own cost for all risks excluding theft. There is a buy-back guarantee at minimum support prices, but the farmer is free to sell his produce on the market to any other buyer should he so desire (Wimco, August 1988).

The Central Board of Forestry has advocated import of wood to stop further forest fellings in India. As an interim measure or to meet deficits this may be in order. But it would be imprudent to conceive of wood imports as long term conservation measure. In the first place, there is no reason why even reserved forests should not be scientifically worked except in ecologically fragile areas. That apart, the cost of imports would constitute a serious and mounting foreign exchange drain and entail a corresponding loss of productive employment and related benefits in India. The R&D element is crucial. It is necessary to select and standardize ideotypes to ensure high productivity planting material for specific purposes. The equivalent of the hybrid seed revolution in cereals is what is needed, based on a careful study of forest genetics. Tissue culture techniques and the use of mist-chambers to propagate hard-to-root species also need to be harnessed. The Haryana Agricultural University, Hissar has started building up a free germplasm bank.

ELICITING COMMUNITY PARTICIPATION

Private and community efforts have a considerable role and striking successes have been achieved. The Sukhomajri experience with social fencing in Haryana has been cited. The work of Annasaheb Hazare in Ralegaon Shindi in Maharashtra is again outstanding. The social forestry and watershed management programmes taken up by the Chipko-oriented Dasholi Gram Swarajya Mandal in Chamoli district, Garhwal have demonstrated a high survival rate of new plantings.

Alienated tribal populations believing that their right s and interests are being disregarded have uprooted sal and teak when planted by the Forest Department without their consent. The Bihar Social Forestry project for Chota Nagpur and the Santhal Parganas, 1985-91, however shows that tribal cooperation can be won. This Swedish assisted project has the rehabilitation of degraded forest lands and farm forestry as its major components though institutional and strip plantations are also being taken up. The forests of the region are overburdened with "rights" and have been depleted over the years for firewood and small timber. Village forest committees have been established for rehabilitation areas under joint management plans drawn up with the Forest Department. All strata of the community are represented in these committees, especially the weaker sections and so-called headloaders , who are generally women. The villagers have to put in 6,900 man-days of work per annum in return for which they are entitled to collect a variety of forest produce in accordance with the management plan. Plant species and the rotation cycle are jointly determined and work is done through chosen contact person who is paid an honorarium. Local involvement guarantees protection of the trees. Under the farm forestry component, the department supplies the seeds and farmers are compensated for their labour and other inputs in stages and receive in all about Rs.1.45 per plant by the end of two years when the young tree is certified to have survived. Grazing is controlled.

The evolution of a suitable legal framework is important if all such programmes are to be sustained. The Indian Law Institute, Delhi, set up a team of experts to study this and submitted a series of reports to the Ministry of Environment and Forests on panchayat forestry, forest cooperatives, NGO participation in forestry programmes and Forestry in Bihar (Singh, Chhatrapati 1987).

The Koran forestry programme has been successful but there are perhaps more lessons that India can learn from China which claims to have reforested 38 million hectares since 1949. Under the new responsibility system, peasant households have since 1981 been allotted 1 mu (15 mu equals 1 hectare) in the plains, 5 to 10 mu on hillsides, and 50 to 100 mu in the mountains for afforestation. According to a National Wasteland Development Board study team that visited China "the trees and grass grown on these plots belong to the allottees who are entitled to manage their plots on a long-term basis of 30 to 50 years. The Forestry Act specifically provides that the right of the individual shall be protected against encroachment and the trees cannot be commandeered. Allotments can be inherited. Young trees and premature trees on allotted plots may be transferred for money. By the middle of 1984, 20 million hectares of barren hills had been allotted 50 million peasant households to set up small family forest farms and orchards" (NWDB Study Team Report, May 1987). It was further reported that the Chinese had selected a few tree species for each agro-climatic zone and no more than 20 species for the whole country. Monoculture had created no problems. Eucalyptus had proved greatly successful and aerial seeding very cost-effective over large tracts of inaccessible wastelands.

The greening of the Basin can only be accomplished with community involvement, participation and support that ensures protection of plants, social fencing, rotational grazing or whatever. In India, retired military personnel have been used in eco-development brigades, one in the Mussoorie hills and another in Rajasthan. But something larger and bolder like the US conservation corps that Roosevelt brought into being during the dust-bowl years in the early 1930s would be a more appropriate model. The Indian Constitution was amended a decade ago to write in a fundamental duty on the part of each citizen "to protect and improve the natural environmental including forests, lakes, rivers and wild life". This is a task that is best ensured through collective action. Its accomplishment will bring its own rewards.

The Tropical Forests Action Plan proposed by the World Resources Institute with World Bank and UNDP support (October 1985) spelt out a five-year programme, 1987-91, with donor assistance. There is a coincidence of national and global interest in such a programme in view of fears of global warming and climatic changes that might soon be manifest. It is in this context that schemes have been mooted and are already being tried out on a limited scale in Central and Latin America to buy up Third World debts in lieu of reforestation programmes undertaken by them (*Newsweek*, August 31, 1987). The world can certainly help and should. But essentially and ultimately it is national governments and peoples that must help themselves.

CHAPTER 9

Energy Abounding

Lenin saw electricity as the key to Soviet development. India gave pride of place to steel. Energy far more than steel is critical to every activity. Poorer nations depend on traditional sources of biomass, especially wood fuel, for cooking and heating and have raided their forests at the cost of environmental degradation. They have to make the transition to commercial sources of energy, whether based on fossil fuels or electric power, hydel or nuclear, or other emerging sources that are no longer entirely futuristic.

The Ganga-Brahmaputra-Barak Basin is endowed with a vast hydro-electric potential of the order of 200,000 to 250,000 MW of which half or more could be viably harnessed today. Large volumes of monsoon flows and snow and glacier melt cascading down the Himalaya and other ranges are a gift of gravity that can be harnessed. Only a tiny part of this immense wealth has been tapped as yet. Why this should be so remains something of an enigma as falling water is a renewable resource unlike fossil fuel which is a depleting asset and unavailable or found only in limited quantities within the basin. Not that hydro-electric development started late. The first hydel station in the Indian subcontinent was built near Darjeeling in 1897. It generated 400 kw for municipal use. The Mussoorie (1909), Simla (1913) and Nainital (1922) municipalities followed with mini-hydel projects. Larger installations were developed in South and West India in the first quarter of this century. In Nepal, the Pharping hydroe-electric station was commissioned in 1911 with a capacity of 500 kw. In Uttar Pradesh falls of one to two metres on the Ganga canals were tapped in the 1930s through a series of micro-hydel projects that generate almost 70 MW today. The availability of this cheap source of power in turn triggered the first development of tubewells in that State.

Nepal and Bhutan have huge hydro-electric reserves which constitute their largest single resource endowment and source of wealth. Not to develop this potential is to accept a self-denying ordinance and lose the income, employment and overall multiplier effect that hydel generation could bring them through area development, manpower training and very considerable export earnings from the sale of power to India and Bangladesh and, in time, even Pakistan. Unlike oil or gas which remain future assets if kept underground, hydro-power is lost if not utilized, even though it can be tapped at a later date. Hydel power is to Nepal and

Bhutan what oil is to the U.A.E. or Kuwait. Not to develop it reasonably fast is to forego the one resource above all others that would propel these countries from poverty to plenty, transform the lives of the people and safeguard their fragile environment. Tibet too is gifted with hydro-possibilities though many of the best sites are in very remote areas far away from load centres. Bangladesh is the one exception. Practically all the headwaters of its rivers are located beyond its territory, mostly in India. But imports of cheap hydel power from India or Nepal would have a dramatic impact on its economy.

India took up a number of large river valley projects soon after Independence and several multipurpose or purely hydel projects were completed by mid 1960s. Thermal projects were also executed and power shortages were modest and limited to certain regions. Energy supply initially appeared to move in step with development. But not for long. The energy gap began to widen, with the green revolution adding a new and rapidly rising demand for energy for agricultural pumping and processing.

HYDRO-THERMAL MIX

Three other factors intervened at this stage. Inter-state disputes on the sharing of river waters slowed down hydro-electric development through the Indian Basin states were somewhat less affected and were able to negotiate interstate agreements sooner than those in peninsular India. Resource constraints resulted in sanctions being more readily accorded to thermal stations with their lower direct capital costs. Admittedly thermal stations do not entail costly dams or tunneling in remote or relatively inaccessible areas requiring prior development of considerable infrastructure even for detailed investigations let alone construction. But the notion that thermal stations entail little or no indirect costs was and remains mistaken. Most thermal plants in India are coal fired and, require highly capital intensive mining and transportation investments to win the coal and carry it to the generation site if not located at the pit-head. If these associated costs are taken into account, as they must, then the capital-intensity of hydro-electric schemes no longer appears quite so forbidding.

A third factor militating against hydel projects was the longer gestation period involved at a time when the cry was for quick-yielding projects that would provide more energy with the least possible delay. A coal-fired power plant takes between three to five years to complete against seven to nine years required by a comparable hydro-electric project. However, if the first couple of years that are primarily given to developing the site and access to it are eliminated, the time differential is seen to narrow appreciably. Moreover, if staggered starts are made in a steady series then hydel projects will be ready for commissioning in an equally steady stream. The time difference is manifest only if two fresh starts, one thermal and the other hydel, are compared. Since the object of planning should be to secure steady incremental growth rather than large, quantum jumps, steady additions to hydel capacity would be both desirable and eminently possible with no net additional investment apart from the initial hydel-priming.

However, the fact is that hydro-electric generation was permitted to fall behind. The hydro component in total generation capacity rose from around 33 per cent at the commencement of planning in 1951 to a high of 45.68 per cent in 1966. Thereafter it started declining, touching 34.1 per cent in 1985 and falling as low as 17 per cent in the Eastern region. It is likely to dip to 30 per cent by 1990 and decline still further in the Eighth Plan unless corrective steps are taken. An optimal mix would have hydro-electric capacity around 40 per cent and this is now stated to be the desired objective.

ADVANTAGES OF HYDEL GENERATION

The reason for wanting a better hydro-thermal mix is easy to see, for hydro-electric power has many significant advantages. It is a renewable energy source and, once commissioned, has no fuel cost. As of 1986, the investment cost of both hydro and thermal generation was about Rs 1,000-1,100 per megawatt of installed capacity. Although hydel capital costs are higher, in view of the cost of the dam and/or tunneling, the stipulated life of a hydel plant under the Electricity Act is 35 years as compared to 25 years for a thermal plant. This means lower depreciation. Operational requirements are minimal, outages are far less frequent, consumption of energy for auxiliaries is around 1 per cent compared to some 9 per cent for thermal stations, and maintenance is far simpler and entails a far shorter down time thus reducing the related reserve capacity that would otherwise be required.

All these factors make hydel power generally far cheaper than thermal supplies. The Biara Siul hydro-electric station with an installed capacity of 280 MW was completed in 11 years in 1981 at a cost of Rs 135 crores. Its cost of generation per kilowatt-hour is 17 paise. In contrast, Badarpur-III thermal, was commissioned in Delhi over a five year period in 1982. It has a capacity of 210 MW and a cost of generation of 51 paise per kilowatt-hour. The comparison is not atypical, hydel power generally being cheaper, by half if not more. Hydel stations are not affected by rising wage, fuel, (coal, furnace oil, gas) and transport costs. The uniform pool price charged by power grids is invariably subsidized by the far lower hydel rates. This has enabled electricity boards with a larger hydro-electric component to show bigger and more consistent surpluses (National Council for Power Utilities, 1986).

Another significant advantage of hydro units is their ability to start and stop and vary their output very quickly. This makes them particularly well suited to meet peak demands as thermal stations, other than those operating gas turbines, take far more time to bank down or build up capacity, an operation that entails an unrequited fuel cost and additional wear and tear. This flexibility of hydel operation eliminates the cost of maintaining considerable reserve capacity to meet peak demands. While this a net system saving, constant base load operations by thermal stations at times of day when the demand for power falls below this output can be used to pump water back into hydel storages from balancing reservoirs that hold the water discharged through hydro-turbines during peaking periods. Such pump-storage systems can be designed in select areas and are economical to operate and extremely useful in meeting peaking requirements. The first Indian pump storage systems have come into operation and many more will now follow.

Hydro-stations do exhibit a seasonality that follows the pattern of river flow and multipurpose storages have to be operated keeping in mind the requirements of irrigation and flood moderation. Yet with all that, firm hydel power is generally a third or more of the installed capacity (which is available for peak requirements) and there is full generation for three to five months during the monsoon period. This secondary power (that is generation above the continuous output) is valuable in so far as it permits shut down of thermal capacity for annual maintenance and overhaul without dimunition of supplies to the grid. Run-of-river schemes are cheaper but in the absence of storage are designed with installed capacities many times the minimum continuous output to avail of higher seasonal generation when the river registers high inflows. The firm power produced by hydel stations may appear to render a significant part of the installed capacity idle over a good part of the year. This is true. But in the case of thermal stations, the plant load factor in India has averaged 5 per cent countrywide with many State Electricity Boards and individual plants registering a much lower figure.

FOSSIL FUELS ARE DEPLETING ASSETS

Another aspect that should not be lost sight of is the fact that Bangladesh, Nepal, Bhutan and Tibet have no exploitable coal resources worth the name. While Bangladesh does have some gas reserves, these are estimated at no more than 450 billion cubic metres and are not likely to last more than a couple of decades on present showing. India has decided to develop gas-based thermal stations over the next decade in view of new gas finds and the continued flaring of associated gas in the Northeast and from the offshore Bombay High structure which is now being piped from Gujarat to Madhya Pradesh and Uttar Pradesh, with further spurs projected. The country's total proven and recoverable reserves of oil and gas as of 1988 were 636 million tonnes and 580 billion cubic metres respectively, a rather modest asset indeed. The prime thermal fuel however remains non-coking coal, the total reserves of which are currently placed at 130,553 million tonnes. Of this, the proven and indicated reserves at depths up to 1,200 metres are only 32,681 and 53,805 million tonnes respectively, the balance being inferred mostly in the South. The coal reserves are concentrated in eastern and central India and large parts of the basin within India are situated several hundred miles away from the collieries at the end of long haulage leads.

India's thermal power stations are currently consuming some 80 million tonnes of coal or almost 50 per cent of current production. This demand is expected to rise to around 243 million tonnes by 2000, accounting for an even larger proportion of overall coal production (CEA, June 1987). Therefore it makes good sense to place maximum reliance on renewable sources of energy such as hydel power and conserve the dwindling reserves of coal. In 1985-86 a hydro generation of 110 billion units "saved" about 72 million tonnes of coal, which saving could rise to over 243 million tonnes on full development of the economically feasible hydro-potential. There is of course the nuclear power option which India is pursuing. The country's resources of thorium oxide, which is derived from monazite sands and can be used to fuel breeder reactors, are far larger than either its coal reserves or currently feasible hydel potential of 101,000 MW that could yield 400 billion units of electrical energy. But nuclear power poses its own problems and is more expensive though it does have a place in the national energy spectrum with appropriate safeguards. The environmental consequences of hydro-electric development with large dams will be examined in the next chapter.

The basin countries have among the lowest levels of commercial energy consumption per capita in the world. The numbers for 1986 in terms of kilograms of oil-equivalent were 23 for Nepal, 46 for Bangladesh and a somewhat better figure of 208 for India. Figures for Bhutan and China's Tibet region are not available but they are obviously very low (World Bank, 1988). The largest part of energy demand is met from traditional non-commercial sources such as fuelwood, agro-wastes, dung, and animal power. The bulk of the demand is also in the rural and household sector for lighting and heating, though kerosene is a preferred illuminant.

CONSERVING GAS AND BIOMASS IN BANGLADESH

The total energy consumption of Bangladesh in 1981 was estimated at 8.3 million tonnes of oil-equivalent, some two-thirds of this being contributed by traditional fuels, mostly in the household sector. Commercial energy use amounted to 2.9 million tonnes of oil-equivalent with oil, all imported, accounting for 52 per cent, natural gas for 41 per cent, coal, again all imported, for five per cent, and electricity for two per cent (World Bank, 1982). The object of the policy has been to curtail the use of imported oil and rely more on indigenous gas. As a result of this thrust, the proportion of gas in relation to total commercial energy use is expected to rise to over 68 per cent by the end of the Third Five Year Plan (1990). What inhibited greater exploitation of natural gas earlier was the location of all the gas fields along the country's eastern border and the absence of any means of moving gas supplies to the western region across the Brahmaputra-Meghna divide. With the commissioning of an electric inter-connector, as-based electrical energy is now moving west and a similar east-west gas inter-connector is contemplated.

At the time of partition in 1947, East Pakistan (as it then was) had a total generating capacity of only 21 MW. On the eve of the liberation of Bangladesh in 1970 installed capacity had increased to 475 MW, including 80 MW at the Kamaphuli hydro-electric station in the Chittagong Hill Tract. This has remained the country's only hydel station, with an augmented capacity of 130 MW, another hydro source with a potential 87 MW being on the Sangu, also in the Chittagong Hill Tract and yet to be harnessed. Possible generation of up to 1000 MW of largely peaking power on each of the proposed Brahmaputra and Ganga barrages have been mooted from time to time. But these remain distant prospects. There may be limited hydro possibilities in the Teesta barrage project and some micro-hydel sites in Sylhet. Altogether, the hydro potential is small. Bangladesh has some 700 million tonnes of coal in Bogra district, northwest of Dhaka. These are at depths of 1000 to 1300 metres and, being expensive to exploit, have remained undeveloped thus far. A shallower, 150-metre deep, 125 million tonne coal deposit has also been located in Dinajpur and further investigations are in progress. Some 125 million tonnes of dry peat has been found near Dhaka, an eight million deposit near Khulna, and another small deposit in Sylhet. Their commercial significance has yet to be established.

Prospecting for oil in Bangladesh started early and in 1955 gas was struck. There are today 13 gas yields in the eastern region including one off-shore field. The total estimated reserve (proven, probable and inferred in equal proportions) is placed at around 12 trillion cubic feet or 260 million tonnes of oil-equivalent. Of the 1140 MW of electrical energy being generated in 1987, about 60 per cent was gas-based. Load forecasts made by the Bangladesh Power Board place the demand for power at 4000 MW by 2000 and 5900 MW by 2015. If the additional generation is to be fuelled with gas to the same extent as at present, the prospects do not look very promising. Power Board sources fear that proven gas sources may not be available beyond 1995 unless there are fresh finds. There has been an oil show in Sylhet but no firm potential has been established thus far. The Planning Commission too has warned that "no power and fertilizer plants can be planned and constructed after 1990 on known indigenous gas reserves" (1985). Alternative sources must be tapped. A nuclear power station was planned at Rooppur, near Khulna, but has made no progress as donors find this an expensive option. There is some tidal power available in the Sunderbans in West Bengal and there could be a somewhat larger potential in Bangladesh. But nobody has looked at this as yet. Apart from continuing exploratory efforts and seeking to utilize such coal and peat resources as may be feasible, one obvious answer lies in importing energy from Northeast India which has been unexploited potential of over 40,000 MW of hydel power. Northern Bangladesh could also be supplied hydro power from Sikkim as well as from Bhutan to eastern Nepal through an eastern subcontinental grid.

By 1985 only 7,888 of Bangladesh's 85,650 villages had been electrified and it was planned to cover 22,000 villages by 1990. The agricultural pumping demand has grown steadily. The main constraint on the power sector remains the stringency of financial resources, large system losses of 37.5 per cent (gross), and low tariffs. The 132 kv trunk transmission system which was in two separate halves until the eastern-west inter-connector was commissioned is now being raised to 230 kv. It is expected that this will make for greater system efficiency and reliability.

Limited availability of commercial fuel has aggravated the biomass crisis. Some 83 per cent of all the energy consumed in Bangladesh comes from non-commercial sources. The bulk of this goes into household consumption. The percentage shares of a variety of feedstock in the country's non-commercial fuel budget was estimated some years ago as follows: cowdung 25, rice husk 24, rice straw 18, firewood 13, jute sticks 6, bagasse 5, and others 9. Projections indicated a shrinking per capita availability of these traditional fuels to the detriment of the most poor. The development of bio-gas, community woodlots and social forestry, solar energy, and improved stoves and other means of conserving energy were accordingly recommended (World Bank).

In order to look at the situation in the round and project a longer term strategy, the Government of Bangladesh commissioned a comprehensive study. The National Energy Plan (1986) offers no panacea as there is none. Conservation along a less energy-intensive path of development would be one option. But there is no reason for Bangladesh to forego the other option of sharing the huge hydro resources of the Ganga-Brahmaputra-Barak system.

CHUKHA ENEGY TRANSFORMS BHUTAN

Bhutan is more happily placed. Its major source of energy has traditionally been firewood (and charcoal) which is still abundantly available. This is not a resource to be indefinitely or indiscriminately exploited if it is to preserve its fine forest stands and retain a 60 per cent forest cover. Fortunately it has an abundance of hydro-electric potential, estimated at 20,000 MW. This is its true wealth. As of March 1987, Bhutan was generating 3.5 MW in seven micro-hydel stations and another 10.5 MW at a number of diesel stations. But its first major hydro scheme, the 336 MW run-of-the-river Chukha project, partially came on stream that year and is now fully commissioned. Bhutan is able to absorb no more than about seven MW from Chukha as yet, partly owing to the absence of transmission facilities that could connect small and scattered load centres. Apart from supplying the capital, Thimphu, and Phuntsholing, the main roadhead and budding industrial centre on the Indo-Bhutan border, the bulk of Chukha power is exported to India, the sale proceeds solidly buttressing both the Kingdom's balance of payments and budgetary resources.

The Chukha project, on the Wangchu river, as first investigated in 1961 and taken up under an agreement signed in 1975. India undertook to build and fund the Rs 825 crore project, with 60 per cent of the cost given as a grant to Bhutan. The balance is being treated as a loan at 5 per cent interest repayable over 15 years from the completion of the project (1988), inclusive of a three year grace period. The project cost includes a 66 kv transmission line from Chukha to Thimphu and another to Phuntsholing and 220 kv lines from Chukha to Birpara in West Bengal. A 40 metre high diversion dam at Chimakothi provides diurnal storage in a little two-kilometre pond to provide peaking power to Calcutta and other areas from 6 to 10 p.m. The top of the dam is at 1845 metres and a 6.5 kilometre tunnel drops the water 300 metres into an underground power station at Chukha.

A power line communication system connects Chukha to Siliguri in North Bengal via Birpara and on to Calcutta where the load dispatch centre and the Eastern Region Electricity Board is located. Chukha power is shared within India by West Bengal, Sikkim, Assam, Orissa, Bihar and the DVC. Built by the National Hydro-Electric Power Corporation of India, the 1237 circuit-kilometre 220 kv network, with an 84 kilometre 400 kv DC link from Malda to Farakka, connects the Northeastern and Eastern India regional grids. It also constitutes the first international grid in the sub-continent linking as it does the Bhutanese and Indian power systems. Only a narrow tongue of territory separates this line from Bangladesh and Nepal, making it the forerunner of a future eastern sub-continental grid.

Operating at 60 per cent load factor, the Chukha hydro station will generate 1944 million units of saleable power, including 832 million units of firm power priced at 27 paise per unit and 1112 million units of secondary power initially priced at half that rate but equalized in 1989. India has guaranteed to purchase all the energy that is available for export. In a full year, Bhutan's export earning from this source at the old tariff was expected to be of the order of Rs. 34 crores gross or around Rs. 20 crores net during the period it takes to pay off the loan capital and interest thereon. There was some bargaining over the price at which Bhutan should sell surplus power to India. The matter was amicably settled and the agreement, valid for 99 years (though subject to amendment), provides for a tariff review every two years. The project is overseen by a Chukha Project Authority, an autonomous body with high-level representation on both sides and chaired by the representative of the King of Bhutan, a position currently held in an acting capacity by the Bhutanese Foreign Minister. The authority enjoys the powers of government and has therefore been able to act decisively and expedite construction which nonetheless did witness some slippage and escalation on account of accidents, labour problem and a rise in wage and material costs. The general manager is from India.

Bhutan's energy demand is rising and the electricity tariff has been lowered to 40 paise per unit and may need to be further lowered to 25 paise to encourage people to switch from firewood to electricity. The cost of generation of micro-hydel and diesel units is far higher, but large input of Chukha power has enabled the government to charge a lower national pool price. An experimental ropeway has been developed and another more ambitious ropeway alignment from Thimphu to Phuntsholing has been investigated. Unless traffic builds up and ropeways can act as feeders to the highways, they may not be immediately economic. Further prospects are, however, not unattractive but care will need to be taken in planning and transportation network and locating activities that will generate traffic.

Bhutan has only a small deposit of low grade coal in the southeast which is being mined for briquetting after washing. It has requested Indian assistance in oil and gas exploration. However, hydro power will be its principal commercial energy base. More micro and mini-hydel units are under construction or planned; especially in remote areas with small loads and in the far north where it would be uneconomic to extend transmission lines to reach isolated hamlets. A larger 45-60 MW project on the Kuri chu has been investigated by India to supply eastern Bhutan and is to be taken up with Indian assistance. Another run-of-river project has been investigation which might yield up to 1000 MW on the Wang-chu below Chukha. Competing with this are proposed storage dams on the Wang-chu and Amo Chu rivers which could yield 600 MW and 250 MW respectively for the development of industry in southern Bhutan and for export. The Bhutanese government is evaluating these projects and may thereafter pose one or the other to India for assistance and execution. The Sunkosh and Manas, further east, have much larger potentials. But only preliminary studies have been conducted and the Royal Government will have to take a view about how fast and to what extent it would like to proceed in hydel development.

One view is that power could stimulate the industrialization of Bhutan which has some mineral deposits and could attract energy intensive industries. The other view is that industries and concomitant transport facilities could be polluting and that the country would be better off developing and exporting maybe up to 25 per cent of its hydro potential or around 5000 MW, the income from which would enable it to finance infrastructural and human development. The King would hasten slowly at this juncture. He places high value on Bhutan's identity and culture, which should not be lost or corrupted, and on contentment rather than mere material gain.

PROMISE OF KARNALI

Nepal initiated its hydro-electric development in 1911. Further progress was slow on account of the insularity of the Kingdom, limited demand and lack of resources and trained personnel. Reliance was placed on diesel generation to meet growing requirements. After the eclipse of the Rana regime in 1951, Nepal launched on a programme of modernization and some hydel development took place with international assistance. The Trisuli (21 MW) and Devighat (14 MW) projects were financed and constructed by India, and the Sunkosi project (10.5 MW) by China. In a bid to accelerate progress and develop indigenous capabilities, a Water and Energy Commission was set up in 1976 under the Water Resources Ministry with Canadian assistance to back up the technical secretariat. By 1983-84, total generation capacity had grown to 126 MW with the addition of Kulekhani I (60 MW) and a number of thermal and micro-hydel plants. Kulekhani II (32 MW) has now come on stream and Marsyandi (66 MW) is nearing completion. Demand was initially slow to pick up but now Nepal has entered an era of power shortage. The Seventh Plan envisages an installed capacity of 240 MW by 1990. Load forecasts suggest that this capacity will suffice to meet demand until 1993 and that Arun-III (402 MW) on one of the seven arms of the Kosi, expected to come on stream by 1996, will take care of domestic demand until 2004.

Nepal's development of its assessed 83,000 MW hydro potential could have got off to a far more significant start but for misunderstandings and suspicions that have divided it from its giant southern neighbour. India's own indifference to the exploitation of this vast potential must also be noted (Advisory Board on Energy, May 1985). Its interest in the Chisapani project on the Karnali was for long desultory and it posed the Pancheshwar project (2200 MW) on the Mahakali to Nepal only relatively recently.

The Karnali project has been under study since 1964 by various international consultants – Japanese, Australian and Norwegian. Yet another Canadian-US consortium was invited by Nepal in 1986 following an understanding with India and with the good offices of the World Bank, to prepare a feasibility report. A preliminary optimization report by the Himalaya Hydro Consultants settled the site and proposed raising the height of the dam to generate 10,800 MW as against the 3600-4500 MW earlier contemplated. With related developments upstream on the Karnali bend (a run-of-the-river scheme that will supply energy for the construction phase) and storages on the Bheri and Seti rivers feeding into the Karnali reservoir, total capacity could ultimately go up to 16,000 MW. Hopes of accomplishing the main project by 2001 at a cost of $ 4.4 billion at 1987 prices seem unduly optimistic. But Karnali could transform Nepal's economy and the energy scene in northern India, which would be the market for this huge block of power. What it will take to negotiate an Indo-Nepal agreement, which alone will ensure international funding, is discussed in a later chapter.

Nepal must meanwhile improve its transmission and distribution system. The Seventh Plan called for a reduction in system losses from 30 per cent to 20 per cent by 1990. It is also felt that lowering the electricity tariff, recently raised, would encourage a switch from petroleum products and firewood to power which would be to the nation's advantage. As of 1980, Nepal's overall energy consumption, inclusive of non-commercial sources, was 3.3 million tonnes of oil-equivalent and is expected to rise to a little under 4. million tonnes by 1990. Even at that stage, however, firewood and other traditional sources are expected to account for over 93 per cent of energy needs, the commercial fuel proportions being 1.22 per cent for electricity, 4.55 per cent for petroleum products (imported) and 1.12 per cent for coal (imported) (National Planning Commission, Nepal June 1985).

MICRO-HYDEL UNITS AND WATER TURBINES

The Water Resources Ministry has been concerned with this problem and conducted five energy workshops in 1985 dealing with small and micro-hydel generation, bio-gas, improved cookstoves and fuelwood demand. The problem with small and micro-hydel development, especially with regard to the former, was found to be uncertain stream flow data, cost of transportation of cement and equipment to remote sites through difficult terrain, and the low initial load factor until small industrial loads develop. But there are solutions too. The Namche micro-hydel scheme in the Sagarmatha (Everest) National Park employs a dual circuit for lighting and cooking and sealed home circuit breakers as an alternative to meters. These devices control excessive energy use and ensure that the available power supply goes round. Fluorescent bulbs of nine and 18 watts, equivalent to 60 and 100 watt incandescent bulbs, have been introduced.

About 27 small hydro units have been commissioned or are under construction with installed capacities ranging from 32 to 2000 KW. A special fleet of helicopters and skyvan planes has been used for transport of equipment and materials and VHF communications system have been installed at each site. Local manpower is being trained to take over operation and maintenance functions. The cost of completed small hydro projects varies from Rs 27,000 to Rs 73,000 per KW, depending on the site. Larger projects are more economical. While the cost is high, there are savings on transmission costs as distribution is limited to a small radius. Even otherwise, the equivalent cost of diesel generation would be four to five times higher (Ibid).

Experiments are afoot with small water turbines and improved water mills. The Planning Commission estimates that if Nepal's 25,000 traditional water mills or pani-ghattas could be fitted with cross-flow turbines or small multi-purpose power units (MPPUs), they could generate up to 10 KW each on an average and replace the traditional mills with greatly improved efficiency for hulling, milling and grinding grain, oil pressing and saw milling. But local water rights would need to be defined and enforced. The first water turbine was installed in Nepal in 1961 but the movement developed in the 1970s with institutional finance. Cross-flow turbines can generate between five and 20 KW of energy. Subsequently an improved adaptation of the traditional water wheel was designed. These so-called multi-purpose power units can develop between three to five kilowatts of mechanical energy and can be used for mini agro-processing activity or power generation. By 1988 some 400 water turbines and MPPUs had been installed and a larger programme is under way with Asian Development Bank support. The average cost of water turbine works out to NRs 1.1 lakh and that of an MPPU to around NRs 80,000 (Ibid). Enterpreneurs who have installed such turbines/MPPUs have found them an attractive proposition. Biogas plants are also being encouraged and women are being sought o be interested in this programme. The target for 1990 is about 4000 units, including some community plants.

While both Nepal and Bhutan can augment their energy output through conventional and non-conventional means, their prime asset, hydro-electric power, cannot be exploited to its fullest without the benefit of the Indian market, India's load growth, more especially in the northern, eastern and northeastern regions, and plans and strategies for meeting this over the next few decades will therefore largely govern the growth of hydro-electric generation in these two countries.

SYSTEM GROWTH IN INDIA

Until Independence in 1947 very little hydel energy had been tapped in the Indian part of the Basin, barring some micro-hydel developments on the Ganga canals and a few smaller schemes. But thoughts had begun to turn to exploiting the large hydro potential available and multipurpose projects such as Bhakra and the development of the Damodar Valley, already on the drawing boards, were taken up as harbingers of planned development. Other projects followed: Chambal, Rihand and lesser schemes in West Bengal, Assam and UP. The country's hydel potential was initially placed at 45,000 MW (1950) but was revised to 85,000 MW (1980) and seems set for further upward revision which will take it above 100,000 MW. Yet only 12 per cent of the potential had been harnessed by 1985, the percentage of various river systems within the Basin being 12.2 in the Ganga, 10.3 for the Central Indian rivers, and a mere one per cent in respect of the Brahmaputra.

Organizationally, while the private sector participated in the development of power generation prior to independence, the Industrial Policy Resolution of 1956 reserved the generation and distribution of electricity almost exclusively for the public sector. The Electricity Supply Act, 1948, created State Electricity Boards (SEBs) and provided a Central Electricity Authority (CEA) which was set up as a part time body in 1951. With the bifurcation of the Central Water and Power Commission in 1974, the CEA was made a full time body with a coordinating, regulatory and technical role. Constitutionally, electricity is included in the Concurrent List but it was not until 1976 that the Electricity Act was amended to facilitate the creation of two Central generation companies, the National Thermal Power Corporation (NTPC) and the National Hydro-Electric Power Corporation (NHPC) as well as a regional Northeastern Electric Power Corporation (NEEPCO). To foster the development of grids, five regional electricity boards were set up in the 1960s, the Northern, Eastern and Northeastern Regional Electricity Boards among them spanning the Basin. The Damodar Valley Corporation was statutorily created in 1948 on the model of the Tennessee Valley Authority with what was supposed to be a monopoly of generation (and irrigation storage) within the Damodar Basin. There is additionally today a Nuclear Power Board for the exclusive development of atomic power.

As of March 1987, all-India generation capacity (utilities only) totaled just under 50,000 MW and was expected to reach a little over 64,000 MW by 1990. As against this the corresponding figures for the regional grids are 13,365 MW and 18490 MW for the northern region (including Punjab and Jammu & Kashmir), 7766 MW and 9666 MW for the eastern region (including Orissa), and 873 MW and 1215 for the northeastern region, inclusive of Central generation. While the agricultural load had risen to 9.1 per cent all-India by 1985-86, it was 28.3 per cent in the northern region, but only 6.3 per cent in the eastern region and a mere 1.6 per cent in the northeastern region. The peak load in 1985-86 was 26,762 MW, being over 8000 MW in the northern region and under 3500 MW in the eastern region. However, the system load (defined as the ratio of the average load to the peak load of the system) was 66.9 per cent all-India, being lower in the northern region than in the eastern on account of the far higher seasonal agricultural load. The proportion of hydel power, which imparts a greater measure of flexibility to the system, is falling and the hydro-thermal mix in the northern grid by 1990 is expected to be 33.8 per cent hydro, 61.5 per cent thermal and 4.7 per cent nuclear (Rana Pratap Sagar in Rajasthan andNarora in Uttar Pradesh), the corresponding figures for the eastern region being 16.9 per cent hydro and 83.1 per cent thermal by that date.

The demand for power has clearly outstripped supply in practically every part of the country and existing surpluses in certain areas are likely to be shortlived. The position in the Northeastern region taken as a whole is a little different on account of other development constraints that have suppressed the growth of energy demand. According to the Advisory Board on Energy (December 1986) there is likely to be an overall peaking deficit of around 7800 MW all-India in 1990, assuming that the thermal plant load factor improves to 57 per cent by that date as against the 64 per cent considered feasible (Committee on Power, September 1980) and exceeded by the Andhra SEB (68 per cent in 1988), and as much as 80 per cent in the U.K. As it is, the ABE points out, the country is already experiencing load shedding, power cuts of the order of 10 per cent costing the country approximately Rs. 7000 crores per annum in tems of losses in industrial production alone. Power shortages have compelled resort to increased reliance on oil resources such as diesel pumping sets and the installation of captive power units by industry, the total capacity of which may reach 7000 MW at an investment of Rs.10,000 crores by 1990.

NATIONAL POWER PLAN 2000

The Central Electricity Authority's generation expansion programme, 1985-2000, based on optimization studies suggests a "desirable-cum-feasible" plan to add 46,684 MW of capacity in the Eighth Plan and 61,307 MW in the Ninth Plan, making a total addition of 108,000 MW between 1990-2000 which would raise the overall installed capacity to just under 175,000 MW by that date. Such a programme is calculated to cost Rs. 203,000 crores at 1985-86 prices, a little over 63 per cent being for generation and the balance for transmission and distribution. However, keeping in mind the very substantial cuts in investment that had to be imposed on the power sector during the Seventh Plan on account of resource constraints which have, if anything, worsened, the CEA envisages a capacity induction of 38,000 MW and 55,000 MW in the two ensuing Plan periods, or 15000 MW less than the desired figure. The conclusion is somber. With these reduced capacity inductions the era of power shortages must continue with peaking deficits averaging 18 per cent and 16.8 per cent in the Eighth and Ninth plans. In order to mitigate the impact of such a development the CEA recommends curtailment of peak demand by suitable measures of demand management and energy conservation; an overall improvement in thermal performance with greater operational efficiency, renovation and modernization; and "accelerating development of hydro-electric projects for overall reduction in the capacity induction requirement"

The National Power Plan suggests that reducing the energy demand over the next decade by 10 per cent would reduce capacity requirements by 15,690 MW and investment by Rs.28,000 crores. Likewise, were the forced outage rate of thermal plants reduced from 32 per cent to 24 per cent this would further bring down capacity requirements by 8000 MW and investment by Rs. 14,000 crores. Improvements in the system load factor by lowering peak requirements would also bring about appreciable savings. Energy conservation is possible by reducing transmission and distribution (T&D) losses which rose from 16.8 per cent in 1969-70 to 21.5 per cent in 1987-88, reducing auxillary losses in the process of generation, and improving the energy efficiency of end-uses, whether these be motors and engines or appliances, pumps and lamps. Co-generation, using both steam and heat energy, could also yield 1500-2000 MW of additional power. Peak load could in turn be lowered by a variety of administrative and fiscal measures such as staggering work over the day or week, and introducing certain incentives and disincentives through time-of-day tariffs. Flat rate tariffs as for agricultural uses are also not conducive to economy. Daylight saving may have some benefit during certain seasons, but dividing India into two time zones could certify lower the national peak demand by staggering the peak.

PROBLEMS OF SUPER-THEMAL STATIONS

Thermal generation has been the preferred method of augmenting power capacity over the past two decades. A number of super-thermal stations have been developed by the NTPC and SEBs at pit-heads or coal washery sites where large quantities of middlings are available. One of the largest of these concentrations, with some 10,000 MW commissioned, under construction or planned, is sited within the Basin near the Singrauli coalfield in Madhya Pradesh and around the Rihand hydel reservoir which provides the necessary cooling water. The large quantities of water required make reservoirs and pondages, canals and large rivers ideal sites for such super-thermal stations. The Narora nuclear plant is on the Ganga caal near Delhi and the Kahalgaon station on the Ganga near Bhagalpur. Other large thermal stations have been sited at Farakka. Rana Pratap Sagar (nuclear), and around the DVC reservoirs. Land and water scarcity are becoming problems in siting new large-sized thermal units. A 2000 MW plant for instance requires up to 1800 hectares for the generating station, township and ash pond where the fly ash is dumped. Every tone of coal contains 35 to 40 per cent ash, or more, the disposal of which requires large dumping grounds. Water availability is becoming another constraint. According to the CEA, under Indian conditions the consumptive requirements per megawatt of installed capacity range from 9.4 cubic metres of water per hour for open systems, in which the water is recycled, to five cubic metres per hour for open systems, in which the water is returned to the source of origin. The open system however requires a source that can supply a continuous stream of 155 cubic meters per hour per megawatt of installed capacity.

The other increasing constraint on expanding thermal capacity is that of moving huge quantities of coal to power stations located at load centres, especially when large quantities of ash have to be hauled. Over short distances merry-go-round systems and unit trains are being operated, but such is the regional concentration of coalfields in India that many existing and up-coming thermal sites call for moving coal over long leads. In view, of all these difficulties, the new approach is to plan to establish large new thermal stations along the coast where land may be more easily available. Coal may be moved by inland and coastal waterways and sea or tidal water could be used for cooling purposes. Hence plans for new stations at or near Madras, Tuticorin, and along the West coast.

It is in consideration of some of these problems that the next two Plans are likely to see an acceleration in the development of gas-fired and nuclear stations, the indicated target for nuclear generation being around 6000-7000 MW by 200. Among other possible sources, geothermal and ocean thermal energy offer little prospect at present. India is said to have a tidal potential of up to 9000 MW, a small part of this in the Sunderbans at Pitts Creek in West Bengal. A larger 900 MW tidal station in the Gulf of Kutch is being designed for execution by the NHPC.

Non-conventional options arc opening up, linked to solar energy and biomass, and energy plantations. These are considered later. But in the short-run, no great additionality can be expected from these sources though it is important to press forward with them in view of their future potential. Which leaves a large block of hydro-electric power awaiting exploitation.

In addition to India's hydro potential of 85,000 MW at 60 per cent load factor as officially assessed at present, the country has another 5000 MW of micro-hydel energy of which only 200 MW is in operation and another 218 MW under construction. This has great possibilities for independent generation in remote regions and for catering to small, isolated loads which is also where sources such as bio-gas, biomass and solar energy show great promise. There is little doubt that India's hydel potential will continue to be upgraded in the wake of further detailed surveys.

The CEA has for the first time estimated the prospects of pumped storage for peaking purposes. A systematic survey has revealed a large number of possible sites. Keeping in mind more immediate needs, the National Power Plan identifies 56 major pumped storage schemes with high heads that offer the most economic development with a total potential of 94,000 MW. Of this 13,000 MW would be located in the northern, 9000 MW in the eastern and 17,000 in the northeastern regions. Nagarjunasagar in Andhra Pradesh (500 MW) was the first pumped storage scheme to be commissioned in India and Kadana in Gujarat (240 MW) is under construction. The Tehri project (Uttar Pradesh) will be among the next lot of large pumped storage schemes with a potential of 1000 MW.

CONSTRAINTS ON HYDRO DEVELOPMENT

The National Power Plan envisages an additional hydel generation of some 39,000 MW by 2000 inclusive of sanctioned schemes (6800 MW), schemes cleared by the CEA (9600 MW), and new schemes (23,000 MW). Even if all these projects are implemented, the hydro-thermal mix will be 34:66 as against the desirable 40:60 ratio and may well be much lower if quick-gestation gas turbine thermal stations with peaking capability are substituted for hydel projects on account of resource constraints. Quick-yielding and economic renovation and modernization programmes to improve plant load factors and reduce transmission and distribution losses could also temporarily depress the hydro ratio. The hydro mix in the northern and northeastern regions is however likely to be comfortably above 40 per cent. Not so in the Eastern Region unless this is inter-connected to the northeastern region in an inter-regional grid.

According to optimization studies conducted by the CEA, there would be a clear advantage of maximizing hydro generation in all Regions. Unfortunately hydel development is beset by three problems: time and cost overruns which have added to the higher capital cost; a lack of new starts or even adequately investigated schemes in view of the turning away from hydel projects in recent years for lack of resources; and environmental objections, which will be considered in a later chapter. At the commencement of the Seventh Plan it was decided to avoid fresh starts and to expedite the completion of on-going schemes. As a result a project like Naptha Jhakri (1500 MW) in Himachal, cleared in 1972, took 16 years to get started. Likewise, Tehri was only partly stalled by environmental considerations. The Uttar Pradesh Government simply did not have the funds to go ahead despite a cumulative outlay of something approaching Rs. 300 crores on the project since the early 1970s. The Soviet Union agreed to underwrite the project in 1987 and it is now moving forward.

The constraint of funds has been paramount. Projects yielding benefits within a single Plan period tend to be favoured and restraints on new starts during successive Plan have resulted in even sanctioned projects remaining on the shelf. Divided organizational responsibility for hydel schemes between Irrigation Departments and SEBs has been an aggravating factor. Problems of land acquisition and construction management in isolated and inhospitable sites and related contractual difficulties are other impediments. The National Council for Power Utilities however argues that the investment needs of hydel schemes are rather small during the first two years and that if this preliminary period is taken out, the additional time required to complete a hydro project may not be more than a year or two at the outside except in the case of very large and complex projects or if there are geological surprises, which are not infrequent in the Himalaya. If therefore a special funding strategy can be evolved to take care of the first two years of hydro schemes, the global investment requirements of hydro and thermal projects may not be very different as their investment cost per megawatt is approximately the same at around Rs. 1 crore (1986) and double that and more today.

Long gestation has often been a product of inadequate investigation of hydel projects for lack of adequate funds or the availability of personnel to spend arduous months in difficult environments without due recompense. It has time and again been recommended the technical personnel assigned such tasks should be given incentives such as higher allowances, in order to be able to maintain a double establishment or to place their children in boarding school, and other fringe benefits including longer leave. Access to the site is often difficult and delays on this account can be overcome by use of helicopters and good telecommunications. There is need for strengthening the cadre of engineering ecologists and enhancing the level of geological investigations even at some added cost in order to mitigate uncertainties and provide for unforeseen contingencies. This may entail special procedures for deciding on alternatives and meeting consequent costs, including procurement of material. Better construction planning and the evolution of more practical and flexible contractual norms to take account of uncertainties that go with tunneling, landslides and similar contingencies is very necessary. Contractors may also need to be funded to procure special equipment like tunnel boring machines and jumbo drills or to draw upon a special equipment bank so that delays are minimized. Advance procurement of materials like steel and cement might also be necessary so that the rhythm of work is not upset for lack of supplies. Land acquisition for hydel projects is also a more complex process as land has to be acquired at different sites and not in a single compact block as in the case of thermal plants. Submergence and displacement also pose delicate human issues. Project planning must anticipate many of these issues.

ADVANTAGES OF BASIN DEVELOPMENT

There are several advantages in developing whole cascades on a river system and a basin development approach is, therefore, being increasingly advocated. Upstream development invariably improves the economics of downstream projects because of regulated discharges or silt control, whereas downstream projects open up access and provide a base infrastructure for tackling upper valley schemes. Labour, skilled personnel and specialized equipment can also be phased from one project to another. This would reduce movement and assembly time and prevent the inevitable losses and disruption occasioned by dispersal at the conclusion of a single project. Watershed management and rehabilitation programmes can also be carried out more effectively and at less cost if done as part of a single, phased programme rather than as a series of ad hoc schemes. This basin approach is indeed now being followed in the upper Ganga and Yamuna valleys, the Sharda and Sone basins, the Sutlej and Chenab basins and so on. There may be a problem of investment concentration in a finite area while many would prefer a wider spread of benefits. But the time and cost overruns inherent in dispersed development also has an opportunity cost which cannot be left out of the reckoning.

There is a potential of almost 3000 MW available in the Yamuna basin in Himachal and Uttar Pradesh and may be double that in the Upper Ganga basin from Haridwar to the glaciers, and some more again in the Sharda basin. The Vindhya and Satpura rivers flowing into the Ganga from Middle India would have a potential of maybe another 5000 MW. Sikkim and North Bengal have a potential of between 2000-3000 MW. Uttar Pradesh also shares a potential of over 2000 MW with Nepal on the Mahakali river. All these are however dwarfed by the immense 40-50,000 MW potential of the Brahmaputra and Barak basins in the Northeast. Of the 41,000 MW potential of the Brahmaputra, less than 500 MW has been commissioned or is under construction in Meghalaya and Assam. Other giant schemes have been mooted in discussions with Bangladesh since 1978 but so far only some medium-large projects have been cleared for construction, Ranganadi (405 MW) and Kameng (600 MW) in Arunachal Pradesh being the two largest. The Brahmaputra Board, a statutory body set up to prepare a master plan for the Northeastern basins has so far submitted two reports. The first deals with the Main Stem of the Brahmaputra (1986) and the second with the Barak basin (1988). A third part is to follow on the tributary streams of the Brahmaputra. Though primarily concerned with the flood problem, the Board has advocated several multipurpose storages which would generate huge blocks of power while moderating floods as well.

DIHANG, SUBANSIRI, TIPAIMUKH

Pride of place among these projects is the Dihang Dam on the main stem of the Brahmaputra above Pasigha where the river enters the plains. A 296 metre high rockfill dam will store 4.70 million hectare metres of water in a 490 square kilometre lake with an installed capacity of 20,000 MW which would make it the largest single hydro-electric station in the world, surpassing the Itaipu Dam on the Parana between Brazil and Paraguay (12,600 MW) and the proposed Three Gorges Project on the Yangtze in China (15,000 MW). The project would be capable of yielding 6370 MW of continuous power year round, with huge quantities of secondary power during the monsoon season. Though estimated to cost Rs.8600 (1983 prices) the economics is extremely attractive, the cost per megawatt installed being Rs. 43 lakhs even if the entire outlay is debited exclusively to power, and the cost per unit being 19.05 paise. Construction is estimated take 13 years with power generation commencing in the seventh year. The project will give a substantial flood benefit and will both improve and augment navigation. It would also facilitate irrigation downstream. The firm power generated would have an energy equivalent of 27.5 million kilolitres of oil valued at Rs 7,150 crores or 66 million tonnes of coal valued at Rs 1,980 crores per annum.

A second project which is also highly favoured is the Subansiri Dam with an installed capacity of 4500 MW. The construction of the Subansiri and Dihang projects would require six million tonnes of cement, a considerable quantity of construction power, and the strengthening and extension of transport links to move the weight and volume of materials required. The very construction of the projects together with related soil conservation and watershed management programmes would itself constitute a massive area development programme that would quite transform the region. There would be a displacement of some 42,500 people on account of both projects, a figure that is as small as it is, despite the huge lakes to be formed behind the proposed dams, because of the low density of population in Arunachal. The Brahmaputra Board recommends that the Subansiri project be taken up first as this would enable the project engineers to garner valuable experience while allowing time for detailed engineering and design work on the Dihang dam.

The master plan for the Barak Valley has as its centerpiece the Tipaimukh dam (1500 MW) on the Barak where it makes a V-turn just south of the tri-junction of Manipur, Mizoram and Assam. It again offers very considerable benefits in terms of flood moderation and navigation both in India and Bangladesh and could also conveniently export power. The Loktak project (105 MW) is currently the only major hydel scheme in the southern tier of India's northeast, but some others are under investigation.

The bulk of the power generated at Dihang and Subansiri would need to be evacuated through extra-high voltage systems to load centres in Bihar and West Bengal where it would serve peaking requirements. A study undertaken by Bharat Heavy Electricals Ltd. suggests that this would be entirely economic. India has graduated to 400 kv transmission lines and BHEL is currently developing a 500 kv HVDC (high voltage direct current) transmission line from the Rihand super-thermal complex to Delhi. With India now moving to 765-800 kv systems the Dihang transmission line would qualify as a candidate. Additionally, it would be possible to develop electrochemical, electrometallurgical and other energy-intensive, industries in the northeast, using cheap river haulage up and down the Brahmaputra system to move raw materials and finished products into and outside the region or to Bangladesh. India was at one time examining the possibility of sending alumina to Zambia for processing into aluminium. There is no reason to go so far when abundance of cheap power can be made available within the country.

There are significant potentials on some of the other major Brahmaputra tributaries: Lohit (300 MW), Dibang (2500 MW), Kameng (2600 MW), Manas in Bhutan (5000 MW) and Teesta (2000 MW). The aggregate potential of all the projects on the southern tributaries of the Brahmaputra, however, is no more than 1600 MW. There are problems in taking up these projects – environmental objections and lack of resources among them. The environmental issue is discussed later, but the question of funding is a misconception for after some initial priming, the hydro-option is still clearly the most favourable for developing large blocks of cheap, renewable, bulk energy with the advantage of adding stability and flexibility to the system. The other options are not without their own constraints and problems, some of which may be even more onerous than those affecting hydel generation. And a situation of continuing load shedding is the most expensive alternative of all, with a considerable negative multiplier effect on productivity, employment and growth.

TAPPING THE BRAHMAPUTRA BEND

China has possibly the largest hydel reserves in the world, the bulk of it in and around Tibet. The giant U-bend on the Tsang-po as it breaks through the Namche Bawra-Gyala Peri gorge and turns first north, then east and finally south to cascade 2500 metres from Tibet into India has long excited the imagination of "engineer dreamers" as far and away the biggest single concentration of energy anywhere in the world. In 1977, Masaki Nakajima, founder and currently special adviser to the Mitsubishi Research Institute of Japan conceived by a $ 500 billion plan for reversing world depression (Sneider, Daniel February 1982). This envisaged a series of super and, possibly, supranational "global infrastructure" projects that would have the effect of pump-priming global economic recovery and initiating a "global new deal". This was to be financed through a Global Infrastructure Fund (GIF) at the rate of $ 25 billion per annum over 20 years with contributions from Japan, the US, the EEC and OPEC, but starting with a $ 13 billion core fund. Among GIF projects conceived of from the start and short-listed at the first GIF international conference under Japanese-American sponsorship at Anchorage, Alaska in July 1986, was the Himalayan Hydropower project.

A preliminary desk-top study done by the Electric Power Development Company of Japan envisages the construction of up to 11 large dams around the Brahmaputra loop to harness the cascade. At either of two sites a shorter or longer 80 to 240 kilometre tunnel through the Himalaya would drop the water into India to generate in a variety of combinations a fabulous quantity of power from a series of hydel stations with an overall installed capacity of 70,000 MW, the tunnel-drop power station itself having an installed capacity of 48,000 MW. An $ 18 million pre-feasibility study of the project has been suggested including a regulating dam on the Tsang-po about 100 kilometres southeast of Lhasa which would generate 1000 MW and form a lake stretching some 200 kilometres up the Tsang-po and Lhasa rivers (EPDC, 1988). The proposed Dihang Dam reservoir would incidentally back up to a point not too distant from the lowest dam in Tibet in the EPDC concept. Practically no displacement of population is expected in view of the remoteness of the area. The principal market for the power, which could be developed in stages, would lie in India as the Chinese load centres in Sichuan are some 1500-2000 kilometres distant and far more difficult to access.

The GIF now has the backing of Keidanren, the Japanese national business federation, and has aroused interest in the World Bank and many industrially advanced nations. It was said to be in the process of formulating and forging an international structure and secretariat and the first steering committee meeting was held in Tokyo in March 1987. The Himalayan Hydropower Project was reportedly mentioned in conversation with Mr. Rajiv Gandhi and, earlier, with Indira Gandhi. It is also within the knowledge of the Chinese authorities.

MODERNISING TRANSMISSION AND DISTRIBUTION

While this may be peering a little further into the future, there is a more immediate problem of overcoming the long neglect of transmission systems which are adequate and outmoded. For quite some time transmission bottle-necks have precluded moving available supplies to load centres. It is reckoned that the ratio of investment as between generation, transmission and distribution (including rural electrification) should be 4:2:2 in order to ensure proper integration. An analysis of actual outlays between 1952 and 1980 however indicates a backlog of about Rs. 2100 crores on transmission and distribution. The Committee on Power (1980) hoped that it would be possible to reduce T&D losses to no more than 15 per cent by 2001 which it felt was an achievable figure even with the losses that initially go with rapid rural electrification. The trend since the Committee reported has not been reassuring with losses actually rising steadily to 21.5 per cent in 1986-87. The significance of this can be gauged from the fact that every percentage point of T&D losses saved some years ago was equivalent to adding about 380 MW of capacity or an energy saving of about Rs. 90 crores per annum assuming a price of 50 Paise per unit (Advisory Board of Energy, December 1986). The savings would be greater today – nearer 500 MW on a larger system.

Transmission systems have been plagued by neglect and delay with available funds being siphoned into generation. There has been failure to keep pace with rapidly changing transmission technology and to go in for higher and more optimal transmission voltages and modes, to develop grids with regional inter-connectors and run neighbouring systems synchronously in parallel to facilitate interchange of power. Regional load dispatch centres were slow to come up and the process has only now been completed. To overcome this problem the Committee on Power had recommended that adequately empowered regional electricity authorities should bee established in place of the existing and some-what powerless regional power boards, which should own and operate inter-State high-tension and extra high tension transmission lines and regional load dispatch centres. This has not yet been done, though the NTPC and NHPC have been constructing EHV lines of 400 kv.

Many power engineers have been critical of the delay in deciding to what higher transmission systems India should have moved from 220 kv. The argument about whether to adopt 400 kv or the more efficient 500 kv system was prolonged and 400 kv was finally adopted. A 500 kv high voltage direct current (HVDC) line is, however, now being constructed from Rihand to Delhi. The same delay should not occur in moving up to 765/800 kv systems. One such line is being planned to evacuate Tehri power to Delhi around 1996. The National Power Plan, 1985-2000, has projected certain bulk transmission corridors with a capacity of evacuating 1000 MW and above from generating stations to load centres in all regions within a time-frame related to generation schedules. HVDC systems are more economical than AC for transmission over long distances. They entail lower transmission losses and are more economical in right-of-way requirements. Once these systems are developed and regional grids suitably inter-connected in a national grid it would also be possible to switch large blocks of secondary power from major hydel stations during the monsoon months with considerable advantage. Super-conductivity, when and if it comes, will result in very considerable long distance transmission savings.

The distribution system taking off from the main transmission lines is equally in need of modernization, upgradation and strengthening. The wide and destructive voltage fluctuations that are so common are a sure sign of overloading and short supply. Long rural leads over low tension lines to meet tiny, isolated loads are expensive and entail high losses. Better demand management and the clustering of energy-using devices would help. Rural electricity cooperatives have proved successful in some places in southern and western India in ensuring greater efficiency and better customer service at lower cost. The Committee on Power listed several well known techniques of reducing distribution losses such as optimal sizing of conductors and transformers, installation of capacitors, improved instrumentation in sub-stations, and stricter vigilance to prevent pilferage which is high in certain areas. The ABE pointed out that 60 to 70 per cent of all distribution losses take place in the distribution transformers and that line losses can be reduced by 90 per cent in 11/15 kv systems.

Many urban distribution systems too are outmoded and operate low tension feeder lines with large losses. Changeover to higher voltage systems would not merely reduce these losses but improve the quality of supply and reduce theft.

Renovation of the Kanpur distribution system is expected to cost Rs.61 crores and of all urban centres in Uttar Pradesh about Rs.500 crores. But the savings would be very considerable. Though the CEA has been insisting on it, many SEBs have yet to introduce energy audit system. South Korea has a very good record in reducing T & D losses from 26 per cent in the 1960s to around 7 per cent today, despite far higher generation, by adopting a dynamic process of upgrading voltages as the system load increased and adding more sub-stations. Such innovations pay for themselves.

ASSISTING ELECTRICITY BOARDS IN DISTRESS

The State Electricity Boards are weak and, many of them, in dire straits. Barring a few – and those with a better hydro ratio – most are losing money. Their accumulated losses were likely to be of the order of Rs.12,000 crores cumulatively during 1985-90 and 1985 tariff levels though they were expected to earn Rs.7000 crores net during the Plan period. Some SEBs have indeed raised their tariffs but efforts to increase agricultural rates have met with strong resistance, as in Uttar Pradesh. The Punjab SEB subsidized the state's farmers to the extent of Rs.82 crores in 1982-83. But it was argued that this subsidy was justified in view of the cost-price squeeze on farmers whose terms of trade had been deteriorating. The recommendation made therefore was that rather than revise the agricultural tariff upwards, the government should levy a cess on every tonne of grain procured from the farmer and reimburse this to the Electricity Board (Punjab SEB Expert (Johl) Committee, May 1984). Although the Electricity Supply Act mandatorily requires every SEB to earn a stipulated surplus, now three per cent net of the fixed assets n service, few have complied. Low tariffs, low operating efficiencies, high overheads on account of project delays and overstaffing are among the factors that have kept SEBs in the red. Every one per cent improvement in plant load factor would today make available an additional 500 MW of power. Expanding rural electrification into remoter areas has also added to their burden. According to official figures the average cost of generation and supply in India through 1988 was 83.8 Paise per unit, whereas the average realization was only 65.3 paise per unit, with agricultural consumers being heavily subsidized (Indian Express, January 24, 1989).

Quicker systems of project clearance would help. Power projects costing over Rs.5 crores have to be cleared by the CEA and Central projects costing more than a certain figure require approval from both the Public Investment Board and the Cabinet. Quicker clearances would in turn be possible if projects were better investigated and more rigorously formulated. SEBs started out as departmental organizations without equity. Karnataka took the lead in setting up a power development corporation and other States such as West Bengal have followed suit. Many SEB's now have corporate status and should be able to float bonds, like the

National Thermal Power Corporation has done, provided their performance evokes public confidence.

The Power Finance Corporation of India was incorporated in 1986 to make available supplementary project finance to SEBs over and above their Plan allocations and to provide long-term finance free of annual uncertainties with regard to budget allocations. It has an authorized share capital of Rs.100 crores of which barely a third has been paid up. But the PFC has entered the market and hopes to be in a position to disburse Rs.1400 crores by 1990. It lends at 12.5 per cent interest with repayment periods of three to eight years depending on the nature of the project which could include renovation and modernization. The PFC hopes to use its financial leverage and monitoring role to get the SEBs to put their house in order and secure more expeditious completion of schemes. The Corporation is approaching the World Bank and ADB for funds so as to be able to lend a critical Rs.3500-4000 crores in bridging finance over the next four to five years.

Meanwhile the Faridabad industrial association has been permitted to set up a 100 MW thermal unit for its own members and have this distributed by the Haryana SEB. This however looks like a limited opening for the private sector and the task of augmenting power requirements remains essentially that of the government. Small States such as Himachal, Sikkim and those in the Northeast have large hydro potentials but limited resources. Even other States are facing problems in taking up larger schemes. Himachal has tried negotiating joint projects with some of its neighbours on the basis of cost and power sharing. A memorandum of understanding has been executed with Punjab for two schemes. Such arrangements have possibilities but clearer parameters need to be evolved. The Centre could play a larger role and has been willing to do so through the NHPC and NTPC. But States are reluctant to surrender projects to the Centre and would prefer to undertake joint projects with it. The first such collaborations has been worked out in regard to the 1500 MW Nathpa Jhakri project in the Sutlej basin in Himachal. The agreement stipulates that the Centre will provide 75 per cent of the investment in this Rs.2000 crore project. Himachal will receive 12 per cent of the power generated free of cost as royalty to the home State under a new formula evolved for Central projects in 1983. This is more attractive to the States than the earlier formula gave the home State 10 per cent of the power produced at cost price plus 1.5 per cent of the unit cost of the quantum of power generated. The Water Resources Ministry is however reported to favour abolition of royalty to the home State for power generation as States may demand similar compensation for irrigation from storages. Considering that storage sites are "depleting" natural assets on account of siltation, payment of royalty to the home State is not unreasonable and is likely to ensure earlier starts on such projects. The economics of future hydel projects may improve in many cases if, as recommended by the Committee on Power, all schemes are designed to operate at 40 per cent load factor, instead of the 60 per cent norm adopted in the past, so as to exploit their peaking capability to the fullest extent.

For run-of-the-river projects this would entail modest 24-hour pondages to meet diurnal peaks.

DECENTRALISED NON-CONENTIONAL ENERGY OPTIONS

The demand for electrical energy is galloping. And there is also pressing need all over the developing world to protect the environment by switching from non-commercial to commercial fuels and more fuel-efficient systems. India's per capita consumption of electricity is as low as 180 KW. Though this is somewhat higher than the figure for its neighbours in the basin it is only a fraction of the average figure for more developed societies. A study made a decade back anticipated that it might be possible to electrify all the 560,000 villages in India and provide a connection to every household by 2000 and recommended that this be done in order to improve the quality of life and bring economic and other benefits to the rural populace. It estimated that the cost would come to Rs.5000 crores in public investment (at 1979 prices) in addition to Rs.2250 crores of private investment at the rate of Rs.300 per household. The country would save some Rs.200 crores of kerosene annually at 1979 prices (Working Group on Energy Policy, 1979). Any such target date is unlikely to be met but the obvious desirability of the objective remains. The resource constraint can be mitigated in a number of ways, one of which would be to go in for decentralized generation through low-head micro-hydel units wherever possible and through non-conventional means. Dispersed generation based on local natural resource endowments would be invaluable in itself and would minimize transmission costs and losses.

Apart from conventional power there are other forms of energy that can be tapped: solar, wind, bio-gas and biomass. A perspective plan for the development of these and other sources of energy suggests the development of 250 million tonnes of coal-replacement (mtcr) in India by 2001, a figure estimated to represent 20 per cent of the level of energy demand by that time (DCNE, February 1987). The listing includes generation of 6000 MW from biomass, 5000 MW from wind, 2000 MW from solar systems, 2000 MW from micro-hydro units, and 50 MW from sewage sludge. Also mentioned are 100 million improved chulhas or cookstoves (as against an estimated 150 million households using fuelwood in 2000 according to the Advisory Board on Energy), 12 million bio-gas plants, 2.5 million hectares of energy plantations yielding an average of 20 tonnes/ha, solar thermal systems, 50,000 photovoltaic umps, 50,000 wind pumps, small battery chargers and stand-alone systems, and energy from distillery and solid municipal wastes.

The Department of Non-Conventional Energy estimates an annual biomass production of 1250 million tonnes and believes that 1000 hectares of land can yield three MW of power. Large quantities of agro-wastes are available and the quantity will increase with the growth in farm production. A 10 MW thermal station based on rice straw fuel is being constructed near Patiala in Punjab at a cost of about Rs.35 crores, the fuel-stock being collected from within a radius of 15 kilometres beyond which cartage becomes uneconomic. Rice straw is at present burnt in the fields in Punjab causing environmental nuisance. Sugar cane wastes offer another of several options and current availability would suggest a theoretical potential of 2000 MW from this source. It would be unrealistic to suggest that all agro-wastes can be converted into power as there are competing uses and energy sources within any economic radius of action. Nor can all wastelands be put under energy plantations. Nevertheless, there is a significant realizable potential.

The concept of integrated energy plantations and power programmes (EPPP) has been advocated under which non-farm land can be planted to fast-growing species of trees with a four-year rotation cycle. One fourth of the area under plantation could then be harvested every year for conversion into power or to be gasified to produce both power and charcoal. Farmers would be offered a guaranteed market at remunerative prices (Dayal, Maheshwar April 1984 and October 1986).

The Department of Non-Conventional Energy (DNCE) has also designed a 30 MW solar thermal station using parabolic concentrators and it is proposed to put up such a unit, perhaps near Jodhpur in Rajasthan, at a cost of Rs 90 crores. Power from these systems is estimated at around 75-160 paise per unit which would compare favourably with the delivered cost of power from centralized systems or diesel generation at such distant places. Small photovoltaic systems are already being used for lighting and powering small communication and TV sets in remote border areas in Rajasthan and Mizoram.

Over a million biogas plants, many of them of improved design, were operating in India in early 1989 apart from larger community-sized units. A variety of animal, human and agro-wastes have been successfully used as feedstock, either singly or in combination. The gas is being used for cooking and heating as well as to operate small engines and motors. Water hyacinth, a nuisance over large parts of Eastern India and Bangladesh, is being utilized in biogas plants and experiments are afoot to recover methane from paper and pulp waste, apple waste and other waste materials (DCNE, 1988). Conversion of gas into electricity and storage of gas in balloons for use away from the point of generation are both possible.

Wind mapping studies indicate the possibility of using wind power in several regions in the mountains and along the coast in particular. Wind-electric and wind-pumping systems are being developed and a number of experimental wind farms are under operation. Concepts of multiple energy systems are also being developed so that local communities can meet their energy needs from a variety of sources operating as integrated systems. China too is experimenting with the development of such energy villages. Briquetting of agro-wastes and biomass, coal dust or blends of these would again seem an attractive proposition. Some experimentation is in progress. Hydrams could be used to lift water in hill regions. These are simple and economical to construct and entail virtually no running or maintenance cost. If water could thus be lifted to suitable mini-storage sites that naturally exist or could be created at higher elevations, some of the water could be dropped back to generate micro-hydel power. The conversion of town wastes into energy is also likely to yield good dividends while ensuring improved sanitation and health. Delhi has some schemes in operation and more are planned elsewhere.

Other technologies are under development for basing thermal power generation on coal gasification and the underground gasification of deep coal seams; magneto hydrodynamics (MHD), production of methanol from certain types of biomass, and hydrogen energy. These are for the future. None of this however detracts from the fact that the Basin is extraordinarily well endowed with cheap hydro-electric potential which, as a renewable source, is running to waste when it could and should be generating wealth. Admittedly there are both financial and environmental problems with hydel generation, as there are with the exploitation of other energy sources. Run-of-the-river hydro projects are very attractive and all hydel power is clean, being free from the greenhouse gases emitted by fossil fuels. The country's fossil fuels are in short supply and, being depleting assets, should be conserved for purpose where substitution is not possible or efficient. There is a cost to hydro-electric generation. But the cost of avoiding this option is considerably greater.

CHAPTER 10

From Displacement to Opportunity

Environmental issues have long been a matter of varying concern, but largely to the specialist, Gandhi was an exception, being an early environmentalist who advocated a pattern and pace of development that ensured harmony between man and nature. Popular awareness of environment developed rapidly after the Second World War with the dawn of the nuclear era, the burgeoning of new technology, an extraordinary burst of industrialization, exploding populations, runaway urbanization, a looming end to the seeming inexhaustible reserves of natural resources that resulted, in the doomsday "Limits to Growth" thesis, writing such as Rachael Carson's "The Silent Spring", the oil crisis, and a whole host of more basic land and water management problems associated with the emerging Third World. The World Environment Conference at Stockholm in 1972 brought these issues into global focus and the United National Environmental Programme was launched. That same period saw the birth of the Chipko movement and the establishment of environmental cells within governments, as in India.

The environment movement in South Asia is less than two decades old. But it has caught the imagination of the poor who see a certain causal relationship between the growing degradation of the environment and the periodic disasters that afflict them. The concept of sustainable development has gained ground and both national governments as well as donor nations and international lending agencies such as the World Bank have come to place increasing emphasis on the environmental dimension of development and the quality of life. Environmental impact assessments are becoming standard practice. Projects are only cleared subject to safeguards and compensatory action, the costs and benefits of which are sought to be built into programmes and schemes from their very inception.

FALSE DEMONOLOGY

Dams and large water resource development programmes have understandably come to attract the close and critical attention to environmentalists in view of a variety of considerations: submergence, displacement of population, loss of forests and cultivable land, and the ecological effects of damming rivers, questions of dam safety, salinity and water logging, sedimentation, floods, health impacts and the incidence and sharing of costs and benefits. There is a somewhat extreme view that large projects are somehow iniquitous and bad in themselves as they are too big, complex and multi-faceted to be controlled and managed by small, local communities. More so projects in tribal areas, especially those entailing displacement of considerable numbers of people and loss of forests, habitations and traditional livelihood patterns. Some skeptics see nothing good coming out of such projects and cite past experience around the world as testimony to the ill-effects of large dams whether in human, economic, social or environmental terms (Goldsmith and Hilyard, 1984). "Doomsday" people in India and abroad reach their altogether grim conclusions as they tend to be somewhat narrowly selective and overly emotional. For them, small is beautiful and big is bad by definition. At the other end of the scale and those who believe that anything goes. They are so imbued with technological arrogance and taken with monumentalism that they will brook no opposition. Neither of these extremes has much credibility.

Many others suffer from the excessive zeal of new converts. Their concern for the environment amidst visible evidence of its degradation is understandable. But some of them have developed somewhat over-simplified explanations for whatever they see around them and have become victims of a mythology and demonology of their own. They would appear to romanticize the "noble savage" living close to nature, and fantasise about an exaggeratedly idealized past unmindful of the fact that it cannot be recalled even if it ever existed. The sheer fact of population growth and the pressures this continues to generate is ignored. These are the great preservers who would maintain the status quo or at best plead for slow, incremental change. They too are sometimes prone to take too narrow a view, as if life and development can be neatly and absolutely compartmentalized, and are not always able to indicate an alternative. "Stop the World, I want to get off', the title song of an old musical, "It's A Mad, Mad World", is seldom a viable option, especially for deprived populations in desperately poor nations. And the Abominable No-Man, quick to say "No" or "Not yet" comes dangerously close to pitting development against environmental preservation despite Indira Gandhi's salutary reminder at Stockholm in 1972 that "poverty is the worst polluter".

Of course things have gone wrong in the past – out of ignorance, haste, carelessness, lack of coordination, poor management or implementation, bad maintenance, lack of experience, wrong technology, corruption, or whatever. As the saying goes, good judgement comes from experience, and experience comes from bad judgement. There have been vast improvements in technology though it would be folly to imagine that technology is everything or is foolproof. The answer therefore does not lie in doing nothing but in acting prudently. So while eco-fundamentalism is damaging, it is obvious good sense to ensure meticulous environmental impact assessments, reasonable environmental safeguards, a careful monitoring of change, and constant re-valuation of the meaning and distribution of costs and benefits over time and space and even across national boundaries so that there can be enriching, sustainable development for all with equity.

The headwaters of many major river systems in Middle India and the Northeast, the Chittagong Hill Tract and eastern Tibet lie in what are residuary tribal homelands. Middle India is also a large and sometimes exclusive repository of mineral wealth. Water resource development and mineral-based industrialization must therefore necessarily impinge on tribal domains. This cannot be prevented and need not be lamented provided the tribal people are not made victims but become partners in development whose benefits are theirs to share. That tribal homelands have been ravaged in the past without thought to their sensibilities or welfare does not mean that this must inevitably happen, but that it must not be allowed to happen again. This is possible. To suggest that the tribal people can be cocooned in their pristine state and kept away from development is to treat them as unequal citizens. But they can surely be shielded from economic trauma and culture shock and enabled to develop in a manner and at a pace that avoids social injury. They too want change and improvement without loss of identity.

Let us then look at the indictment of large dams and examine the evidence.

A. Displacement

Displacement is perhaps the single-most important problem. Dams cause submergence resulting in displacement of people who must be suitably compensated and rehabilitated so that they are quite soon, certainly ultimately, better off than they were earlier. While submergence is unique to dams, displacement of populations from lands acquired for development is commonplace. Lands are required for the dam site itself and for canals or transmission lines, just as much as they must be acquired for roads, railway systems, mines, telecommunication lines, industry, ports, urbanization or habitation, airports, schools, hospitals, and warehouses. Large submergence losses in the upper catchments are particularly distressing because it is fertile, habited, gently sloping valleys that are inundated in what is otherwise a perpendicular landscape.

How much land has been submerged behind dams? According to official figures, 4.24 million hectares of forest lands were diverted to all non-forest uses between 1951 and 1980 and 46,850 hectares thereafter (Forest Survey of India, 1987). These figures do not include loss or submergence of non-forest lands and no overall figure of submergence appears to be available. But some broad orders of magnitude emerge from the break up of the figure of forest diversion until 1980. The largest amount of forest lands, 2.62 million hectares, was lost to agriculture, 134,000 hectares to industry and townships, a million hectares to miscellaneous uses, 61,000 hectares to roads and transmission lines, and half a million hectares to river valley projects, including dams and canals. The right of way required for power transmission lines varies in width from 7 metres in the case of 11 kv lines to 15 metres for 33 kv, 18 metres for 66 kv, 22 metres for 110 kv, 35 metres for 220 kv, and 52 metres for 400 kv. In other words, the higher the voltage the less the right of way proportionately required (Chandra and Kumar, October 1987). According to another estimate, production of every megawatt of hydro-generation on an average entails the submersion of 22 hectares of land (Advisory Board on Energy, December 1986). Calculating on 15,000 MW of installed hydro-capacity in 1986, some 330,000 hectares would have been submerged and a further 600,000 hectares may be submerged by 2000 should another 30,000 MW of hydro-capacity be added. Submergence behind purely irrigation dams would of course be additional, by about the same order.

No estimates of the overall numbers displaced by dams is available, though these figures can be had for individual projects. Some 30,700 hectares of land were acquired for the Pong Dam and 20,722 families were displaced according to the Himachal Government. The Tehri Dam in Garhwal is officially estimated to displace 46,000 persons, about 12,000 of them from Tehri town which will go under. The proposed giant Dihang Dam in Arunachal on the main stem of the Brahmaputra will submerge 490 square kilometres and displace 35,000 people, a relatively small number on account of the remoteness and sparse population of the area. The Subansiri Dam, also in Arunachal Pradesh, will have a lake spread of 193 square kilometres and will displace 7,500 persons. Figures of area submerged (in square kilometres) and population displaced by some other major dams are as follows: Bhakra 168 and 36,000; Rihand 461 and 55,000; Lakhwar Vyasi (on the Yamuna) 14 and 3600; Hirakud 283 and 17,700; Nagarjunasagar 282 and 13,227 and the DVC dams, 344 and 93,874. As a matter of interest, approximately 50,000 persons were displaced on account of acquisition of land for coal mines after coal nationalization between 1972 and 1987.

Maybe about a million persons may have been displaced by major and medium irrigation and hydro-electric projects and multipurpose dams in India since Independence. The numbers will increase in future as the population increases. This is not a small figure and it is a tremendous emotional and economic wrench for those who are compelled to move. The trauma is greater when displacement is attended by lack of information, uncertainty, long waiting, niggardly compensation, social dislocation and the cultural shock that accompanies any diaspora when cohesive rural and particularly tribal communities are scattered and resettled away from their kinship and linguistic groups. Therefore, those who are displaced need to be treated with the greatest consideration, sympathy and generosity.

MALTHUSIAN REFUGEES

Two factors must, however, be noted in relation to the numbers displaced by dams. The first is that displacement on account of other factors is cumulatively far greater though generally unnoticed as the magnitude involved in each case is usually far smaller. So, displacement is not caused exclusively by dams but by development generally. Secondly, most dams are located in remote hills and forests which are invariably backward regions. Being disadvantaged areas, they suffer from the lack of development and employment opportunities as well as environmental degradation which is often accentuated for that very reason. This in turn results in falling agricultural productivity and the out-migration of young and able-bodied men to the cities and plains for employment or better income-earning opportunities in the armed forces, government service, trade and industry. These "Malthusian refugees" are involuntarily displaced and are forced to move, not out of choice but by economic compulsion. Most do not migrate on taking a job elsewhere but migrate in the hope of finding employment which in the main is unrelated to the land. These "refugees" crowd into noisome squatter settlements and shanty towns that girdle the metropolitan cities and industrial centres. Later, if and when they make good, their families join them. Otherwise, they live separately. This movement has nothing to do with dams but is independent of them. Indeed, out-migration from the Middle Himalaya belt in Nepal has gathered momentum over the years, spilling over into the Terai and beyond into India from areas where there are no major or medium water resource projects at all and from a country where there is as yet virtually only a single (small) storage dam at Kulekhani. The numbers involved in such out-migration are not easily estimated but would already be many times greater than the total displacement likely to be caused by all the dams that have been built or are likely to be constructed in the Ganga Brahmaputra-Barak basin over the next 50 years. It is important to keep these proportions in mind.

Poverty is far larger and far more cruel displacer of populations than dams. Sensible dams, sensibly managed, with elements of upper-catchment equity built into the projects, could conceivably be a potent means of reversing this trend and bringing about a return flow of numbers to build and share a new prosperity that these neglected hill areas have perhaps never known.

According to the Nepalese geographer Bal Kumar K.C., Nepali migrants cite lack of food, inequality, poverty and miniscule land holdings as reasons for migrating. In the hills, six persons must share a hectare of land and Nepal's Planning Commission's analysis of the 1981 census data indicates that "the scarcity of cultivable land is one of the major reasons for the exodus of the (hill) people". The Hills live on a money order economy, but remittances are modest as the émigrés (to India) occupy the lowest economic rungs. Prof. Ashish Bose, President of the Indian Population Studies Association, notes that Nepalis in the Delhi area fill the lowest paid jobs. But, he adds, "even this poor situation…is an improvement over the alternative. After all, migration is a human endeavour to improve the quality of life." Harka Gurung, a noted Nepali geographer and planner, comments that most out-migrants from the Nepal highlands are "survival migrants-they leave for the sheer necessity of survival" (Dixit, July 1988).

The Uttar Pradesh Hill Development Department estimates that 18 to 25 per cent of the total population of the Uttar Pradesh Hills has migrated on account of poverty, low family income, and lack of suitable employment opportunities. A study entitled *Migration from U.P. Hills and its Consequences* by R.S. Bora of the Institute of Economic Growth, Delhi, sets out the findings of a survey of 10 villages in Pithoragarh (Kumaon) and Tehri Garhwal (Garhwal) districts. He found that 46.2 per cent of the total male workers had migrated. These are telling statistics.

The mounting increase in rural-urban migration is evident throughout the Third World and is manifest within the basin. Cities are growing inexorably as refugee camps with the exodus from the countryside. This rural push is spawning what has been well described as the inadvertent city. It is the remote, isolated, neglected and backward regions, by-passed by development and economic opportunity that send out most migrants. These same regions also typically exhibit high birth rates and the resultant pressure of increasing population (and livestock) results in accelerating environmental degradation as people deplete their natural resource capital for very survival. Development of these regions, appropriately planned and executed, is therefore not to be seen as a disaster but as a harbinger of opportunity and revival. To say that some numbers, even if they be quite large, will be displaced cannot be an unassailable reason for rejecting development or needlessly postponing it. This can only lead to further environmental deterioration and loss of productivity and an even greater subsequent displacement of these very people through involuntary migration.

The related notion that the hill people, like forest dwellers, can or should live a separate existence uninfluenced by all that is happening around them in the country at large is unrealistic. No man, no more than any region, is an island. He cannot be relegated to live in an anthropological museum. Hill and plain, forest and farm, city and countryside are interactive systems, each dependent on and drawing sustenance from the other. It cannot therefore be argued that the hills are being plundered through dams, submergence and displacement to benefit the plains and that each region or segment of the population must live apart. Each has its own natural resource and other endowments and must contribute what it best can to the whole for the well being of all. Certainly, development must be genuinely productive, well ordered, humane and equitable. But this can be said of education and industrialization as much as about dams or anything else.

B. Rehabilitation: To Invest with Dignity

The real issue is not displacement. It is compensation, resettlement and rehabilitation. A displaced person is not a mere statistic or number but a person, a member of a family and of a larger kinship or social group, with a home and economic and cultural rights and interests which cannot be lightly dismissed without due recompense. If land is acquired in the public interest then those whose lands, homes and livelihoods are lost or affected must be adequately compensated and resettled so that their subsequent condition is better than or at least as good as it was previously. This was the philosophy underlying the Indian Land Acquisition

Act of 1894. But, as in much else, the letter of the law has long superseded its spirit. Compensation has often been parsimonious and limited in many ways and has until recently been largely related to material loss with little or no reference to emotional trauma and social and cultural deprivation. In the case of innocent tribals or other underprivileged and unlettered groups, the transactions involved in notification, land acquisition, payment of compensation, valuation and resettlement have been totally baffling and individuals and communities have been tortured by uncertainty and doubt without knowing where to turn. The vocabulary used is itself demeaning and dismissive. The Pong Dam "oustees" as they are officially termed were offered lands to be broken under the plough in the distant Rajasthan desert in the Indira Gandhi Canal command. Some of these displaced by the Rihand Dam were resettled in areas from where they were displaced again and again as new lands were acquired for coal mines, super-thermal stations, townships, roads, transmission lines and other infrastructure (Sharma, Suresh 1985).

Giving an illiterate tribal "oustee" or backwoodsman "market" value for lands in remote interiors, where a rare or random land sale can scarcely be regarded as indicative of a market price, can itself be unjust. Offering a market price related to sale values in a neighbouring command area may not also be wholly satisfactory in all cases as recorded sales are often undervalued in order to save on registration fees and stamp duty. However any money will seem big money to an impoverished villager largely accustomed to a subsistence-barter level of living. And there are liquor contractors, tradesmen and touts of all descriptions waiting to sell their wares and relieve him of his money through every kind of enticement. So compensation may well be paid in a fashion, with little to show by way of rehabilitation. Or land and a dwelling may be provided to displaced families but not the supporting infrastructure that would enable them to settle into their new surroundings. Communities may be scattered and separated from their kith and kin and transplanted into a very different, strange or even hostile milieu where they might feel rejected and alone. Cultural genocide or ethnocide may be excessively strong words to describe such situations, but they do convey something of the human tragedy that displacement may entail. This must not be allowed to recur. However, the fact is that this has happened not merely in the case of dams or water resource projects but in respect of the development process generally.

The word "rehabilitate" in its pristine sense means to invest with dignity. This is a noble and humane concept and it is to this high purpose that we must return. Whether land has been acquired for steel plants, mines, ports, new townships, railway systems, dams, irrigation works or any other public purpose, there has been little rehabilitation in its truest sense.

In Bangladesh, there was a similar failure in the sixties to treat with adequate consideration the tribal Chakmas and others displaced by the Kaptai Dam on the Kamaphuli river in the Chittagong Hill Tract. This, coupled with a policy of settling "outsiders" in the region during the seventies, sowed the seeds of what has grown into the present Chakma insurgency (Zaman, January 1982). If in India every project entailing substantial land acquisition, whether for a dam (Koel Karo in Bihar) or a missile range (Baliapal in coastal Orissa) or a mine (Gandhamardan, again in Orissa), tends to degenerate into a wrangle if not a law and order problem at the very inception, it is all least partly because off ears about rehabilitation.

FALLACY OF LAND FOR LAND

Rehabilitation has in respect of water resource development projects come to imply replacement of a dwelling place and, in the case of agriculturists, the grant of land for land, preferably in the command area (if an irrigation scheme) or in the vicinity of the acquired properties. That displaced persons should be rehabilitated in their chosen livelihoods as far as possible as understandable. Where land is available, even landless agricultural labour has been promised and given land on relocation. While this may be a viable policy in certain areas or to a certain extent, any firm or binding commitment to give land for land is unwise and impracticable and could and, indeed, has aroused expectations that may not be easily fulfilled if at all. The Narmada Water Disputes Tribunal Award, 1978, contains a chapter on "Directions to Madhya Pradesh, Gujarat and Maharashtra as Regards Submergence, Land Acquisition and Rehabilitation of Displaced Persons". This too uses the unfortunate term "oustee families" and provides that "every displaced family from whom more than 25 per cent of its land holding is acquired shall be entitled to and be allotted irrigable land to the extent of land acquired from it subject to the prescribed ceiling in the State concerned and a minimum of two hectares (five acres) per family ... Of the price to be paid for the land a sum equal to 50 per cent of the compensation payable to the oustee family for the land acquired from it will be set off as an initial instalment of payment. The balance cost of the allotted land shall be recovered from the allottee in 20 yearly instalments free of interest."

The principle of land for land on the Maharashtra and Gujarat models is now being repeated everywhere. As a refinement, some would seek not just land for land but "soil for soil" in terms of quality. This again is prima facie entirely reasonable except for the fact that there is insufficient land to go around as it is and holdings are rapidly diminishing in size with the passing of every generation as sons partition their inheritance. This has resulted in fragmentation and uneconomic holdings. There is already an army of landless in every part of the country and marginal to small farms are the norm. hence to promise land for land to "outsiders" at the relocation site is to invite trouble. If some landholders in the host area are willing to sell their lands then it may be possible to form a land pool for distribution to the displaced persons. This has been done in some cases. But the amount of land that may become available in this manner is likely to be limited and will most often be in scattered holdings in widely separated villages which would mean resettling the displaced persons in a dispersed fashion among envious, hostile or indifferent strangers which would militate against the social and cultural norm of group rehabilitation. *The Times of India* reported on August 14, 1984, that five persons were killed in police firing in Sabarkantha district in Gujarat "when people from three villages adjoining Tarudi (village) attacked the police party which had gone there for supervising the land allotment process to some displaced villages." The incident has a moral that it would be unwise to forget.

Village common lands have already been rashly distributed by State governments, increasing pressure on the remaining commons and the neighbouring forests to the common detriment. Persons likely to be displaced by the Tehri Dam in Garhwal have ben allotted land and resettlement sites in the Doon Valley after clear-felling hundreds of hectares of beautiful sal forest in what can only be described as an act of sheer official vandalism in fulfillment of a populist political promise rashly made earlier. In November 1983 the Union Ministry of Agriculture placed a complete ban on release for land is not a sound policy and should not be routinely pursued although it might offer a partial option in some cases.

THE NARMADA AND TEHRI PACKAGES

However, following Gujarat's lead in respect of the Sardar Sarovar project, Madhya Pradesh has adopted legislation for compulsory acquisition of land for rehabilitating displaced persons in the "benefited area" on the lines of the Maharashtra Act of 1977. The Madhya Pradesh Act provides that restrictions will be placed on the transfer, sub-division or partition of land in the benefited zone. Efforts will be made to purchase land for resettlement of displaced persons by agreement. Should this not succeed, land for resettlement will be acquired under the Land Acquisition Act and placed in a land pool in the command area (Varma, S.C. July 1985A). The Maharashtra government had been able to acquire no more than 1946 hectares of land in eight years up to 1985. The Act has since been challenged in the High Court and the decision cold be taken to the Supreme Court in appeal. The Madhya Pradesh Government hopes that on account of its ceiling on holdings, placed at 22 hectares of dry land or 7.28 hectares of irrigated land, many landholders will have to part with their excess lands once irrigation commences in the Narmada command. But actual experience in the neighbouring Tawa command shows that "much before public irrigation is introduced, the owners manage to parcel out their holdings to others in such a way that hardly any land remains to be taken over under the ceiling law" (Ibid).

Displaced persons may be willing to accept allotments in the drawdown area along the upper contours of the submergence zone as the reservoir progressively recedes with the onset of the dry season. Tank-bed farming is lucrative and widely practiced. Opportunities for drawdown cultivation may be limited in the narrow and steeper Himalayan Valleys but is a distinct possibility in Middle India and Bangladesh. The DVC has permitted what it calls reservoir foreshore farming with encouraging results. Foreshore farming is also practiced in the Chambal reservoirs between December and June. Some 6000 hectares of public land and additional areas of private land are estimated as likely to be available for drawdown farming around the Narmadasagar reservoir with irrigation provided through simple lift schemes. Since 64 of the Madhya Pradesh Irrigation Act regulates drawdown farming. Allotment of such rights would obviate some displacement. But displacement there will be.

The provisions made for rehabilitation and settlement of displaced persons in Madhya Pradesh is elaborately described by S.C. Varma, former Chairman of the Narmada Valley Development Authority who resigned his office as he felt that the State administration was disciplined to honour some of the rehabilitation commitments made by the Project authorities. These by and large follow the award of the Narmada Water Disputes Tribunal which stipulated Gujarat's obligations towards those displaced by the Sardar Sarovar which submerges areas in M.P. and Maharashtra as well. These include a resettlement grant and a grant-in-aid to each family and civil amenities of a certain standard at the rate of one primary school per 100 families; a panchayat ghar, seed store, children's park and village pond per 500 families; a drinking water well with trough for every 50 families; an approach road and a platform or meeting place around a tree for every 50 families; a place of worship per 100 families; and power lines and street lights at the rate of two kilometres per 100 families. Certain norms were also prescribed for the provision of social amenities for townships. Each family is entitled to a free house site measuring just over 18 x 27 metres (and 100-150 square metres in the case of Narmadasagar). The work of rehabilitation in Madhya Pradesh is being supervised by committees at the divisional, district and sub-divisional level with representation for displaced families, officials, MPs and MLAs, panchayati officials and NGOs. The interests of women and disadvantaged groups is to be specially protected. Compensation is to be given three years before submergence, with a transportation allowance for movement to the new site. In calculating compensation for land that may be submerged, the price of similar land in the command area will be taken as the basis.

The Tehri project will displace 46,000 persons, 12,000 of them from Tehri town which is being rebuilt some distance away on a higher ridge in consultation with the townsfolk. The Tehri reservoir will submerge 23 villages completely and 72 villages partially according to official figures. Compensation for the land acquired is being paid overall at the rate of Rs. 43,000 per acre – Rs.1.06 lakhs if irrigated, and Rs.51,890 and Rs.35,335 per hectare for Class I and Class II unirrigated lands, respectively. If a family prefers cash compensation it will receive Rs.40,000. Each displaced family is entitled to Rs.1000 as a displacement grant and a like sum for movement. Those opting for land for rehabilitation are being given a minimum of 0.81 hectares in lieu of their existing holdings in the Doon Valley or Saharanpur district. The new sites are being provided with irrigation, drinking water, electricity, roads, dispensaries, schools, post offices and panchayat ghars. As far as possible entire villages are being relocated collectively at a single site so as to minimize any social or cultural deprivation. Cement, steel and other building materials are being provided at the new sites at controlled prices for construction of houses. By the end of 1986 over 1200 families had been resettled at the new sites. Even so some of them continue to cultivate their old fields as well since submergence is yet some years away.

PROPOSED KOEL KARO FORMULA

The Koel Karo hydel project in south Bihar (710 MW) has been stalled for over 16 years since the detailed project report was first prepared and sanctioned. The project was initiated by the State authorities but was taken over by the National Hydro-electric Power Corporation in 1980 with a sanctioned estimate of Rs.390 crores. A population of some 25,000 persons, 70 per cent of them Scheduled Tribes and Castes, in 42 villages will be totally affected. This population is not unduly worried about environmental considerations nor does it now seek land for land. It is more concerned about the quantum and mode of compensation and resettlement. Tribal sentiment was deeply hurt by the callous displacement of considerable numbers with the acquisition of 24,000-28,000 hectares of land in Ranchi. Recalling this, hostile tribals gathered at the dam site to hold off project personnel and successfully prevented any activity. The Jan Sangharsh Samiti that was formed petitioned the Supreme Court in 1984 and obtained a stay order. The Directorate of Land Acquisition and Rehabilitation of the Koel Karo Project has meanwhile prepared a rehabilitation plan after close consultation with the tribal population and the Sangharsh Samiti. This has reportedly found wide acceptance (October 1986).

The new philosophy is based on "total rehabilitation" that ensures a life at least as satisfying if not more so than before. The concept is defined to include economic and occupational as well as social and cultural rehabilitation and satisfactory integration in the new settlement. Since land is all but non-transferable under the Chota Nagpur Tenancy Act, except with the permission of the District Commissioner, there is no true market price. Land values are therefore proposed to be determined by capitalizing the net yield from the land over 15 years which would give a compensation ranging from just under Rs.80,000 per hectare for the best land to Rs.15,815 per hectare for fallow land, at 1985-86 prices. Additional compensation is payable for fruit and other trees, wells, tanks, structures or facilities and, of course, for houses, including the cost of labour computed at official minimum wages. Since compensation is estimated to be not less than Rs.1.5 lakhs per family, and knowing that the tribals are unaccustomed to handling such large sums of money which would be easily squandered or swindled, the compensation amount is to be placed in fixed deposits with banks or in national savings bonds. A plan of investment is to be drawn up for each beneficiary by the Directorate of Rehabilitation subject to approval by an advisory board.

In not a few cases, compensation may yield a monthly interest income of Rs 6,000-12,000. Each family will therefore be paid a monthly sum to meet all living and other expenses while the balance will be ploughed back into approved investments that will give the family a steady lifetime income. Deposits may not be withdrawn without the approval of the District Commissioner who will need to be shown a convincing investment plan. Land prices will be frozen so that those wishing to purchase land may do so at reasonable rates. The Patna High Court is to be requested to set up a special court as near the project as possible to hear land acquisition cases pertaining to Koel Karo.

More than the monetary compensation, the rehabilitation scheme emphasizes education, training and skill formation so that each displaced family is able to take up some gainful occupation or self-employment with provision of raw material, tools of trade and marketing arrangements. Special attention is to be paid to the needs of women. Roughly 4,000 hectares of land out of the 14,000 hectares submerged will be available for drawdown cultivation for six to eight months. Preference in allocation will be given to landless tribals and others liable to receive less compensation. While efforts are to be made to provide a job to a member of each family in the project or in the local or state administration or elsewhere, training will be provided to set up tribal families in vegetable and fruit farming, animal husbandry, trade and small industries, or in the service sector such as in the transport business. An industrial estate is to be set up in the project area to stimulate industrialization in the region. The two large reservoirs formed behind the Koel and Karo dams will provide opportunities for fish culture and tourism.

A special organization is proposed to be set up to manage the rehabilitation and compensation programme with a degree of decentralization and popular participation at various levels. There will be special cells for each activity and a public grievance cell. Village committees will select and approve each new village location, site plan and its development. Voluntary agencies and local institutions are to be closely involved and two respected tribal leaders of the area are to be appointed permanent advisers with an honorarium and a vehicle so that they are mobile and can maintain close contact with the settlement sites and programmes.

The host populations are also to be associated with the rehabilitation programme and will benefit from the provision of various social amenities. Each displaced family will get a residential plot of 0.25 acres and will receive up to Rs.15,000 with materials, and wages for its own labour input in constructing its dwellings. A tree plantation programme is proposed around each settlement site. The old village names will be retained and kinship groups will be settled together. The Sarna or sal groves in which each *gotra* or "*killi's*" forest goddess is enshrined will be re-created at each new site and the spirit will be invoked with traditional rites. Likewise the Sasandiri or abode of departed ancestors in each village and the bones of the dead will be ceremonially transferred. All other places of worship will also be rebuilt in the new sites. This consideration for cultural continuity and tribal and religious sentiment is important.

The Koel Karo rehabilitation and compensation plan has been explained to the tribal leaders and others affected and there is said to be a broad consensus on its acceptance. The compensation payable and the rehabilitation plan is expected to cost Rs 127 crores (as against the Rs 12 crores initially provided). This amount has been built into the overall project estimate which has been cleared by the CEA at a revised figure of Rs 1,037 crores following considerable escalation in the cost of materials and wage rates since 1980. The Supreme Court has vacated the stay order on an assurance that the revised compensation and the rehabilitation plan will be honoured. The cost of Koel Karo power is now likely to be about Rs 1.60 per unit which will still be economic for a peaking station. However, an investment decision has been held up pending environmental clearance which has in turn been linked to preparation and approval of a total catchment area conservation plan!

WHO IS ELIGIBLE?

Figures of those affected are often disputed by non-official observers. All manner of interlopers seek inclusion. This apart, definitions of the "affected" vary. Vasudha Dhagamwar's critique of current rehabilitation, resettlement and compensation policy with special reference to the Narmadasagar project in Madhya Pradesh has wide applications (April 1988). She notes that generally for every project compensation awards and rehabilitation plans are made piecemeal. Madhya Pradesh and Maharashtra however do have Acts. The character of the affected population – poor, illiterate, tribal – is not adequately taken into account. People are not adequately informed and consultation may be little more than notional, if at all, eligible for compensation. Others such as landless, traders, artisans, women, cowherds, nomads who depend on common property resources and so on are not compensated for loss of livelihood but only for loss of houses.

Little consideration is given to the emotional trauma suffered by the affected population. The concept of "displacement" is also limited to physical movement. "In fact displacement begins when its possibility is mentioned and ends only when people are integrated in their new homes". Again, the reference to displaced persons should extend to a broader category of "project-affected persons" who lose their employment, markets, kinship groups and so on. Cash compensation does not secure rehabilitation as "money disappears like water in a sieve". Nor is land for land a viable policy in all cases as the experience of the Pong Dam and Ukai project indicate. Tribal people want rehabilitation in groups or clusters near forests with access to their kinsfolk. Many of these problems might be mitigated or overcome if, apart from timely information and consultation, there is actual participation of project-affected persons in planning their future resettlement. Education and technical training and a job per family would be more appropriate in many cases. All this is more likely to be achieved if rehabilitation is entrusted to a separate agency or permanent department of government and if the entire process is planning in detail as part of the original project.

A survey pertaining to the Sardar Sarovar project cites instances of encumbered private lands being allotted to displaced persons and cases of land costs and titles awaiting finalization even after three to six years. In other instances, high costs of land development have put the settlers in debt. There have also been delays in providing the promised or necessary community amenities (Medha Patkar, December 1987).

In yet another critique, Enakshi Ganguly Thukral (1988) comments that the history of rehabilitation in India shows that what starts as a fight for just compensation soon becomes a prolonged struggle for survival with displaced persons moving from a state of poverty to pauperization – this being her assessment of rehabilitation processes in the case of the Hirakud, Rihand, Pong-Bhakra and Ukai-Kakrapar "oustees".

A second report on resettlement of persons displaced by the Srisailam dam across the Krishna in Andhra Pradesh refers to payment of commissions and bribes from out of the compensation received. It speaks of good housing and amenities but a sharp decline in income and work, difficulties in finding fuel and fodder, and problems for special categories like toddy tappers and fishermen. The study recommends that the statutory 30 per cent solatium paid for involuntary resettlement is reasonable but the limits should be raised to range between Rs 5,000 and Rs 1 lakh. It notes that 20,137 cases have been filed in the district courts challenging the quantum of compensation. Of the 3,358 cases decided, not one has gone in favour of the government which has been asked to pay significantly larger amounts by way of compensation (Chowdry, K.H. et al., 1985).

SETTING NORMS

The World Bank has laid down certain norms in the form of an operational manual pertaining to social issues associated with involuntary resettlement in projects financed by it. The Bank's approach is to ensure that the displaced persons are at least enabled to regain their previous standard of living and that they are as far as possible socially and economically integrated into the host communities. The Bank now insists that planning and financing resettlement should be an integral part of the project since there is growing recognition that those to be relocated feel powerless and alienated when uprooted from familiar surroundings which could result in the disruption of community structures and social networks and a weakening of social cohesion. At the same time care should be taken to avoid paternalism and "the syndrome of settler dependency" leading to a feeling of having become "permanent wards of the state". Likely hostility of resettlement on the part of the host community must be overcome through consultation and provision of equal benefits so that the settlers do not appear to be privileged and pampered community. The Bank guidelines include a special section on tribal populations who must be given time and appropriate conditions for acculturation in their new surroundings.

The Home Ministry in Delhi has also set out guidelines for the rehabilitation of tribal people who may need to be resettled. It is emphasized that displaced tribals must be resettled as a community and not as individuals. If land cannot be provided then employment must be guaranteed to at least one member of every family after whatever education and retraining might be necessary.

Not all States have legislation governing resettlement on the lines of the Madhya Pradesh Rehabilitation Act, 1985. In the case of many projects, such as the Tehri Dam, rehabilitation is governed by executive orders. A statutory basis has some advantage in being generally applicable and justiciable and not the subject of a project by project bargain. But there must be room for flexibility in view of rapidly changing circumstances, unexpected contingencies, and the need to learn from experience.

One important aspect that should not be overlooked is the long gestation period associated with river valley projects even prior to their sanction. Inter-state river disputes have aggravated this problem as in the case of the Narmada project with the result that Sardar Sarovar and Narmadasagar have been on the anvil for over a generation. The very announcement that a dam is contemplated or a visit by surveyors sends out a signal of doom to those who may be in the submergence area. Such is the psychological shock that few new investments and improvements are undertaken while there may actually be some disinvestment. Such attitudes are reinforced by a policy of studied neglect of the area by the State and local authorities as even normal repair and maintenance, let alone fresh development, is likely to be soon overtaken by submergence. Such a situation has been known to engender stagnation and regression which is hurtful to the local population.

Writing about the Narmada dams, one study notes that "development activities in the entire submergence area have been delayed because of this (30 year) uncertainty. While there is a ginning unit in Harsud (M.P.) both the baling unit and a unit for the extraction of oil from cottonseed have been located at Khandwa. Private investors of capital have not been keen to risk their investment. Banks have not been enthusiastic about giving loans under the plea that immovable assets will be submerged. In the villages, roads and infrastructure have also suffered in the face of the same inexorable logic. In town and village, construction activities have come to a halt, evidenced by a number of unfinished house. One direct consequence of this has been that local masons are on the verge of starvation…." (Environmental Service Group, World Wildlife Fund-India, September 1986).

C. Upper Catchment Area Development

If the best features of the Koel Karo, Narmada and Tehri rehabilitation plans are taken as a norm then a displaced person will no more be an "oustee" but a well cared for citizen with renewed hope and opportunity. He will indeed be "invested with dignity". As such, rehabilitation programmes could become triggers for area development and poverty alleviation and should be so regarded. Whole area or regional rehabilitation programmes, whatever the cause of displacement, could be integrated into mutually supporting overall rehabilitation plans. Given a rolling 10 to 15 years perspective plan as a development norm, with advance planning for the location of industry and infrastructure around growth centres along transport corridors, it should be possible to anticipate displacement to some degree and prepare long range programmes of development into which rehabilitation schemes could be fitted. The present unplanned and ad hoc manner of dealing with rehabilitation must end.

Indeed, water resource development should increasingly be based on larger basin plans and an integrated view taken of soil conservation, reforestation and watershed management as well as of rehabilitation. In fact, there is no reason why rehabilitation should not dovetail into the former activities. Watershed management to arrest ecological degradation caused by any form of human intervention is necessary whether or not a dam comes up in a particular valley. Should a dam be proposed then prior watershed management will be an essential or useful pre-investment. On this understanding, indicative basin plans with upper catchment components should be prepared as a guide to development. Anticipatory rehabilitations should indirectly or more obviously commence with the initial decision to build a dam or project and be complete by the time submergence, land acquisition or displacement takes place. The very gestation period entailed in the planning and construction of a medium or major dam might range from six to 12 or 15 years. This offers ample opportunity for education and retraining of would-be-displaced persons, especially youth, and for developing alternative forms of employment and land use in situ that benefit the project to follow while improving the lives of the local population. This would also get over the feeling that upper catchment populations, upstream of dams, are only and always condemned to submergence and displacement while all the benefits of electricity, flood control, irrigation and related employment go downstream communities. There must be equity not only between people but between communities and regions.

This is not a utopian idea but can be realized through the establishment at the very inception of large water resource projects of upper catchment authorities (UCAs), in the manner of command area development authorities (CADAs). These bodies could be separate organizations, with their own funds, personnel and a clear charter, with statutory backing if necessary, to achieve their objectives. Why should not every major dam have an upper catchment authority charged with responsibility for soil conservation, watershed management and compensatory afforestation as well as rehabilitation. This is not a task to be left to overburdened chief engineers but requires a very different and dedicated agency with a mandate and the wherewithal to deliver the goods. Nor need the mandate be limited to upper catchment conservation and rehabilitation. It should extend to developing alternative sources of fuel and fodder; promoting stall feeding of animals and hill dairying; horticulture and the processing and marketing of fruit, vegetables, medicinal plants, herbal extracts and minor forest products; floriculture; developing and other alternative sources of energy (and hill irrigation), fostering appropriate industrialization; constructing ropeways; developing pisciculture in the reservoirs formed behind dams; promoting tourism; and undertaking manpower training. These would then become avenues of rehabilitation even without being thought of as such and would generate a quantum and quantity of employment that would not merely arrest the present out-migration from the hills but possibly facilitate a reverse movement from the plains.

UPPER GANGA CONSERVATION PLAN

The Tehri project has a provision of Rs.35 crores for soil conservation and afforestation and about Rs.175-200 crores for rehabilitation and compensation. But why consider Tehri-Koteshwar in isolation when there are a whole series of projects either already completed or under construction or under investigation in the upper Ganga above Rishikesh along the Bhagirathi, Alaknanda and their tributaries. The Upper Ganga Valley comprises an area of 21,373 square kilometres, over 30 per cent of it under perpetual snow, with a population (1981) of 1.32 million and 1.12 million head of cattle. At least 18 hydel projects are envisaged in all with an installed capacity of 8000 MW at a cost of Rs.8010 crores (plus Tehri-II) at 1985 prices. Recognizing the need for an integrated basin plan, the former Tehri Dam Organisation itself some years ago drew up an overall plan for catchment area development of the entire valley above Rishikesh embracing forestry, agriculture, horticulture, minor irrigation, soil conservation and animal husbandry at a cost of Rs.305 crores (August 1986). It is proposed the constitution of a separate catchment area authority, a multi-disciplinary organisation under the Department ofEnvionment. For funding it proposed a levy of 1.5 per cent of the total cost of all water resource projects in the Upper Ganga which would yield Rs.121 crores (less Tehri-II), the balance coming from the concerned Departments of the State Government under the hill areas development programme. No rehabilitation component was included.

The blueprint divided the Upper Ganga Catchment into eight watersheds, namely, the Bhagirathi, Bhilangana, Alaknanda, Pindar, Mandakini, Lower Alaknanda, Nayar and the catchments of other streams directly flowing into the Ganga. Priorities were assigned, starting with the upper Bhagirathi-Bhilangana catchmens, immediately relevant to the Tehri project, followed by the Alaknanda catchment as the Srinagar hydel project (200 MW) has also been taken up for construction. Overall, some 100 square kilometres were proposed to be forested (including planting of blanks) and another 500 square kilometres brought under fodder. Some 200 square kilometres were also proposed to be planted to fruit trees and 950 square kilometres brought under vegetables.

The scope of the proposal needs to be widened to include planning for energy, communications, industry, health, education and training, and to build in mechanisms of community participation and involvement of local institutions and voluntary agencies. There is surely a role here for Chipko groups, such as that under Chandi Prasad Bhatt which is already engaged in a watershed management project in the Alaknanda Valley. Cost reduction would be possible if some of the proposed conservation and afforestation were executed through food-for-work, with part of the additional grain production in the U.P. plains from irrigation provided by Upper Ganga storages being returned to the Hills. Grain could also be given to hill farmers willing to restore marginal crop lands on steeper slopes to tree crops or grass at a rate equivalent to their estimated loss of production over a period of say three to five years by when their new land use should have begun to yield an income.

Such a plan with food-for-work would entail building small grain storages in each valley or at nodal hamlets to ensure assured access to supplies during the monsoon or winter when landslides and snow drifts can cut off while areas. The existing eco-development battalion deployed in the Mussoorie Hills could be the model for establishing more varied eco-development brigades of ex-servicemen from the Garhwal (and Kumaon) Regiments. A certain fraction of the firm power produced by each hydel project should also be committed in kind or in value to the to the upper catchment through cross-subsidies so as to electrify the Hills through mainline or mini-hydel sources and provide cheap energy for agro-processing, industry and ropeways.

According to an expertestimate, it would be practical to aim at reforesting or regeneration 10,000 hectares of Himalayan terrain annually. The cost may be around Rs.1700 per hectare and the employment potential would be one man-year per hectare for the first five years and one man-year per five hectares thereafter. The raising of seedlings by the local community would generate employment and save on costs. The species planted would depend among other things on the soil, altitude and aspect. The employment potential in reforesting 1000 square kilometres or 100,000 hectares under the proposed Upper Ganga Catchment plan would therefore be considerable, even on a permanent basis.

An investment of Rs.305 crores or more over 20 years would entail an annual burden of no more than Rs.15-20 crores, though disbursements would follow programme requirements. But some income and revenue returns would accrue after five to eight years so that the actual net outgo would be smaller. A programme of this kind would take care of rehabilitation through regeneration of the Hill region would provide in situ or local employment and obviate the trauma of long distance displacement or the need to hold out unrealistic promises of land for land. Area development offers scope for creating a variety of off-farm employment. Upper catchment area plans would transform backward and neglected regions. Far from destroying the Hills, dams might well be their salvation.

The Tehri Dam Organisation forwarded its Rs.305 crores Upper Ganga catchment area conservation plan in 1986 to the U.P. Government which has since approved it in principle. The plan allocates Rs.138 crores to the Bhagirathi-Bhilangana valley in which the Tehri complex (incuding the Koteshwar dam) is located and the balance of Rs.167 crores to the Alaknanda Valley and the area between Devprayag, where the Bhagirathi and Alaknanda meet to form the Ganga and Rishikesh. The CWC however has only approved Rs.35 crores for soil conservation under the Tehri Dam project on the ground that the balance of Rs.113 crores allocated to the Bhagirathi-Bhilangana Valley should be debited to other hydel projects in that same Valley and to other sectoral departments such as agriculture, forestry and so on. However, at the insistence of the Union Ministry of Environment that there must be a specific authority to implement the Tehri soil conservation programme if the Tehri project was to get environmental clearance, the U.P. Government constituted a Bhagirathi-Bhilangana Valley Authority. With the Centre having agreed to co-finance the Tehri project to the extent of 75 per cent, a Centre-State joint venture, the Tehri Hydro Development Corporation Ltd., was subsequently incorporated in July 1988. its jurisdiction extends to the Tehri Dam and Power Stations I and II and the Koteshwar Dam, and a 765 kv HVDC transmission line from Tehri to Meerut at a total cost (including catchment and treatment, rehabilitation and transmission) of about Rs.2700 crores. The Memorandum of Association charges the Corporation with responsibility for the investigation, design, construction, operation and management of dams and transmission systems in the Bhagirathi-Bhilangana Valley as may be entrusted to it by the State Government, along with environmental protection, afforestation and rehabilitation works. The Corporation's mandate has since been widened to include construction of the Vishnuprayag project (400 MW) in the upper Alaknanda valley. At present, on-going works on Maneri Bhali-II (above Tehri) and the Srinagar project (on the Alaknanda) are being carried out by the U.P. Government

The relationship between the Bhagirathi-Bhilangana Valley Authority (headed by the State's Chief Secretary) and the Corporation have yet to be defined, as also that between the Corporation and the existing Tehri Control Board of which the U.P. Chief Minister is chairman. Any dichotomy can only cause duplication and confusion. There would be some merit in the Corporation undertaking soil conservation and catchment area treatment, compensatory afforestation and rehabilitation, which it is in any case required to fund (the first element only to a limited degree), and integrating this into its programme. But the concept of a larger upper catchment area development programme into which rehabilitation (currently under the Commissioner Garhwal Division acting under Government orders) and catchment conservation would mesh, is probably better implemented by a separate upper catchment authority set up by the State Government, with appropriate representation for the Corporation, as so many sectors and Departments of Government are involved.

The Naptha-Jhakri and Kol hydro projects on the Sutlej, above Bhakra, have been similarly entrusted to the Naptha-Jhakri Corporation, a joint venture in which the Centre and the Himachal Pradesh are partners. This Corporation is independent of the Bhakra-Beas Management Board.

D. Forest Loss and Bio-diversity

The loss of forests to submergence behind dams has sometimes aroused even greater passion than the displacement of population. Certainly, there is a loss of some forest in upper catchments. But in not a few cases, the forests may already be sparse or degraded on account of other factors, or the loss may be relatively small or even minute in relation to the total area under forest in the region or the catchment itself.

As noted earlier, more forests have been lost and are being lost for reasons of poverty than on account of dams or even development generally. And unless development is accelerated to keep ahead of and, in time, decelerate population growth, the devastation of forests over the next three or four decades will be even greater than before. Those who wish to save forests must therefore aid the process of development (though certainly the right kind of development) and not get lost in utopian nostalgia. The notion that most catchment area forests are pristine is a gross exaggeration. There are very few forests within the Basin that have not been jhummed, fired or otherwise felled. Many have regenerated. Even newer plantations of monocultures will, if left alone, attract mixed species over time and become "natural" if situated near a mixed forest. Other species can also be introduced by planting. In most of the Central Himalaya, regeneration in the mid-hills will tend to yield chir pine in the first succession with broadleaved species following later in favourable circumstances.

Bio-diversity could well diminish though it need not be lost as few species are endemic to finite submergence areas. Silent Valley in Kerala comes closest to a climax tropical rain forest in India and was saved from submergence in the 1970s when popular protest resulted in the shelving of a proposed hydro project. Barring some very rare pockets in the southern reaches of the Western Ghats and in the eastern Himalaya, Silent Valleys are not to be found everywhere except in population imagination. The Botanical Survey of India is called on to survey submergence areas before river valley projects are taken up so that rare and endemic species, if any, can be identified and sought to be preserved in biosphere reserves or gene-banks. The BSI has undertaken a number of such pre-project surveys, the Tehri and Narmada inundation areas being among them.

It is now a national requirement under the Forest Conservation Act in India that any project entailing loss of forests must undertake compensatory afforestation of an equivalent area in an adjacent area if possible, or elsewhere if necessary to the extent of double the area submerged or felled. It is true that compensatory afforestation cannot fill the ecological niche that it is intended physically to replace. But, barring the most exceptional cases, this must be accepted and cannot be described as an irreparable loss. There may be often be no degraded or waste land or forest blanks near a submergence site for compensatory afforestation, necessitating such replacement to be undertaken at a more distant site. About 2583 hectares of forest land has been or will be taken for the Tehri project. To make good the loss, the Tehri Dam authorities have acquired and transferred to the U.P. Forest Department 4595 hectares of non-forest land in Lalitpur and Jhansi districts, 500 kilometres away. These forests will not green the Himalaya, but they are not to be despised for that reason as Bundelkhand is as much in need of greening and the benefit will be to Uttar Pradesh in either case and to the country. This compensatory afforestation scheme is estimated to cost Rs.5.67 crores which will be defrayed by the Tehri project.

At Koel Karo, 870 hectares of forest are likely to be lost. The NHPC is to deposit Rs.56 lakhs with the Bihar Forest Department for undertaking compensatory afforestation in the same general area on non-forest land.

The Sardar Sarcvar reservoir will submerge 2732 hectares of forest land in Madhya Pradesh and the Narmadasagar dam a further 40,332 hectares. Against forest loss of 44,000 hectares, a plan to reforest an area of 97,000 hectares has been proposed at a cost of Rs.162 crores at Rs.15,000 per hectare over 12 years (Revised Action Plan, December 1986).

In the Chamera hydel project in Himachal, as against 40,000 trees to be lost, the project authorities plan to plant 2.3 million trees within the same general area. The environmentally-stalled Bodhghat hydel project on the Indravati, a tributary of the Godavari, in Bastar, Madhya Pradesh, will submerge 5704 hectares of sal forest as against which 11,000 hectares are to be afforested. Some 1000 hectares had already been planted in 1988.

There was at one time controversy over the valuation of forests by the Ministry of Environment and Forests which, following what is said to be an FAO norm, and estimated the ecological value of a hectare of forest with a density of one (i.e. total forest cover with a complete crown canopy) to be of the order of Rs.126 lakhs over a 50 year period, or Rs.2.52 lakhs per annum. If this yardstick is applied in calculating project costs in relation to forest loss (Rs.30,923 crores for Narmadasagar) the results are likely to be distorted. Closed forests under Forest Survey of India norms have a crown cover of 40 per cent or more. Reduced by this factor, the "value" of good forests might be placed at Rs.50 lakhs and a degraded forest at half that figure. This works out to Rs.1 lakh to Rs.50,000 per annum. If compensatory afforestation is undertaken in double the area of forest submerged or acquired then this ecological "loss" might be recouped in five to ten years, depending on the species, and the new forest may be twice as "vulnerable" as the original forest in double that period. These calculations are misleading. So is the theorem, as the esoteric norms prescribed can be assumed only in a purely notional sense. And how is one to calculate the likely forest "savings" from incremental substitution of non-commercial with commercial energy as a result of income and employment generation triggered by irrigation or hydel development? And who will count the additional trees growing today along the Rajasthan Canal and in its command and estimate, the ecological "credit" to be attributed to the Bhakra Dam. These are exercises in futility. Logic pushed beyond a point is sometimes reduced to absurdity.

The Dihang and Subansiri reservoirs will have a combined spread of 683 square kilometre should those two dams be built. Three-quarters of this area is forested. In relation to Arunachal's 51,500 square kilometres of forest area the forest loss from submergence behind these two dams would constitute a little over one per cent of the total forest in the State. Other things being equal, would this be a disaster? Surely not – not in relation to the gains. However, the two projects also propose compensatory afforestation and replacement of jhum cultivation with tree farming.

The influx of large numbers of construction labour at dam sites has often been cited as being responsible for despoiling the forests for fuel and other purposes and for introducing diseases hitherto unknown to these areas. These matters certainly require attention and can be taken care of with some little planning and foresight.

E. Impact on Fauna and Flora

The impact of submergence and forest clearance will necessarily vary from case to case. Environmental impact studies are now mandatory and the services of expert bodies like the Zoological and Botanical Surveys of India and the Wildlife Institute of India, Dehra Dun, are being availed of for assessing the consequences and advising on ameliorative measures. Forest corridors need to be provided to enable wildlife to migrate to other areas so that loss or dimunition of habitat has little or no adverse effect. In other circumstances it may be necessary to remove animals, especially rare or endangered species, to parks and sanctuaries, or to relocate them if possible, may be in areas of compensatory afforestation.

The regional circles of the Botanical Survey of India similarly undertake ecological impact studies in respect of various developmental projects and report on their vegetational and floristic status. Such studies were submitted on the Teesta Valley hydro-electric project in West Bengal and Sikkim, the Dhaleshwari hydel project in Mizoram and other projects in UP, Madhya Pradesh and elsewhere during 1986-87. Floral surveys have been made of the upper and lower Subansiri, of

Arunachal and Nagaland and of Jammu and Kashmir, with parties visiting hitherto botanically unexplored areas.

Typical of a botanical environmental assessment is the one done by the Botanical Survey of the Tehri Dam (October 1982). The report notes that "the vegetation in the area under direct impact is rather scantly and mostly dominated by dry sub-tropical to temperature shrubby components including a few exotics. Due to various biotic factors and land utilization practices operating in this region since long, the natural vegetation is considerably altered at many places in the lower valleys .. A large number of exotic invaders have secured a permanent footing … (and) many broad-leaved species are being constantly lopped for fodder". Again: "The surrounding mountains overlooking the large reservoir are mostly devoid of natural forest vegetation and much disturbed due to constant biotic interference". Then, "few rare and economically interesting species in the area have been located which are going to be lost in the inundated reservoir…The total number of trees to be engulfed by the reservoir is estimated to be more than one thousand (sc)…". Further "about 64 species of economic and medicinal importance could be located in the submersible area, which of course have wide distribution in the Himalaya and no special conservation is immediately required. However, about 12 rare and threatened species which are likely to be disturbed by the inundation have been indicated in the enumeration list (of 462 plants under 99 families) and their preservation in other localities of the Himalaya needs special consideration".

F. Sedimentation and the Life of Dams

Sedimentation, whether on account of natural or manmade factors, is inevitable in some degree and all storages provide for a certain amount of "dead storage" within which silt will accumulate over the life of a dam. This is generally assumed to be 100 years in India for hydel projects under the Seventh Schedule of the Electricity Act of 1948. Dead storage is notionally provided along the deepest contours of the reservoir which would invariably be that portion nearest the base of the dam and extending back along a flat plain. In point of fact, silt is not deposited evenly or necessarily sequentially, contour by contour from the base of the dam. Different grades of sediment get deposited at different locations. More often that not, the slope of the river above the dam suddenly levels at the point of commencement of the lake and heavier sediment is deposited at the upper fringe of the reservoir in a delta formation, with ridges lowering into the depths. Subsequent distribution may be affected by floods, tributary flows into the reservoir, such flushing action as may be possible by reservoir operations, and so forth. Dredging is not a viable option except in marginal cases as it would be too expensive and there would generally be nowhere to dispose of the spoils.

In many instances the observed rate of sedimentation after the closure of the dam has been found to be 50 to 400 per cent more than the assumed rate, thus substantially reducing the number of years it would take to fill up dead storage. The Irrigation Commission (1972) reported sedimentation studies that forecast filling of the dead storage of the Maithon Dam (DVC) in 50 years, the Mayurakshi dam (Bihar) in 25 years and the Ramganga (U.P.) in 44 years. Soil conservation and afforestation of the upper catchments and the construction of check dams upstream can make a significant difference. Watershed management and soil conservation programmes in critical catchments have produced positive results. However, the Irrigation Commission also recommended that the rate and pattern of sedimentation and the configuration of its deposition in reservoirs be surveyed every three years to assist appropriate management decisions and practices.

The Bhakra reservoir's live storage depletion period was estimated to be 585 years. But irrigation could be affected after 25 per cent depletion which would normally take about 135 years. It was however expected that soil conservation works apart, upstream storages and check dams would reduce the depletion rate. This in fact is now beginning to happen. The Naptha-Jhakri project on the Sutlej is under way and the Kol Dam is to follow.

The rate of siltation of the Bhakra reservoir is currently around six hectare-metres per 100 square kilometres of catchment per annum. This is the level to which the sedimentation rate of the Tehri reservoir is also expected to decline with soil conservation works as against a present figure of 13.5 ha m/100 square km per annum. Silt load measurements at the Tehri dam site between 1973 and 1985 show wide variations in the quantum of silt transported from one year to another. The silt load in 1978 was exceptionally high on account of a massive landslide 150 kilometres above Tehri, a most unusual occurrence according to the project authorities but not to be disregarded for that reason. The rate of siltation for the 12-year period, excluding and including the data for 1978 works out to be 13 ha m/ 100 sq km and 15 ha m/100 sq km per annum respectively as against an assumed rate of 13.95 ha m/100 sq km. as road and other construction was in progress during the period of data collection, the siltation analysis is believed to have been influenced by the debris brought down by such works in progress which will conclude with the completion of the dam around 1996 when filling of the reservoir will commence (Agarwal P.P. et al December 1985). A far more pessimistic view is taken by Vijay Paranjpye (1988) who estimates the economic life of the Tehri dam at 61.4 years on the basis of calculations said to have been made by the Department of Environment indicating an annual rate of sedimentation at 16.53 ha m/100 sq km. However, check dams are being constructed on streams carrying excessive silt loads and an elaborate watershed management programme is proposed.

Despite all these measures, should a reservoir silt up, as ultimately it must, what then? Dams of all kind, concrete, earthen, rock fill, etc. technically can be raised. This is not uncommon by any means (Varshney, 1988). The Grand Dixene dam in Switzerland was raised thrice after it silted up by a total of 100 metres to attain its present height of 286 metres. The Aswan Dam on the Nile, originally built in 1902, was twice raised in 1912 and 1933 to increase its storage capacity five times. In India, several dams have been raised and strengthened including the Koyna, Panshet and Tansa dams in Maharashtra. The Machkund dam (Orissa) was raised by some four metres. Consideration was also given to raising the height of the Bhakra Dam by four metres while it was under construction so as to augment storage. But this was not undertaken. Examples of raising dams can be found in the proceedings of the 6th, 7th, 10th, and 13th Congress of the International Commission on Large Dams. However, some structures like the Tehri Dam may not be amenable to raising for site-specific and other reasons. Sound watershed management suggests that the shoreline of all reservoirs formed behind high dams should be kept grassed or wooded up to some appropriate higher contour. This is a matter of contemporary prudence but could also come in handy should it be necessary to heighten certain dams a hundred years hence.

G. Ecological Effects of Dams

The closure of a dam can obviously greatly alter the regime of the lower reaches of th river by regulating flow and changing its natural rhythm. At the same time it stems the flow of the river to create a new lacustrine condition above the dam. These changes influence floods, sediment, fish migration, other aquatic life, and water quality. Reduction of headwater flows with abstraction of water for irrigation could induce salinity in the estuary or delta region, affect mangroves and lead to coastal erosion. Changes in the nutrient budget of the river after impoundment could also have a bearing on marine life and coastal fisheries.

Few of these factors are unmanageable. They require understanding, approximate regulation and periodic monitoring (Interim Mekong Committee, 1982). Salinity intrusion on account of diminished headwater supplies is a problem in many areas. Ndia constructed the Farakka Barrage to flush the Hooghly and, among other things, prevent salinity creeping up to Calcutta. This diversion of headwater supplies to the Bhagirathi-Hooghly has left Bangladesh protesting about the injury that it feels has been caused to it with salinity intrusion in the southwest region. Pakistan's Indus basin master plan incidentally reserves 566 cumecs for salinity control. With regeneration, the actual quantum of water flowing into the Arabian Sea is believed to be of the order of 990 cumecs.

Project designs often envisage periodic releases from dams to flush the river. In planning the DVC reservoirs it was provided that a discharge of up to 2830 cumecs would be released for two or three days in a year exclusively for flushing. This has not been done regularly as a result of which the river regime has deteriorated badly and the outfall into the Hooghly has almost completely silted. The river now flows through the Mundeshwari spill channel which falls into the Rupnarayan. The old Damodar channel has been occupied and built upon (Sinha; Basawan, 198).

H. Cultural Loss

Dams or waterlogging and salinity caused by faulty irrigation can damage or destroy cultural property. In a sense, Mohenjodaro and the ruins of Babylon are sad reminders of bad water management in river valleys that cradled great civilizations. However, submergence could drown and rising water tables behind barrages undermine the foundations of nearby monuments or historical sites.

The Archaeological Survey of India (ASI) is routinely notified of all river valley projects but is essentially the State Archaeological Departments that are directly involved in recording and salvage operations. Archaeology is not well funded in India and the concerned departments are too weak to be effective in many areas. A U.P. Government proposal to construct a barrage in Agra to pond the Yamuna in order to embellish the waterfront was forestalled by a timely reference to Roorkee University. This might have affected the foundations of the Taj Mahal. The site of the Maurayan palace at Kumrahar in Patliputra (Patna) is threatened by a rising water table. This needs to be treated by means of an appropriate drainage scheme.

The Tehri Dam will submerge Tehri town but the design, site and heights of certain other projects proposed in the Upper Ganga Valley have been reviewed to avoid or mitigate damage or threat to such pilgrim centres as Karanprayag and Rudraprayag as well as the lovely Valley of Flowers in the Bhyunder Valley east of Badrinath.

The Bhakra lake submerged the little town of Bilaspur with its palace containing murals by Nandlal Bose. The township was relocated. There was more controversy when the ancient site of Vijaypuri, capital of the Ishkvaku dynasty that ruled the lands between the Krishna and Godavari in the 3rd and 4th centuries, was to be submerged behind the Nagarjunasagar Dam. This was a great centre of Buddhist learning under Nagarjunacharya and an authentic site of the ashwamedha or horse sacrifice. The site was quickly surveyed and excavated and such treasures as could be removed are now housed in a museum located on an island in the Nagarjunasagar lake.

The most famous archaeological rescue operation was of course the lifting of the Abu Simbel Temples above Lake Nasser with the construction of the Aswan High Dam, a project led by UNESCO. Some 24 temples were similarly translocated above the Srisailam lake in Andhra Pradesh when that project was taken up.

The proposed Polavaram Dam on the lower Godavari will submerge areas in Andhra Pradesh, Orissa and Madhya Pradesh. An archaelogical survey has revealed several pre-historic survey has revealed several pre-historic sites and 80 sculptures have been identified for relocation at a cost of Rs.1.50 lakhs. Another 24 sites are to be excavated for Rs.12 lakhs and four temples are to be transplanted at a cost of Rs.10 lakhs. While it is possible to mourn the loss of some sites and treasures, it is equally true that decades or centuries of neglect and absence of funding for even the most minimal upkeep have been ended by water resource projects of this kind which have compelled prompt and ameliorative action and have restored many sites, monuments and artifacts to the mainstream of cultural life.

The Kadana Dam submerged areas in Gujarat and Rajasthan, Galiakot, a centre of Muslim pilgrimage, was inundated but the Dargah (Shrine) was protected by constructing a ring embankment at a cost of Rs.1.50 crores.

The Narmadasagar project will inundate a region that saw the evolution of early man in Indian Gondwanaland. But none of this will affect the extraordinary cave settlements carved into rock at higher contours. The Archaeological authorities, both Central and Madhya Pradesh are surveying and excavating stone-age tools and historic mounds. Several temples and structures of historical interest are being listed for relocation. But the most famous pilgrimage sites will not be affected.

The Mekong Committee is assisting the Thai government in salvaging important sites that may go under various proposed reservoirs. But apart from surveying cultural sites, environmental archaeology can help uncover much valuable information about ancient land and water developments as a tool for modern development planning. A document published by the Mekong Committee in 1973 noted that archaeological study could provide the Project authorities with needed information on climatic oscillations and their repercussions on vegetation and soil formation. "If changes in climate, rainfall, flooding patterns or river courses influenced early civilizations to the extent of causing significant migrations or leading to new land use patterns, there are important lessons planners can derive".

CONCLUSION

Environmental impact assessments are now mandatory. The World Bank has laid down stringent norms which must be satisfied before it will fund water resource programmes. Suitable guidelines for environmental impact assessments were prescribed for river valley projects by the Department of Environment in India (January 1985). These are now being revised and updated in the light of experience. The factors that should be considered in such studies include impacts on or aspects pertaining to health, plant genetic resources, aquatic resources, waterlogging and salinity, deforestation and soil conservation whether in the planning, construction or operational phases. The data that is to be collected and collated and the agencies that should be entrusted with the task are spelt out.

The U.S. Water Resources Council has set out "principles and standards for planning water and related land resources". This requires alternative options to be examined from the point of view of economic efficiency and environmental quality. Canada drew up a set of environmental assessment guidelines in 1976 which calls for an examination of alternatives, a listing of adverse environmental effects and the relationship between local short-term uses of man's environment and the maintenance and enhancement of long term productivity. ESAP too has been advocating environmental impact studies and has collated regional environmental experience as a guide for action. Public meetings have been recommended and could be a useful means of securing both public participation and public education in evolving a consensus (September 1986). Environment groups of the Central Water Commission and the Water and Power Consultancy Services (India) Ltd. are jointly engaged in developing guidelines for India.

Much useful work on conserving Nepal's rare flora and fauna and preserving unique wilderness sites is being done by the King Mahendra Trust for Nature Conservation (1988). It has now begun to take an interest in the environmental impact of large water resource development projects such as Arun-III and the Karnali dam in respect of which Himalayan Hydro Consultants has prepared an elaborate environmental status and impact report. Nepal well realizes that economics and ecology must go together.

The Bruntland Commission's Report, "Our Common Future", has also come to influence current thinking on sustainable development everywhere.

Environmental issues arouse strong emotions. Here is one view: "The nation has to develop; it has to become modern, grow strong, seek its rightful place among the community of nations. It has a self-proclaimed "tryst with destiny" towards which it must move inexorably as the chariot of Lord Jagannath. It is said about the chariot that those amongst the devout who are crushed beneath its wheels attain moksha forthwith. Such perhaps will be the case with Indira Sarovar (Narmadasagar). Only time will tell" (Environmental Services Group, September 1986).

"What we need today is an ecological religion – one that makes it clear above all that if God created the world of living things, then its annihilation by means of science, technology and industry can only be the work of the devil. God, it must teach us, can only be served by helping him to reconstitute his creation". This from Edward Goldsmith, co-author of "The Social and Environmental Effects of Large Dams" (Spring 1987). Goldsmith quotes Ivan Illich as saying that development has not eliminated poverty but only modernized it. The ecological movement, he says, denies the desirability of industrialism itself, whether capitalistic or Marxist. "It is only if we adopt a totally materialistic and technological view of the world that we can regard an Amazonian Indian or a tribesman from NEFA territory (Arunachal Pradesh) as poor. He may not have electric toothbrushes nor plastic Mickey Mouses – but he has a family, he has a real community, he has a wonderful life, full of ritual and ceremony. He eats a varied and rich diet consisting of all sorts of fresh foods. His life is, in fact, very fulfilling"? Is it? For whom? There can be no return to Genesis.

Many will echo M.G. Padhye, a former Indian Irrigation Secretary, who exclaims that "if the environment were static, we would (all) have remained tribals" (January 1987). Yet, administrators, planners and engineers alike have come to develop an ecological conscience with growing awareness. Safeguards are there and can be refined where necessary. Over and beyond that, implementation can and must be monitored. Apart from the financial audit that is even now conducted, a process of social audit of large dams would appear to be desirable so as to ensure that the social and human objectives set for every project are met in letter and spirit. A Council for Social Audit was mooted to monitor the National Technology Missions on rural drinking water, immunisation, adult literacy and so on. The Council has been described as a mechanism to increase people's participation, conduct qualitative assessments, perform concurrent evaluation through independent channels, suggest improvements for delivery, and heighten public awareness. This suggests a model that can be suitably structured and adapted to the intended purpose. Public hearings on the environmental, human and cultural effects of large water resource projects would also be an important means of confidence-building, public participation and feedback, with openness.

Who dare think today of an India without Bhakra, though it has entailed every "cost" ascribed to dams? Environmental prudence and care is the path of wisdom in water resource development as in all other forms of sustainable development. Not eco-fundamentalism.

CHAPTER 11

Dam Safety Despite Seismic Hazards

Earthquakes can be among the most frightening and devastating of natural visitations. And since they have been known to tear the earth apart and destroy large structures it is understandably fared that they might bring down dams and unleash horrendous floods that would sweep everything before them. The filling of reservoirs too has been found to set off what is known as reservoir induced seismicity (RIS), a factor that has added to the alarm about the possible dangers emanating from large dams.

Globally, about a million earth tremors of varying intensity may be experienced annually. Some are so slight or remote that they pass unnoticed. About 20 or so are major events and liable to cause considerable damage to life and property. The geological theory of plate tectonics, now widely accepted, suggests that earthquakes are caused by the sudden release of slowly accumulating stresses at the boundaries of the vast rocky plates that glide over the underlying warmer and yielding atmosphere. In the case of converging plates, continued compression causes the rocks to first deform and then to fracture and slip along the weak planes when the accumulated strain budget reaches the breaking point thereby releasing tremendous amounts of energy. It is this phenomenon that is manifested in earthquakes.

Most earthquakes are concentrated in two long, narrow seismic belts which are now recognized as boundaries of lithospheric plates. The first of these is the circum-Pacific belt that rings the Pacific Ocean. The second is the Alpide belt which joints the former in a T junction at the Celebes (Suluwesi) and runs westwards through the Indonesian archipelago, Asia and southern Europe to the Atlas mountains in northwest Africa. The northward movement of the Indian Plate that started the process of Himalayan orogeny continues 40 million years after the continental Indian Plate first encountered the southern margin of Asia, still pressing and denting the Asian Plate to the north at a rate of five centimeters per annum. "Apparently, about half this displacement is still being accommodated by deformation within the Himalayan belt which is makred by prolific seismic activity" (Gaur, October 1984).

The magnitude of earthquakes in terms of the released energy is measured on a scale of one to nine on the basis of a system devised by Richter. Each unit step in magnitude represents a tenfold increase in ground motion and about a thirtyfold increase in the energy released by the earthquake. In terms of energy release, a Hiroshima-type bomb would crudely measure six on the Richter scale and a Nagasaki-type hydrogen bomb eight. The truly cataclysmic seismic events, categorized as "great earthquakes", register eight and more on the Richter scale. The intensity of damage caused is however measured on the MM (Modified Mercalli Intensity) Scale of 1931 with values from I to XII ranging from scarcely felt tremors to situations of total damage. It is important to keep the two measurements distinct to avoid confusion. The Tehri Dam is being designed to withstand earthquakes within the broad parameters of magnitude 7.5 and MM-IX intensity.

There are early records of historic earthquakes from China, Persia and Lisbon. The first available record of an earthquake in the Indian sub-continent is that experienced in the Delhi-Agra area area on July 15, 1505 (Hukku et al., August 1986) The Mughal historian, Khafi Khan, reports that during Friday prayers on June 27, 1720, a severe earthquake shook Delhi. "A noise under the earth was heard, doors and walls shook, and roofs rattled". Parts of the ramparts of the Red Fort and the parapets of Fatehpuri Mosque were damaged. "It was very amazing that for a month and two days the shocks continued, and were felt four or five times in the twenty-four hours (sic). Many persons were so alarmed that they would not sleep under a roof. After this time the force of the shocks decreased; but for four and five months the earth and the houses were found to shake occasionally, until the arrival of the blessed feet of His Majesty, when the shocks gradually ceased" (Khan, Khafi). Another earthquake on September 1, 1803 around Mathura, measuring M6.5 "caused intensive figures in fields through which water rose with considerable violence (Srivastava, 1983). The tremors were felt in Delhi and topped the cupola atop the Qutab Minar. Bengal, and more particularly Assam, and Darjeeling, Nepal, Kumaon, Kangra, Kashmir and Kutch experienced earthquakes of severe intensity through the 19th century. Earlier some 300,000 persons were reported killed in the great earthquake that shook Bengal in 1737.

Thomas Oldham of the Geoloical Survey of India prepared the first catalogue of Indian earthquakes in 1883. In 1890 the Indian Meteorological Department commenced making instrumental measurements of seismic events. Earlier historical data and newspapers were canned to prepare a homogenous and systematic catalogue that now goes back some 200 years. Archaeological and paleo-seismic evidence have also been sifted to reconstruct past seismicity. Two scientists of the GSI examined old temples to establish the occurrence of a 6.6 magnitude earthquake in Bastar in the 12-13th century. Even rings on trees offer evidence of seismic events. An examination of old Peshwa archrival material after the Koyna earthquake of 1967 brought forth evidence of earlier seismic history in the region, an earthquake of 6.5 magnitude having been felt in southern Maharashtra in 1764.Likewise, there was a newspaper report of an earthquake in Hyderabad in 1876, preceding the latest earthquake of about the same magnitude, M5, in 1983.

FOUR 'GREAT' EARTHQUAKES

Four "great earthquakes" have occurred in the Indo-Nepal Himalayan belt over the past one hundred years. Possibly the very greatest ever recorded anywhere in the world was the 1897 earthquake in the Shillong Plateau measuring 8.7 in the magnitude and felt over a vast area of 4.48 million square kilometres. It caused extensive fissures and landslides and took a toll of 1542 lives. There was a 10 metre vertical displacement over a length of 20 kilometres along the Chedrang fault and groundwaves were clearly visible. After-shocks continued for ten years. The Kangra earthquake of 1905 recorded 8.5, with an epicentral intensity approximating MM-X. it took 20,000 lives and was felt over 4.16 million square kilometres and apparently uplifted Dehra Dun by 12.70 centimetres. The North Bihar-Nepal earthquake of 1934 was felt over 916,000 square kilometres and measured 8.4 with an intensity of MM-X. About 10,000 people were killed. The most recent of the Great Himalayan earthquakes occurred on August 15, 1950. It measured 8.6 on the Richter scale, placing it among the five greatest earthquakes known in historic times. The shock was felt over 2.9 million square kilometres. It savaged the eastern Himalaya and altered the drainage of the upper Brahmaputra system.

A narrative volume on the 1950 Assam earthquake published by the Central Board of Geophysics (Ramachandra Rao, 1953) contains detailed scientific data as well as graphic personal accounts. The main shock was variously said to have lasted about four to five minutes with an energy estimated at 3×10^{27} ergs – "several million tines the energy released in an explosion of an atom bomb" (Parmanik and Mukherjee, 1953). From aerial reconnaissance it appeared that abut 15,550 sq kms were affected by severe landslides. Taking an average depth of 10 feet, I.P. Mathur, a Central Water and Power Commissin geologist estimated the total volume of earth removed to be of the order of 6×10^{10} cubic yards. Extensive landslides blocked the Subansiri and other rivers, the dams bursting a few days later to cause immense flood havoc. A huge block of rock "about four miles in length and a quarter mile in width" dammed the head waters of the Tidding 120 kilometres up the river from Sadiya which was itself obliterated as the Dihang changed its course. The Lohit was dammed; bombing the dyke to mitigate the flood from a possible dam-burst was abandoned as infeasible. The speed of the current flowing down the angry Brahmaputra at Pasighat was estimated from 45 to 75 kilometres per hour for some time after the earthquake and waves of four to six metres were noticed. The rivers were choked with silt and the bed of the Brahmaputra rose on an average by 1.5 metres in the vicinity of Dibrugarh. Rivers changed course and navigation was totally disrupted over a distance of 64 kilometres below Dibrugarh. The Ranganadi, Dihang, Dibang and Lohit Valleys were most affected, landslides and erosion extending up to 5000 metres on the MacMohan Line along a 300 kilometre arc.

The well-known plant explorer, F. Kingdon-Ward, and his wife were camping beside the Lohit river near Rima in Tibet when the earthquake occurred, starting with "an·appalling noise". The "first feeling of bewilderment – an incredulous astonishment that these solid-looking hills were in the grip of a force which shook them as a terrier shakes a rat – soon gave place to stark terror… The din was terrible; but it was difficult to separate the noise made by the earthquake itself from the roar of the rock avalanches pouring down on all sides into the basin… Within two hours, the air was so thick with dust that every star was hidden; we breathed dust, it gritted our teeth, filled our eyes … The destruction extended to the very top of the main ranges – 15,000-16,000 feet above sea-level. No wonder the mountain torrents began to glow (sic) intermittently as the gorges became blocked, followed later by the breaking of the dam; whereupon the wall of water 20 feet high would roar down the gully, carrying everything before it and leaving a trail of evil-smelling grey mud. Everywhere the scraped cliffs glistened while in the sunshine" (January 1951). Kingdom-Ward concludes: "It would be incautious at this stae to state categorically that the annual burning of the pine forest for the last fifty years between Walong (in Arunachal) and Rima (in Tibet) was responsible for the huge damage done in the arid Lohit valley; but it seems that any further burning will prove completely disastrous". The forests were presumably burnt to practice jhum cultivation.

Damage to plant and animal life, fish and birds was enormous. The very topography of Upper Assam was recast and the morphology of the Brahmaputra underwent dramatic change. E.P. Gee, the distinguished naturalist noted : "The silted-up river beds in the plains areas could not contain the flood water, and consequently vast tracks of adjacent land became inundated, some for the first time in recorded history. The gradual westward movement of the colossal silt deposits down the Brahmaputra Valley may be completed within a decade or two … And until new and deeper channels can be formed by the rivers of these alluvial plains, the widespread flooding experienced in 1951 will be an annual occurrence – and may even worsen".

ZONING AND PREDICTION

More than 650 earthquakes in excess of magnitude 5 have been recorded in India since 1890. these have been plotted on maps and indicate that abut 56 per cent of the country's land area is at varying degrees of risk. Five levels of probable seismic intensity have been delineated at a macro level in a seismic zoning map. Zone V is liable to experience tremors of the highest intensity and is the most vulnerable area. This covers the entire Northeast, Darbhanga in North Bihar (extending into Nepal), Kumaon and Garhwal, the Kangra belt, an area around Srinagar in Kashmir, Kutch and the Andaman and Nicobar Islands. Zones IV and III represent areas in which earthquakes can cause moderate damage to well designed structures but could be dangerous for poorly built edifices. Zones I and II are liable to feel light to minor tremors and are regions where damage is improbable. Zone IV covers the remaining Himalayan belt and the adjacent Indo-Gangetic plain along a line roughly running through Amritsar, Gurgaon-Delhi-Mathura, Bareilly, Gorakhpur, Patna and the Rajmahal Hills, taking in North Bengal and Sikkim.

The seismic zones were delineated in 1975 on the basis of past earthquake history in various regions. The Himalayan catchments all lie in Zones IV and V and many of the potential dam sites fall in areas that have experienced earthquake intensities of MM-VIII, IX and X. For any given location, the intensity of the shock measured in MM units is more relevant then the magnitude of the earthquake on the Richter scale in considering the safety of large structures such as dams. The expected intensity at a site depends on the distance of the structure from the epicenter, the depth of focus (the hypocentre), the length of the underlying fault and the extent of displacement, and more importantly on the nature of the foundation or soil. Alluvial soils are more prone to liquefaction and consequent instability in contrast with firm rock.

How then is the question of dam safety in seismic-prone regions to be approached? Earthquake prediction or forecasting is still rather tentative though the behaviour of earthquakes and swarms of minor tremors have been studied to reveal emerging patterns. The Chinese successfully predicted a major 7.3 magnitude earthquake that destroyed the city of Heicheng in Liaoning province on February 4, 1975. A timely warning to evacuate high-risk buildings saved an estimated 100,000 lives but industrial and residential property suffered heavy damage. The forecasting experience started with regional earthquake studies during 1970-73 in this risk-prone region. Intensified observation of precursory phenomena during 1973-74 foretold a significant earthquake that must be soon expected. There followed concentrated observation of short term precursors such as unusual animal behaviour, changes in water levels in wells and increases in the radon (gas) content. The occurrence of two precursor shocks measuring 4.7 and 4.2 on February 4 was the signal to alert the populace to move outdoors and to place disaster prevention system in a state of full preparedness. Some hours later the main earthquake occurred (Adams, March 1976). Euphoria was short lived. Triumph turned to tragedy on July 27, 1976 when a severe earthquake struck the Tangshan-Tienstsin region in which some 650,000 lives are sad to have been lost.

SEISMIC GAP THEORY

A hypothesis that has increasingly come to be used in defining high risk areas and predicting major earthquakes is that of so-called seismic gaps. The tectonic theory of earthquakes postulates that when plates move against one another, strains accumulate along their boundaries. These may be temporarily absorbed in crustal deformation and locally manifested in landslides or through swarms of minor to medium shocks which are however only precursions to a major rupture that must follow to release the pent-up energy as it builds up to breaking point. Mapping these signals in space and time has provided useful clues to future events. The related earthquake cycle hypothesis holds "that two comparable-size earthquakes rupturing the same section of fault will be separated by a period of time sufficient to re-accumulate strain by an amount equal to the elastic-strain drop accompanying the first earthquake...Specific stages within the earthquake cycle have been recognized for major earthquakes: a long period of seismic quiescence following a major earthquake and its immediate aftershocks, a shorter (and varying) period of enhanced seismicity as elastic-strain accumulation approaches (and, locally, exceeds) the critical strain level, and a very short (hours to days) but commonly non-existence period of immediate foreshocks, all followed by the next major earthquake" (Hanks). Segments of plate boundaries whose flanks have been ruptured but which themselves have exhibited quiescence for decades to centuries are recognized as seismic gaps. From the 1970s these seismic gaps have been identified globally and ranked according to their "seismic potential". Between 1968 and 1980 ten major plate-boundary earthquakes were correctly anticipated by means of the seismic gap hypothesis (Ibid).

Using such scientific tools, the U.S. National Earthquake Hazards Reduction Programme now knows where to look for earthquakes and predicted a moderate earthquake near Parkfield, California, a segment of the notorious San Andreas fault system, sometime before 1993. This impending earthquake was the subject of an elaborate prediction experiment and occasioned no surprise when it occurred in October 1989. Impending great earthquakes, with less certitude with regard to timing, are also forecast in Alaska and at a more critically stressed section of the San Andreas fault. In California, two major projects in earthquake preparedness planning are in progress. These are the Southern California Earthquake Preparedness Project and the bay Area Earthquake Study. These exercises in "real-time geology" are aimed at disaster mitigation through the adoption of prudent land-use policies and improved earthquake design and construction (Ibid).

Put differently, "averaged over a sufficiently long period of time, the sum of (the) various slippages or displacements – the slow aseismic fault creep, the fault displacement accompanying earthquakes, and inelastic deformation such as crustal folding – must equal the displacement between two plates. This leads quite naturally to the idea of long-term earthquake prediction based on what might be called a slip budget" (Wesson and Wallace, February 1985). Further, "certain laboratory experiments and theoretical models of the earthquake process suggest that accelerated deformation – called pre-seismic slip – is intrinsic to earthquakes. The idea is that the failure of crustal rock is preceded by the development of small cracks or weak spots, which then grow into the catastrophic rupture. The identification of earthquake precursors within the background of crustal deformation, which fluctuates continually, remains a chief objective of earthquake-prediction research". The growing reliability and capability of advanced instrumentation, computer hardware and software, the ability to exhume the past through new techniques of paleo-seismology and repeated surveys provide the means for purposeful study.

The tragic 8.1 earthquake that devastated Mexico City on September 19, 1985 occurred in "the Michoacan seismic gap which had been identified as a zone with high seismic potential by several investigators though with … speculation that the gap was permanently aseismic" (Anderson et al., September 1986).

STRAIN-ENERGY RELEASE MEASUREMENTS

A strain-energy release map of the Himalaya prepared by R.K. Verma, R.K. Mukhopadhyay and B.N.Roy in 1977 identified three separate segments, the Punjab Himalaya, Kumaon Himalaya and Nepal Himalaya, as active seismic zones with little intervening seismic activity (Wadia Institute of Himalayan Geology, 1986). More specifically in the Indian region two seismic gaps have been identified, one in Himachal along the plate boundary between the earthquakes of Kangra (1905) and Kinnaur (1977) and the other in the so-called Assam gap in northeast India between the great earthquakes of 1897 and 1950.

"Given the abundant evidence for convergence of the Indian sub-continent toward the rest of Eurasia, we can reasonably expect that… large and destructive earthquakes (similar to the four great earthquakes of 1897, 1905, 1934 and 1950) will occur in the Himalaya in the future. Moreover, by analogy with subduction zones, the likely areas to rupture in 1897, 1905, 1934 and 1950. It follows that an important first step in evaluating the earthquake hazard in India is to estimate the extent of ruptures associated with those great earthquakes" (Molnar, February 1987). Molnar disputes deductions by scholars that the entire Himalaya ruptures by slip during great earthquakes in 180 to 240 years and that the recurrence interval for earthquakes with rupture lengths of 300 kilometres is between 200 and270 years. He believes they have overestimated the extent of rupture and consequently the uncertainty in the recurrence interval is greater than postulated by them. His own analysis of the Kangra earthquake of 1905 leads him to state that "in anticipatin the next great earthquake in the Himalaya, one probably could assume safely that the rupture zone will not include the area from Dharamshala to a few tens to a hundred kilometres southeast. At the same time, it probably would be foolish to assume that the next great earthquake will not rupture the segment of the Himalaya that includes Dehra Dun".

Moving further east, Prof. K.N. Khattri et al observed that the "Garhwal Himalaya forms the western segment of the 700 kilometre long seismic gap that intervenes (between) the rupture zones of the Kangra (1905) and Bihar (1934) earthquakes. It is not known to have experienced a major earthquake (greater than magnitude 8.0) in recorded history, and unless it happens to be an exceptional segment on the Himalayan collision zones distinguished by aseismic strain release, the ambient stresses here must be fairly high" (August 1987).

In Assam, a NE-SW rectangular slip, 150 x 100 km, "continues to be comparatively quieter. This zone, lying in the northeastern segment of the suspected seismic gap between the great Assam earthquakes of 1897 and 1950 could be the quiescent phase of a major earthquake and will be investigated more intensively..." (NGRI, 1987).

The Soviet academician Igor Gubin opines that "the focus of an earthquake is not a hypocenter, a point within the earth's crust, as many experts in instrumental seismology believe; shock waves propagate from the fracture (fault) caused by the differential displacement of rock around it. The fault zones vary in length, throw and dip. Very intense earthquakes occur in seismogenic fault zones only, which are from tens to thousands of kilometres long and contain both manifest and latent sources. Intense earthquakes migrate along such a fault (and) occur ... mostly in the so-called seismic gaps." Using Gubin's Law of Seismotectonics based on the size and type of seismogenic structures of crustal blocks of the Earth moving against one another along a fault, Gubin has drawn up several multicomponent tectonic maps. His "Earthquakes and the Seismic Zoning of the Indian Subcontinent" was published some years ago (Gubin, May 1987).

HIGH DAMS IN SEISMIC ZONES

The fact that practically all of the Indo-Gangetic-Brahmaputra-Barak catchments fall within seismic zones and that the Himalaya is a highly dynamic tectonic region does not preclude the construction of dams. "The argument that dams should not be built in highly seismic zones is not only unsound from the point of view of national economy, but also not supported by the trends of seismic activity as in the case of high dams already built in similar regions elsewhere" (Srivastava). The Brahmaputra Board is of the same view in the context of proposals to construct high dams on the Dihang and Subansiri in Arunachal. "The advisability of building high dams in this region which is prone to severe earthquakes has been under serious consideration and several experts of international repute, both Indian and foreign, have been consulted in the matter. Their advice has been that safe high dams can be constructed at suitable sites provided due allowance is made for the seismic factor in designing the various structures" (Brahmaputra Board, 1986).

Dr. Jai Krishna points to scientific developments and the advancement of knowledge that have enabled high dams to be built with confidence at Nurek and Rogun (325 metres high) in the Soviet Union, Sussodha in Alaska (280 m), and Mica in Canada (245 m) although they are located in highly seismic zones. A number of earthquakes have been recorded in epicentral areas" so that we are now aware of the type of intensity of ground motion that could be expected in a region. Similarly the science of soil mechanics and also the development of compaction machinery has enabled engineers to achieve 90-100 per cent compaction of the rock and earth-fill mass. The rock-fill dam, therefore, should be considered to be the equivalent of a natural hill with easy slopes on both sides". His conclusion is that a suitably designed rock-fill dam is as safe as a natural hill and that "taller dams are no less safe in seismic region that shorter dams" (Ibid). Dams may slump or be deformed by violent shocks but will not necessarily break.

The question of the seismic risk surrounding the Tehri dam has been the subject of considerable controversy. Earthquake engineers are however confident that the design parameters ensure more than reasonable safety. The Soviet Union which is collaborating in the construction of the project has carried out further investigations based on recent Soviet technology. But it has basically accepted the Indian design. Nevertheless, on-going research to safeguard the Tehri dam and other large structures in that general region would be desirable. Vinod Gaur has suggested a number of research goals to this end such as taking in situ stress measurements in deep boreholes at depths of up to 500 metres to refine the Tehri-Himalayan tectonic model as well as measuring the slip rate of the Lesser Himalayan Block relative to the Indian shield through the Global Positioning System making use of satellite signals along a given Himalayan axis received simultaneously at a point somewhere along the Narmada (October, 1984).

The cost of such research and the other programmes suggested in the 15 year Perspective for the Study of Himalayan Seismicity and Seismotectonics (DST) is miniscule in relation to the cost of the Tehri Dam and other large structures proposed to be built in the Himalaya over the next couple of decades. The returns in terms of scientific knowledge, better prediction capability, a more careful appreciation of design parameters, and greater safety are likely to be obviously so much greater as to render this an urgent and most worthwhile investment. High dams in the Himalaya are even now not unsafe. But there is every reason to make them safer over the projected century and more of their expected life. Even with regard to study of reservoir induced seismicity in general, a regular set of investigations has been proposed and should be followed (Rastogi, December 1984).

STRENGTHENING RESEARCH AND OBSERVATION

Seismic observation and studies were initiated in India over 90 years ago and the work undertaken by the Indian Meteorological Department and Geological Survey of India was given a sharper focus and inter-disciplinary thrust with the launching of the All-India Coordinated Project on the Study of Seismicity and Seismotectonics in the Himalayan Region by the Department of Science and Technology (DST) in 1982. This involves 15 organisations including Government departments, national laboratories and universities. The principal objectives of the project were to mitigate seismic hazards, understand the mechanism of earthquakes and seismotectonic activity, and prepare different types of seismic and seismotectonic maps of social relevance (DST December 1984).

It was recommended in 1982 that during the Sixth Plan (1980-85) studies should focus on Tehri Garhwal and Kumaon in the Western Himalaya and the Shillong Plateau in the northeastern Himalaya. Cooperation with Nepal and Bhutan was suggested. Nepal already had some seismological stations at the time and it was proposed that some stations be located in Bhutan. Further, in order to cover Tibet, the establishment of collaborative research proposals and exchange of data with China was advocated. The central data centre located in the Department of Science and Technology in Delhi was seen as growing into an Institute of Seismology. A 1984 Workshop recommended that during the Seventh Plan (1985-90), the Kangra-Sutlej-Beas region and the Dawki-Haflong area should be priority areas of study in the Western and Northeastern Himalaya.

What are known as strong motion earthquake instrumentation arrays have been set up in the Kangra and Shillong regions and are being enlarged and strengthened within a larger all-India network of accelograph stations. In 1968 the Indian Standards Institution formulated IS: 1967-1968 containing recommendations for the instrumentation of river valley projects following which a number of dams and catchments have been instrumented: Bhakra, Ramganga, Koyna, Yamuna, Tehri, Pancheshwar, Sallal, Idduki, Srisailam, Narmada and the Brahmaputra Valley.

The number of seismological stations and arrays are proposed to be extended and enhanced in sophistication. Existing stations can monitor earthquakes of magnitude-5. The object is to be able to monitor lesser earthquakes of 4 and even 3 as a basis for more elaborate modeling studies. "The earth being heterogenous and complex, it becomes necessary to have a high density of observation points to achieve the desired level of accuracy. For example, in the western United States along the San Andreas fault system there are over 600 seismic stations. By similar standards we might deploy about a thousand seismic stations in the Himalayan seismic province" (Khattri, August 1986).

The National Geophysical Research Institute is engaged in a Deep Seismic Sounding Project. This adopts a recent technique to echo-sound the earth by sending down seismic waves generated by exploding large charges (placed a few metres below the surface) and recording the up-coming waves. It enables study of the outer 50 to 60 km of the earth's interior including the Mohorovicic discontinuity (Moho), the density and chemical boundary between the quartz-rich rocks of the crust and the iron-magnesium-rich rocks of the underlying mantle.

Relatively modest funds have so far been expended on earthquake research in India. The Department of Earthquake Engineering in Roorkee Univesity has installed a shake table that can simulate earthquake motions, including the recorded motions of actual seismic events, as an aid to testing the designs of various structures and their ability to withstand shocks of different intensities. Seismic response calculations of several large dams, nuclear plants, thermal stations, bridges and other structures have been made.

A committee of Experts under the Department of Science and Technology has advocated five basic strategies (June 1987) relating to preparation for an earthquake, including contingency plans for warning, response and recovery; land use planning on the basis of seismic risk; the evolution and revision of building codes, standards and design practices with regard to earthquake resistant structures; the provision of a data base for moderating the adverse impacts of earthquakes through insurance, loan programmes and relief efforts; and the mounting of systematic educational, training and awareness programmes. A five to 10 year proposal for earthquake disaster mitigation studies includes preparation of micro-zoning maps for cities such as Srinagar, Delhi, Patna, Calcutta, Guwahati and Shillong and the creation of two regional centres for holistic studies on earthquakes and disaster mitigation in the Northwest and Northeast Himalaya.

A series of tremors over the past few years have underlined forecasts of a possible or probable major earthquake in the Western and Northeastern Himalaya in the foreseeable future. The Dharamshala earthquake in Himachal on April 26, 1986, though of no more than a magnitude of 5.7 took a considerable toll and evoked suggestions for earthquake disaster mitigation procedures for the future (Arya et al, July 1986). Tremors of 4.5 at Idduki in June 1988 caused some panic but were authoritatively denied as being reservoir induced. A minor tremor of 2 was recorded in the Nagarjunasagar area some weeks later. In August 1988 two shocks of a magnitude of 6.5 to 7.3 shook Northwest India and Northeast India respectively closely followed by the damaging earthquake that rocked eastern Nepal and parts of North Bihar. A number of houses weakened by the previous year's flood collapsed, taking a heavy toll of lives. Based on continuing research, the ISI brought out Indian Standards IS; 4326-1976 (first revision) and IS; 1893-1975 (third revision) incorporating guidelines for the design and construction of earthquake resistant buildings in various seismic zones. However, more research needs to b done to formulate an Indian Standards code for so-called lifeline structures relating to water supply, sewage, transportation, electrical power, communications, and gas and liquid fuel supply.

RESERVOIR INDUCED SEISMICITY

Earthquakes have been induced by human activity such as construction of large reservoirs and mining operations. The Klerksdorp Mine in South Africa recorded a mine-associated earthquake of a magnitude of 5.5. Reservoir induced seismicity (RIS) was first noticed with the filling of Lake Mead behind the Hoover Dam in the Untied States. Other major instances of RIS were reported from the Kariba Dam on the Zambezi, Kremasta in Greece, Lake Oroville in California (5.7), Nurek Dam on the Vaksh river in Soviet Tadzhikistan, Kurobe Dam in Japan, Hsinfengkiang Dam in China (6.1), and the Aswan Dam in Egypt (5.6). A large dam like Bhakra, located in a highly seismic zone, has not shown any evidence of

RIS but Bhatsa Dam, near Bombay experienced an earthquake of 4.5 while minor tremors have been felt in the region of Hirakud, Nagarjunasagar, Ukai, Idduki and Mula dams (Srivastava). However, there was consternation when an earthquake of a magnitude of 6.5 shook Koyna in 1967, killing 117 people and causing some damage to the dam in an area regarded as seismically quiescent.

Detailed investigations of earthquakes in the vicinity of non-made reservoirs show that small magnitude earthquakes (say up to magnitude 3) can be caused as a direct consequence of reservoir loading through settlement of the basin. Larger magnitude earthquakes cannot be caused by impoundment of water as the stresses caused by reservoir impoundment are much smaller compared to the stresses released by earthquakes of magnitude 5. The reservoir impoundment provides only a trigger. The triggering is mainly caused by an increase in pore-fluid pressure. "It is therefore a necessary condition for the occurrence of reservoir-induced earthquakes of magnitude 4 or larger than the region to be stressed close to the critical (level) before impoundment of the lake" (Gupta, Harsh, K). Gupta notes that a thrust-fault environment is not conducive to RIS. Investigations at some sites have even shown reduction of seismicity consequent to reservoir impoundment as at Tarbela Dam on the Indus in Pakistan. Nevertheless, Gupta warns that it is essential to carry out seismic surveillance at the site of large reservoirs at the planning stage. Further, since all dams built on Himalayan rivers have a probability of occurrence of a magnitude 6 or larger earthquake in their immediate vicinity, "all efforts should be made to guarantee `slope stability' to avoid ... the kind of disaster experienced at Lake Vaiont in Italy in 1963".

The danger of slope failure along the rim of dam impoundments on account of reservoir erosion caused by drawdown of the lake and landslides is often mentioned (Valdiya). Both RIS and possible over-toping of the dam by wave action as a result of a hill-slide caused by slope failure have been cited by wave action as a result of a hill-slide caused by slope failure have been cited among the risks confronting the Tehri Dam. Vinod Gaur however points out that the Tehri region "being under compression, the effect of pore pressure due to impounding of water would be to reduce the effective compressive stress, while the vertical stress remains unchanged .. Impounding of the reservoir would thus have the effect of delaying fracture. However, it must be borne in mind that draining of the reservoir would have the opposite effect" (October 1984). To this Devendra Kumar (1988) adds that investigations show that the hills rising above the rim of the Tehri reservoir are in general stable. "No area has been noted where a large scale hill slide could occur which would generate a high wave in the reservoir resulting in over-topping of the dam or filling the reservoir with rock debris. It is also significant that no such phenomenon of large scale movement of soil mass has been reported from any of the existing reservoirs like Bhakra and Ramganga located in similar conditions in the Himalaya".

DAM FAILURES AND DAM SAFETY

Despite the fact that many dams have stood for years and others have been built in the most complex terrains, the possibility of dam failures remains and dam safety must ever be a prime concern. Inadequate investigations invite trouble. An analysis of dam failures in the United States made in 1959 attributed as many as two-thirds to geological factors. A further study of these failures concluded that a third of the failures were on account of foundation defects, a third due to inadequate spillway capacity, and the remaining third because of other factors (Ahmad et al, May 1986). The International Commission on Large Dams (ICOLD) made a study of failures of or incidents relating to large dams in 1965. As against 8925 large dams around the world at the time, 535 incidents were reported, 202 being total failures. In India the number of failures was 13 and incidents or accidents 27, making a total of 40 in respect of 435 large dams. Australia reported 29 cases, Canada 11, Britain 32, Japan 16 and the United States 331, including 117 failures.

ICOLD's 1973 analysis of 236 failures mentioned insufficient study of potential floods and inadequate investigation of foundation as major factors. In the case of the Ramganga Dam, a fault zone was discovered after the project report was approved and sanctioned in 1959, necessitating design changes. Still later, it was realized that the order of floods had been underestimated as a result of which further design changes had to be incorporated to increase the capacity of the spillway and provide for certain training works (Ibid). Here the problems were anticipated and overcome in time though some delay and cost escalation inevitably resulted.

Dams may face distress after construction or on ageing and a number of instances of this kind have been reported (Murty, 1978). Problems include "excessive leakage through gate seals during operations". The Bhandara Dam built around 1929 across the Pravara river in Maharashtra started leaking badly in 1969. The Vir Dam suffered two cracks in its earthen segment within 10 months of its completion in 1961. These dams were repaired in good time. Others failed. The most notable failure was that of the Panchet Dam in Maharahstra after is first filling in July 1961. The flood this released caused by Kadakvasala Dam downstream to fail as well. The Nanak Sagar earth dam in U.P. failed in September 1967 due to settlement in a reach of 1.5 km caused by piping of the foundation. The Chikahole masonry dam failed in December 1972 due to tension caused at the dam base as the water level rose to the top of the dam. The Aran earth dam failed in 1978 as the foundation gave way on account of seepage pressure. The Vaiont dam (Italy), the Malpasset dam (France) and the Teton dam (U.S.) are among some contemporary international dam failures. Murty states that detailed investigations indicated that many of these failures could have been avoided by proper design, construction and regulation.

Dam technology has of course advanced greatly since these failures were reported. Nonetheless, accidents have sensitized engineers and policy-makers alike to the vital need for design reviews and an independent check of construction and operational procedures which is now ensured by legislation in many countries. In India, the CWC's Dam Design Directorate has been acting as a review agency in matters relating to dam safety and the 1975 Conference of State Irrigation Ministers recommended the establishment of an advisory dam safety service. Among the steps proposed are installation of early warning instrumentation in dams to sound an alert with regard to a variety of contingencies, including ageing and measurement of deformations, especially in the foundations. Periodic inspections would help enforcement under an independent national authority.

Given adequate care, state-of-the-art research and instrumentation, and rigorous monitoring, large or small dams may be constructed with reasonable assurance of safety even in hazardous areas. The fact of risk, whether from seismicity or flood or whatever, is no reason to avoid construction of dams. It implies a higher order of design safety and surveillance and a preparedness to bear the attendant costs. Certain dams should obviously not be built in any circumstances – where the risks or the costs of overcoming them are too high. In all other cases, not to go ahead would be to mortgage the future.

CHAPTER 12

To Your Good Health

The manifold uses of water are essential to living. Yet, the manner of its use and disposal have a close bearing on health, sanitation and the quality of life. Diverting water to distant fields and habitations affects the microclimate and is conducive to transporting or hosting pathogens, vectors and pests that may have been previously unknown. To criticize water resource development on this count per se, as some have done, is perverse as water management is as important for health and pollution control as it is for sound irrigation.

Bringing (protected sources of) drinking water supplies to rural and urban habitations lacking them is to fulfil an urgent and basic human need. Yet, water supply programmes have been pursued without related drainage facilities of the most elementary kind, leading to diseases that never existed before. Dr. V. Ramalingaswami summed up the problems some years ago. There is, he said, "a host of water-related diseases, some of which are water-borne like typhoid and cholera, some water-washed like skin infections and trachoma, some water-dependant like schistosomaiasis and guinea worm. An impact on these disease is dependent not only upon the quantity and quality of water (available) but also on improved personal hygiene (which again requires water) and life-styles, on drainage of excess water and efficient water management, on excreta disposal and environmental sanitation … (which) must be viewed as components of an integrated sanitation package" (1980). Malaria has of course long been endemic in many parts of the sub-continent. So was it in southern Europe, along the Mediterranean regions of France and Italy until the marshes in these areas were drained in the 19th century and the land developed for agriculture.

The early 19th century saw the Indian subcontinent swept by epidemics of cholera and plague, products of impure water and insanitation. Cholera took a high toll of troops in various parts of the country and though medical literature was apt to cite cholera as originating in Bengal, it was endemic in several areas and spread along the trade routes (Visaria, Leela and Pravin 1982). A series of malaria epidemics reportedly halved the population of Hooghly district between 1850 and 1870. Irrigation works were taken up to combat famine and the railway system also saw considerable expansion during the second half of the 19th century. Both developments soon came to be associated with the spread of malaria as railway and canal embankments impeded the natural drainage. "During the 1870s, the incidence of the disease (malaria) increased alarmingly throughout the canal-irrigated districts where the saturation of flush irrigation coincided with the obstruction of natural drainage lines. In spite of a series of minor drainage operations begun by the Irrigation Department, fever continued to be a frequent cause of death, and worse still for a large number of cultivators, a frequent cause of debilitation, especially in districts with large irrigated areas". (Whitcombe, 1971). Between 1901 and 1911, cholera and plague ravaged Punjab and the United Provinces. Looking back, the Census of India 1951 recalled that "epidemics of malaria fever decimated the irrigated tracts of the eastern and central Punjab, and the Ganga-Jamuna doab in the United Provinces, where in 1908 alone the reported mortality from fevers was nearly two millions." The construction of the Sarda canal in U.P. between 1920 and 1929 had to be periodically suspended due to the outbreak of malaria in the labour camps. A conference on irrigation and malaria convened by the National Institute of Sciences in India in 1938 established a correlation between the two, though not without much disputation between medical and engineering personnel.

In reverse, the drainage of swamps over 77,000 hectares of U.P. Terai after 1948 led to the reclamation of dense jungle for cultivation and refugee resettlement. Land clearance was accompanied by the spraying of pools and marshes to eliminate malaria from that tract. This was the beginning of what was to become a nation-wide malaria control programme.

Before malaria control commenced in the country, nearly 100 million cases and almost 0.8 million deaths were reported annually, with mortality peaking sharply during epidemic years. The National Malaria Control Programme was launched in 1953 and was in 1958 converted into an eradication programme (NMEP). The results were dramatic and by 1965 the incidence had been reduced to 100,000 cases with no deaths reported. Inadequate and interrupted supplies of DDT at a crucial juncture and failure initially to include urban areas, which were left to the municipalities, resulted in some malaria vectors developing resistance to DDT before total eradication was achieved. Lack of vigilance and surveillance were contributory factors. As resistance to DDT increased there was a change over to BHC but by 1970 vector resistance to both necessitated use of malathion as a replacement insecticide.

RESURGENCE OF MALARIA

The resurgence of malaria in India appeared to coincide with the green revolution as the new hybrid varieties demanded more intensive irrigation. This in turn augmented and enlarged the area of breeding sites along the entire canal network. These mosquitoes could be vectors of malaria, filariasis or Japanese encephalitis. V.P. Sharma noted that "in many areas of the country it was, and still is, observed that the construction of canals brings malaria to healthy areas. The commonly encountered reasons for irrigation-associated malaria are the rise in sub-soil water resulting in waterlogging, poor drainage, minor engineering aberrations such as leaky sluice gates, seeping canal banks, burrowpits, defective distribution chambers, improper delivery of water, poorly maintained canals, banks and beds ... absence of a controlled system of field channels, increased wet cultivation and lack of coordination between different agencies" (September 1987). However, Sharma also quotes Russell (1938) to the effect that it is not irrigation per se, but defective and untidy irrigation which, by misplacing water to the advantage of certain species of anopheline mosquitoes, generates malaria. Irrigation also increases average humidity thus enhancing mosquito survival and the basic reproduction rate of the vector. The gross area under irrigation increased from 29 million hectares in 1960 to 60 million hectares in 1980 and continues to expand rapidly.

By 1977, malaria eradication had become a forlorn hope and the Modified Plan of Operation was adopted with the immediate objective of reducing morbidity and preventing mortality. The incidence of malaria, which had peaked to 6.4 million cases with 59 deaths in 1976, declined to 1.76 million cases, though with 277 deaths, in 1986.

Out of 51 anopheline species of mosquito, six are primary vectors and four others are of more limited regional importance. While the urban problem lies in the emergence of certain chloroquine-resistant strains, the rural situation has been affected by the use of fertilizers and pesticides which have brought about a succession of new anopheline species (Sharma V.P.). In India *A. culicifacies* is the main malaria vector, especially in the rural areas, and is responsible for up to 70 per cent of all cases in the country. This breeds profusely in irrigated areas wherever there are stagnant pools.

It might be inferred that rice-cultivation favours malarial breeding. This is in fact not necessarily so. A comparative study of paddy cultivation shows that whereas the resurgence of malaria in Punjab paralleled the expansion of acreage under rice, Bihar has a very low incidence of malaria despite a high acreage under rice. The same contradiction is to be found between Haryana and western U.P., areas of active malaria transmission, and eastern U.P. and elsewhere which suggests that *A. culicifacies* "have different vectorial capacities in different areas" (Subbarao, 1988). Unlike Punjab which is afflicted by species A of this vector, Eastern U.P., North Bihar and Nepal have species B which has a low vectorial capacity. Thus eastern UP and North Bihar show little malaria transmission despite high rainfall, flooding and waterlogging. On the other hand, Punjab which once experienced malaria only after the rains has now become an endemic foci on account of relay cropping of high-yielding varieties of wheat and rice with a high intensity of water use. Tubewell areas are less prone to malaria.

Migration of agricultural labour and other populations and the concentration of labour at work sites, such as dams, has also been responsible for transmitting malaria and other diseases.

In Bangladesh too malaria has once again become a major health problem and was reported to be on the increase in 1986. In Bhutan and Nepal, as in the Himalayan region in India, the incidence of malaria is largely limited to elevations below 1,000 metres although the vector has been found even up to 3,000 metres. Like India, Nepal had tremendous success in combating malaria after the launching of an eradication programme in 1954. The number of cases fell from around two million per annum to 2,500 cases in 1971. The same constraints as in India led to a rise in the incidence of the disease in the 1970s and there was a further resurgence in the 1980s with 29,000 cases detected in 1984 as a result of expanding irrigation in the Terai. There are however signs of decline.

India has been spending about 45 per cent of its health budget on the control of malaria alone. But the strategy is undergoing change in view of the rising cost of spraying insecticides and ecological objections to their use, especially in the case of stronger chemicals with increasing vector resistance. DDT, though banned in several countries, is still widely used as it is the cheapest insecticide, costing Rs.33 lakhs per million population covered. As many as 210 million people are still covered by the DDT programme as compared to 110 million and 22 million each under BHC and malathion programmes which cost Rs.37 lakhs per million population and Rs.200 lakhs per million population respectively. Attention is, therefore, now turning to integrated systems of environment management for vector control.

INTEGRATED VECTOR CONTROL SYSTEMS

An experiment in vector control of malaria in Kheda district Gujarat, a highly endemic area, was successfully conducted in 1985 through source reduction by elimination of all breeding sites. Small ponds were filled, drains cleaned, containers emptied and a larvivorous fish, Guppy, introduced into water troughs, wells and ponds. Soak pits, tree planting, chemotherapy, and a host of other measures were also instituted. Definite improvement was noted at modest cost. The bio-environmental control method was estimated to cost under Rs.5 per capita as against over Rs.6 in the case of DDT and BHC spray techniques and as much as Rs.23 if malathion was used. Indeed, the community was able to generate an income by cultivating fish and prawn in what were once malaria breeding ponds, and marshy lands were drained by growing eucalyptus. Smokeless *chulahs*, bio-gas plants and solar cookers were popularized (Sharma, V.P. et al. December 1986).

At a different level, another experiment was conducted at the Bharat Heavy Electricals Ltd. township near Haridwar. Burrow pits and depressions were filled with fly ash and land leveled. Drains were unclogged and sources of stagnant water treated or removed. It was estimated that the total loss to BHEL from malaria, including man-days lost, hospitalization, absenteeism and loss to the affected families, was of the order of Rs.57 lakhs per annum as against an expenditure of Rs.3.5 lakhs on bio-environmental control which has reduced the incidence of malaria by over 80 per cent(ICMR Bulletin July, 1987).

The Malaria Research Centre of the Indian Council of Medicinal Research in Delhi has now launched a larger project on integrated vector control of malaria, filarial and other vector borne diseases in collaboration with a number of other Departments and agencies (1988). The country has been divided into seven zones within which malariogenic stratification is to be attempted on a district-wide basis as a means of introducing malaria control through appropriate bio-environmental methods. In Haldwani in the U.P. Terai for example, gambusi a larvivorous fish and other commercial species have been introduced in village ponds and in eight storage reservoirs. The idea is to breed small non-edible larvivorous fish which can be released into canals and would be able to enter tiny channels and grassy margins which are vector breeding grounds. Experiments have been conducted in mine areas in various parts of the country including U.P., Delhi, Madhya Pradesh and Assam since 1986 and in two years the estimated savings/earnings on not spraying DDT, prevention of cases, and from edible fish production and tree plantations is placed at over Rs.4 crores. Efforts are now on to locate larvivorous fish suited to rivers, streams, canals, drains, rice fields and other water bodies through systematic study.

Like malaria, filarial, Japanse encephalitis and schistosomaiasis are caused by vectors that breed in water. Filarial, whose mosquito vector breeds in insanitary water conditions, has spread alarmingly. The population at risk increased from 25 million in 1953 to 342 million in 1985, the bulk of this rural, with significant concentrations in U.P., Bihar, West Bengal, Assam and Madhya Pradesh. As of 1981 there were over 15 million diseased persons in the country and more than 21 million microfilaria carriers. The opening up of agriculture in the U.P. Terai and Assam through migrant labour from endemic areas such as Bihar, West Bengal and Orissa has imported filarial into those regions. Intensive agriculture promoted by irrigation has caused growth centres to develop without sewerage and sanitation which has created favourable breeding sites for the filarial vector Culex quinquefasciatus. With the vectors already present, the arrival of migrant labour carriers from endemic regions has transmitted the disease as in the case of malaria. In 1969 the Government of India directed all State administrations to make adequate arrangements for disposal of sewage and sullage, prevent filariogenic conditions in new settlements and ensure recurrent anti-larval measures under the National Filariasis Control Programme. Action did not match the alert.

The Vector Control Research Centre, Pondicherry, has shown that integrated vector management is possible with community participation through a combined strategy of environmental management, biological control and chemical control. Gambusia and Tilapia fish were successfully released in wells and the transmission of the disease was sharply reduced (Rajagopalan and Das, 1986).

Japanese encephalitis or brain fever is new to India and entered the country from Japan via Southeast Asia in the mid-1950s. It moved up from south India into the Ganga-Brahmaputra plain after an epidemic in West Bengal in 1973. The vector is the *Culex vishnui* group of mosquitoes, especially *C. tritaeniorhynchus*, which breeds in paddies and other deep irrigated areas with a warm, humid climate. The vector transmits the virus to pigs but the more potent carrier in India has been birds such as cattle egrets and pond herons that are attracted to new water bodies that tend to accompany untidy irrigation. The Japanese developed a vaccine for both humans and pigs and alerted irrigation practices by draining paddy fields every week to kill the larvae. Unlike the malaria vector, which comes indoors, the JE vector remains outdoors but is susceptible to the DDT, BHC and malathions prays used in anti-malaria fogging operations.

Dengue fever is also caused by mosquito, the *Aedes aegypti*, but is almost entirely an urban disease. The vector breeds in water tanks and cisterns attached to desert coolers. The Gangetic cities have suffered dengue epidemics and Delhi has become an endemic focus (Centre for Science and Environment, 1985).

Schistosomaisis (bilharziasis), caused by a snail, is endemic in certain parts of the world, especially southeast Asia and Africa. It did quite some damage in the Aswan High Dam project until brought under control. It is fortunately not found in India though there have been some reports of a focus of schistosomaisis in Ratnagiri in Maharashtra and in the Narmada basin where a coordinated health study was conducted by the National Institute of Communicable Diseases, Delhi in 1985 for the Sardar Sarovar reservoir area. A vector-snail and alternative host surveillance programme has been recommended.

Kala Azar, once thought to have disappeared had staged a come back in Bihar and West Bengal and though stray cases have been reported in Assam, U.P. and elsewhere. This is not a water-borne disease but is caused by the sandfly which breeds in dung and can be controlled by DDT. In Bihar, 26 districts are now endemic and over 66,000 cases and 264 deaths were reported between 1985 and 1988.

More than 12 million people live in villages endemic to guinea worm in India and half a million cases are reported annually. Communities dependant on ponds, cisterns and stepwells for drinking water are at risk as the water becomes contaminated when guinea worm infected persons use those sources for drinking and bathing (Elding, 1986). Conversion of stepwells into draw wells and provision of standpipes are among the prophylactic measures being taken. Guinea worm occurs in areas where the water surface temperature exceeds 19 degrees Celsius. In the semi-arid endemic areas of India, including Rajasthan and Madhya Pradesh, its peak season coincides with the April and September harvest season and it affects agricultural operations by spreading disability. The number of cases had however been halved to under 23,000 between 1983 and 1986 and only 5600 villages were reported affected in 1988.

WATER-BORNE PARASITIC AILMENTS

As lethal and debilitating and more widespread in the entire Ganga-Brahmaputra-Barak Basin than vector borne diseases are water-borne parasitic ailments such as diarrhea, dysentery, cholera, hepatitis and typhoid. These ailments come from polluted sources of drinking water and by oral-faecal contact. Delhi's cholera epidemic in 1988 was caused by use of shallow handpumps for drinking water in insanitary colonies resulting in heavy pollution of the upper layers of a high water table. It is mandatory that drinking water be drawn only from aquifers that lie below at least the first impervious rock and clay strata; but this is often violated, sometimes on the plea that such shallow pumps will only be used for non-drinking purposes. Distance and accessibility factors however drive hapless families to use these sources for all purposes. Leaking water mains and pipes in proximity to drains or other sources of faecal mattes are liable to get contaminated. Nullahs and drains often discharge into ponds and rivers from which people draw drinking water. Floods can also contaminate wells, tanks and other normally-safe sources which are not always properly decontaminated before being restored to community use. The only sure remedy is the provision of protected water supply and proper sewerage and sanitation.

Dams and irrigation storages can result in the absorption of fluoride content in drinking water above the permissible levels, causing fluorosis. This has taken the form of knock-knees (genu valgum) in areas around the Nagarjunasagar Dam in Andhra Pradesh. Fluorosis has also affected pockets in Rajasthan (Jaipur, Jhunjhunu and Churu districts), Haryana and Punjab where the fluoride content of water in semi-arid areas exceeds the permissible limit of one part per million, even in wells. Defluorinisation of water is however possible and is being done in Andhra.

Goitre, which is endemic in the sub-Himalayan belt, including Nepal, is related to iodine deficiency which may be caused by leaching and erosion of naturally-occurring iodine in soils in heavy rainfall and flood prone regions. Iodised salt offers a simple remedy.

Still other diseases can be caused by the incremental ingestion of chemical residues from fertilizers, pesticides and insecticides like DDT through the food chain. Agro-wash flowing into streams and rivers or seeping into groundwater can contaminate fish, crops and milk. Some of these chemicals deposited in vital organs of the human system can cause serious maladies over time.

Careful and sustained water planning, a protected water supply, good water management, an environmental sanitation accompanied by health education and awareness, especially among women, and personal hygiene are necessary to prevent a variety of skin and 'water-washed' diseases such as scabies, yaws, leprosy, typhus, conjunctivitis and trachoma. The toll on children and pregnant women is particularly tragic. Nepal, Bhutan, Bangladesh and India are prey to these same poverty-associated disorders that not merely impair the quality of life but operate as a terrible and costly drag on economic progress.

Water resource development on any scale should be preceded by epidemiological studies of the region so that anticipatory measures are built into the overall programme. Unfortunately public health with community participation was too long downgraded and is only now being given some attention. Disease hazard mapping related to migrant labour streams and changing socio-economic parameters must be developed to cover vulnerable areas at first and the entire country in due course. This will have to be done not for large regions but for villages and city-wards ultimately. Surveillance and sentinel systems should also be developed on the basis of regular feedback so that preventive measures can be initiated in good time as soon as a rising incidence of any particular disease is noticed. This has been done in Delhi for meningitis.

HEALTH MAINTENANCE IN WATER RESOURCE DEVELOPMENT

The Indian Health Ministry has advocated a health component for all water resource projects but there is little or no "health maintenance" in reservoirs and canal systems. Cleaning and weeding of canals, their periodic flushing during the off-season when stagnant waters facilitate vector breeding, provision of culverts to prevent breaches and spills at channel crossing, plugging of leaks and seepage points, and lining of certain canal reaches to eliminate grassy margins where mosquitoes breed would make for better health. Health surveillance of migrant labourers on large projects who may carry unknown diseases into new areas would be an important preventive measure. The Parallel Ganga Canal in U.P. for example is being constructed in sections and will accumulate stagnant water which could be a health risk. One answer would be to breed larvivorous and other fish until the canal is completed and ready to be run.

Elaborate studies are being conducted on the Accelerated Mahaweli (irrigation and colonization) Project in Sri Lanka to define the engineering aspects of irrigation development in relation to vector breeding. "In this survey a matrix approach has been applied, linking potential breeding places with specific disease vectors, the location of these breeding places with the phase in the irrigation cycle, and the occurrence of these breeding places with water management practices. A number of characteristics in System C (of the project) have been pinpointed as being of direct relevance to vector production. First and foremost is the discrepancy between the calculated need of water and the actual intake. Clearly, the level of excess water in the system gives rise to collection of water in depressions, thus creating suitable breeding places. Of the other factors considered important in vector propagation, lay-out of tertiary canals, improper land leveling, and disruption of the natural drainage system all relate to the subject of water management" (Bos, December 1986). Designing irrigation systems to high flow velocities has also been suggested.

Again, land reclamation for irrigated agriculture can create favourable conditions for malaria transmission. "Wild animals disappear as vast tracts of forests are cleared. *A. culicifacies*, which is usually in zoophilic species having a preference for cattle blood, is forced to turn to man for its blood meals, leading to an increased man-vector contact. The vast network of irrigation channels, if not properly maintained, will further increase the breeding potential of this species ... Agricultural practices have been changing during the past 20 years. The tractor is replacing the buffalo, particularly in the newly-opened lands under the Mahaweli Development Project. As the buffalo population rapidly decreases, the vector mosquito is diverted from animal to man" (Samarasinghe, December 1986).

The health impact of the green revolution in Punjab and the paddy-wheat cycle as in Haryana and Western U.P. have not been evaluated. Agriculturally, diversification of the cropping pattern is now indicated and a different crop rotation would alter the environmental background and disrupt established vector breeding cycles. Such a change would be facilitated were the intensive rice production programme in Eastern UP and Bihar to take off as the A. culicifacies vector that has played havoc in northwestern India does not transmit malaria in these two eastern regions.

DRINKING WATER CRISIS

Diarrhoeal diseases are high throughout the basin and their incidence is said to be the highest in Bhutan. Gastro-intestinal infections and parasitic infestations seriously impair health as they reduce an already low protein-calorie nutritional intake and are debilitating. Proper disposal of human wastes is as yet limited to a few towns but the Bhutanese government hopes to universalise sanitary latrines by the end of the century. A three-phase rural water supply programme envisages 60 per cent coverage by 1991, 87 per cent coverage by 1996 and total coverage by the turn of the century (UNICEF, October 1986).

About 44 per cent of all child deaths in the 0-4 age group in Nepal are diarrhea-related on account of poor sanitation and polluted water. The traditional water sources on which most people depend are not protected and are further polluted by multiple use. About 22 per cent of the total population had access to piped water in 1985, most of these urban dwellers. Worm infestation is high. A programme to introduce sanitary latrines was initiated in the Seventh Plan (1985-90) and the sewerage system is being extended in Kathmandu and being introduced and strengthened in other larger towns (UNICEF, October 1986).

In Bangladesh an estimated nine million people were served by shallow tubewells in 1986 but the vast majority of the rural population still used ponds or other surface sources and were exposed to faecal pollution. In 1984 only between two and four per cent of the population had a sanitary latrine. A rising water table in the monsoon complicates sanitation technology and in 1983 there were over 57 million episodes of diarrhea among children under five causing an estimated 200,000 child deaths (UNICEF, December 1986). Most rivers also show high coliform levels during the period of lean flow.

The Indian situation is not much better, especially within the basin. The time taken in fetching water, firewood and fodder by women and the high incidence of water-related diseases reinforces a vicious circle of poverty, ill health and illiteracy. It has been said with some justification that greater access to protected water supply would improve school attendance and school results.

India's drinking water crisis has worsened from year to year with physical shortages being reported through all the summer months in town and country. It is being found necessary to supply communities with water through carts, tankers, trains and even by coastal tankers. Heavy pumping has lowered groundwater levels in many regions leaving traditional wells and shallower tubewells high and dry. Drought and environmental blight has resulted in scarcities, the drying up of springs, sedimentation and reduced stream flows with greater abstractions upstream. It was to tackle the rural segment of this problem that a national technology mission on drinking water was mounted a few years ago (Rural Development Department, January 1988). As of 1985-86 there were approximately 154,000 villages with an identified drinking water scarcity and another 73,000 problem villages remained to be covered. The mission involves locating and developing water sources and systems together with a maintenance plan; the establishment of a network of water quality testing facilities at various levels and a plan for establishing desalination and defluoridation plants, units for removing excess iron, and converting wells into sanitary wells.

The technology mission was in a sense in continuation of the National Master Plan drawn up in implementation of the international drinking water supply and sanitation decade, 1981-90 (Works and Housing Ministry, July 1983). Since the object of national saturation is not going to be achieved by 1991, the Decade programme is proposed to be extended up to 2001 consistent with the commitment to achieve Health-for-All by that date.

Under both the Decade Programme and the Indian National Water Policy drinking water gets first priority amongst water uses, water irrigation, hydro-electric power, navigation, industrial and other uses following in that order. The policy statement further provides: "Adequate drinking water facilities should be provided to the entire population both in urban and in rural areas by 1991. Irrigation and multi-purpose projects should invariably include a drinking water component wherever there is no alternative source. The drinking water needs of human beings and animals should be the first charge on any available water" (Water Resources Ministry, September 1987). The State irrigation departments have been advised to keep this in mind in planning and executing all water projects and to liaise in this regard with appropriate State-level and local authorities. However, only Andhra Pradesh had till 1988 issued orders in this regard, adding that all irrigation systems should make available drinking water supplies free of cost in rural areas and at nominal cost for urban consumption. Since the water supply norm is 40 to 70 litres per capita in rural areas and a graded 100 to 220 litres per capita in urban areas depending on city-size, and only a little part of this is consumed as drinking water, the quantities involved are quite small in an absolute sense. Tubewells supply a considerable part of the urban demand too. However, the problems are of availability at given locations, even within cities, accessibility, equity and water quality.

URBAN SEWERAGE AND SANITATION

Rapid urbanization has posed enormous problems. The Delhi master plan initially envisaged an ultimate population of 5.4 million. This has long been exceeded Delhi's population is today over eight million and is estimated to peak at round 12.8 million by 2001. The city's water supply system in 1988 provided 1860 million litres per day (4.55 litres equals one gallon) of which 182 mld goes to industry. With the schemes under execution this is expected to increase to 2320 mld by 1990 and will have to more than double again to 4660 mld by the turn of the century to match the city's anticipated population. As of no some 136-160 mld comes from Ranney wells (in the Yamuna) and tubewells, 455 mld from the Eastern Ganga Canal from Muradnagar in U.P., and the balance from the Yamuna and the Western Yamuna Canal. Delhi is currently fighting for a larger allocation from new storages in the Yamuna (Kishau Dam) and Ganga (Tehri Dam) catchments. Part of the additional demand in Delhi and other urban centres can be met by recycling. Of the standard maximum 200 litre average per capita per day water supply to metro-cities, only six litres or 3 per cent is consumed in drinking and cooking. The rest runs off as untreated sewage flows into various rivers, causing pollution. If sewage is fully treated, as now proposed, then all non-consumptive urban water waste can be recycled and used for non-potable purposes or, less expensively, led into sewage farms. If the additional waste waters treated in Delhi were used for downstream irrigation then Haryana, the beneficiary, could be requested to release an equivalent quantum of raw water from the Yamuna upstream for use in the capital. Many industrial uses too are non-consumptive except where high temperatures or pressures cause evaporation losses. Otherwise, unless waste waters are highly toxic, effluents can be treated and recycled.

Toilet cisterns normally empty about 12 litres each time the pan is flushed. As against this, pour-flush latrines and a simple low-volume cistern of Swedish design use about 1.5 litres. But these are only good for limited static sanitary systems. Water-borne sewage in larger city systems require about 132 litres per day toilet to move faecal matter with a self-cleaning velocity.

Most Indian city systems suffer water losses of up to 30-40 per cent on account of leakages according to a sample study. This figure compares unfavourably with the international norm of 10-15 per cent for what is termed unaccounted for water. Water conservation and better maintenance would work wonders for most urban systems.

The demand for augmenting water supply has been so pressing and enjoys such high priority that, given limited funds, it is no surprise that sewerage has taken a very low place. The pattern of Central Government assistance also puts a greater burden on States and in turn on local bodies to generate their own resources to finance sanitation and sewerage schemes. Water supply programmes are treated more generously. These priorities obviously need to be brought into better balance. Again, water rates are low, being 35 paise per 1000 litres in Delhi against a production cost of a rupee and an additional distribution cost that could be as much. However, sewerage charges are even more nominal at one per cent of the property tax in Delhi whereas the cost of sewerage would be about 20 paise and that of treatment about Rs. 1 per 1000 litres. Delhi is of course a highly pampered city. The Maharashtra Water Board operates some 65 waterworks and produces water at Rs.0.60 to Rs.2.70 per 1000 litres. It sells this at a pooled price at Rs.1.50 per 1000 litres which enables it to recover its overall costs. Rajasthan too charges Rs.1.50 to Rs.2 per 1000 litres whereas U.P., Bihar and West Bengal levy very low rates. World Bank aided projects have a financial covenant that binds the loanee authority to charge a price that meets the operational costs and servicing of the loan. This has been done in Bombay and Madras.

The tradition of open air defecation that prevails over much of the basin area is not merely insanitary and a health hazard but a human indignity. The existence of about six million dry bucket privies throughout India, of which half a million are located in Delhi, altogether employing about 200,000 night-soil scavengers is another disgrace. Assuming an average cost of Rs.2000 for conversion of a dry latrine into a low-cost pour-flush toilet, it will take about Rs.1200 crores at 1998 prices to eliminate scavenging from the country. A further sum of Rs.400 crores will be needed for the training and rehabilitation of those relieved of the demeaning task of scavenging (Sulabh International, July 1988). The Sulabh organization took up the challenge under a Gandhian, Bindeswari Pathak, in 1970 and has done excellent work in Bihar and elsewhere in converting dry latrines into low-cost pour-flush water seal toilets, constructing several pay-and-use urban community toilet complexes with bathing and washing facilities and linking these to biogas plants (Ribeiro, 1985)

The problems of urban water supply, sewerage and sanitation have received inadequate attention and funds – as noted by the National Commission on Urbanisation (August, 1988). The Commission reported; "A major feature of our urban scene is the misery and serious health hazards caused by lack of water supply and sanitation. Almost all our urban centres, even those which at one time had reasonably adequate water supply, are now suffering from crippling shortages. It is a matter of national disgrace that, in 1988, there were prolonged periods when Hyderabad and Madras received piped water supply for only about 20 minutes a day – with many localities doing without water for days on end. Delhi, too, had to face severe problems in the summer of 1988. On the one hand there is no long-term planning for urban water needs; on the other, there is a constant paucity of funds. The Ministry of Water Resources has gradually evolved basin development plan for our major rivers for the purpose of irrigation and hydro-electric development; but urban water supply is looked upon as a totally residual item … The Commission recommends that unified plans should be drawn up for all water resources and their utilization, both for agriculture and urban use. The allocation of water resources should be done in an integrated manner, which means that the funding of water development utilization schemes should treat all uses on an equal footing". This should not remain a cry in the wilderness. India is fast moving away from being a predominantly agricultural society. The urban-industrial sector and ecological needs are acquiring a salience they lacked before. An irrigation-led tradition or water development must therefore yield to more comprehensive integrated planning for the future.

RISING GANGA AND YAMUNA POLLUTION

Comprehensive urban sewerage, treatment and disposal systems came into vogue in Europe and the United States only in the mid-19th century and were introduced in Calcutta, Bombay and Madras in the 1870s. These systems have not kept pace with urban expansion and in many cases have deteriorated on account of lack of maintenance. Half of Delhi, for example, has no sewerage facilities and the capital's waste water treatment capacity is less than half that required today. The city has 17 storm water drains which now also carry sullage from unplanned and unauthorized colonies and empty into the Yamuna. With ever-increasing abstractions of water upstream for irrigation, even the Ganga below Haridwar and the Narora, where the Upper and Lower Ganga canals take off, is reduced to a waste water drain in the lean season until replenished at the Holy Sangam at Allahabad by the Yamuna, which is itself only rejuvenated at Etawah by the Chambal. River pollution, with a heavy load of untreated sewage and industrial effluents, has emerged as another major health hazard. On one estimate, disease spread by Ganga pollution alone deprives the country of nearly 40 million man-days on account of ill-health. The loss in terms of mortality and economic injury is incalculable (Environment Folio, 1986).

The Ganga, particularly, and the Yamuna are among the most sacred rivers in India or possibly anywhere in the world. Like the Himalaya, they have held saints, poets, writes, sculptors and artists in their spell and are closely woven into epic legend. Who does not know the story of the descent of the Ganga through the labours of Bhagirath. The Mahabharata and Ramayana were enacted along and astride these rivers. It was Jawaharlal Nehru who wrote: "The Ganges, above all the rivers of India, has held India's heart captive and drawn uncounted millions to her bank since the dawn of history. The story of Ganges, from her source to the sea, from old times to new, is the story of India's civilization and culture, of the rise and fall of empires, of great proud cities, of the adventure of man…"

Concern over rising pollution in the Ganga became manifest with growing environmental consciousness in the 1970s. The Committee on Studies for

Cooperation in Development in South Asia, held in Delhi in October 1980, suggested an exploratory investigation into the impact of human settlements and developmental activities on the Ganga river system in India with, a similar study hopefully to follow in Bangladesh. The result was a book (Chphekar and Mhatre, 1986). Meanwhile, following a proposal in India's Sixth Plan that universities be associated with eco-development and a study of environmental problems, a coordinated action research project for the integrated study of the Ganga was launched under the auspices of the Planning Commission involving 16 universities situated on or near the Ganga from the Garhwal to Calcutta and 14 scientific and technological institutions (March 1982). The river was divided into given reaches and the programme of studies included a baseline inventory of all natural resources and human activities, water quality and pollution, and ecological modeling.

A little earlier, the Central Board for the Prevention and Control of Water Pollution, Delhi, took up a study of the Yamuna and Ganga basins as part of its Assessment and Development Study of River Basin Series. Three monographs were prepared by the Board, Part I pertaining to the Yamuna sub-basin (1978), Part II to the Ganga basin (1984), and Part III to the West Bengal stretch (1981).

The Yamuna sub-region supports a population of 57 million. The study noted that 80 per cent of the river's 100 million cubic metre run-off is in the three monsoon months. Consequently, the fair weather flow for beneficial uses and pollutant dilution, dispersion and assimilation are rather small, going down to 0.1 million cubic metres per day (mcm/day) or 1.2 cumecs in Delhi and 0.3 mcm/day in the Mathura-Etawah reach. Ingress of untreated sewage, wading by large herds of buffaloes, and mass ritual bathing on festive days introduce heavy bacteriological loads. On special bathing days, numbering over 20 major fairs are listed at Delhi, Mathura, Agra, Etawah, Kalpi and Allahabad on the Yamuna, Orcha on the Betwa, Ujjain on the Kshipra, and Kota on the Chambal "when thousands or sometimes even hundreds of thousands of people bathe in the congested stretch of river within the span of a few hours". The stream-reaches needing immediate steps for upgrading quality to satisfy current best use classification comprise those immediately downstream of the large industrial and urban centres of Delhi, Mathura, Agra and Indore. Apart from the pollution load from these centres, a build up of salinity is reported in the Yamuna between Wazirabad (the northern end of Delhi) and Etawah over a stretch of nearly 350 kilometres on account of return flows from agricultural activities.

The main directions of pollution control effort cited is augmentation of lean season flows in critical reaches, particularly along the Yamuna from Wazirabad to Etawah. "It has to be brought out to the planners and administrators of agriculture and irrigation that while meeting the rising irrigation requirements is extremely important, this cannot be done by diverting most of low water flows except at the cost of severe environmental degradation. The only practical approach is to store more and more of the monsoon run-offs both for various beneficial uses and for release in the critical reaches during lean periods. Such flow regulation and equalization can be achieved either by building large storage projects (and the Kishua dam on the Tons, a tributary of the Yamuna is specifically mentioned for this role), or by ensuring enhanced percolation to the underground reservoir. A balanced mixture of both these will be advisable. In any case, the current spurt in pumped canals and small irrigation schemes does not seem very desirable from an environmental point of view as they tend to reduce stream flows during critical periods. An indepth study of the irrigation system, and particularly all new irrigation projects, to ensure optimal use of water with minimum adverse impact on the environment should be insisted on".

The Ganga Basin Study (Part II) also mentions the problems of very low seasonal flows, after abstractions for irrigation, in certain critical stretches below Haridwar and upto Kannauj where the river is joined by the Ramganga. Very numbers of people bathe daily in the river at Rishikesh, Hardwar, Garh-Mukhteshwar, Kannauj, Allahabad, Mirzapur, Varanasi and Nawadwip. From the point o view of water quality, the stretches from Kanpur to Patna and from Nawadwip to Diamond Harbour were found to give cause for concern. With intensive irrigated agriculture being practiced in Western U.P., a rising salinity and alkalinity trend is evident in the river between Haridwar and a point near Badaun. However, "on the whole, the salinity level in the Ganga is somewhat lower than what is found in the Yamuna".

The Ganga transports 83 million tonnes of dissolved solids, the highest for all Indian rivers, and the Brahmaputra another 35 million tonnes to the Bay of Bengal. The Ganga is twice as saline as the Brahmaputra and it is said to account for 2.5 per cent of the global flux of sodium to the oceans (National Environmental Engineering Research Institute, 1987).

Given adequate stream flows, the Ganga is able to dilute and assimilate sewage and other pollution loads within 20 kilometres of large cities except in vulnerable low-water stretches during the lean season and below major industrial urban and bathing centres. The river is resilient and belief in its purity is sustained by its unusually good keeping quality as testified by devout pilgrims who have taken home Ganga jal. Faith in the curative quality of the water possibly stems from its high radon content (86.5 pci per cent on a sampling reported to have been done by the Uranium Corporation of India at Jaduguda in Bihar).

River quality is normally measured in accordance with three standards. The dissolved oxygen (DO) level should not be less than five, the bio-chemical oxygen demand (BOD) provides an index of pollution and should not be more than three, and the most probable number (MPN) of coliform or harmful bacteria should not exceed 500 per 100 millimetres of water. The Ganga has a good DO rating, averaging a count of 9 to 10. But the BOD and MPN counts in vulnerable stretches leave a great deal to be desired.

GANGA ACTION PLAN

Concern over the degradation of the Ganga led the Department of Environmental on the basis of the findings of the Central Pollution Control Board to prepare an Action Plan to combat pollution in the river. Addressing the nation early in January 1985, the Prime Minister lamented the pollution of the river and declared "we will restore the pristine purity of the Ganga".

Thus was launched the Ganga Action Plan (GAP), one of the greatest and most significant river cleaning operations carried out anywhere in the world. A separate Central Ganga Authority was set up in February 1985 with a commitment of Rs.292 crores for Phase I of the programme covering 27 Class I cities (with populations exceeding 100,000), Rs.240 crores being earmarked for the Seventh Plan (1985-90). The Authority is a high-level body with the Prime Minister as Chairman, and the Chief Ministers of U.P., Bihar and West Bengal, and the Deputy Chairman of the Planning Commission as members. Detailed guidance under the policy directions of the Authority is provided by an inter-departmental and inter-disciplinary Steering Committee of which the three State Chief Secretaries are members. Actual executive authority vests in a Project Director who also draws upon the services of a number of universities and specialized institutions (Environment Department, July 1985). The Central Ganga Authority is not an organization as much as an empowered committee backed with an unusual degree of political will, a firm and adequate budget, high visibility and able, it would seem, to command a great deal of emotional support. It has provided a unique platform for integrated river management cutting across political, economic and socio-cultural domains and unobtrusively promoting a number of valuable linkages with wider implications than the immediate objective in hand.

Of the 692 towns within the Ganga basin, there are actually along the river 27 Class I cities, 23 Class II cities (population between 50,000 and 100,000) and 48 towns (less than 50,000 population). The Class I cities have been taken up first as 82.3 per cent of the total urban population living along the banks of the river from Gangotri to Sagar Island in the Bay of Bengal live in these centres which also generate 88.5 per cent of the total volume of sewage produced. Fifteen of these cities have at least partial sewerage and six of them sewage treatment plants. Optimization of benefits from existing systems was therefore considered the best course to adopt.

The Ganga Action Plan falls into three broad categories. The first is to intercept and treat the raw sewage flowing directly into the river causing gross pollution. The second is to ensure and enforce proper effluent treatment of industrial wastes. The third is to promote and assist programmes for supply of protected drinking water, drainage, construction or conversion of existing dry latrines into sanitary pour-flush toilets, renovation and improvement of bathing ghats, construction of electric crematoria, improvement and illumination of streets, plantation and limited erosion control measures, removal of unauthorized "dairies", relocation of dhobi ghats, development of facilities and services such as community toilets and washing places, lighting, water-front development, and establishment laws (as at Varanasi where 30 million pilgrims bathe annually). These tasks are being carried out through local and State institutions and are linked, in part, to World Bank and other aid programmes.

Another important task is monitoring the river for water quality throughout its length and undertaking, coordinating and collating a host of studies pertaining to all relevant aspects. Water quality is being monitored at both macro and micro levels for up to 42 parameters at 27 stations covering physio-chemical, biological and heavy metal indices.

India has as yet no statutory norm for water quality such as those set by the WHO and the Environmental Protection Agency and the United States which are very stringent. However, the Central Pollution Control Board has fixed standards for different uses in India such as Class A (fit for drinking with chlorination), Class B (fit for mass bathing), Class C (fit for drinking after full treatment), Class D (fit for aquatic life), and Class E (fit for receiving wastes). The object of the Ganga Action Plan is to upgrade the river quality to Class B against the Class C and D quality that largely prevailed at the commencement.

IMPROVING WATER QUALITY

Of the 260 or so schemes taken up, 45 have been completed with very positive results. During the Haridwar Kumbh in 1986, 500 youths participated in a Ganga Sewa shivir and prepared 30,000 pits for planting trees in a badly eroded portion of the Mansadevi Hills adjoining Hardwar and constructed and repaired some check dams. Over 9,000 pilgrims who had come to the Kumbh were persuaded to trek to Mansadevi and plant a sapling; subsequently 20,000 more pilgrims completed the task. More dramatically, pilgrims to the Maha Kumbh at Allahabad, which attracted up to 10 million persons on some of the peak bathing days in January and February 1989 were able to bathe in a pollution-free Sangam at the confluence of the Ganga and Yamuna. This was accomplished with the interception and diversion of 13 major drains that formerly carried 90 million litres per day of untreated sewage into the Yamuna just above the Sangam. This sewage is now taken across the Yamuna from where it is pumped into two large sewage farms. The waste water not so used is released into the Ganga at a point 7.5 kilometres below the Sangam. With the assistance of Sulabh International, over 43,000 low-cost sanitation conversions have been completed and 900 scavengers are being rehabilitated in other occupations. The sewage system is being designed against a long-term perspective up to 2020 when Allahabad's population, now approaching a million, may have doubled or tripled.

At Varanasi, seven major drains that used to flow into the Ganga have been plugged and diverted with the result that there is no floating excreta and dung to be seen any more. The dumping of garbage along the river has been reduced and the waterfront is being greened. A 545 million litres-per day capacity sewage treatment plant is proposed. Existing treatment plants here and elsewhere are recycling waste, extracting methane gas and manorial sludge and irrigating sewage farms with organic-rich residual flows. As many as 24,000 low-cost sanitation pour-flush latrines are to be converted by 1990 and the task is well in hand (GAP, Varanasi 1987).

Two electric crematoria are being built after initial opposition from the Dom Raja who heads the caste group that traditionally performs the last rites for the dead. It is the wish of the pious to be created at Varanasi. About 40,000 bodies are cremated at the city's burning ghats and some 5,000 unburnt or partially burnt bodies and 8,000-10,000 animal carcases are thrown into the river every year along with bodies of children and sadhus which are consigned to the Ganga. Because of the crescent shape of the river at Varanasi, dead bodies and other pollutants would hug the city bank during periods of lean flow. Few can afford a traditional funeral which costs up to Rs 1,000 for firewood, dakshina (fees), and boat charges for immersion of the ashes. The municipal authorities spend about Rs 400 in cremating each unclaimed body. Huge quantities of firewood are consumed (an estimated 12,000 tonnes per annum at Varanasi) and large amounts of ash Rs 50 and it takes only about two to three hours to collect and immerse the ashes. Today at Varanasi floating bodies are fished out and cremated by the Municipal Corporation while carcasses are push-towed to a point below the city. An animal waste rendering plant is proposed to be installed to utilize the carcasses.

At Kanpur the major problem is the toxic waste from 70 odd tanneries which cause severe pollution. An integrated sanitation scheme to treat the tannery wastes and improve drainage and garbage disposal has been initiated. (GAP-Kanpur, 1987). Likewise, industrial pollution along the Hooghly in and around Calcutta is being tackled alongside solid waste management and sewerage. The West Bengal Government has examined and laid down norms for 32 hazardous industries in the State (January1987).

A committee set up to survey the magnitude and sources of industrial pollution of the Ganga identified 68 units in the public and private sectors as "gross polluters" on the basis of the toxicity of their effluents or a volume of discharge into the river in excess of 1000 kilolitres per day. Notices were issued and by July 1989 it was reported that 70 out of 76 units had installed primary effluent treatment plants with or without assistance. Some plants had closed down.

Turtles, once plentiful, were no more to be seen around Varanasi on account of poaching and increasing pollution despite being valuable scavengers. Large numbers of turtles were bred and reintroduced into the river in 1989 at Varanasi and other places. The Gangetic dolphin, the only mammalian species native to the Ganga, is also said to have reappeared near Varanasi in 1988 after it too had disappeared for several years. The dolphin is found lower down the river in Bihar, above Farakka and all the way to Sahebganj, and is recently reported to have found its way up the Brahmaputra to a point near the Kaziranga rhino reserve below Jorhat. These are encouraging bio-indicators of the recovering health of the Ganga with urban improvement.

The problem of the Class II and smaller towns and the rural areas will presumably be tackled in the Eighth and subsequent Plans, beyond 1990. Rural water supply and sanitation programmes are being undertaken by the States.

More important, from the point of view of water quality including that of groundwater, will be controls on fertilizer application, stricter regulation or the banning and substitution of more toxic pesticides and insecticides, and the moving over to bio-fertilisers, organic manures, systems of integrated pest control and the bio-environmental management of disease vectors.

India currently uses around 120,000 tonnes of pesticides in agriculture and public health and manufactures 55 varieties of pesticide, of which DDT, BHC and malathion account for half the output. As indiscriminate or excessive use of pesticides can be harmful, safe tolerance levels in foodgrains have been prescribed for each variety. While these limits may not be exceeded in a single dose, there is danger to health from incremental accumulation in the body system of pesticide residues ingested through the food chain. An Indian's daily diet is estimated to contain 0.27 mg of DDT and the accumulated DDT in the body tissue of an average Indian is said to range between 12.8 and 31 parts per million which would rank among the highest in the world. Not all this is communicated by or through water. But above a certain threshold, every incremental unit of consumption through whatever source must be a matter for concern (Gupta, Y.P. February 1989).

RIVER MODELLING AND STANDARDS

A sophisticated two-dimensional model of the Ganga has been developed to enable pollution loads and the pollution status of the river to be forecast on the basis of 19 parameters measured both along the river bank and across the width of the river. One-dimensional modeling along the river bank is the norm. Measurement across the river under the 2-D model provides a better understanding of the rate of dispersal and mixing of sullage. The basic data is being developed and the model will thereafter be applied experimentally city by city, starting with Allahabad and Varanasi. Nine auto-river quality monitoring units have been ordered and two were installed on the Yamuna at Allahabad just upstream of the Sangam prior to the 1989 Kumbh. No significant concentrations of heavy metal have been noticed anywhere along the river except in some stray pockets. This, as well as chemical wash from fertilizers, pesticide, and urban insecticides used for malarial spraying, is however being closely watched (Industrial Toxicology Research Centre, 1988).

The condition of any river depends on a dynamic balance between the quality and quantity of river flow and of sedimentation, which not merely adds to turbidity but can alter important parameters. This is being studied by an inter-departmental-cum-inter-State Committee on minimum flow requirements along different stretches of both the Ganga and the Yamuna and how this is to be achieved. Factors such as navigational needs, the siting of proposed new river ports at Allahabad and Patna and the implications of dredging by the Inland Waterways Authority of India are also being looked at. Sediment quality monitoring and the impact of the Ganga outfall on marine life in the Bay of Bengal have also been posed as areas of future study. International experience has been garnered and external collaboration sought in specific areas. A twinning agreement between the Central Ganga Authority and the United Kingdom Water Authorities Association is envisaged. This may cover a number of specialized programmes such as estuary modeling, city master planning and so on. The cleaning up of the Thames and the on-going Mersey estuary clean-up project at Liverpool offer two successful models.

The Ganga Action Plan has its critics. There have been problems in getting prompt compliance with the law in regard to discharge of industrial effluents into the river. Installation of effluent treatment plants takes time and costs money and peremptory closures can displace workers and cause industrial unrest. Nevertheless, there is little doubt that it is a programme of profound importance and will invigorate and encourage a number of linked activities along an innovative chain. Its implications for public health, city planning, recycling of wastes and river environment are obvious. An expert of the Thames Water International associated with the Gap believes that some of the quality norms set are questionable or may be unattainable as they follow standards adopted by the West where millions do not bathe in rivers as they do in India. He feels India may be trying to achieve too much in too short a time. Over 900 million litres of sewage is dumped into the Ganga daily, which is only a fifth of Jhat received by the Thames which was cleaned up in 15 to 17 years. But the GAP is perhaps better described as a "spiritual mission", for the Ganga is not just another river, "it is Ma Ganga" (Rai, Usha December 1987). Even so, extensive sampling of five critical parameters under the auspices of the Central Pollution Control Board between 1983 and 1988 has established improved river quality up to the programmed Class B standard (fit for mass bathing). This is a considerable achievement which other more advanced nations have taken more time to realize in relation to their river conditions and objectives.

As the implications of the Ganga Action Plan are realised, demands are beginning to be made for similar programmes on other rivers. A Narmada rehabilitation programme, a Cauvery clean-up, a hill springs recovery plan in the Himalaya, and a lake development authority have been mooted. Indeed, a Loktak Lake Development Committee was set up in Imphal in 1987 under the chairmanship of the Chief Secretary, Manipur to preserve and develop its unique eco-system. A three-State Krishna Action Plan (Maharashtra, Karnataka and Andhra Pradesh) is also fairly well advanced as well as a Gomti Action Plan which the U.P. Government is desirous of pursuing in view of the pollution load from Lucknow and Jaunpur.

Following the cholera epidemic that hit the trans-Yamuna areas of Delhi in the summer of 1988, a Yamuna abatement programme has been drawn up to cover the river from Tajewala, where it enters the plains, to Etawah. The Yamuna carries more toxic wastes than the Ganga because of industrial effluents from Jagadhri, Panipat, Sonepat, Delhi, NOIDA, Mathura and Agra as well as effluents poured into it from the Hindon and Kali Nadi. Moreover, the Yamuna carries less water than the Ganga. Haryana, U.P. and Delhi are involved. Good ideas have legs.

THE LEGAL FRAMEWORK

The Indian Constitution from its commencement called upon the State "to raise the level of nutrition and the standard of living and to improve public health". With rising environmental consciousness, the Constitution was amended in 1976 to insert a further Director Principle enjoining the State to endeavour "to protect and improve the environment and to safeguard the forests and wild life of the country". At the same time, a list of so-called Fundamental Duties was added. Article 51A(g) now requires every citizen "to protect and improve the natural environment, including forests, lakes, rivers and wild life, and to have compassion for living creatures". The Ganga Action Plan is in fulfillment of that Directive Principle and Fundamental Duty. A number of regulatory measures had of course been earlier instituted. The Water and, subsequently, the Air (Prevention and Control of Pollution) Acts of 1974 and 1982 require governments, local bodies and industry alike to seek the consent of pollution control boards and comply with various "consent conditions" before discharging effluents into the water or air. After the Union Carbide disaster at Bhopal, the Environment Protection Act and a rigorous amendment to the Air Act were brought into force in 1986 and 1987. The Supreme Court of India has ruled that managing directors of companies and "occupiers" have a personal liability under various pollution laws. Public interest litigation has also been entertained against municipalities, public bodies and industry in prevention of and securing compensation for injury under various environmental laws (Goswami, 1988).

In a landmark judgement on a public interest suit brought against the continuing discharge of untreated and toxic tannery wastes into the Ganga at Jajmau, Kanpur, despite efforts by the UP Pollution Board under the Ganga Action Plan, the Supreme Court of India on September 22, 1987 ordered the closure of 30 tanneries and gave another group of tanneries six months within which to install primary effluent treatment plants. Justice E.S. Venkatramiah, sitting with Justice K.N. Singh, ruled that "just as an industry which cannot pay minimum wages to its treatment plant cannot be permitted to continue to be in existence, for the adverse effect on the public at large which is likely to ensue by the discharging of trade effluents from the tannery into the River Ganga would be immense; and it will not outweigh any inconvenience that may be caused to the management and the labour employed by it on account of its closure". The Court found that the Kanpur tanners were not taken by surprise and that the cost of installing a primary treatment unit did not appear to be excessive. Yet, as subsequent events have shown, counter availing pressures to export leather are diverting investment resources away from further environmental improvement measures. However, new tanneries are being required to face stricter environmental standards.

The rising number of environmental cases coming up before the courts under various laws and the need to develop suitable expertise on the very complex issues that are to be adjudicated has led the Indian Supreme Court to recommend the constitution of environmental courts consisting of a judge assisted by two experts to be drawn from an ecological sciences research group which it is suggested should also be established. Appeals would lie with the Supreme Court. The U.P. Government has since, in consultation with the State High Court, named a special judicial magistrate in Lucknow exclusively to hear cases pertaining to the prevention and control of pollution.

GREENHOUSE WARNINGS

While water pollution is indeed a worrying problem, air pollution is beginning to cause greater anxiety in terms of its likely consequences in impelling macro-climatic changes through the so-called greenhouse effect with major impacts on the timing and distribution of rainfall.

Recent scientific studies, reinforced in the popular mind by aberrant weather around the world over the past few years, appear to suggest the possibility of global climate changes some of which could have very adverse consequences for mankind. The effects of acid rain on forests and water bodies caused by excessive emissions of sulphur dioxide, particularly in Europe and North America, drew a warning from the International Union for the Conservation of Nature, UNEP and the World Wildlife Fund (1980). In 1987 it was reported that Switzerland would that winter begin the first evacuation of people from villages no longer protected from avalanches because the forests above them are dying; thousands of lakes in Scandinavia and North America are without life; and in Greece, the Acropolis and other marble monument are turning to gypsum (MacNeill).

The World Commission on Environment and Development recalled that Nature is bountiful but also fragile and finely balanced and that "there are thresholds that cannot be crossed without endangering the basic integrity of the system". One such threat to life-support systems to which it called attention was the greenhouse effect. The accelerated burn-up of fossil fuels and the cutting and burning of forests has resulted in an accumulation of carbon dioxide and other gases which trap solar radiation emitted from the earth's surface, causing global warning (1988). The unprecedented growth in population and ever-increasing consumer demands have resulted in widespread destruction especially of tropical forests, which are a natural sink for carbon dioxide, and increasing gaseous emissions (carbon, sulphur and nitrous) from thermal power plants, automobile exhausts, etcetera. These developments threaten within the next 30 to 40 years to raise the concentration of carbon dioxide to approximately 550 parts per million or double the level that prevailed before the industrial revolution. This could raise global temperatures by 1.5 to 4.5 degrees Celsius which in turn could result in a rise of the sea level by 40 to 140 centimetres which would swamp many low-lying coastal areas around the world. Coral reefs such as the Maldives might disappear while a one-metre sea-rise would submerge a land area inhabited by over nine million people in Bangladesh. The lower Sunderbans in West Bengal would likewise be inundated. The higher base line for storm surges would also extend the marine "flood plain". Other greenhouse effects could be more frequent tropical cyclones such as sweep up and around the Bay of Bengal, and changes in atmospheric circulation impacting on the pattern of winds, ocean currents and the timing and distribution of rainfall, rendering some drier and others wetter (Mintzer, 1988).

According to one estimate, forest felling has since 1860, added 90,000-180,000 million tonnes of carbon dioxide to the atmosphere as compared with 150,000-190,000 tonnes from the burning of coal, oil and gas. At present "deforestation is believe to add between 1000 million and 2600 million tons of carbon to the atmosphere annually, or between 20 and 50 per cent as much as the burning of fossil fuels" (Postel and Heise, 1988). Global climatic changes, it is feared, could also create a horrendous new problem of environmental refugees.

Greenhouse warming is however not the only problem. A British research team in 1985 reported a sharp decline in the level of ozone over Antarctica. This "ozone hole" in the earth's protective shield will let more of the sun's ultra-violet radiation filter through, thereby causing an increase in skin cancer, impairing human immune systems and retarding crop growth (Brown and Postel, 1987). The prime cause of ozone erosion is attributed to chloroflurocarbon (CFC) emissions. These synthetic chemicals are used in aerosol cans, refrigerants, fire extinguishers and in a number of other products and processes such as blowing plastic foam. Concerned over the impending danger from continuing and possibly more rapid ozone depletion as a result of increased manufacture and use of CFCs, 24 nations met in Montreal in 1987 and decided to secure a 35 per cent global reduction in CFC production by 1999. Current worldwide production of CFCs is estimated to be around a million tonnes and there being but a limited number of manufacturers facilitated agreement. About 56 nations signed the Montreal Protocol under the aegis of UNEP and it came into force with effect from January 1, 1989 following ratification by a third of signatories, which did not include either India or China and many other developing nations as on that date. Under the agreement, developing countries were expected to freeze consumption at 300 grams per capita or the actual level reached, whichever is less, by the end of 1989 while the industrialized nations were called upon to reduce their consumption to 500 grams per capita by that date and to halve this by 1993.

A National Conference convened by the Indian Ministry of Environment and Forests in Dehra Dun in December 1988 considered the upper atmospheric environmental problem among other things and recommended that India address the following issues on a priority basis: measurement of various problem gases in the upper atmosphere through regular monitoring; adoption of policies to limit carbon dioxide emissions through energy conservation, improved fuel efficiency, appropriate energy pricing policies and shifting the energy mix more towards renewables; the undertaking of fundamental studies to establish the sources and sinks of pollutants; development of alternatives to CPCs; use of Antarctica expeditions for ozone studies; and the development of costal management, agricultural and other development strategies to minimize greenhouse damages and cope with its negative effects. A large continental sized country like India with a wide variety of agro-climatic and altitudinal regions is possibly better placed to cope with macro climatic changes than others; but this by no means certain. Existing experience however offers some insights into adaptation strategies (Jodha, 1988). The issue of food security in the changing global climate must also be addressed. The implications for research and policy have been spelt out by scholars (Sinha S.K. et al, June 1988).

Not all experts are agreed about the extent and impacts of global warming and there are sceptics. Nevertheless, the implications of global change are so far-reaching that it is best to be forewarned. The World Meteorological Organisation hosted a meeting some years ago in Villach, Austria, which concluded that a temperature rise of 1.5 to three degrees Celsius from the greenhouse effect mightbe apparent by 2025. And that is not so far away. An international conference on "Global Warming and Climate Change: Perspectives from Developing Countries" held in Delhi made a whole series of recommendations and concluded that "no further time should be lost in initiating action, although debates on the qualitative and quantitative dimensions of global warming and climate change will always continue among professionals". It reinforced this injunction by stating that many measures recommended were in any case essential for promoting sustainable development (Tata Energy Research Institute, February 1989).

TOWARDS REFORESTATION AND RENEWABLE ENERGY

Two lessons that prospective global warming holds out among others relate to the need to stop and, indeed, reverse the process of deforestation as also to switch to renewable sources of energy. Awareness of the hazards of further deforestation is already widespread, but developing nations are desperately in need of resources to speed development and provide the poor other means of survival than destroying their resource-capital base. One means of placing more resources in the hands of developing societies and directing these funds towards preserving existing forests and greening wasteland would be to build on the so-called debt-for-nature swaps that have been tried out in Central and Latin America. The Third World currently owes $ 1320 billion to various international donors and debt servicing is becoming an increasingly crippling burden. In one of the earliest debt-for-nature swaps in July 1987, an American conservation organization, Conservation International, purchased $ 650,000 of Bolivia's commercial debt through Citicorp Investment Bank at a discounted value of $ 100,000. In return for this redemption of its debt, Bolivia agreed to earmark 1.5 million hectares of tropical forest around an existing biosphere reserve as a protected area and to establish a $250,000 fund in local currency to manage the reserve with assistance from Conservation International. Larger swaps have been entered into by the World Wildlife Fund with Ecuador, Costa Rica and Philippines. Other debt-for-nature swaps have been negotiated with Argentina, Brazil and Venezuela, with the debtor nation offering the creditor some equity in domestic enterprises. As of mid-1987 such debt-for-equity swaps totaled around $ 6000 million and was expected to grow to $10,000 million by 1988. The U.S. Government has amended its laws to allow lenders tax deductions for such swaps and the World Bank too has evinced interest in such mechanisms (Fuller, 1988). U.S. Senator Albert Gore has gone further in advocating a "new Marshall Plan for sustainable development and environmental preservation" and suggests are afloat to draw Japan into a new International Bank for Environmental Protection (Sancton, January 1989).

The greening of the Himalaya and preserving its bio-diversity, as in the rest of the Ganga-Brahmaputra-Barak Basin, would be a fit candidate for international arrangements of this kind, suitably adapted to fit in with its special needs and circumstances. Growing new forests on lands laid bare would also absorb some of the carbon dioxide being exuded into the atmosphere and fuelling the process of global warming. A hectare of woodland (100 trees) is said to absorb about 3.7 tonnes of carbon-dioxide while releasing 2.5 tonnes of oxygen into the air (Khoshoo and Ahmed, 1981). Climate changes will affect the entire world, though different regions and latitudes may be affected differently. So the industrialized world would be serving its own interests and redeeming both a historical and ecological debt it owes the developing world for past colonial exploitation and current resource extravagance.

Coal, oil and even gas-fired thermal station emissions have adverse environmental impacts. The smoke plume of the Obra thermal station in Mirzapur district, U.P., monitored by the Remote Sensing Applications Centre, Lucknow, forms an ellipse measuring 40 by 28 kilometres. This defines its zone of polluting influence. Measures to mitigate adverse effects on the environment from thermal stations have been prescribed in guidelines issued by the Department of Environmental (1987). Electrostatic precipitators are useful only up to a point and, apart from gaseous emissions, fly ash from thermal stations totaled 25 million tonnes in 1986-87 and may be of the order of 90 million tonnes by the end of the century. Proper disposal of this waste, beyond stocking in ash-ponds, is necessary if air and water pollution are to be avoided. Fortunately, fly ash lends itself to a variety of by-product uses. Certain trees are good filters and can metabolise pollutants such as sulphur dioxide emitted by thermal stations. Some plants act as bio-indicators of pollution while others are mitigators. A number of such species has been identified and such trees could be planted in green belts around thermal stations as a means of pollution abetment (Singh, Nandita June 1986)

Hydro-electric power is in contrast, absolutely clean. It does of course entail submergence losses. These can, however, more often than not be adequately compensated in terms of the overall environmental balance. Solar, wind, and biomass energy certainly merit encouragement. So does the enormous hydel potential of the Ganga-Brahmaputra-Barak Basin which it would be folly to waste. As the Delhi global warming conference was told, even if each of India's 600,000 villages is to be provided a mere 100 kw of power (or 0.5 kw per household) to satisfy minimum needs over the next 20 years, this will require 60,000 MW, most of it in additional generation. If the hydel option is foreclosed on environmental grounds, the environment may be sooner doomed for prolonging poverty which is the greatest threat to the forests and sustainable development.

CHAPTER 13

More Fish to Fry

The erosion of its human capital poses as great a threat to the prosperity and well-being of the people of the Ganga-Brahmaputra-Barak basin, and of South Asia generally, as soil erosion. Both are by-products of poverty and perpetuate this condition by lowering productivity in a vicious cycle. Malnutrition is widespread. Aggravating the basic problem of under-nourishment in terms of calories, is the qualitative inadequacy of protein intake among vast segments of the population, especially pregnant and lactating women and children.

Fisheries can provide some of the food, protein, employment and income needed to reverse this trend. The natural resource base for fish is especially rich in the Ganga-Brahmaputra-Barak Basin and the unique Sunderbans eco-system, quite apart from what can be harvested from the sea. Yet, poor maintenance and exploitation of the region's water resources, or their gross abuse in some cases, has depleted fish catches, endangered certain species and resulted in failure to develop the full potential of agriculture as a whole, and not just of fisheries alone. Crustaceans, shell-fish, frogs duck, a variety of water-plants and certain weeds are of considerable economic value.

The possibilities in Tibet and the Himalayan uplands are limited to certain cold-water fish varieties. But Nepal and Bhutan can develop fisheries in the Terai as well as in the lower reaches of certain rivers and in such reservoirs that might be created as a result of water resource development. The scope in Bangladesh and India is however enormous. Bangladesh is the third largest inland fish producer in the world after China and India. Fish accounts for almost 80 per cent of the animal protein in average Bangladeshi diets, but per capita availability declined from 12 kilograms in 1962-63 to 7.5 kilograms in 1979-80 as a result of population increase and falling production. Overall production, inclusive of the marine catch, is planned to be raised from 774,000 tonnes in 1985 to a million tonnes by 1990.

India's fish resources are extremely rich. Over 1200 species are found in its inland and coastal waters, a third of them commercial. The country's 28,000 kilometres of river run through a wide variety of climatic and altitudinal zones and biotypes.. the entire range of diversity is found in the Ganga and Brahmaputra systems, the former alone extending over 12,500 kilometres. The Brahmaputra sustains 126 species of fish belonging to 26 families. Both rivers and the Barak-

Meghna enter the sea through the Sunderbans with its brackish waters and tidal creeks where there is a blending of freshwater and marine species and through which migratory fish must transit on their journey from upland waters to the ocean or the other way around for spawning. The Hooghly-Matla estuary in West Bengal spreads over 800,000 hectares and has a tidal impact that travels 295 kilometres inland. These eco-systems and the fish fauna they harbour have been catalogued by the National Bureau of Fish Genetic Resources in Allahabad (NBFGR, 1985; and Jhingran, 1984).

FAUNAL WEALTH AND DIVERSITY OF THE GANGA

The first scientific account of the faunal diversity of the Ganga was published in 1822 by a retired surgeon of the East India Company, Francis Hamilton Buchanan, who described 269 species of fish. In addition, the river is home to the Ganges dolphin (the susu or susuk), which once extended from the Himalayan foothills up to the estuary, the Malay dolphin, large Indian porpoise, and Indian otter; the gharial, estuarine, crocodile and mugger (a smaller version of the gharial that inhabits canals, lakes and marshes); huge monitor lizards (in the estuarine mangroves); 11 varieties of freshwater, mud and estuarine turtles, and the small Olive Ridley marine turtle which comes into the Sunderbans to lay eggs; frogs (some of them edible) and toads; eel, four varieties of estuarine prawn, apart from a freshwater species; crab, jellyfish, and a whole range of shell-fish or mollusks (Ghosh, A K July 1986).

The volume of water (shallows, deep pools, rapids), temperature (altitude), bio-chemical and bio-physical characteristics (oxygen content, turbidity, pollution load), and nutrient status (phytoplankton and zooplankton, aquatic vegetation and organic matter) are among the factors that influence fish stocking in any river. Barrages and dams can obstruct the migration of certain fish like the hilsa, catfish and mahaseer in the lower, middle and upper reaches while flood embankments or channelisation of rivers can affect spawning in limpid pools, ox-bows and depressions along the river or in its floodplain. Similarly, polders or closures of estuarine or tidal creeks as in the Sunderbans can disturb or destroy the rich interaction of mangroves is known to have a negative effect on the foodchain that sustains prawn and other valuable species.

The confluence of the Ghaghara, Gandak,Burhi Gandak, Kosi and Sone with the Ganga within a 250 kilometre stretch of river between Chapra and Kursela makes this an extraordinarily rich fishing ground. The importance of the Ganga in India's fisheries is evident from the fact that its lower reaches between Patna and Farakka alone contribute almost 90 per cent of the country's total riverine carp seed production for seeding ponds, tanks, reservoirs and other water bodies under fish culture. It is, therefore, in every sense the mother-river for aquaculture in India while being a prime source of inland capture fishery (Jhingran and Ghosh, March 1978).

India's overall fish production went up from 752,000 tonnes in 1950-51 (218,000 tonnes inland and the rest marine) to over three million tones in 1987-88 with 1.38 million tonnes representing the inland catch. Some baseline data was collected by the Central Inland Fisheries Research Institute, Barrackpore (Calcutta) for various stretches on the Ganga, Yamuna, Narmada and Godavari for the period 1958-69. In terms of tonnes per kilometre the catch averaged 0.643 on the Yamuna at Agra and Kanpur, Varanasi and Buxar, to a peak of 1.608 at Patna, declining thereafter to 0.700 at Bhagalpur. The values for the Narmada and Godavari came to 0.364 and 1.125 tonnes per kilometre respectively in given stretches. Based on these figures it is estimated that the riverine catch in India is of the order of one tonne per kilometre or about 25,000 tonnes per annum for the country as a whole (NCA, 1976).

A census of the Ganga from Bulandshahr in U.P. near Delhi, to Lalgola in West Bengal, just before the river enters Bangladesh, was made in 1956-57. This showed 1577 fishing villages along that 1580 kilometre stretch, the density increasing in the lower segments. The concentration of fishermen in the upper reaches was about four per village, gradually going up to 680 per village downstream. A population of 24,608 fishermen was found to possess 7859 boats. A similar survey of 730 kilometres of the Yamuna from Agra to Allahabad showed 573 fishing villages and 119 boats but only 148 active fishermen. However, some part-time fishermen were also found to be engaged in operating boats fixed with a certain type of engine called Rok in the upper stretches (Jhingran and Ghosh). Declining trends of catch were observed in many or most reaches.

The Ganga has traditionally been the source of carp seed for culture fisheries. Estimates for 1966 placed the spawn collection at 2010 million in Bihar, 1200 million in West Bengal and 122 million in U.P. Riverine spawn yields from all three States have since declined on account of the heavy and indiscriminate catch of juvenile carp and fingerlings after the floods, sometimes by erecting barricades on spawning streams, and in the lower reaches of the river in West Bengal supposedly on account of the Farakka Barrage. Destruction of juveniles implies a lower rate of recruitment of spawners. The implications of this are apparent from the fact that 10 tonnes of spawners are sufficient to produce 500 million spawn. Embankments have also prevented the inundation of carp spawning grounds including depressions (jheels) and beels (ox-bows) which are impregnated with fish seed by flood waters.

THE BHAGALPUR PANIDARI

Spawn production and destruction are greatest in the most fertile reach of the Ganga between Patna and Farakka, the richest stretch within which remains under an extraordinary zamindari or panidari ever since fishing rights were given to the then kanungo of Bhagalpur, entitled Mahashay by the Mughals in 1604 during the reign of Akbar. According to the family's version, the Mughals vested Taraknath Ghosh and his successors from generation to generation with the right to hold the *jalkars* (water body) Gangapath to Chanah free of revenue. The rights extended between the "high banks" of the Ganga from Sultanganj to Kahalgaon, a stretch of about 80 kilometres. This right was challenged by the East India Company's khas mahal officer and later by others at various times but was validated by the Board of Revenue in 1805 and again in 1810 under the Regulations of 1773. Almost a century later, the Calcutta High Court again upheld this right on the ground that since the fish follow the water and fishermen follow the fish, Mahashay Ghosh enjoys the right to fish between the high banks of the Ganga in spate.

Following Independence, the Bihar Government enacted legislation to abolish zamindari and sought to appropriate the "estate". It argued that jalkar rights were included in the land records and constituted an encumberance on the land. The family challenged this interpretation and the lower court, and subsequently, the Patna High Court ruled that a "fishing right" was not an estate or immovable property under the Land Reforms Act. The matter is now pending in appeal before the Supreme Court. Meanwhile, as far back as 1930, the then Mahashay, the present incumbent's father, dedicated the income from this fishing right or panidari to a trust in the name of a family deity by a deed of endowment and appointed himself the first shebait. Some years earlier, in 1923, the family had settled the lower half of the panidari (towards Farakka) on one Haji Aziz Pramanik who acquired this portion of the jalkar mahal by a registered sale deed. Abdul Aziz's successor, Musharraf Hussain and his brother, Jalip, died in quick succession in 1978, bequeathing the jalkar mahal to their heirs, some of whom are in Bangladesh. Confused titles and family rivalries are said to have aggravated existing tensions resulting in violence on the river.

This historical interlude is significant for the Bhagalpur jalkar mahal is probably the only surviving example of panidari anywhere in the country. There are reportedly still some exclusive ferry rights extant along the Ganga at certain points which also derive from Mughal grants. What is of far more relevance is the fact that Mahashay Ghosh's panidari, extending over both flowing water and adjacent jheels and ox-bows between the 'high banks' of the river in spate, covers far and away the richest riverine fishing and spawning ground in the country, constituting as it does a priceless treasure house of fish genetic resources. That a single family should exclusively control such a national asset is anomalous and that the jalkar should be recklessly exploited and unscientifically managed can only be a matter for deep concern.

Mahashay Ghosh lets out segments of his jalkar mahal on contract and the contractors in turn lease out these waters to group of fishermen. Sipahis or agents move along the waters to detect and punish encroachments and infringements.

The panidars and the sub-lessees are said to collect tolls and taxes from the hapless fishermen who are not merely restricted in movement but to certain types of gear. Carp varieties in particular spawn in quiet waters and depressions that fill as the river rises. Surviving spawn, juveniles and fingerlings are washed back into the mainstream with the ebb floods. It is on this return journey that streams are often barricaded and juveniles, future spawners, are netted or killed in huge numbers thus depleting the size of catch by weights as well as future stock. Pollution has added to the destruction or deterioration of stock with effluent discharges from a large above factory and distillery near Mokamah and from the oil refinery and fertilizer plant at Barauni. Unless there is proper waste water treatment, further damage may ensue from thermal pollution from the Kahalgaon super-thermal power station which will draw its cooling water from and return it to the Ganga.

Distress among the fishing communities living along the river on account of poverty, exploitation and oppression, led to the formation in 1982 of the Ganga Mukti Morcha (Ganga Liberation Front) to fight the Ganga panidari by elements of the Bihar Chhatra Sangharsh Samiti, a youth volunteer corps inspired by the late Jayaprakash Narayan. The andolan or struggle has taken the form of organizing the fishermen, initiating a no-tax campaign which has enraged the panidars and their agents, agitating against pollution of the river and bank erosion affecting both fishing villages and fishing, and calling for an end to the Ganga zamindari. A 13-day procession of 100 fishing boats from Kursela (the Kosi outfall) to Patna in April 1987 was mounted to mobilize public opinion which was further aroused in November that year when 12 fishermen, moving up-river from the lower jalkar (under Pramanik) to the upper jalkar mahal, were killed by person unknown in Bhagalpur district.

The Ganga Mukti Andolan leaders claim that the panidars collect over Rs.60 lakhs in taxes from some 60,000 fishermen in the Sultanganj-Pirpainti Jalkar. Mahashay Ghosh dismisses all this as a figment of the imagination. He admits to leasing out the waters on annual contract – official sources cite a figure of Rs.4 lakhs as rental – but denies levying any tax. By his estimate only between 300 and 500 fishermen are involved and, far from exploiting anybody, he and his sub-lessees protect fishermen who earn the ire of landowners who cultivate the jheels and beels as the flood waters recede. Moreover, he has to regulate the fishing as different varieties of fish require the use of different types of net or other gear, which are hired out to the fishermen, and entail riverbank fishing or midstream fishing in the boats. Finally, the income he earns from the jalkar goes to temples under the trust deed that governs the endowment of the mahal.

Among the casualties of the indiscriminate fishing that has gone on in this rich fishing ground is the Ganga dolphin which is being killed as its fat and flesh attract other fish. Apart from the panidari dispute, which has been in court for years, jalkars in Bihar as a whole were under the State's Revenue Department and were only transferred to the Fisheries Department as of April 1, 1987 for conservation and development.

MENACE OF FISH GENETIC EROSION

The process of fish genetic erosion in the Ganga has been studied by Bhagalpur University under the Man and Biosphere programme (Bilgrami and Datta Munshi, April 1985). A survey of the Patna-Farakka stretch between 1982 and 1985 established indiscriminate fishing as a grave threat to aquaculture as a result of "removal of fingerlings and concomitant reduction of spawn production potential which is like `a floating gold mine of spawn' from May to September. Every possible effort should be made to conserve the diversity of fish fauna of the River Ganges and there is urgent need for more regulated and restrained fishing in this great riverine system". Pollution control, mesh-size regulation, closed fishing seasons during the monsoon to protect breeders, and the establishment of fish seed farms to rear juveniles caught in bari or jhanga fishing (through netting along water barricades) are among the recommendations made. It was suggested that a number of microbial organisms could be employed for bio-monitoring water quality. The Report noted that many Ganga fish have a highly specialized ecological niche and have zonal preferences in the river. It therefore concluded that "the management of the Ganga ecosystem requires an ecological approach and not merely an economic one". The greatest threat is to the fish as the impact of urban and industrial pollutants on the food chain as well as on their breeding, spawning and growth has not been properly evaluated. Indeed, even from the commercial point of view, mass capture and sale of juveniles reduces the potential fish yield by more than a hundred times and also diminishes the number of future spawners. The Report also speaks of the mass destruction of the sting ray (*Dasyatis sephen*) in the Sahebganj-Farakka reach. This endangered species is said to be the sole representative of the genus Dasyatis "which was originally a marine form and has now adapted itself to the Ganga system". Likewise the Ganges dolphin, turtles and tortoises whose numbers are fast declining.

Civic and industrial pollution pose a threat to fish and other aquatic life. Tannery discharges into the Ganga at Kanpur have resulted in toxicity levels that are inimical to fish. Fishermen report virtual absence of fish in certain reaches. Effluents draining into the Yamuna via the Hindon from Ghaziabad have from time to time resulted in mass fish-kills at Okhla in Delhi. Pollution destroys fish directly by poisoning and indirectly by reducing the oxygen content, killing fish food and affecting spawning grounds. Some species of air-breathing fish might survive in polluted waters but bottom dwellers find the water devoid of plankton and benthos. Persistent pollution can cause mutations and bring about genetic changes. Arsenic, mercury, chromium and other heavy metal pollutants are dangerous as they tend to accumulate in fish tissues and can enter the human system through the food chain. Bandel to Budge Budge on the Hooghly at Calcutta is yet another badly polluted stretch. Fortunately both civic and industrial pollution is being tackled under the Ganga Action Plan and water quality should increasingly improve over the next few years to the benefit of aquatic life all along this great river system.

Other factors too are at work. A survey of the waters of the Doon Valley in 1976 revealed dynamiting of rivers and electrocution in power canals as among the other reasons for the decline of the dominant mahaseer fishery. A ban on the use of explosives, establishment of sanctuaries and fish farms for culture and breeding, and inter-departmental coordination were suggested (NEERI, 1987). Poisoning of rives through toxicity and transplantation of exotic species are two other factors that have been cited for declining catches of mahaseer and snow trout in Garhwal (Sehgal K.L. April 1986).

FARAKKA AND THE HILSA RUN

The Farakka Barrage has posed a threat to habitats and biota in the lower Ganga. It is a barrier, as are all anicuts, barrages and dams, to the passage of migratory fish of which the hilsa (*Hilsa ilisha*) is a particularly important species and a delicacy of high commercial value. So too the (freshwater) prawn which used to migrate from as far as Varanasi to Diamond Harbour, below Calcutta for spawning in estuarine waters. Prawn catches at Varanasi and from the Gomti and Ghaghara have now virtually disappeared. The hilsa has its natural home in the estuarine segment of the Ganga but makes two spawning runs up-river post-monsoon and in the winter and has been known to migrate as far afield as Hardwar. The Farakka barrage, under construction from 1960-61 and commissioned in 1975, has two fish locks of 8 x 36 metre size which are operated thrice a day for 30 minutes each. Although engineers maintain that fishery experts were consulted, the fish locks are clearly inadequate despite additional openings to let Departmental boats pass through the barrage from time to time. The Barrage does not store any water, but it ponds up the river with the back-fill stretching back 100 kilometres to Sahebganj. This too has changed the character of the river from a flowing stream into a partially lacustrine system, altered the current velocity up to Buxar, and the flood regime.

The hilsa catch has declined in the middle reaches of the Ganga. Barring a bumper catch of 350 tonnes at Allahabad in 1954, the average hilsa landing at this point averaged 19 tonnes over a 30-year period until 1971. Thereafter, the hilsa catch declined dramatically to around one tonne between 1972 and 1982 following the commissioning of the Farakka Barrage. There was a similar drop in hilsa landings at Buxar and Bhagalpur. However, Farakka has had some positive effects too. The hilsa requires a minimum column of water for its migratory run. With the Barrage now diverting water into the moribund Bhagirathi-Hooghly, the hilsa has begun to move up that river. As the salinity line in the Hooghly on account of tidal ingress has been pushed down, the hilsa, which at first found only sufficient freshwater to breed to Barrackpore, north of Calcutta, is now breeding almost 90 kilometres lower down, at Diamond Harbour. It is the judgement of the Central Inland Capture Fisheries Research Institute at Allahabad that while the distribution of the hilsa catch has been affected by the Farakka Barrage, overall landings have not diminished as the increase in the Hooghly catch has compensated the loss of the freshwater hilsa catch above Farakka. There is now a new recruitment pattern. The Durgapur Barrage and DVC dams have similarly affected the hilsa run up the Damodar river.

The hilsa offers lucrative fishing in the Brahmaputra up to Guwahati and even Tezpur in Assam as well as in the Barak in Cachar, catches declining with progress up-river. More encouraging has been the evidence of sustained hilsa landings from a number of depressions and ox-bows in lower Assam which suggest a certain lentic adaptability of the species which could be exploited (Yadava et al., April 1986).

Dams and barrages pose problems which can be overcome up to a point by constructing fish ladders, fish locks or fish lifts. This calls for a good deal of research both into the behaviour of specific fish species and design parameters. The model of the Pacific salmon which migrates up the North American rivers is unique and not representative. Years of effort went into research and experimentation before appropriate fish passes were designed for it. These designs cannot be replicated at random. River conditions, currents, the swimming energetics of particular fish and other relevant factors will have to be taken into account in evolving workable designs. It is not evident that this kind of detailed case by case research has been conducted in India. In view of the large water resource developments under way, this would seem to be a necessary requirement. There are not too many species that undertake linear migration up or down river. Movement from the sea into estuarine waters or vice versa can be facilitated by providing suitable sluices in polders and coastal embankments. Other species such as Indian carp 'migrate' literally to breed in depressions and ox-bows in the flood plain or other quiet waters. In this case, the spawn is generally washed back into the river with the receding flood waters. Flood embankments have precluded such lateral movements and thereby affected fishing in many areas. This again can be remedied by fitting embankments with sluices or appropriate fish passes.

It is also now possible to induce spawning of migrant fish captured below a dam, rear the juvenile to sizes at which they would naturally migrate and then release them into the river above or below the dam. Such techniques are said to have been successfully employed in the case of the Volga sturgeon and other species and similar methods have been proposed to deal with endangered species in the Lower Mekong (Mekong Committee, 1972).

DEVELOPING RESERVOIR CULTURE FISHERIES

Nevertheless, despite such measures, riverine fisheries are liable to suffer some loss on account of dams. But reservoir fisheries hold out considerable promise. The Mekong Committee reports that in the case of the Nam Pong dam, fish production increased remarkably from negligible harvests in the streams prior to impoundment to about 1700 tonnes annually from the reservoir. This experience is not uncommon. The Aswan High Dam has trapped phytoplankton and zooplankton and other nutrients which no longer fertilise the Mediterranean, thereby resulting in a significant decline in the oil sardine catch from the sea. But the reservoir fishery developed in Lake Nasser in far greater in volume and value though the beneficiaries are not Mediterranean but Nubian fishermen.

This has been the Indian experience as well. Closure of dams on tropical rivers, however, brings about radical changes in the physical and chemical properties of the water body as the system changes from riverine to lacustrine. With inundation and the decay of organic and vegetative matter on the bed of the newly-formed lake, nutritional enrichment of the reservoir occurs, with the further addition of minerals from leached soils under and ringing the impoundment. This invariably results in a rapid multiplication of the fish population, though here again there is soon a shift from rheophilic (flowing water) species to lacustrine varieties. Luxuriant algal blooms or the growth of aquatic plants or floating vegetative mats, such as African sudd, or other organisms under water can either diminish sunlight penetration or alter the thermal gradient or deoxygenate the lower and bottom layers with repercussions on the subsequent distribution of the fish population (Interim Mekong Committee, 1982). Sediment flows and their distribution can also have a profound effect on water quality. Appropriate reservoir planning and management can mitigate some potentially adverse repercussions.

Reservoir filling therefore follows a cycle. An initial surge of fish-food productivity is followed after some years by saturation and trophic (nutritional) depression which tends to stabilize at a given level. Thereafter, fertility again rises as the reservoir attains a certain ecological stability and the fish adapt to these conditions (Jhingran, 1984). Cultured stocks of given species of fish may be released into the reservoir and in certain cases exotic varieties may be introduced with advantage to fill unoccupied ecological niches, though only after due care and study so that valuable indigenous species are not eliminated by predators or crowded out by more prolific and competitive breeders.

Different reservoirs exhibit different post-filling phases depending on the geo-chemical, vegetative and other characteristics of the lake basin. Fish production rises with the initial efflorescence of fish food in the reservoir. In Rihand (Sone basin) this early peak was reached in the fourth year after filling while in the Gandhisagar (Chambal) this was only reached in the thirteenth year. Therafter, with stock manipulation, production has increased again to a degree and then stabilized. Studies on the ecology and stock dynamics of large reservoirs commenced in 1963 with the Tungabhadra reservoir, followed by the DVC reservoirs.

A wider all-India coordinated project was launched in 1971 under which several reservoirs were studied in West Bengal, Uttar Pradesh, Himachal and other States. This has yielded valuable data on eco-systems, productivity characteristics, fish food organisms, and stock characteristics of economic fishes including their breeding, recruitment and size, vulnerability to gill nets, and management. Cyclical drawdown of reservoirs was found to discourage proliferation of large aquatic plants. The food habits of different species also revealed distinct preferences. Thus medium-finned catla preferred phytoplankton and large-finned catla favoured zooplankton; catla-rohu hybrids subsist mostly on detritus, and pangasius species on mollusks (Natarajan A.V., December 1984). The productivity of various reservoirs also showed marked differences after attaining a stable state. Thus, the level of production was found to be 200 kg/ha in Gandhisagar (Chambal), 220 kg/ha in Ukai (Tapi), 70 kg/ha in Govindsagar (Bhakra), and 187 kg/ha in Rajsamand (Rajasthan). Production at Rihand (which has a very large water-spread), Getalsund (Bihar) and some other reservoirs was found to be low. "In most cases the reservoirs are under-stocked, under-exploited, and ill-managed, resulting in low yield rates of less than seven kg/ha. It is possible to achieve higher levels of production in the range of 75-100 kg/ha in reservoirs which are above average category" and managed in an appropriate ecological frame (Ibid).

The Narmada Valley Development Authority is making elaborate preparations to optimize reservoir fisheries. It is estimated that the entire Narmada complex of dams and reservoirs will achieve the norm of 40 kg/ha on full development within 20 years in the major reservoirs as envisaged by the National Commission on Agriculture, with good stocking and management, and 80 kg/ha in smaller reservoirs. Altogether an output of 10,000 tonnes of fish per annum is anticipated, valued at Rs.10-15 crores from some 225,000 hectares of productive waters. The four major dams contemplated are Narmadasagar, Omkareshwar, Maheshwar and Sardar Sarovar. On full development these four projects are expected to yield 3900 tonnes of fish and employ 2500 active fishermen. Equivalent numbers are likely to be employed in allied and ancillary occupations such as hatchery management, seed production, marketing, net-making, packing, ice factories, bost-building and operation, basket making and transport of fish. Some 974,000 mandays of well-remunerated employment is expected to be generated. Besides the reservoirs, approximately 100 kilometres of the main Narmadasagar canal will be available for intensive fish culture. Cage culture will also be possible in other running canals while the network of distributaries will be able to replenish ponds and depressions for pisciculture. A massive stocking of 14 million fingerlings per annum is envisaged in the Narmadasagar reservoir alone. To plan all this will require considerable expertise. So too its operation and management. Hence the project authorities plan to establish a multi-level, multi-disciplinary training-production complex at Narmadasagar (Varma S.C, July 1985).

INDUCED BREEDING

Fishing in rivers, estuaries and the ocean entails capture by man of fish stocked by nature. In reservoirs, lakes, ponds, tanks, ox-bows and inundated depressions (jheels, beels, hoars, etc), the stocking has to be done by man. These culture fisheries as they are called have a vast potential and, though traditionally exploited, need careful seeding and sound management if they are to be really productive. The Basin region, especially Bangladesh and eastern and Northeastern India and the Nepal Terai, is particularly well endowed in this regard.

The production of fish seed from riverine spawning grounds needs to be properly managed. The lower Ganga, as earlier stated, is uniquely productive and as yet been cruelly vulnerable to the destruction of spawn, juveniles and spawning grounds. This must obviously be set right. Fortunately however, techniques of induced spawning of carp have been developed which have given inland fisheries a new reach. Traditional carp culture dependent on naturally occurring fish spawn of major carps was long practiced in eastern India. But mortality was high and yields low in the absence of scientific management. The Central Indian Fisheries Research Institute was able to ensure considerable improvement in this situation with the introduction of a package of practices in nursery management with inputs of fertilizer and feed to raise yields and enhance survival rates. This was followed by induced breeding of carps in 1959 through administration of pituitary gland extracts (hypophysation). Carp normally breed in quiet monsoon-inundated waters to which they migrate laterally during June-September. By environmental manipulations, such as regulating water temperature, it has been possible to advance gonadal (reproductive) maturation to mid-March and thereby permit off-season breeding which in turn makes for greater fish seed production. Similarly, hatchery techniques have been refined resulting in a vast improvement in hatching rates.

The establishment of pituitary banks has further enhanced the flexibility of breeding operations (Natarajan). Cross-breeding to impart hybrid vigour or certain characteristics has become possible through genetic manipulation which also now permits sex reversal. The catla-rohu hybrid is better than both parents. Selection of advantageous traits such as faster or larger growth is being done by mating the best varieties to enhance heritable characteristics. Change of sex, generally from female to male, is useful as many male fish species grow to a larger size (not the trout) and therefore ensure higher yields and stocking up to the carrying capacity of the water body. Genetically female "males" can be crossed with genetic female fish to get a 100 per cent female progeny. This mono-sex technique is being applied to the common carp. Since this breeds in confined waters, it is necessary to limit its numbers so that each fish attains optimum size. Procedures are by now well established for the culture of air-breathing fish like magur, singhi, koi and murrell by induced breeding as these thrive in weed-infested ponds, beels and jheels with low dissolved oxygen which dot eastern and Northeastern India and Bangladesh. Efforts are on to culture the giant freshwater prawn and catfish. Initial success has attended the artificial culture of hilsa and nursery-raised hilsa fingerlings have been introduced in the Ukai (Tapi) reservoir. Pen and cage culture in still and running waters is also being developed, pens being especially suited to season wetlands and for culture of tiger prawn in estuaries and lagoons.

HABITAT PRESERVATION AND NEW HABITATS

Another technology that shows great potential is composite fish culture. This entails the simultaneous exploitation of all the available ecological niches in a water body as different species variously prefer the top, upper, middle and lower layers. Previously, fish production from small water bodies averaged 500-600 kg/ha. Under the composite culture technology the six species selected are the three major Indian carp (catla, rohu and mrigal) and three Chinese carp (silver carp, grass carp, and the common carp). Given some supplementary feed and fertilizer, organic and inorganic yields have increased dramatically to averages of 5000 kg/ha, which peak production touching double that figure.

All these improved practices are creating an ever-increasing demand for more fish seed. A ten-year Indian aquaculture plan drawn up in the mid-seventies envisaged a production of 6000 million fish seed. This has been exceeded and the Seventh Plan target is to attain production of 12,000 million by 1990. West Bengal in particular has made remarkable progress in fish seed production. Creation of deep pool sanctuaries in rivers, charting and protection of seasonal water-bodies, such as beels and jheels by preserving their inundation channels, and tapping potential sources of fish seed in hitherto unexploited areas such as the Rapti in eastern U.P. and the Banas (a tributary of the Chambal) in Rajasthan, would yield dividends. Habitat preservation is important.

The aquaculture development programme is being fostered through the establishment of a network of Fish farmer Development Agencies in India and 200 such agencies will be in operation by 1990. The FFDAs arrange required inputs of fish seed, credit, feed and equipment and subsidise pond and tank development together with the first year's cost of inputs. Training is also imparted. By the end of 1987 almost 180,000 hectares had been brought under intensive fish culture and fish production from village ponds and tanks was estimated at about 217,000 tonnes that year. Yields too had gone up from 50 kg/ha to 1950 to 1330 kg/ha by 1988 (Agriculture Department, 1988). Grass carp is a good agent for the biological control of weeds as it consumes noxious aquatic plants. Mahua oilcake can in turn be used to clear ponds of unwanted fish whether they be carnivores or uneconomic or otherwise unwanted species. This fish poison of vegetable origin has a toxicity of 15 days after which the water body in question can be safely stocked.

An interesting experiment now on the threshold of commercial exploitation relates to the cultivation of marine prawn varieties in brackish water in Haryana. Ponds dug in saline (usar) soils are filled from tubewells drawing on brackish aquifers. The salinity content of the water is in the range of 12 to 15 parts per million. Common carp has also been successfully raised in saline water and has been found to grow to economic size from August to January. These experiments hold out new opportunities for profitable fish culture and employment in usar-saline tracts in the semi-arid regions of western U.P., Haryana, Rajasthan and Punjab (Dwivedi, 1984).

Waterlogged paddy fields have been converted into highly remunerative fish seed farms in Andhra where profits of up to Rs.30,000 per hectare have been earned. Farmers are being trained in this technology and demonstration programmes have been conducted in Haryana, Madhya Pradesh and Rajasthan with a view to extending this practice in waterlogged command areas with vegetable and fruit cultivation along the embankments (Central Institute of Fisheries Education, 1986). Some of these programmes are being promoted through fishery estates in U.P., Rajasthan and Madhya Pradesh under the FFDA scheme and the same institutional pattern is now being advocated for the use of coastal saline soils and estuarine waters through the cooperatisation of poor fishermen. It is proposed that these coastal fishery estates should include fish seed farms and hatcheries, windmills to pump water, cold storages, storm shelters, housing and civic amenities.

LEASING OF WATERS, ORGANISATION AND MARKETING

The productivity of the Brahmaputra system in Assam is lower than that in the Ganga because of faster currents generated by its greater slope, the geo-physical characteristics of the terrain, and the volume of plankton occurrence. A more critical factor has been the jacketing of the Brahmaputra within flood embankments which has affected auto-stocking of the river as carp and other varieties cannot migrate laterally into still waters to spawn. Further, there is no free fishing as the entire network of rivers, ox-bows and other water bodies are auctioned by the Revenue Department for two to five years at a time. These leases are in turn sub-let and tributary streams are often fragmented into separate holdings with bamboo screens erected by lessor out to maximize their own catch to the common detriment. The numerous beels and jheels are choked with weeds, especially water hyacinth. An Assam Beel Fisheries Development Corporation was set up in 1970. Most beels (both ox-bow and lake types) are registered with the Revenue Department but there are additionally a number of unregistered water bodies in the forest. Some 53 beels had been leased out to fishermens' cooperatives by 1979 on a longer term basis so as to avoid slaughter fishing. Beels constitute the primary fishery resource of Assam, spanning about about 100,000 hectares. Inter-connecting them back with spawn-bearing riverine waters and their subsequent flushing with floodwaters has been advocated by the Corporation (Mahanta and Lahon, April 1986).

The situation in Northeastern India is unusual in so far as the population of this region, especially those living in Meghalaya, Tripura and parts of Assam, used to depend on what is now Bangladesh for much of their fish supply. The region was estimated to produce around 65,000 tones of fish in 1985 as against a demand approaching double that figure. Some 60,000 hectares of beel and lake area is available in the Northeast, excluding Assam, for pisciculture and the North Eastern

Council is promoting several developmental programmes to establish adequate fish seed stock, hatcheries and trained personnel in the region. One project relates to prawn culture in 14,000 hectares of the Loktak and other lakes in Manipur to produce 1000 tonnes of prawn and lobster by the early 1990s (North Eastern Council, 1985).

The problem of leasing of waters needs streamlining. Water bodies are owned by disparate authorities: the Departments of revenue, irrigation, forests and panchayats, the Railways, local bodies, public sector corporations like the Steel Authority of India, etcetera. These are often auctioned to the highest bidder, which means that poor fishermen or infant fishermen's cooperatives cannot hold their own against contractors and middlemen. The fisheries cooperative movement is no stronger than it is as no fisherman is going to join a society that does not have sure access to a productive water body. The Central Board of Fisheries in India has recommended that water bodies of up to two hectares in areal extent should in principle be leased to individuals and larger water bodies to fishermen's cooperatives for at least 10 years. This salutary recommendation has not been uniformly implemented (National Federation of Fishermen's Cooperatives Ltd., January 1988).

The fishing community is poor and unorganized and needs to be assisted in a variety of ways to modernize and compete following the breakdown of the simple traditional structures on which it once depended. Marketing is also a problem, as well illustrated by the uncontrolled development of silver carp in the Gobindsagar (Bhakra) reservoir. Consumer preferences being such, the market for this species is in Calcutta and other distant regions. However, the silver carp deteriorates after six to eight hours on ice, while ice slabs are generally replaced only after 24 hours in transit. The marine catch being larger, more regular and more lucrative, presumably on account of its export orientation, the domestic marketing infrastructure for fish has received less attention. Reservoirs are not well connected to railheads and refrigerated rail-vans are not available in requisite numbers.

The National Federation of Fishermen's Cooperatives was started in 1980 and currently has over 800,000 members in 7857 primary societies. The Cooperative is spotty in coverage but is growing steadily with new schemes such as fish pond insurance and pond fish insurance. An estimated seven million fishermen are involved in inland and, mostly, marine fishing. But it is the Central Inland Fisheries Research Institute's estimate that the new technologies of inland fishery hold out the promise of employing about eight million persons. As both fishing as well as fishermen must be developed, the challenge to the cooperatives and other associations of fishermen is enormous.

INTEGRATED FISH FARMING

Some deep water areas do not drain sufficiently early to grow a productive paddy crop in many parts of North Bihar and elsewhere. Here fish could be the kharif crop. But deep water paddy can also be grown with fish over wide areas in the eastern and Northeastern region of India and in Bangladesh through highly remunerative integrated fish farming systems. A perimeter trench is dug along deep water paddy fields and fingerlings are released into the fields with the kharif sowing. As the crop matures for harvest, the fish move into the flooded trenches until the fields are watered again with the sowing of the winter paddy crop. The fish is subsequently harvested with the paddy, having attained a commercially marketable size. In parts of West Bengal, where this has been tried, yields have been of the order of 5.5 tonnes of paddy (in two crops) and 700-800 grams of fish per hectare which ensures a handsome return to the grower. The fish eat harmful insects and need not be affected by pesticides if only bio-degradable varieties are used.

Similar integrated farming systems in the form of duck-and-paddy or pig-and-paddy cultures offer equally good returns as experiments in West Bengal have once again established. Ducks live on flooded paddies which they fertilise with their droppings while they feed off the water. The yield includes ducks egg and meat in addition to the harvest of paddy. Where pigs are raised, the piglets are housed on bamboo platforms above the field and are fed there so that their droppings wash down to fertilise the paddy. Pig-cum-paddy cultures could be popularized among tribal communities with advantage as they are given to rearing pigs and the combination would confer both an income as well as a dietary benefit. One variant of the fish-cum-paddy culture in the neighbouring cities could be the rearing of fish in treated sewage ponds, the manured water being subsequently led into farms for irrigation. All these are profitable and practical systems based on the principal of recycling wastes.

With projects to build dams in the Himalaya, and even otherwise, there is need to develop cold-water fisheries which have been relatively neglected. Snow trout and other trout species have been introduced into a number of Himalayan streams but natural recruitment is limited by the low fertility of the females which require very special conditions for spawning. Hence the need to develop hatcheries as trout are good both for food and sport. Mahaseer are indigenous and inhabit the lower hills and foothills of the Himalaya. These migratory fish have fund barrages and dams a serious impediment to their breeding runs up river, just as much as snow trout which move to lower altitudes. Research is needed to design suitable fish passes for these and other species. There could also be other exotic cold water fish whose suitability and adaptability to Indian conditions would be worth study the cold waters of the Tsangpo and Lhasa rivers in Tibet also support fishing which has been encouraged both as a major occupation as well as a sideline activity after the introduction of the household responsibility system in 1980 (Xinhua, July 10, 1989).

ESTUARINE-MARINE TRANSITION ZONE

There is a far greater potential at the other end of the river system in estuarine and brackish water fisheries not only on account of the extent of the Sunderbans in

Bangladesh and West Bengal but because of the high value attached to prawn and shrimp exports. Estuarine waters also constitute a transition zone between freshwater and marine fisheries and are therefore of great economic importance. Tidal creeks have been closed and ponded, with sluices, to culture prawn, beckti and other species. The tides bring in micro-organisms and oxygenate the ponds. Prawn being more profitable than paddy, there has been a tug-of-war between fish and paddy farmers, between polderisation and flooding. In some areas, paddy-cum-brackish-water fish culture has been found to be viable with saline-tolerant paddy being raised on monsoon precipitation, followed by prawn and fish. In other areas the Government has stepped in to encourage paddy cultivation in the higher and shallower estuarine reaches which are easier to close within polders, leaving the deeper segments nearer the sea for fish culture.

Mullets and milk fish are among the marine fish which breed in estuarine waters. Sardines, anchovies, hilsa and many other varies are found off the West Bengal coast where fishing is influenced by the fact that the Bay of Bengal is closed to the north and receives a large discharge from the Ganga-Brahmaputra-Barak rivers. Fishing ports and ice-factories are being set up in the Sunderbans region and fishermen are being assisted to equip themselves with powered boats with mini-freezers on board. However, the lure of high export profits has brought in a good deal of trawling by large operators resulting in tensions between this sector and the traditional small fishermen who feel threatened not merely in terms o catch but in respect of the preservation of these rich in-shore fishing grounds. The small fishermen complain that ground trawling for prawns disturbs the water column which gets churned up thus scaring away hilsa, pomfret and other fish as well.

Trawlers are alleged to damage drifting gill nets. And since the trawlers are only looking for prawn, they throw away all the other marketable species which are killed in the process to the detriment of the local fishermen. The mono-culture of tiger prawn is also leading to the scooping up of post-larval prawn in tidal creeks. Micro-mesh scoop nets are used to supply the burgeoning prawn seed market. Here again, "the incidental catch composed of the whole range of resident and migrant fish and crustaceans at the early stages in the estuarine nursery ground" and constituting 95 per cent of the total, is discarded and destroyed. Such practices and overfishing can affect the future potential and care will need to be taken, as in the Ganga, to ensure that the estuarine eco-system, a most valuable renewable resource, is not endangered (Ray, Pranab April 1988).

Destruction of the mangroves is also likely to affect the Sunderbans fishery. Conservation measures are called for to protect these estuarine nursery grounds. While complete prohibition of shrimp fishing in these nursery areas of the lower Sunderbans may be infeasible, enforcing certain closed seasons, mesh-size regulations, banning or phasing out the use of certain fixed gear, and restrictions on the export of shrimps below a minimum size are among the method suggested (George M.J., July 1988).

Among the products of aquaculture, and a valuable export, is froglegs. Between 3000 and 4500 tonnes of froglets worth about Rs.8-12 crores were being annually exported until a few years ago when a conservation quota system was introduced. This has now promoted smuggling. Frogs are captured from wet paddies in West Bengal and Bangladesh as well as in Orissa, Andhra Pradesh and, especially, Kerala. There was at one time a fear that the growing frog-catch was likely to affect its role as a past controller in paddy fields as well as of mosquitoes. This was investigated by the frog culture department of the Central Inland Fisheries Research Institute and was established to be without foundation. Of the 150 species of frog found in India only three varieties, constituting about one per cent of the entire species, are exploited for frogleg exports. Even the three commercial species are not simultaneously caught in all parts of India and any imbalance caused in nature is highly insignificant. It was also found that the three frog species caught do not feed on mosquitoes. A reduced frog population, however, is said to have brought out more snakes in search of food. In any event, the development of hatcheries to produce frog seed and for fast-rearing them to marketable size should take care of any conceivable problem (Mondal et al., 1986).

LEGAL AND GENETIC SAFEGUARDS

One of the issues facing fishery development in India is the inadequacy of the legal base. The Indian Fisheries Act of 1897 is still extant. A model bill for its revision is still under discussion. The law provides for closed areas and closed seasons for habitat an species protection, regulation of mesh net size and so on. But juvenile fishing and many other infractions are widespread and fishery officers often find they lack the power to act effectively. Water bodies are not necessarily under fisheries departments but are controlled by many different agencies. Traditional fishing rights too need to be codified in the interests of proper stocking, management and conservation. Some States have intervened with local legislation. The West Bengal Fisheries Act, 1984, empowers the administration to acquire derelict water bodies and lease these out to fishermen's cooperatives.

The National Bureau of Fish Genetic Resources was established n 1983 with a mandate covering the collection, classification and evaluation of fish genetic resources, their maintenance and preservation, cataloguing of genotypes, introduction of exotic species in Indian waters, and the conservation of exploited and endangered species. The Bureau has four approved centres for freshwater, brackish water, cold water and marine fisheries. A first list of endangered and threatened Indian freshwater fish enumerates four endangered, 21 threatened and 20 rare species, all of which need special attention. Destruction of fish habitats diversion of waters, engineering structures, alterations in flow patterns, over-fishing, and pollution are some of the factors involved. Arising out of this, measures have been suggested for in situ and ex situ conservation, the latter by means of creating gene pools and germ plasm banks. Habitat identification of endangered shell fish and surveys and cataloguing of genotypes are also being undertaken (Das P et al., September 1986).

With the rapid growth of aquaculture the danger of in-breeding has to be kept in mind. Exotic species have been introduced over the years, but such introductions must be effected without detriment to native species. The Bureau is now charged with testing exotic fish, their compatability with indigenous species, adaptability and proneness to disease before they are introduced into Indian waters. The Bureau is required t quarantine all live fish imports and issue disease-free certificates if they are to be propagated in the country. Hyacinth was introduced into India early this century from Brazil by a lady who was struck by its ornamental qualities. It has since become a menace, choking water bodies. Recently however some economic uses have been found for it as a bio-gas feedstock. The lesson is salutary.

PRODUCTION STRATEGIES IN NEPAL AND BANGLADESH

Nepal's fish development programme envisage increasing production to around 8300 tonnes by 1990, with priority being given to the Terai and inner Terai districts and by reliance on integrated fish culture with ducks and pigs. Efforts are also being made to study ad promote fisheries in the country's many rivers and streams and in the pondages and reservoirs coming up under water resource development programmes. Since Nepal and India have many common rivers, as do India and Bangladesh, it would be desirable to concert programmes so that the migratory runs of several varieties from the waters of one country to the other are not impeded to their common detriment. They can also cooperate in monitoring and combating fish disease such as epizootic ulcerative syndrome which affected both Bangladesh and Northeast India in 1988.

Bangladesh of course has immense possibilities. Inland waters suited to aquaculture are estimated to spread over 136,000 hectares, including nearly 1.8 million village ponds, and 16,000 hectares of ox-bow lakes. Over 2.8 million hectares of paddy fields also get inundated and retain water for four to six months, offering opportunity for seasonal fish culture. The potential culturable waters in the coastal and estuarine belt including mangrove and tidal flats is of the order of 630,000 hectares while the country's 500 kilometre coastline provides about a million hectares of territorial water with extended economic zone beyond. Fish production in 1985 was 774,000 tonnes of which over 70 per cent came from the inland catch including 308,000 tonnes of prized hilsa. The fisheries sector contributes about five per cent to the GDP, over six per cent of export earnings and employs six per cent of the population directly in fishing and allied occupations (BADC, 1981).

Bangladesh's waters contain around 250 species of fish but it has faced problems of poor management and over-exploitation in some segments, very much as in India. The strategy for fisheries development in the Third Plan (1985-90) was postulated on increasing overall fish production to a million tonnes, three-quarters of this from inland and estuarine sources and the generation of an additional million jobs in this sector. Great store is being set on development and export of shrimp and frog-legs. The Fish Conservation Act of 1950 has been revised to augment fish stock and protect habitats. The breeding and nursery grounds of major commercial species are being identified, charted and brought under protective management. Since most fresh water fish breed between mid-May and mid-August, the use of agricultural pesticides in farmlands contiguous to rivers, canals, depressions (haors) and beels are being sought to be regulated during this season. Likewise, spraying of pesticides in mangroves between January and March when post-larval shrimp enter the Sunderbans estuaries and tidal creeks is being controlled. Deep water paddy fields and all other seasonal water bodies are being provided with sluices and inlets so that natural stocking of fish occurs during the monsoonal inundation. The practice of harvesting hilsa at river mouths during up-river migration is also being discouraged in the interest of stock conservation. A large number of derelict water bodies are being reclaimed for culture fishery and efforts are being made to provide the requisite stocking material and to organize fishery cooperatives (Planning Commission, 1985). Many of these programmes are being coordinated by the Bangladesh Fisheries Development Corporation which was set up in 1964. The Corporation has been engaged in developing the infrastructure for inland and marine fisheries and providing training and processing facilities.

MANGROVES AND COASTAL MANAGEMENT

The Sunderbans, as mentioned earlier, is a critical transition zone and has high economic importance for the productivity of fisheries in Bangladesh and West Bengal. Its mangroves, covering almost 6000 square kilometres, constitute the largest single such block in the world. The mangroves thrive on the estuarine-marine tidal interface and are fertilized equally by the organic material washed down by the great river system criss-crossing it in an intricate web and that brought inland by the ides. Detritus from the mangroves in turn are a rich source of nutrients for both marine and estuarine fish which abound in the coastal and in-shore region for this very reason. The empoldered lands and mangroves of the Sunderbans provide a livelihood to an estimated half a million or more persons in Bangladesh alone in agriculture and fishing as well as in the extraction of fuelwood and timber, thatching material, beeswax and honey, shells and other produce. Reduced upland flows on account of abstractions as well as diversions at Farakka have, according to Bangladesh sources, aggravated salinity which has affected the distribution of sundari, the main Sunderbans tree species, and led to its top-dying. A mangrove forest inventory made in 1983 is reported to show a 40 to 45 per cent decline in the standing volume of sundari and gawa since 1958 on account of human activity within the region. Reduced vigour and regeneration has also occurred from reduced lean season discharges and increased siltation as a result of external interventions (Anwar, October 1988).

Further construction or raising of coastal embankments, polderisation and schemes to construct cross-dams to close certain estuarine or tidal channels could also have an effect on the coastal ecology with repercussions on mangroves, fish and their migratory runs. In West Bengal, demarcation of the northern forest limit along the so-called Dampier-Hodges line in 1830 was the signal for permitting reclamation of areas within the forested tidal swamps to the south in lots for the purpose of cultivation. One half of the 7000 square kilometres of forest had been cleared by 1911 when further clear-felling was banned. However, fresh reclamation was permitted in the 1960s for refugee resettlement. Proposals for closure of the Saptamukhi estuary, as a first phase of a larger Sunderbans delta development programme, have been under consideration off and on.

In Bangladesh too, there has been discussion on the Sandwip cross-dam project, abutting the Meghna outfall, to control erosion of Sandwip char and the recently formed Urichar, which was the scene of a huge cyclonic-tidal flood in 1985. An accretion of 18,000 to 22,000 hectares of land has been mooted as an additional benefit. However, issues of land ownership and land use will need to be determined with care to ensure equity and stability. Afforestation and agriculture are competing uses but the former would appear to be more benign environmentally as this would not merely promote stabilization of the reclaimed area over a critical 15 to 20 years period but also benefit coastal fishery if the plantations are of mangrove species. At the same time, closure of estuaries could affect the migratory passage of hilsa and the net balance of advantage would need to be studied with care (Asaduzzaman, February 1987).

In any scenario, what emerges is the importance of proper coastal area management for both inland and in-shore fisheries and the role of mangroves in this interaction.

CHAPTER 14

Restoring the Waterways

In any consideration of water resource development and transportation inland navigation has only received marginal and fitful consideration. This is particularly surprising in eastern India and Bangladesh where the lower Ganga, Brahmaputra and Barak-Meghna have been major arteries throughout the ages into recent times. Bangladesh could not exist without inland water transport, so formidable are the barriers formed by the great rivers and estuaries otherwise. And India has turned its back on history in neglecting these same waterways.

Megasthenes, ambassador from Seleucus Nicator, King of Syria, at the court of Chandragupta Maurya in Patliputra found a well ordered department of navigation headed by a superintendent of ships. Kautilya's Arthasastra spoke of an extensive system of navigation and referred to different sizes of boats assigned to different sizes of rivers, river tolls, port charges, ferries, shipping regulations, treatment of foreign merchants, spoilage charges, and piracy.

Jataka texts of the third century B.C. tell of voyages down the Ganga from Banaras, an ancient and prosperous city, to the mouth of the river and thence to Burma and beyond (Randhawa December 1980). The bustling port of Tamluk stood on the Rupnarayan river near modern Haldia. It was mentioned by Ptolemy and visited by the Chinese pilgrims Fa-Hien and Hiuen Tsang (Archaeological Survey of India, 1964).

SLOWLY DOWN THE GANGA

By Mughal times, boats of 100 to 500 tonnes plied on the Ganga and Yamuna as far as Agra according to Bernier, Manrique, Tavernier and other travelers. River traffic was more pronounced below Patna with barges sailing down to Hugli. Some of the smaller rivers wee bridged, including the Gomti at Jaunpur. But ferries had to be used to cross the major rivers, with boat bridges across the Yamuna at Delhi and Agra (Habib, 1982).

An English merchant, Ralph Fitch, writing at the close of the 16th century, notes that he "went from Agra to Satagam in Bengala, in the companie of one hundred and fourscore boates laden with salt, opium, hinge (asafetida), lead, carpets, and divers other commodities, downe the river Jemena" (Barns 1940). Satgaon (above modern Calcutta) was found by Caesar Frederick, an earlier traveler, to be a busy port visited by 30 or 35 ships great and small, laden with rice, lac, sugar, myrobalam, long pepper, oil and other merchandise. Merchants would buy or hire boats which sailed up and down the Ganga to fairs, "buying their commoditie with a great advantage, because that every day in the week, they hafe a faire, now in one place, and now in another..." (Hakluyt).

As water transport was relatively cheap, a great deal of inter-regional trade in bulk commodities like grain and salt moved on inland waterways or along the coast. The Ganga, Yamuna, Indus and their tributaries linked a large number of markets and though movement by water could be slow it reached out in many directions (Raychaudhuri, 1984). The Ganga was navigable by smaller vessels right up to Hardwar; larger vessels plied the lower Ganga system. Mirzapur was the entrepot for cotton and cotton-goods from the Deccan, and Anupshahr (on the Sone) for up-country cotton and indigo. Pride of place went to Banaras, India's second city, which handled a flourishing and wide-ranging import and export trade totaling about Rs.2.4 million, much of it waterborne.

Commerce along the Ganga was greatly stimulated after 1757 especially with the ris of Calcutta with its insatiable demand for indigo, cotton, silk, grain and opium which it traded in world markets. Manchester cotton piecegoods began to flood Indian markets through the port after 1824. The overall volume of trade multiplied manifold after 1785 and river traffic alone accounted for an estimated 3.2 million tonnes between Mirzapur and Calcutta and Mirzapur and Delhi by the 1948s (Kessinger, 1984). The demand for specific commodities in the international market resulted in shifts in land use and agricultural patterns along the Gangetic riverine tracts. Calcutta was the magnet. The mode of water transport changed, from smaller boats using sails as they rode the current downstream and bank haulage by crew using tacklines going upstream, to faster and more capacious steamboats which were introduced in 1834. The East India Company had a flotilla of ten steamboats and nine special barges by 1852 on the Ganga system, an enterprise stimulated by the deplorable state of the roads (Ibid).

Steam navigation on the Ganga between Calcutta and Allahabad was advocated by H.T. Princep in evidence before the House of Commons in London in 1828 in which he argued the case for inland navigation in India versus railroads drawn by animal power (not locomotives). There was no river in the world, he said, except those of China, on which there was so much navigation as on the Ganges. Thirty thousand boatmen found their livelihood on that river as far back as 1780 (Rennell) and the number had since increased. Princep estimated the cost of an irrigation-cum-navigation canal and that of a single railroad using animal power at £900 per mile, the returns on the two, however, being £190 and £175 respectively (Dutt Ramesh 1960 edition).

So cheap was water transport, especially for long distance haulage of bulk commodities, that larger merchants were even prepared to warehouse foodgrain and salt until the arrival of the monsoon when the navigable network would be greatly extended in reach. In 1849 the cost of transporting goods per ton-mile was 1.2 pence downstream and 1.6 pence upstream by country-boat (and 25 per cent more by steamboat), and double that by overland transport. Rennell found the Bhagirathi deteriorating in 1781. The silting of the river and the rise of Calcutta both as a port and as an administrative centre also led to the decline of Murshidabad and Dacca. The Hooghly was the main artery of river trade (Bhattacharya, 1984).

The growth of international trade had meanwhile increased the demand for hemp which was used for making sails and rope and for packing. Not wishing to be dependent on Baltic and Russian sources, the British began to experiment with jute the manufacture of which was perfected in Dundee in 1832 giving rise to jute cultivation in Bengal and, half a century later, to the growth of a thriving jute industry along the Hooghly around Calcutta (Morris, 1984).

RAILWAY COMPETITION

The rapid development of railways in India from the mid-1850s followed an Indian government guarantee of a minimum return to the private companies constructing the railroads. This was soon to introduce a strong policy bias in favour of the railways leading to a steady decline in the inland waterways and coastal shipping. Romesh Chunder Dutt has graphically recounted the heated debates in England and India on the relative priority that should be accorded to railways and irrigation through canals that might also be navigable. Famines were on the increase. One view was that the extension of railways would enable the government to rush grain to needy areas and avert starvation. The other school argued passionately for the extension of canal irrigation to tackle the root cause of the recurrent cycle of drought and famine caused by wayward monsoons.

Irrigation canals had no greater champion than Sir Arthur Cotton, architect of the high productive Cauvery and Godavari delta project. Addressing a parliamentary committee in London he declared that "what India wants is water carriage; the Railways have completely failed; they cannot carry the quantities; and they cost the country three million (pounds) a year, and increasing, to support them ... Steamboat canals would not have cost more than one eighth that of the Railways; would carry any quantities at nominal prices and at any speed; would require no support from the Treasury and be combined with irrigation". Listening to Cotton's eloquence, a member inquired why anyone should fear cheap transit. Because, replied Cotton, "it would stultify the Railways; that is the sole point". The navigation routes Sir Arthur Cotton urged in 1872 were from Calcutta to Karachi, up the Ganges and down the Indus; from Coconada (Kakinada) to Surat, up the Godavari and down the Tapi; a line up the Tumbhadra (Tungabhadra?) to Karwar on the Arabian Sea; and a line up the Ponang (Ponnani) by Plaghat and Coimbatore.

The Select Committee recorded Cotton's evidence in these terms; "Sir Arthur Cotton proposes the summary and indefinite suspension of nearly all Railways schemes and works. He would, however, devote ten millions (sterling) for the next ten or twenty years to irrigation works, mainly canals, the main canals to be of such dimensions as to permit navigation. By such an expenditure he estimates that ten thousand miles of main line navigation would be constructed at a cost of thirty million sterling, dealing with the most populous districts, while the remainder of this vast sum was to be spent on feeders or subsidiary works". Cotton had not provided any details regarding cost of materials or interest rate though he was confident of a "large return". The Select Committee concluded: "It is evident to your Committee that this scheme, though of gigantic dimensions, if o too shadowy and speculative a character to justify their noticing it, except for the purpose of emphatically rejecting it" (Romesh Dutt).

The Select Committee's fear that irrigation canals would be uneconomic was soon dispelled by the findings of the Madras Famine Commission. The Committee had also ignore the role played by inland navigation in developing commerce not only within the Gangetic plain but along the Brahmaputra. David Scott was witness to the mobility and power of the Burmese fleet on the Brahmaputra in1822 as the East India Company pushed into Assam to destroy Ahom power. He feared that Burmese command of the river routes into Bengal placed Dhaka and other districts at their mercy. However, Assam was subdued and Scott turned to commerce. Silk, then tea and possibility of a river-cum-land route to China fired his imagination and the discovery of coal in Upper Assam led him to urge the introduction of steamboats on the Brahmaputra up to Sadiya. Scott died before a commercial vehicle steamed up the river in 1841 to carry tea for export. But by 1830 gunboats were stationed at Sadiya to keep off Singhpho and Khampti raiders as it was proposed to hold a fair at Sadiya where an assorted consignment of cloth, opium and other items might be traded for ivory, amber, musk and copper. The boat hire from Calcutta to Sadiya, with insurance, was estimated at Rs.312 (Barooah, March 1970).

In 1834 there commenced a regular service on the Ganga from Calcutta to Allahabad under the East India Company. Within 30 years two steamer companies had come into existence, the Indian General Steam Navigation Company Ltd. And the River Steam Navigation Company. Both these sterling companies subsequently combined to form the Joint Steamer Companies which continued to ply the Ganga and Brahmaputra for over a hundred years. By 1842 a regular fortnightly service operated from Calcutta to Agra on the Yamuna and by 1863 there were similar services to Assam. River services up the Ganga extended as far as Garhmukteshwar, 645 kilometres above Allahabad, and Ayodhya 325 kilometres up the Ghaghara. Waters that powered craft could not negotiate were served by country boats which ran feeder services from Delhi and the Nepal border. At the peak in 1877 as many as 180,000 country cargo boats were registered at Calcutta, 124,000 at Hooghly and 62,000 at Patna.

TURNING AWAY FROM THE WATERFRONT

Decline had however set in from 1860 with the extension of the East Indian Railway (and the Bengal Nagpur Ralway). As the Railways grew, new centres of economic activity moved away from the rivers and coastal waterways to this new artery of commerce, and later to the roads as a result of state policy. Abstraction of river supplies for irrigation, increased siltation on account of deforestation, and neglect the maintenance of the waterways aggravated their decline (National Transport Policy Committee, May 1980).

The Joint Steamer Companies were fighting a losing battle. The great Assam earthquake of 1950 disrupted navigation along the upper Brahmaputra, the river bed having risen by some metres above Dibrugarh. Sadiya was wiped out. The RSN Co Ltd "had in fact reached a point of no return by early 1964 and was only kept going for another year by the payment of River Holdings of its outstanding debt on the purchase of the RSN investment in (East) Pakistan ... In the end it was agreed that the Government (of India) should take over the equity shares of the RSN for the nominal consideration of £ 1" (Griffith). Partition in 1947 also partitioned the river and isolated Calcutta from its upland riverine hinterlands in Bihar and U.P. as much as in Assam. The Bhagirathi was shoaled up for most of the year and could not be navigated to the Ganga except through East Pakistan or Bangladesh until the Farakka lock and feeder canal were finally commissioned in 1987. Likewise, Northeast India virtually became a landlocked region, connected to the mainland by a hurriedly constructed Assam Rail Link and national highway traversing the Siliguri corridor. The river service to Assam continued through East Pakistan. It was interrupted in 1965, but was restored in 1972 after Bangladesh came into being. The assets of the Joint Steamer Companies in India were meanwhile transferred to the Central Inland Water Transport Corporation which was incorporated in 1967 as a government undertaking.

The Government of India professed a commitment to inland navigation and the technical organization set up to deal with all aspects of water resource development in 1945 was named the Central Water and Inland Navigation Commission. It was only in the mid-1950s that the name of this body was amended to Central Water and Power Commission, and "navigation" was dropped. Some of the early post-Independence irrigation canal were designed to be navigable. Among these were the Tungabhadra left bank canal, the Rajasthan canal and, mostly notably, the Damodar canal which was fitted with 22 locks to pass vessels. None has worked. Neglect in the pursuit of the larger aims of irrigation and power, lack of an organization to develop inland navigation and network these canals into larger systems, and the absence of an industrial location policy that would encourage development of the waterfront combined to scuttle any real hope of inland water transport coming into its own. IWT is energy-efficient, land saving, employment oriented and well suited to the long distance carriage of bulk commodities like grain, salt, construction materials, and the like. But it has the disadvantage of low seed (which need not matter in many cases) and limited spatial accessibility. Seasonality need not be a crippling constraint. But one factor that can and does handicap IWT (as any other mode of transport) is transshipment, which greatly adds to costs.

Public expenditure on IWT in India's first six Plans, 1951-85, came to just Rs.100 crores or less than 0.1 per cent of the total outlay on all forms of transport. Despite under-funding, allocations could not be fully utilized for lack of a purposeful organization. There was some improvement in the Sixth Plan and a further step up in proposed outlays in the Seventh Plan (Rs.226 crores). The earlier benign neglect was manifest despite the reports and recommendations of a number of expert committees and commissions. The National Transport Policy Committee (1980) lamented this, describing coastal shipping as the Cinderella of the transport industry "whom neither shipowners nor Government is willing to own and operate". The Committee referred to lack of any river conservancy programme or nodal agency to develop the necessary infrastructure. It recommended the declaration of certain stretches as national waterways and the establishment of an Indian waterways authority. Fortunately the Prime Minister gave public support to the development of IWT and the Hoghly-Bhagirathi-Ganga from Haldia to Allahabad was designated National Waterway No. 1 upon the creation of the Inland Waterways Authority of India (IWAI) by statute in 1985. The other national waterways projected are the Bahmaputra in Assam, the Sunderbans, the Mahanadi-Orissa system, the Krishna and Godavari canals, the West Coast Canal (Kerala), the Mandovi-zuari-Cumbarjua Canal system in Goa, the Narmada and the Tapi. This list by no means exhausts the country's navigable rivers and waterways. These extend over 10,240 kilometres of river and 4300 kilometres of canal and are currently used by country boats and ferries.

On being declared a national waterways, the financial responsibility for development of that stretch becomes that of the Central Government. The criteria for selection as a national waterway is that it should have a channel width of at last 45 metres, a depth of 1.5 metres and a length of at least 50 kilometres except in case of urban centres or intra-port traffic. It should generally serve more than one State or a significant hinterland or strategic area, or connect areas not served by any other mode of transport.

INLAND NAVIGATION ELSEWHERE

While India has long neglected IWT and coastal waterways, these have continued to play a major role in Europe, the Americas, China and elsewhere. The Danube connects eight countries over 2300 kilometres and in the later 1970s carried a traffic of 80 million tonnes per annum. The Rhine is navigable over 900 kilometres and serves five nations. It handled over 300 million tones of traffic in the early

1980s with the great Dutch port of Rotterdam as its ocean outlet. French waterways in 1982 moved over 76 million tonnes of merchandise over 6700 kilometres of rivers and smaller link canals. More ambitiously, until a few years ago only a small link remained to join the Rhine and Danube systems to complete a trans-continental waterway from the Black Sea to the North Sea and the Arctic Ocean.

The Soviet Union has a huge 150,000 kilometre waterway system linking the Caspian Sea to the Black Sea in the south and joining these to the White Sea and the Baltic Sea in the north. The system is being expanded by various basin boards. Substained efforts have paid rich dividends. The draft of the Belaja river, a tributary of the Kama, just east of the Ural Mountains, was improved from 0.8 metres to 2.25 metres between 1931 and 1975. In the case of the Nadym River in the northern part of West Siberia, the draft was improved by three times to 1.8 metres over 10 years by dredging. What is interesting is that the Beleja is navigable for just 215 days and the Nadym for no more than 130 days, both rivers being ice-bound for the rest of the year. Despite this seasonality, both routes have proved viable.

The United States and Canada share the Great Lakes and St. Lawrence Seaway. The Seaway was modernized between 1954 and 1959 and one of its key links, the Welland Canal lifts vessels of up to 25,000 DWT over 100 metres to by-pass the Niagara Falls through eight locks in 44 kilometres. In addition, the U.S. moves some hundreds of billion tonne-kilometres of cargo along the Mississippi River system and three major coastal waterways along the Gulf of Mexico, the Atlantic and the Pacific.

Brazil and Egypt, both developing nations, have exploited inland waterways to the full. In China, inland waterways and coastal shipping accounted for 65 billion tonne-kilometres and 106 bn/t/kms. As against this it plans to carry 580 to 670 bn/t/kms of traffic by inland waterways or 21 per cent of the inter-modal split by 2000, a third down from 1960 on account of other water resource development programmes. But there has been a policy to locate industry such as steel mils and fertilizer plants along waterways such as the Yangtze (World Bank, 1985).

FACTORS IN REVIVAL OF INTEREST

Two factors have turned India's gaze back to its lost inland and coastal waterways. The Transport Policy Committee (1985) noted that India's transport sector uses nearly a third of the country's total energy and more than half of its oil supplies. It accordingly recommended choice of modes with the highest energy efficiency. This puts IWT at a considerable advantage as one horse-power of energy moves 150 kilograms by road, 500 kilograms by rail and 4000 kilograms by barge. Put ifferently, the energy intensity of different modes in terms of BTU per tonne-kilometre works out to 1587 by diesel, 2765 by steam train, but only 166 and 106 by diesel and electric traction respectively. As against this the figure for barge movement is 328 (Planning Commission, April 1988). This indicates that while barge movement is cheaper than carriage by road or steam traction, it is not as economic as diesel or electrically-powered rail haulage. However, barge haulage is estimated to be more economic than diesel-rail movement if barge sizes are increased from 1000 tonnes to 1500 tonnes (National Transport Committee, 1980). Since railway rates are subsidized for bulk goods over long hauls, barge or coastal movements enjoy an economy of scale-cum-distance if there is no transshipment. Moreover, it is estimated that while the initial investment per kilometre of rail track is about Rs.10 lakhs, it is only Rs.4.5 lakhs in the case of roads and Rs.2 lakhs for waterways (Public Undertakings Committee, Lok Sabha, 1976).

The other factor that has come into play is the realization that while the Railways are likely to carry an estimated 345 million tonnes of freight in 1989-90 or 245 billion tonne-kilometres (as compared with 307 bn/t/kms moved by road), they may be expected to carry about 542 million tonnes and roads 396 million tonnes of freight by 2000 (Planning Commission, April 1988). An earlier estimate indicated that freight movement in India by the end of the century was likely to be of the order of 600 billion tonne-kilometres. With existing transport corridors already greatly congested if not saturated it would be necessary to develop alternative routes and modes of traffic (Consulting Engineering Services, March 1987). This would be particularly true of coal movements to super-thermal stations which are proposed to be located along the coast where they will have no problem about availability of cooling water or, hopefully, carriage of coal from Talcher in Orissa and elsewhere by IWT or rail-cum-coastal waterway, with the possibility of importing coal as well if necessary.

Despite the revival of interest in IWT in India, planning for it continues to be sequential. The Farakka Barrage was from the very start designed to restore a direct link between Calcutta and the Ganga. The Barrage was completed in 1971 and the feeder canal in 1975 but the navigation lock was not inaugurated until November 1987. Even so, little traffic moves because the infrastructure for IWT is only now being developed. Meanwhile little has been done as yet to lay down a policy framework for developing and attracting traffic by providing locational and other incentives as has been done for the past 50 to 100 years in the case of the roads and Railways. To create an expensive IWT infrastructure and then have no traffic to move would not merely be wasteful but would discredit IWT in the yes of potential developers and consumers. The DVC navigation canal is an outstanding example of mismatched "planning", though that waterway could perhaps even now be revived.

DEVELOPING NATIONAL WATERWAY NO.1

National Waterway No. 1 falls into three sectors: Haldia-Farakka, 500 kilometres, Farakka-Patna, 480 kilometres, and Patna-Allahabad, 600 kilometres. The lowest 100 kilometre of the waterway between Haldia and Nawadwip (above Calcutta) is a tidal reach and presents no problems for barges which do not require a draft of more than 1.5 metres. Between Nawadwip and Farakka however, some dredging or conservation measures may be required near Murshidabad. Farakka Lock is part of the national Waterway but was in 1989 still being operated by the Water Resources Ministry. The Farakka complex consists of a 2.245 kilometre long barrage across the Ganga, a 38.3 kilometre one feeder canal diverting up to 40,000 cusecs of water to Jangiur where the Bhagirathi takes off from the Ganga. The Bhagirathi offtake is choked with silt and headwater supplies from the Ganga only enter it during the monsoon months. A barrage of the Bhagirathi at Jangipur prevents the waters fed into the feeder canal at Farakka flowing back into the Ganga. A lock has been built at this point to provide a navigation link from the Hooghly-Bhagirathi into the Ganga-Padma and Bangladesh. The Farakka lock "bridges" the difference between the bed level of the Ganga and the pond level of the Farakka "reservoir". The lock has two chambers, each 25.15 metres wide and 180.7 metres long, sufficient to pass craft or a barge train of up to 1500 tonnes. Provision has been made for adding a second lock at a future stage if necessary. The feeder canal has a minimum draft of four metres. The lock tool is Rs.200 per country boat and Rs.20 per GRT in respect of powered vessels which seem rather excessive at this promotional stage. Trial operations through the lock have established that unit sizes too large for the Railways or any truck to handle can be moved through the lock. A single 450 tonne piece of equipment for a fertilizer plant under construction in UP was in fact shipped through the lock without difficulty soon after it as opened.

The hydrographic survey of the middle sector between Farakka and Patna has been completed and conservancy works are in progress with bandalling to divert river flows to scour a deep channel to provide a freeway with the requisite two metre depth and 45 metre width. There is up to a nine metre difference in river levels between the lean season and the floods and the deep channel keeps changing course. The IWAI will have to see how far channel fluctuation can be moderated and a fairly constant fairway maintained and appropriately marked for safe navigation. Five terminal sites have been selected for the location of floating jetties-cum-warehouses pending more permanent construction at Rajmahal, Munger, Bhagalpur, Mokameh and Kahalgaon. A major inland port is planned at Patna which the IWAI estimates could develop a cargo potential of over five million tonnes by 1991 and 10.5 million tonnes by 2006 within a radius of 110 kilometres between Mokameh and Ballia. The facilities envisaged include port-related industrial an commercial infrastructure and container handling capacity.

The 600-kilometre sector between Patna and Allahabad is being developed with Dutch assistance and know-hw. Dredgers, survey vessels, instruments and especially designed cargo carriers are being obtained as art of a pilot project. Above Patna the lean season draft in the Ganga varies between 1.2 and 1.5 metres. About

20 shoals have been identified of which five may require dredging while the others may be overcome by bandalling. Seven terminals are planned at Chapra, Ballia, Ghazipur, Varanasi, Chunar, Mirzapur and Allahabad.

The type and mix of craft that should be used is also being given careful consideration. Push-towing has an advantage insofar as the prime mover is in constant use and can be employed to move a number of dumb barges in trains of four units of 125 tonnes each. A self-propelled barge of say 600 tonnes with a 460 horse-power engine can move independently. Modular-sized deck-loading barges or flats could carry containers while barges with holds may be required for certain types of cargo that need safer handling.

FEEDER SYSTEMS AND INTERCONNECTIONS

Navigational studies on the Ganga tributaries are being left to the States for the moment. Many of them have a transport potential which could be augmented by water resource development and river conservancy works. The Arrah, Patna and Buxar canals takin off below the Sone Barrage were fitted with locks and were opened to navigation between 1876 and 1880. Together with Sone escape channel discharging into the Ganga near Patna they were in use for local navigation until Independence. Country boats could operate feeder services along these and other routes, though most country boat traffic is at present short-haul ferry movement over distances of 10-20 kilometres with 10-20 tonnes of freight per trip. Mechanization would make for higher speeds and a greater range but would cut into employment as each boat carries four to five boatmen.

The DVC was designed to permit navigation by 250-tonne barges along is main left bank irrigation canal over a length of 120 kilometres from Durgapur in the coal-steel belt to a point on the Hooghly 55 kilometres above Calcutta. Unfortunately, on account of a relatively small transshipment lead from the coalfields and industrial area to the canal, the waterway has remained practically unused. Consequently more water came to be diverted for boro (winter) irrigation thus reducing the draft available for navigation. The West Bengal government is now concerned that were navigability to be restored, lockage losses may affect established irrigation. In any event the water loss on account of navigation is estimated to be no more than 12,300 hectare-metres as against a provision for double that amount in the original DVC design. Meanwhile the canal lock gates have rusted for lack of maintenance and the entire system will require to be renovated if IWT operations commence. Some time back French experts suggested building a lock around the Durgapur barrage to extend navigation upstream in stages to the lower Raniganj coalfields around Asansol as a means of moving coal to Calcutta. The idea does not appear to have been seriously pursued. But it would be worth examining once again and also looking at the feasibility of building locks around the two main DVC dams at Maithon and Panchet Hill.

If IWT is to be revived, there would appear to b a good case for rejuvenating and modernizing some of the old waterways of lower Bengal. The Hijli Tidal Canal and the Orissa Coast Canal are linked to the Buckinghgma Canal further south in Andhra Pradesh and carried a significant traffic until the Bengal-Nagpur Railway took over. Likewise the Krishopur Khel system linking Calcutta with the Sunderbans which is still used by non-mechanised craft.

TRANSIT THROUGH BANGLADESH

The Brahmaputra and Barak-Meghna systems were the main arteries of transit and outlets to the sea for Northeast India until Partition severed this lifeline. Until 1946 water transport was paramount in Assam and other modes were relatively undeveloped and circuitous. Substantial tonnages were moved by water. River conditions were much better and IWT services were fairly well organized. Partition dealt this a body blow. The Assam Inland Water Transport Department operated a small flotilla and moved about 300 tonnes of traffic in 1986-87 from Guwahati to Calcutta, with the CIWTC moving a larger share. Political uncertainties regarding relations with Bangladesh and the renewal of the IWT protocol between the two countries has been an inhibiting factor. Within Assam and the Northeast generally, rail movements beyond Siliguri are subsidized and this further handicaps river services in competing for traffic. The IWT cost has been estimated at 10 paise per tonne per kilometre. As against this, thc cost of rail carriage works out to 30 P per tonne/km. But with the transport subsidy given to it, the Railways is quicker. It takes 10-15 days to move a wagon from Guwahati to Calcutta and about the same time to cover the distance by barge, the different in upstream and downstream movements being about three days. With only limited river training and maintenance of the fairway, soundings have to be taken and pilots taken on boarding both the Indian and Bangladesh stretches. There is as yet no night navigation. Use of sails on powered barges could enhance speed ad improve energy efficiency. But there is no R&D organization. Manning requirements for barges and tugs under the Indian Vessels Act are excessive and outdated. Despite all this, IWT has met with strong opposition from both the Railway and road lobbies. There is no corresponding lobby for IWT anywhere in the country.

Indian vessels are cleared to operate on about 1,300-1,500 route-kilometres of transit waterways in Bangladesh while moving from Calcutta to the Northeast. The route takes vessels from Calcutta through the Sunderbans and into Bangladesh waters at Raimangal and then on to Khulna and Chandpur at the confluence of the Padma and the Meghna. From here, barges bound for Guwahati move up the Brahmaputra (Jamuna in Bangladesh) to Bahadurabad-Chilmiri and on to Dhubri in Assam, while those bound for Cachar travel up the Meghna-Kushiyara-Barak via Jakiganj, Sherpur and Karimganj in Assam. Some of these waterways are not greatly used by Bangladesh vessels which implies investment by that country in conservancy, charting and other works in aid of navigation primarily to facilitate transit by Indian vessels. India has accordingly been paying Bangladesh a subvention for these services and investments as negotiated from time to time under IWT protocols. The latest navigation protocol signed towards the end of 1987 recognises IWT as an instrument of Indo-Bangladesh trade and a means of enabling each country to develop its natural resource in the mutual interest. It has been agreed that bilateral trade cargo be shared equally by Indian and Bangladesh bottoms and that Bangladesh will charge India the same tariff and pilotage fees as it levies on its own domestic traffic. Development of container traffic, inland container depots, night movement, facilities to help ships in distress, and R&D programmes for IWT have also been proposed and would make a difference if operationalised.

The Brahmaputra has sufficient draft year-round in Bangladesh though some conservancy works may be necessary to canalize the lean season flows of this greatly braided river. The Kushiyara-Barak however does not have sufficient draft for at least four lean months, with the draft diminishing as one travels up-river into northeast India. This situation will change once the proposed Tipaimukh dam and irrigation barrage are constructed on the Barakabout 100 and 40 kilometres, respectively from Silchar. The reservoir will back up another 80 kilometres along the Barak, the Tuvai river in Mizoram and the Makru and Irang in Manipur. A steady tailrace discharge of 15,000 cusecs from the Tipaimukh hydel turbines (1500 MW) is also expected to provide ample draft down-river into Bangladesh. This would not merely improve the IWT transit route from Calcutta to Karimganj-Silchar and beyond but also open up a considerable hinterland that is at present bottled up for lack of communications which has in turn severely impeded development, giving rise to unemployment and a host of social and political problems in the entire region.

OPENING UP THE NORTHEAST

A power dam on the Dhaleshwari (160 MW) at Bhairabi on the Cachar-Mizoram border was investigated by the National Hydroelectric Power Corporation in 1984. The lake formed behind the dam will spread about 80-100 kilometres south to Sairang in Mizoram, barely 25 kilometres by road from Aizawl on the ridge above the waterway. This stretch will be navigable and the waterway could extend another 100 kilometres further south to Lungleh were another dam built near Sairang as tentatively proposed. With power generation, Sairang port could be linked to Aizawl by ropeway. The tail-race discharge from the Dhaleshwari hydel station would also permit navigation down the river to Silchar. The Mizoram government has a feasibility report on navigation between the proposed Dhaleshwari Dam and Sairang, as well as on the upper Tut river (a tributary stream), with Ro-Ro or roll-on, roll-off facilities whereby laden trucks will simply move on the barges, move along the waterway, and then roll-off and make for destinations such as Aizawl under their own power by road (North Eastern Council, March 1985).

A power dam, with a possible irrigation component has also been investigated on the Kolodyne (Kaladan) river which runs south through eastern Mizoram into Burma and falls into the sea at Akyab. This route was used for improvised river movements by Wingate's Chindit force under Mountbatten's command in the Arakan operations during the Second World War.

Agartala in Tripura is 2100 kilometres from Calcutta by road and is still to be connected by railway. It is within five to ten kilometres of navigable routes and a railhead to Chittagong and elsewhere across the border in Bangladesh. Even before Bangladesh came into being, the Karnaphuli river was dammed at Kaptai in the Chittagong Hill Tract to generate hydro power. Bangladesh was at one time keen on raising the height of the dam in order to augment the power potential. India objected as the backflow of the Kaptai lake already threatens to submerge Indian territory in Mizoram during high flood. Even now, construction of a lock of ship-lift, around the Kaptai Dam could enable barges to move through Demagiri in Mizoram down the Karnaphuli to Chittagong where the river meets the sea.should the Kaptai dam's height be raised, some submergence in India would be well compensated by improved navigation both above Demagiri and below Kaptai to Chittagong and the restoration of Mizoram's traditional outlet to the sea.

The possibilities are immense and with storage on the Brahmaputra system in Arunachal a stable deepwater fairway would be available along the entire length of the Assam Valley and into Bangladesh. The Farakka-Padma link would even now provide a shorter and better navigation route between Calcutta and Guwahati. The NEC's transport research division identified 2.26 million tonnes of traffic that could profitably be moved by water in the Northeast in 1985 and recommended a matching Rs.291 crore IWT development programme (Ibid).

The lack of communications in Northeastern India is so crippling, despite a massive road development programme by the Border Roads Organisation, that a special study was mounted some years ago to augment all forms of communication. There was a specific proposal for constructing a series of Railway spurs to provide a railhead in each of the seven units in the Northeast, and undertake conversion of certain sections from metre to broad guage. The Lumding-Badarpur hill section links Assam Valley with Cachar, Manipur, Mizoram and Tripura and serves an area of about 50,000 square kilometres. This metre guage section is a big bottleneck but its conversion to broad guage up to Silchar is estimated to cost Rs.680 crores. A further BG spur to Dimapur in Nagaland would cost Rs.400 crores. Another alternative discussed is a second metre guage link from Haflong to Badarpur along an easier alignment through the hill sector. The existing Lumding-Badarpur section (185 kilometres) has 37 tunnels and 586 bridges. Most of the track is along sharp curves which entails reduced speeds. Cost estimates for new tracks go as high Rs.2 crores per kilometre in certain segments of this region which is subject to torrential rainfall and landslide-prone. Even roads destabilize the hills and are expensive to bridge and maintain whereas the railways can at best establish a token presence in many of the States.

It is against this background that the development of water transport needs to be viewed. Railways and roads obviously have a place; so has water transport which is better suited to the Northeast and would have a greater reach at less cost while serving the needs of power generation, irrigation and flood control as well.

With water resource development in Bhutan, the Manas and other rivers falling into the Brahmaputra could at some stage be rendered navigable, at least during certain seasons. Dhubri in Assam could become a useful transshipment point for carriage of Bhutanese cargo to and from Calcutta or Bangladesh.

The Dhubri-Sadiya reach of the Brahmaputra (891 kilometres) is soon to be designated a national waterway. Terminal facilities are being planned en route at Jogighopa, Guwahati, Silghat, Tezpur and Neamati. A terminal is also proposed at Karimganj and other ports will no doubt develop along the Barak system.

R&D FOR FAIRWAY AND FLEET

The working group on IWT for India's Seventh Plan recommended that the development of inland waterways should form part of an overall transport plan with the advantages of each mode being maximized. Apart from big and small rivers that could be trained and channelised to secure the requisite drafts, there could even be a case for multipurpose barrages on certain rivers to pond up flows during the lean season. For example, the deep channel of the Ganga at Kanpur has strayed seven kilometres away from the southern bank thus creating municipal water supply problem sin that city. Efforts to canalize the Ganga have proved unavailing and expensive and the local authorities have been pressing for a barrage across the river, which would also augment cooling water supplies for thermal generation. A number of committees have suggested construction of a barrage. Such a proposal, to pond up the river by about two metres and channel flows beside the city at a cost of some Rs.130 crores, has been approved. Once completed, a lock (not so far envisaged) might facilitate navigation along this stretch. Barrages certainly entail substantial outlays, especially on large rivers. But costs can be allocated over multiple uses and must be compared with the cost of augmenting transport capacity by other means.

Canals afford another means of extending navigation or connecting waterways. The Planning Commission's IWT consultants lament the fact that the parallel Ganga Canal now under construction in UP, like the 500 kilometre long Sharda Sahayak canal, is being constructed without a navigation component. Most often the sponsoring department – Irrigation in this case – is not concerned with navigation and its reluctant to think of larger dimensions while struggling to get approvals for its own project in the face of resource constraints. If planning were better integrated and had a longer perspective, some of these problems might be avoided, at least to the extent of not preempting future options, at marginal cost:

The Narmada Valley Development Authority envisages movement of up to 49 million tonnes of coal from the Central India and Western Coalfields via Jabalpur and Hoshangabad to Gujarat to feed existing and future thermal power stations. The return cargo could consist of fertilizers, salt, edible oils and industrial goods. Construction of the Sardar Sarovar, Narmadasagar and other dams there would create a 1000-kilometre waterway from Jabalpur to the sea provided passage is provided through the dams (IWT Working Group, 1985). A feasibility study on locks or ship-lifts around the four major Narmada dams, and costs and methods to pass certain other difficult stretches of river, has been done by Indo-Dutch consultants (Haskoning and CES April 1985) and found remunerative.

There have been considerable advances in the engineering and design of locks so as to save water losses and reduce transit time. Alternatives such as ship elevators and waterslopes (that propel a vessel in a water container up or down as incline) are in operation in France, the Soviet Union and elsewhere.

Canals and other waterways may need pitching or other forms of protection to prevent bank erosion from the wave effect caused by the passage of vessels. A reduction in speed can mitigate the erosive force, and where speed is not a determining criterion this could prove to be a viable option. More efficient lock arrangements could compensate for some time lost. A French observer has expressed surprise that Indian canals, many of which are the size of European rivers, are not more effectively and intensively used for navigation. In the case of older waterways with sufficient traffic and route-mileage, it may be necessary and even desirable to design special types and sizes of barges to negotiate them. Fortunately thought is now being given to rejuvenating and modernizing the Andhra, Godavari and Krishna canals, and the Buckingham canal, that hug the east coast for some 1500-2000 kilometres.

Development of waterways also depends on ensuring horizontal and vertical bridge clearances. Surveys, charting and dredging or training of fairways must be accompanied by installation of buoys and markers, lights, navigational aids, terminal and warehousing facilities, both fixed and floating. Also cranes, conveyor belts and other handling equipment where manual handling will not suffice, bunkering facilities, refuge harbours for bad weather or for vessels in distress, repair yards, patrol services and so on. Vessels too will have to be selected and designed to suit a variety of Indian waters or specialized needs with different unit sizes of powered vessels for given tasks. Newer propulsion systems are making it possible to operate with lower drafts or higher energy-efficiency. A strong research and development thrust is necessary and skilled manpower will need to be developed in various cadres. The IWAI is taking steps to set up a national training institute at Patna.

Ship design, navigational equipment including radar and echo-sounders, and VHF communication systems are variously necessary if safe, efficient and competitive water services are to be operated. Newer materials are being used in place of wooden and other traditional construction material: ferrocement, light alloys, marine hardboards, fibre glass and plastics. The CIWTC's fleet is being augmented and modernized and its Rajabagan Dockyard at Calcutta is being developed for both shipbuilding and repair. Standardisation is important to keep down costs and ensure compatability with Bangladesh and other systems so that future interchange is not hampered. Equally, there must be a rigorous classification of waterways (including locks) so that compatability is maintained.

WINNING BACK TRAFFIC

It is estimated that 18 million tonnes of traffic and 186 million passengers were carried by mechanized and country craft, including ferries, in India in 1985-86. The IWT forecast for 1995 and 2000 envisages carriage of 45 to 69 million tonnes of cargo and 223 and 242 million passengers, respectively (Vasudev, August 1988). CES Ltd. However estimates that 54 million tonnes of traffic may be on offer by 2000 AD, much of this being coal (March 1987). These estimates appear rather conservative and flow from the diffidence with which IWT continues to be treated.

The pre-independence Joint Steamer Companies operated a triangular traffic between Bihar, Bengal and Assam. Rice, sugar, pulses and other agricultural producer was carried from Bihar to Assam from where jute, timber and some tea would be lifted to Calcutta. Here, manufactured products would be loaded for Patna and destinations beyond. A study undertaken some years ago indicated that 18 items of cargo, including both agricultural produce and manufactures like steel, fertilisers, non-ferrous metals and cement, accounted for 78 per cent of the total traffic moved by all modes of transport between Calcutta and its hinterland as far as Bihar and eastern U.P. The IWT rates for these items between pairs of points were for most part significantly less than those charged either by the railways or roadways, with the exception of cement where the chargeable Railway freight rate (as distinct from the cost of carriage) was lower (NCAER, July 1976).

If traffic is to be attracted to the waterways, then new industries must be located along existing or prospective waterfronts. This calls for a deliberate review of location policy with appropriate regulations to control water pollution through untreated effluent discharges. Incentives could be offered such as making available power at waterfront sites, developing industrial estates around inland ports with captive jetties, offer for financial inducements by declaring selected waterfronts as backward areas, permitting established units to expand or diversify if they locate new investments in waterfront zones and so on. IWT should also be declared an industry for attracting soft loans from financial institutions. State Governments are now being given additional loan assistance for IWT development (IWT Working Group, 1985). None of this is special pleading for IWT as comparable facilities have long been enjoyed by the railways and roadways. At another level, consideration should be given to extending canals to nearby traffic-generating centres so as to link them with established waterways where viable.

The private sector is not debarred from engaging in IWT but will not be induced to do so unless a whole package is developed that ensures a reasonable return.

CONTAINERISATION AIDS INTER-MODAL SYSTEMS

The concept of transport has changed with the development of inter-modal systems. The quickest and cheapest movement may well be achieved by a combination of different modes. Containerization and the development of modular vehicles and vessels have given great impetus to this trend. The system has further developed with the establishment of inland container depots (ICDs) or "dry-ports" to which goods can be shipped for import or export in sealed or bonded wagons, vessels or containers moving under the combined transport document or a single inland bill of lading, irrespective of the mode or modes of transport employed and acceptable to both domestic and international carriers. India has established a number of ICDs, some of them at inland ports like Guwahati and Patna, and efforts are afoot to adapt the Foreign Exchange Dealer's Association of India's documentation, which has been approved by the Reserve Bank of India, to the widely used International Chamber of Commerce standardized documentation. The main problem is to clearly define the liability regime in case of loss, damage or misdirection of cargo. Rather than adapt an Indian document that may not be entirely or universally acceptable in international commerce, India should adapt its laws and practices to well-established international usage so that trade and exchange are stimulated. It is certainly most important that India, Bangladesh, Nepal and Bhutan and the other SAARC nations adopt uniform systems of documentation.

Containerised barges, containers that can be loaded on to barge flats, or trucks laden with containers that could move along given stretches of waterways on roll-on, roll-off barges are some among possible combinations. Self-propelled or dumb barges could also be loaded on to LASH (light abroad ship), Seabee or Bacat (barge aboard catamaran) vessels, permitting an inter-modal transfer from inland to marine ships. Another combination that would have obvious advantages for India and Bangladesh would be fluvio-coastal as much as fluvio-maritime vessels. These could then navigate inland waters to the sea and travel along the coast to re-enter some other inland waterway. Thus a barge from Guwahati or Allahabad should be enabled to move through Calcutta-Haldia to Kakinada and up the Godavari. The Indian Inland Vessels Act at present bars an inland vessel from venturing beyond tidal limits. Thereafter, different scantalling, freeboard draft and other specifications are required to negotiate occan waves and currents. This is a matter of design and suitable systems could be designed at least for seasonal operation excluding the rough monsoon months. Such systems would give IWT a range and flexibility that could make it ever so attractive for certain movements.

Studies on inter-modal movement of coal have been undertaken in response to the decision to locate a number of super-thermal stations along the Indian coast at Vishakapatnam, North Madras, Tuticorin, Kayamkulam (Kerala), Mangalore, Karwar and other sites. A RITES study has found movement of coal from the Talcher collieries in Orissa to North Madras and Tuticorin via Paradeep or Dhamra (a potential new port at the mouth of theBrahmani-Baitarani river further north) to be feasible and economic whether by a rail-coastal shipping or by IWT-coastal shipping. This would however require some investment in the missing Railway or IWT link from Talcher to the port.

Cutting a passage through the Palk Straits, the old Sethusamudram project, would reduce the distance between points south of Pondicherry on the east coast and west coast destinations by several hundred kilometres by obviating the circumnavigation of Sri Lanka. This has not been looked at seriously in recent times but would merit re-examination should movement from the east to west coast be likely to develop substantially. The Central Electricity Authority has estimated a possible requirement of over 33 million tonnes of coal movement from Talcher to coastal super-thermal stations by 2000 of which as much as 25 million tonnes might lie below or around the Palk Straits (CES Ltd., March 1987).

CRITICAL ROLE OF IWT IN BANGLADESH

If inland water transport has increasing role to play in meeting India's future transportation needs, it has always been crucial for Bangladesh, criss-crossed as it is by rivers, derelict streams and tidal creeks too wide and numerous to bridge. In 1985, Bangladesh had 2,892 kilometres of railway, 4,827 kilometres of paved arterial and feeder roads and 5,632 kilometres of inland waterways (about 14 per cent of this being seasonal). The modal split shows that IWT moved 5.73 million tonnes of freight in 1984-85 or double that carried by rail, though not quite as much as by road. By 1990, IWT is expected to move 8.7 million tonnes of freight and 212 million passengers or 28 and 32 per cent of the total as against 13 and 25 per cent by rail and 59 and 41 per cent by road (Planning Commission, December, 1985). The Bangladesh Railways are in decline and are losing heavily. Arterial roads too can cost $650,000 a kilometre to construct and are expensive to maintain. Stone is not easily available for metalling (and is an item that India could supply economically by water). Inland water transportation is very competitive but despite its salience has not received financial allocations commensurate with its potential (Choudhury, Mahiuddin, June 1986) and comparative cost advantage.

The waterways link the country's two main ports of Chittagong and Chalna with five major inland ports at Dhaka, Narayanganj, Chandpur, Barisal and Khulna and serve the rural heartland. Ferry services interconnect roadways across the principal north-south river divide. The waterways are classified into trunk routes (625 kilometres) with a 2.8 metre draft, transit routes (1,352 kilometres) with a draft of a little under 2 metres, secondary routes (1,454 kilometres) with a one metre draft, and estuarine waters (990 kilometres). These are maintained by the Bangladesh Inland Water Transport Authority. Maintenance and development dredging efforts are also under way to resuscitate some dead and dying waterways.

THE COUNTRY BOAT SECTOR

The critical importance of IWT in the life and economy of Bangladesh becomes strikingly apparent if non-mechanised transport systems are also considered. These account for about 95 per cent of all vehicles and craft, 80 per cent of all employment in transport, and 75 per cent of the value added by transport operations. Within this sector, country boats are the single most important mode with a combined carrying capacity of around one million tonnes. They provide a vital rural-urban link and are of the utmost importance for the distributive trade as they are often the only means of reaching certain areas. Yet the country boat sector has been left to fend for itself and has, as in India, suffered from a "tradition or policy neglect" (Netherlands-Norway Study, February 1984).

The country boat sector is dominated by small owner-operators though there are a number of owner-supervisors and absentee boat owners who rent out their vessels, each class being closely related to the land structure. Growing siltation of rivers, reduced dry season flows and the impact of certain engineering structures such as barrages and embankments has resulted in a deterioration of available drafts. In the circumstances, country boats are assuming a greater importance in some ways as they alone can negotiate these shallow waterways. After a careful analysis of the problem the Netherlands-Norway study outlines a programme of development and research built around a new policy orientation regarding the place of country boats in the development of human resources, employment, transport services and rural development generally in Bangladesh.

It recommends manual dredging of country boat feeder routes through food-for-work during the dry season when agricultural wages are low; introducing technologies for seasoning and preserving timber for boats and experimenting with new boat-building materials such as ferro-cement and marine plywood; improving boat designs; awarding transport contracts to country boat cooperatives which should be assisted with credit and given preference in the carriage of public sector cargo such as goodgrains and jute; construction of storage at riverside markets and ports that would enable country boats to get a return cargo; provision of line-towing by tugs (rather than manually) on difficult stretches and known "trouble-spots" where delays occur; and construction of shelter stations to insure again adverse weather conditions. Other recommendations relate to construction of improved boat-to-shore facilities especially designed for country boats; introduction of a system of demurrage for country boats which are detained (partly to provide free storage until merchants are ready to clear the goods) as in the case of mechanized boats at present, the provision or improvement of gates and sluices in embankments in the delta region to ensure country boat mobility; and careful consideration to labour displacement and other possible effects of mechanization of country craft without necessarily serving the overall needs of transportation any better (Ibid).

HOPES AND POSSIBILITIES IN TIBET AND NEPAL

Strange as it may seen, inland navigation is not unimportant in Tibet where the Tsangpo (Brahmaputra) is navigable for about 6,000 kilometres west-east along the roof of the world at an altitude of 4,000 metres. This stretch embraces some of the richer agricultural lands and more populous parts of the region. Should a high barrage be built across the river, as conceptualized by the Electric Power Development Company, Japan, navigability would improve and be greatly extended both along the main stem of the Tsangpo and into some tributary streams such as the Lhasa river, thus connecting the Tibetan capital and Shigatse, the second largest city to the region.

There is little scope for conventional navigation in Nepal. However, quite apart from the sportsman's interest in white water rafting, shooting down Himalayan rapids, the possibility is emerging of moving stores and equipment to remote upper valleys by shallow draft jet barges. These high-powered craft are capable of carrying loads of up to 12 tonnes, or more than what can be hauled by gas-guzzling trucks snorting laboriously up and down winding hill roads. There is a proposal to use jet barges to move personnel and equipment to the site of the Arun-III run-of-the-river hydro-electric project in the upper Kosi valley pending construction of a project road. The site is otherwise difficult to access at present. In order to facilitate jet barge movements it may be necessary to clear certain rocks in limited stretches by blasting or other means, a proposition that has met with some environmental objections. The fact is that new technologies are emerging which might render it possible to use at least some hill rivers as waterways, even if for limited or temporary purposes such as project construction, in preference to the building of more expensive and ecologically destructive roads which are not easily maintainable. Bhutan and India will watch any experiment to use jet barges for Arun-III with considerable interest.

The reservoirs that form behind projected high dams in Nepal, such as Karnali, also hold out possibilities of navigation not just to ferry people across the lakes but longitudinally as well. These hydro projects are quite likely to open up hitherto sequestered valleys for horticulture, small industry and settlement, apart from recreation and tourism. Man-made lakes would offer a means of transportation and marketing or of bringing hill produce down to processing centres or cold storages near townships where electricity would be available in plenty from hydel generation. It is also not conceivable that small aquaplanes might be able to land and take off from these lakes to provide a net network of air links that would stimulate development and make for better administration and national integration.

As a landlocked country whose geography and population distribution orients it overwhelmingly to the south, Nepal is vitally interested in transit to third countries and the sea. Its trade and transit treaties with India provided for access to Bangladesh and, most importantly, to the port of Calcutta which is the entrepot for not merely all of eastern, northeastern and east-central India but Nepal and Bhutan as well. Indeed, until the deterioration of Sino-Indian relations in the late 1950s, Calcutta was Tibet's port of entry and still remains the closest ocean outletto Lhasa, far nearer than Shanghai or Guanzhou (Canton) or even the Sichuanese capital, Chengdu. No surprise, therefore, that the 1981 trade and payments agreement between Nepal and China stipulates that overseas trade between the two countries shall be "on the basis of C.I.F. (or F.O.B.) Calcutta or other port to which both parties have agreed". It would probably also be cheaper to move bulks cargo to and from Lhasa and other parts of Tibet to the Chinese heartland via Calcutta and Kalimpong than by any other route.

In the circumstances, it is understandable that Nepal should want an inland navigation route by river or canal to secure access to the sea from its own territory if possible. The establishment in time of such an IWT link to Calcutta and Bangladesh ports would be of considerable advantage to Nepal and fits in well with India's own interest in developing navigation up and along the Ganga system. The techno-economic feasibility of the project would, of course, need to be established.

CHANGING ROLE OF PORTS

These have been a welcome even if modest turn around in Calcutta's port operations over the past few years. This is clearly of significance as the prosperity of the port and its industrial hinterland are interdependent. Historically, European settlements came to develop along the Hooghly as it commanded a rich up-country trade with a large export potential. The rise of Calcutta gave stimulus and new direction to the economy of the Gangetic valley. That same interactive process can be made to work again and the revival of inland water transport with a coastal and inter-modal range with containerization offers new opportunities.

What is needed is a new concept of transportation in India and the region. It is more important to meet the demand than worry about the mode of carriage. This should certainly be competitive, but also complementary to the extent that modal advantages and economies are maximized and harmonized as far as possible. As transshipment is being limited and its costs curtailed, a port is becoming less a terminal than a point of interchange. Major ports are tremendously expensive to build and Nhava-Sheva, Bombay's twin port on the mainland, is estimated to have cost Rs.900 crores. India has today 12 major ports but as many as 145 minor ports or roadsteads and 23 intermediate ports which are so classified if they handle over 100,000 tonnes of cargo per annum. The major ports each handle 35 or more million tonnes of cargo which means that road and rail systems of at least equivalent capacity must radiate out from them to move this traffic. The pre-emption of large investments is in creating and catering to these few nodal centres has inevitably resulted in the starvation or neglect of the minor and intermediate ports and their hinterlands which have remained backward areas. This regional imbalance has an economic as well as a political and social cost.

This trend could be corrected by the development of inland-cum-coastal waterways as inter-connected systems. Japan, admittedly an island nation, has used port development as a means of area development. India could do likewise. This would not merely make for more balanced spatial development but relieve pressure and congestion at the major ports and the transport corridors emanating from them.

NEED FOR NEW TRANSPORT CORRIDORS

This last point is one of substance as the existing transport corridors are saturated and duplicating them is likely to cost far more than diversification and dispersal. With India's population likely to exceed 1200 million in another 25 years and with the economy growing at a rate of 6 per cent, the volume of freight and passenger movement must multiply rapidly. If the existing high density corridors are alone used to move this traffic, the congestion will be enormous and will also to some extent imply ribbon development alongside existing routes resulting in the neglect of other regions with their resource endowments. The anticipated modal split in 1989-90 in terms of million tonnes of freight carried or handled is 345 for railways, 307 for roads, 145 for ports, and 0.52 for IWT, (excluding non-mechanised systems and short haul traffic). By 2000 the modal split in the movement of inter-regional traffic is likely to be 542, 396 and 14.4 for railways, roadways and coastal shipping (POL and coal only in respect of the last category). With average leads of 851 kilometres, 397 kilometres and 1690 kilometres in each case the modal share in terms of tonne-kilometres is expected to be 77.77 per cent, 24.25 per cent and 3.78 per cent respectively (Planning Commission, April 1988).

The high or superior energy efficiency of water transport, especially over long leads is well established. Yet one finds that the place of IWT even in the medium term in official discussions of policy issues and perspectives for transport planning is minimal if not altogether absent. Despite lip service, IWT, coastal shipping and ports continue to be seen in somewhat limited, traditional terms. The National Transport Policy Committee (1980) urged the need for a centralized pricing authority to recommend a common criteria for fixing fares and freight rates for different modes and suggested a national transport commission as a nodal agency in which the functions of transport pricing, investment and regulation are vested for effective and meaningful coordination. Transport planning requires both a long term and an integrated view reinforced by an equivalent industrial location and, thereby, unbanisation policy.

India has moved away from its inland and coastal waters and needs to come back to them for optimal regional and inter-modal transport development. A fraction of the investment made in the Railways and roadways diverted to water transport would yield handsome dividends. The decay of once-flourishing riverine and coastal towns represents underutilized urban and infrastructural capacity which could be put to good use. Traffic congestion in metropolitan centres with waterfronts like Calcutta and Delhi is leading to experimentation with intra-city water transport services and fast ferries which could have roll-on, roll-off facilities. In Bombay, development of the Thana Creek-Ulhas River and related waterways could greatly decongest the city and improve transport and environmental quality by a considerable factor as studies have demonstrated (Saggar, September 1979). However, entrenched vested interests and inertia govern transport planning. Goa's highly productive barge traffic operations are being driven out of business.

There has to be both vision and will to reverse this trend. The Ganga-Brahmaputra-Meghna-Bay of Bengal waterway once again offers a highway to progress.

CHAPTER 15

Water Laws and Compacts

Water is such a precious thing that rights to it have always been zealously safeguarded. The Buddha is said to have intervened to settle a water dispute while still a Prince of Kapilavastu in Nepal. In early times, however, populations were limited and it was often possible for individuals or communities to settle differences in many cases by simply moving on and exploiting a new source. The scale of water resource development in times past was modest in relation to the plentitude of water available in most situations and consumptive uses, even for irrigation, seldom threatened others with deprivation. Customary use regulated most transactions.

Transport, whether for irrigation or the floating of timber, provided the most obvious and important inter-regional or international water use. Rivers often formed natural boundaries or flowed through successive domains or territories and came to be used as common highways open to all for communication and commerce, though kings and conquerors often barred passage and levied taxes. River piracy was, of course, another matter. Conventions pertaining to the Danube between Austria and Turkey in 1619, and the Rhine between Germany and France in 1697 were among early landmarks in the making of modern International law on navigation. Inland navigation was again an item on the agenda of the Congress of Vienna in 1815 at the close of the Napoleonic wars.

From Boundary Rights to Water Sharing

It was, however, from the latter part of nineteen century onwards that water law for non-navigational uses saw rapid development especially in north America but elsewhere too as a result of colonization and new settlement, and rival claims to apportionment of rivers flows. This trend followed the application of new technologies of dam construction and storages of multiple uses and increasing diversions for consumptive or conflicting uses. These issues arose as inter-state problem within federations such as the US and Australia as well as in the form of international issues between the US and Mexico, the US and Canada and among other sets of nations sharing trans-boundary waters there were agreements on the Nile between Egypt and the Sudan, and concerning common rivers and lakes in

South America, Africa and Europe. With the growth of irrigation India too witnessed disputes and agreements between the provinces and the princely states under the aegis of the Raj and, as we shall see, the evolution of water law here was not uninfluenced by developments abroad.

Political issues of boundary alignment along wayward rivers tended to be settled on the principle of the median line or *thalweg* (a line purporting to demarcate the deep water course of a river). However, braided rivers and those prone to make large erosive invasions of territory on either bank have continued to pose problems of jurisdiction. In the temperature regions, irrigation has not quite the same imperative quality as in much of the Third World today and other concerns such as fisheries, timber floating, hydro development, flood control to some degree, industrial uses, the municipal demands of large urban agglomerations, recreational needs and, of course, navigation have most often been of greater relevance. In more recent times pollution and ecological considerations have assumed great importance. Witness the US Supreme Court decision to prohibit a dam to preserve what was at that time believed to be the only habitat of a fish, a snail darter (subsequently located in other waters as well), and the international furore over the deadly chemical spill from an industrial plant at Basel in Switzerland that poisoned the Rhine in November 1986 killing fish and all living organisms over a stretch of 300 kilometres.

While issues of water quality rather than water quantity have come to the fore in the industrially advanced nations, the old fashioned problems of apportionment and conflicting uses have not disappeared; nor is the Third World unaffected by or unconcerned about water quality. It, however, needs to be noted that earlier settled international law is largely based on the experience of temperature societies. While there are many universal principles to be found here, Third World development is tending to spawn many current water disputes which must be seen in the context of tropical societies confronting a different hydrological rhythm, exploding populations and few new frontiers to offer refuge.

Who owns water? This was well answered by Wall writing in the *Harvard Law Journal* in 1909: Running water in a natural stream is not the subject or property but is a wandering, changing thing without an owner, like the very fish swimming in it, or like wild animals, the air in the atmosphere, and the negative community in general". This is the principle in English common law. A joint committee of the British Parliament on Indian constitutional reforms leading to the Government of India Act, 1935, held that "The Government of India always possessed what may be called a common law right to use and control in the public interest the water supplies of the country". Punjab's claim to own the waters of the Ravi and Beas in their entirety was on these grounds set aside by the Eradi Tribunal (Ravi and Beas Water Tribunals, 1987).

Groundwater was until fairly recently not controlled, partly because limited drafts were made on it on account of technological limitations, the availability of surface flows, and lack of knowledge of its characteristics. The common law right of every landowner exclusively to appropriate groundwater for his use found recognition in the Indian Easements Act, 1882. This however applied only to percolating water (or the upper water table in practice), but excluded "water under the land which does not pass in a defined channel" or in other words, underground flows which are governed by riparian laws (Jain, S.N 1981).

Various principles have been advocated or asserted in the apportionment of flowing water. A proposal by the Princely state of Patiala to draw waters from the Sutlej, through what was to become the Sirhind Canal, was disputed by Punjab. The matter was referred to the Inspector-General of irrigation Works who offered this opinion in 1867: "… Such a project will be best which, while it provides a reasonable supply of water to the British territory, shall also given an equitable share to the foreign states whose country can be irrigated from the canal. The project should be so designed as to give the greatest aggregate advantage under the above conditions, with the smallest outlay" (Gulati, 1972). However, since the Sutlej was wholly within British Indian territory, the Punjab Government pointed out that the surrender of any part of the flow would be a "favour" which might nevertheless be granted, provided Patiala state paid a seigniorage which, it was advocated, "should be made a sine qua non before diverting the waters of our rivers from our own territories to those of Native Chiefs." (Ibid). Seigniorage was levied under several agreements thereafter. Mysore paid a royalty to Madras Presidency on hydel generation on the Cauvery, a boundary river. Seigniorage was only abolished after Independence.

HARMON DOCTRINE

A clash of international water rights was bound to occur sooner or later. This happened in 1896 in the controversy between the U.S. and Mexico over the Rio Grande. The then American attorney general, Harmon, speaking on behalf of the upper riparian, which wanted to abstract water from the river for irrigation, rejected "a servitude which makes the lower country dominant and subjects the upper country to the burden of arresting its developments and denying to its inhabitants the use of a provision which nature has supplied entirely within its own territory." According to the Harmon Doctrine "the fundamental principle of international law is the absolute sovereignty of every nation, as against all others, within its own territory". The U.S. did not press the point and ultimately accommodated Mexico's interests under U.S.-Mexico Convention on the Rio Grande in 1906. But it insisted that it did not "in any way concede the establishment of any general principle or precedent by concluding this Treaty". It was not until 1922 that the U.S. Supreme Court disowned the Harmon Doctrine in a ruling on Wyoming vs Colorado. In fact, the Harmon Doctrine, though asserted by many off and on, was only once applied in international law by the Imperial Royal Administrative Court of Austria in 1913 in a dispute between Austria and Hungary which were then both part of the Austro-Hungarian Empire under the Hapsburgs (Krishna Raj, 1979).

The Indus Waters Treaty, 1960, stipulates that "nothing in this Treaty shall be construed by the Parties as in any way establishing any general principle of law or any precedent" (Article XI (2). Some commentators have noted that "though India has taken the position that as an upper riparian owner it has absolute supremacy over the Indus River flowing from India to Pakistan and its tributaries originating in India, (it) has conceded certain rights to the latter" (Jain S.N. et al. 1971).

If the Harmon Doctrine represented one extreme, some jurists advocated the theory of territorial integrity which went to the other extreme. Under this theory, every lower riparian is entitled to the natural flow of streams entering its territory. Egypt tried to assert this right over the Sudan in 1925, but the Nile Waters Commission rejected the proposition (Ibid).

FROM PRIOR TO EQUITABLE APPORTIONMENT

With the settlement and irrigation of arid lands in the northwestern part of the United States, subsequent users, especially if lower riparians, found that they had been pre-empted. In Wyoming vs Colorado, the U.S. Supreme Court ruled (1922) that "priority of appropriation gives superiority of right". However, as far back as 1906, the Calcutta High Court refused to apply the doctrine of prior appropriation in a dispute between two private parties and stipulated "reasonable use" by the upper riparian in Balbhadar Pershad vs. Sheikh Barkat Ali (Ibid).

The Indus Commission set up under B.N. Rau to adjudicate on Sind's objection to Punjab's Bhakra dara proposal in 1942 fell back on another American decision, Kansas vs Colorado (1907), which enunciated the doctrine of "equitable apportionment". The Krishna (1971), Narmada (1978) and Ravi-Beas (1987) Water Dispute Tribunals in India all adopted equitable apportionment as a fair doctrine in considering the allocation of waters of inter-state rivers. The Ravi-Beas Tribunal specifically adopted this in preference to the theory of community interested as defined by Prof. F.J. Berber in his "Rivers in International Law". Under this, rights are either vested in the collective body of riparians or are divided proportionally, or any other kind of absolute restriction on the free usage of the waters by the riparians is created in such a way that no one state can dispose of the waters without positive cooperation of the others" (Ravi-Beas Waters Tribunal).

Community of interest in the river basin as a whole was reflected in some measure in the U.S.-Canada Columbia River Treaty (1961) and in that between Egypt and the Sudan on the Nile (1959). The Columbia River Treaty notes the desire of both the U.S. and Canada to develop the resources of the Columbia River "in a manner that will make the largest contribution to the economic progress of both countries and to the welfare of their peoples" and recognizes "that the greatest benefit to each country can be secured by cooperative measures for hydro-electric power generation and flood control, which will make possible other benefits as well".

A related issue that Courts found necessary to determine early on was the quantum of flow that was to be equitably apportioned. The U.S. Supreme Court spoke of "fairly dependable and continuous flow" in Wyoming vs Colorado. The Indian Irrigation Commission confirmed that "the existing practice in Indian conditions of planning irrigation schemes on the basis of 75 per cent dependability should continue. Where carry over (from one season to another in the case of storages) is provided, the 75 per cent dependability can be figured out taking into account the carry over water" (Irrigation Commission, 1972).

In expounding the doctrine of equitable apportionment or equitable utilization, the Narmada Water Disputes Tribunal (1978) insisted that this implied "beneficial uses", avoidance of waste, and "the duty of efficiency in the use of such waters which is commensurate with (the parties') respective financial resources". That a transitional period be permitted to less developed states to improve the efficiency of irrigation or other uses was settled by the Rau Commission (1942) when Punjab protested deprivation on account of Sind's wasteful inundation (flood) canals. The commission opined: "Undoubtedly inundation canals are a wasteful anachronism and the sooner they are replaced by weir-controlled systems the better. But many miles of such canals are still in existence (in Sind) … and large numbers of people have for generations depended on them for their livelihood. It may be that they and their Province cannot yet afford to install a better and, in the beginning, more expensive system of irrigation. In the meantime, are they to be deprived of their living merely because an Upper Province needs water? If the Upper Province wishes to take the water, let it pay adequate compensation in cash or kind". The Commission pointed out that the Nile Commission of 1925 had recommended a similar gradual transition away from flood irrigation on the lower Nile and a corresponding delay in the development of conservation works in the Sudan (Ibid).

STRESS ON EFFICINECY IN BENEFICIAL USE

The Narmada Tribunal, like the Krishna and Ravi-Beas Tribunals, excluded groundwater from a consideration of equitable apportionment although it recognized that underground water may furnish an alternative source from which to satisfy States' needs. It, however, opined that groundwater flow could not technically be accurately estimated and was, therefore, "not fully cognizable as yet from the legal point of view". The Tribunal quoted Teclaff's "River Basin in History and Law", 1967, as follows: "Groundwater drainage divides do not necessarily correspond to surface watersheds. An example is the subterranean ridge that runs beneath the basin of the Chenab river … This ridge affects the distribution of groundwater, its direction of flow, and differences in the chemical composition of the water. The water beneath the basin's surface thus may drain into more than one river system ... A case in point is the Upper Danube mainstream in southern Germany: water lost from the Danube here by percolation eventually re-emerges in the River Aach, which belongs to the drainage basin of the Rhine. The derivation of stream flow from underground sources is thus very complex and can often be traced only by detailed study of the geology of the basin".

The doctrine of equitable apportionment was eloquently stated by Justice Oliver Wendell Holmes in the U.S. Supreme Court in a case concerning the Delaware River. A river, he said, "is more than an amenity; it is a treasure. It offers a necessity of life that must be rationed among those who have power over it. New York has the physical power to cut off all the water within its jurisdiction. But clearly the exercise of such a power to the destruction of the interests of lower states could not be tolerated. And on the other hand equally little could New Jersey be permitted to require New York to give up its power altogether in order that the river may come down to it undiminished. Both states have real and substantial interests in the River that must be reconciled as best they may. The different traditions and practices in different parts of the country may lead to varying results but the effort always is to secure an equitable apportionment without quibbling over formalas" (McCaffrey, March 1987).

The Delaware River Basin Compact fashioned in 1961 between four States and the U.S. Federal Government was built on the principle of common or community interest. It declared that "the water resources of the basin are functionally inter-related, and the uses of these resources are interdependent. A single administrative agency is therefore essential for effective and economical direction, supervision and coordination of efforts and programmes ... Ever increasing economies and efficiencies in the use and reuse of water resources can be brought about by comprehensive planning, programming and management ..." (Ibid).

The notion of the unity of a river system was spelt out by H. Smith on his work on the Law of International Watercourses. In his view, "the first principle is that every river system is naturally an indivisible unit, and that as such it should be so developed as to render the greatest possible service to the whole human community which it serves, whether or not that community is divided into two or more political jurisdictions. It is the positive duty of every government concerned to cooperate to the extent of its power in promoting this development, though it cannot be called upon to imperil any vital interest or to sacrifice without full compensation and provision for security any other particular interest of its own, whether political, strategic or economic, which the law of nations recognizes as legitimate" (Ibid).

STATUS OF TRANS-BASIN DIVERSIONS

Another question that arose was the area to which the doctrine of equitable apportionment should apply. Some jurists have argued that diversion of the waters of a river outside its basin is illegal or at any rate improper. The Narmada Tribunal dismissed this argument. It suggested that "there may be a situation in which there are arid or drought areas of a State which, though technically lying outside a basin, require for development waters from and inside the basin. It may also be that the inhabitants of such ... areas ... have no alternative source of water supply ... It is manifest that in determining what is an equitable share of such a state in the waters of an inter-state river, a most relevant factor is the use that can be made of it by such State as a whole and so diversion to arid areas from the river system ought to be considered and the watershed line cannot be treated as a strict and impassable legal barrier". In support of its stand, the Tribunal cited Article IV of the Helsinki Rules of the International Law Association which reads: "Each basin state is entitled, within its territory, to a reasonable and equitable share in the beneficial uses of the waters of an international drainage basin". It also cited Justice Oliver Wendell Holmes, speaking for the U.S. Supreme Court in New Jersey vs New York: "The removal of water of a different watershed obviously must be allowed at times unless states are to be deprived of the most beneficial uses on formal grounds".

The Narmada Tribunal went further. It not merely certified inter-basin transfers as legal, but asserted that "the need for diversion of waters to another watershed may ... bea relevant factor on the question of equitable apportionment in a particular case". It held that the question of diversion of the waters of an inter-state river outside its basin "is not a question of law but is a question of fact to be determined in the circumstances of each particular case". A caveat may however be entered that since governments draw their power from the people, "the representatives of the people would not be justified in using, or permitting, the use of, the waters of a river outside its basin, until the needs of people of the basin have been met – at least as known at the time" (Gulati 1972).

What emerges quite clearly from this discussion is the fact that Indian municipal law on river waters, as laid down by Tribunals and Commissions or through legislation, has borrowed substantially from U.S. and other municipal law as well as from international law at various times. And prior to Partition, Bangladesh and India were one and shared a common municipal law.

Indian practice has in some instances been contemporaneous or in advance of that in other countries. Thus in 1884, the Government of India approached the British Government in London to approve the Periyar project "to utilize a portion of the superabundant rainfall on the western slopes of the Ghats (in Travancore) for the purpose of irrigation in the district of Madura (in Madras Presidency) to the east of the watershed, where the rainfall is completely scanty and very often uncertain, and where famine has in consequence been severely felt on more than one occasion". The project was sanctioned and the work, incepting 300 square miles of the Periyar catchment by means of a dam and tunneling the water westward into the Vaigai river for irrigation, was completed in 1893. By a separate agreement with the Travancore state, a hydro-electric component was added to the Periyar project in 1954 (Gulati, 1972).

STEPS TOWARDS CODIFICATION: HELSINKI RULES

Feeling the need to codify national and international experience in a unified statement on international river law, the Institute of International Law turned its attention to this problem in 1911. After setting out various formulations over the years, the Institute adopted a Resolution on the Use of International Non-Maritime Waters at its session at Salzburg in 1961. It stressed the principles of equity and adequate compensation for loss or damage done and spelt out a process of conflict resolution within "hydrographic basins" through resort to technical expertise, negotiations "in good faith", judicial settlement or arbitration (United Nations, 1974). In 1979, the Institute followed this up with a resolution at Athens on The Pollution of Rivers and Lakes in International Law.

Meanwhile, the International Law Association had also turned to the subject of international water law in 1954 and after a number of intermediate stages adopted a widely-acclaimed set of principles at its session at Helsinki in 1966. The Helsinki Rules moved from the concept of an international river to that of an "international drainage basin", including underground waters, and covered the areas of equitable utilization, pollution, navigation, timber floating, and dispute settlement procedures. To these the ILA added further Articles on Flood Control and Marine Pollution of Continental Origin (New York, 1972); Maintenance and improvement of naturally navigable waterways separating or traversing several states (New Delhi, 1974); Protection of water resources and water installations in times of armed conflict as well as proposals for the establishment of an International water resources administration (Madrid, 1976); and Regulation of the flow of water of international watercourses and the Relationship between water, other natural resources and the environment (Belgrade, 1980) (Hayton, December 1981).

Article I of the Helsinki Rules refers to "the general rules of international law ... applicable to the use of waters of an international drainage basin". Art. II defines an international drainage basin as "a geographical area extending over two or more states determined by the watershed limits of the system of waters, including surface and underground, flowing into a common terminus". Art. III likewise describes a "basin state" as one "the territory of which includes a portion of an international drainage basin".

The Rules of Equitable Utilisation of the waters of an international drainage basin are set out in Arts. IV to VIII. Thus, "each state is entitled within its territory to a reasonable and equitable share in the beneficial uses of the waters of an international drainage basin". The operational words are "reasonable and equitable", and "beneficial uses" within its territory and not just within the basin. What is reasonable and equitable is to be determined in the light of "relevant factors" such as the geography of the basin and the extent of the drainage area in the territory of each basin state; basin hydrology and the contribution of water by each basin state; climate affecting the basin; past utilization including existing uses; the economic ad social needs of each basin state; the population dependent on the basin's waters; comparative costs of alternative supplies; availability of other resources; avoidance of unnecessary waste; practicability of compensation as a means of adjusting conflicts among uses; and the degree to which the needs of a basin state may be satisfied without causing "substantial injury" to a co-basin state. The weight to be given to each factor is to be determined by its comparative importance, all relevant factors being considered together and a conclusion reached on the basis of the whole.

The Rules provide that no category of use is entitled to inherent preference over any other and that no present reasonable use shall be denied to reserve waters for any future use by another co-basin state. An existing reasonable use may continue until it is outweighed by a balance of factors favouring the accommodation of a competing incompatible use. While a use comes into being with its relevant construction or implementation, a use will not be deemed an existing use "if at the time of becoming operational it is incompatible with an already existing reasonable use".

The Helsinki Rules have been cited by jurists and tribunals around the world. But it has not escaped criticism. Thus, the definitional clause of an international drainage basin as one in which surface and underground waters flow into a common terminus has been questioned. In the Indus basin for example, "whereas all the surface waters drain into the Arabian Sea, southeast of Karachi, the ground waters have a terminus in the Rann of Kutch" (Gulati, 1972). A similar divergence between mainstream and underground flows has been cited earlier with regard to seepage from the Danube being regenerated in the Rhine basin.

A special sub-committee of the Asian-African Legal Consultative Committee in 1973 submitted a series of Draft Propositions on the Law of International Rivers to the 14th session of the Committee in New Dehi. These Propositions closely followed the Helsinki Rules but suggested some variations and additions. The Sub-Committee called on basin states to act "in good faith … in accordance with the principles governing good-neighbourly relations". In determining preferences between competing uses it urged that "special weight … be given to uses which are the basis of life, such as the consumptive uses". In modifying or discontinuing any existing use on a balance of more recent factors prevailing, it suggested that this be done only to accommodate "a competing but more important incompatible use" (Hayton, 1981). The significance of these recommendations was that they came from an inter-governmental body.

UN MANDATE TO INTERNATIONAL LAW COMMISSION

Even though the Helsinki Rules commanded a great deal of attention, they had emanated from a non-governmental organization, however eminent. There was accordingly pressure on the United Nations to codify the rules of international law relating to watercourses. Finland raised the question in 1970 and suggested that the Helsinki Rules be adopted in the interim and be used as a starting point for US codification. This was resisted, and the Sixth Committee of the General Assembly instead recommended that the International Law Commission should as a first step take up the study of the law of the non-navigational uses of international water courses "with a view to its progressive development and codification".

The International Law Commission was established in 1947 in pursuance of a resolution by the U.N. General Assembly. The regulations it finally adopts will bear the stamp of the widest possible international discussion and approval at the governmental level, taking cognizance of all the work done by a variety of non-governmental, regional and scholarly bodies and authors. The ILC's current membership, elected by the General Assembly for a five year term, with effect from January 1987, consists of 34 members including an Indian representative.

The ILC took up the task assigned to it at its 23rd Session in 1971. Its procedure has been to appoint a Special Rapporteur whose role has been to frame draft articles with detailed commentaries on each and recalling other statutes, formulations and judgements for consideration by the Commission. Six draft articles were provisionally adopted at the 32nd Session in 1980. Since its charter enjoined it to frame a law for "international watercourses" rather than an international drainage basin which the Helsinki Rules had adopted, the Special Rapporteur decided to set out a working hypothesis of the term. The hypothesis said "a watercourse system is formed of hydrological components such as rivers, lakes, canals, glaciers and groundwater constituting by virtue of their physical relationship a unitary whole; thus, any use affecting waters in one part of the system may affect waters in another part. An 'international watercourse system' is a watercourse system, components of which are situated in two or more states." However, it was further stated that to the extent that part of the waters in one state are not affected by or do not affect uses of waters in another state, they shall not be treated as being included in the international watercourse system. Accordingly "there is not an absolute but a relative international character of the watercourse" (Schwebel, December 1981).

If the ILC preferred the expression "watercourse" to "drainage" it equally preferred to adopt "system" in place of "basin". This was because of an apprehension among some that the basin concept might be extended to include the territories falling within the basin rather than on the waters and their relationships. It accordingly decided to eliminate any suggestion implying regulation of land area (Ibid).

The articles provisionally adopted defined "international watercourse system states" and system agreements, which might relate to all or part of the international watercourse without adversely affecting any other system state "to an appreciable extent". They called for negotiations in good faith; entitled each system state to participate in negotiations to any system agreement applicable to an international watercourse as a whole or, if appreciably affected, to negotiations on a particular project or programme thereon; and stipulated that if the use of waters in one state affects the use of waters of that system in another state, the water shall be deemed to be shared natural resource. Further, it was provisionally agreed that without prejudice to the requirement that system states negotiate in good faith, the present articles would not affect treaties in force relating to the whole or part of an international watercourse system or a particular project, programme or use.

DRAFT CONVENTION AND FURTHER PROPOSITIONS

At its 36th session in 1984, the commission had before it a complete draft convention prepared by the then Special Rapporteur consisting of 41 draft articles in six chapters setting out introductory articles, general principles, rights and duties of watercourse states, cooperation and management in regard to international water courses, environmental protection, pollution, health hazards, natural hazards, safety, peaceful settlement of disputes, and final provisions (McCaffrey, March 1987).

A summary of the views of the Special Rapporteur at the ILC's 38th Session showed overwhelming support for the doctrine of equitable utilization involving a balance between the needs of the system states in such a way as to maximise the benefit and minimize the detriment to each, the balance being struck by taking into account all relevant considerations. Also discussed were the duty to refrain from causing appreciable harm in relation to the principle of equitable utilization. The implementation of all these principles was found to rest on good faith and cooperation which, it was felt, should be established through appropriate institutional mechanisms and procedural rules for the prevention and resolution of conflicts (ILC, May 1987).

A recitation of the descriptive headings of the proposed Articles broadly conveys the primary concerns underlying the propositions advocated:

Equitable participation aimed at optimum utilisaton.

Equitable use determinations are to be posited on an objective valuation of various factors as well as the possible adverse effects on the other party.

Responsibility for appreciable harm with procedures of notification, consultation and negotiation.

Duty of states to provide other system states with information and data for planning rational utilization of the water resources of international systems, including data required for conflict resolution.

Environmental protection and pollution, including avoidance of irreversible environmental degradation; steps to be taken in case of an environmental emergency, and protection of the maritime environment from polluting discharges from international watercourse systems.

Prevention and mitigation of hazards through cooperation on an equitable basis in dealing with floods, erosion, sediment transporation and saltwater intrusion exchange of information, monitoring systems, and development of early warning systems.

Regulation of international water courses for beneficial uses through hydraulic works or other measures.

Water resources and the safety of installations such as dams, including the prevention of poisoning of waters, attacks on hydraulic installations in peace or during armed conflict or by means of terrorist sabotage of the destructive release or withholding of waters in order to swamp or damage the civilian population or environment downstream (Schwebel, December 1981).

Some of these proposed articles derive inspiration and support from earlier conventions or regulations adopted, for example, under the UN Law of the Sea regarding maritime pollution from mainland discharges, two protocols adopted by the International Committee of the Red Cross in 1977 relating to attacks on or willful damage to drinking water installations and supplies and irrigation works, and the protection of works and installations "containing dangerous forces", namely, dams, dykes and nuclear power stations unless these are (mis)used in furtherance of military operations; and the International Law Association's report (1974) on the protection of water and water installations in times of armed conflict.

The ILC's drafting committee was at the end of 1988 working on a set of graduated procedures "in order to allow States involved to preserve or to arrive at an equitable system-wide allocation of watercourse uses or benefits while preventing the escalation of disputes". This is sought to be done through initial requirements concerning notification of proposed actions, information exchange and consultation leading on, where necessary, to negotiation and further measures that might bring about a settlement (McCaffrey). These further measures were tentatively spelt out to include a call for an international commission of inquiry (into a charge of appreciable harm), renewed negotiations on the basis of that report, conciliation and, finally, arbitration or adjudication (Schwebel). Among the issues not yet addressed are diversions outside the international watercourse system, rules governing shared groundwater resources, equal access to information and to the administrative and judicial process by nations of co-system states, and preservation of wild and scenic watercourses (Ibid).

The International Law Commission is still a long way from adopting a final draft for presentation to the General Assembly. Certain terms and definitions, even that of a watercourse "system", are yet to be settled. But the trend of discussion brings together the emerging contours of international river law.

OTHER PROTOCOLS AND WORLD BANK MANUAL

The commission and its special rapporteurs have from time to time taken note of propositions or protocols adopted by various other international, regional and non-governmental bodies. Among these, are considerations relating to health and water-related diseases adopted at the fourth meeting of the Foreign Ministers of the Plata river basin countries in South America in 1974 and echoed in the Treaty for

Amazonian Cooperation (1978); the concerns of the European communities on the environment pertaining to risks to human health; the principles laid down in the Action Plan adopted at the UN Stockholm Conference on the Human Environment (1972); the UNEP Draft Principles of Conduct in the Field of Environment for the Guidance of States in the Conservation and Harmonious Utilisation of Natural Resources by Two or More States (1978); the Code of Conduct with respect to shared water resources adopted by the UN Water Conference in 1978; and many more.

Much recent water resources development has its locus in developing countries in the Third World where numerous contentious issues have begun to surface regarding equitable apportionment and prior appropriation. Lending agencies, notably the World Bank, have accordingly attempted to formulate guidelines for their own funding activities in relation to projects and programmes that bear no such sensitive issues.

The World Bank's Operational Manual Statement relates to projects on international waterways which may affect relations between the bank and its borrowers or between states. The guidelines cover rivers and their tributaries, canals and lakes which form a boundary or flow through two or more countries and all types of projects, whether irrigation, hydro-electric, flood control, navigation, drainage, sewerage, or involving industrial uses or possible pollution. The bank believes that cooperation among riparians best ensures that efficient utilization of international waterways. It therefore seeks to encourage riparian states to enter into agreements or understandings for utilization of part or all of the waterway, for which its good offices are available if requested. Procedurally, the bank advises project or beneficiary states to notify any or all other concerned states about the proposed project along with sufficient data so as to enable the other party to ascertain whether the project may do it appreciable harm in terms of water quantity or quality. The notified riparian should be allowed up to six months to respond. Should that state raise any valid objections, the bank advocates negotiations in good faith through any suitable institutional framework and, if necessary, may seek independent expert opinion. The bank may not insist on notification of the other party or parties if the project entails no more than rehabilitation or modernization of any existing work without any implication of additional abstraction of water that may affect a lower riparian (World Bank, April 1985).

International codes and protocols are instructive insofar as they enunciate principles or propositions which offer useful guidelines, even though they may not be legally binding. There is as much to be learnt from municipal law and from agreements and treaties between co-riparians from which emerging international law has generously borrowed.

India, with the largest tribal population in the world, and Bangladesh, Nepal and Bhutan, which also have tribal communities, should find instruction in recent Canadian and US practice in dealing with aboriginal water rights. The Canadian

Supreme Court recognizes aboriginal title as a common law right extending to the water of the traditional territory of the aboriginal people. American courts have similarly held that Indian water rights extend to the irrigation of all practicable acreage. The rights include consumptive and non-consumptive uses and both quantitative and qualitative aspects. Aboriginal rights are therefore prior and paramount to other uses. The so-called Northern Flood Agreement (presumably relating to submergence) arrived at between the Manitoba Hydro-electric Board and five aboriginal groups constituting the Northern Flood Committee has established a pattern for mediating between resource development and aboriginal rights. This concedes the aboriginals certain substantive rights, an inter-governmental process in furtherance of community-based plans, and an arbitration procedure to resolve all differences (Aboriginal Water Rights, 1987).

RIO GRANDE AND COLORADO SETTLEMENTS

Many precedents can be derived from U.S. experience. Amongst the earliest water-related international settlements arrived at by the United States was the 1889 Treaty with Mexico which established the U.S.-Mexico International Boundary and Water Commission to implement an earlier treaty of 1884 laying down procedures for determining national jurisdiction over tracts of land falling into adverse possession on account of the changing course of the Rio Grande and Colorado rivers which mark two thirds of the 300 kilometre long boundary between the two countries. This mechanism has served admirably well to resolve a number of contentious issues that have arisen in the past century over issues of irrigation, flood control, hydel generation and water quality.

A Treaty in 1906 apportioned the waters of the Rio Grande in the uppermost 140 kilometre reach of the river, recognizing Mexico's existing irrigation uses. A convention in 1933 facilitated joint works to stabilize the river boundary and control floods upstream. With growing population and urbanization on either side and related demands for irrigation, municipal and industrial water supplies, the demands on the Colorado and Rio Grande began to outstrip overall water availability, totaling 2.71 million hectare-metres plus small flows from the Tijuana, a tributary stream. A Treaty, signed in 1944, fixed and delimited the rights of the two countries and provided for deliveries from two new storage dams on the Rio Grande to be jointly constructed. The cost of the dams was divided between the two governments in proportion to their respective benefits. The two dams are to this day jointly operated and maintained and the hydel power generated is equally divided.

The 1944 Treaty also apportioned the waters of the Colorado river. Although all the waters of this river originate in the U.S., Mexico is guaranteed, a delivery of 185,000 ha m of water plus an additional 25,000 ha m in a "surplus" year. A proportionate reduction is made by the U.S. in its consumptive uses in years of extraordinary drought or in the event of a serious accident. In the case of the Rio

Grande, Mexico is guaranteed an average amount of 43,000 ha m per annum averaged over cycles of five years, taking good years with bad. Two of the most recent agreements were signed in 1965 and 1979 for water quality improvement in the lower Rio Grande in Mexico to benefit the U.S. and for action by the U.S. to maintain the salinity of the Lower Colorado below an agreed threshold.

The U.S.-Mexico International Boundary and Water Commission has wide jurisdiction and has been able to settle all contentious issues that have arisen over the decades. The Commission, headed by engineer commissioners, has the status of an international body and directly constructed the two international storage dams on the Rio Grande under the 1944 Treaty. Although the Harmon Doctrine was first stated by the U.S. at the very commencement of the U.S.-Mexico water dispute, it was in fact never invoked and the machinery of the Boundary Waters Commission was devised instead.

US-CANADA BOUNDARY WATER TREATY AND COMMISSION

The United States shares an even longer border with Canada, much of this made up by the Great Lakes and boundary rivers such as the St. Lawrence, and traversed by innumerable rivers. Conflict was inevitable, especially, during the formative years and, whether or not as a result of the U.S.-Mexico model, a Boundary Waters Treaty was signed between the U.S. and Canada in 1909. The preamble set out the primary objectives of the Treaty as being "to prevent disputes regarding the use of boundary waters and to settle all question which are now pending … involving the rights, obligations or interest of either (the U.S. or Canada) in relation to the other, or to the inhabitants of the other, along their common frontier and to make provision for the adjustment and settlement of all such questions as may hereafter arise". The instrumentality for addressing both boundary and trans-boundary water issues was an International Joint Commission (IJC) composed equally of Canadians and Americans. The IJC acts only upon a reference or applications by the two governments. The governments then decide whether or not to act on its recommendations, with or without IJC involvement. Several issues are dealt with bilaterally. Nevertheless, the IJC has enjoyed great success over the past 80 years of its existence (United Nations International Law Commission Year Boo, 1974; Canadian Government, 1984).

In the 1909 Treaty there was a special provision concerning the trans-boundary St. Mary and Milk Rivers which were to be treated as a single unit for purposes of equal apportionment. In other words, the principle of grouping adjacent rivers was adopted in the interest of maximizing overall beneficial use.

On an evaluation of its own experience, the IJC set out a series of principles which it presented at the Inter-Regional Meeting of International River Organisations at Dakar in 1981. These advocated, first, the provision of an on-going, permanent joint commission within which there is absolute parity between countries in spite of the very significant disparity in the size of their population and of their economies. Thus governments are assured of a balanced forum. Second, the development of a commission structure to provide a broad network within which a great deal of information can be exchanged formally and informally between governments and which encourages officials from both sides to work together and get to know one another. Third, the commission process permits governments to depoliticize issues that are difficult to resolve, acting as a buffer, which processes a joint fact-finding provide governments with a common data base. And fourth, the commission provides a mechanism which can alert governments to matters of concern which may or may not be fully appreciated by them (Schwebel, December 1981).

The Boundary Waters Treaty and IJC mechanism has dealt with issues of diversion of flows for irrigation and power generation, reduction of municipal and industrial waste discharges, and sharing of project costs and benefits. Of 100 cases referred to the IJC until 1984, unanimous decisions were arrived at in all but three cases and the two governments invariably accepted the recommendations. The cooperative relationship this engendered resulted in other bilateral agreements, Among these, two outstanding agreements relate to the 1972 accord on the Great Lakes water quality, in which the IJC had been assigned a role, and the seminal Columbia River Treaty, 1961, in which again the IJC had a key role to play by conducting the necessary engineering and technical investigations and by formulating a set of principles for determining the likely benefits and their apportionment between the two countries.

COLUMBIA RIVER TREATY

The Columbia river rises in the Rocky Mountains in British Columbia. Only an eighth of the basin lies in Canada but this is where the bulk of its hydro-electric potential is located. The Columbia River Treaty, signed in 1961, calls for the construction in Canada of three major dams providing 15.5 million acre feet or two million hectare-metres of storage to be operated in accordance with operating plans designated to serve increased power production and flood control benefit in the downstream reaches in the United States. In return, Canada is entitled to receive one half of the additional power benefits accruing to the U.S. as a result of the Canadian storages and a sum equivalent to one half of the estimated flood damage prevented in the U.S. Canada is liable to provide an additional flood cushion up to certain defined limits "on call" from the U.S. For each such call the U.S. is required to pay Canada a pre-determined sum, together with a further amount equal to the hydro-electric power lost to Canada as a result of reservoir operations to meet flood control objectives over and beyond the primary flood control objectives.

The estimated value of half the flood loss saved to the U.S. was calculated and commuted for a sum of US $ 64.4 million which has been paid to Canada. Likewise, the Treaty permitted Canada to sell its entitlement of downstream power benefits to the U.S. if it so desired. Canada decided to exercise this option in 1964 for a period of 30 years from the dates of completion of each of the three dams it was called upon to construct. It accordingly sold its downstream power entitlement for a sum of U.S. $ 254.4 million, that being its then present worth discounted at 4.5 per cent per annum. The condition was that Canada would use this sum to finance part of the cost of the three dams. Since energy prices rose sharply some years later, following the oil crisis, Canada may not have made a good deal in hindsight. What is interesting, however, is the application of the principle of equal apportionment in terms of cost and benefit sharing.

The Columbia River Treaty provides for the establishment of a Permanent Engineering Board consisting of two members from either side. This assembles flow records, reports on the deviations from agreed operating plans and recommends remedial action and compensatory adjustments. It carries out periodic inspections and submits an annual report to the two governments. Differences are to be settled by the International Joint Commission and, if they persist, by resort to arbitration in accordance with agreed procedures or by reference to the International Court of Justice.

The Treaty stipulates that barring some specified diversions, neither side may divert the Columbia's waters for a period of 60 years without the consent of the other. This is because both sides had planned diversions for their own exclusive benefit prior to the conclusion of the Treaty (Columbia River Basin Treaty, 1961).

PRINCIPLE OF DOWNSTREAM BENEFITS

The principle of downstream benefit evolved by the U.S. Canada International Joint Commission in 1959 and incorporated in the Columbia River Treaty two years later, is a valuable addition to evolving water law. Elements of this principle had been embodied in the U.S. Federal Power Act, 1935, and in certain other U.S. and Canadian River compacts. But its true flowering came with the Columbia River Treaty and it was appreciatively cited and adopted by the Narmada Water Disputes Tribunal (1978). Indeed, the principle was even earlier recognized in Section 15(4) of the Indian River Boards Act of 1956. This provides that in the preparation and execution of schemes by the Board it shall take into account the costs likely to be incurred in constructing and maintaining such works; and the costs shall be allocated among the interested governments in such proportion as may be agreed or, in default of agreement, "as may be determined by the Board having regard to the benefits which will be received from the scheme by them."

What is perhaps implicit here was made explicit by the Yadav Mohan committee appointed by the Government of India in 1961 to examine the levy of charges for utilization of water on a downstream project. The committee recommended as follows: "When an upstream project is constructed later than an existing downstream project, the latter shall be liable to pay for the benefit obtained from an upstream project irrespective of the period that has elapsed after its construction; but when the downstream project is constructed after the upstream project, the downstream project may need pay for the benefits received only if it is conceived within 20 years of completion of the upper project. In either case the charge will be borne only if it is clearly established that the downstream project has been benefited by the changes in flows or otherwise by the construction or operation of the upstream project. The lower project will bear the cost to the extent the actual additional benefits are made available to it and as and when these benefits actually accrue." (Ibid).

The Narmada Tribunal applied the principle of downstream benefits and concluded that Madhya Pradesh was entitled to payments for such benefits from Gujarat for regulated releases of Narmada waters from the Narmadasagar dam for Gujarat for the benefit of the Sardar Sarovar project down the river in Gujarat and for flood control benefits, if any, obtained by Gujarat due to construction of upstream reservoirs in Madhya Pradesh. On an examination of the Narmadasagar, Omkareshwar and Maheshwar dams in Madhya Pradesh, the Tribunal found that no exclusive flood cushion had been provided and that any flood benefit was unregulated and incidental. Madhya Pradesh would thus be incurring no cost nor any inconvenience to justify charging any downstream benefit to Gujarat for flood control. However, Sardar Sarovar would benefit greatly in terms of both irrigation and power generation as a result of the Madhya Pradesh dams and would thereby be able to et the expected benefits with a reduced height of dam at Sardar Sarovar.

The cost apportionment of additional downstream benefits to Sardar Sarovar was calculated as Rs.4.77 crores and Rs.12.05 crores on account of power and irrigation respectively, or a total of Rs.16.82 crores at 1975/76 prices or 17.63 per cent of the cost of the Narmadasagar dam. As the actual cost of constructing the Narmadasagar dam would be different from the estimated cost, the Tribunal ruled that "Sardar Sarovar should credit to Narmadasagar each year 17.63 per cent of the expenditure in the financial year commencing from the year of taking up the construction of Narmadasagar Dam. This will be initially credited on the basis of budget allotments to be adjusted at the end of the year on actual expenditure. The post-construction expenditure on maintenance is not to be considered as a cost of construction" (Ibid).

With regard to apportionment of cost and allotment of reservoir storage space in multipurpose projects, the Ministry of Irrigation and Power (India) wrote to all State Governments on April 17, 1967. The letter explained that the cost of multipurpose river valley projects should normally be allocated only to three main functions, namely, irrigation, power and flood control. Other functions like water supply for domestic or industrial uses, navigation, pisciculture recreation, wild life protection, etcetera, should be included in one of these three functions. The share of cost and any revenue derived by the project from these "subsidiary" functions, should be accounted for in the share of the same main function. However, where the cost of any of the subsidiary functions exceeds 10 per cent of the total cost of the project, such a function should be treated as an "additional main function" and costs allocated to it separately. The letter recommended the "facilities used" method of allocation of joint costs in preference to the "alternative justifiable expenditure" or "separable costs, remaining benefits" methods. The reservoir capacity or the quantity of water used for each purpose should be the basis for allocation of common costs. Such cost allocation should be done for each component like dam, canal, weir, etcetera, separately (Ibid).

BINATIONALS AND COORDINATION IN DEL PLATA BASIN

Binational agreements and those bringing a larger number of countries together in river basin agreements lay down certain principles and provide a variety of mechanisms for fostering mutual cooperation. Among these is the agreement between Argentina, Uruguay, Paraguay, Brazil and Bolivia on the Del Plata (River Plate) Basin encompassing the basin of the Parana, Uruguay and Paraguay system which, incidentally, is the fourth largest in the world. As elsewhere, these rivers initially formed a grand north-south highway through impenetrabe forest but have latterly acquired greater importance for their enormous hydro-electric potential. However, even today, Paraguay and Bolivia, being landlocked, find navigation along these rivers of vital importance in gaining access to the sea. By 1986, over 38,000 MW of hydro power had been developed on the system, ninety per cent of this on the Parana, with the great Itaipu project (12,600 MW) being the largest hydro station in the world today. Other projects totaling 1000 MW were under construction and a further 14,000 MW under design. Almost 25 per cent of the power developed is in Paraguay for whom electricity exports to Brazil and Argentina have become the mainstay of its economy. Itaipu's output is shared equally between Paraguay and Brazil, the project being on the common boundary along the Parana. Yacyreta (Argentina-Paraguay, 3980 MW, under construction); Corpus (Argentina-Paraguay, 3400 MW); Salto Grande (Argentina-Uruguay, 1890 MW); and two Argentina-Brazil projects (Roncador, 3000 MW and Garabi, 2196 MW) are other major shared projects within the basin (Cano, September 1986).

To coordinate and harmonise basin development, the five Del Plata nations have formed an Inter-Governmental Coordinating Committee (CIC) with a permanent secretariat in Buenos Aires at which the ambassadors of the other four countries to Argentina take their seat. While this meets frequently, the CIC takes instructions from and implements policy decisions taken at annual meetings of the five Foreign Ministers. The CIC has a secretary, elected for a two year term, and is assisted by expert groups drawn from the staff of the respective governments. Funding is organized through Fonplata, an agency set up in 1976 with a capital that had grown to $200 million by 1986. The Fund is managed by a Board of Governors on which the Five Economy Ministers or Central Bank Presidents are represented. Fonplata, headquartered in Bolivia, is empowered to grant 15 year loans (with a two to three year grace period) at seven to eight per cent interest on the directions of the Foreign Ministers meeting. Two loans had been sanctioned until 1986 but navigation improvement and silt control through afforestation have not been funded as yet.

The Dal Plata institutions were set up by the Brazilia Treaty of 1968 and subsequent understandings and provide for exchange of information, agreement to refrain from causing willful damage to another state, prior consultation, and joint and integrated action (Ibid). The mechanisms provided have helped resolve a number of conflictual situations.

The Itaipu Treaty between Brazil and Paraguay was signed in April 1973 culminating many years of negotiations and a show of force by Brazil in 1962. The Treaty establishes the principle of parity under which the Itaipu Binactional was formed. Membership, costs and benefit sharing in equal proportions were set out together with rules to determine the price of electricity, royalties and compensation. The Itaipu Binactional established guidelines for a conservation plan to safeguard the ecology around the 1350 square kilometre Itaipu lake. This covers all flora and fauna, fish, soil, erosion, health problems, reforestation, monitoring of climatological changes, wildlife preservation, health surveillance and environmental sanitation, and cultural preservation through archaeological mapping and relocation of artifacts in a museum (Itaipu Biacional, 1980).

The Yacyreta Treaty between Paraguay and Argentina signed at the end of 1973 adopted somewhat similar terms, with parity in cost and benefit sharing and construction and operation through a binational Yacyreta entity (EBY). Argentina has loaned Paraguay $ 50 million towards the latter's subscription to EBY which is required to engage 50 per cent Paraguyans in all contracts by a "mirror law" in a somewhat mechanical fulfillment of the parity principle. However problems have arisen since Paraguay does not always have the skilled personnel required in sufficient numbers.

The Amazon Pact signed in 1978 by eight basin states aims to promote harmonious development of the river and just sharing, keeping in mind regional development, cooperation and environmental preservation. Exchange of information, improvement and monitoring of public health, "the total integration of each country's Amazon region into that country's economy", preservation of the ethnological and archaeological heritage of the Amazon region, and freedom of commercial navigation through the Amazon river and its international tributaries were among the objectives spelt out. Foreign Ministers' meetings were expected to provide guidelines for a high-level diplomatic Amazon Cooperation Council to consider initiatives and projects, frame rules and implement decisions. The contracting parties agreed to set up permanent national commissions and to create special commissions to study specific issues, raise capital for projects and function on the basis of unanimity (Amazon Pact, 1978).

WATER COMPACTS IN AFRICA

The Nile has been the subject of various agreements as a prelude to further stages of development. The first agreement between Egypt and Sudan in 1929 was followed 30 years later by the Agreement on the Full Utilisation of Nile Waters which allocated the available waters, protecting Egypt's prior uses, and providing for the construction of the Aswan High Dam. Sudan agreed to construct various projects in the upper basin to increase the river yield by prevention of water losses in several swamps and through storages. The net yield of these projects and their costs were to be divided equally between the two countries. Sudan was compensated, for submergence of lands under the Aswan High Dam reservoir (Lake Nasser) and the two sides agreed to set up a Permanent Joint Technical Commission to develop the basin, supervise execution of projects and prescribe fair arrangements for sharing low river flows. Since the Nile basin is shared by seven other countries (Ethiopia, Zaire, Tanzania, Kenya, Uganda, Rwanda and Burundi), Egypt and Sudan agreed to discuss claims by any of the others and Sudan agreed to share the deduction in equal proportions (Egyptian Ministry of Irrigation, 1981).

A proposal to constitute a Nile Basin Commission in which all nine co-riparians would be represented was made a decade back to provide a means for rational planning, conservation, development and (future) allocation of basin waters, to conduct surveys, compile and collate data and determine operational schedules, and to recommend measures to combat flood and drought and protect the environment. But such a body is yet to be set up. A hydro-meteorological survey of the upper catchments and Lakes Victoria and Nyanza has been undertaken with Zaire, Kenya, Uganda, Tanzania, Rwanda and Burundi collaborating. A Kagera Basin Organisation was also established in 1977 with Tanzania, Rwanda and Burundi as partners in the development of the Kagera basin in the upper Nile.

Nine nations joined to sign an agreement on navigation and economic cooperation in the Niger basin in 1963. Four of these states also formed a (Lake) Chad Basin commission a year later. A River Niger Commissions was constituted in 1964 and in 1980 the signatories determined to form a Niger Basin Authority for the harmonious development of the basin (United Nations, 1984).

Another model is that of the Organisation for the Development of the Senegal River (OMVS) set up by Mali, Mauritania and Senegal in 1972. The charter of the OMVS provides for a conference of Heads of Government/State, a Council of Ministers, a Secretariat-General and a Standing Commission. The Council is the principal organ and meets twice a year and acts on the principle of unanimity. The Secretariat is led by a High Commissioner through stages of data collection, planning, implementation, review and synthesis (McCaffrey, 1987). Among other regional initiatives in Africa is the draft agreement on an action plan for the environment management of the Common Zambezi River embracing eight basin states.

THE MEKONG COMMITTEE AND INDUS TREATY

Among the more successful experiments in river basin planning and development and unique in Asia is the Mekong Committee, first established in 1957 and dedicated to the coordinated development of the basin's resources on the basis of reasonable and equitable sharing between the riparian states. The charter covers the Lower Mekong Basin with Laos, Thailand, Vietnam and Kampuchea as members, though Kampuchea's seat has been vacant in recent years on account of the Kampuchean imbroglio. Acting through National Committees and a Mekong Secretariat located in Bangkok, the Committee for Coordination of Investigations of the Lower Mekong Basin produced an indicative plan for the short term (1971-80) and long term (1981-2000) development of the basin. With war, development and social and technological change the Mekong Secretariat commissioned a revised indicative plan which was presented in a document entitled Perspectives for Mekong Development (1988). The investment plan suggested for 1988-2000 covers 26 national and three international projects with irrigation and hydro-electric components. The 1970 plan proposed a cascade of seven major dams with a storage of 136,000 million cubic metres of water and a 23,300 MW power potential. This has now been recast and full development of the basin's 37,000 MW potential is unlikely to be realized until well into the 21st century. Incidentally, half this total potential lies in Laos and a third in Kampuchea, both of which, like Paraguay, Nepal and Bhutan, will have a considerable power export capability. With careful and detailed investigations, supported by international consultancy, the projects and proposals developed by the Mekong Committee enjoy national acceptance among the basin partners and international credibility which has been an important aspect in securing donor support in implementing basin development programmes.

The Indus Waters Treaty of 1960 is perhaps the outstanding example of the success of World Bank good offices in conflict resolution. This certainly helped in securing a peaceful settlement and an agreed water allocation as between India and Pakistan, including the Mangla and Tarbela Dams. The Permanent Indian Commission it established has survived two wars and provides an on-going machinery for consultation and conflict resolution through inspection, exchange of data, and visits and, failing agreement, by reference to a neutral expert, mediation and arbitration. The Treaty provides for its own modification by a duly ratified treaty concluded between the two governments at any time.

BARCELONA CONVENTION ON NAVIGABLE WATERWAYS

Until the end of the 19th century the most important use of international rivers was for navigation. When a watercourse was primarily used for navigation the border-line on boundary rivers was defined as being the middle of the main navigable channel (thalweg) as set out in the Treaty of Munster (1648) with regard to the frontier between France and Germany along the Rhine (Caponera, August 1985). The Convention of Mainz (1831) and the Convention of Mannheim (1868) provided the basic texts for navigation on the Rhine which was further developed and extended to non-riparian nations by the Treaty of Versailles (1919). The Central Commission for Rhine Navigation and special Rhine navigation tribunals are the principle regulatory mechanisms (Ailleret, 1979). Other protocols were developed to regulate navigation on the Danube and other European rivers.

In 1919 a convention of imperial powers preserved subsisting freedom of navigation on the Niger, Congo and all other rivers and lakes in a specified zone in Central Africa to all signatories. More important, in 1921 a General Convention, Statute and Additional Protocol on the regime of Navigable Waterways of International Concern was opened for signature at Barcelona. The Barcelona Convention declared as "navigable waterways of international concern" all such naturally navigable waterways separating or traversing different states and natural or artificial waterways expressly placed under the regime of the General Convention. Tributaries are classified as separate waterways but lateral canals coming parties are to be treated equally and no distinction is made between riparians and non-riparians. States may however reserve local transportation (cabotage) to their own flags. A waterway "naturally navigable" is so defined if currently used for ordinary commercial navigation or is capable by reasons of its natural conditions of being so used (Barcelona Convention). India was a signatory to the Convention, but denounced it in 1956.

In a case concerning the River Order, the Permanent Court for International Justice in 1929 ruled that "community of interest in a navigable river becomes the basis of a common legal right, the essential features of which are the perfect equality of all riparian states in the user of the whole course of the river ..." (Narmada Water Disputes Tribunal).

The International Law Association's Helsinki Rules (1966) devoted a chapter to codify the law of navigation applicable to the waters of an international drainage basin. The Rules adopt the Barcelona definition of what constitutes a navigable waterway and provides for free navigation thereon. Each riparian state is to the extent of the means available to it, required to maintain in god order that portion of the navigable course of a river or lake within its jurisdiction.

WATER TRANSFERS OLD AND NEW

Inter-basin water transfers from areas of existing or potential surplus to deficit regions for purposes of irrigation, hydel generation, municipal and industrial uses and even for navigation have long been in vogue. An outstanding example is the California state water project transferring four cubic kilometres of water from the northern to the soutern part of the state. This was completed in 1973, sixty years after the Los Angeles Aqueduct, and subsequently extended to provide municipal and industrial water to this burgeoning metropolis from Owens Valley on the eastern side of the Sierra Nevada mountains. The Soviet Union too has made several inter-basin diversions from the Volga, Amu Darya, Dnieper and Irtysh. Israel's National Water Carrier, which pumps Jordan inflows into the Sea of Galilee southwards into the Negev desert (1953-64), is another notable example (Arlosoroff, 1977). China has a number of inner-basin projects, among the oldest of these being the Linguà canal linking the Xianjiang and Guijiang rivers for shipment of armaments during war (214 B.C.) and the Grand Canal, linking the Chang Jiang (Yangtze) and Huang He (Yellow River) for navigation and irrigation (605 A.D.).

Far more ambitious futuristic plans for major water transfers have been pıoposed in the United States. The North American Water and Power Alliance (NAWAPA) is a $100 billion project proposed in 1964. This would tap the surplus waters of northwestern Canada and the United States, including Alaska, and transfer these south for uses in Canada, a large number of American States and parts of northern Mexico. Strong Canadian environmental and economic objections stalled it. Likewise, the Texas Water Plan (1965) proposed diverting water from the Mississippi and eastern Texas to western Texas and New Mexico. This too was halted by opposition. Similar mega-projects were planned in the Soviet Union for turning the Siberian rivers, principally the Ob and Yenisi, southwards to Kazakhistan and other parts of Soviet Central Asia. Another proposal envisaged diverting certain north Russian rivers into the Volga to compensate for increasing water uses in the Caspian Sea of Azov basins. All these projects have been scrapped in the wake of controversies and a reassessment of priorities (Golubev and Biswas, June 1979).

China has a problem of little arable land and an abundancc of water in the south and the opposite in the north. The Chang Jiang (Yangtze) and Zhu Jiang (Pearl) rivers in the South account for just about half the total run-off of all the rivers in China while many northern cities are faced with acute water shortages. A major project to divert Yangtze waters north to the Hunag He (Yellow River) has been under study for some time. Three possible routes are being investigated: a west route (which is mountainous and therefore more difficult), a middle route, and an eastern route (where the diversions could be partly effected through a modernized Grand Canal). A test siphon under the Huang He was completed in 1988 and is now to be expanded to 200 cumec capacity to provide a trans-Huang He link to the arid North China Plan beyond (Li Rongxia, June 1988). China is separately investigating different designs for a dam across the Yangtze. The so-called Three Gorges Project has aroused much controversy in view of the very large submergence and displacement that will be involved should the dam be raised to the full height proposed and its possible impact on the Shanghai coastline (Han, Baocheng, July 1986). Further study has been proposed.

Inter-regional diversions do indeed cause the liveliest concerns to the exporting regions in view of the elemental importance of water for life and the economy. To this must be added mounting ecological cautions. Nonetheless, even in South Asia, inter-basin transfers have been made since long and will continue to take place in view of the compulsions of growing demand, with population growth and development, and the high degree of imbalance in water availability over space and time.

In India, the Periyar diversions across the Western Ghats to Tamil Nadu established the principle of inter-basin transfer a century ago. Since then, the Ghaghar ahas been diverted to the Sharda (Sharda Sahayak project) although within the same larger Ganga basin, and the Ravi-Beas into the Yamuna system through Bhakra. Krishna basin waters have been transferred to the Godavari basin and vice versa and inter-basin transfers have been made from the Mahanadi, Cauvery, Tapi and Mahi (Gulati, 1972).

PROPOSED WATER GRID

A much larger grand design inspired K.L. Rao in 1972 to propose a Ganga-Cauvery Link and certain westward diversions as part of a national water grid. Dr. Rao's proposal envisaged the diversion of 1.85 million hectare-metres (15 million acre-feet) of Ganga water from a point near Patna where a barrage would be constructed across the river. It was proposed to pump 1410 cumecs (50,000 cusecs) south through the Sone, Narmada, Tapi, Godavari, Krishna and Pennar basins to the Cauvery basin over 150 days during the high flow period, with a lift of 335-400 metres, and 290 cumecs to the southern parts of Bihar and U.P. within the Ganga basin itself. Also envisaged were a barrage across the Brahmaputra at Dhubri in Assam and a 320 kilometre link canal from there to Farakka to transfer 1.49 million hectare metres of water (12 million acre feet) to the Ganga with a lift of 12 to 15 metres. Dr Rao estimated the cost of his project with certain adjuncts at Rs.12,500 crores, with a power requirement of 7200 MW. It would have an irrigation potential of four million hectares. The Central Water commission found the plan technically feasible but not economically viable. The costs were believed to have been under-estimated while benefits were likely to be reduced by seepage and other losses en route (National Water Development Agency, 1988).

A team of U.N. experts endorsed the project in these terms: "India's national economy in its development and growth will be confronted with the problem of increasing scarcity of water within the next 30 years. From basic compilation of water demands and water yields is becomes evident that by the year 2000 or so, the National Water Grid will be a vital necessity. No time should be lost to start the very complex and difficult investigations today so that plans will be matured and prepared in due time and the facilities will become operative when the need and will have come. The project of the Ganga-Cauvery Link Canal has been developed by Indian engineers on a national level … The Mission believes that the project is technically feasible and presents no insurmountable engineering or construction problems, but requires continuing study and refinement during several years to come … Thorough investigation of water yields and demands, of technical features, and of availability of low-cost pumping is needed to determine the economic feasibility of the project" (Ibid).

A few years later, Captain D.J. Dastur, a former airline pilot, submitted another proposal for the total harnessing of almost the entire run-off of the country in what he called a Garland Canal Project. His proposal postulated a 2400 kilometre-long Himalayan canal from Jammu to Sadiya and a further 1700 kilometre spur to the south at a constant elevation of about 350 metres to hold the water of all the Himalayan rivers, including those flowing down from Nepal and Bhutan, with a view to their redistribution. There was to be an inter-connection with a similar 9332 kilometre long Garland Canal around the Central Indian peninsular plateau with two giant storages of the order of 37 million hectare-metres (300 million acre feet) near Nagaur in Rajasthan and in the Sone basin. Captain Dastur priced his project at Rs.24,100 crores but a technical examination by a committee of experts estimated the cost at 500 times that figure and pronounced it technically unsound and economically prohibitive (Ibid). It is extraordinary that such a totally unrealistic concept, ecologically disastrous and politically and socially unacceptable from any viewpoint, should have been seriously entertained and allowed to pre-empt consideration of more rational proposals for two to three years because the then Prime Minister thought it should be examined. The Garland Canal was finally laid to rest, though its ghost still haunts the uninitiated.

INDIA'S NATIONAL PERSPECTIVE PLAN

Committed to finding a more realistic alternative, the Central Water Commission proposed a conceptual variant of Dr. Rao's National Water Grid (Irrigation Ministry, August 1980). The new National Perspective warned that by the turn of the century "water will be a critical resource to mankind" and noted that of India's total surface water resources of 178 million hectare-metres (1440 million acre-feet), only 27 m ha m (220 m.a.f.) was currently being used. It assessed that the plans evolved by the State governments would use no more than 66.5 m ha m (540 m.a.f.). however, "if we take a national view and harness major inter-state and international rivers in the larger interest of the country as well as neighbouring countries, the benefit would increase considerably. At least 22.2 m ha m (180 m.a.f.) more water could be utilized to provide an additional 35 million hectares of irrigation (as against the currently estimated surface and groundwater irrigation potential of 113 m ha) and generate another 40,000 MW of energy in India and Nepal.

The National Perspective has been broken down into a Himalayan Rivers component and Peninsular Rivers component. The Himalayan component envisages storages on the Ganga and Brahmaputra and their main tributaries in India and Nepal to conserve monsoon flows for flood moderation, irrigation and hydel generation. The object would be to transfer these stored monsoon surpluses west to the upper Yamuna-Chambal basins and thence to Rajasthan, Haryana and Gujarat.

A Brahmaputra-Ganga link (again based on stored monsoon-diversions) would facilitate upstream withdrawals from the Ganga without affecting uses in the lower Ganga and Brahmaputra basins in India and Bangladesh. An estimated 14.8 m ha m (120 m.a.f.) of additional water would be available to irrigate 22 m ha in Nepal, Bangladesh and India and or generate an additional 30,000 MW of power. The cooperation of Nepal and Bangladesh would be essential for the fruition of this project (NWDA, 1988).

The Peninsular component is in four parts: a Mahanadi-Godavari-Krishna-Pennar-Cauvery link (diverting 3.7 m ha m); diversion of the west-flowing rivers of Kerala and Karnataka eastwards across the Western Ghats; storages on and links between small west coast rivers north of Bombay and south of the Tapi, partially releasing some Narmada and Tapi waters to extend irrigation in Saurashtra and Kutch, meet the future water needs of the Bombay metropolitan area and irrigate the coastal areas of Maharashtra; and inter-linking the southern tributaries of the Yamuna, Ken and Chambal in particular, with small storages on intermediate streams, with a dam on the Yamuna at Panchnad, below Etawah, to provide irrigation to the Indore-Ujjain region in the Malwa plateau of Madhya Pradesh as well as parts of Rajasthan. This fourth sub-component of the Peninsular project would only entail redistribution of Ganga basin waters within the basin. The Peninsular component would facilitate additional utilization of water to irrigate 13 m ha.

The National Water Development Agency was set up in July 1982 to promote the optimum utilization of the country's water resources. In view of the sensitivities involved in working on the Himalayan component of the National Perspective without first coming to an understanding with Nepal and Bangladesh, the NWDA is for the moment charged with confining its attention solely to the Peninsular component including transfer of surplus waters of the Yamuna, Ken, etcetera, within the Ganga basin itself. It has been called upon to carry out detailed surveys and investigations of possible storage sites and inter-connecting links in order to establish the feasibility of the Peninsular component of the National Perspective Plan. To this end it will make detailed studies of the quantum of surplus waters that might be available for transfer after meeting all reasonable needs within the exporting sub-basin in the foreseeable future and will prepare feasibility reports of the various elements that might fit into the Peninsular component (NWDA, 1986).

WATER BALANCE STUDIES AND GUIDELINES

The NWDA has divided the Peninsular components into 137 basins and sub-basins. Water balance studies had been completed in respect of 50 sub-basins by the end of 1988 based on ideal cropping patterns in relation to soil and climatic conditions and on sound water management practices. The water balance studies project the population of the sub-basin up to 2025 and provide for drinking water, livestock, irrigation and industrial needs in relation to resource endowments and regional location policies. Groundwater potentials are being assessed but are being reserved as a non-transferable asset. It is assumed that irrigation efficiency will improve, and ecological requirements and minimum water flows for salinity control are being taken into account. It is on the basis of such exhaustive studies that the water balance is ascertained and a calculation made of the likely deficit that might need to be met by conservation and import of water or the extent of surplus out of which some quantum might be exported. Each water balance study is being done in cooperation with the concerned State government and the draft reports are being sent to them for comments before being put up to the NWDA's governing council and technical advisory committee for approval.

As an aid to the NWDA, an expert committee has set out certain guidelines. Since the capital cost of irrigating one hectare of land by long distance water transfer is estimated at Rs.80,000 (exclusive of drainage and compensatory environment outlays) as against Rs.25,000 and Rs.13,500 per hectare of irrigation by conventional surface and groundwater schemes, it is recognized that in-basin potentials need to be exhausted before inter-basin transfers are contemplated. As the development of remaining in-basin potentials is likely to cost Rs.100,000 crores, investments of this order will take another 20 to 30 years to complete. Meanwhile, conservation and greater efficiency in the use of water must receive the highest priority, including modernization of older projects and the adoption of appropriate cropping patterns and crop calendars. Preference should also be given to short links rather than long distance transfers.

Nevertheless, many sub-basins are already beginning to face water shortages and in view of the long lead time involved in conceptualizing, investigating, designing, financing and executing inter-basin links and transfers, the NWDA has been advised to continue its studies pertaining to the Peninsular component.

Additionally, there might be possibilities of using secondary Himalayan power to pump some of the Ganga's monsoon flows from around Varanasi and points lower down, as well as from the Yamuna, above Allahabad, to the Rihand dam (which seldom fills to its full capacity) and other storages, existing or potential, or natural depressions in the Vindhyas and Kaimur and Chota Nagpur plateaus beneficial uses, and generating power over the reverse drop. Such recycling projects appear worth investigation.

Bangladesh has off and on contemplated a Brahmaputra-Ganga transfer within its own territory and Nepal has likewise identified certain deficit zones which might at some stage import water from surplus basins.

Water law on inter-basin transfers is still evolving. There is clearly no bar on it and it is widely practiced around the world. But the principle of equitable apportionment will surely apply in terms of fulfilling all reasonable in-basin needs before catering to beneficial uses outside them. Availability of agreed data is a precondition to understanding and a resolution of differences over water use and sharing within and between basins and nations. But the will o cooperate remains paramount.

CHAPTER 16

Cooperate or Beggar My Neighbour

The Ganga-Brahmaputra-Barak/Meghna represents one of the greatest and potentially richest river systems in the world. No basin encompasses the same magnitudes of arable land, water availability and energy on which the lives and aspirations of such large and growing numbers of people depend, 480 million today, 600 million by 2000. In the water dispute India earlier had with Pakistan, it was possible to divide the Indus waters. The three eastern rivers of that system were allotted entirely to India and the waters of the three western rivers given more or less exclusively to Pakistan, barring some limited Indian consumptive uses in Jammu and Kashmir. The Ganga-Brahmaputra-Barak system cannot be so divided. It must be shared.

All the five nations that share this system have witnessed significant political and social changes within the past few decades. New forces of modernization, development equity, ecological security and the desire for a better quality of life are at work and will not be denied. The enormous diversity within the region, the different stages of development in which the basin states and people find themselves, and the divergence in social and political institutions are obvious. But there are many ties of shared history and cultural tradition and common resource endowments whose benefits can only be optimized through cooperation. Interdependence is compatible with independence and fraternity no enemy of sovereignty.

Prior to 1947, Bangladesh and India were one country. For various reasons, East Bengal was the less developed part of undivided Bengal, the economic life of which pivoted around Calcutta. East Pakistan, as it then was, emerged to independence handicapped. Partition did something else too. It severed Northeast India's natural riverine links with Calcutta and Chittagong, separating this region from its traditional markets, road and railheads, and outlets to the sea. The Northeast is an extraordinary mosaic of tribal-ethnic entities that had been long sequestered in what were constitutionally "partially or totally excluded areas" fringing the Brahmaputra and Barak Valleys. Now, joined to the Indian heartland through the tenuous Siliguri neck, this homeland of the youngest members of a newly independent nation-in-the-making came to be all but landlocked. "Distancing" from heartland-India has meant economic hardship and isolation for this rich and resurgent region. It remains a "partially or totally excluded area" in a new geo-political situation which would be most easily and effectively ameliorated by cooperation with and transit through Bangladesh.

Nepal and Bhutan, both truly landlocked, were even otherwise hermit-kingdoms until they opened their doors to the world in 1951 and 1959 respectively. Nepal had experienced some limited water resource development by way of small hydro-electric and irrigation projects during the first half of the 20th century under the Rana regime; but Bhutan not at all. Tibet too did not depart from traditional practice until the mid-fifties when the Chinese initiated some development. India inherited a well developed system of irrigation. The Yamuna, Ganga, Sone, Sharda and other canals were long extant and the Ganga canal hydro-electric system had triggered tubewell development in Uttar Pradesh in the 1930s. There was, however, virtually no storage on the Ganga until after Independence and there is even today only limited storage on the Himalayan Ganga though various developments like the Tehri Dam are under way.

The major contribution to the annual flow of the Ganga comes from the Nepal. Himalaya rivers, principally, the Karnali (Ghaghara), Gandak and Kosi. These, with the Mahakali (Sharda), are snow-fed and, along with other rivers rising in the Mahabhaat Lekh, provide 45 per cent of its lean season discharge. India has long diverted these waters in the plains. Further benefits of irrigation and flood control and, particularly, of power can only be had from large multipurpose storages in Nepal. Discussions on these possibilities were slow to commence and have not progressed very far or fast on account of a number of sensitivities on the part of Nepal and the lack of any agreement as yet on the allocation of costs and benefits from these projects between itself and India. Meanwhile, these potentials remain unused whereas they could generate wealth. Hydro-power is to Nepal what oil is to Kuwait, except that oil is a depleting asset while hydel energy is a renewable resource.

In the case of Bangladesh, the lean season flow of the Ganga at Farakka is inadequate to meet its full requirements as well as those of India. It is Bangladesh's complaint that diversions at Farakka to resuscitate Calcutta port constitute an unfair depletion at its cost. Talks on augmenting the lean flows at Farakka have proved infructuous and even such ad hoc arrangements as prevailed off and on since 1976 for sharing the dry weather flow of the Ganga between India and Bangladesh expired at the end of December 1988. Severe floods in Bangladesh in recent years, especially 1988, have also accentuated Bangladesh's sense of helplessness and frustration in dealing with what it regards to be a callous and overbearing upper riparian. India, on the other hand, is of the view that both Nepal and Bangladesh have exaggerated claims. The rival views are set out later in this chapter.

Underlying the deadlock, however, are political rather than merely techno-economic considerations. The political, social and financial commitments involved are so large, the ramifications so great and the consequences so long-lasting that political factors are likely to override technical ones though the latter are not unimportant. The political framework is therefore of prime importance and any discussion of the course of water resource development negotiations between India and its neighbours will be incomplete or simplistic without some understanding of this aspect. India speaks as an upper riparian when it addresses Bangladesh and turns the argument around and takes its stand as a lower riparian when it talks to Nepal. The United States and other large countries have done likewise. International water law is not yet sufficiently precise or universally binding in all respects as to be mandatory, but it nevertheless offers valuable guidelines and cannot be lightly disregarded. International public opinion would certainly not be uninfluenced by the emerging consensus on water law.

I – NEPAL'S CONCEPTS AND CONCERNS

Nepal, like Bhutan, is listed among LDCs or least developed countries by the World Bank. The 1981 census placed the population of this mountainous landlocked nation at 15 million. With a rate of growth of 2.66 per cent, this is estimated to double by 2004. At the commencement of its Seventh Plan in 1985, about 60 per cent of the population was below the poverty line, the domestic savings rate is low and has declined in recent years, with up to half the entire development outlay being financed through external assistance. It is the object of policy to meet the basic needs of all the people by 2000.

Ecological degradation has resulted in a decline in agricultural productivity in the populous mid-Himalayan region and ha compelled migration to the Terai which has been extensively cleared and settled in the past two to three decades. In this situation, with increasing pressure on the land, Nepal sees its water resources, and hydro-electric potential in particular, as a saving grace.

The first official study by the Department of Electricity assessed Nepal's hydel potential to be 83,000 MW. It described this resource as Nepal's "greatest asset" since "power means progress" (Shah, P.P. June 1971). A decade later, King Birendra said that water resources was the "magic key" to and a "catalyst" for all round development (Water Resources Ministry, 1981).

The policy document that the King's words prefaced spoke of a marked regional imbalance in development. It saw water resource development as an answer to the country's problems and the "leading edge for overall national growth". Three types of water resource projects were envisaged. First, small-scale schemes directly benefiting the rural populace and providing opportunities for self-reliance. Secondly, medium-sized projects designed to meet national needs in relation to energy, irrigation and water supplies. And, thirdly, large scale projects to satisfy expanding national requirements in the future but primarily for export and to be undertaken "on a cooperative basis with neighbouring countries". Among the benefits likely to be conferred on lower riparians by water resource development were flow regulation and flood control from storages and energy exports. The attainment of navigational rights on downstream waterways or the development of alternative navigable water routes to the sea within a framework of regional cooperation was also seen as likely to ease the difficulties caused by Nepal's landlocked status. Sediment control (through watershed management and soil conservation programmes) was cited as another area of cooperative endeavour. Other possibilities envisaged were the development of an international power grid, the establishment of a regional transportation network based on waterways and "electrically-propelled land transport" where feasible, the creation of a regional cold storage and refrigerated transport facility, and the better utilization of the primary resources of the region, "namely, water, coal and natural gas" (Ibid).

PARAMETERS OF INTERNATIONAL COOPERATION

Several prerequisites to water resource development were spelt out such as building up a sound database; studies on international water laws and practices and of international treaties on the cooperative development of water resources; manpower and institutional development; improving accessibility to project sites; and funding, including innovative organizational arrangements for financing giant projects. Pursuant to these aims, the Department of Electricity initiated a programme to train 250 Nepalese engineers at Roorkee University in India by 1989 in addition to other cadres, and a series of basin studies were planned.

A couple of years later, Nepal set out the parameters of international collaboration in the development of its water resources on a Himalayan watershed which "represents one of the world's last great frontiers of development" and "a unique opportunity for breaking the vicious poverty trap currently confronting the country" (Water Resources Minsitry, September 1983). This defined a "feasible" power potential of 27,000 MW as against which only 88.5 MW had been developed while another 800 MW might be harnessed by 2000 assuming a load growth of 10 to 13 per cent per annum. Karnali and Pancheshwar were mentioned as two export possibilities on the anvil.

More interesting was the approach spelt out for basin development: "Nepal, realizing that it has a water resource asset of mutual value to the nations of the region, is desirous of capitalizing on the development of that asset to increase its role and improve its economic significance within the region. To protect its interest and facilitate financing of the internationally important water resource projects, Nepal will require guidance and assistance from organizations such as the United Nations in studying, implementing and managing the developments". It sought active cooperation either bilaterally or multilaterally with other co-riparians in basin-wide water resource development "based on sharing of the costs and benefits with its neighbours and through the medium of trade". The complexities of management and organization and the magnitude of investments involved were made strikingly apparent in the statement that in contrast with Nepal's development budget of $ 406 million in 1983-84, the estimated cost of the Chisapani Project on the Karnali, as then conceived, would be of the order of $ 3.7 billion at 1983 prices.

Pursuant to its plan for basin studies, the Snowy Mountain Engineering Corporation (Australia) completed a Gandak River Basin Power Study, Basin Master Plan in 1979. Nippoa Koel, with UNDP funding, had studied the Karnlai basin 1962-66 and identified 10 sites for hydro development. The Snowy Mountain Authority reviewed the two most promising Karnali sites in 1968. This was further reviewed by Norçonsult A.S. and Electrowatt of Norway (Feasibility Study of the Chisapani Hydroelectric Project of the Karnali River, Nepal, 1977). These, together with the latest optimization report on the Karnali and associated projects by Himalaya Hydro Consultants, provide the outlines of a Karnali basin plan. A Kosi basin study was completed by Japanese consultants in 1986. All these basin studies identify projects and potentials and have been useful in determining their techno-economic ranking. An index of water resource development projects for all of Nepal's river systems was prepared in 1971 and had been refined and updated periodically, the most recent compendium being published by the Ministry of Water Resources in 1985. Canadian assistance has also been available to Nepal on basic water resource surveys.

DISENCHANTMENT OVER KOSI AND GANDAK

If against this background of great possibilities and high expectations actual progress has been limited, the reasons have to be sought in certain other factors and developments affecting Indo-Nepal relations. There appears to be a widespread feeling in Nepal that the first two Indo-Nepal projects taken up after the democratic revolution of 1951 were not entirely in favour of the kingdom. These relate to the Kosi and Gandak projects, both diversion schemes on the international border, agreements in respect of which were signed in 1954 and 1959. In both cases, it is felt that Nepal would have received greater benefits all round had the barrages been sited further upstream. This would necessarily have placed them wholly within Nepal which it believes would have given it a greater say in the management and control of these projects and ensured fairer sharing of the costs and benefits. A Kosi barrage located upstream of the present site would have enhanced its river training capability and reduced the attacks upon it by wounded river.

The Kosi is highly silt-laden and wayward and had over the past century migrated over 100 km west from the point where it debouches into the plains. Its annual floods had devastated north Bihar and it had come to be known as Bihar's "River of Sorrow". The coarse silt it spread over the flood plain rendered vast areas unfit for cultivation and the westward swing had continued unabated. The great 1954 flood was a dreadful calamity and there was great pressure on the Government of India to adopt immediate preventive measures. Expert consultations since the last part of the 19th century had not yielded any agreed solution other than the palliative of soil conservation works in Nepal. The newly formed Indian

Central Water and Power Commission in 1950 proposed a 239 metre Kosi High Dam at Barakshetra and a barrage lower down at Chherta, both within Nepal, to regulate the river, control silt flows, generate 1800 MW of power, irrigate large tracts in Nepal and Bihar and provide an element of navigation in the reservoir as well. The proposed 850,000 hectare-metre (6.9 million acre-feet) storage would have moderated a peak flood of 24,050 cumecs (850,000 cusecs) to a more manageable 5,660 cumecs. The idea was dropped as even a flood of 5,660 cumecs would require embankments in Bihar and it was believed that it would be difficult to find a market for 1,800 MW of power or to utilize the very large irrigation potential that would be created (Sain, Kanwar 1978). Variants such as a lower dam and different combinations of sites were explored and abandoned.

A new proposal was evolved in 1953 to anchor the river by means of a regulating barrage below Chherta and it was this scheme, with some modifications and a pair of embankments to jacket the Kosi within its existing course, that came to be adopted in answer to the 1954 flood. The Kosi embankments were completed by 1959 and the barrage four years later. The entire cost of the Barrage and appurtenant works were borne by India. Nepal got a measure of flood protection, some irrigation (partly through an inundation canal), an estimated 10 MW of hydel power generated on a canal drop, and a valuable bridge over the barrage which opened up east-west communications in that sector (Ibid). In the Indian view, it had not done badly by Nepal.

The Nepalese perception is different. Likewise on the Gandak project, which India again financed in toto, it has been pointed out that Nepal got only 56,650 hectares of irrigation and 15 MW of hydel power (again from a canal drop) while a huge irrigation benefit went to India. "Some Nepalese feel that had Nepal been economically strong, it would have constructed the entire system and sold the benefit at a fair price to India by utilizing her terrain as a resource site", says Chandra K. Sharma (1983), currently Executive Director of Nepal's Water and Energy Commission. He adds: "It is felt that at present the entire watershed of Nepal is working to tap water for the benefit of the lower riparians ... any lean (sic) towards extra benefit to Nepal at the time of the (Kosi and Gandak) agreements would have helped to solve all the prevailing misunderstandings which unfortunately have permeated down to the people. Now the situation is such that no political or bureaucrat will ever dare to stake his career and fame in dealing (with) the sensitive issue of water resources which involves the question of sharing between and among (the) co-riparians."

OTHER PROJECTS HALTED

The Nepalese are sore that the planning of the Chhatra Canal, built with Indian aid as an adjunct to the Kosi project, was defective and resulted in its having to be renovated with an IDA loan after Nepal took over its operation in 1976.

An earlier grievance relates to the agreement reached between Nepal and the then British Indian Government in 1920 pertaining to the Babassa barrage across the Sharda (Mahakali) which marks Nepal's western boundary with India in Uttar Pradesh. Under this, Nepal traded 1,658 hectares of its territory required for the project for an equivalent area in five fragments in three Indian districts. Nepal was conceded a right to a minimum of 11.3 cumecs for its own kharif irrigation and 9.25 cumecs in the rabi season with a proviso that the kharif supply may be augmented to 28.3 cumecs in the future when Nepal's own Mahakali irrigation system might have developed. But when Nepal was more recently able to organize credit for an expanded Mahakali irrigation project it found itself unable to get an increased supply over and above the minimum 11.3 cumec commitment on account of prior appropriation by India which also controls the barrage (Ibid).

There are other projects too on which there have been differences. Following the completion of a feasibility study of the Kankai multipurpose project in eastern Nepal in 1978 with West German funding, Nepal posed this to the Asian Development Bank for project financing to develop about 38 MW of energy and extend irrigation over 57,000 hectares. The ADB suggested consultation with India as it was already using Kankai waters for irrigation in Bihar. On such a reference being made, India sought a formal project report on the basis of which it might evaluate the impact of the Nepalese project on its existing Kankai uses.

Irked by this, and anxious to meet an emerging energy deficit in the Biratnagar industrial region, Nepal instead posed the Mulghat hydro-electric project on the Tamur, an arm of the Kosi, as a replacement. This was located in the same general region and promised a comparable energy output of up to 60 MW. India, however, raised an objection on the ground that the Mulghat dam would be submerged should the Kosi Dam, in which it had once again become interested, be constructed. The Nepalese in turn were reluctant to discuss the Kosi project as their Kosi basin study was still in progress. In any event, the High Dam would submerged the Mulghat site as well as the Dharan-Dhankuta highway built with British assistance and some experimental farms, apart from displacing a substantial population. The Kosi High Dam proposal had in fact been revived by India in 1974 after a fresh review which indicated that its energy and irrigation potential could now be beneficially used. Moreover, the dam would check sediment flows, stabilize the river and moderate its erosive attack above the Kosi barrage. In the result, neither Kankai nor Mulghat went through and the Nepalese felt doubly deprived.

INADEQUATE CONSULTATIVE MACHINERY

Further consultations might have yielded a via media and some harmonization of plans. Unfortunately, this did not happen. The existing mechanism available in the Kosi Coordination Committee, set up under the earlier Kosi agreement, was functioning fitfully while the corresponding Gandak committee had virtually become defunct. Nor did India take any great interest in the Kosi catchment treatment programme earlier agreed upon. The opportunity of gradually developing the Kosi and Gandak (barrage) project agreements into larger and more meaningful cooperative basin agreements with a watershed management component in a spirit of mutual accommodation for mutual benefit was lost by default.

While India is quick to suggest that Nepal should consult it before taking up projects on various boundary and border rivers so as to protect prior uses or adjust conflicting demands, Nepal complains that it was not consulted by India in regard to the major Sharda-Sahayak project or the Kamla-Jayanagar barrage. On the other hand, external funding for Nepal's Bagmati project was initially discouraged on account of Indian objections, though Saudi funding was available at a later stage. Indian objections to reduced boundary water flows are countered by Nepal which says that some dimunition may have taken place on account of deforestation and sedimentation and should not necessarily be attributed to additional abstractions by Nepal which is modernizing and renovating some of its traditional schemes. At the same time it protests India's claims to prior appropriation, especially on the smaller and medium rivers on which it is able to design and undertake projects on its own for local benefit without running into the engineering and financial complexities attending the harnessing of the bigger rivers. The Indian response is that it cannot prevent Indian villages from using available stream flows for local uses nor deprive them of these waters to favour a smaller neighbour as the Indian villager is as poor and deprived as his Nepali counterpart just across the border. Again, a suitable mechanism for dealing with this problem is not really available and there is the added complication that Bihar and U.P. are involved in the matter of the smaller streams and local projects. The Central Government had to intervene when a hydel-cum-irrigation project was planned near Tanakpur in Kumaon which would have diminished flows in the Mahakali for Nepalese uses. The project was recast to ensure that Nepalese interests were protected.

Alternative proposals have been put forward by Nepal and India with regard to the Rapti multipurpose scheme. A revised project is now under implementation and India hope's that its interests will be suitably accommodated through appropriate phasing so that planned diversions in Nepal coincide with and do not precede the construction of a projected dam which will provide the storage to meet the requirements of both countries.

The recently formed Indo-Nepal Joint Commission has a sub-commission on water resource development which supplements the earlier Water Resource Secretaries-level committee. This has worked out a joint programme, with Indian assistance, to improve Nepal's hydro-met infrastructure and upgrade its flood forecasting and early warning systems which would greatly benefit U.P. and Bihar. However, the sub-commission is a sub-system of a larger mechanism for Indo-Nepal consultations on a variety of issues and is to that extent not insulate from the slings and arrows affecting Indo-Nepalese relations as a whole. Isolating water resource developments from other aspects of Indo-Nepal relations may be both useful and desirable in view of their enormous complexities, technicalities and ramifications. Long gestation periods should not also be allowed to be needlessly prolonged by any sudden freeze in political relations as occurred when trade and transit arrangements between the two countries ruptured in the spring of 1989. The durability of the Indo-Pakistan Indus Commission through periods of political acrimony and even war perhaps has a moral.

KARNALI AND PANCHESHWAR

Negotiations on the proposed mega-projects, the Chispani Dam on the Karnali, the Pancheshwar project on the Mahakali (Sharda), and the Barakshetra High Dam (Kosi) have been even more tortuous. Discussions on the Kosi High Dam commenced 40 years ago though it must be said that India lost interest between 1954 and 1976. A high dam at Chisapani was first investigated by the Japanese in 1966 and this has been on the anvil practically ever since. Nepal's mistrust of India after the raw deal it feels it got on the Kosi and Gandak barrage agreements, particularly the former, have led it to keep out Indian consultancy and design skills and instead to opt, indeed to insist, on engaging international consultants. Here again, there was a time when Nepal may have been willing to go ahead with the Chisapani project in the 1970s. But there was a fear of being too dependent on Nepalese power in some Indian circles. With an installed capacity of 3600 to 450 MW as estimated at that time, Chisapani would certainly have been a major contributor to the Northern Indian grid by the early eighties had it been taken up then. But despite the lesson of Bhakra – that power generation creates its own demand – and the emerging energy shortage, nobody had the vision or the will to seize the opportunity. India also exhibited an excessive antagonism towards all international consultants or even international interest in the belief that this would necessarily load the dice against it if for no other reason than to favour the smaller country or to foster the sinister designs of that "foreign hand". President Carter, Prime Minister James Callaghan, the World Bank et al were spurned when they expressed willingness to support Himalayan water resource development. A minority would even quote the Indus Waters agreement, mediated by the World Bank, as being unduly generous to Pakistan, though this has never been a vocal contention. Furthermore, until the mid-eighties, the Indian Planning Commission had never looked at the Himalayan potential in Nepal and Bhutan in terms of long-term energy planning. The Chukha project in Bhutan (336 MW) has however made a significant difference to the Eastern Indian grid which has not gone unnoticed.

Conversely, some would attribute Nepal's diffidence about Karnali and similar projects at various times to an unspoken fear among sections of the ruling elites that a massive development programme of this kind might create alternative power centres and change the political balance within the kingdom. Mortgaging such a massive investment to a single buyer, India, might also be dangerous were excessive interdependence to erode independence. Yet another view is that hydro-electric development like other development efforts in Nepal "have largely failed because they have concentrated too heavily on the hardware and ignored or downplayed the changes needed in the social software", with elites viewing development as a zero-sum game (Gyawali, 1989). All these fears, as much as India's, are exaggerated. Any regime leading Nepal into this altogether new era of development and progress would surely be acclaimed. Any major water resource development project today must be conceived as both an area development as well as a human development programme rather than as a simple power project. The benefits would be enormous and transforming and the return to the exchequer, after payback on the investment, could be ploughed into balanced regional development.

Both sides have moved haltingly when the other was willing. But the growing energy shortage and the need to utilize more fully the water resources of the Himalayan Ganga encouraged them to pick up the threads again in the 1980s. The quiet good offices of the World Bank were available in coaxing acceptance of agreed terms of reference for a prefeasibility study of the Karnali project in the new context. An agreed firm of international consultants was appointed in 1986 from out of a list prepared by the bank, the contact going to a consortium of four Canadian-US firms, the Himalayan Hydro Development Company.

Impatient at the slow pace of progress on Karnali, India had started pushing Nepal for consideration of the Pancheshwar project on the Mahakali, a boundary river, to generate 2000 MW and provide irrigation benefits in the plains below. Having already investigated the Pancheshwar site from its side of the border and being in possession of much of the hydrological and other data, India believed that this might move ahead. Nepal did express interest but dragged is feet because it feared that if Pancheshwar, a shared Indo-Nepal project, was to get off the ground, then India might slow down on Karnali, the larger and wholly Nepalese project. With the result that despite India also agreeing to refer Pancheshwar to international consultants, this has not been done as the Nepalese are still completing investigations on their side of the border.

The Himalayan Hydro Development Company (HHDC) submitted an optimization report on the Karnali project in the latter half of 1988. It proposed raising the height of the dam from 240 m, as previously suggested, to 262 m in order to augment the power potential from 4500 MW to 10,000 MW. Further, by dovetailing this with an upstream run-of-the-river hydel project (240-270 MW) on the Karnali bend (which will generate the power required for construction of the Chisapani dam), as well as two related storages on the Bheri and Seti rivers, both by an additional 5400 MW in subsequent phases. The benefit-cost ratio is said to be exceedingly favourable. Setting a timetable for study of the feasibility report, preparation of a detailed project report and commencement of construction by 1992, HHDC thinks it might be possible to get the first two turbines spinning by

2001. This seems a somewhat optimistic schedule. While expedition is desirable there are a number of issues that remain to be settled on cost and benefit sharing, funding, organization and management. The project cost is currently estimated at $ 4.4 billion at 1988 prices but would probably be more, escalation apart. India must guarantee to buy all of the Nepal-surplus Karnali power, which will be 95 per cent or more, if the project is to be internationally funded with a credible repayment commitment. On what terms ?

SHARING COSTS AND BENEFITS

Karnali, like Pancheshwar, is a multipurpose project with hydel, irrigation and flood control components. Nepal would like to sell the power to India at the alternative thermal or nuclear replacement cost. This obviously sets the maximum price that Nepal might seek while the cost of generation and transmission to the Indian border would establish the floor. The price will have to be set in between these two limits with a formula for periodic revision in the light of changing circumstances. A compromise suggested by some Nepalese observers is that India's current thermal replacement cost plus Karnali's generation cost divided by two would suggest a fair price. This might provide a negotiating basis but there will obviously be a cut of price which India would not be willing to exceed as it would then find it prudent and economic to develop its own hydel, thermal or nuclear options.

In respect of irrigation, Nepal appears to be asserting ownership of waters stored behind its dams. This is not a principle in international law and is unacceptable to India which may, however, be willing to bear the entire capital cost of the irrigation component of Pancheshwar or Karnali and allow Nepal first use of whatever water it requires for irrigation. Nepal is also asserting the downstream benefit principle built into the US-Canada Columbia River Agreement, on the ground that storage beneficially regulates the timing of water delivery to match the crop cycle during the lean season. This is a legitimate consideration and could be settled in terms of a commuted value inclusive of a "royalty" for the dam site, a scarce and wasting natural resource, which is liable to silt up within a certain time. Indian dams are normally depreciated over 50 years or so which takes into account the finite life of the site.

The Nepalese also cite the Columbia Treaty regarding the manner of calculating downstream benefits in respect of flood control and additional power from hydel projects located in the Lower Columbia basin within the United States (Sharma, C.K., 1983). Canada receives free of cost half the additional power generated in the US downstream on account of its Upper Columbia storage as well as half the flood damage saving to the US over a period of 30 years. The quantum of downstream benefit is a matter for assessment depending on the circumstances of the case. But it is the principle that Nepal is advocating.

However, with regard to flood moderation, it is India's case that it has already ensured complete flood protection along the Ghaghara (Karnali) in normal years by building and maintaining embankments that jacket the river. It cannot, therefore, now be called upon to pay twice over for the same degree of protection. This is a valid consideration. Nevertheless, some benefit might still accrue in terms of floods beyond the discharge that the Indian embankments can contain, or moderation or elimination of normal floods in the floodway within the embankments on account of the cushion provided by the Chisapani dam, or because it is no longer necessary to maintain or even retain the embankments in their present state of readiness because of the insurance provided by the Dam. A resolution of this question should not present any insuperable difficulties.

India would however have reason to be concerned over any effort to load excessive flood benefits on the dam. This follows the suggestion that with the raising of the height of the Chisapani dam, it will be able to moderate a 10,000 year return flood with an added safety margin. Such technical details are capable of fairly precise measurement and there are well-established principles for allocating the cost of multipurpose dams as between various functions or benefits. India also has some doubts about the wisdom of raising the height of the dam to the extent proposed in view of seismic hazards and would if necessary counsel some lowering despite a reduction in the power output.

If there are benefits to be shared in terms of the proportionate cost of services rendered, there are "disbenefits" that could be debited to the upper riparian. Prime among these in the case of Nepal would be erosion as a result of deforestation and "faulty" land use or watershed management (as opposed to mass wasting on account of natural factors), resulting in sedimentation, floods, and loss of navigability. Likewise, certain structures might impede fish migration or the natural fertilization associated with flooding. Pollution might be yet another factor. The complexities of measuring and managing these factors and allocating "costs" can well be imagined. The lesson, therefore, is that settlements must follow reasonable assumptions and values reasonably negotiated, especially since some factors, such as man-made erosion, are evident even where there is no dam or other water resource development.

BINATIONAL ORGANISATIONS

The Nepalese say they have their hands full with Karnali and that Pancheshwar will have to follow. Pancheshwar is a border project and so costs and benefits will be shared equally. But the same issues will have to be settled as in the case of Karnali. The two countries even now exchange power at a few points along their common border, with Nepal being a net buyer of electricity from India at varying rates going up to 76 paise per unit. This situation will change, with bulk sales of power by Nepal to India.

Some of the issues pertaining to the pricing of Karnali energy may be resolved sooner arising out of Nepal's interest in developing Arun-3, a run-of-the-river hydro project on the Arun (Kosi) which is estimated to generate 400 MW, hopefully by 1996. A cascade of seven projects has been identified on the Arun with an installed capacity of something in excess of 1185 MW. Arun-3 is an attractive proposal and, once developed, will open up the upper Arun valley for exploitation. Commissioned in stages after 1996, Arun-3 is expected to meet Nepal's electricity demands until after the turn of the century when Karnali should be ready for commissioning. But on completion Arun-3 will have surplus power for several years for which the immediate market lies in India. The economics and phasing of the project partly turns on the disposal of this surplus power which is why the question of pricing of power exported to India might come to be expedited.

While Nepal plans to build Arun-3 on its own some Nepalese observers have advocated a binational organization for the construction of Pancheshwar, a boundary river project, on the model of the Brazil-Paraguyan Itaipu Binacional and the Argentina-Paraguyan Binacional that has been entrusted with the responsibility of constructing and managing the Yacyreta Dam (Sharma C.K. 1983). This could be a possible organizational form on the lines of the autonomous Chukha Project Authority set up by the governments of Bhutan and India for the development of the Chukha hydro-electric project. A binational entity of this kind may not only be less bureaucratic and less prone to red-tape but could also impart a greater sense of equality among the two corporate partners although their sponsoring governments are very unequal in size. Such possibilities should be open to discussion though, when everything is said, these mega projects in Nepal are unlikely to get off the ground without some kind of Indian guarantee. Karnali's likely cost of around $ 5 billion is more than double Nepal's GDP ($2.35 billion). As a wag put it, "Will Nepal own Karnali; or will Karnali own Nepal". Understandably, Nepal will proceed with great caution.

ACCESS TO THE SEA

Nepal is greatly interested in a possible navigation route from within its territory, or the Indo-Nepal border to the sea as this could partially mitigate the handicap it experiences as a landlocked country. Navigation on the Gandak and Kosi, via the Mahananda and Korotoya and thus into the lower Ganga-Brahmaputra system has been proposed by Bangladesh. The Indo-Nepal Gandak Agreement in 1959 does indeed provide for a lock in the Gandak Barrage. Such a navigation route, with Nepalese cargo being handled through an inland container depot-cum-port and using inter-modal systems would be of benefit to India as well in sustaining any waterway developed for this purpose through its territory. But apart from its technical feasibility, any waterway must be economically viable in terms of a minimum volume of traffic to support its development and maintenance along with the related infrastructure. This remains to be studied. India is, however, not prepared to countenance Nepalese assertions that the Ganga is an "international" river over which other nations have a prescriptive right to navigation. Nor is it willing to consider any suggestion of a Nepal-Bangladesh navigation link aligned through the strategic Siliguri neck.

The proposed Kosi High Dam may or may not by itself be sufficient to rescue the present Kosi barrage. There has been discussion earlier about constructing a second barrage across the Kosi below the first, at Dagmara, to flatten the gradient of the river as a means of dealing with continuing siltation and erosion problems. Should this be built at any time, an improved waterway might be a by-product. The Himalayan component of India's National Perspective on a water grid may be a long way away. But should it ever materialize, a diversion barrage is envisaged across the Ganga below Patna which would cause the pondage to back up the Gandak. Navigable links could be constructed to complete a continuous waterway if warranted by overall regional transport economics. Such ideas are not amenable to here-and-now decisions. At the same time, these options should not be foreclosed as their time may come 10 or 20 or 30 years from now with on-going water resource development and the generation of traffic.

TRADE-OFFS BETWEEN RIVERS

The preceding narrative suggests the contours along which Indo-Nepal discussions might sensibly proceed, especially with regard to energy and navigation. Irrigation presents an easier problem insofar as India would in principle have no difficulty in agreeing to Nepal's using all the water it needs. The only problem would arise in certain border localities or common boundary streams where prior appropriation by one side or the other taken with prospective uses has created or is likely to create shortages for the other. Storages on the large and some medium rivers such as the Rapti, could make good the deficit. For the rest, the answer would appear to lie in exploring three possible lines of action, especially with regard to smaller common or boundary rivers which provide local benefits. First, India might phase out certain existing surface withdrawals and replace these with groundwater, or compensate Nepal for developing groundwater resources on its side of the border wherever available and assist it in so doing. Some of the compensation could take the form of an electricity debit to India from among any "joint" projects. Secondly, both countries might agree to group clusters of local rivers along with a medium or large river and allocate the waters between themselves or undertake small basin transfers to even out local surpluses and deficits. Thirdly, India might draw on storages on the four large rivers (Mahakali, Karnali, Gandak and Kosi) to develop replacement works for existing uses in deficit locations if feasible.

A survey of existing and prospective needs and uses would indicate areas of surplus and deficit groundwater availability and replacement possibilities and costs on either side within a given time-frame. Once this is done and the magnitude of the problem is known, suitable agreement could be worked out, sector by sector, cluster by cluster. There will certainly have to be some give and take on both sides and there may be other elements that could be brought into the bargain to ensure appropriate trade-offs. Something in the nature of a boundary rivers agreement on the U.S.-Canadian pattern with suitable adaptation to fit local conditions would also provide a mechanism for problem identification, problem-solving, cooperative management, and adjudication as and when necessary.

There could also be a broad trade-off, with India accommodating a larger measure of Nepalese interests in so-called local and medium rivers in return for greater leeway on the four major rivers, an arrangement that would appear to fit well with geo-national development interests. India's interest in the Kosi High Dam, for instance, must obviously exceed the stakes it has in the smaller rivers in the eastern Nepal region.

COLLABORATION IN WATERSHED MANAGEMENT

Even while studies and negotiations are in progress on various aspects of water resource development, there is an urgent and necessary task that needs to be accomplished right along the Himalaya, in India as much as in Nepal, in the form of soil conservation and the adoption of moral rational land use and cropping patterns or improved watershed management. Soil conservation and reforestation are essential prerequisites for water resource development in view of the fragility of the Himalayan eco-system and the degradation of the environment visible all around. Soil conservation arouses less passion and fewer issues of competing national interest than dams. All the more reason to use this as a means of confidence building and working together for the common good, and as a valuable pre-investment measure. This would also be the most effective way of overcoming environmental objections and providing for the rehabilitation of persons like by to be displaced by submergence which would then be seen and must be conceptualized as area development programmes for the rejuvenation of remote and generally neglected upper catchments.

India threw away an opportunity by showing no more than a minimal interest in the earlier Kosi soil conservation programme in the 1960s. It has now proposed a more ambitious watershed management programme in a couple of the most erosion-prone districts in the Kosi catchment which it would be prepared to finance. Preliminary discussions have taken place. It would, however, be unwise for India to make this condition on Nepal's agreeing to the Kosi High Dam. It should be taken up as a separate programme that could in time mesh with the Kosi High Dam. One means of funding this would be through partial payment payment through food-for-work, the grain being provided by India, probably as a distinct development-cum-employment support component of SAARC's food security reserve. Seasonal farm labour could be engaged under village labour cooperatives or other associations working alongside permanent, professional eco-development corps made up of Gurkha ex-servicemen, many hundreds and thousands of whom are drawn from the Kosi and Karnali regions in particular, like the Kumaonis and Garhwalis in U.P.

Grain could be given to families that agree to abandon crop farming on marginal lands in favour of horticulture, grass, medicinal plants, or forestry in order to see them through the gestation period. Forward and backward linkages would need to be established through marketing, processing, cold storages, transportation, development of alternative sources of fodder and fuel, micro-hydel stations, ropeways or whatever in consultation and participation with local communities. The logistics of food supply in the hills is difficult. But this can be overcome by building regional depots and local sub-depots during fair weather, micro-hydel stations, ropeways or whatever in consultation and participation with local communities. The logistics of food supply in the hills is difficult. But this can be overcome by building regional depots and local sub-depots during fair weather. India's long and proud association with Nepal's splendid Gurkha fighting men would continue a bond and draw on a vast reservoir of goodwill in ensuring another kind of security.

Such an Indo-Nepal programme would be best managed on the Indian side by a non-governmental organization like the officially-supported Society for the Promotion of Wastcland Development. This has experience in working with local communities and voluntary agencies and enjoys an easy flexibility that could not be replicated in a governmental agency. The Nepalese too would probably feel happier dealing one to one with an NGO of this kind than with the Government of India or the Indian Embassy in Kathmandu.

THE POLITICAL DIMENSION

The course of Indo-Nepal negotiations on water resource development has unfortunately been affected by the general state of political relations which have been marked by mistrust and have at times been abrasive. No two countries in the world, not even the US and Canada or the members of the EEC, have such a close relationship as India and Nepal. Indian currency can be freely used in Nepal. Citizens of one country are entitled to national treatment in the other in terms of residence, ownership of property, movement, employment and participation in trade, commerce, industry or contracts. Even so, an open border and free movements have generated political sensitivities as both countries are developing societies with burgeoning populations.

As a land-locked country, Nepal is particularly concerned about transit rights and has struggled to separate transit from trade which India long resisted, accepted for a decade after 1978 but reversed in 1989. Nepal has a large Rs.300 crore deficit in its trade with India which in itself accounts for 48 per cent of its total international trade. There was a sudden rupture in trade relations in March 1989 with India declining to sign a fresh trade agreement, initialed six months earlier, on grounds of non-fulfilment of certain conditionalities that Nepal disputed, and permitting the Transit Treaty to lapse against Nepalese protests. This does not imply an "economic blockade" as alleged by Nepal but it has caused economic disruption and does end a number of privileges granted to Nepal by India the years as part of a "special relationship" which, India claims, was not being reciprocated. Nepal has introduced work permits for all foreigners employed in the organized sector in Kathmandu Valley which India asserts has also been extended to other regions. This Nepal denies. There has been vague talk about reviewing the citizenship certificates granted to non-nations over the past 12 years. India sees these as a steps that could result in squeezing Indians out of the kingdom. Nepal also imported some arms from China in 1988 in order, it says, to modernize its armed forces and combat terrorism, a development that India protests is out of line with the security relationship between the two countries. India had earlier objected to Nepal awarding a contract to China to complete the last segment of the East-West Highway which runs parallel to but quite some distance away from the open Indian border. But Nepal protests that the Chinese won this contract in open competition on a tender floated by the World Bank which was funding the project. India subsequently bought out this contract for Rs.50 crores. Nepal in turn has its own list of grievances about delays and dilatoriness on the part of India on various counts and its high-handedness in dealing with a small neighbour. It is aggrieved by India's refusal to recognize it as a "zone of peace" despite acceptance of this status by 108 other nations. India dismisses this as a ploy to play it off against China in negotiation of the spirit of the Indo-Nepal Treaty of Peace and Friendship, 1950. And so it goes with minor or even trivial issues being blown up emotionally far beyond their true worth.

There is also the big country-small country syndrome at work with Nepal wishing to emphasise its identity at every turn and exhibiting what has been termed the tyranny of the weak. Nepal's economy is heavily aid-dependent and India feels that its interests have at times been subordinated to those of international donors although it is among the largest of Nepal's benefactors with an aid budget of Rs.20-30 crores per annum. Indian assistance to Nepal has been of the order of Rs.350-400 crores over the past 35 to 40 years, a figure that would be considerably more at current prices.

DELAY IS DENIAL

It is in this larger context of Indo-Nepal relations that water resource development must be seen. Nepal would be unwise to rehearse ancient grudges, some of them exaggerated, for little purpose and India would do well to be less over-bearing on occasion and to deal with Nepal in a more relaxed and understanding fashion.

There is no basic conflict of interest between the two and India can afford to be generous in dealing with its smaller neighbour. Delay in developing Nepal's vast water resources in a denial of the kingdom's own best interest, and equally denies India optimality in the development of its shared water resources. Nepal's trade deficit with India could be more than offset by electricity exports to India in the first place and then, with the development of an international grid, to Bangladesh and Pakistan. Islamabad from the Chisapani (Karnali) dam is no more distant than Calcutta from the proposed Dihang dam in Arunachal. Maximizing the use of Nepalese and Indian manpower, material and equipment as well as design and consultancy services in water resource development would lower the foreign exchange/dollar cost and make debt servicing that much easier. Some Nepalese have argued that while Nepal will need convertible currency payments from India to service its international debt on Karnali et al, over and beyond that, much of Nepal's "profit" could be paid in rupees and this, in turn, could finance extended trade and development imports from India. A SAARC project development fund has also been suggested. India must however be able to compete in terms of quality and price in bidding for hydro-electric development in Nepal.

The kinds of arrangements devised with Nepal would also apply to Bhutan and to some extent to Bangladesh. Bhutan too has a considerable Himalayan hydel potential with flood control and irrigation benefits as well. Projects on the Torso and Raidek are already being appraised, with larger possibilities on the Manas and Sunkosi. These will all take time as each country will want to rank its projects in relation to its own priorities while India will need to rank these international projects alongside its own developments. Apart from exporting power, Bhutan and Nepal could also process and sell electro-chemical, electro-metallurgical and other power products to India and the world.

Addressing the SAARC summit at Kathmandu in 1987, King Jigme Singye Wangchuk of Bhutan said that political will was required to ensure the environment South Asia needs to make it one of the most prosperous regions in the world with its rich endowments of water, land and manpower.

The current Indo-Nepal impasse, however, constitutes a most unfortunate setback to Himalayan water resource development. The Karnali consultant's feasibility report, possibly delayed for reasons other than the Indo-Nepal contretemps, was still awaited that commencement of 1990. Agreement on its techno-economic and operational parameters will be necessary before the preparation of a detailed project report can go forward. With a new National Front Government assuming office in Delhi there is some prospect of early talks between the two countries to restore normalcy. Hopefully these discussions will prove fruitful and the Karnali schedule will not be further delayed. Should the delay be prolonged, the self-injury suffered by the two sides will ultimately be seen by both to be far greater than the slights and dangers against which they are so determinedly defending themselves today. Nothing can bind these two neighbours more closely and to greater mutual benefit than the harnessing of Nepal's Himalayan rivers. It would be a strange diplomacy on either side that sets about zealously to maximize losses.

As by far the larger and more resourceful partner and the one with the widest options open to it, it is clearly for India to give a lead. The rude jolt given to Indo-Nepal relations following the break down of trade and transit negotiations in the spring of 1989 will have served a purpose, howsoever painfully, if it brings about a realization that Nepal as much as India has acquired a new personality over the years. Traditional relationships have assumed a new dimension and new aspirations among their people preclude either side taking the other for granted.

King Birendra has often spoken of Nepal's water resources being available for regional benefit. He has said that "Nepal is willing to cooperate in such a joint venture that will lead not only to planning prosperity together but also emphasise our independence through independence". It is this vision of shared prosperity through independence in independence that Nepal, Bhutan and India with Bangladesh and others must jointly translate into reality.

II – THE PORT OF CALCUTTA

Sentiment over Farakka has run particularly high in Dhaka with the graduated diversion of up to 1132 cumecs (40,000 cusecs) into the dying Bhagirathi-Hooghly, for the preservation of the port of Calcutta, now a city of 10 million and eastern India's gateway to the world. With the dry weather flow of the river falling to 1558 cumecs (55,000 cusecs) in the last part of April, these abstractions at Farakka have come to be regarded by Bangladesh as a serious and unfair deprivation causing it manifold injury.

The Farakka dispute has a hoary background, closely associated with the rise of Calcutta. Bengal's ancient port of Tamluk was located on the Rupnarayan near modern Haldia. With the gradual silting of its channel after the 10th century, other ports arose, pride of place going to Saptagram or Satgaon, above Calcutta, at the confluence of the Old Damodar with the Bhagirathi. Satgaon reached its acme between the 14th and 16th century. Thereafter the Damodar moved away towards its present channel, further west and south, but not before the Portuguese had arrived at this trading centre which they named Porto Pequeno. By 1570, the Portuguese had moved their factory from Satgaon to nearby Hugli which is where the Mughal Governor had his residence. The Dutch had meanwhile moved further up river to Chinsura and the French to Chandernagore. The English were latecomers to Hugli and a quarrel with some Mughal retainers caused them to move away to a new and, at first, unpromising site down river. Job Charnok founded Calcutta in 1690 on a swamp sufficiently inland to be reasonably out of reach of marauding river pirates who were reluctant to venture too far up the labyrinth of estuarine tidal creeks. The Bhagirathi-Hooghly was still the main or at least a major arm of the Ganga delta with its apex at Farakka.

EARLY GROWTH AND ALARMS

Calcutta grew rapidly and was soon the principal point of exchange for goods brought down the Ganga and Brahmaputra from upper India and Assam and for British manufactures which were in turn distributed up and along these rivers. By the time of the Battle of Plassey in 1957, the Hooghly was not yet quite fordable in the dry season though the Ganga had begun to favour its more easterly channel which takes on the name of Padma in Bangladesh after its confluence with the Brahmaputra, locally known as the Jamuna. As trade with Britain increased, so did the size of vessels. Meanwhile drafts had begun fluctuate if not decline, causing alarm to shippers and the port authorities from time to time.

The first of a series of expert committees set up to examine the problem of the navigability of the Hooghly met in 1853. Nothing came of it, but continuing concern over the fate of Calcutta led to a brief but abortive experiment to establish Port Canning on the Matla River, nearer the sea. The opening of the Suez Canal in 1869 gave an impetus to trade and witnessed the transition from wooden to ironclad vessels of larger dimensions. The Calcutta Port Trust was established in 1870 soon after the failure of the River Trust set up under the municipality to improve the port. Yet it was not long before proposals were afloat to dredge a ship canal from Chitpur, just below Calcutta, to a point below Port Canning or to establish an auxiliary port at Diamond Harbour. Earlier, proposals had been made for locating a coal dock at Geonkhali. Nothing came of these ideas either but dredging operations commenced at Calcutta. Yet another inquiry committee was appointed in1891, a couple of years before Kidderpore Dock was opened to provide sanctuary to vessels that were otherwise lashed by tidal bores in open moorings. King Georges Dock was opened some decades later in 1928.

There followed further proposals for a ship canal, this time to Diamond Harbour to avoid problematic bars and bends in the river, and suggestions for improvement in headwater supplies to the Bhagirathi. This had been proposed by Sir Arthur Cotton as far back as 1854 by means of a diversion barrage across the Ganga, though his main purpose was to facilitate navigation up-river. The Port Commissioners were torn between assuring shippers that all was well with Calcutta and persuading the government to do something to save it by calling attention to the growing peril of falling drafts, limiting bars and larger and more frequent bore tides sweeping up the channel. Discussion of this would fill a book and details are available elsewhere (Mukherjee N. 1968; and Crow, 1980).

As the Bhagirathi became moribund for all but the few monsoon months, its capacity to flush the river of silt deposited in its bed began to decline. So did its ability to prevent the tidal carriage of silt further upstream. The Port's official historian reports that "in 1938, 26-feet draft vessels could come to the Port for about 291 days a year. In the next 25 years, the number of days the Port has been open to such vessels has continued to decline and in fact in 1961 the Port could not be kept open for a single day for vessels of this type. The fall in depth has been alarming. In general there has been fall of about seven feet navigable depth in typical localities during this period" (Mukherjee N.). If the tonnage moving through the Port increased, it was only because of the fact that there was no alternative to serve the vast hinterland of Calcutta and that bulk cargo vessels, especially those carrying foodgrains, sailed up the river after being considerably lightened by off-loading at Madras or Visakhapatnam.

The complex factors interacting on river conditions at and below Calcutta because of both upland and tidal circumstances were the subject matter of elaborate model studies and analyses over the years up to and after India's independence. There were differences on the causative factors and the possible results of the prescriptions proposed. The idea of a diversion barrage across the Ganga to resuscitate the Bhagirathi was moved to the forefront by Webster in 1946 and the Man Singh Committee in 1952 (Crow).

THE RADCLIFFE AWARD

Meanwhile, with the approach of Partition, the question arose as to the line along which Bengal should be divided. A Boundary Commission was appointed with Sir Cyril Radcliffe as chairman. As the four Indian and Pakistani members divided equally, Radcliffe was compelled give his own decision on August 12, 1947. The demarcation of the boundary would, in his opinion, depend on answers to certain basic questions, two of which pertaining to Calcutta. These were "to which state was the city of Calcutta to be assigned, or was it possible to adopt any method of dividing the City between the two (successor) States? (Further), if the city of Calcutta must be assigned as a whole to one or other of the States, what were its indispensable claims to the control of territory, such as all or part of the Nadia river system or the Kulti rivers, upon which the life of Calcutta as a city and port depended". Radcliffe decided that Calcutta could not be divided and awarded the Nadia-Kulti headwatrs (the Bhagirathi, Jalangi and Nadia) along with Calcutta to India. This entailed transferring the Muslim-majority Murshidabad district to India and, balancing this, the Hindu-majority district of Khulna and certain other areas to Pakistan (Radcliffe Awards).

Radcliffe assigned no detailed reason for his award. The Farakka site, some 15 kms above the point where the Ganga becomes the boundary river, falls in India. The only other site for a barrage would have been further upstream at Rajmahal, which was considered and rejected, or a little lower down at Lalgola at which point its two ends would have been in India and what is now Bangladesh, respectively. Indeed in May 1953, India suggested to Pakistan, which had queried its plans to build a barrage, that the water resources of Ganga be developed cooperatively by the two countries on a reciprocal basis. Pakistan responded favourably, but nothing came of it (Gulati, 1972). The proposal was revived at the

Nehru-Ayub meeting in 1960 at the time of the signing of the Indus Water Treaty and was formally proposed by Pakistan a year later. India replied by stating that Farakka had by then become irreversible (Crow).

EARLIER DOUBTS DISPELLED

Before taking a look at the course of negotiations on Farakka. It would be best to dispose of the doubts expressed as to its efficacy by various observers. Kapil Bhattacharya, an Indian engineer, argued that Farakka begged the real question as the deterioration of the lower Hooghly had been caused by the reduction of the discharges from the Damodar and Rupnarayan rivers below Haldia as a result of the DVC and other water resource developments. Earlier, two American consultants engaged by Pakistan, A.T. Ippen and C.F. Wicker, had expressed considerable scepticism about the anticipated flushing effect of Farakka diversions and had, in fact, forecast new problems. Even on the eve of the commissioning of the Farakka Barrage the idea of the ship canal to the sea was again mooted (Roy L.B. 1974). This was not considered viable as there would be no way of preventing heavy siltation, especially of the seaward entrance.

The Indian decision to go ahead with Farakka was based on prolonged and careful studies and model tests and was certified by an international tidal hydraulic expert from Germany, Dr. Walter Henson (Framji, May 1975 and Mookherjee, 1975). Suggestions that dredging would solve the problem were found wanting. About eight million tonnes of silt were removed from the Hooghly annually by dredging between 1926 and 1956. Yet the draft kept declining and each loss of one foot in draft (30 cms) meant a loss of 600 tonnes of cargo carrying capacity. Indeed, even finding place to dump the spoils was becoming a problem (Framji, 1962).

Simultaneously with the decision to construct the Farakka Barrage, it was decided to go ahead with the establishment of an auxiliary deep draft port at Haldia, 85 kilometres down the river, commencing with the Haldia anchorage in 1959.

POSITIVE IMPACT OF FARAKKA DIVERSIONS

The hope that regular flushing of the Hooghly by means of diversions at Farakka would carve out a stable deep channel has not been belied and the Ippen and Wicker argument that this would not happen on account of the so-called saline wedge created by incoming tidal waters, challenged at the time, has been disproved. Between 1976 and 1988, drafts up to Calcutta improved by about 1.2 to 1.5 metres. even between 1986 and 1988, the number of days on which the draft at Calcutta and Haldia was more than 6.7 m and 8.2 m respectively rose from 75 to 167 in the case of Calcutta and 95 to 144 in the case of Haldia. It is now aimed to improve drafts to 7.9 m and 10.4, respectively, through various means. Farakka has worked. But any improvement of draft beyond 7.9 m (26 feet) at Calcutta will be of little avail as the size of the Port's dock gates and bends in the river will not admit of larger and longer vessels.

Leaving aside for the moment the benefit to Calcutta from Farakka in terms of improved drafts, reduced salinity in respect of drinking water and industrial uses, and less dredging, the issue was how Pakistan/Bangladesh saw its interests being affected. On one view, the real purpose of the Farakka Barrage was not the preservation of Calcutta port, which many in that country had long persuaded themselves was not technically feasible or otherwise credible, but "to control the river for supplying Ganges water to the Indian states of Uttar Pradesh and Bihar" (Abbas 1982). More recently, a thesis has been propounded that "experts of Bangladesh guess that the Barrage is part of India's greater national plan for irrigational development" which the author quotes a former Indian Irrigation Minister, Dr K.L. Rao, as describing as the "Farakka-Dhubri Project through Teesta" to irrigate areas in Assam (Khurshida Begum 1988). This clearly rests on a total misunderstanding of a proposed Brahmaputra-Ganga link canal through an all-India route which had occasionally been canvassed. The notion of diverting the Ganga to irrigate areas in Assam would prima facie be absurd.

Although the Farakka feeder is designed to carry 40,000 cusecs (1132 cumecs) for flushing the Bhagirathi-Hooghly, the quantum of discharge required for this purpose has been a moot point. The Man Singh Committee on the River Hooghly and the Improvement of its Headwater Supply (1952) fixed the discharge from the Farakka feeder at 20,000 cusecs. The Farakka Project as sanctioned by the Government of India n April 1960, "took note of various viewpoints with regard to duration of head discharge and made provision for moderated discharges at Kalna … It was proposed to run the Feeder Canal at 40,000 cusecs practically for 10 months, and for two months, mid-March to mid-May, with lesser discharges up to 20,000 cusecs" (Public Accounts Committee, January 1976).

Two study groups of the Public Accounts Committee visited Calcutta to discuss this matter with the Port authorities. The Port Trust reiterated a minimum demand for 40,000 cusecs on the basis of model and analytical studies. It concluded: "If the above-mentioned discharge of 40,000 cusecs through the Farakka network into the Bhagirathi-Hooghly can be ensured for seven years, particularly during the lean months, the deterioration in Calcutta Port could be effectively stopped. If this discharge, even at the rate of 32,000 cusecs, was continued for a further period of seven years, it was hoped that the draft of 28 feet may become available in Calcutta Port for a major portion of the year, as was the position in 1938" (Ibid).

FURTHER OUTLOOK

Fourteen years back passed since that was written and although 1132 cumecs (40,000 cusecs) have not been continuously diverted into the Bhagirathi-Hooghly during the lean season, drafts have improved. It should now be possible to make a firmer forecast of the quantum of diversion required in the light of actual experience. An expert committee should be appointed to make a critical examination of this issue or suggest a series of controlled experiments on the basis of which alternative hypotheses can be tested to determine by when and by how much, if at all, headwater discharges into the Bhagirathi-Hooghly can be reduced during the lean period through diversion at Farakka.

A harmonized modulation of Bangladesh and Indian requirements was in fact projected by some Indian experts at the time the Farakka Barrage was commissioned. K.K. Framji, who had a very long and intimate association with the Farakka Project and participated in the earlier negotiations, had this to say: During this (initial) period of relatively low water demand in Bangladesh, full withdrawals for effective operations of the Farakka Project (for the benefit of Calcutta Port) should be allowed to take place, so that when the projects in Bangladesh come up and are sufficiently developed to require increased supplies, the Farakka Project may be susceptible of some adjustments ..." (May 1975).

Trying to restore Calcutta's pristine position as a great ocean port is to attempt the impossible. The evolution of large, deep draft vessels in the post-Seuz era and of containerization has changed the mode and concept of international shipping. Calcuta has had its day. It has had to yield to Haldia which came up 20 years ago as an auxiliary port but has now become the principal port. Haldia too has its problems even though it lies just below the Balari bar, long the troublesome governing bar in navigating the Hooghly to Calcutta, which is to be subjected to a major capital dredging cut. Even with Haldia, Sagar Island, at the mouth of the Hooghly is being used as a lighterage point for vessels seeking to visit Calcutta.

Round the world, river ports have tended to migrate towards the sea. London is a classic example. Calcutta is another. Its future lies in becoming a major port for inter-modal exchange, handling smaller ocean going vessels but more and more barges and coasters, reliving its earlier role as the focal point at the head of a great system of inland and coastal waterways with an ocean interface.

The preservation of Calcutta port and its resuscitation in a dynamic new role is entirely compatible with India's interests and the larger development of the eastern waters.

Meanwhile, the problem of erosion along the right bank of the Ganga upstream and over a distance of 94 kms downstream of Farakka merits greater attention. This threatens the National Highway, Eastern Railway line and the Jangipur navigation (feeder) canal. Over 28,000 hectares of land had been eroded between 1931 and 1978 along this stretch and a further 1700 hectares was swallowed by the river between 1979 and 1987 rendering large numbers homeless and creating a problem of rehabilitation. A Rs.198 crore anti-erosion project was suggested by the Ganga Erosion Committee (at 1980 price). This is being implemented piecemeal by the West Bengal government and various Central authorities. This is not a satisfactory arrangement and a concerted programme of action is required.

III – THE BANGLADESH CONTENTION

The sharing of costs and benefits rather than the allocation of waters is the principal bone of contention in the matter of water resource development between Nepal and India. In the case of Bangladesh and India, however, the sharing of the lean season flows, especially of the Ganga, and augmentation below Farakka are the main points at issue. Of the overall annual discharge of 148 m ha m (1200 million acre-feet) of all Bangladesh rivers (to which local rainfall contributes 12.3 m ha m (100 m.a.f.) the headwater flows from India to 56 common rivers account for about 94 per cent. All but a tiny part of this huge discharge is contributed by the Brahmaputra, Ganga and Meghna in the proportion of 5:4:1. The flow is highly seasonal, about 80 per cent occurring during the monsoon months, causing floods with peak discharges rising to as much as 141,560 cumecs (five million cusecs) while there is a graduated insufficiency of water from January to May. It is during this 150 day lean period, Bangladesh protests, that excessive abstractions by India, especially from the Ganga at Farakka but on certain other rivers upstream as well, has created problems with regard to water availability for irrigation, salinity control (against tidal ingress), navigation, fisheries, and sustenance of the mangrove forests of the Sunderbans. At the other end of the scale, India is accused of not being sufficiently cooperative with regard to flood control.

THE PAKISTAN PERIOD

Discussions on the Farakka Barrage commenced in October 1951, with a letter from the Government of Pakistan querying the project, and followed a tortuous course thereafter. Pakistan expressed apprehensions about the impact of these projects on its eastern wing while India showed concern over the implications of East Pakistan's Ganges-Kobadak project, which made exaggerated claims to prior or prospective water uses, and the Karnaphuli hydel project which it was feared might submergence Indian territory in Mirozam.

On March 17, 1956, India denounced the Barcelona Convention on the Regime of Navigable Waterways of International Concern in a letter to the UN Secretary General. Article 10 of the Barcelona Statute provides that "Each state is bound, on the one hand, to refrain from all measures likely to prejudice the navigability of the (international) waterway, or to reduce the facilities for navigation and, on the other hand, to take as rapidly as possible all necessary steps for removing any obstacles and dangers which may occur to navigation". Pakistan protested on the ground that the Indian action was intended to enable it to proceed with the Farakka project unmindful of its consequences in East Pakistan. The Indian response was that this apprehension was unfounded and that the inland navigation purposes of the Barcelona Convention had been superseded by GATT (Abbas, 1982). The Indian contention was not only unconvincing but was seen as a setback to Nepal's dream of "Free access to the sea" (Sharma C.K. 1983). More than that, it revealed the lack of thought or comprehension of the role of inland navigation, communications and transit in the integration and development of India's Northeast.

Pakistan proposed the intervention of an agreed U.N. body to assist in the cooperative development of the eastern rivers, presumably with the World Bank's good offices with regard to the Indus waters in mind. But India was not to be persuaded. It did however agree to initiate expert level meetings in the course of which it announced commencement of construction of the Farakka Barrage. India sought ever more data and clarifications while Pakistan kept urging upgradation of the talks to a political level. Among the clarifications India asked for was the reason why Pakistan had discontinued use of Ganga discharge data gathered over decades at Hardinge Bridge in East Pakistan in favour of readings at a completely new site at Paksey, further downstream, which entailed a complicated and controversial reconstruction of a new time series by extrapolating and interpreting Hardinge Bridge readings. This was linked to a protracted argument about the quantum of regeneration between Farakka and Hardinge Bridge which India assessed as between 283 to 425 cumecs (10,000 to 15,000 cusecs) which the Pakistanis felt was exaggerated. Five expert level meetings (1962-68) were followed by five Secretaries level meetings (1968 to July 1970) with a further meeting scheduled to consider the quantum of water to be supplied to Pakistan below Farakka and to resolve other outstanding issues. That meeting never took place. The liberation of Bangladesh intervened.

Meanwhile, during this long series of negotiations, Pakistan's statement of requirements for its own irrigation projects kept growing in scope from 100 cumecs (3500 cusecs) in 1961 to 1642 cumecs (58,000 cusecs) by the end of the last round, an investigations proceeded and new possibilities were envisaged. India questioned the technical and irrigability aspects of the Pakistani proposals and concluded that it was totally unreasonable and unrealistic that the lower riparian should lay claim to the entire lean season flow of the Ganga to service a fraction of the irrigable area and population in India with an irrigation intensity of 210 per cent (Mathrani, 1969/1986). The Indian position was summed up by the Indian Irrigation Secretary leading to Indian delegation to the 1970 talks in Islamabad: "Our dependence on the waters of the Ganga is so overwhelming that whatever portion of it we may forego will involve a sacrifice on our part. Before we agree to a sacrifice of this nature, it is but just that we should know what the extent of sacrifice should be and how it can be justified, having in view the importance of the Ganga to India and of the Padma to Pakistan" (Chari, 1970).

Another reason suggested by Indian publicists for what were seen as no more than propagandist machinations over Farakka was Pakistan's need to invent as emotional an issue for East Pakistan, vis-à-vis India as Kashmir was for West Pakistan (Rangaswami, 1969). The idea that the Ganga might ever run short of water had also quite genuinely not occurred to most Indians, such being the inspirational power of that river. Bangladesh nationalists admitted a Kashmir factor in reverse: Pakistan was soft-pedalling the Farakka issue in order not to prejudice the gains it sought in Kashmir which was also simultaneously the subject of intense negotiation with India.

Differences had also surfaced during the early years on other issues. Pakistan felt rebuffed when its requests for information on Indian projects that might abstract Ganga water higher up the basin, as on the Kosi and Gandak, were not answered to its satisfaction. A Ganga Barrage below Hardinge Bridge and, at one time, even a dam on the river coupled with a Brahmaputra storage dam just below the confluence of the two rivers had been mooted in Dhaka. The UN (Krug) Mission that visited East Pakistan primarily to study the severe floods of 1954, 1955 and 1956 found these propositions infeasible and advised against them (UN Technical Assistance Mission Report, 1957). A revised Ganga barrage proposal submitted by Pakistan in 1969 met with Indian objections to its back-water effects on India. On the Teesta too, a pre-partition scheme for a dam upstream and a barrage in Jalpaiguri district (now in India) to irrigate areas in both Bengals was abandoned. Both sides prepared to develop separate schemes, sacrificing optimality and economy for independent control of the truncated parts.

NEW CLIMATE RESULTS IN 1977 AGREEMENT

The birth of Bangladesh held out brief hope of a new beginning. An Indo-Bangladesh Treaty of Friendship, Cooperation and Peace was signed on March 19, 1972. Pursuant to that and the joint declaration of the Two prime ministers, the Indo-Bangladesh Joint Rivers Commission (JRC) was established. The preamble to its status spoke of the desire of the two parties to work together "in harnessing the rivers common to both countries for the benefit of the peoples of the two countries" (Indo-Bangladesh JRC Statute, 1973). Priority areas for cooperation were identified but Bangladesh's plea that it would be useful to have a full time secretariat for the JRC with expert backing was not favoured by India.

The Farakka Barrage and the Feeder Canal for diverting Ganga waters into the Bhagirathi were by now ready and India started pressing for trial running of the channel. B.M. Abbas records the brief he was given as leader of the Bangladesh delegation in the negotiations that followed. Bangladesh expected at least 1132 cumecs (40,000 cusecs) in any sharing of the lean flows of the Ganga at Farakka out of the 1598 cumecs (55,000 cusecs) available on a basis of 75 per cent dependability. To use this water, Bangladesh proposed to construct a Ganga barrage within its territory with a pond level that ensured avoidance of any submergence in India. Further, it reserved the right to seek reasonable compensation for any loss as a result of water sharing, whether through financial assistance from India in executing its barrage of for "any other replacement works that might be necessary". The terminology seemed faintly to echo the Indus Treaty.

The two sides agreed to a 41 day test-run of the Farakka Feeder on the basis of a certain schedule from April 21 to May 31, 1975. The repercussions if ay on Bangladesh were to be monitored. India, however, continued to run the Feeder after May 31 and Bangladesh protested at the onset of the next lean season in January, 1976. The acrimony this generated, especially after the assassination of Sheikh Mujibur Rehman and the ensuing down-turn in Indo-Bangladesh relations, was soon politically internalized on both sides. Maulana Bhashani, the National Awami Party leader, organized a long march on Farakka, and Bangladesh went to the United Nations. This produced no result (as all upper and lower riparians divided within the General Assembly), but definitely embarrassed India. The consensus resolution adopted recognized the urgency of the question, urged ministerial negotiations, called for establishment of an atmosphere conducive to talks, asked the parties to give due consideration to the most appropriate ways of utilizing the capacity of the U.N. system, and got the two sides to reaffirm their adherence to the Declaration of Principles of International Law concerning Friendly Relations and Cooperation among States in accordance with the U.N. Charter in settling their disputes (Abbas 1982).

Bangladesh's protests and complaints about Farakka rested on the alleged adverse repercussions on its economy. India found its claims, including that of desertification, to be excessive and unsupported by evidence gleaned from the 100 kilometres below Farakka along which the Ganga is either a wholly Indian or boundary river. Bangladesh had its own version. This was supplemented by an elaborate "Special Studies" funded by the World Bank and produced by the Bangladesh Government in collaboration with a U.S. firm, International Engineering Company Ltd. Though classified, those with access to it concluded that the operation of the Farakka Barrage did cause damage to Bangladesh in 1976 and 1977. whereas the Bangladesh Government "exaggerated the extent, seriousness and, in some cases, the nature of the damage ... the Government of India under-estimated the damage". Some questions remained unresolved on account of the complexities involved resulting in "technical uncertainty providing a "freedom of movement' to political dispute" (Crow, 1980).

The election of the Janata Government in India brought about an improvement in Indo-Bangladesh relations and on September 30, 1977 the two sides initialed an Agreement on Sharing of the Ganga Waters at Farakka and on Augmenting its Flows. Ministerial signatures followed at Dhaka on November 5, 1977. This was something of a breakthrough. The accord defined the lean season as the 150 day period from January 1 to May 31 and allocated the flows below Farakka over 10-day segment with an understanding that during the leanest period between April 21-30, when the Ganga discharge troughs at 1158 cumecs (55,000 cusecs) at Farakka, India would divert no more than 20,500 cusecs (580 cumecs) and permit 34,500 cusecs (977 cumecs) to flow to Bangladesh. Should however there be unusually low flows below 80 per cent of the assumed values in any 10-day period,

India guaranteed Bangladesh 80 per cent of its stipulated share. The Agreement provided that the JRC would meanwhile investigate and study proposals that may be made by either relating to augmentation of the dry season flow of the Ganga with a view to finding an "economical and feasible" solution. The JRCF was to submit its recommendation within three years from the Agreement would be reviewed. The accord however had a life of five years, subsequent to renewal by mutual agreement (Verghese, 1978). The Agreement was to be implemented in good faith and included side-letters stipulating that augmentation proposals "do not exclude any scheme or schemes for building storages in the upper reaches of the Ganges in Nepal".

AUGMENTATION PROPOSALS

The two sides set to work on their augmentation proposals which were exchanged in March 1978. The overall lean season deficit at Farakka had earlier been identified as being of the order of 923,645 ha m (7.5 million acre feet). This was now found to have undergone considerable upward revision with Bangladesh taking account of present and future irrigation needs as well as industrial, municipal, navigational ecological and other requirements from Nepalese storages and India making a correspondingly large bid for transfer of waters from the Brahmaputra through a gigantic link canal from Jogighopa in Assam across northern Bangladesh to a point above Farakka. Bamgladesh also proposed a canal along the Terai "conveying water from the Gandak and Kosi to augment the dry season flows of the Mahananda in West Bengal in India and the Korotoya in Bangladesh as well. Such a waterway and its connecting route through India and Bangladesh thus created for increased dry seasons flows could also serve as an international navigational water route" (Power, Water and Flood Control Ministry, Bangladesh, March 1978).

Unfortunately the response of each country to the augmentation package put forward by the other was negative. Desultory exchanges continued even as the 1977 Agreement began to run out. A meeting between President Ershad and Indira Gandhi paved the way for a further interim agreement for 18 months (covering the dry seasons of 1983 and 1984) on the basis of a revised sharing formula with marginal differences in allocation but with only a promise of consultation and no guarantee of a minimal 80 per cent allocation should assumed flows dip abnormally (October 7, 1982).

Negotiations on augmentation were revived and in October and December 1983 India and then Bangladesh presented their "Updated Proposals" following which they exchanged their comments on these in February 1984 (Indo-Bangladesh Joint Rivers Commission, May 1985). Bangladesh's updated proposal entailed the construction of 12 dams in Nepal including storages at Chisapani (Karnali), Kali Gandaki I and II, Trisul Ganga, Seti, Sapt Kosi (Kosi High Dam), and Pancheshwar (on the Mahakali/Sharda). The proposal claimed that it would be technically feasible to raise the height of the seven dams named to augment dry season flows at Farakka 7 m ha m (70,000 million cubic metres). Given the existing dry season flow at Farakka of 2.6 m ha m and releases from existing and other proposed storages in Nepal and India within the Ganga basin, there would be a total dry season availability of 19.55 m ha m as against a requirement of 18.97 m ha m overall made up of 5.5 m ha m for Bangladesh, 2.9 m ha m for Nepal and 10.57 m ha m for India, inclusive of 1.47 m ha m for flushing Calcutta port. It was settled that 5.2 million hectares of south-west Bangladesh is dependent on the Ganga and that existing and planned irrigation developments in the region would cover 3.2 million hectares. The cost of the seven specified high dam sin Nepal was estimated at $ 17.1 billion.

The Indian Updated Proposal in brief comprised two parts. First, a barrage across the Brahmaputra at Jogighopa in Assam combined with a 324 kilometre long link canal across Bangladesh to a point just above Farakka in West Bengal. The link canal would have a capacity of 2832 cumecs (100,000 cusecs) at its head and would not only augment the lean season flows of the Ganga at Farakka to meet the requirements of both countries, but also irrigate some million hectares en route in northern Bangladesh and improve navigation, fish culture and groundwater supplies in the dry 'V' between the Brahmaputra (Jamuna) and the Ganga in that country even while providing for some irrigation in India as well. The canal would also provide a direct navigation link between West Bengal and Assam.

The second phase of the Indian proposal envisaged the construction of three dams. The first on the Dihang, the main stem of the Brahmaputra in Arunachal Pradesh (with a net storage of 35.5 billion cubic metres and an installed generating capacity of 20,000 MW); the second on the Subansiri, also in Arunachal Pradesh (10 billion cubic metres of net storage and 4800 MW); and the Third at Tipaimukh on the Barak, on the Mizoram-Manipur border (nine billion cubic metres of net storage and 1500 MW). The Dihang and Subansiri dams were estimated to lower the flood peak in Bangladesh by some 1.3 m while the Tipaimukh dam would make a significant contribution towards mitigating floods in the Meghna basin in Bangladesh. India would be in a position to offer large blocks of cheap power to Bangladesh. The cost of this package was placed at Rs.16,196 crores. And once the Dihang and Subansiri storages were commissioned, the diversion from the Brahmaputra would be limited to the monsoon surplus without any dimunition of its dry season flows.

RIVAL VETOES VITIATE TALKS

As mentioned earlier, India virtually vetoed the Bangladesh proposal not only on techno-economic considerations but on the ground that it could beneficially use all available Ganga storage in Nepal and India, whereas the far larger flows of the Brahmaputra with a smaller land surface and population dependent on it were untapped and running waste to sea. Bangladesh in turn vetoed the Indian plan on techno-political grounds. It was said to go beyond the terms of reference of the JRC in not fully exploiting the available and sufficient waters of the Ganga and, instead, sought to harness and divert the flows of a totally different river basin whose waters were not in super-abundance and would barely meet the legitimate needs of its own basin.

The official Indian critique of the Bangladesh proposal would have it that the maximum additional storage in Nepal, realistically calculated, would not yield more than 25 billion cubic metres. All of this would be required for uses in Nepal and India and would therefore not be available for uses below Farakka. Bangladesh had raised the proposed height of the seven Nepal dams it specified to rank them among the very highest structures in the world. This it had done without any firm data or estimate of submergence and displacement costs and their acceptability to Nepal. Moreover, it had pegged its own irrigation demand at an intensity far greater than it would allow for India despite the higher rainfall in the Ganga-dependent area of Bangladesh which would make such excessive watering counter-productive. The Bangladesh updated proposal would allow India only 0.15 units of water per unit of irrigable area or just about a twelfth of what it was claiming for itself. The Indian view was that the Ganga-Brahmaputra-Meghna constitutes "one single system" within which water availability per capita in the Brahmaputra-Meghna "sub-basins" was four to 12 times that in the Ganga sub-basin. On the principle of equitable utilization India said it claimed the predominant share of the lean flows of the Ganga of which it was the major riparian, accounting for 99 per cent of the catchment area, 94 per cent of the population and 94.5 per cent of the area dependent on its water in relation to Bangladesh.

On the contrary, Bangladesh estimated its own present and planned dry season uses of Brahmaputra water at 5100 cumecs (180,000 cusecs) for irrigation alone. This wuld exceed the lean flows of the river which dipped to 3965 cumecs in February-March. Even with storages on the Dihang and Subansiri there would be no dry season augmentation of the Brahmaputra at Bahadurabad (in Bangladesh), but rather a reduction by almost a third should what was mistakenly stated to be an Indian proposal to irrigate 3.5 million hectares in Assam and Arunachal be implemented. This, it was said, was unacceptable since half the population of Bangladesh is heavily dependent on the waters of the Brahmaputra and 70 per cent of the country's rice and 65 per cent of its jute is grown in the region served by the river. It seemed India was seeking to transfer the deficit in the Ganga basin to the Brahmaputra basin, whereas the Brahmaputra itself was in need of augmentation in the dry season. Further, India's proposed net diversion through the Brahmaputra-Ganga link canal would fall far short of south-west Bangladesh's dry season requirement of 4248 cumecs (150,000 cusecs) for agriculture, navigation, water supplies, etcetera.

Bangladesh was clearly labouring under a misunderstanding as India had never proposed to irrigate 3.5 million hectares (net or gross) in Assam and Arunachal under schemes listed in its Updated Proposal. In fact the net area sown in these two States is about 2.8 million hectares of which 600,000 hectares were already irrigated at the time, while another 350,000 hectares are under shifting cultivation. Moreover, about 160,000 hectares of the net area sown in Assam lies in the Barak basin.

Bangladesh also listed a number of technical and other objections to the Link Canal. This would be 266 metres wide in Assam and narrow down to 100 metres at its outfall above Farakka, with a uniform depth of 9.1 metres throughout. It would require much cutting and filling in accordance with the intervening terrain. It claimed that such a huge diversion through a gigantic 324 kilometre long canal (125 kms in Bangladesh) running against the natural gradient was unparalleled. Cross drainage would be extremely difficult and chancy. The Indian proposal for "level crossings" with gates to pass four major north-south rivers, including the Teesta, was to invite siltation and all manner of other troubles. The Link Canal would impede drainage and accentuate flooding over 1.09 million hectares and condemn 97,000 hectares of fertile land in northwestern Bangladesh to permanent waterlogging. Diversion of the dry flows of the Brahmaputra into the Link Canal would render the river unable to serve its many distributaries in Bangladesh. This would have serious implications for groundwater recharge, navigation and fisheries in entire region. Agriculture would suffer. Reduced Brahmaputra flows would increase salinity in a number of southern districts on account of tidal ingress, affecting 280,000 hectares of agricultural land. The feeder navigation routes to the ports of Chittagong and Chalna would be affected. The river morphology and ecology of the region would be adversely affected and the Sunderbans mangroves would suffer with the diminution of freshwater supplies which in turn would affect fishing and forest-based industry, water quality and public health.

To add to all these woes, the Link Canal would divide the country into two. It would require acquisition of 256,750 hectares of land and displace a population of over a million people. Finally, the storage dams proposed would be infeasible on account of seismic risk and would provide virtually no flood moderation. In sum, the financial, ecological and human cost of the Indian proposal would be prohibitive. The package was dismissed as disastrous.

JOINT APPROACH TO NEPAL

With the approaching expiry of the 1977 Agreement, the water sharing accord was given an ad hoc extension with this difference that the guarantee of 80 per cent of the flow values earlier allocated to Bangladesh was omitted.

In pursuance of the memorandum of Understanding signed by President Ershad and Mrs. Gandhi on November 7, 1982, the JRC set to work to evolve a mutually agreed formula for augmenting the lean season flows of the Ganga in Farakka. The emphatic rejection of the other's updated proposal by either side confirmed the deadlock. The Brahmaputra-Ganga Link Canal had by now become anathema in Bangladesh kept insisting that the only way to establish the feasibility of its proposal would be for both sides to approach Nepal for data and cooperation with regard to storage dams in that country. India continued to demur, insisting on bilateralism and opposing any multilateral approach to a resolution of what it perceived to be an issue exclusively between itself and Dhaka. It was already negotiating with Nepal on a number of projects of Indo-Nepal benefit and expanding this into a triangular or multilateral discussion would, in its judgement, only confuse and complicate matters as the Indo-Nepal and Indo-Bangladesh issues were distinct and separate. Bangladesh, however kept harking back to the reference to Nepal storages in the exchange of letters accompanying the Memorandum of Agreement of 1977 and saw no other way to proceed. It seemed for while that Bangladesh might be willing to consider a variant of the Indian Brahmaputra-Ganga link were these structures to be constructed wholly within its own territory. An Indian expression of interest in this proposition as parallelling its own earlier proposal in this regard was however sufficient for it to "flounder" as a section of the Bangladeshi leadership feared a backlash at home if the government was seen to be going in principle with something that it had hitherto strenuously rejected (Crow and Lindquist, October 31, 1989). The Bangladesh Water Resources Minister, Mr. Obaidullah Khan, resigned some months later. The discussions within the JRC remained stalemated.

The then Indian Prime Minister Mr Rajiv Gandhi sought to end the impasse soon after assuming office and progress was registered in discussions with President Ershad at the Commonwealth Heads of Government Conference at Nassau in October 1985. The outcome was a Memorandum of Understanding signed the following month extending over a three year period. It provided for continued sharing of the lean season flow of the Ganga below Farakka, more or less on the 1982 basis. The MOU, details of which were not formally published, covered "river waters common to India and Bangladesh" and provided for a joint study of alternatives for sharing and augmentation (Crow and Lindquist, 1989). This was clearly a wider charter. In order to by-pass old tangles, Bangladesh also proposed a new forum. Thus was created the Joint Committee of Experts (JCE), alongside the JRC, headed by the two Irrigation Secretaries, with a life of 12 months. The idea of augmentation from the Brahmaputra was discussed and found technically feasible, subject to further studies, the Bangladesh Irrigation Minister, Mr. Anisul Islam Mahmud informally informed his counterpart that Bangladesh would be willing to consider a barrage across the Brahmaputra at Bahadurabad with a canal linking this to the Ganges near Hardinge Bridge.

Meanwhile, India finally agreed that the JCE might approach Nepal for the limited purpose of eliciting data on the feasibility of augmenting lean season flows at Farakka from storages in Nepal. If this was found infeasible then further discussions on this matter would necessary have to remain bilateral. The Indian and Bangladesh Resource Secretaries accordingly visited Kathmandu in November 1986 to meet their counterparts. The Nepalese officials recalled their country's commitment to regional cooperation and wanted to know the extent of Nepal's participation in and benefit from the proposed storage dams. They were not concerned about augmentation at Farakka and found the JCE mechanism unsuited to their purpose. Secondly, - though this was not stated at the time – they wondered why only the listed dams and other projects were being proposed, presumably indicating that there could be other priorities and that they might well prefer a basin approach to random schemes. Thirdly, they sought time to respond to the request for data. The Indo-Bangladesh delegates however wished to report back to their leaders at the forthcoming SAARC summit in Bangalore a few days hence when the term of the JCE was also due to expire. The visitors promised to send a more detailed statement elucidating Nepal's benefit and setting out the terms of reference within which they sought Nepal's preliminary response and departed. India was responsible for preparing such a note but baulked at actually doing so. Despite an extension of the JCE's term, no further communication was sent to Nepal.

NEW PREFERENCE FOR OVERALL SHARING

Apart from other reasons for this loss of interest in trilateral discussions, Bangladesh's attitude apparently underwent a change. The Kathmandu visit had a somewhat chilling effect on Dhaka. It brought home realization that Nepal had its own ideas, problems and priorities and that previous Indian cautions against assuming Nepal's instant readiness to fall in with Bangladesh's very ambitious plans for damming all its rivers was not just bluff. Augmentation also suddenly appeared to be an iffy question, distant and dependent on many factors including vast international funding. Thus it might take 20 to 30 years before any augmentation materialized whereas Bangladesh's needs were here and now.

The Indo-Bangladesh Memorandum of Understanding November 1985 had extended the ad hoc sharing of the lean season flows of the Ganga below Farakka until June 1988, with India agreeing to let down 977 cumecs (34,500 cusecs) during the leanest 10-day segment at the end of April. If these supplies, or even a larger quantum were to be effectively and beneficially used, Bangladesh would need to build a Ganga barrage somewhere below Hardinge Bridge to pond up the river within embankments in order to divert water into the moribund Gorai spill channel by gravity flow for irrigation, groundwater recharge and salinity control in the southwest region. In order to design the structures that would have to be built on the Ganga and Gorai, it would need to know the precise quantum of water it could expect from India. Without some understanding on this no international funding would be forthcoming either.

It is against this background that an influential section of opinion within Bangladesh argued the case for separating immediate lean season sharing of the

Ganga, a riparian right, from future augmentation in whatever degree, which could only be a matter of goodwill and political understanding. The proponents of this view advocated a Ganga barrage below. Hardinge Bridge to divert sufficient headwater supplies into the Gorai in order to control salinity along the Khulna-Bhola axis, irrigate a million hectares of Ganga-dependent farmland in the south-western region during the critical moisture-stress weeks of April, and use the ground water recharge to extend the area under irrigation through conjunctive pumping (Verghese, March 1987).

The proposed Ganga barrage, headworks, regulatory structures on the Gorai, canals, afflux bunds, and other appurtenant works might take up to 12 years to complete and was to be followed by a similar barrage on the Brahmaputra. A possible third phase envisaged some transfer of water within Bangladesh itself from the Brahmaputra barrage to the Ganga barrage through some old spill channels and inter-connecting links, together with such augmentation of Ganga flows below Farakka as might occur in course of time.

According to informed observers, those advocating certainty in immediate sharing as a basis for firm planning, design and investment decisions were prepared to settle for 25,000 or even 20,000 cusecs of the lean season flow of the Ganga which, with regeneration, would meet all targeted requirements in the southwest region. This however was contingent on the 3,964 cumec (140,000 cusec) lean season flow of the Brahmaputra being similarly divided. India was to be allocated 25 per cent of the lean flows from Bangladesh a similar quantum for agricultural and other beneficial uses, with the remaining half being allowed to flow into the sea primarily to maintain the salinity balance in the southeast region and on other ecological considerations. Likewise, there could be a 50:50 sharing arrangement in respect of all or clusters of the remaining 54 common rivers, (excluding the Teesta on which separate negotiations were in progress), and the Barak-Meghna.

BANGLADESH NATIONAL WATER PLAN

Thinking on these lines was influenced by the National Water Plan, 1985-2005, that had just been submitted to the Bangladesh government (Master Plan Organisation, December 1986). This was prepared with the aid of international consultants under the guidance of the Ministry of Irrigation, Water Development and Flood Control in cooperation with the UNDP and World Bank.

The National Water Plan makes a sober appraisal of needs and possibilities and has none of the extravagant over-statement to be found in Bangladesh's 1983 Updated Proposal. For the purpose of this study, the country was divided into five planning regions: northwest (Ganga, Mahananda, Teesta etc.), northeast (Meghna-Brahmaputra), southeast (Meghna-Karnaphuli), south-central (Ganga-Brahmaputra) and southwest (Ganga). These regions were further broken down into 60 planning areas. As far as the southwest region is concerned the relevant figures are as follows (in million hectares) with the combined SW and SC totals in brackets: net cultivated area, 1.67 (2.70); land suited for irrigation, 1.28 (2.00); water availability, 1.21 (1.84); presently irrigated, 0.27 (0.36); and potential for development, 0.94 (1.48). Taking the country as a whole, the NWP estimated that water was available to irrigate 91 per cent of the land suited for irrigation. Certain active flood plain areas were excluded in these calculations.

The NWP envisages irrigation of 72 per cent of the irrigable area of 6.90 million hectares by 2005 using both surface and ground water. This figure is expected to go up to 91 per cent thereafter with fill development of the three main rivers with the construction of barrages and large gravity schemes. As an immediate strategy, while barrages are under investigation and planning, small diversions of the large rivers into their distributaries advocated through pumping and by dredging offtakes as a means of quickly enlarging the area under irrigation at relatively modest cost. During the lean season, it is suggested that 40 per cent of stream flows and all static waters be reserved for fisheries and navigation. The importance of electrical and diesel energy for pumping and of in situ storage are emphasized. According to the NWP, "the groundwater reservoir possesses the single major potential within Bangladesh to store excess monsoon rain and floodwater for use during the dry season". A 10 per cent improvement in irrigation efficiency is considered possible by optimizing channel layouts and lining to save 1,180 million cubic metres of water. Water conservation by amending cropping patterns and the crop calendar is also advocated.

The NWP prescribes storage to augment main river stream flows in the lean season, especially in the Ganga where reductions have been observed after the commencement of Farakka withdrawals. Augmentation of the Ganga to feed the Gorai and other moribund distributaries is found to be very necessary to control salinity ingress. The problem is to achieve critically needed industrial water quality in the southwest without greatly sacrificing agricultural development.

The investments proposed under NWP up to 2005, excluding main river barrages, is estimated to cost $ 6.6 billion in 1986 prices. It recommends pre-investment works leading to the development of barrages on the Ganga and Brahmaputra early in the Third Five Year Plan (1985-90). Additional water supplies made available as a result of the Ganga barrage would render it possible to expand irrigation in the southwest from just 18 per cent to 66 per cent of the irrigable area and to reduce salinity around Khulna and in the smaller rivers and the shallow aquifer in that region to tolerable levels. Significant storage potentials to resolve still longer term problems are seen to exist in the upper catchments of the Ganga and Brahmaputra basins in Nepal, Bhutan, India and China.

The Bangladesh water sharing formula mooted in 1987 met with considerable opposition from domestic critics and was never pressed. Abandonment of Ganga augmentation was strongly resisted. India too, though approached on this basis, did not respond to informal soundings in a manner that might have strengthened the hands of those in Dhaka who wished to explore this avenue. Unofficially it was hinted that a permanent sharing arrangement could be discussed provided Bangladesh clearly gave up any claims to augmentation in the future. It could not be allowed two bites at the cherry.

INDIA UNWILLING TO FOREGO AUGMENTATION

In the upshot, the JCE and the interim agreement for sharing the lean season flows of the Ganga that had continued in one form or other since 1976, lapsed at the end of December 1988. The 1989 dry season opened without any agreed schedule of releases below Farakka, leaving it to India to determine what amount of water it would divert into the Bhagirathi up to the full 1,132 cumec capacity of the Farakka Feeder. Presumably India did graduate its withdrawals to coincide with actual availability so as to ensure Bangladesh sufficient supplies to meet its reasonable requirements. There was unhappiness in Dhaka over this situation but no public protest despite reports of drought in late April after which flows improve.

Mr Rajiv Gandhi informed Parliament in the summer of 1988 that India would be compelled to take "a tough line" if Bangladesh merely moved from one temporary sharing agreement to another without seriously discussing a permanent settlement. It is perhaps in pursuance of this directive that no ad hoc sharing agreement was concluded for 1989. Instead, even the interim sharing agreement on the Teesta was permitted to lapse. Both countries are constructing Teesta barrages on their side of the border and it would appear that whoever completes its project first will seek to establish claims to prior appropriation. Another controversy is in store here. Similarly, no progress has been achieved in resolving issues pertaining to sharing of any other of the small border rivers flowing into Bangladesh from India's Northeast.

On one reading, it would now seem that India is more interested in Brahmaputra-Ganga augmentation than in merely sharing the lean season flow of the Ganga. Seasonal and absolute water shortages are beginning to be felt in many sub-basins of the Ganga and in many other river basins such as the Ravi-Beas-Sutlej, Cauvery, Krishna and so on. The Godavari and Mahanadi have some residual long term surpluses beyond their basin requirements. This is what the National Water Development Agency is planning to divert southwards under the National Perspective Plan.

This apart, the only true long-term sub-continental surplus lies in the Northeast, in the Brahmaputra and Barak basins, which account for a third of the entire Indian run-off. There are only minimal uses for the waters of the Brahmaputra in the relatively small Assam Valley which receives high rainfall and possesses considerable groundwater resources, while topography permits little utilization in Arunachal Pradesh, Nagaland and Meghalaya. The monsoon surplus of the Brahmaputra system stored behind a series of dams is therefore seen not merely as a vast storehouse of energy but as a standby reservoir to meet at least some of the future needs of a water-short Indian heartland without any prejudice to Bangladesh's requirements. It is this larger facet of national augmentation rather than merely augmenting the lean season flows of the Ganga to make good the current deficit below Farakka that is perhaps beginning to loom large in the new policy perspective.

DEADLOCK DEEPENS WITH FLOODS

Indo-Bangladesh relations took a beating in 1988 on another account when there was an unprecedented 100-year return flood in the Brahmaputra and a 50-year return flood in the Meghna that devastated both Assam and Bangladesh. In Bangladesh, the Brahmaputra, Ganga and Meghna peaked around the same time causing the Meghna to back up into the Sylhet depression as normally happens in this kind of situation. Although the Ganga flood was not as severe as in 1987, which was also a bad year, the 1988 flood was unprecedented with almost two-thirds of Bangladesh being submerged. The situation was aggravated by heavy local rains and high tides which accentuated drainage congestion and greatly extended the retention time of the spill. The combination was devastating and the loss of crops, livestock, property and infrastructure grievously high, with attendant problems of public health, reconstruction and restoration of productive employment. As usual though, residual flood moisture over an extensive area yielded a richer harvest from the ensuing winter crop.

In 1988 the Brahmaputra peaked on August 30 with a discharge of 99,500 cumecs and the Ganga three days later with a discharge of 72,300 cumecs. The Meghna had peaked earlier on August 11 with a discharge of 19,800 cumecs. The agony of Bangladesh was real and India was among the first of a large number of nations that rushed to its aid. However, many public statements and media comments appeared to hold India and the Farakka Barrage in particular responsible for the deluge. The Indian Air Force helicopter rescue and relief mission in Dhaka was suddenly told that it was no longer required, provoking a reaction in India.

Bangladesh mounted an international campaign calling for regional cooperation in solving its flood problem which originates outside its own boundaries. President Ershad visited India for talks with Mr Rajiv Gandhi and there were similar high-level missions to Kathmandu, Thimphu and Beijing. Various international agencies and industrially advanced nations were addressed to help find and implement a permanent solution.

The Ganga in 1988 registered a lower peak value than in 1987 "and as such Farakka cannot be considered as a cause of the 1988 flood". Nor some small research experiments conducted by Indian scientists during the 1987 drought artificially to augment glacier melt in a couple of places in the western Himalaya (Shahjahan, February 1989). The Brahmaputra and Meghna were the major offenders in 1988.

The fact is that floods in Bangladesh can certainly be mitigated but simply cannot be eliminated, Bangladesh has been built by the floods and occupies the greatest delta in the world that discharges a uniquely large volume of flood waters through a densely occupied flood-plain. A third of this lies below the high tide level which is whipped up to greater heights as a result of monsoon storm surges. This combination admits of no absolute flood control. Apart from flood mitigation measures, the answer lies in better flood management and planning to live with a certain level of inundation which is or could be rendered beneficial.

What then is the solution? Soil conservation and catchment area treatment in India, Nepal and Bhutan would help. Also improved flood and flood-plain flood management within Bangladesh itself with better flood forecasting and early warning systems from all these countries and China, but especially India. Augmented flood-plain storages in existing depressions could provide useful relief. However, a massive 20-year, $ 6 billion comprehensive river embankment project recommended by the UNDP (May 1989) may not be cost-effect or viable in the long run. Others have independently expressed skepticism about such an approach including an U.S. team which favours simpler "soft" flood-proofing measures and more data collection and research before environmentally costly heavy engineering solutions as Himalayan storages are taken up (Peter Rogers et al. April 1989). Mere flood-proofing without some effort to moderate flood peaks in turn may not suffice in a densely population flood plain like Bangladesh. Hence there would appear to be merit in multipurpose storages in the upper catchments to hold some of the monsoon flows and redistribute this over time for beneficial uses during the lean season while producing energy and assisting navigation as well. The average peak flows of the Ganga, Brahmaputra and Meghna amount to 14,1600 cumecs while the estimated 100 year return period peak is estimated by the Master Plan Organisation to be of the order of 169,000 cumecs. "A significant reduction in flooding in Bangladesh can be achieved if 10 per cent of these flows can be stored for about a month. Naturally this has to be done in the upper reaches by building reservoirs. Any other method is not going to work against the type of flood we had in the last two years" (Maniruzzaman Miah, February 1989).

The Indo-Bangladesh task force set up to examine all aspects of flood management and flood moderation in the wake of the 1988 flood reported some headway on short-term measures. India has been reluctant to provide Bangladesh all the very detailed data it seeks to develop a dynamic river flood routing model which it is engaged in setting up. According to one report, Bangladesh is developing this facility with World Bank assistance as part of a mathematical and physical model of the Brahmaputra. When completed, "it will be one of the world's most elaborate hydrological models and will allow planners to posit the full range of possible flow conditions and test simulated engineering works" (Kaye, February 1989). The Bangladeshis say they are willing jointly to operate and monitor this model along with Indian personnel in Dhaka. India is however wary of the implications of such a model being extended into the Indian catchment in complete detail as it fears this could be manipulated against its interests by third-powers who may gain access to it, especially in view of Bangladesh's recent efforts to internationalise the eastern waters question. Such apprehensions appear excessive but could in any case be obviated by appropriate safeguards.

International concern over the recurrence of catastrophic floods in Bangladesh was reflected in the Economic Declaration issued by the Group of Seven Summit in Paris on July 16, 1989: "We stress the urgent need for effective, coordinated action by the international community in support of the Government of Bangladesh in order to find solutions to this major problem which are technically, financially, economically and environmentally sound". The Summit noted the different studies on flood alleviation initiated by the U.S., France, Japan and the UNDP, and welcomed the World Bank's agreement to coordinate these efforts. An action plan to control floods in Bangladesh was discussed and broadly approved at a World Bank-sponsored meeting of the Bangladesh was discussed and broadly approved at a World Bank-sponsored meeting of the Bangladesh Aid Group consisting of 15 nations and 11 international funding and technical agencies held in London on December 11-12,1989. Envisaged is a series of pilot projects and studies costing $ 150 million as a first stage of a comprehensive programme leading to further investments totaling over $ 500 million. The action plan includes support for technical, socio-economic and environmental impact studies and entails measures to strengthen and extend embankments along the main rivers, improve drainage and water control, rehabilitate and construct coastal embankments against cyclones and tidal surges, town protection schemes (notably for Dhaka), strengthening the flood forecasting and early warning system, and development of a flood preparedness programme.

All these projects are intended to dovetail into Bangladesh's development programme and an integrated water management and irrigation system. It is noteworthy that all these proposals envisage measures that are to be undertaken wholly within Bangladesh. The one exception relates to a study of the northeast Sylhet region, "leading to a regional water management programme" implicitly with Indian collaboration which as proposed the Tipaimukh Dam to regulate the Barak/Meghna (World Bank News, December 14, 1989).

India should not ignore this global interest but rather would have much to gain by associating itself with what could grow into an internationally-aided effort of regional flood and water resource management.

POLITICAL PULLS AND PRESSURES

As in the case of Nepal, there is little doubt that the overall climate of political relations has a great bearing on the course of water-related negotiations between India and Bangladesh. The goodwill evident at the creation of Bangladesh was soon spent and relations soured. Bangladesh water diplomacy got caught up in internal politics with those favouring a more flexible and accommodating approach to India in the interests of a fair settlement fearful of being accused of selling out.

India's failure to this date to honour its commitment under the Indo-Bangladesh Boundary Agreement of 1974 to grant Bangladesh a 150 m-long "corridor" through Tin Bigha in perpetual lease that would give it access to two tiny enclaves, Dahagram and Agoropata, in Cooch Bihar, Jalpaiguri district, is indefensible despite the plea that the matter has been tangled in litigation. All the more so because India has absorbed South Berubari which was the quid pro quo. Even a subsequent understanding that the Indian commitment might be met by the construction of a fly-over or tunnel across Tin Bigha, an area no larger than a cricket field, has not been implemented. Inability to live up to a solemn treaty on such a trivial matter erodes India's credibility when it asks Bangladesh to take its word on such a spectacular projects as the Brahmaputra-Ganga Link and associated storage dams.

There is a dispute over rival claims to a newly-formed deltaic island, New Moore as India calls it, or South Talpatty as Bangladesh would describe it. The island, which is in India's possession, is at the mouth of the Raimangal River in the Sunderbans, which marks the international boundary. Disagreements on the basis of demarcating the maritime boundary between the two countries remain unresolved. How this is drawn will define Bangladesh's extended economic zone which is tightly sandwiched between the EEZs of India and Burma in the Bay of Bengal, Bangladesh sees possible satisfaction of its protein requirements from marine fisheries and the possibility of off-shore oil as strong reasons for warning to enlarge its EEZ.

The "infiltration" of land hungry peasants from Bangladesh into Northeastern India and West Bengal is protested by India and strenuously denied by Dhaka which has objected to Indian moves to build a barbed wire fence along the Assam-Bangladesh border. India has also expressed concern over the exodus of minorities to India following the proclamation of Bangladesh as an Islamic State. This has been compounded by the movement of Chakma refugees into Tripura and their reluctance to return home despite Bangladesh assurances regarding their safety and well-being. Recent legislation conferring local autonomy on the tribal people in the Chittagong Hill Tract has made no difference. Bangladesh had earlier accused India of giving aid and comfort to the Shanti Bahini insurgents, which the latter denies. The problem initially arose following settlement of tribal lands by "outsiders" who still remain and cannot now be ousted any more than they can be from Tripura.

Difficulties in promoting trade, transit and mutual economic cooperation between India and Bangladesh despite periodic negotiations have also caused frustration. Proposals with regard to joint ventures and complementary investments have stalled. Bangladesh's efforts to regionalize and internationalise the water issue have been thwarted by India. This is resented in Dhaka. Much will have to be done on both sides to improve the political climate so that mistrust yields to cooperation.

MYTH AND MISTRUST

On the eastern waters question too, each side has been put off by what it regards as the unreasonable and devious attitude of the other. Myths have been so long and so assiduously propagated by official negotiators that these have become realities in public perceptions making both sides prisoners of their own propaganda.

An objective analysis would suggest that over the years both sides have taken certain inflexible positions and made extravagant proposals and inflated claims without adequate technical, socio-economic or ecological data or sufficient regard for the other's reasonable needs. They have got locked into their own past rhetoric or perceptions, viewing enormously complex and diverse sets of propositions and aspirations in simplistic terms. Limited vision has precluded any meaningful consideration of potential tradeoffs. Mistrust has hardened and none has calculated the opportunity costs of delay.

Basically and ultimately, the eastern waters question, which includes water sharing and augmenting the lean flows of the Ganga as much as Indo-Nepal water resource development, is not just an engineering problem but a political question enveloping the long-term relationship between the co-riparians. The magnitudes, complexities, vast investments, huge populations, ecological implications, priorities and planning horizons involved are such, the gestation periods and consequences so great, and the linkages so numerous that only a genuine willingness to accept mutual interdependence can unlock the door to opportunity. To leave this task almost exclusively to engineers and avoid open and informed discussion on the subject, rendered the more difficult because of excessive data classification (at least in India), is self-defeating. The problem is by no means incapable of a solution that is just and fair to both sides.

AN INTERACTIVE WATER SYSTEM

It is not necessary to get bogged down in the technicality of whether or not the Ganga, Brahmaputra and Meghna constitute two or more watercourse systems or a single international drainage basin as under the Helsinki Rules. The fact is that they are interactive rivers, especially in Bangladesh where what might be regarded as distinctive drainage basins flow into a common terminus. The Teesta flowed into the Ganga until 1787 when, following a great flood, it migrated east and joined the Jamuna, at that time the less favoured arm of the Brahmaputra which preferred a more easterly course past Mymensingh through what is now known as the Old Brahmaputra channel. The vigour imparted to the Jamuna by the Teesta capture soon led to its becoming the principal channel of the Brahmaputra. This in turn stopped the eastward movement of Ganga which had abandoned the Bhagirathi-Hooghly, and pushed that river south. Although a Ganga distributary, the Baral, taking off near Rajshahi, falls into the Jamuna above Goalando Ghat where it joins the Ganga to become the Padma. The Old Brahmaputra spills into the Meghna at Bhairab Bazar, well above the confluence of the Padma with the Meghna just above Chandpur.

When the Padma is in spate, the waters of the Meghna back up well over a hundred kilometres to flood Sylhet depression which forms a vast detention reservoir. And when the Ganga and Jamuna (Brahmaputra) peak at the same time, that again aggravates the flood. These are significant interactions which cannot be ignored. Likewise, the Ganga and Brahmaputra have different seasonal rhythms. The Brahmaputra's flow troughs in February after which the river starts rising, whereas the Ganga's discharge is lowest during the last 10 days of April, two months later. This asymmetry immediately suggests the possibility of diverting Brahmaputra waters into the Ganga to meet critical shortfalls at this time.

Indeed, the idea of constructing barrages across the Brahmaputra and the Ganga within Bangladesh had been mooted in the mid-1950s and found subsequent expression from time to time in official and non-official literature. The 1987 debate within official circles in Bangladesh in the matter of trading future augmentation of the Ganga with immediate, firm, long-term agreements for sharing its lean season flows as well as that of the Brahmaputra, envisaged the construction of barrages on both rivers and a possible subsequent diversion of surplus flows from the Brahmaputra to the Ganga along certain spill channels and inter-connecting links. This admitted the principle of water transfer between the two rivers. The logic of this is inherent in the fact that the Ganga and Brahmaputra, respectively, carry 16 and 67 per cent of the total dry season flow of all rivers in Bangladesh between February and April (Khan, Hamidur Rahman August 1985). This is the unspoken logic of the National Water Plan as well.

EACH SIDE CAN DO WITH LESS

What quantum of Ganga supplies does each side say it requires below Farakka? India claims 1132 cumecs for flushing the Bhagirathi-Hooghly and for the preservation of Calcutta port. Bangladesh has defined its present requirements as 1558 cumecs (excluding regeneration). This is the minimum to which the low season flow dips on the basis of 75 per cent dependability, and that too only during only one ten-day segment between April 21-30. However, authoritative Bangladesh spokesmen have asserted the country's "right" to the entire "natural flow" of the Ganga during the dry season which has been defined as the 150-day period between January 1 to May 31 (Abbas, 1982). Bangladesh's future requirements are pitched even higher and West Bengal too seeks 425 cumecs from the Ganga for irrigation requirements.

On the other hand, the NWP suggests that Bangladesh can make do with its existing post-Farakka dry season availability (presumably based on the last MOU sharing formula) until 2005 to produce 27.5 million tonnes of grain nationally, after which reliance will have to be placed on the proposed Ganga and Brahmaputra barrages within the country, and any available augmentation from upper catchment storages thereafter.

The informal Ganga-Brahmaputra sharing plan that was advocated by a responsible section of Bangladesh officials and technical experts early in 1987 stemmed from the NWP strategy. At that time it appeared that Bangladesh was willing to settle for 566 to 708 cumecs (20,000-25,000 cusecs) of the lean season flow of the Ganga at its lowest 1,158 cumecs (35,000 cusecs) out of a minimum flow of about 3964 cumecs (140,000 cusecs) in he last part of February, with India being given an equivalent share and the remaining 50 per cent flowing into the sea to maintain the ecological balance. In a sense this would have meant allocating 991 cumecs to India and 2,973 cumecs to Bangladesh during the leanest period from out of the river's natural flow.

India should be able to live with this order of sharing. If 566 to 708 cumecs of Ganga water are released below Farakka in the last 10 days of April, this would still permit the diversion of 850-990 cumecs into the Bhagirathi-Hooghly. This is 270 to 410 cumecs more than what India was entitled to divert under the 1977 Agreement and 1982 MOU which virtually subsisted until December 1988. With that schedule of flushing, salinity has been reduced to safe limits below Calcutta while drafts at Calcutta Port have improved to 6.7 m. Efforts are on further to improve the draft to 7.9 m (26 feet) but, as earlier explained, any deeper draft will not admit bigger or longer vessels into the port on account of the dimensions of the dock gates and bends in the river. A higher rate of flushing during the lean season may however help Calcutta regain a maximally useful 7.9 m draft over the next five to seven years.

CHANGING PARAMETERS WITH TIME

During this period, three other things will have happened. Bangladesh will be able to execute its short and medium term NWP programme for the southwest region. A detailed study of rainfall, stream-flows and salinity conducted by the Bangladesh Water Development Board and its international consultants. IECO, between 1975 and 1980 indicates "that a minimum discharge of 5000 cusecs (142 cumecs) down the Gorai distributary of the Ganga at Karnarkhali is necessary to keep salinity penetration below Khulna" (Nishat and Chowdhury, August 1985). The Indian Updated Proposal of 1983 also assigns 5,000 cusecs for the River Gorai, presumably for this same function, as this is in addition to a larger allocation assigned for irrigation in Bangladesh's Ganga command. This quantum of water could even come out of the regenerated flows between Farakka and Hardinge Bridge which are not less than 5,000 cusecs at their lowest. Simultaneously, with a firm figure of lean season sharing, Bangladesh will be able to commence designing its proposed Ganga Barrage and be able to negotiate whatever assistance it may require for its funding.

Secondly, by the time Bangladesh is ready to divert large flows into the southwest region from its Ganga Barrage by the turn of the century, sustained flushing of the Bhagirathi-Hooghly may have stabilized a 7.9 m draft fairway between Calcutta and Haldia which could possibly thereafter be maintained with smaller withdrawals at Farakka during the period of maximum water-stress in March and April.

Thirdly, the basis will have been laid for augmentation of the lean season flows of the Ganga in a variety of ways. India's Ganga-Brahmaputra System Study, conducted by the Central Water Commission (corresponding for this region to Bangladesh's NWP) and completed a few years ago, is believed to have indicated that water resource development programmes projected into the 21st century largely on the basis of storages and groundwater will not diminish the lean season flows of the Ganga at Farakka. But by then it is already envisaged that very considerable savings could and, indeed, must be made throughout India by improving irrigation efficiency from its present sorry level of 40 per cent to at least 60 per cent. This is a perfectly realizable target and vitally necessary to achieve to prevent India's huge and growing irrigation system – far and away the largest in the world – from becoming an increasingly "sick industry", burdening the exchequer with crippling losses. There is corresponding scope for water conservation and greater use-efficiency in Bangladesh.

The vast groundwater potential, particularly in eastern U.P., Bihar, West Bengal and Assam, will be and must be more effectively tapped. Increased irrigation and enhanced groundwater pumping will by itself augment recharge and permit a larger draft being made on underground storage which is a dynamic element that grows by its very use in the kind of circumstances prevailing in the Gangetic plain. Normal groundwater recharge would be further enhanced by afforestation, soil conservation and improved macro and micro-watershed management as well as by schemes of induced recharge and groundwater storage as advocated by Prof. Rama of the Tata Institute of Fundamental Research, Bombay, and variants of the Ganga Water Machine thesis of Roger Revelle and V. Lakshminarayana (1975) discussed in earlier chapters.

A study done by Revelle and Herman in 1972 suggested that 'if all evaporation of groundwater in the three States (of U.P., Bihar and West Bengal) could be prevented by lowering the water table, the amount of presently unused groundwater that could be applied to irrigation without reducing river low flow would be of the order or 20 million acre feet" (2.46 m ha m). even allowing for some exaggeration here, such possibilities need to be carefully re-examined.

It was waste to seek unquestioning increases in irrigation capacity without related improvements in a host of other systems such as agrarian structures, on-farm development, extension, credit, marketing and food storage that would increase farm yields and post-harvest returns. The productivity of irrigated land in India is very low. Its currently irrigated 70-75 million hectares should by themselves yield a minimum of four tonnes per hectare at least. The resultant produce (assuming all this acreage to be under foodgrains) would yield a crop of 280-300 million tonnes (not counting output from dryland farming) or 110-130 million tonnes in excess of the nations 1988-89 bumper harvest.

There is also a prediction of a vast deep aquifer underlying parts of the Ganga plain in India, Nepal and Bangladesh. This remains to be proven and established as a viable source with no adverse ecological or other consequences. Even fossil water, if available in significant quantities, can be subjected to controlled mining to meet marginal shortages in critical seasonal water-stress situations. The Libyans are planning to exploit such a fossil water aquifer under the desert and to pipe it for irrigational and municipal use along the Mediterranean on the basis of a 50-year budget (Associated Press, September 1988). Yemen has been less prudent in the unscientific exploitation of fossil water that could be anything up to 20,000 years old to augment water supply to the capital city of Sana (Walker, April 1988). Variations in yield in Australia's Great Artesian Basin over the period 1880 to 1970 have now leveled off to a steady state (Habermehl, M.A. 1980), but some artesian basins in the U.S. as in Texas, are in trouble from over use. All that this implies is due caution and proper modeling.

KOSI-BRAHMAPUTRA OPTIONS

The lean season flows of Ganga could also be augmented from the Kosi High Dam and to some extent even from Gandak storages. India is anxious that an early start be made on the Kosi Dam as this, together with check dams and soil conservation works upstream, is considered essential for flood and sediment control and in order to save the existing Kosi Barrage and re-anchor the restless Kosi. Nepal has its own difficulties regarding submergence and displacement, environmental impacts, and loss of infrastructure in this populous and well forested basin. These factors will obviously have to be taken into account in the sharing of costs and benefits. Bangladesh would benefit from flood moderation and augmentation and could share some of those costs. It could purchase a block of Kosi power which Nepal should be glad to offer to break India's monopoly as an otherwise single buyer of its energy. The development of a navigable waterway from Nepal to Bangladesh through Indian territory, if techno-economically feasible, would be an added attraction for both, especially Nepal which has been chafing at its landlocked status. Should all these arrangements – flood control, augmentation, navigation and electricity exports – admit of duplication in the Gandak basin development, this would be a double benefit.

Far from viewing a Nepal-Bangladesh nexus with suspicion, India should promote its development. The promptings of each one of these smaller neighbours would encourage the other to overcome its fears of cooperating with India. They would also find it easier to confront internal opposition to these projects at home and be able to point to a lessening of sole dependence on India. International funding would no doubt be facilitated by such regional arrangements and the eastern sub-continental power grid that emerges (with Bhutan included) would be a boon to all.

Although Bangladesh has been focusing almost exclusively on the Ganga, realization has begun to dawn that a far larger land area, population and proportion of its economy lies within the Brahmaputra basin and that this weightage greatly increases if the Meghna basin is also taken into account. The devastating 1988 flood has again demonstrated the enormous stake it has in the harnessing of the Brahmaputra-Meghna systems. In turn, India has in a sense subordinated or mortgaged the interests of its Northeast to Aryavarta (Bihar and U.P.) in its zeal to reserve all but 1132 cusecs of the lean season flow of the Ganga in the middle and upper Gangetic basin above Farakka. Witness the panic denunciation of the Barcelona Convention, an instrumentality that could have helped secure transit rights for the Northeast in pursuance of its historic uses of international waterways. Conversely, Bangladesh has exhibited similar amnesia about the problems and prospects of a large part of the country in bestowing almost exclusive attention to the relatively smaller Ganga-dependent southwest region below Farakka in its prolonged parleys with India. Both countries have adopted negotiating positions that confuse a part with the whole and both are the poorer for it.

COMBINING ALTERNATIVES IN AN OPTIMISED SYSTEM

The Brahmaputra has much the greater discharge and by far the smaller utilizable potential. As mentioned earlier, the principle of an internal Brahmaputra-Ganes transfer within its own territory has been mooted off and on in Bangladesh for years and is now beginning to shape into an optimized systems policy. But on leaving the somewhat narrow confines of the Assam Valley, the mighty Brahmaputra becomes more difficult to manage as it opens out into a wider braided channel in Bangladesh. Finding a suitable barrage site will not be easy and the investment will be high. The NWP estimates the cost of the Brahmaputra and Ganga barrages separately up to 2005 and says an additional $ 1.25 billion will be required thereafter to complete the two barrage systems. Splitting this additional cost equally, and adding this to the upto-2005 estimates, the Brahmaputra barrage is likely to cost $ 3.60 billion and the Ganges barrage some $ 2.39 billion (in 1986 prices).

There could be many permutations and combinations of Brahmaputra barrage sites and link canals in Bangladesh to transfer different quantities of water to the Ganga. India had originally proposed a canal to a link a Jogighopa Barrage in Assam to the Farakka Barrage. This is now in cold storage. Bangladesh might propose a transfer along old spills and inter-connecting links from its Brahmaputra Barrage, somewhere in the vicinity of Bahadurabad, to its Ganga Barrage. India has also toyed with the idea of a link canal Jogighopa to Farakka entirely along

Indian territory by short links, first to the Teesta, then to the Mahananda and finally to the Ganga. The route would be circuitous and would involve a life of 60 metres with an attendant pumping cost. In any event, the volume of water that could be transferred would be modest. A Teesta-Mahananda canal is however already under construction as part of India's Teesta Barrage project in North Bengal.

A water transfer within Bangladesh from its projected Brahmaputra Barrage to its proposed Ganges Barrage could permit India to transfer some current releases below Farakka for uses upstream should Dhaka agree. The BB-GB link canal could also have an additional spur that delivers a given quantum of water to India at any given point, if this is techno-economically viable. A conceptually attractive and cheaper alternative may be for Bangladesh to save itself the cost of building a Brahmaputra Barrage and instead use India's proposed Jogighopa Barrage, estimated to cost Rs.357 crores plus another Rs.292 crores for a 300 MW power plant (1983 Updated Proposal), and share a link canal through various Bangladeshi rivers and inter-connecting links to its Ganges Barrage with or without spurs to India.

This alternative and its advantages are spelt out by S.K. Guha and S.B. Sen Sarma. They would align a canal from the Jogighopa Barrage "to the drainage heads of the Korotoya-Atrai river systems within Bangladesh ... for conveying the water on to the Padma upstream of the Sara-Hardinge Bridge" and so to GB. They would also effect "channel improvements for the Korotoya-Atrai systems in Bangladesh and the Jalangi, Bhairab, Mathabhanga systems in lower Bengal (straddling both West Bengal and Bangladesh) in sections adequate to carry the augmented flow from the Barrage". This proposal, it is claimed, would permit diversions of part of the augmented flow into the Bhagirathi-Hooghly and resuscitate various moribund distributaries in both countries. It would also provide "better scope for flood moderation within Bangladesh by stage reduction, by introducing the relay system of flood water routing through the widely spaced Korotoya-Atrai rivers, thereby delaying (the) on-rush of flood water into the Brahmaputra (Jamuna) – Padma confluence and their effects down below: (1985).

Incidentally, the augmentation from Nepalese storages proposed by Bangladesh also envisages a Gandak-Kosi canal along the Terai to feed the Mahananda, Atrai and Korotoya and serve as "an important international navigation route to the sea" for Nepal (Abbas 1982). Any navigation canal through the strategic Siliguri neck would however be unacceptable to India.

MUTUAL TRADE-OFFS

If the diversion from Indian benefit along whatever alignment or combination of alignments is made from monsoon storages on the Dihang, Subansiri and other rivers, there should be no reason for Bangladesh to apprehend any adverse dimunition of the Brahmaputra lean season flows, at least beyond any agreed India dry flow allocation. The Dihang-Subansiri projects would generate considerable energy and, even discounting official Indian claims, could moderate floods below Jogighopa by perhaps half to one metre, both of which would obviously greatly benefit Bangladesh as well.

Bangladesh flood analyses reveal that up to two-thirds of the country is flood prone in one year or another, though in an average year no more than 9.35 million hectares may be affected. According to a flood depth classification, inundation does not exceed a depth of 0.3 metres over an area of 2.55 million hectares of 27 per cent of the affected area. Another 3.68 million hectares, or 39 per cent experiences shallow floods of between 0.3 and one metre. About 1.6 million hectares, or another 18 per cent, would be under one to two metres of water; while deep flooding in excess of two metres is limited to 1.5 million hectares or 16 per cent of the flood affected area (Khan, Akbar Ali August, 1985). The Tipaimukh dam on the Barak would likewise moderate the Meghna flood in Sylhet, while the proposed Teesta dam in Sikkim would provide relief to Rangpur district. No dams in Nepal can mitigate the floods that ravage the largest part of Bangladesh when the Brahmaputra, Meghna and Teesta are in spate. Storage on the Manas in Bhutan would however make a contribution. It would also enable Bangladesh to diversify its power supply from that source, through an eastern sub-continental electricity grid, and possibly develop another international waterway as well.

The Dihang and Subansiri dams are likely to be viable propositions even if the entire cost is loaded on to the power component and the electricity generated is evacuated to the major load centres in Bihar and West Bengal through a 765 kv transmission line. Flood mitigation in Assam would be an added benefit and would absorb a proportionate share of the cost of these projects. Even so, India feels that unless it can transfer some of the stored monsoon flows of the Brahmaputra which is the country's long-term reserve reservoir of last resort, it will be forfeiting a very major resource. There is merit in this contention and Bangladesh should not face any real conflict of interest were this to be conceded in principle, subject to techno-economic validation.

It is certainly arguable that the proposed Indian Brahmaputra-Ganga Link Canal suffers from giganticism. The 1132 cumec Bhakra and ndia Gandhi (Rajasthan) canals are among the largest in the world. But even these would be dwarfed by the proposed 2830 cumec B-G Link Canal. This capacity was related to the theoretical possibility of transferring the entire monsoon storage of the Dihan and Subansiri dams. A transfer of up to half that amount would be a more practicable proposition and a most valuable insurance for the future.

However, even this quantum need not be transferred in full or part along the proposed Indian B-G Link Canal alignment but could be broken into smaller components and undertaken in phases as and when required. Initial transfers, as discussed earlier, may be made within Bangladesh by a BB-GB link with or without spurs to India, or from the Jogighopa Barrage in Assam to the Ganges Barrage in

Bangladesh, again with or without extensions to India. These canal alignments could also be navigable. A smaller all-India alignment from the Jogighopa Barrage to the Teesta-Mahananda-Ganga might conceivably prove economic for a supplementary transfer of water. All these formulations would need careful investigations and analysis on technical, environmental and economic considerations and a combination of transfer options could be implemented as part of a larger integrated programme in phases under an Indo-Bangladesh accord as and when or if ever necessary.

In such a situation India could offer flood control, irrigation, navigation and energy benefits to Bangladesh in exchange for water transfers aligned through that country together with transit and transmission rights. The same would apply to Tipaimukh where the Indian interest would lie in navigation and transit plus the facility of transmission of electricity to the heartland via Bangladesh's new east-west connector spanning the Brahmaputra. Such an extra high voltage transmission line could form part of the proposed eastern sub-continental grid and supply power to Bangladesh as well. It could also evacuate much of the 840 MW of energy to be generated at the gas turbine thermal station under construction in Agartala, electricity from which would otherwise have to move 2200 additional kilometres around Bangladesh to reach the nodal grid station at Farakka. The additional capital and maintenance costs and the line losses are avoidable-given an agreement with Bangladesh. An Agartala-Calcutta gas pipeline could also be laid through Bangladesh. In all this there would be many possible trade-offs, including additional allocations of water to Bangladesh from some of the smaller common rivers, or concessional energy supplies in exchange for road, rail and water transit facilities and access to Chittagong port.

NOT A ZERO SUM GAME

Bangladesh has developed 130,000 MW of energy at the Kaptai dam on the Karnaphuli in the Chittagong Hill Tract. A further 100 MW could perhaps be added for peaking purposes by raising the height of the dam. But this would submerge areas in Mizoram. There are certainly delicate problems of tribal displacement and resettlement that would need to be negotiated on both sides of the border, and with the Chakmas in Bangladesh in particular. Nevertheless, the Government of India and people in Mizoram might be willing to accept some submergence and displacement in return for construction of locks or a ship lift or other ship transfer arrangement around the Kaptai dam to permit navigation from Mizoram down the Karnaphuli to Chittagong. An outlet to the sea for barge traffic would transform Mizoram and Tripura's economic prospects.

There is yet another possibility that might bear techno-economic scrutiny. This envisages a navigation-cum-irrigation canal taking off from the left bank of the Farakka reservoir into Bangladesh as part of a larger, optimized Indo-Bangladesh water exchange. Would it likewise, be too late even now to marry the Indian and Bangladesh Teesta Barrage projects? Could they even at this juncture be run in tandem? As far as the other 50 odd common rivers are concerned, they could be grouped in suitable clusters and water sharing agreements worked out in which storages in India could play a part. Very senior Bangladesh water resource development officials have advocated that in the light of the National Water Plan, "a comprehensive agreement for permanent sharing of all rivers should be made with the co-riparian countries (Khan, Amjad Hossain and Khan Akbar Ali, August, 1985).

Apart from other trade-offs, India may need partially to finance certain replacement works in Bangladesh. An obvious candidate would be any canal links that transfer Brahmaputra waters to the Ganga to make good additional abstractions by India above Farakka or for conveying the Brahmaputra's monsoon surplus from India's Northeast to the heartland.

In none of this should or need Bangladesh suffer. Nor India. Both would gain immeasurably by cooperation. So would Nepal and Bhutan

It is reassuring that as doughty a champion of Bangladesh's water rights and the doyen among its water resource engineer-administrators, B.M. Abbas, should write that 'the long term objective should be the optimum development of the water resources of the river basins and not the narrowly defined purpose of augmenting the dry season flow of the Ganges". Such a plan, he continues "should provide a broad outline for the harmonious development of various works in relation to all reasonable possibilities in the basin. These include irrigation and drainage, electric power generation, navigation, flood control, watershed management, and industrial and domestic uses of water. The entire river basin should be treated as one unit and its water as the property of all the people living in the basin, to be equitably allocated, taking into account the availability of water, the requirements of the different areas and their ecological needs". He concludes: "The key to the solution of the water problem is integrated river basin development ... The future of 250 million people living in the flood plains and delta of the Ganges and Brahmaputra river systems rests on this effort" (August 1985).

It is this wisdom that must prevail over any more wasted years of strife. To exchange the prospect of cooperative synergism for a zero sum game would be a barren alternative.

CHAPTER 17

Waters of Hope

As the nations that share the Ganga-Brahmaputra-Barak Basin enter the 1990s, they commence new five year plans that postulate an end to the sorrow and indignity of destitution by that magic year 2000. The third millennium beckons. What will it bring?

It all depends on what those living in the Basin and their governments will and do. The glaring contradiction of the largest concentration of the world's most poor unable to garner the bounty of one of the world's richest natural resource regions in which they live is an indictment that can no longer be evaded. Not a little has been achieved over the past 40 years. But not enough. Political stability and the social fabric are threatened as populations multiply and justly demand equity and opportunity.

The Basin can quite easily more than feed itself with appropriate land use and crop planning and better drought and monsoon management in accordance with the agro-climatic and ecological capability of its distinct regions. The new agriculture will entail diversification and regional specialization on the basis of beneficial mutual exchange. Hill and plain are interactive systems and each must support the other. A new complementary must be developed. On a large canvas the Basin has to become an ecologically responsible region which alone will secure ecological security for all.

Food production initially increased through extensive agriculture. That option was exhausted. Irrigation and the so-called green revolution technology dependent on it then became the "leading edge" of agricultural growth. This has paid handsome dividends and remains to be fully exploited. The groundwater potential of the eastern region awaits intensive development and the scope for harness in surface flows is still large as there are as yet few monsoon storages in the Himalaya. Water and flood-plain regulation is again of paramount importance in the eastern Basin which has to contend with floods alternating with drought. It is no paradox that agricultural stability and productivity should be greater in the semi-arid western portion of the Basin where there is better water control and fewer problems of drainage though greater risk of salinisation.

SETTING NEW SIGHTS

However, although the basin boasts a very large and growing irrigation system, it is characterized for the most part by low yields and low use-efficiency averaging no more than 40 per cent. Irrigation has become another "sick industry" and various problems of soil and water management, on-farm development, mainline canal operation above the farmgate, maintenance, modernization of older systems and conjunctive use of water cry out for attention. As in the case of energy, emphasis must shift from projects to policy, from hardware to software, from capacity creation to effective utilization at 60 per cent efficiency at the very least. Farmer participation through water user associations would do much do improve system-reliability, accountability and equity.

Iniquitous agrarian relations are, however, a strongly inhibiting factor and have impeded the adoption of technological innovations and greater labour absorption in obvious tasks of land and water conservation and the creation of farm capital assets through a land army partly financed through food-for-work. A fascination with ceilings legislation, badly drafted and indifferently implemented for the most part, has combined with a not-so-benign neglect of the oppressive tenurial condition of millions of small farmers and share-croppers, thus denying them sufficient incentive to realize the full potential of available land and water resources. Consolidation has not been pressed, except in some parts. Despair is turning to violence. The situation can be retrieved with political will and administrative underpinning through community participation. Were this to happen, the multiplier effect would open up whole new employment opportunities in agricultural services and processing, biomass conversion and by-product utilisation and give a tremendous fillip to the whole economy.

Faulty land use planning has resulted in environmental degradation and out-migration from the hills. This human erosion is as devastating as the soil erosion that is more frequently addressed. With the growing pressure of population and livestock on the land, the poor are eating into their own capital resource base for survival. The forests and rangelands have been despoiled. While this is obviously a matter for deep concern, the answer does not lie in slowing down development but in accelerating the process. Poverty is the greater polluter endangering the environment. And so development, carefully and humanely conceived, must be encouraged even if it means losing some more forest initially in the process until a real dent is made on poverty and a new and more satisfactory balance is attained between population, ecology and income generation through productive employment. Better lose a few trees today than have people involuntarily cut many more tomorrow. The gains of development, such as they are, have been neutralized by high fertility within the basin. Accelerated development could be the best contraceptive.

FALSE TRIALS

The whole environmental debate has got overheated. Emotion has come in the way of rational judgement. Various myths have been engendered and causal linkages distorted by excessive simplification and generalization.

It is true that water resource development has caused displacement of people and loss of valuable croplands and forests. Displacement however is an attribute of almost all land acquisition for development and is not peculiar to submergence behind dams. Indeed, in all the years since the commencement of planning, less land or forest has been lost to dams than to agriculture, human settlements and other developments. Illustratively, over 25,000 hectares of land have been acquired for Delhi's urban expansion since 1957. At the same time, poverty had displaced far larger numbers through forced migration than have water resource projects. Unfortunately, the record of resettlement and compensation in South Asia has been poor. The whole concept of rehabilitation has to be thought of afresh, taking social and cultural as much as material factors into account. The persisting tendency to offer land for land is mistaken and unviable. There is no land to give away for the most part. Rehabilitation has to be ensured, through alternative off-farm employment and in upper catchment area development programmes which should be an integral part of water resource projects in the manner of command area development downstream.

The notion that aboriginals affected by dams should be left alone in splendid isolation is to romanticize a certain kind of deprivation and condemn tribal populations to less than equal treatment. Likewise, the notion that the commercial exploitation of forests, even if scientifically and equitably undertaken, is somehow wicked and therefore to be avoided is to exclude a valuable partner in organizing, funding and executing an enormous and urgent exercise. The level of productivity of the Basin's forests and rangelands is abysmal. It must be improved.

The huge hydro-electric potential of the basin is a priceless renewable energy resource. Hydel power is cheap, clean and flexible, contributes greatly to system-efficiency and is invaluable for peaking purposes. Hydel development and exports can transform the economy of Nepal and Bhutan in particular. The hydro-thermal mix, which should ideally be around 40:60, has been allowed to fall but must be restored over the next two decades. This will call for bold decisions and regional cooperation in marketing the huge blocks of Himalayan power that could be brought on line through a subcontinental grid. The real environmental cost of thermal power stations, especially those fuelled by coal, is seldom calculated. Current concerns with global warming on account of accumulating greenhouse gases in the atmosphere should, however, dictate greater resort to renewable energy sources.

The world may in the next quarter or half century be moving from an energy crisis to a water crisis. Much of the Ganga-Brahmaputra-Barak Basin is even now critically water short seasonally. Water availability and conservation are becoming increasingly important.

Water resource development, or national planning for that matter, cannot also afford to neglect issues of water quality. River and groundwater pollution have an intimate relationship with drinking water, sanitation and public health. The spread of water-borne and water-related diseases is avoidable with integrated planning and in-built prophylactic measures. The Ganga Action Plan is a major initiative whose significant for public health and urban improvement has not been fully appreciated.

Water policy has thus far been largely concerned with irrigation. While this is obviously important, greater provision must be made for other uses. Thinking water admittedly accounts for but a tiny fraction of available supplies. But reaching it to everybody over time and space ensuring the requisite quality is another matter that has perhaps not yet received due priority. The ecological and recreational uses of water have only just begun to attract attention and the growing demands of industrial and municipal uses can no longer be ignored. India's national Water Policy requires water zoning of the country with economic activities guided and regulated in accordance with such zoning. The injunction has not been sufficiently heeded. Emphasis will need to shift from quantitative to qualitative aspects of water availability and use and its pricing.

Fish might seem a minor element in the basin's food budget. Not so. It is a significant source of protein, employment and income and has a huge potential. Inland, estuarine and coastal waters and deep water paddies can nourish thriving culture and capture fisheries, as well as duck and frogs, in integrated systems.

It is almost forgotten that only a little more than a century ago, the Ganga Brahmaputra and Barak were the great highways of commerce. Sadly, the promotion of the Railways by the state, and subsequent road development, killed inland and coastal navigation. India, though not Bangladesh, moved away from the waterfront. The waterways are now to be revived and could make a great contribution in opening up new transport corridors within an appropriate policy frame.

Containerization and inter-modal systems offer interesting new opportunities, especially for river-cum-coastal movements. The energy-efficiency of inland water transport is an answer that can be turned to good account as existing rail and road routes attain saturatic.. and require heavy investments to augment capacity.

There has to be a grand vision which, worked backwards could spell out what must and must be done from now on in order incrementally to fulfil that dream. Small is beautiful; but big is not necessarily evil and can be broken down into smaller components that can be grasped and managed by local communities as partners in a larger enterprise.

CREATING APPROPRIATE MECHANISMS

It is not that none of this is being done; but there is no over-arching design that comprehends all these manifold aspects in consummating what is already and over the next few decades going to be far and away the largest water resource development programme in the world. Each activity, every programme should be mutually reinforcing rather than inconsistent with the other. But how is this to be accomplished when Department and federal jurisdictions are compartmentalized and scattered, when the gestation period of even medium-large water resource projects cannot be encompassed within the span of a single five year plan, which is the political and financial time-frame within which the nations of South Asia function, and when the basin is divided by sovereign jurisdiction? Even setting apart the international aspects for the moment, there is no national mechanism, not even within planning commissions, to undertake this task.

Arising out of a national seminar conducted in 1978 (Gandhi Peace Foundation), the Committee of Secretaries, Government of India, decided to set up an inter-Department and inter-disciplinary Focal Technical Group at the Centre to study the integrated development of the Ganga-Brahmaputra-Barak Basin in its totality. The Group was to work under a Committee of Direction of which the Secretaries in the Ministries of Agriculture, Irrigation, Planning, Power, Finance and External Affairs and the Chairman of the Central Water Commission were members, with other departmental heads being associated as and when necessary. The Government fell some months later and this nodal organization never got off the ground.

Even the existing departments are inadequately structured. Take the Indian example. The Central Water Commission and the Central Groundwater Board are separate organizations. The CWC remains primarily an engineering body on which economics and ecological expertise is not represented at sufficiently senior rungs. The whole mode of project investigation and sanction as between the States, the concerned Central Departments and the Planning Commission leaves much to be desired and has resulted in ruinous time and cost overruns aggravated by under-funding. Conjunctive surface and groundwater use needs to be more closely integrated with project planning and design from the very inception, rather than as an add-on. Nor can drainage be relegated to an afterthought. Emphasis on irrigation and energy hardware has resulted in lack of attention to and funding for operational systems, training, management and maintenance. The Central Electricity Authority likewise lacks real autonomy. Transmission and distribution have been neglected.

The high-powered National Water Resources Council has not been reconvened after its inaugural meeting in 1985 although it recognized water as a precious national asset and a scarce natural resource whose utilizable potential might be more or less exhausted by the turn of the century. Meanwhile, the Ministry of Water Resources has been down-graded.

There has been a certain conservatism in developing construction technology and in modernizing and upgrading tendering systems. Construction by corporate bodies whether in the private or public sector is much to be preferred to Departmental construction which is limited by bureaucratic regulations and protocol. The concept of basin development would also appear to have many advantages over random project planning in terms of overall planning, deployment and phasing of skilled manpower and equipment, and in reducing overheads. Shifts are taking place in these directions but need to be further systematized.

Education and training programmes need to be diversified and upgraded with whole new areas of specialisation (Jagdish Narain, 1985). There is a shortage of engineering geologists. Today's civil engineers must know more than what it takes to design and construct a dam or canal. Irrigation layouts, conjunctive use planning, management and a host of other disciplines, and related research, are required. The irrigation engineer must know something of agricultural practice. Agricultural and forestry too can no longer be kept apart. Nor a study of ecology from any of these. Support services such as agro-meteorology and seismology in relation to dams must be rapidly developed to impart the necessary sophistication to the more complex phase of design and management that lies ahead. Basin development boards and implementing authorities such as the Brahmaputra Board, and even the Tehri Project Development Authority and the Damodar Valley Commission may have to be more adequately staffed, funded and mandated so that they are able to move beyond broad conceptual planning to more rigorous project design, appraisal and execution. It is a pity that the Sone Commission, which prepared a comprehensive overview of basin development extending over Madhya Pradesh, U.P. and Bihar, was disbanded. Admittedly inter-state basin authorities like the DVC confront certain difficulties. But they are also able to overcome problems that might otherwise get locked in inter-governmental pulls and pressures, especially between bigger and smaller states or upper and lower riparians, or even Centre and States. A professionally oriented corporate body is more likely to be guided by techno-economic considerations than by political or electoral advantage. The scope for organizational reform all round is real and urgent considering the very large investments proposed.

INDIA'S CATALYSING ROLE

Water resource development lies at the heart of what the Basin states must accomplish soon and well if they are to escape from poverty and move towards securing a better life for their people. But none, not even India, can do this in isolation. Tibet may be in a somewhat different category, but all the others constitute a single geo-political entity, divided by territorial sovereignties but bound together by the monsoon and the common river system that drains the Himalaya.

India has insisted on bilateralism and has viewed any effort to look at the Ganga-Brahmaputra-Barak Basin as a whole with deep suspicion. This is not the best way to develop an optimized systems approach that will provide least-cost solutions for the common good. India's apprehension that it will be numerically isolated, with international consultants and donors necessarily siding with its smaller neighbours, is greatly exaggerated and has proved counter-productive. And it has become needlessly paranoid about classifying water resource data pertaining to the Basin. This has merely sown suspicion and undermined credibility. It has also inhibited relevant research and scholarly analysis and precluded informed debate on important policy issues. This is scarcely in the public interest. Being by far the largest partner, and placed centre-stage, India enjoys a commanding position and should have little to fear. Indeed there is a strong case for data-gathering and data-sharing on a multi-disciplinary basis within and beyond the basin and encouragement to joint studies and research as a confidence-building measure. This will also provide the necessary unpinning for cross-boundary techno-economic decision-making and international funding.

India has on occasion seemingly been somewhat unmindful of the genuine concerns and aspirations of its smaller and less well endowed neighbours. It should not appear to be over-bearing, uncaring, and unresponsive towards these countries which ultimately look to it for a lead India has a high stake in the political stability and economic progress of the Basin states and its own long term security interests are best served by underwriting their well-being. Unequal size does give rise to complexes among smaller partners, but they in turn cannot ignore the fact of interdependence either.

The magnitude of regional water resource development contemplated or desired is so overwhelmingly large that this simply cannot be considered in isolation from political relationships. SAARC offers a promising frame but cannot meaningfully develop without an improvement in bilateral relations between each of the constituent units and India, which alone shares a common border with or is most proximate to each of the others. Hence India's catalyzing and cementing role is paramount.

A TIME FOR STATESMANSHIP

The Indo-Bangladesh dispute on the eastern waters question is clearly capable of resolution. It was, however, a strategic error to call on irrigation engineers to settle what was and is essentially a major political issue affecting long term political and economic relations between the two countries. Even the technical issues were and remain far too narrowly focused as the prime negotiators are neither conversant nor officially concerned with the totality of the multiple interests involved. There are a whole range of important trade-offs that have not even been put on the *tapis*. The Indian Planning Commission was for years not aware of the augmentation proposals that were being mooted, though the entire plan perspective for the country, and most certainly for the eastern region, would undergo a complete metamorphosis were the Indian Updated Proposal to fructify. As the political situation in each country and the relations between them kept changing from time to time, there were periods when there was a favourable constellation of various internal and external circumstances calculated to promote a constructive dialogue. But the opportunity was never seized, possibly because clarity of purpose and a calculus of longer overall national and regional interests was lacking. This has been a failure of statesmanship and diplomacy and is not because of any technical impasse.

Even on the limited issue of irrigation, both sides overstated their claims, cited uncertain data as suited them, and were totally dismissive of the other's legitimate interests and apprehensions. Neither was prepared to listen to the other and it is no surprise that a dialogue of the deaf yielded no result. India unwisely questioned every demand for water put forward by Bangladesh (or East Pakistan) even when this was initially pitched at no more than 100 cumecs (3,500 cusecs). It always sought more data, a further clarification. Pakistan's demand was inflated to an extent where it would appropriate even more than the entire 1158 cumecs (55,000 cusecs) low season flow of the Ganga by 1968, a proposition that Bangladesh inherited and made its own, convinced that Farakka diversions were irrelevant to Calcutta and an evil design to harm it.

These might have been regarded as rival statements of maxima and minima typical to all political bargaining, but for the fact that each side has to no small degree become a prisoner of its own public opinion which, after long years of indoctrination, has come to accept the myth for the reality. Each is now in a political bind, hoist with its own petard.

The subsequent argument as to whether augmentation of the lean flows below Farakka should be wholly from the Brahmaputra, as India insisted, or from the Ganga, as demanded by Bangladesh, was equally unreal. Bangladesh may have had an arguable case against the specific Brahmaputra-Ganga Link Canal proposed by India on technical and political grounds and in view of its gargantuan dimensions. But its objection to the very principle was untenable. Similarly the Indian proposition that the Ganga is essentially an "Indian river" from which Bangladesh can at best hope to receive only marginal lean season flows and certainly no augmentation from any storages, whether in India or Nepal, is highly questionable and must sound arrogant and menacing to Bangladesh ears. Moreover, it ignores the significant "augmentation" to be had both from improved irrigation efficiency, which India like Bangladesh must realize in its own best interest, as well as from a variety of known and potential groundwater sources.

Juxtaposing the Ganga and Brahmaputra as mutually exclusive sources of lean season augmentation is mistaken and suffers from narrow, compartmentalized thinking. Both river systems must be harnessed for the overall benefit of the peoples of the entire region. At the same time it would be unrealistic to ignore the fact that the huge monsoon surplus of the Brahmaputra does constitute an invaluable regional reserve whose utilisation outside its basin and when required in phases over the 21st century should be accepted in principle, though assuredly in a manner that benefits Bangladesh as much as India.

Harnessing the tremendous hydro-electric potential of the Nepal and Bhutan Himalaya is equally in the common interest of the region which cannot find riches by scorning its own great wealth. The issue of designing, constructing and managing water resource projects and related works and that of energy pricing are amenable to rational discussion and settlement. Here again, cooperation can only be constructed within an appropriate political frame. All the more tragic that Indo-Nepal relations should have ruptured in 1989, hopefully only very temporarily. It will serve either side little to rehearse the past. They would be better off to overcome their current pique and enter into an altogether new and dynamic phase of mutual cooperation that Karnali and other projects signify.

INTERNATIONAL COOPERATION

In respect of both Nepal and Bangladesh as well as in the case of Bhutan suitable instrumentalities and corporate or inter-governmental mechanisms will have to be established. The existing structures have failed either because they were too narrowly conceived or were not given a fair trial. The institutional basis of bilateral and multilateral cooperation must [illegible] laid and backed by treaties, self-actuating procedures for conflict resolution and a strong and agreed data. Ultimately, something like a Himalayan Rivers Commission might emerge, not excluding China [illegible] a significant upper riparian in Tibet, bringing together many strands of [illegible]ive endeavour. The possibility of diverting some Tsangpo flows south into the upper Gandak or Arun by tunneling through the modest ridge that divides these rivers in Tibet, merits study.

The task of developing the Himalayan watershed will require international funding and other assistancein view of the massive investments and technical complexities involved. India does not have to be suspicious about every show of interest in this challenging task by other countries and international agencies. It must get this chip off its shoulder. Admittedly, more than altruism is involved as prize contracts are going to be on offer. This is perfectly understandable. But paralyzing fears of subversion and "destabilization" need to be firmly put aside as India is not a hapless banana republic. Otherwise too, the Himalaya is a world heritage resource, like the Amazonian forest, and its ecological preservation and regeneration is a matter of considerable concern. Far from baulking at the prospect, India should therefore take the initiative to invite international interest and participation in the development of the region's Himalayan resources as part of a global infrastructure project to liquidate the largest remnant of world poverty.

Entry into the 21st century must mean something more for the deprived millions of the Basin than merely turning over yet another page in a dreary calendar. India must take the lead. And it must be not just fair but generous in dealing with its neighbours. It will gain by giving. Many national solutions lie in regional cooperation which is the wave of the future. Ultimately boundaries do not matter; people do. The vision of SAARC is perhaps most strongly embodied in a collaborative endeavour to harness the potential of the Ganga-Brahmaputra-Barak waters. These are waters of hope.

CHAPTER 18

Postscript

Much has happened while this book has been under printing. A general election in November 1989 brought a new National Front government into office in India pledged to establishing good neighbourly relations. This aroused hopes of an early end to the impasse between India and both Bangladesh and Nepal on water resource development, trade, transit and other issues. There has indeed been a significant improvement in the political climate following high-level talks on overall relationships. Substantive negotiations on water-related questions are now likely to get under way but will require a quantum jump in thinking rather than a search for mere incremental gains if real headway is to be achieved.

India and Bangladesh have renewed their inland water transit and trade protocol for a further period of two years until October 1991. In May 1990 the Indian Supreme Court decided that a perpetual lease to Bangladesh by India of a tiny corridor through Tin Bigha in West Bengal under the terms of the Indo-Bangladesh Boundary Agreement of 1974 would not entail ceding territory. This obviates a constitutional amendment and should facilitate expenditious implementation by India of a long-standing obligation, thereby removing a major emotional irritant in Indo-Bangladesh relations.

Bangladesh's hopes of massive external aid or quick relief from the flurry of ambitious flood embankment and drainage schemes advocated by a World Bank-led consortium of donor nations last December have only found limited fulfillment. Funds have been committed for 26 studies and further decisions will rest on their outcome some years hence.

The Indo-Bangladesh Joint Rivers Commission and Task Force on Flood Control have been reactivated. But Bangladesh's efforts to secure a fresh Ganga water sharing agreement below Farakka even if only for the 1990 January-May lean season proved infructuous. Hence, for the second year running, Bangladesh had to do with ad hoc releases by India below Farakka. The 30th meeting of the JRC in mid-April 1990 directed the two sides to take early steps to complete the work of the Task Force on linking inter-country flood embankments where desirable and feasible and arrangements for communicating river discharge data in real time for all common rivers so as to ensure Bangladesh a better early-warning system. It was also decided to expedite Secretary-level discussion on sharing Ganga and Teesta flows before the commencement of the 1991 lean season.

Long term augmentation or more immediate sharing proposals await a bolder political initiative. There was a hint of this on the occasion of the visit of the Bangladesh Foreign Minister, Mr. Anisul Islam Mahmud to Delhi in the last week of May for a meeting of the Indo-Bangladesh Joint Economic Commission. He proposed an agreement on permanent sharing of the lean season flows of the Ganga below Farakka on the lines of the tentative proposals made to India early in 1987 but not pressed at that time on account of strong internal opposition within the government in Dhaka.

Mr Anisul Islam Mahmud revived the suggestion that the two countries share the dry season flows of the Ganga in agreed proportions through a series of 10-day stages, with Bangladesh receiving up to 708 cumecs (25,000 cusecs) in the last ten days of April when the river discharge at Farakka troughs at around 1158 cumecs (55,000 cusecs) which, incidentally, is the minimum demand of either side. Considering this to be a concession, Bangladesh desires in lieu thereof that it be allotted 75 per cent of the far larger Brahmaputra flows (50 per cent of this ostensibly required for salinity control and other ecological reasons) and a 50 per cent share in al the other common rivers.

This package foregoes augmentation altogether and is conceived in terms of enabling Bangladesh to make effective use of the minimum flows in excess of the 708 cumecs that it had in fact been receiving below Farakka for the past many years. This it would do by constructing appropriate structures on the Ganges. The larger sharing package would in due course further enable it to make internal diversions from Brahmaputra surpluses if and as required to irrigate its south-west region and hold the salinity line south of Khulna.

The Tipaimukh dam on the Barak at the trijunction of Assam, Manipur and Mizoram is likely to be tak en up for constriction in 1992-93 primarily as a power project (1500 MW) with considerable potential for flood moderation in Cachar (Assam) and Sylhet (Bangladesh). Phase II of the project envisages construction of the Fulerthal barrage and canal system which could be extended into Bangladesh by agreement to provide considerable irrigation and navigation benefits to both countries. This could appropriately find a high place in any early agenda of talks and is illustrative of one of the many trade-offs that could be negotiated by India and Bangladesh to mutual advantage.

The latest Bangladesh package offers a viable basis for negotiation, though India will obviously need to seek the consent of the concerned riparian states within its part of the basin. The West Bengal Chief Minister has already been consulted and has offered to cooperate. Both sides would have a sufficient margin for adjustment through improved water use efficiency and groundwater pumping. Nor does the package preclude subsequent Brahmaputra-Ganga transfers by any or several of the possible links discussed in Chapter 16, with storages in Arunachal and/or Bhutan.

In fact, the Water Resources Ministry's Performance Budget for 1990-91 states that "office studies" conducted by the CWC confirm the feasibility of a barrage across the Brahmaputra at Jogighopa with a canal linking this to the Teesta barrage "and then on to the Ganga at Farakka" (New Delhi, May 1990). It is presumed that such a link canal with a capacityof around 283 cumecs (10,000 cusecs) would be aligned via the Mahananda and entail a lift of approximately 50 metres. Such a project might become viable 15 to 20 years from now. A possibly simpler alternative could be to transfer this quantum of water from Manas and/or Sunkosh storages in Bhutan to Farakka should Bhutan accede to such an arrangement.

Large parts of India, including significant regions and urban conglomerisations such as Delhi within the Ganga basin, are already water short and the crisis is likely to deepen with population growth and related developments. The National Water Development Agency, which has hitherto confined its attention to the Peninsular segment of India's National Water Perspective Plan, has now been authorised to consider the feasibility of inter-basin transfers north of the Vindhyas, in the Ganga-Brahmaputra basin. The Ghaghara and Kosi have surpluses that can be diverted west and south. But the largest surplus by far is available in the Brahmaputra basin which explains India's long-term interest in diversions from this virgin source with its huge potential for monsoon storages that would yield multi-purpose benefits to Bangladesh, Bhutan and India. A larger political understanding is clearly necessary between these three countries and Nepal so that a wider perspective plan for integrated regional water resource development can be conceptualised and studied in all its techno-economic, benefit-cost, environmental, organizational and investment aspects. The approaching water crisis is likely to be even more severe than the current energy crisis. This therefore is the time for planning and preparation. The NWDA has to this end wisely decided to expedite the formation of river boards for the better planning and development of inter-state rivers.

India's new Eighth Plan, 1990-95, is yet to take shape. The resource crunch and the possibility of converting significant gas finds into quick-maturing power projects suggest that the additional hydro capacity likely to be added to the national grid will probably be less than what the CEA's National Power Plan has recommended. The Chairman of the Japanese Employers' Federation, Keidanren, held out the prospect of a possible funding source when he told a gathering of world businessmen at Davos, Switzerland in February that the Global Infrastructures Fund, first proposed to lift the world out of global recession in the early 1980s, could be a "constructive way of using surplus resources resulting from arms reductions." This clearly seems a worthwhile avenue to explore for an ambitious programme of Himalayan hydro-cum-ecological restoration in the Ganga-Brahmaputra-Barak basin. Such a programme would fit in with Japanese political and economic interests in the wake of the superpower détente and the rapid movement towards One Europe in close partnership with the U.S.A.

There was a flicker of hope after the Indian elections for a positive renewal of Indo-Nepal relations which remained frozen after their trade and transit treaties lapsed in March 1989. However, no sooner had negotiations commenced when the launching of a grassroots movement for the restoration of multi-party democracy in Nepal in place of the Palace-controlled partyless panchayat system brought further developments to a halt. Pro-democracy human rights elements in the Kingdom made strong appeals to the Indian leadership to avoid concluding fresh treaties with the Panchayati regime as this would tend to consolidate the Panchas position as against the democratic movement under the banner of the Nepali Congress and the Left. With the abrogation of the Panchayati system by the King in mid-April 1990 and induction into office of a Nepali congress-led interim government under Mr. K.P. Bhattarai with United Left Front and Palace representatives, the stage has been set for constitutional reform and open elections.

The emerging democratic regime will, hopefully, possess the political will and social base that enables Nepal to move into a new phase of modernization and development encompassing decisions on water resource development with ecological safeguards, regional balance and equity. The petroleum fuel crisis and the consequent pressure to secure compensatory fuelwood supplies caused by the lapse of its subsisting trade and transit treaties with India in March 1989, has stimulated fresh interst in Nepal in developing electrically-powered transport systems including trolley lines and ropeways. The 69 MW Marsyangdi hydel project in the Gandaki zone was inaugurated in February 1990 bringing Nepal's total generating capacity to 230 MW. Construction on the 12 MW Jhimruk project is now being taken in hand while preliminary work continues on the more ambitious Arun-3.

A White Paper published by the interim government (Finance Ministry, Kathmandu, May 25, 1990) under the signature of the new Finance Minister, Dr. Devendra Raj Pandey, exposes in stark detail the extremely parlous state to which Nepal's economy and exchequer have been reduced "as a result of public resources and property abuses to fulfil the interests of the powerful during (three decades of) Panchayat rule". The document states that population growth has outstripped both agricultural productivity and food supply, resulting in ecological degradation, regional imbalances and a deepening and widening of the poverty gap with large pools of unemployment. Large funds have been diverted to luxury consumption, while smuggling and leakages in all spheres of development expenditure have crated distortions and aggravated the debt problem. The non-renewal of the Indo-Nepal trade and transit treaties after March 1989 for 15 months further disrupted economic development, adversely affecting costs and prices.

This sorry chapter in Indo-Nepal relations fortunately appears to have closed with the recent visit of Mr. Bhattarai to Delhi for talks with the Indian Prime Minister, Mr. V.P. Singh. The status quo ante has been restored on trade and transit with mutual concessions by either side. The joint communiqué issued at the conclusion of the visit on June 10 was upbeat and makes specific reference to cooperation in the fields of water resource development and the environment.

The severity of Nepal's resource crisis makes hydro-electricity exports its best long-term option. The Kamali feasibility report has just been submitted to the Nepalese government by the Himalayan Hydro Consultants and is under examination. It envisages generation of 6,500 MW of firm power, virtually all of which is t be exported to India. It is designed for a seismic coefficient akin to that provided for Tehri Dam. While discussions on this mega-project are yet to commence, the Nepalese have informally expressed interest in selling surplus Arun-3 power to India from around 1996-97 until the domestic load grows over the ensuing five years or so when the entire output can be absorbed internally. The initial, but as yet very tentative, asking rate of Rs. 1 per unit has raised some eyebrows. However, there is a real possibility for agreement here, not merely as a point-to-point sale but in the makings of an extended eastern sub-continental grid, though some would consider this premature.

In Tibet, the Chinese have announced plans to augment electricity production from 140 MW in 1989 to 360 MW by the end of the century. The additional capacity is likely to come in large part from a 90 MW hydro station at Yamzho Lake and an expansion of the Yangbajain geothermal power station, apart from smaller projects in the Tsang-po, Lhasa River and Nyang Qu basins. A report on Tibet's new development strategy for the 1990s issued last April stated that the autonomous region is importing 150,000 tonnes of grain, equal to a third of its own output, from other parts of the country to feed its population which is growing by 30,000 annually. A more recent report however claims that Tibet harvested 530,000 tonnes of grain in 1989 (Xinhua, Lhasa, April 1 and May 21, 1990).

Throughout the region, population growth has belied expectations of fertility decline and the numbers living within the basin may exceed a billion within the next quarter century. As the Basin states launch their next five year plans, 1990-95, the outlook for food production and employment remains challenging.

The Approach to India's Eighth Plan (Planning Commission, New Delhi, May 1990) has employment as its central thrust and aims to create over 100 million new jobs by 2000 to attain full employment through decentralized planning. With two-thirds of the labour force occupied in the agricultural sector, (and farm labour per hectare perceptibly declining in many areas), the strategy advocated is expanded irrigation and diversification from paddy-wheat to more high-value crops, especially vegetable gardening and horticulture, as both entail a higher labour intensity in agriculture and are water saving as well. A large, localized land and water conservation programme is also envisaged. Agrarian reform, better water management, sustainable development, and expeditious completion of and enhanced productivity from on-going schemes are emphasized.

In a bid to protect land reform legislation, the Indian Government has just enacted a constitutional amendment including recent agrarian legislation in the

Ninth Schedule of the Constitution which places these Acts beyond challenge in any court of law. A more basic problem however lies in the poor recording of land rights and their maintenance. The computerization of land records is being pushed. More important is the acceptance in principle of changing over from merely registering land records, and up-dating them from time to time, to the registration of land titles as in Australia, Canada, the U.S., Malaysia, Kenya and elsewhere. The difference is between "record and reality", between facts on the ground and the fiction recorded (or not recorded/updated) in the official record of land rights. England accomplished a meticulous record of land titles with legal sanctity with the compilation of the Doomsday Book under William the Conqueror as far back as 1086. The need for a changeover from registration of deeds to registration of titles to land, known as the Torrens system from an Australian innovation, has been documented in a report on "Guaranteeing Title to Land" that has won official endorsement (D.C. Wadhwa, Bombay 1989).

Some confusion has been created by recent reports that the country's groundwater potential has magically doubled to a little over 80 million ha m. This is not so. As the Water Resources Ministry's Performance Budget indicates, "the country's total replenishable groundwater resource works out to 45.23 million hectare metres keeping the provision for drinking, industrial and other uses as 6.93 m ha m." This leaves 38.34 m ha m for irrigation which appears to have been shown as representing an "ultimate irrigation potential from groundwater" of the order of 80.38 m ha. From this it is clear that it is not the groundwater potential that has increased but its supposed applicability through a sharp reduction in the delta or intensity of irrigation depth per hectare to half the figure assumed by the national Agriculture Commission in 1976. This would appear to be a somewhat exaggerated estimate, even with desired changed in the cropping pattern over the country as a whole, and probably stems from the states' anxiety to cash in on agricultural pumping credits on offer from NABARD.

The development and political problems of the sequestered Indian northeast remain an urgent priority. A report on the Economic Development of Assam (Planning Commission, New Delhi, 1990) brings out the problems of that state and, inferentially, of the northeast as a whole. It notes that an estimated Rs 700 crores of the limited purchasing power of this impoverished State flow out to the heartland by way of procurement of foodgrains, edible oil, fish, etc. including "enormous" transport costs. The bill for all of the northeast on such imports by rail alone is of the order of Rs 1,500 crores annually. The remedy prescribed is enhanced agricultural production and productivity in the entire region by improved farming and fisheries. It is sought to move away from jhumming to horticulture and plantations, including rubber and tiny tea estates, with Java citronella and other intermediary crops being cultivated during the gestation period. Better communications and flood control are advocated through a reinvigorated Brahmaputra Board, rail extensions and conversions, and a fourth bridge over the

Brahmaputra at Bogibil near Dibrugarh in Upper Assam (following the third bridge coming up at Jogighopa). The report, however, makes no mention of the possibilities of negotiating use of the proposed World Bank-aided road (and ultimately, cum-rail) bridge across the Jamuna (Brahmaputra) in Bangladesh, near Shirazganj, whose economics would improve by diversion of Indian traffic moving from West Bengal to Cachar by avoiding the circuitous North Bengal loop via the Siliguri neck.

Construction of the Tipaimukh Dam on the Barak (commencing 1992) and the Paglidiya flood control-cum-irrigation dam are strongly recommended. Alongside these, techno-economic and environmental "processing" of the larger Subansiri multipurpose dam (4,800 MW) is also proposed so that infrastructural works on this project can commence in the Eighth Plan itself, with the mighty Dihang project reserved for subsequent consideration.

With the Sadiya-Dhubri stretch of the Brahmaputra having been declared a national waterway, and with improved navigation on the Barak in Cachar resulting from the Tipaimukh project, the Committee sees worthwhile prospects for inland water transport in the region, including transit traffic through Bangladesh on the basis of projected freight estimates over a 15-year perspective.

Nevertheless, inland water transport remains an orphan in the absence of any lobby to push its development against the pressure of powerful Railway and road interests. The Expert Committee on Assam, just cited, would allocate as much as Rs 1,500 crores for new rail lines and gauge conversions in the Assam Valley and strengthened links to Çachar over the next decade. This represents more than what is likely to be spent on inland navigation over half a century since Independence. Indeed, the Eighth Plan Approach Paper does not even mention IWT in its section on transport.

Meanwhile, furious debate continues on whether or not India should proceed with the Tehri and Narmada projects, both of which have long been under way. Both have been assailed by environmental activists with passionate arguments, strong on emotion but often weak on facts and ground realities and offering would almost suggest retreating to a mythical arcadia.

It is nobody's case that better project planning and implementation and sound management, operation and maintenance are not required. It is also now widely accepted by engineers and planners and by the community generally that effective and generous rehabilitation programmes for the displaced are absolutely necessary. No political authority can ignore this aspect any more. Nor will the international funding agencies permit backsliding on this issue. International knowledge and concern in relation to all aspects of dam safety and environmental impacts is being continuously codified and upgraded as guides to action, nationally and in terms of multilateral funding responsibility (World Bank, February 1990). These are in many ways general imperatives and by no means limited to water resource development.

Tehri has fortunately all but cleared what seems to be last of a series of "final" techno-environmental hurdles and appears poised to move ahead. The Tehri catchment includes some 8000 ha of erodible area for which a treatment plan of Rs.30 crores has been built into the project estimates. During the lat round of the official Tehri environmental debate, there was pressure for a watershed management programme for the entire Bhagirathi-Bhilangana Valley. While this is very properly a national concern, the cost of such a programme, which goes beyond the ambit of any one single water resource project, cannot be unilaterally or exclusively debited to the Tehri Dam. Hence it was separately agreed by the Energy Ministry that it would as a national service be wiiling to provide a sum of Rs 300 crores for the "greening of the (Indian) Himalaya" in respect of various projected hydel catchments by loading the estimated cost of Rs 4 lakhs per MW on the price of power to be generated.

Protests against submergence of forest lands continue unabated. It is instructive to note however that the recent Nepalese White Paper indicates the loss of 570,000 hectares of forest over the past 26 years "due to reasons as varied as growing population pressures, indiscriminate deforestation, as well as the illegal felling and trade perpetrated by Pancha powers and their contractors..." Water resource development simply does not figure at all as no significant storages have yet been constructed in Nepal. Nearer home, official sources reported the loss of 22,000 hectares of forest in Baster, Madhya Pradesh from felling and encroachment over the past 12 years over and above 30,000 ha of forest encroachment by tribals in this same area prior to 1976. Compare this with the 5704 hectares of forest that would have been submerged by the Bodhghat hydel project which was approved, funded by the World Bank and then dropped following strong environmental objections about three years ago (*Times of India*, New Delhi, May 21, 1990). Ironically, the project authorities had already undertaken some compensatory afforestation before the project was abandoned. A growing tribal population with no other economic opportunity is converting forests to farmland. Some young tribals of 1990 wear jeans but have no jobs. Impeding development will therefore only accelerate the disappearance of the remaining forests.

In a more hopeful hill development programme, the World Bank has sanctioned an integrated horticulture development project in the northwest Himalaya, including Garhwal-Kumaon and Jammu and Kashmir. The Himachal component provides for Rs. 75 crore outlay spread over seven years to develop and replant 18,600 hectares with apples, pears, citrus, mango, litchi and flowers, with agrotechnical and marketing support.

A second *State of Forest Report*, 1989, recently published throws further light on the status of India's forests. Whereas the 1985-87 satellite-based assessment placed forest cover in the country at 64.20 million ha the new 1989 assessment put this at 64.01 million ha. This implies a loss of 0.19 million ha of forest between 1985 and 1989 or an annual loss of 47,500 ha. However, the area under dense forest, with over 40 per cent crown cover, has increased by 1.70 million ha to 37.84 million ha. Some increase in mangrove forests is also reported. The next survey will be in 1991 by when, hopefully, replantation may exceed forest loss due to land acquisition and deforestation for various development purposes.

In the area of water pollution, the Comptroller and Auditor General of India has in a report presented to the Lok Sabha (May 1990) pointed out lack of coordination and delays in implementation of certain aspects of the Ganga Action Plan. The programme is being continued into the Eighth Plan and the Environment Ministry has proposed launching a wider National River Plan primarily to deal with pollution from untreated urban sewerage and effluents and take up catchment area treatment in all major river basins.

In what could be a major development of wide significance, the Department of Science and Technology made its third pre-monsoon forecast in February 1990, with an update in May. Earlier, forecasts proved remarkably accurate in both 1988 and 1989. In all three years good monsoons were forecast on an analysis of 16 parameters in a monsoon model prepared by the Indian Meteorological Department which has been refined to permit of both quantitative as well as qualitative assessments. Past rainfall records over four decades indicate that whenever more than 55 per cent of the parameters measured are favourbale, as this year, the monsoon is expected to be not just normal but good, normal rainfall being defined as plus or minus 10 per cent of the long-term average for the country as a whole (*Indian Express* and *Times of India*, New Delhi May 25 and June 2, 1990).

The global warming debate continues, with the Third World seeking more generous assistance from the advanced industrialized countries for access to and funding for technologies that would eliminate or mitigate greenhouse gases or chloroflurocarbon emissions. Dire warnings about the forthcoming apocalypse are however even now discounted by some eminent researchers on the basis of scientific measurements of ocean temperatures and land-based data pertaining to the United States over the past century (Brookes, December 25, 1989). Nevertheless, insurance is useful and prudence always wise.

Climatologists are now seeking to run atmospheric and dynamic ocean models simultaneously to achieve more assured results of possible global warming or other climatic changes. The developed, industrialized nations bear a historical responsibility for by far the greater part of greenhouse gas emissions over the past 150-200 years. While the North may be able to adapt to new technologies or prefer to wait and see the outcome of more accurate and certain climate research, the developing, semi-arid, tropical South is likely to be far more vulnerable to climatic changes. This aspect is beginning to receive attention.

Peter H. Gleick, (Stockholm June 1989) notes that nearly 50 countries in four continents have more than three-quarters of their land area within international river basins. India, Bangladesh, Nepal and Bhutan fall in that category. But in a measurement of per capita freshwater availability within these countries in terms of 10 cubic metres per person, Bangladesh and Nepal fall among the high water availability nations with indices of 35.2 and 9.4 respectively, whereas India ranks rather low, even below Pakistan, with an index of 2.3. These are of course crude estimates as much depends on seasonality, location, topography and storage capability. And it is precisely this seasonality and uncertainty that regional cooperation within the Ganga-Brahmaputra-Barak basin could even out in space and time for the good of all. Such action would anticipate more difficult times to follow whether by climatic changes or sheer population growth, about which there is no uncertainty, or both.

The Himalaya-Ganga-Brahmaputra-Barak region constitutes an interactive mountain-plain system that is home to more than a tenth of mankind. Every imperative therefore to tap more fully its vast unexploited potential within a frame of sustainable development. The world too has a high stake in such a well-conceived integrated programme designed to uplift the marginal man in what remains the largest concentration of global impoverishment despite being blessed with great gifts of nature. Opportunity beckons. Seize it.

CHAPTER 19

From Vision to Reality

Eight years ago, when "Waters of Hope" was last published, the prospect it unfolded was, for many, more or less visionary rather than immediately practical. No more.

It was against a growing awareness of time lost and opportunity squandered that the Power Trade Agreement and Mahakali Treaty between Nepal and India and the Ganga Waters Treaty between India and Bangladesh were concluded in 1996. This has broken the prolonged impasse that impeded progress in developing the shared water resources of the Ganga-Brahmaputara-Meghna basin.

The alarm bells have been ringing more insistently with rising census figures and the annual portrayal of the region's abysmally low quality of life indices. The GBM quadrant has sunk below large parts of sub-Saharan Africa despite its rich human and natural endowments. Further, growing seasonal water stress, and even actual scarcity or contamination in certain areas, has spread distress. Social stability is threatened.

The causal relationship between population growth, shrinking land-man ratios, low agrarian productivity and energy shortages on the one hand and unregulated water flows, poverty, unemployment, a degrading environment and migration on the other is now more widely understood. Harnessing the bounty of available primary land and water resources is central to rescuing the ninth of mankind habiting the region from the coils of poverty.

The Mahakali and Ganga Treaties are fruit of patient effort. While addressing specific issues that had remained deadlocked for decades, both set them within a wider framework of water resource development and regional cooperation. They constitute landmarks insofar as they have truly transformed state relationships.

GUJRAL DOCTRINE

The Preamble to both agreements is couched in language that speaks of a political rather than a narrow technical approach towards resolution of what had become crucial obstacles in any improvement of inter-state relations. Both reaffirm their common determination to promote and strengthen a relationship of friendship and close neighbourliness. The political setting is important as Ganga water sharing in the case of Bangladesh had cut across other matters to become the "core issue" blocking progress or even consideration of anything else. Likewise for Nepal, the water issue as epitomized by the Tanakpur controversy, had become a marker for assertion of sovereign equality and national integrity.

The political basis for a mutually beneficial accord between India and its neighbours was buttressed by the so-called Gujral doctrine, named after India's then United Front Foreign Minister, I.K. Gujral, who subsequently became Prime Minister, noting that equality between unequal partners need not be based on strict reciprocity, Gujral declared that India would not necessarily seek a quid pro quo in situations of asymmetrical relationship. He saw this as a confidence building measure in promoting regional cooperation, especially in South Asia. India should therefore be willing to make political concessions to meet the understandable fears and aspirations of its smaller neighbours. The motive underlying the doctrine was not pure atruism but a shrewd realization that accommodation will yield dividends over the long run in terms of goodwill and synergy.

The political and emotional overtone surrounding years of disputation cut across partly lines and in both cases constituted an inescapable reality that had to be confronted. The earlier stages of negotiation have been well described (Iyer and Rangachari, 1993). Linking sharing (a right) with augmentation (a future hope) only complicated matters. Separating the two was an act of statesmanship and of faith. The Gordian knot was cut.

Commending the Ganga Treaty, the Indian Prime Minister, Deve Gowda told the Lok Sabha that the visit of his counterpart, Sheikh Hasina Wajed, to Delhi to sign the Agreement "has placed our relations on an entirely new footing". This would be "of immense benefit to India in the long term in all areas of bilateral relations including security, trade and other areas". The Nepalese Water Resources Minister, Pashupati S.J.B. Rana, for his part, saw water as a "strategic resource" for the Kingdom and Mahakali Treaty as safeguarding that vital interest. Surya Bahadur Thapa, Chairman of the National Democratic Party and subsequently Prime Minister, said that with the Treaty "Nepal-India relations will now enter a new age".

The analogy with West Asian Oil and Central Asian gas underlines Nepal's conviction that water for it is a strategic resource that must be zealously safeguarded. This sentiment was embodied in the new Nepalese constitution of 1990, Article 126 of which provides that "ratification, accession, acceptance and approval of a treaty or agreement" shall require passage by a two-thirds majority of members of both houses of Parliament present and voting in a joint session is respect of matters concerning "(a) peace and friendship; (b) defence and strategic alliances; (c) the boundaries of Nepal; and (d) natural resources and distribution in the utilization thereof". The last category especially includes water resource development. Hence the prolonged deliberations, first over Tanakpur and then Pancheshwar. The Kingdom's deepest concerns and interests were carefully embodied in the Mahakali Agreement which was only then ratified by the requisite two-thirds majority.

Water looms large for wider development and social change. So the twin Agreements may understandably be viewed not merely as having removed a couple of intractable roadblocks but as providing an instrumentality for catapulting each of the partners and the region as a whole into a new growth orbit.

MAHAKALI AGREEMENT

The Mahakali Agreement resolves the controversy that had arisen over India's Tanakpur project. The story begins with an Indo-Nepal agreement entered into in 1920 which provided for a small territorial exchange that enabled India to construct the Sharda barrage at Banbassa at the southern end of the common boundary segment of the Mahakali river which assumes the name Sharda after fully entering Indian territory. This Upper Sharda Barrage was commissioned in 1927 and irrigates 1.6 ha in India but was also intended to provide some kharif and rabi irrigation for specified but limited commands in Nepal, depending on water availability. Nepal only commenced developing its command after 1976 and its grievance is that the residual water available to it falls short of the 1927 commitment.

The ageing of the Banbassa barrage and opportunity to generate 120 MW of power a little above this point, where the Mahakali river leaves the boundary and makes a westward loop into Kumaon, led India to construct the Tanakpur barrage. This also provided some additional to water availability but entailed anchoring the eastern aflux bund to high ground in Nepal, causing some marginal riverbed flooding in Nepal. Between them, these Indian uses of Nepalese territory extended over 11.9 ha. The Nepalese, however, felt that their territorial integrity had been impugned without adequate consultation or compensation.

Following prolonged discussions, the compensatory package offered Nepal was upgraded twice over the ensuing years. But by now the issue had become totally politicized and enmeshed in the Kingdom's domestic politics. It was finally resolved in the larger Mahakali Treaty which envisages the construction of a high dam at Pancheshwar and subsumes the earlier Sharda and Tanakpur agreements and further enhances the compensation package offered to Nepal.

Nepal continues to exercise sovereignty over the 12 ha of land used for flooded by the Barrage and has been guaranteed that its water requirements from the Mahakali will be fully met and accorded prime consideration at all times. This is specified to include its stipulated irrigation needs from the Sharda and Tanakpur barrages and Pancheswar storage during both the kharif and rabi seasons as well as a substantial command of 93,000 ha in the terai. To this end, India is to construct head regulators at the related off takes and a canal from the Tanakpur barrage to the Nepalese border.

Further, Nepal is to receive 70 million units of energy per annum free of charge from the Tanakpur power station, with a transmission link to its border. Half the incremental power generated at Tanakpur following augmentation of river flows with the commissioning of the Pancheswar dam will also be supplied to Nepal which will, be required to bear half the operational and any additional capital cost.

Finally, India will construct an al-weather link road connecting the Tanakpur barrage to the Kingdom's East-West Highway, including several bridges en route.

The Treaty takes as its domain the portion of the Mahakali river that "is a boundary river on major stretches between the two countries". From this follows the principle of equal partnership and equal entitlement to the utilization of its waters without prejudice to the respective existing consumptive uses. The detailed project report to be jointly prepared by the two sides envisages implementation as an integrated project designed to produce the "maximum total net benefit" in the form of power, irrigation and flood control. While benefits are to be equally apportioned, "the cost shall be borne by the Parties in proportion to the benefits accruing to them".

The Agreement has a life of 75 years and envisages basin development under the aegis of a Mahakali Commission which shall be guided by the principles of equality, mutual benefit and no harm to either Party. India is committed to maintaining a minimum flow of 10 cumecs (350 cusecs) below Banbassa in the Mahakali river "to maintain and preserve the river ecosystem".

A Pancheshwar Development Authority is to be negotiated and both sides shall jointly seek funding for the project which is presently estimated to cost Rs.12,000 crores (at 1995 prices). This has been broken down into roughly 80 per cent for power and 20 per cent for water, with a one per cent component included in the latter for flood moderation.

The major benefit envisages is peaking power, with a planned installed capacity that could go up to 6480 MW. The Letters exchanged with the Agreement set out the principles of cost-benefit sharing. While the power and augmented discharge form the Pancheshwar reservoir are to be equally shared between the Parties, the net power benefit "shall be assessed on the basis of, inter alia, saving in cost to the beneficiaries as compared with relevant alternatives available"; the irrigation benefit on the basis of "incremental and additional benefits due to augmentation of river flow"; and flood control on the basis of "the value of works saved and damage avoided". However, should either side not utilize its share of the augmented flows, it is precluded from making any claim on the other in any form.

These principles will inevitably apply to all future water resource agreements between Nepal and India. The fact that the Mahakali is a boundary river made it possible to enunciate equal sharing which in turn simplified negotiating procedures by psychologically creating a level playing field. Provision for independent arbitration of disputes, with the chairperson being named, if necessary, by the Secretary-General of the Permanent Court of Arbitration at the Hague, should again provide reassurance to Nepal.

There have been some hiccups in proceeding with the preparation of the joint DPR. The issue is one of interpretation and would have been sooner resolved but for political uncertainties in either country that precluded bolder action. However, there is little reason to fear any insuperable difficulty.

EXISTING USES

The differences are basically three. The first relates to defining the "existing uses" that must be deemed to be protected by the Treaty. Nepal's water demands present no problem and are to be met in full. India's Upper Sharda command of 1.6 m ha supplied from Banbassa is also protected. Nepal, however, argues that the 2 m ha irrigated from the Lower Sharda Barrage, 160 kms further downstream, is outside the scope of the "Mahakali" agreement and not a protected existing use. This system primarily depends on water diverted from the Karnali (Ghaghra in India) at Girjapur through the Sharda Sahayak link for over ieght months in the year. But it indents on Sharda supplies during the monsoon between July and October when the Karnali carries a lot of silt.

With unutiiized flows from Nepal's Pancheshwar half-share, further supplies from the catchment between Pancheshwar and Tanakpur, additional free inflows below Banbassa and regeneration, there should normally be enough water to meet all requirements at Banbassa (with some increased intensity of irrigation as proposed) and of the lower Sharda Barrage except for an occasional marginal deficit in July and possibly in October in lean years. On the normal calculus of 75 per cent dependability of river flows, such a shortage in the lower Sharda system may only occur once in four years. This too only after Nepal's stipulated irrigation uses are fully developed to attain the high intensity prescribed, which could take 20 or more years to realize. Meanwhile, it should be possible for India to tap the abundant groundwater to be found along the adjacent *bhabar* springline to the extent necessary.

Nepal, however, claims a half share in the incoming river flows between Pancheshwar and Banbassa on the "equal entitlement" principle within the common boundary segment of the Mahakali. It is here vaguely asserting the right to ownership of the natural flows of the river, or the discarded Harmon Doctrine, which is an untenable principle in emerging international water law. One must distinguish between water rights and water ownership. And the Mahakali Treaty clearly states that Nepal forfeits the right to augmented and other flows that it does not utilize. Equally, India cannot make any absolute claim to prior appropriation with regard to existing uses if this results in expropriation rather than equitable apportionment and reasonable use.

Granted that both sides are perhaps pressing a misplaced claim, the real issue is one of sharing the cost of the Pancheshwar project on the basis of the benefits accruing to either party. Hence if India uses more than its half-share of Pancheshwar/ Mahakali waters (having conceded that Mahakali waters are to be equally shared), it should be prepared to pay a proportionately larger part of the irrigation/water component of the project. This may entail an additional Indian liability of around Rs.600 crores, more or less, or about Rs.1,800 crores out of the Rs.2,400 crore "water" component of the Pancheshwar project at 1995 prices.

There could, however, be a case for awarding the host state(s) a commuted royalty on the dam site, a depleting natural resource, whose life must at some stage come to an end with sedimentation of its live storage capacity. In the case of Pancheshwar, this could be notionally spread over the 75 year life of the Treaty. In India this principle is met by awarding 12.5 per cent free power to the host state from whatever is generated.

PHASING AND TARIFF FIXATION

The second issue relates to the phasing of the project. India initially conceived of an installed capacity of 2000 MW, rising in one or two further stages to anywhere between 5000 to 6000 MW. This was related to the need to investigate and construct a re-regulating dam below the main dam to store and make controlled releases of the water passing through the Pancheshwar turbines to meet the irrigation schedules of the commands below. Nepal, however, favors maximizing the estimated 6480 MW potential in one go to secure the "maximum total net benefit".

There are two possible sites for the re-regulating structure. The first, at Rupali Gad, would generate 240 MW and have limited storage on account of its lower height (60 m) and proximity to Pancheshwar. The Indian view is that the storage this offers will not meet the irrigation demand and that it is accordingly better to site the re-regulating dam further downstream at Poornagiri which would permit construction of a 180 m high dam, provide adequate storage and support a power plant with an installed capacity of 1000 MW.

The Nepalese first opted for Rupali Gad on cost considerations, believing that the Poornagiri investment over and above that on Pancheshwar might be unaffordable. They are, however, now approaching the Indian view that Poornagiri offers a greater "maximum total net benefit". The re-regulating dam sites can be investigated, detailed project reports prepared and work completed within the eight years it will take to complete the Pancheshwar dam. Given this, India would be willing to go along with the principle of maximizing the peaking benefit from Pancheshwar. The final figure of installed capacity and unit sizes will depend on available cavern sizes at the projected power house sites on either bank and the ability of the transport system and bridges on the access road to carry heavy equipment beyond a certain size.

Finally, there have been some differences on power tariff fixing. The Nepalese are right in saying that this be best calculated when the final design parameters and financing details are available. As far as calculation of the avoided or replacement cost is concerned, senior Nepalese spokesmen themselves have come forward with the suggestion that thermal alternatives fuelled by coal, gas or a nuclear reactor be considered and the average unit cost of production be split in agreed proportions (Jha, Hari Bansh, 1996). The Indian side is prepared to go along with this but would wish alternative hydropower costs also to be taken into account as India has considerable unutilized Himalayan hydro capability that awaits harnessing and will very soon have a national power grid to transfer large blocks of power regionally as soon as some inter-regional grid links are completed.

Indeed, the first inter-regional grid links in India were established in 1998 and limited quantities of power flowed hundred of kilometres from east to west and north to south. As the national grid develops, the marginal cost principle of pricing will emerge, linked to optimized system efficiency and time of day tariffs to even out peaks. A power trade corporation is mooted. Altogether then, there is no insuperable hurdle. Minor irritations could recur from time to time and could be insulated from political pressures and uncertainties were the Pancheshwar Development Authority and Mahakali Commission soon constituted and enabled to get on with the job in a professional manner. There is a fourth difference, one of four "strictures" or concerns listed by the Nepalese Parliament when it ratified the Mahakali agreement. This, however, is not a water related but a territorial issue, though tenuously linked to the matter of which of three converging streams is the true source of the Mahakali river. Survey and revenue officials of both sides are meeting with maps and historical records to resolve this issue. But no water issue or allocation of shares turns on this resolution. The disputed Kalapani area is small and given the will, a determination of the facts should not take long.

GANGA TREATY

The Ganga Treaty relates to "sharing of the Ganga/Ganges waters at Farakka" between India and Bangladesh but goes beyond this particular concern. It delinks lean season sharing from augmentation of flows but at the same time enjoins both parties separately to address the long term problem of dry season augmentation. Again, while focusing on the Ganga, it speaks of sharing the waters of (all) international rivers flowing through the territories of the two countries. It goes on to place this in a broader regional context by referring to optimal, integrated river basin development for flood management, irrigation and hydropower generation on the principles of mutual benefit, mutual accommodation, equity, fairness and no harm to either party.

The 1977 Accord and subsequent ad hoc sharing agreements until 1988 were based on 75 per cent dependable flows of the Ganga at Farakka. The 1996 Agreement rests on a 40-year (1949-88) 10-day period average availability of water, or 50 per cent dependability, which India is to make "every effort" to protect against additional upstream abstractions. The change from 75 per cent dependability to average flows notionally enhances the figures of water arrivals that are to be shared at Farakka in order more nearly to meet the numbers desired to give political satisfaction to both sides.

The actual sharing of dry season flows is set out in a formula at Annexure 1 of the Treaty. In brief this assures both sides half the flow when the availability is 70,000 cusecs or less; 35,000 cusecs to Bangladesh and the balance to India when availability is between 70,000 and 75,000 cusecs; and 40,000 cusecs to India and the balance to Bangladesh when the availability is 75 per cent or more. This formulation is subject to the condition that both parties are guaranteed 35,000 cusecs in alternate 10-day periods between March 1 and May 10 when the flows trough just as the boro (winter) crop ripens.

While Annexure I sets out the actual sharing formula. Annexure II provides an "indicative schedule" of the respective shares "if actual availability corresponds to actual flows of the period 1949 to 1988". It is easy to see why this Annexure was included. It spells out the political requirement for India to show that it has safeguarded Calcutta port's 40,000 cusec flushing requirement as far as possible while enabling Bangladesh more particularly to show that it has got 35,000 cusecs (or 500 cusecs more than the minimum provided under the 1977 Accord) during alternating 10-days periods of critical plant growth in March-April. Bangladesh spokesmen also coyly claim that the Gorai river, which serves the Ganges-dependent southwest region, can only take upland water when the Ganges carries more than 30,000 cusecs which is clearly not so.

Finally, the treaty provides that both sides will hold emergency consultations should Ganga flows drop below 50,000 cusecs. In their contingency, 90 per cent of Bangladesh's illustrative share as shown in Annexure II shall be released by India until such time as agreed emergency flows are decided upon through official consultations. This minimum emergency guarantee is 22,500 cusecs.

RESIDUAL FLOW OR FAIR SHARE?

Critics have argued that al the accords reached thus far do not fairly share the waters of the Ganga but only the residuary flows at Farakka after unfettered abstractions by various upper riparians within India. The fact of upstream uses and diversions is undeniable, but the fairness of the quantum being delivered to Bangladesh cannot be seriously questioned. While current average lean season arrivals at Farakka are known, there is no firm estimate of what would be the corresponding virgin flow were there to be no upstream uses at all.

One rough and ready means of computing this may be to make a comparison with the far larger Brahmaputra which flows into Bangladesh below Dhubri in western Assam with very little diversion or consumptive use in its entire upper catchment. The average lean season arrivals at Dhubri are known to be not less than 110,000 cusecs. If this figure is generously assumed to apply to the Ganga at Farakka, then the lowest averaged 25,000 cusec share of water normally flowing into Bangladesh during March-April represents an allocation of 23 per cent of the overall river flows for a Ganges-dependent area with less than a twelfth of the population and a twentieth of the culturable area as compared with that part of the Ganga basin lying in India, much of it semi-arid. This cannot be regarded as unreasonable by any means.

This calculation obviously offers no more than a crude estimate that does not take account of groundwater withdrawals and regeneration. Nevertheless, it provides some idea of the orders of magnitude involved on either side.

There is also need to disaggregate what Bangladesh calls its Ganges dependent area (GDA). This consists of the Southwest Region (SWR) and the South-Central Region (SCR) lying on the right bank of the Padma (as the river is known after the Ganges and Brahmaputra meet). These two regions are together known as the South West Area (SWA) which has a population is 30 million. The SCR is, however, well-watered as it is supplied by the Padma through the Arial Khan and its effluents. The SWA and a strip of the Northwest Region (NWR), lying along the north bank of the Ganges between Hardinge Bridge and its confluence with the Brahmaputra, constitutes the GDA.

The real problem area is the SWR or Kushtia-Jessore-Khulna region served by the Gorai river. According to official Bangladesh sources this channel used to draw a mean monthly flow of 390 cumecs (13,150 cusecs) in April, the leanest period of the dry season, during the 30 years preceding Farakka from 1946 to 1975 (Government of Bangladesh, March 1998). It is now high and dry through most of the lean season.

The Treaty has a life of 30 years, which may be extended by mutual agreement. It is, however, is subject to five-yearly reviews, though either side may call for an initial review after two years. This long-term accord now permits Bangladesh to go ahead and plan for the development of its Ganges-dependent area on the basis of assured minimum flows. It more specifically enables Bangladesh to approach donors to assist in designing and constructing a long-planned Ganges Barrage below Hardinge Bridge, near Pangsa just below the Gorai offtake, to pond the river to a level that renders it possible for the backwaters to enter the derelict Gorai. Without guaranteed flows, donors, multilateral financial agencies and private investors would understandably be chary of coming forward and either risking their money or tangling with the upper riparian. The Treaty therefore opens a door.

TEETHING TROUBLES

In its actual working over the first year or the 1997 January to May lean season, three problems arise. These generated considerable emotion and heat in Bangladesh and heightened political opposition to the treaty.

In the first instance, given a poor hydrological season, actual Farakka arrivals fell below the illustrative Annexure-II figures of average 1949-88 availability, declining below 50,000 cusecs. The shortfall commenced in the last week of February, coinciding with the unseating of the then Indian government and the absence at the United Nations of the Indian technical adviser dealing with implementation of the treaty. This unfortunately resulted in a slight delay before India could respond adequately to the requirement of emergency consultation. The hiatus was brief and arrangements were made to ensure compensatory deliveries to Bangladesh over the ensuing 10-day periods.

A second problem arose around the stepped deliveries of no less than 35,000 cusecs to either side during the stipulated alternating 10-day periods. If flows were at or near 50,000 cusecs this would mean ensuring shares of 35,000 to one side and 15,000 cusecs to the other in one 10-day period and abruptly reversing these flows during the next 10-day period. The earth-lined walls of the Farakka Feeder Canal require graduated increments or reductions in flow if they are not to suffer damage or even collapse. This safety factor, though known to both sides from previous experience, was not reflected in the letter of the Treaty. However, this was overcome by effecting graduated increases and reductions in flows spread over a few days, thus ensuring the stipulated quantum but with a slightly difference time-cycle. Nonetheless, a technical violation was cited. Once a Ganges Barrage comes up, this problem will be mitigated.

More mysteriously, the releases at Farakka, which swelled with regeneration at Hardinge Bridge in Bangladesh, the other point of joint flow observations under the Treaty, began to show marked degeneration or a deficit at the Hardinge Bridge observation point for some weeks after March. This caused a public outcry with allegations of Indian mala fides through excessive abstractions or faulty releases at Farakka, despite daily joint observations.

It is a hydrological commonplace that there is an interchange from stream flows to aquifers when the groundwater table is below river bed levels and vice versa when river flows fall below aquifer levels. Thus influent conditions cause regeneration while effluent conditions lead to degeneration. Such a possibility was in act forecast by an influential Bangladeshi paper, *Sangbad*, on January 2, 1997.

"Sangbad" reported that "Hydrologists have expressed concern that during the lean period in March-April, the exact quantum of water released from Farakka under the newly-signed Agreement may not be received at the Hardinge point". It went on to quote experts to the effect that approximately 100,000 tubewells had been dug in an area of 7692 sq. km from the point opposite Farakka to Hardinge Bridge under the Borendra Project (in Rajshahi district within the GDA). "A quantum of 31,700 cusecs is being pulled through these tubewells although in 1982 Sir Macdonald and Partners (sic) advised that pulling 15,500 cusecs will b appropriate in this region. In the last five years, the underground water level in this area has gone down from about 25 feet to 60 feet and this has been done intentionally. Due to this condition the whole area is under arsenic pollution".

The evidence is not conclusive and the matter is being jointly investigated by technical experts. There could also be some loss to aquifers along the right bank of the river in West Bengal.

The other issues in contention relate to procedures for emergency consultation and interim releases pending an agreement and amending the stepped-flow schedule to accommodate safety considerations. At the instance of Bangladesh, these mattes have been left for discussion at the first Treaty review that may be convened after December 1998. However, the 1998 lean season witnessed superabundant flows right through to May in reversal of the hydrological situation during the previous year.

At the political level, the Bangladesh Government kept its cool through the 1997 time of troubles and did not give any handle to impatient or motivated critics of the treaty.

GORAI CLOSURE

A more substantial issue that has as yet attracted little notice is the Gorai problem. This major deltaic spill of the Ganges and the Kobadak river to the west of it serve the southwest Ganges dependent region which Bangladesh feels has been devastated by Indian withdrawals at Farakka. These low flow diversion, it is said, have denied sufficient headwater supplies to operate the Ganges-Kobadak river lift irrigation system and have left the Gorai high and dry. This has resulted in a sharp northward movement of the salinity front which reduced freshwater supplies for drinking purposes, irrigation and industrial use and adversely affected agriculture, fisheries, navigation and the Sundari species in the Sunderbans mangrove forest.

Farakka withdrawals can at best only be a secondary cause of this environmental degradation. The entire Ganga system has been migrating eastward over the past century and more. The Bangladesh Water Resources Ministry has this to say: "The river systems of the SWA have evolved as a result of high local rainfall and the historically eastward progression of the mouth of the Ganges. Only two rivers of significance remain connected to the Ganges-Padma, the Gorai serving the SWR and the Arial Khan serving the SCR. Over time the smaller distributaries have been separated from the Ganges and fear now is that the Gorai, the one remaining river flowing through the Southwest, will soon follow" (Ibid).

The Bhagirathi-Hooghly, the westernmost deltaic channel of the Ganga and once the main arm of the river, was the first to bc affected. Its offtake, lying just below Farakka, started silting and ultimately became derelect. The river has since continued to shift eastward, causing progressive deterioration in the other spill channels.

The Bangladesh Land and Water Resources Sector Study, Volume VII, Water Technical Report No. 20 of 1972 has this to say at Para 6.12: "Present dry season flows in the Gorai river are often decreased by sand bars that develop at the Ganges offtake. Without sandbars, the minimum discharge varies historically between 10,000 to 18,000 cfs (cusecs), but with the sand bar the discharge had decreased to 5 cfs in February-May of 1950, 2900 cfs in January 1952, and to 500 cfs in May 1954.

However, the effect of sand bars could be eliminated by dredging and a minimum discharge of some 15,000 cfs could be assured under the present circumstances".

These trends and findings long predate the commissioning of the Farakka Barrage in 1975. More than the stipulated minimum of 34,500 cusecs was released below Farakka into the Ganges between 1978 and 1988 under various agreements. The Gorai problem clearly preceded Farakka which has virtually stopped drawing water as the Ganges recedes after the floods and its discharge falls below something around 50,000-70,000 cusecs, more or less, depending on natural factors. The Gorai outfall has got plugged with a hard silt barrier some 16 feet high and 30 km long, up to the Gorai railway bridge.

GORAI AUGMENTATION AND GANGES BARRAGE

What this means is that very little if any of the Ganga Treaty releases below Farakka will enter the Gorai during the critical dry period from February to April. Capital dredging followed by annual maintenance dredging offers a partial but expensive solution. This Gorai Augmentation Project has been the subject of considerable study and is now proposed to be taken up experimentally with Dutch-World Bank assistance as a measure of interim relief. The long-term solution could be a Ganges Barrage 15 km below the Gorai outfall at Pangsa and 60 km downstream of Hardinge Bridge, to pond the river within its banks and thereby permit headwater water supplies to back into the Gorai.

The Ganges Barrage was investigated in 1963,1964 and 1968 prior to the liberation of Bangladesh and again in 1984 and under the Flood Action Plan (Khalilur, Rahman Feb.1998; FAP-4 August 1993). The National Water Plan Summary Report of December 1986, also stressed the need to have both a Ganges and a Brahmaputra barrage in place by 2005. With the Ganga Treaty in hand the Bangladesh government has now accorded the highest priority to the multipurpose Ganges Barrage. It convened a high level international Seminar in Dhaka in March 1998, with World Bank, ADB and Japanese co-sponsorship, to muster technical and financial support for a detailed feasibility study of the project as a preclude to its construction thereafter with international assistance. Various price-tags have been mentioned but the Bangladesh Government believes that the cost of a multipurpose barrage project might be of the order of $ 1.5 billion.

The concept of the project has undergone change. While the Gorai resuscitation, salinity control, fisheries, navigation (including navigational lock), mangrove restoration and road (and even rail) bridge components remain, the agriculture-irrigation perspective is different. Rather than use the barrage to feed an elaborate state-run canal system, current thinking favors enabling restored Gorai flows to enter and fill a network of moribund spill channels, khals, hoars (oxbows), village tanks and wetlands, with dredging of choked outfalls, regulatory structures, drainage improvements and some restoration of coastal embankments with sluices.

This is expected to restore the former ecosystem of the region, facilitate recharge and enable farmers to irrigate their fields through river lift pumps and shallow tubewells. Further, this would protect drinking water supplies currently affected by arsenic contamination. The modest hydropower generation (11 MW) planned at the barrage is expected to serve the farm demand for lifting water. It is estimated that there will be sufficient water to irrigate 670,000 ha apart from providing assured supplies for the sick Ganges-Kobadak scheme and its expansion further west.

Such a strategy is seen as encouraging the development of a water market, people's participation through water-user associations, lower capital costs and overheads, and avoidance of bureaucratization. The Jamuna Multipurpose Bridge project (JMBP) across the Brahmaputra at Siraganj, completed ahead of time in 42 months through use of precast structures, has instilled confidence in Bangladesh that it can build the Ganges Barrage in less than the eight years being forecast, through use of similar technologies. With the JMBP, the country now has a legal framework and contracting procedures that should cut down on delays while the proposed Dinajpur hard rock project being taken up with Japanese assistance will provide cheaper stone nearer at hand for the Ganges Barrage and its guide bunds than the huge volume of quarried material imported from Meghalaya and the Rajmahal Hills in India and, further afield, from Indonesia for the JMBP.

The cost-benefit ratio is estimated to be favourable. Positive side-effects include encouraging needed crop diversification, saving the cost of the proposed Paksi road bridge across the Ganges below the existing Hardinge Bridge railway crossing, establishing a new Dhaka-Khulna transport corridor and improving the economics of Mongla port. The project is seen as contributing greatly to poverty alleviation and employment generation in the SWR.

India has shown interest in the Ganges Barrage Project and has offered technical support in view of its long experience in building barrages, including the Farakka Barrage. Some modest financial support for the project.

The Dhaka Seminar in March 1998 on "Water Resource Management and Development in Bangladesh with Particular Reference to the Ganges River" witnessed something of a centretemps. The World Bank, ADB and Japanese, who are likely to lead the donor consortium that might ultimately support the Ganges Barrage Project, balked at going along with an immediate feasibility study. They felt that other options should not be foreclosed and the impact of Gorai augmentation with dredging merited deeper scrutiny alongside further environmental, economic and social studies including people's participation. Basin-wide studies, presumably in relation to assurance of water availability and augmentation and wider regional cooperation, were also advocated.

The final plan of action struck a compromise. The urgency and importance of converting the flows assured by the Ganga Treaty into utilizable supplies for the service of the affected SWR was noted. However, the Water Resources Planning

Organisation (WARPO) which is responsible for the National Water Management Project-III now commencing was asked to prepare an inception report within three months suggesting what further preliminary studies it should undertake on a priority basis before a decision is taken to embark on a feasibility study of the Ganges Barrage project. This procedure is likely to entail a delay of about a year.

SHARING THE BRAHMAPUTRA AND OTHER RIVERS

Though the Ganges Barrage may serve two-thirds of the 40,500 sq. km SWA with 30 million people, the larger part of Bangladesh's land area and population falls in the Brahmaputra and Meghna basins which could also do with better water regulation for irrigation and flood mitigation. The country's almost exclusive preoccupation with Farakka over the past two decades has precluded anything more than fitful attention to these other regions where cooperation with India could again make a significant difference.

It is with this in mind that Bangladesh in 1987 informally proposed an overall water agreement with India that envisaged a minimal share for itself of up to 25,000 cusecs in the Ganga, and an equal split with regard to all other rivers barring the Brahmaputra. It was suggested that both sides use 25 per cent of the lean flows of the Brahmaputra and leave the balance for ecological needs and salinity control in Bangladesh. The Brahmaputra split requires more detailed justification than has been vouchsafed thus far and could be better balanced.

More recently some others have argued that even the river's entire current lean flows, which are scarcely diminished by any consumptive uses, are insufficient for Bangladesh and that any diminution will adversely affect the ecology of the lower Meghna basin. This appears an extravagant claim. This mighty river accounts for as much as 29 per cent of India's total runoff and constitutes the single largest source of virtually untapped surplus that might be available in the future to meet the emerging water-shortage over large parts of the country, without prejudice to Bangladesh interest's.

Planning studies undertaken by the Brahmaputra Board suggest that storages identified for development in the Brahmaputra basin by 2010, 2020 and 2030 could yield an additional live storage of 4.88 b.c.m. and 7.80 b.c.m. respective or 23.21 b.c.m. in all (Mohile, A.D. March 1998). Even if 20 per cent of this storage capacity were dedicated to providing a flood cushion, there would still be a conservation storage capacity of 16.57 b.c.m. to augment lean season flows for purposes of irrigation, navigation and other in-stream and ecological uses.

In accordance with the Ganga Treaty, the Secretary-level joint committee of experts has met to work out permanent sharing arrangements for the other common rivers. Priority is being given to the Teesta, on which both sides have irrigation projects, followed by six smaller rivers, namely, the Manu, Khowai, Gumti, Muhuri, Dharla and Dudhkumar.

In the longer run, some of the commands of these smaller rivers could be subsumed in certain larger projects. For example, the flood moderation, irrigation navigation and power benefits of the 1500 MW Tiapimukh project on the Barak in southern Manipur could extend across the border. A cost-benefit study of the environmental and other impacts in Bangladesh have indeed been proposed and it would be greatly to the advantage of both countries if Tipaimukh were taken up within a cooperative framework.

The Teesta insufficient flows to meet the requirements of the twin Teesta projects. Augmentation would render the barrages in either country more viable. India has investigated a Teesta power cascade in Sikkim and the Darjeeling Hills. One of these dams could provide some modest storage as and when built. But it is diversion from the Brahmaputra system that could really make a difference. Meanwhile Teesta sharing is obviously necessary. The flow data needs to be firmed up and the possibility of operating the two barrages in tandem merits examination. The Indian barrage could in fact irrigate areas that cannot be commanded by the lower Bangladesh system.

Teesta augmentation could come from regulated releases from the proposed Sunkosh dam in Bhutan. This 4000 MW multipurpose project with a re-regulating lift dam (60 MW) lower down would, if approved by the Royal Government, augment lean flows by about 12,000 cusecs. This could be transferred via the Teesta and Mahananda barrages/canals to the Ganga for redistribution at Farakka. This possibility was in fact informally mooted in Indian circles at the Ganga Treaty talks as a candidate for augmenting supplies to Calcutta port and, maybe, to Bangladesh.

This link canal will also provide some irrigation to North Bengal and could supplement both Teesta and Mahananda flows to make good existing deficits in those rivers in part or whole. Environmental objections have been raised, as the originally proposed canal alignment cut through two major game sanctuaries and several tea gardens. A fresh alignment now under examination skirts the southern fringe of the sanctuaries and could provide additional irrigation en route.

JOGIGHOPA DIVERSION

In 1978 and 1982 India's proposal for augmenting Ganga flows at Farakka envisaged transfer of up to 100,000 cusecs of monsoon storage behind the mega Dihang (20,000 MW) and Subansiri (4800 MW) dams in Arunachal Pradesh through a 324 km Link Canal taking off from a Brahmaputra barrage at Jogighopa near Dhubri in Assam where the river makes a southward bend around the Garo Hills into Bangladesh. The idea of a giant Link Canal was dropped over Bangladeshi objections on technical, environmental and political considerations. The two dams aroused strong opposition in Arunachal as they would submerge six of the State's new towns, including Along, Yingkiong and Daparijo, and prime forest areas and displace a significantly large population.

Both projects are with Arunachalese consent being now reworked as a series of three cascades each. The Dihang dam is proposed to be replaced by a smaller dam at the same site just upstream of Pasighat, with two upper dams at Yingkiong on the main stem and another on the Siyom river, a right bank tributary with a total installed capacity of 20,000 MW. Likewise, the originally proposed Subansiri dam is proposed to be substituted by a lower dam at the same site at Gerumukh, with two upper dams at Daporijo on the main stem and another on the tributary, the Kamala river, with a combined installed capacity of 7300 MW. They will between them store almost as much water as originally contemplated. But no towns will be submerged and displacement and forest loss will be smaller. The Brahmaputra Board expects to have the project reports ready in phases within three years. The flood mitigation and navigation benefits in the Assam valley will be substantial and it has now been technically established that it should be possible to evacuate a large block of power through the narrow Siliguri neck without hazard.

The Jogighopa barrage could in this eventuality again come into play to transfer smaller quantities of stored waters west and south through any one or more alignments. These could be entirely through India (which would entail an expensive lift) or aligned through Bangladesh to feed its Teesta canal system, augment the Atrai and Korotoya rivers in Northern Bangladesh or be extended further to the Ganges barrage at Pangsa. A cross link to Farakka might also be feasible. The quantum, alignment (along existing streams and old river channels that could be interconnected) and management of the facilities proposed would of course need to be discussed with and approved by Bangladesh if its territory is involved.

Bangladesh would have a stake in such a package for several reasons. First, it could be a partner in a joint enterprise. Secondly, right and left bank canals taking off from Jogighopa could irrigate large areas in northern and centralbangladesh that could not be commanded otherwise. Such augmentation would take care of the Teesta command and could even obviate the need for constructing the far more expensive and technically complex Brahmaputra barrage at Bahadurabad in Bangladesh that is also under contemplation. With upstream storages in Arunachal, there would be some flood mitigation in Bangladesh while navigation and pisciculture would greatly improve. Any subsequent construction of the Bahadurabad barrage, if still desired by Bangladesh for river training, channelisation and reclamation of the Brahmaputra's vast and braided river bed, would perhaps be rendered simpler by upstream regulation.

The Indian Government set up a National Commission on Integrated Water Resources Development in 1997 to look at the scenario in 2025 and beyond and undertake basin-wise water balance studies to map out areas of emerging water stress and potential surplus countrywide. The objective is to study and design a cost-effective national water grid that would transfer the surplus waters of the Brahmaputra and, in part, the Ganga west and south to the semi-arid and desert areas of Haryana, Rajasthan and Guajarat and to water-short peninsular India, with some additionality from any residual surpluses in the Mahanadi and Godavari.

Far and away the largest surplus is in the Brahmaputra basin and it is essential to work in tandem with Bangladesh if this is to be optimally tapped. Fortunately, there is a fairly close fit between the kind of long term water perspective being developed in India (for moving "surplus" waters west and south) and that being developed in Bangladesh through the Water Resources Planning Organisation WARPO in 1991 inherited the mantle of the erstwhile Master Plan Organisation which had prepared the country's National Water Plan's I and II in 1985 and 1990. The new study stress social and economic issues and participatory strategies over a 25 year time horizon social and economic issues and participatory strategies over a 25 year time horizon of 1997-2023.

It would therefore be logical for India's National Water Development Agency (NWDA), the technical limb of the National Water Commission, to establish contact not only with WARPO but also with Nepal's Electricity Development Corporation, which is looking at long term prioritization of hydro-development in the Kingdom, and its National Water Resources Council. These organizations could usefully exchange data and working plans and move incrementally towards developing the integrated, optimized framework GBM basin plan envisaged by the Mahakali and Ganga Treaties.

As a sidelight, the Chinese Academy of Engineering Physics was informed in 1995 that it was technically possible to divert Tsang-po waters north to the arid Gobi across the intervening mountain ranges through peaceful nuclear explosions (Scientific American, 1996). This seems farfetched. It would possibly be simpler to divert some flow from the Tsang-po into the Ganga system in Tibet through tunneled interconnections with the upper Gandak or upper Arun. This too much at least for now remain in the realm of fancy.

BHUTAN FORGES AHEAD

Bhutan has an assessed hydroelectric potential of 20,000 MW from its many snow-fed rivers, especially the Manas. Development of its water resources commenced with the very successful 336 MW run-of-the-river Chukha project on the Wangchu (Raidek) which was commissioned in 1987 with close Indian collaboration. Harnessing its rich water resources promises it a sustainable pathway of development and environmental conservation but could at the same time give considerable stimulus to regional cooperation as well. With four tariff revisions since its inception, Chukha's power exports to India have earned it an increasing annual revenue which amounted to Rs.121.60 crores in 1997-98 at one rupee per unit. No cost or interest recoveries have thus far been made from Bhutan for this entirely Indian funded project. Instead, these have been adjusted against other ongoing Indian-assisted projects.

Emboldened by the eco-friendly Chukha project and increasing income-generation from periodic tariff revisions, Bhutan has entered into further agreements with India under which two more projects are under construction. The 45 MW Kurichu project was initiated in 1994 in eastern Bhutan. More recently, work on developing the Wangchu cascade has commenced with the 1020 MW Tala scheme (again with 60 per cent grant and 40 per cent soft loan assistance from India). This should be ready by 2005 and is to be followed by Wangchu Stage III (900 MW) and Bunakha (180 MW), upstream of Chukha. If implemented, these projects taken together with Sunkosh could take Bhutan's installed capacity to near 6550 MW, with surplus energy feeding into the Indian grid.

The Bhutanese government has its own views about the pace and pattern of development. Its caution stems from not wanting to open up or modernize too rapidly. This could be culturally destabilizing and, it is feared, impact adversely on the environment. The King wisely places happiness above growth. However, rapid population increase and the new growth impulses in South Asia will generate their own pressures for employment and income generation. Hydro power, bio-diversity and eco-tourism offer Bhutan its best development options. Among these, the stream of benefits that could flow from developing even half the country's 20,000 MW hydro potential may well be the least damaging (Somnath Mukherjee, March 1998).

SAPTA KOSI AND ARUN-3 IN NEPAL

Augmentation at Farakka could also come from the Sapta Kosi-cum-Sun Kosi-Kamala diversion project for which a joint detailed project report is under preparation under an Indo-Nepal Memorandum of Understanding signed in 1991. The Joint Team of Experts set up by the two sides agreed on the broad terms of a revised inception report in January 1997. This replicated the cost benefit principles written into the Mahakali Agreement and emphasized the need for comprehensive river basin planning. India has agreed to fund preparation of a joint DPR.

The joint DPR study is to embrace several elements. These include a Sapta Kosi high dam at Barakshetra (3500 to 4000 MW); the Sun Kosi-Kamala diversion project at Kurule (61 MW) with a re-regulating Kamala dam to irrigate some 17,500 ha in Nepal and possibly additional areas in India; and a feasibility study for developing inland navigation from Chatra down to the confluence of the Kosi with the Ganga, either along the river or through a multipurpose canal to link with India's National Waterway No.1 from Haldia to Patna and Allahabad.

Since the Sapta Kosi High Dam may have a live storage in excess of nine billion cubic metres it could provide a considerable flood cushion, irrigate 700,000 ha in the Nepal terai from the Bamati to the Mechi and another 980,000 ha in India, and yet augment Ganga flows below Farakka. This is a project which India rates highly as an answer to the havoc caused by the annual Kosi floods in North Bihar which the Hanumannagar Barrage and embankments are no longer able to contain. Bangladesh too has expressed strong interest in the project and would like its concerns to be taken into account while settling the design and operational parameters with appropriate participation in cost-benefit sharing.

There are cautions too. Without improving drainage and undertaking a package of agrarian reforms, further irrigation in North Bihar's Kosi command could be problematic.

Nepal was earlier ready to go with its attenuated Arun-3 (201 mw) proposal with World Bank-ADB collaboration. But the multilateral agencies withdrew support at a very advanced stage of discussions. This was largely on economic considerations as it was felt that the cost of the realigned 125 km access road would render the project uneconomic by pricing the power out of the Indian market, where the surplus energy was to be exported, and pre-empt a wider sectoral and regional spread of donor assistance to the Kingdom. This sudden volte face came as a great disappointment to Nepal and underlines the moral that development assistance too needs to be sustainable.

This is a lesson that India too learnt a little earlier with the fiasco of World Bank (and, separately, Japanese) loan assistance to the Sardar Sarovar Project on the Narmada. This followed the blinkered report of an Independent Review Mission appointed by the Bank that compelled it to "step back" from the Project virtually against its own better technical judgement.

POWER TRADE STIMULATES PRIVATE INVESTMENT

The dropping of Arun-3 led Nepal to look for a substitute project to meet its load demand by 2001. This was found in the Kali Gandaki-A project (144 MW), work on which has commenced. But with growing environmental opposition, the increasing difficulty in finding resources for multilateral funding, economic reforms and globalization, the role of private investment and financing has assumed a new importance. Partly in response to some of these impulses, India and Nepal entered into a 50-year Power Trade Agreement in February1996.

Under this, any government, para-statal or private party in Nepal or India may enter into an agreement to trade power between themselves or with third countries. They are free to determine the quantum and parameters of supply, point of delivery and the price of the supply proposed to be traded. The reference to "government" here obviously includes State governments in India and does not preclude marketing of Nepalese power supplies directly to users in India or elsewhere in South Asia.

Private entrepreneurs, including foreign investors, have already entered into the business of developing hydro and thermal power in India. Nepal has followed suit and two projects, namely, Khimti (60 MW) and Upper Bhote Kosi (36 MW) have been taken up by consortia of Nepalese and foreign interests. With Nepal and India unable to reconcile their views on the parameters and phasing of the giant Karnali project (10,800 MW) and the developing Tanakpur controversy that stalled further Indo-Nepal water resource negotiations for a while, Enron, the American giant currently building thermal plants in India, showed interest in Karnali which it may seek to develop in stages if an agreement can be reached.

There has in addition been a keen show of private interest in the Upper Karnali (250 MW) and full Arun-3 (402 MW) projects with Indian bidders also in the reckoning. If the access road to the upper Arun Valley is taken up as a separate highway project, the Arun hydro cascade could become an attractive proposition.

The West Seti project (750 MW) is being pursued by the Australian Snowy Mountain Engineering Corporation. The market for all large Nepalese hydro projects is essentially in India as the Kingdom's own load forecast indicates that domestic demand may not exceed 1002 MW by 2010. SMEC accordingly entered into an agreement in May 1997 with the Royal Government for export of the bulk of the estimated 3137 GWh annual energy output to India through a 77 km 400 KV double circuit transmission line. SMEC has been talking to potential customers in Northern India, especially State Electricity Boards. Terms are being negotiated with regard to the period of validity of the licence and the principle and quantum of a power export tax.

Nepal need not think only of exporting surplus power. It should look at the possibility of value-addition by inviting energy-intensive electro-metallurgical and electro-chemical industries to produce aluminium or nitrogenous fertilizer. The electrolysis route was followed by the Nangal Fertiliser plant at its inception which it was offered very cheap Bhakra power before the present agricultural and industrial loads developed. Secondary power produced during the wet season could be so priced as to attract industry. Nepal needs employment too and should seek to enhance the multiplier effect of its power resource.

The Government of Nepal is also concerned to get a return on regulated releases of water passing through the West Seti turbines. These are expected to augment the lean season flows of that river which in turn falls into the Karnali. Rather than gift an unrequited bonus to India, which might beneficially use these augmented flows in the future, Nepal is informally exploring a trade-off.

It argues that Indian cautions on grounds as prior appropriation in Uttar Pradesh and Bihar have in the past led international donors such as the ADB and Kuwait Development Fund to shy away from funding irrigation projects on the Kankai and Babai. Nepal also has in mind a proposal to divert outside the basin the waters of the Bheri (a left bank tributary of the Karnali) through a project that will generate power and augment irrigation suppliers in the host area. In the circumstances, it is suggested, why should not India informally set off the augmentation of Karnali supplies from West Seti with the roughly equivalent quantum of water Nepal might tap through its Bheri, Kankai and Babai projects.

Such trade-offs would not be inappropriate and should be considered with an open mind. Enveloped within mountain folds, Nepal has fewer options than India if it wishes to irrigate the terai fringe as its lesser rivers debouch from the Siwaliks into the vast Gangetic plain. Since lead times of five to 10 years would be involved before any of these projects are commissioned, India could find alternative or supplementary sources of irrigation in collaboration with or even independently of Nepal. Groundwater lift along the bhabar springline supplemented by regeneration from irrigation at higher contours in Nepal would also be a possibility, perhaps with Nepalese inputs of power from a series of small and medium dams.

Such a pattern of integrated development of the common rivers along the long east-west Indo-Nepal border has not yet been either conceptualized or explored. This should be done and could prove mutually beneficial.

U.N. WATER CONVENTION

There is much that can be learnt by India and others from international experience and various new protocols governing inter-country or regional accords. Framework agreements setting out general principles have been found to be helpful, with specific details being negotiated to meet the particularities of specific projects.

Emerging international water law took a forward stride recently with the adoption in March 1997 by the U.N. General Assembly of the Convention on the Law of the Non-Navigational Uses of International Watercourses drafted by the International Law Commission (U.N. Sixth Committee Report, April 11, 1997; earlier Draft Articles and Commentary). India, Pakistan and 21 other abstained while Nepal, Bhutan and Bangladesh voted in favour. China and a few others voted against.

The Convention is a flexible document which spells out the principles a framework agreement with watercourse states may "apply and adjust" to suit the characteristics and uses of a particular river or part thereof. Yet India had reservations on some articles such as an overly prescriptive formulation o how to reconcile reasonable and equitable use as agreed between two states with avoidance of "significant harm" to a third party (Article 3); reference to the yet insufficiently defined concept of "sustainable", even if optimal, utilization (Article 5); the application of non-discriminatory legal and judicial procedures to trans-boundary persons citing injury, in regions where political and economic integration is lacking (Article 32); and mandatory establishment of fact-finding commissions in the interests of conflict resolution between watercourse states (Article 33).

The Convention replaces the earlier terminology with regard to adverse impacts from "appreciable harm" to "significant harm". This moves the argument from subjective to objective criteria and renders it possible to settle issues through ameliorative action or payment of compensation. The right to consultation in good faith is asserted.

Equitable and reasonable utilization should aim at optimality, with the right and duty of watercourse states to cooperate in the development and ecological protection of the watercourse. An interesting principle was elaborated by the

Rapporteur in his interpretive commentary on the articles as they were being drafted. He opined that the right to equitable utilization or "equality of right" does not mean entitlement to an equal share of the uses and benefits of the watercourse, but depends on the facts and circumstances of each individual case and specifically on a weighing of all "relevant factors" as provided in Article 6 (UN, 1966).

The "relevant factors" include (a) geographic, hydrographic, hydrological, climatic, ecological and other natural factors;(b) social and economic needs; (c) population dependent on the watercourse; (d) effects of uses on other watercourse states; (e) existing and potential uses; (f) conservation, protection, development and economy of use and the cost of measures so taken; and (g) the availability of alternatives, of comparable value, to a particular planned or existing use. This is only an indicative list and does not exclude other relevant factors. Nor is any priority or weight attached to any of them. All relevant factors and circumstances must be weighed and a holistic view taken. In weighing uses, vital needs such as provision of drinking water should take precedence.

Another interesting interpretation of the Rapporteur in respect of the obligation not to cause significant harm (Article 7) is that due diligence will be exercised to avoid such harm and that "this is an obligation of conduct and not of result" (Ibid).

Two other articles are of special interest. Article 24 enjoins consultations regarding the management of international watercourses to promote their sustainable development and rational and optimal utilization, protection and control. And Article 27 calls on watercourse states to prevent or mitigate conditions that may be harmful to other watercourse states whether resulting from natural or human factors such as floods, waterborne disease, siltation, erosion, saltwater intrusion, drought or desertification. Data and information exchange and the need for consultation find special mention.

The Convention is non-binding. Nevertheless it offers a valuable guide to the GBM co-riparians in promoting cooperative regional development. For instances, the Mahakali and Ganga Treaties speak of "no harm" which the Convention can help interpret in terms of no "significant harm" and its mitigation or compensation if unavoidable. However, the Ganga and Mahakali Treaties show a close correspondence with the Convention for the most part.

The Convention underlines the growing concern the world over with environmental and water equality issues. Following the earlier Narmada controversy, the Rio Conference and increasing domestic, awareness of the importance of eco-friendly development, avoidance and mitigation of any harsh environmental impacts through design changes or compensatory actions, and truly caring resettlement and rehabilitation programmes for those displaced or otherwise affected by water resource projects has become mandatory. The Courts have intervened to ensure compliance with stipulated conditions and this has further sensitized governments and project authorities to upgrade standards and secure their implementation.

NEW TEHRI R&R AND ENVIRONMENT PACKAGE

The Tehri Dam in the Garhwal Himalaya in Uttar Pradesh was the subject of prolonged controversy with a series of R&R, environmental and dam safety issues being agitated by the Tehri Bandh Virodhi Sangharsh Samiti and Sunderlal Bahuguna. The Courts intervened while a series of fasts-unto-death by Bahuguna persuaded the Government to appoint two separate Committees consisting of the latter's nominees in the main and others to review all aspects of the project. With the collapse of the Soviet Union which was funding the power component (2400 MW), the financial package had to be reworked and this took time to close. Three years later, the Tehri project appears to be out of the woods and poised to move forward in the light of these many reviews.

The Tehri Hydro Development Corporation (THDC) was incorporated in 1988 as a joint venture between the governments of India and Uttar Pradesh. This followed UP's inability to fund the enlarged project with an installed capacity of 2400 MW comprising 1000 MW at the main dam, 400 MW at the 97.5 m high re-regulating dam at Koteshwar 22 km downstream, and another 1000 MW through pumped storage from the balancing reservoir through reversible turbines at the main dam. A 800 KV extra-high voltage transmission line is, to be built by the Power Grid Corporation from Tehri to Meerut. The augmented water flows will provide additional irrigation to 270,000 ha and stabilize existing irrigation over 600,000 ha.

The project was dogged with controversies that were agitated in Court as well as through coercive fasts and a series of representations. These are well documented (Verghese, 1994). However, as the Government of India continued to receive insistent demands for a further examination of various environmental, rehabilitation and dam safety (seismic) issues, despite several earlier reviews, it decided to remit these to two committees. Thus an expert committee on rehabilitation and environmental aspects of the project was set up under Prof. Hanumantha Rao, former Planning Commission Member, and another expert group on dam safety, both around September 1996. the Supreme Court meanwhile suspended further hearings on long-pending suits on these very issues. The Hanumantha Rao Committee reported in October 1997 and the Dam Safety Expert Group in February 1998, both well behind schedule.

The Hanumantha Rao committee's recommendations (Expert Committee on the Tehri Project, October 1997) are estimated to cost an additional Rs.514 crores, most of this on R&R, over and above the Rs. 503 crores already committed, Rs.414 crores of this on R&R and the balance on environmental tasks.

The new R&R package expands the definition of "family" to include al major married sons and major unmarried sons and unmarried daughters as of July 19, 1990. They will be treated as independent families and entitled to two acres of land. Should these independent families not be rehabilitated by July, 2002, all married sons who have attained majority as of that date will be entitled to get cash grants of Rs. 1.5 lakhs in lieu of the standard land allotment and all unmarried sons and daughters Rs. 75,000 each. The definition of fully affected and partially affected villages is also to be upgraded to benefit additional families.

With regard to urban project-affected families, the Committee recommends that every shop-owner who has rented out his premises should be compensated for the land and structure and additionally be entitled to purchase one shop in New Tehri Town at cost and receive a development grant of Rs.50,000 for each additional shop that he may own. House owners in old Tehri should also be entitled to a house construction grant at rates ranging from Rs.60,000 to Rs.1.8 lakhs, depending on the plot size.

Since these recommendations go beyond the norms being currently formulated under the national rehabilitation policy, they are being reviewed by the Government and will be presented to the Supreme Court as the proposed package.

The Committee's principal recommendation pertaining to the environment is that the Project must be responsible for catchment area treatment of all highly degraded and erodible areas, whether draining directly into the reservoir or indirectly through the river further upstream. THDC has already treated 29,350 ha out of 36,000 ha at a cost of Rs. 32 crores. The Committee, however, would like another 74,015 ha to be covered at an additional cost of Rs. 90 crores. An environment cess on Tehri power is suggested to finance this expenditure. Additionally, the Committee would like 79,077 ha of medium and low erosion micro-watersheds comprising both forest and non-forest lands to be treated in their entirety and not just wherever affected, through not at project cost. All these constitute new national norms regarding which the Government must take a view outside and beyond the Tehri project.

In the matter of flora and fauna the THDC has agreed to go along with the recommendation that a further multi-disciplinary study be carried for two years preceding project completion and a full year after impoundment. Other recommendations on health impacts, dust pollution abatement, water quality, compensatory afforestation (already completed), the command area, downstream impacts, reservoir rim stability, water availability, discharge and sediment load data and preparation of a disaster management plan are mostly hortatory or extramural. A high level coordination committee, a monitoring committee and public hearings are suggested.

Two members believe that the Tehr project was never properly environmentally assessed or costed and that the required studies have not been satisfactorily completed. Their view is that all work be suspended until then and only resumed if the project is found viable. Yet another Member, having signed the report, asks philosophically whether the project is necessary or desirable or viable and if there are no alternative means of realizing its objectives, partially if not wholly. The fact is that various alternatives were examined at the very start and found sub-optimal.

The inexorable pressure of population is going to compel further augmentation of supplies wherever possible alongside conservation and demand management which are important and necessary in their own right.

An old objection once again being pressed with renewed vigor by the Vishwa Hindu Parishad, with which Bahuguna appears to concur, is that the not merely should the Tehri dam not be pursued but that the incomplete structure constructed thus far be dismantled. The plea taken is that it is wrong to artificially obstruct the flow of the sacred Ganga. This, 138 years after the initial diversions of water through the Ganga canal! In any event, water will continue to pass through the turbines and over the spillway.

DAM SAFETY ISSUE

The fierce on the safety of the rockfall Tehri dam on seismic grounds has been recorded elsewhere (Gaur, Decembe 1993; Verghese, 1994; Khatri, February 1996). The Dam Safety Export Group, consisting of some of Tehri's most outspoken critics, re-examined the entire issue in detail. The data already collated was reviewed and further studies were undertaken by the Earthquake Engineering Department of Roorkee University. These were carried out under the directions of the Expert Group on the basis of an idealized 2-dimensional model, with a peak ground acceleration (pga) scaled up to the values of a maximum credible earthquake (MCE) as prescribed by the International Commission on Large Dams.

Based on these studies, all five members of the Group concluded that "the present design of the dam is expected to be structurally safe to withstand the MCE during the economic life of the dam-reservoir system" (Expert Group, February 1998).

However, four members have said that some crucial issues such as slope stability remain to be settled. Keeping in view various parameters such as the pga, duration, frequency content and material properties in the context of a maximum credible earthquake, they believe that "still larger displacements cannot be ruled out". Therefore, "as a matter of abundant caution" they have recommended a 3-dimensional non-linear analysis of the Tehri dam to evaluate its performance against a maximum credible earthquake. Additionally, they have suggested a simulated dam-break analysis "to ensure that in the unlikely event of an uncontrolled release of water, the consequences are minimum".

Three-D analysis is a state of the art process but reportedly untested for large structures such as dams though certain software packages exist. Such an experiment would have to be specially set up. Proponent of the Tehri project, appear to be of the view that a 3-D test may only reinforce the finding that the dam, as designed, is safe. Earlier tests show that even given the worst case scenario of a full reservoir, gale force winds and a maximum credible earthquake of M 8.5 with a focal depth of 20 km right under the dam, the structure will only slump by about 0.5 m, a deformation that can easily be accommodated within the 9.5 m freeboard being provided. Deformation does not constitute failure.

A Disaster Management Plan for the Tehri Dam was prepared by the Centre for Development Studies and submitted to the Government some years ago. This covers flood risks and possible deformation, with pre-warning systems that can be relayed downstream, based on complete instrumentation of the dam to detect distress. The THDC has thus far been reluctant to undertake a dam-break study in order to avoid panic in view of the exaggerated fears that have been spread regarding the safety of the dam by lay critics.

The Government is required to file the twin Tehri Dam Safety and Environment Reports before the Supreme Court which will, after considering their findings, pass final orders. The Court might, however, ask the Government to seek a further opinion on the cautionary recommendations made by certain members of the Dam Safety Committee or to carry them out.

Construction of the dam has, meanwhile, been in progress since 1997 and, though stopped twice, is expected to be completed by 2002 if there is no further interruption. The stage I power house (250 MW x 4) and spillway will also be ready by then.

The Centre and UP are funding the project 60:40 with THDC getting some of the power equipment on suppliers' credit. With escalation owing to enforced delays, the cost of Stage I has gone up from Rs. 2963 crores at 1993 prices to Rs.4650 crores in current rupees. Of this amount, a sum of Rs.1610 crores had been spent until March 1998. the cost of the transmission system is being separately borne by the Power Grid Corporation. The Koteshwar dam (Stage II) will cost another Rs.1100 crores and the pumped storage scheme a further Rs.2000 crores.

The unit cost of power and energy output from each of these three components, which will between them produce 6482 m units of energy annually, is estimated at 125 paise, 80 P and 185 P for each stage, producing 3568 million units, 1460 m. u and 1454 m. u respectively. Augmented flows from Tehri will also enhance the output of the downstream Chilla hydro station by 150 m. u per annum.

A significant part of the R&R work remains to be done under the latest package that is to emerge. There was an upgradation of the terms in 1995. Even earlier, an independent evaluation indicated that those already settled were "undoubtedly better off" than before (Administrative Staff College, December 1992).

New Tehri Town is going to be a magnet with its modern facilities and new Garhwal University campus and will be a focal point of tourism around the Tehri lake. Delhi will receive 300 cusecs of drinking water a day, sufficient for a population of four million, while an additional 200 cusecs a day will be available for towns and villages in U.P.

The State Government has set up a Bhagirathi Management Authority by executive order for the welfare of the upper atchment. The Centre would rather that this be made a statutory body. That would be a welcome measure and a cess or surcharge of 2.5 P per unit of electricity sold would yield an income of over Rs.17 crores per annum which could fund the activities of such an upper catchment authority. Even if a third of the 12.5 per cent free power allocated to the host state is diverted to the upper catchment authority, this would swell its budget by another Rs.30 crores. The development of the larger community around the dam, over and beyond those directly displaced or otherwise affected by it, should be seen as the larger human development project spawned by Tehri. This could well be a prescription for all water resource projects.

With its activities likely to wind down over the next two to three years, the THDC should be given more work so that its organizational capability, experience, manpower and equipment can be put to continuing use. The Maneri Bhali-II run-of-the-river project (304 MW), which the U.P. Government abandoned half way for lack of funds, would be an obvious follow-on candidate, being the next hydel station above Tehri in the Bhagirathi cascade.

OTHER DEVELOPMENTS IN THE GANGA-YAMUNA BASIN

The Srinagar and Vishnuprayag projects have also been taken up in the Upper Ganga catchment, the latter by a private party. The Lakhwar Vyasi project on the Yamuna is still under construction and the Kishau and Renuka projects (both with drinking water components for Delhi) are yet to commence. The old Tajewala Barrage which may be completed by 2000. This is being done under the Haryana Water Resources Consolidation Project which will modernize and strengthen the Yamuna Canal System and enable it to deliver more water to ensure higher intensities and additional coverage once the planned upper Yamuna Valley storages are complete.

The Haryana lift irrigation schemes, however, must largely remain kharif projects pending a resolution of the dispute over the Sutlej-Yamuna Link in which Haryana and Punjab are embroiled. A new memorandum of understanding on the Yamuna between the concerned states allocates a share to Rajasthan for irrigation through extensions of the Gurgaon and Agra canals as a result of additional storages in the upper catchment that are either under construction or planned.

The upper basins of the Ganga and Yamuna lie in Kumaon and Garhwal other than a small part of the latter in Himachal. It would therefore be prudent to heed the lesson from inter-state problems arising out of the redrawing of state boundaries. The Union Government should secure prior agreement on fulfillment of current and prospective water obligations, including resettlement in relation to future projects in these catchments before Uttarakhand is carved out of Uttar Pradesh as a separate state. Not do so would be to risk spawning a whole crop of new water disputes later.

Phase I of the Ganga Canal modernization programme which commenced in 1984 is nearing completion. Not merely was this 140 year old structure ageing and in distress but was being called upon to carry more and more water in response to growing demands. The original design capacity of 7500 cusecs is now 10,000 cusecs. Rabi supplies of this order will become progressively available with the completion of the Tehri dam and, subsequently, of storages at Kotli Behl, Rudraprayag and so on.

The modernization of the first 30 kms of the Upper Ganga Canal will be completed by 2000 with the remodeling of the Solani aqueduct and three other major structures. A Parallel Ganga Canal has had to be dug to permit the renovation works as the UGC, a running canal, cannot otherwise be closed. This task too awaits completion. The Madhya Ganga Canal, taking off from the Bijnore headworks, is also being modernized. The Tehri Utilisation Project will stabilize irrigation up to Kanpur and bring 270,000 ha under irrigation for the first time. An Eastern Bhimgoda Canal is planned to take off from the UGC headworks. Groundwater use in the UGC and MGC commands is also rising on account of additional recharge. Conjunctive use has prevented waterlogging. On the contrary, dry wells have revived.

The Rajghat dam on the Betwa is making better headway with funding under the Accelerated Irrigation Benefit Programme. It is already under partial operation and the gates and power house should be complete by 1999. A Chambal lift project and modernization programme are still under consideration while a detailed project report on the Ken multipurpose dam awaits resolution of differences on hydrology between Madhya Pradesh and Uttar Pradesh.

The Bansagar dam on the Sone in Madhya Pradesh has run into difficulties over the resettlement of those likely to be displaced from Ramnagar town. Further construction has been stalled pending a satisfactory resolution. Other R&R problems include slow payment of compensation. There are lessons to be learnt from each of these events. Good projects preparation and R&R packages in prior consultation with the affected communities is the only basis on which water resource development can proceed in future.

Elsewhere, in response to persistent opposition from Buddhist monks and environmental groups, the Sikkim Chief Minister, P.K. Chamling, announced in August 1997 that the Rathong-Chu hydel project (30 MW) would be scrapped. The scheme was launched in 1991 and Rs. 13 crores had already been spent when it was abandoned in a bid to appease religious sentiment which holds the Yaksom Valley sacred. However, the 60 MW Rangit project is almost complete. Work has commenced on a 500 MW project on the Teesta while a larger 1500 MW project on this same cascade has attracted a bid by an Indo-Canadian-French combine.

As earlier mentioned, opposition from the Arunachal Government has compelled the Brahmaputra Board to recast its plans for harnessing the Dihang and Subansiri through two mega-dams. This will limit urban submergence and reduce forest loss.

TIPAIMUKH PROMISE AND FEARS

The Tipaimukh Dam (1500 MW) on the Barak river has also been on hold for the past two years, ever since the Manipur Assembly unanimously resolved that it be abandoned. The project is located at the point in southwestern Manipur where the river makes a sharp U-bend near the tri-junction with Mizoram and Assam. It envisages a 163 m high rockfill dam with a storage of about 8.32 b.c.m. Half this capacity is dedicated to providing a cushion that could greatly moderate a standard flood of 15,233 cumecs. This will protect Cachar in Assam and Sylhet and Dhaka districts in Bangladesh from the annual ravages of the Barak/Meghna. A proposed barrage 100 km downstream of the dam at Fulertal, near Silchar, is yet to be fully investigated. It will provide considerable irrigation which could also extend into Bangladesh.

Further, the augmented flows downstream and the reservoir backing up along the main stem of the river as well as the Iran and Makru in Manipur (all running north to south) and the Tuivai in Mizoram (flowing south to north) will open up hitherto inaccessible areas to navigation, linking up with the Meghna-Brahmaputra-Ganga waterway.

After some initial hesitation, Mizoram has approved the Tipaimukh project as it only suffers marginal submergence. Assam, the major beneficiary, is very keen that it goes ahead and has agreed to relocate within its territory most of the 2500 persons likely to be displaced by the dam in Manipur. This still leaves over the submergence of village lands in 90 villages in Manipur in which no population will be displaced. Manipur's other objection is to the submergence of the national highway from Silcahr to Imphal under the three prongs of the Barak, Makru and Irang. This has been overcome by an assurance that the highway will be realigned along a higher contour with new bridges. These will add to the distance and corresponding transport costs but can be suitably compensated.

The submergence issue irks Manipur. Some feel that certain problems thrown up by the Loktak hydel project have not been addressed and this experience should not be repeated. It would appear that public opinion may have been led astray on both counts in the absence of timely and complete information. Lack of transparency can be costly. Misperceptions and mythologies are hard to demolish. Matters have got politicized and need to be resolved on that plane. This must be done as the Tipaimukh project holds out great promise for the region. Manipur itself is slated to earn Rs. 50 crores annually from the 12.5 per cent free electricity it will be entitled to as the host state from out of the 4000 million units of energy generated (at current power tariffs). This just about equals the State's current annual revenue collection.

Tipaimukh well illustrates the inherent tension that is built into all major projects between the prime beneficiaries below the dam and those who bear the bulk of the costs living as they do in the catchment above the dam. It is therefore necessary to make catchment populations in their entirety, and not merely those directly affected by the project, stakeholders in such large undertakings. This can be done by establishing a catchment area authority charged with responsibility for R&R, catchment area treatment, development of fisheries and tourism around the reservoir as well as for undertaking the planned economic and social development, watershed management and land use planning of the catchment area. This charge should include education, health, skill-formation and employment generation. These activities could be funded by levying a small cess on the power produced. Since most or all of this is generally sold downstream, such a scheme would introduce inter-regional equity as between the catchment and command areas.

A high-level Commission on Basic Minimum Services and Infrastructural Needs in the Northeast under S.P. Shukla, which reported to the Prime Minister in March 1997 (Planning Commission, March 1997), made such a recommendation. It said a Barak (Valley)-Barail (Range) Upper Catchment Authority should be legislated in relation to Tipaimukh, Tuirial (60 MW) and other projects "as spearheads for major area development in otherwise sequestered and neglected regions". The Commission also urged an early inter-state meeting to be convened by the Centre at the highest level to secure full agreement on and approval for the Tipaimukh project, coupled with public hearings and consultations with NGOs. Further, it suggested that the sum of Rs.50 crores sought by the Brahmaputra Board for initiating work on the project during the Ninth Plan (1997-2002) be made available with the assurance that further funding will not be lacking to accelerate construction.

The Loktak Hydel Power Project (105 MW) in Manipur was completed some years ago. The Ithai barrage, a balancing weir, was constructed to pond part of the Loktak Lake through which the Imphal-Manipur River flows) in order to feed the intake channel of the Loktak power plant. The pondage has affected drawdown farming while the consequent neutralisation of the rhythmic rise and fall of this segment of the lake has reportedly begun to affect and quality of "phungdi" growth which forms unique floating vegetative islands. This could have unforeseen consequences for these floating islands, the fish they sustain and the Keibul Lamjao National Park which is home to the rare brown-antlered deer or Sangai. The Loktak Lake Development Authority (LDA) and the government have been advised by the Shukla Commission to concert action to study the problem and come up with and implement ameliorative measures.

"TRANSFORMING THE NORTHEAST"

The Shukla Commission made a number of recommendations in its Report entitled "Transforming the Northeast" (Planning Commission, March 1997). Land and water related issues figure prominently in its Report much of which should, hopefully, find a place in the ensuing 9th, 10th and subsequent Plans.

All of the Northeast, barring the Brahmaputra and Barak valleys in Assam, Imphal valley and the Tripura plains, lie in the Hills where the objective is to upgrade or replace erosive jhum cultivation with horticulture, agro-silviculture and plantations. Nagaland's Environment Protection and Economic Development through People's Action programme (NEPED), an imaginative jhum upgradation and reclamation initiative for bio-diversity conservation signifies an important new thrust.

Agricultural uncertainty in Assam stems from lack of water regulation. Annual floods combined with little irrigation despite an abundance of shallow groundwater has engendered low-risk farming and undermined economic growth. Flood damage to crops, cattle, housing and utilities in the State between 1953 and 1995 has been estimated at Rs.4400 crores, with a peak loss of Rs.664 crores in a single bad year. Only 1.63 m ha or about half the flood-prone area is protected. Even here, poor maintenance has resulted in a high failure rate of embankments.

The State's Flood Control Department has worked out a Rs.500 crore short term plan (1997-2002) for new embankments, anti-erosion works, drainage improvements, construction of sluices and raised platforms. This is subsumed in the revivified Brahmaputra Board's Phase I master plan costed at Rs.1848 crores, including the Rs.480 crore Pagladiya dam which will benefit the Bodo-inhabited Nalbari area in Lower Assam. Long –term measures up to 2050 have also been proposed, consisting of a series of large multipurpose storages in Arunchal (plus Tipaimukh), with a significant flood cushion and very substantial navigation and energy benefits. This is estimated to cost upwards of Rs. 50,000 crores at 1995 prices. The Prime Minister announced in 1996 that the Brahmaputra flood control programme would be Centrally funded and has allocated Rs.500 crores for the 9th Plan (1997-2002).

Endorsing this approach, the Shukla Commission notes that "the manifold income and employment-generating benefits from the mega storages proposed by the Brahmaputra Board must ride on their power potential if these projects are to be viable. Power development is therefore going to determine Assam's flood and irrigation future to a considerable degree". Manipur's nine flood control schemes to protect the Imphal valley at a cost of Rs.45 crores have also been supported.

Assam's irrigable area is 2.7 m ha of which no more than a third will be irrigated with the completion of ongoing schemes. Additional plans could bring another 1.74 m ha under major, medium and minor irrigation. Manipur's Thoubal and Khuga schemes could be completed in the 9th Plan while Tripura has proposed an outlay of Rs.350 crores for bringing another 68,000 ha under irrigation through a combination of diversions, tubewells and river-lifts. The Tipaimukh-Fulertal barrage project will be a major facility in Cachar while the revised Bairabi multipurpose project on the Dhaleshwari (irrigation, power and navigation) is under investigation in Mizoram.

POWER PERSPECTIVES

The Northeast's per capita availability of power is a low 94 kWh as against the very modest national average of 330 kWh. Yet the region could be the nation's powerhouse. Meghalaya is the only surplus state whereas the rest of the region is deficit in power. Hydropower generation in the Northeast is currently 460 MW to which 745 MW is being added (Ranganadi 405 MW, Arunachal; Kopili Extension,120 MW, Assam; Doyang, 75 MW, Nagaland). Five further projects with a total capacity of over 1100 MW have been sanctioned by the Central Electricity Authority in Mizoram, Manipur, Assam and Arunachal, of which the largest is Kameng (600 MW but which could be upgraded to 1000 MW).

Private investment could further these plans and there has been a show of interest. But, as elsewhere, this will require a reorganization of State Electricity Boards in Assam and Meghalaya and the corporatisation of power departments in the other states. Underpricing of power at levels insufficient to cover even maintenance costs, overmanning, political interference and high transmission and distribution losses are among the prime factors that must be addressed. The establishment of independent regulatory authorities to set tariffs on economic rather than political criteria is central to the proposed reform. Thereafter SEBs could be corporatised or privatized with generation, transmission and distribution becoming independent profit centres.

A western consortium was prepared to take over the Meghalaya SEB with all its liabilities provided it was licensed to harness the State's 2000-3000 MW hydro potential and utilize its coal to produce an additional 1000 MW of power, partly for export to neighbouring Bangladesh. That deal fell through but other parties are interested.

The Fourth National (Indian) Power Plan has estimated an additional capacity requirement countrywide of 150,000 MW by 2012 to meet a peak demand of 176,647 MW or 1058 billion units of energy (Central Electricity Authority, March 1997). It accordingly recommends that 58,000 MW of hydro capacity be added over the next 15 years through national and foreign investment. This is a tall order. But if anything like this target is to be attempted, let alone met, much of the hydro capacity contemplated will have to be developed in the Northeast.

The hydro potential available in the Northeast is just under 35,000 MW at 60 per cent load factor, a figure that would stand greatly enhanced were future projects to be developed basically for peaking power. The bulk of this potential lies in the Brahmaputra basin (3063 MW of this in the Teesta and Jaldhaka/Torsa) and with 3908 in the Barak Valley. This does not take into account the further possibility of a collaborative India-China venture to develop the enormous power potential of the order of 54,000 MW locked in the giant U-bend of the Brahmaputra as the river drops several thousand feet between Tibet and India.

The Brahmaputra Board has developed a planning scenario which envisages peaking capacity in the Northeast rising to 5695 MW in 2010 and 44,442 MW by

2040.This would enable the region to export 2495 MW of peaking power through the national power grid by 2010 and 33,742 MW by 2040 (Mohile, A.D. March 1998).

A regional GBM or sub-continental grid is likely to be a reality by 2010, building on the existing Indo-Bhutan link and smaller local Indo-Nepalese tie-ups. This will happen with Pancheshwar and Tala coming on stream even as the regional grids within India get interconnected over the next five years with zonal load dispatch centres and extra-high voltage AC and/or HV DC lines. This will call for standardisation and careful planning to ensure smooth integration of different systems.

Studies for connecting the Indian and Bangladesh systems were initiated by the Power Grid Corporation of India in 1994. An India-Bangladesh Electricity Exchange project has been launched with the assistance of the ADB. This is to examine the feasibility of two 132 KV double circuit lines, one to link either Durgapur-Bhemara or Jeerhat-Jessore for export of power from India to western Bangladesh and the other from Sylhet and Fenchuganj to Kumarghat and Agartala to facilitate export of gas-based power from eastern Bangladesh to India's Northeast (Sambamurti, 1997).

Power exchange possibilities could be exploited leading ultimately to more sophisticated energy exchange planning and trade. Bangladesh is gas-rich whereas Eastern and Northeastern India have a plenitude of hydel potential and coal.

Private investment and foreign capital will not be attracted unless the entire Indian power sector is reformed. This would incidentally also minimize if not altogether obviate the need for counter-guarantees in seemingly "difficult" regions such as the Northeast.

The tariff currently charged on electricity remains below the cost of supply. The all-India gap averaged 37 P in 1996-97 with the agriculture and domestic sectors being heavily subsidized. The average agricultural and domestic tariff that year was 21 P and 92 P as against an average supply cost of 186 P. the hidden power subsidy to the farm sector in 1996-98 was estimated at Rs.17,285 crores. If the tariff were raised to a minimum of 50 P the additional revenue mobilization is likely to be of the order of Rs.2418 crores. Industrial and commercial users subsidise agricultural power consumption. Even so, the State electricity boards' commercial losses in 1996-97 were anticipated to be Rs.10,491 crores, with rates of recovery well below cost (Planning Commission, 1998).

Over 40,000 MW capacity is proposed to be added during the 9th Plan, just under 13,000 MW of this hopefully being hydro power and almost 43 per cent of this segment in the private sector. These are all-India figures; but a good part of this will need to come up within the Northern, Eastern and Northeast grids which serve the GBM region. Private entrepreneurs are interested in the hydro sector but want a level playing field vesting them with greater autonomy. Power sector reform is crucial.

What comes through clearly is that major systemic improvement is required in the irrigation and power sectors if the huge investments already made are to be sustained and if the remaining potential which the nation urgently requires is to be harnessed funds will be forthcoming. Hardware development is relatively simple; getting the software right is what is important and that will take political will and social discipline.

CATCHMENT AREA DEVELOPMENT AUTHORITIES

Large dam and barrage projects inevitably entail establishing a variety of infrastructure and services including roads, telecommunications, electricity, water supply, townships, markets, hospitals, engineering workshops, etcetera, even before construction of the dam commences. Thereby they open up remote valleys, create market linkages and trigger area-development. This should make it possible to relocate and rehabilitate project affected persons in situ within their own milieu without disrupting traditional social and cultural networks, instead of plucking them out of this environment and resettling them on the land in alien surroundings.

The concept of necessarily resettling project "oustees" on the land is mistaken as culturable land is not easily available. Host populations too, many of them landless or marginal tenants, resent being crowded out by "outsiders" who are rehabilitated on the basis of standards that they themselves simply do not enjoy. Employment and training for new vocations is increasingly going to be the answer, not land for land, except where culturable land is available. Area development through catchment area authorities therefore offers an attractive alternative for rehabilitation through wider employment generation, poverty alleviation and environmental upgradation through better watershed management and land use planning.

The concept of catchment area authorities should therefore be built into water resource development. This will end the dichotomy and tensions between communities living above and below the dam and create a common interest in the project and its early and efficient completion. At present, project affected persons, particularly those suffering displacement, are grudging, involuntary partners and are easy prey to those who would opposite these dams. The far larger catchment communities not directly affected or liable to rehabilitation or compensation, are understandably indifferent to the project as their relative neglect seems likely to persist.

Postulating a catchment area concept that promises social and economic development to these disadvantaged communities would translate them from mere bystanders into avid stakeholders as much as those likely to garner downstream benefits such as irrigation, flood control and additional power. R&R, catchment area treatment (project related) and pisciculture and tourism (post-dam opportunities) could be made part of a larger, participatory upper catchment development programme financed initially from project budgets and subsequently from project revenues through a cess or surcharge on power paid into a catchment area fund and a share in the 12 per cent (site) "royalty" paid to the host stage in terms of free power. The Pancheshwar and Tipaimukh projects would be good start-up candidates for such a programme.

The state is committed to poverty alleviation, provision of basic minimum services for all, conservation of the environment and improvement in the quality of life of all citizens. Catchment area authorities would be mandated to undertake this task. In so doing, regional equity would be enhanced and the environment more often than not improved though better land use and cropping patterns and employment and income generation these could lift people above the level of mere subsistence in situations where survival economics inevitably prevails over thought of sustainability.

Area development can and must also be seen in a wider context. Water resource planning is obviously only a means of levering overall development. Land and water are primary assets with varied linkages. Water supply is linked to food security, rural prosperity, health and sanitation; hydro power as a clean energy source drives industry and generates employment; inland navigation facilities transport and communication. Together they influence the environment.

Water resource development in the vast Ganga-Brahmaputra-Meghna region or its Northeast India component, is therefore a means of realizing larger goals as much as being an end in itself. Thus, hydro power with its peaking facility can impart stability and flexibility to power systems, especially if enhanced by transmission grids.

INLAND WATERWAYS

The restoration and extension of the once bustling Ganga-Brahmaputra-Barak waterway could likewise, restore regional communication through eco-friendly fuel-efficient, land-saving inland-cum-coastal navigation. The Inland Waterways Authroity of India (IWAI) has responsibility for National Waterway No. 1 on the Ganga from Haldia/Calcutta through the Farakka Lock to Patna and Allahabad, and NW No. 2 along the Brahmaputra from Dhubri to Dibrugarh. The fairways and infrastructure have to be restored, night navigation facilities established, barge fleets rebuilt and traffic attracted to the waterfront, unless canal spurs are built to connect with existing freight nodes.

The approach to the Farakka lock gate has shoaled, as has that to the Jangipur lock on the Bhagirathi which joins the Ganga below the barrage. Both will require some river training and dredging to restore navigation. The construction of the Ganges Barrage in Bangladesh (with a lock system) combined with the releases being made into the Ganga below Farakka will improve the fairway between the two barrages. The Tipaimukh dam and Fulertal barrage on the Barak will in turn improve this waterway both above and below the dam into Bangladesh, Manipur and Mizoram.

The IWAI has prepared a Rs.134 crore blueprint for development of the Brahmaputra waterway as well as of some Mizoram rivers during the 9th Plan. Among the latter is the Chhimtuipui or Kaladan/Kolodyne which falls into the sea near Sitwe (Akyab) in Myanmar. The river is even now navigable below Paletwa, a third of the way down to the ocean from the southern tip of Mizoram. Two hydro projects on the Chhimtuipui are slated for investigation and should either or both of them materialise, the augmented flows they generate could assist navigation up to Paletwa. Mizoram would also be greatly interested in the restoration of navigation down the Karnaphuli from Demagiri to Chittagong, a proposition that might be revived following the Chittagong Hills accord signed in late 1997 between the Bangladesh government and the Parbattya Chattagram Jana Sanghati Samity to end the Chakma insurgency.

Looking further ahead, some engineers envision the possibilityof jacketing the Brahmaputra at selected points to coax the braided river to flow through a single channel in course of time. This would require elaborate mathematical modeling of water flows and sediment transport (Mohile A.D. March 1998). Such transformations have been effected in the Rhine, while the winding Mississippi has been straightened out, thus improving drafts and general navigability. Low barrages with locks and fish ladders along the Ganga and Brahmaputra could also pond these rivers or major tributaries, where techno-economically feasible, in the interests of improving and extending navigation in India and Bangladesh. Environmental impacts would need to be carefully studied, including those from increased navigation. But such an investment would only be justified if a certain minimum traffic were guaranteed.

The Indo-Bangladesh protocol on Inland Water Transit and Trade of 1980 was renewed in November 1997 for a period of two years. This covers routes up the Brahmaputra and Meghna/Barak from Calcutta to Dhubri/Karimganj, Karimganj-Dhubri and Rajshahi-Dhulian or such others as may be prescribed. Acknowledging that certain routes in Bangladesh are being maintained only to serve Indian traffic, the Government of India has agreed, as before, to bear the cost of such works including night navigation facilities. India is currently paying Bangladesh Rs.1.8 crores annually for channel maintenance.

Vessels may only carry commercial traffic and shall while in transit not engage in inter-country trade. However, inter-country trade is permitted separately "on an equal tonnage basis". This is a very limited agreement and needs to be expanded in keeping with the possibilities.

Nepal is keenly interested in an outlet to the sea. RITES India has done a navigation study on the Gandak for the Nepalese government while the detailed project report for the Sapta Kosi project speaks of a canal link from Chatra to the main stem of the Ganga.

RECONCEPTUALISING "CALCUTTA PORT"

Containerization has fostered inter-modal transport. Customers desire reliability and cost-effectiveness and are not otherwise necessarily concerned with speed or the mode of carriage, which could well be inter-modal. Containers can move from road to barge to rail in any combination to complete a freight movement in the cheapest or most convenient way possible. Likewise, roll-on roll-off trucks can move on barges over shorter or longer distances, and not merely over ferry crossings. Such flexibility would make for integrated transports systems operating on the basis of a single, combined transport document.

Coupled with changes in freight composition and in the nature of shipping and ship sizes, and with the development of alternative ports, this has rendered Calcutta port obsolete. Drafts have been maintained by flushing the river with headwater supplies diverted at Farakka and with considerable focused dredging. Nevertheless, there is a limit to the size of vessel that can ply the Hooghly up to Calcutta and enter the docks and this has long been reached. Additional flushing can scarcely help. The efficacy of current flushing has been diminished by "theft" of up to 8000 cusecs of water from the Farakka feeder-cum-Bhagirathi by farmers using hose-pumps to irrigate adjacent lands. At the same time, the opportunity cost of diverting water for draft maintenance is fast rising.

The Calcutta docks only handled around six million tonnes of mostly containerized and general cargo in 1995-96 as against some 17 m t by the "auxilliary" Haldia docks, which is misleadingly designed as part of Calcutta Port. Calcutta is probably the country's most expensive and least efficient major port. Haldia expansion, a possible new deep sea port at Sagar Island, a single-buoy mooring 45 kms out to sea with a liquid cargo terminal linked to a landfall point on the coast, are proposed. Smaller private container ports below Calcutta, as already investigated at Kulpi, opposite Haldia, are being canvassed. Some or all of this must happen if "Calcutta Port" is to handle 30 m t of freight by 2000, 50 m t by 2005 and may be 100 m t by 2025.

Calcutta's future lies in becoming a decentralized, poly-nodal, inland barge port stretching on both sides of the Hooghly from Haldia to Farakka. It might still receive some small ocean going vessels, but principally barges and cargo river coasters traversing the Ganga-Brahmaputra-Barak and adjacent coastal waterways. Such a network could develop into a vibrant regional facility. This would decongest Calcutta, which has long been overstretched, and enable it to regain its élan as a dynamo of regional growth and an eastern sub-continental hub.

Given such a role, Farakka waters could be more useful redistributed to serve higher-value alternatives, including some augmentation below the barrage. Here again, one would need to focus on a larger vision of regional development looking at energy, not just power, at inter-modal transport, not just railways, road or inland navigation, and at the urban and spatial environment. This would spell synergy.

LAND AND WATER MANAGEMENT IMPERATIVES

Water resources development is after all only an entry point to the larger question of poverty alleviation and a better quality of life. Since the eastern quadrant of the sub-continent is so abjectly poor and its burgeoning population so heavily dependent on the land for basic sustenance and employment, land and water management constitutes a critical resource base which must be developed to feed the millions, provide them gainful occupation and generate the surpluses and markets that stimulate industry and the service sector. But this development must be sustainable and not self-destructive through environmental degradation.

This necessitates appropriate land and water management and environmental care. Eastern and Northeastern India, Nepal and Bangladesh could do better in terms of farm productivity and output per unit of land and water which, more efficiently managed, would enhance the labour-intensity of agriculture and reduce current levels of poverty and migration. Agrarian relations in the eastern Gangetic plain and Brahmaputra Valley are a matter of concern. West Bengal has pushed tenancy reform, but the situation in Assam, Eastern U.P. and especially Bihar is truly depressing. Land records are outdated and tenurial relations, especially in respect of sharecroppers, unsatisfactory. This has had a negative bearing on both canal and groundwater use, on-farm development and other investments as farming remains a high-risk, feudal venture in the hands of oppressive absentee landlords. Even irrigated yields remain abysmally low while agrarian violence is taking an increasingly bloody toll.

The Kosi and Gandak irrigation systems remain incomplete and run down and there can be little irrigation benefit from the proposed Sapta Kosi high dam in North Bihar unless agrarian relations are significantly improved. Assam faces a similar problem. Insecure marginal farmers and sharecroppers have no collateral against which to borrow. The cooperative credit structure is completely choked with overdues. Only a small part of the groundwater potential has been tapped thus precluding multiple cropping over considerable areas.

Water use efficiency remains low region-wide, with created potential slow to be fully utilized, partly for the reasons mentioned. Water management in India cries out for attention. Irrigation systems are deteriorating as the investments are not being properly maintained. Irrigation pricing is archaic and does not even suffice to recoup operation and maintenance costs let alone the true cost of water.

The Draft 9th Plan (1997-2002) has some telling figures which apply nationwide but would be true to the GBM basin as well. Though an irrigation potential of 90 million ha has been created, and irrigated agriculture rightly continues to enjoy the highest priority, water use efficiency is still 38-40 per cent for canal irrigation and 60 per cent for groundwater. The Planning Commission estimates that a 10 per cent increase in water use efficiency could bring an additional 14 m ha under irrigation (Planning Commission, 1998). The implications of this become strikingly apparent in view of the fact that the cost of creating a hectare of irrigation potential is estimated at Rs.66,570 at current prices, as against Rs.1200 in the first Plan when admittedly drainage costs were excluded and the distribution system did not go below 40 ha blocks (Water Resources Ministry, 1996).

Waterlogging and salinity have taken their toll owing to poor drainage and management, lack of conjuctive use and over-irrigation in the absence of price restraints. It is again estimated that 21 m ha have gone out of irrigation, partially or fully, 13 m ha of this from lands irrigated by pre-1947 major and medium projects and the balance from projects constructed during the first 25 years of Independence. These systems require renovation, upgradation and restoration in varying degree at a cost of Rs.20-30,000 crore.

Water is still prone to be seen as a free, social good rather than as an economic good with a definite and increasing scarcity value as prescribed by the 1987 National Water Policy (NIPFP, December 1997). This has encouraged waste and profligacy. Though this is done in the name of the poor, the underprivileged are the worst sufferers. Others have the means, muscle or influence to get by. The poor go to the wall.

The 10th Finance Commission (1995-2000) suggested an O&M charge of Rs.300 per ha if the irrigation potential was utilized and Rs.100/ha if unutilized, with a 30 per cent increase in hilly tracts and some indexation of inflation. By such a reckoning the O&M budget should be around Rs.2500-3000 crores per annum for the country as a whole, whereas the actual allocations aggregate no more than a quarter of this figure.

The (Vidyanathan) Committee on the Pricing of Irrigation Water (1992) inveighed against "subsidizing such a user-oriented and capital-intensive infrastructure as irrigation" and noted that water rates are a user charge and not a tax.

It should therefore be perfectly possible to capture some of the established productivity gains from irrigated farming. The Vaidyanathan Committee recommended linking revision of water rates with improvements in the quality of service; introducing farmer group management systems through user associations that might retail water below certain outlets; switching over to volumetric pricing; setting up high-level autonomous boards in the States to review policy ad reassess credible maintenance costs and outlays; and set this process in motion during the 9th Plan.

Private sector participation under build-operate-own/transfer/lease arrangements have also been mooted and even initiated. In some large projects, the Sardar Sarovar Project in Gujarat for one, the State Government has successfully floated bonds which were over-subscribed. Betterment levies were advocated in the early Plan days as a means of returning to the state a slice of the unearned increment in land values as a result of irrigation and infrastructure development.

Little was actually collected. Nevertheless, the idea remains valid and, given quality service to meet a real need, even the poorest farmers will be prepared to pay their share.

LARGE DAM DEBATE

Over the past few decades, opposition has steadily mounted against the construction of large dams. The Aswan Dam was an earlier target but nothing as fiercely fought over as the Sardar Sarovar Project on the Narmada (Independent Review Mission, World Bank,1992; Verghese, 1994) and only to a somewhat lesser degree, the Tehri Dam. The Chinese are going ahead with the massive 18,200 MW Three Gorges Project on the Yangtze, displacing one million people and costing $ 27 bn. The 2400 MW Bakum dam in Sarawak, Malaysia, has also evoked harsh criticism.

Patrick McCully of the International Rivers Network is among the more impassioned critics of large dams (McCully, 1996). In North America, the movement for de-commissioning dams has won some victories while a number of hydro or inter-basin projects have been blocked or curtailed. The U.S. Bureau of Reclamation, one of the largest dam-builders in the world, has gone into reverse gear in the belief that "the dam building era in the United States is now over. We no longer can count on public or political support for construction projects" (Beard, Daniel 1994). Medha Patkar of the Narmada Bachao Andolan and Sunderlal Bahuguna of the Tehri Bandh Virodhi Sangharsh Samiti are at the barricades in India. These doomsday forecasts have been answered by "The Economists" (Dec. 20, 1997) and Gret Esterbrook (1996).

The comparison between highly developed Western nations and tropical, semi-arid monsoonal lands more typical of the developing world is not on all fours on many counts. The former have by and large their dam building behind them, have stable or low-growth populations and are mostly located in temperate climates and enjoy well distributed rainfall throughout the year. They are prosperous, highly industrialized and technologically advanced nations with small farming populations and a low agricultural dependency. Contrast this with the developing world with its burgeoning populations, high dependence on agriculture, highly seasonal rainfall, high evapo-transpiration and lower technological threshold. The United States may today forego dams or even tear down some; not so South Asia or China. Better dams and greater environmental safeguards, yes. No dams or only small dams fly in the face of grim reality.

The global debate was joined at Gland in Switzerland at an international workshop convened by the International Union for the Conservation of Nature-World Conservation Union and the World Bank. The outcome, recorded in "Large Dams" (IUCN-World Bank, April 1997) was a series of findings and a recommendation favoring the constitution of a World Commission to examine the issues involved and work out a set of international guidelines. A 12-member World

Commission on Dams was established in February 16, 1998 under Prof. Kader Asmal, South Africa's Minister for Water Resources. It will report in 2000.

GLOBAL WARMING TO EMISSIONS TRADING FOR HYDRO

An important factor that has more recently influenced the debate is danger of global warming and climate change from greenhouse gases. "Large Dams" states that one of the most pressing issues today is how to internalize the cost of greenhouse gas emissions. "Most project economists, whether the project is for coal, gas, or hydro, resolutely persist in externalizing these costs. While development agencies, in principle, seek to internalize environmental and social costs … the World Trade Organisation stringently promotes free trade .. and (is) resolutely against any country seeking to protect an efficient national policy of internalization of environmental costs" (Ibid). Irrigation and fast growing urban/municipal requirements do not even find a mention.

"Large Dams" also notes that "there is limited scope for a rapidly industrializing country to meet its energy and needs through non-hydro renewable energies … Non-hydro renewables are positive contributions in many countries, but do not yet contribute substantially to any industrialized nation", let alone to any developing society. Coal is a dirty fuel, especially in India where much of it contains 20-40 per cent ash or has a high sulphur content as in the Northeast. According to "Large Dams", proponents claim that "GHG emissions resulting from the manufacture of the dam's cement and steel, plus the energy used in the construction, amount to less than 10 per cent of the annual carbon dioxide emissions of the fossil-fuel equivalent". Hydro power is cleaner than coal, oil or even gas and nuclear energy and while demand management and energy conservation are very important, the gains they offer are modest in relation to rapidly growing demand.

Concern over climate change crystallized with the signing of the UN Framework Convention on Climate Change at the Earth Summit in Rio in June 1992. This set certain time-targeted goals for emission reductions by the energy-guzzling industrialized nations which are the worst offenders. These targets had not been met by the time the Third Conference of the Parties to the UN Framework Convention on Climate Change met in Kyoto, Japan in December 1997. The US, the European Union and Japan proposed enhanced targets in varying degree. One of the propositions adopted was that of emissions trading and joint implementation projects under this, high-emitters can buy carbon quotas from low-emitters who enjoy a margin of grace as a means of balancing global emissions within a given threshold (Prakasam, January 1998)

Thus high emitters can fund clean energy projects in developing countries through a newly-established Clean Development Mechanism, thereby earning credit for the carbon emissions "saved". This approximates at another level with the earlier debt-for-nature swaps under which donor nations wrote off debt if the debtor nation agreed to invest the amount forgiven in afforestation or other "green" programmes. Emission trading and joint implementation projects, properly understood and prudently applied with appropriate safeguards, could enable countries in Asia, Africa and Latin America like Nepal, Bhutan and even India to raise funds for Himalayan hydro development. South Asian nations need to concert thought and action to get the fine print right and make carbon trading and joint implementation work to their advantage when negotiations are resumed at the Next Conference of Parties to the UN Framework Convention on Climate Change to be held in Buenos Aires at the end of 1998.

GROWING WATER STRESS

Storage remains an important element in overall national and global water management and conservation. Renewable water supplies are increasingly coming under pressure with population growth and are fast approaching the limits of sustainability in both quantitative and qualitative terms. India, particularly, and Pakistan fall within that category within South Asia. If water scarce countries are defined as those with an annual per capital freshwater availability of below 1000 cu m and water-stressed countries those with a per capita annual availability of 1500 cu m, then India will be moving from "water-abundant" in 1990 (2464 cu m) to "water-stressed (1496) by 2025 under the UN's medium population projections (Englcman and LeRoy, 1993). Pakistan will be better off (1803); Bangladesh much more so (10,558). All the west, including Australia and Japan, will remain "water-abundant" barring Israel and Poland.

The Special Session of the General Assembly convened to review and appraise the implementation of Agenda-21 in 1997 had before it a U.N. study making a comprehensive assessment of global freshwater resources prepared by the Commission on Sustainable Development and a companion study on "Global Change and Sustainable Development : Critical Trends" reviewing key issues since the first World Environment Conference in Stockholm in 1972. The prognostications were sobering (U.N., June 1997).

The Comprehensive Assessment Report focused on growing population, poverty, urbanization, water stress, pollution and water-related health in a situation of inadequate and inefficient water management. It noted that high variability of water flows over time and space "unless captured by reservoirs" and drew attention to differential rates of evapotranspiration, it recalled the Dublin Principles recapitulated in Agenda-21, namely, freshwater is a finite and vulnerable resource; water development and management should be participatory; women play a key role in managing and safeguarding water; and water has an economic value in all uses and must be recognized as an economic good.

It counseled countries with low per capita water availability that "the allocation of water to the highest value uses is a necessity ... to maximize the socio-economic value of water rights and permits in allocating water.

MANAGING RIVER BASINS

Some other recent international agreements have a close bearing on the optimal and integrated development of the GBM basin. The need for trans-boundary or regional cooperation in managing international river basins is now widely accepted, not least in controlling pollution. The European Convention on the Protection and Use of Transboundary Watercourses and International Lakes came into force in October 1996. It applies the polluter-pays principle. The Integrated Water Management Working Group at the Delft University of Technology in the Netherlands in evolving a framework for sharing lean season flows of transboundary rivers with a legal and administrative component and a computer model aid-to-decision system with reference to the Meuse and Guardiana rivers.

Finally, the establishment of multi-national commissions for the Pilcomayo river basin (Argentina, Bolivia and Paraguay) and the upper basin of the Bermejo and Rio Grande de Tarija rivers (Argentia-Bolivia) to establish data banks as a preliminary to erosion control in the first case and the construction of a series of dams in the other (U.N. IRL Newsletter, December 1996).

The inadequacy of data and its classification as confidential information is a major impediment to sound water resource development and management in the GBM basin. The lack of transparency has hampered investment, come in the way of rigorous prioritization of projects and subsequent evaluation and, sadly, impeded stakeholder participation. Various UN specialized agencies have now come forward to support and strengthen hydrological networks, flow regimes of international rivers, water supply monitoring programmes, and rural water use (U.N. 1997).

International concern over competition for water and deteriorating water quality resulted in the formation in 1997 of the Global Water Partnership. Institutional and policy initiatives, water demand management and pollution control feature in the concept of Integrated Water Resources Management. An Indian Water Partnership (IWP) was constituted in February 1998 as an affiliate of the global body.

FLOOD MODERATION AND POLLUTION CONTROL

Land and water management and water quality have assumed increasing importance with the passage of time. Groundwater pumping in the GBM basin affects stream flows and has caused arsenic poisoning both in West Bengal and Bangladesh. The problem of floods, landslides, erosion, sedimentation, waterlogging and salinity are well known. The provision of safe drinking water supply an sanitation has come to the forefront with growing urbanization in particular. And it is noteworthy that the Mahakali Treaty specifically provides for minimal ecological flows.

While detention reservoirs and embankments have their place in flood moderation or river management, emphasis is being given to augmenting and improving non-structural measures. Among these are flood forecasting and warning services; flood plain management/zoning/proofing coupled with disaster preparedness; flood fighting, including health measures; and flood insurance (Rangachari and Baweja, 1997). Data collection and transmission in real time, automated systems, modeling studies, and transboundary networking and cooperation between India, Nepal, Bhutan and Bangladesh are all in process of being improved.

A research action plan named Sentinel was mooted for management of water-related disasters in the GBM region at an international flood forecasting and warning seminar held in Dhaka (ICID, December 1997). The project was intended to strengthen capability to predict and forecast major floods through hydro-meteorological modeling, establishment of gauging stations on land and in the Bay of Bengal together with satellite observations. The issue was not clinched but suggests the direction in which regional efforts might move with international support.

A major exercise in controlling river pollution was the ambitious Ganga Action Plan that India launched in 1985. The Central Pollution Control Board prescribed quality standards for various designated uses such as drinking water (raw and treated), river bathing, fisheries and wild life, and irrigation, industrial and waste disposal. Twentyseven Class-I cities with a population of 100,000 and above were monitored from source to sea over 2500 kms for a variety of physio-chemical and bacteriological parameters including heavy metals.

An analysis of observations made between 1985 and 1996 showed an overall upward trend in water quality, certainly with regard to dissolved oxygen and in biological oxygen demand except below Kanpur, with its heavy tannery effluent discharge, and a few other locations. Coliform content remains high while heavy metal pollution has so far not been a problem (Sivaramakrishnan and Dalwani, 1997). Phase II aims to complete unfinished tasks and extend water quality monitoring to the Yamuna, Hindon, Gomti, Western Yamuna Canal and Damodar. GAP-II will additionally take up monitoring of the Betwa, Kshipra, Chambal and other rivers outside the GBM basin.

These programmes are being assisted through the monitoring network established after 1977 under the Global Environmental Monitoring Systems (GEMS) and Monitoring of Indian National Aquatic Resources (MINARS) programmes (Hasan et al. IWRS 1997).

CAPACITY AND INSTITUTION BUILDING

The developments being proposed require the countries of the GBM region to build up their capabilities and not remain overly dependent on foreign consultants or equipment. India has a good deal of experience but needs to equip itself further for the more complex and challenging tasks ahead. Nepal, Bhutan and Bangladesh are lower down on the learn in curve and will need to develop their equipment and material capability as well to the extent possible.

The new projects proposed offer an opportunity. Foreign consultancy should not become a crutch that slows down movement from dependence to greater national self-reliance. It would therefore be appropriate were all concerned to resolve and prepare to face the tasks ahead. The strategy should be to maximize national inputs of manpower, technology and material and only thereafter seek regional and, finally, international support in designing and constructing the next generation of projects. Manpower training programmes should be taken up ahead of time and understudies positioned to take over from expatriate consultants wherever the latter are inducted. This will reduce costs, build national confidence and experience and enable these countries to move faster and more assuredly along their chosen path.

Institution building is necessary. The importance of developing good data banks and exchanging information has been stated. Transparency will facilitate the growth of participatory structures. Cross-border mechanisms exist, mostly at the project level. Not many may have worked too well. India for its part should not be too chary of moving from bilateralism to more multilateral approaches. At the same time, Nepal and Bangladesh would be rash to believe that multilateralism is a panacea. The Indo-Bangladesh Joint Rivers Commission could be strengthened and given a small secretariat for a start so that it functions as a clearing house. A similar Indo-Nepal Rivers Commission could in due course bring together the many project oriented structures that obtain. Institutions can be encouraged to grow to fulfil evolving needs within the GBM region.

There should be no inhibitions in exploring new ideas. After decades, India now accepts that there may be deep aquifers underlying part of the eastern north-Ganga plain and Bengal basin. These could be a series of layered freshwater aquifers under artesian pressure and being recharged. The hypothesis remains to be established through test drilling. Bangladesh, however, remains sceptical about a similar deep aquifer in the eastern region adjacent to Tripura.

TOWARDS TOMORROW

All these many issues, seemingly remote to some at first sight, are of the greatest relevance to the millions who inhabit the GBM basin. This region has been condemned to suffer abject poverty and privation when it is essentially well endowed. What has been lacking is sound, integrated land and water resource management and detailed planning for its optimal development. That could transform the lives of much of mankind.

Water resource development cannot be an isolated thrust. It has been and still remains an entry point and prime lever for a larger design of overall regional and area development. What is involved is not merely a shared resources but the shared future of what has come to be known as SAARC's GBM sub-region, linking this to lands beyond in Southeast Asia, Southwest China and Tibet.

Doing this requires vision, resolution, broad participation within and across boundaries, capacity and institution building and sensitivity to issues of equity and the environment. Problems there will be; there always are. There is a cost for doing anything. The cost of doing nothing can be far greater. In this case it is. Comparisons with unlikes over time and space can only confuse. There is, however, much to learn from relevant experience, our own and that of others.

Ten years ago, *Waters of Hope* may have been an ideal. Times are changing. Today it is a reality that could be ours tomorrow and, indeed, Our Tomorrow.

CHAPTER 20

Hope Remains
Emerging Water Stress

If one looks at the national scene as it might unfold in the decades ahead, the National Commission for Integrated Water Resources Development (September 1999) estimated that India would have a population of between 1335 million and 1581 million by 2050, out of which urban numbers might total between 646 million and 791 million. Current trends suggest that the higher figure might be the nearer approximation, especially on account of continuing high fertility rates in the GBM basin. It also indicates that by mid-century, India will no longer be a predominantly agrarian or rural society though the GBM basin might still remain largely ruralised. Bangladesh and Nepal are likely to exhibit a similar trend.

The commission projected a national foodgrain requirement of 420 to 494 million tonnes (high and low demand), including 38-45 m.t. for seed, feed and wastage.

Assuming rising requirements for surface and groundwater irrigation (with canal irrigation efficiency improving from 40 per cent to 60 per cent), drinking water and sanitation, industry and power, navigation and, not least, ecological uses, it estimated the water demand to increase from 629 cu km in 1997-98 to 973-1,180 cu km by 2050, allowing for evaporation losses.

As against this, it reassessed surface water availability at 1953 cu km, but placed the utilisable quantum at no more than 690 cu km. While GBM flows account for 1204 cu km, their utilisable quantum is no more than 274 cu km. This makes for no more than 23 percent of total basin flows though as much as 48 per cent of total utilisable national surface flows. The reason for this huge discrepancy is because only 24 cu km of the 667 cu km combined annual discharge of the Brahmaputra and Barak is utilisable in and through an almost landlocked Indian Northeast, which being mountainous has limited arable cropland. Cooperation with Bangladesh could improve the figure of utilisable flows.

To complete the water equation it is necessary to add the *dynamic* groundwater resources that may be available. The National Commission assessed the replenishable aquifer resource at 431.89 cu km per annum, with just over 89 cu km of this coming from canal recharge. It is noteworthy that whereas the GBM boasts rich groundwater resources, recharge values from canal irrigation rise dramatically moving east to west, with surface irrigation contributing 12, 14, 24 and 45 per cent of replenishable groundwater resources in West Bengal, Bihar, Uttar Pradesh and Haryana, respectively.

FOOD-WATER BUDGET

The commission's national water budget for 2050 shows that water demand may be of the order of 973 to 1,180 cu km as against the net availability of 1,086 cu km of surface and ground water. These are no more than prognostications based on reasonable assumptions. But they paint the need for careful conservation and management of the country's water resources of which a large segment is part of an internationally shared GBM system. The bulk of the water utilised is for irrigation; but farm consumption will have to come down and cropping patterns amended to accommodate other uses that make for sustainability, higher growth and a better quality of life.

The country is currently producing around 205-215 m.t. of foodgrain from 142 m ha of net sown area, with 80 m ha under gross irrigation in 2000, as against an ultimate irrigation potential of 140 m ha. The Inter-Linking of Rivers (ILR) concept envisages raising this figure to 175 m ha. Even at the present level, India is probably the largest irrigator in the world but needs to improve water use efficiency and pay greater attention to demand management instead of relying overly on supply-side augmentation.

With anything up to 80 per cent of river discharge occurring during the monsoon, storages are essential to avail of these waters during the ensuing lean season. Despite ranking among one of the greatest dam builders in the world, India's total storage capacity until 2004 was no more than 174 BCM from several thousand dams (with another 76 BCM under construction) as against a single storage of 180 BCM in the Kariba Dam reservoir on the Zambesi River, straddling the Zambia-Zimbabwe border. Given the precipitous gradients of Indian rivers, especially in the Himalaya, large, high dams have relatively limited storage.

While the national food reserves are more than comfortable and famine a thing of the past, deaths still occur from poverty and malnourishment and hunger is widespread. These are problems of distribution and income and regional disparities. The GBM-Indus command region, the country's breadbasket, needs to go in for crop diversification, rather than persist with the current intensive, chemicalised paddy-wheat or paddy-cane cycle which, though lucrative (given guaranteed and ever rising minimum support prices), spells danger from soil exhaustion, mineralised return flows and depleting water tables which are being mined. Use of bio-fertilisers, integrated pest control and organic farming (as is becoming popular in the Northeast) could be one answer to moving from a threatened green revolution to an evergreen revolution.

Biotechnology is coming to the aid of agriculture and genetically modified seeds have entered the market. The impact of the System of Rice Intensification (SRI) on rice yields is being evaluated in different parts of India, including Purulia in West Bengal, and appears promising. (Sinha, Shekhar Kumar and Talati, 2005). The International Rice Research Institute in the Philippines, however, is sceptical. SRI is a new technology developed in the 1980s from indigenous practice in Madagascar and is now being tried in some parts of the world. It entails considerably wider spacing of paddy seedlings to achieve far more prolific tillering. It appears to be water saving (only needing protective irrigation) and requires fewer inputs of seed, fertiliser and pesticides but intensive labour, though overall there could be some labour saving too. Trial yields in India have been significantly higher than in the case of conventional methods of paddy farming. Should it become a proven technology in Indian conditions, this could have an important bearing on the national farm economy.

The striking feature of this thumbnail sketch of India's water resources is the dominant role of the GBM basin with its snow fed rivers in terms both of irrigation and hydroelectric potential. Not to convert this water into wealth is to forego the gift of one of the world's greatest natural resources. To postpone the fuller development of this potential is to pay a very high opportunity cost of delay. Agricultural costs and prices will have to be brought down and productivity increased without heavy subsidies on fertilisers and water and electricity rates, in order that India remains competitive in a WTO-regulated globalised farming regime.

Drip and sprinkler irrigation can be used for less water intensive but high-value crops and are now being mandated, especially in regions of water stress. Water sector reforms have started a process of pricing up water so that all direct costs, including those of operation and maintenance are met. System modernisation with regulated outlets and volumetric sales to water user associations (WUAs) is being increasingly canvassed. Such participatory systems assure equity (as between those at the canal head and tail-enders within irrigation systems), satisfactory O&M and drainage, greater accountability and better bill collection. These institutions could also be used to develop collateral or linked facilities and become focal points for crop planning and demand management.

Most irrigation comes from groundwater though it must be properly understood that a large part of replenishable groundwater comes from canal irrigation. With the availability of cheap credit, the number of irrigation pumps has increased exponentially, touching 28 million from under a million 45 years ago. Bangladesh saw a fivefold increase in pumpsets with their numbers going up from under 100,000 to half a million in the 18 years between 1982 and 2000. Nepal too has witnessed a similar trend. Subsidised electricity rates have been a great incentive towards using electric pumps in place of more expensive diesel pumping. Groundwater markets have begun to thrive, oftentimes under the auspices of larger landholders but not infrequently on the basis of small farmer initiatives.

In the absence of groundwater regulation and its enforcement there has been gross overuse of water. This has resulted in small farmer distress from depleting aquifers and falling water tables. In parts of West Bengal and other areas of Eastern India and more particularly in Bangladesh, this has also resulted in arsenic contamination, which has become a health hazard and is now having to be vigorously combated.

All said, a cautious caveat is in order. Are foodgrain requirements being pitched too high, even with regard to the "low estimates"? Although food production is trailing behind earlier projections, offtake has not been moving along the assumed trajectory. This is partly because the better off are consuming less grain and more vegetables, fruit, dairy products oilseeds, sugar and so forth as incomes rise. But for millions of others food demand is suppressed for lack of purchasing power. However, farmers persist with the paddy-wheat, wheat-cane or paddy-paddy cycle, all of which are water intensive, as the minimum support/procurement prices for these crops are not merely the most profitable of any package but whatever quantity is brought to the market must be mandatorily procured. Further, the prices of these grains keep going up every year as State governments invariably enhance the amount fixed by the Agricultural Cost and Prices Commission by adding various bonuses. Fertiliser and electricity subsidies artificially depress costs while free or giveaway power tariffs encourage the mining of water, drawing down aquifers to danger levels. At the same time, the production of pulses, oilseeds and "inferior" grain such as ragi and bajra is stagnant or falling. These are rainfed or dry land crops and the "inferior" grain constitute the poor man's diet. Overall, national agricultural production and productivity have stagnated over the past 10-15 years. Altogether, this is an unsustainable situation in every way and calls for early remedial action if disaster is to be averted.

Land Records, Agrarian Reform and Naxalism

It does not appear that the problem of poorly maintained and inaccurate land records that prevail over much of the former permanently settled areas of eastern India has seen significant improvement. Governance has been poor in the eastern region and in Bihar, Assam and eastern U.P. in particular. Sharecroppers and small tenants face insecurity and privation, much as before, and continue to practice low-risk subsistence farming as they have no incentive to invest and enhance their productivity. Frustration has turned to anger and then to violence under the Naxalite banner. Sporting a variety of names, these armed groups now spread across nine states from Bihar, Jharkhand and West Bengal down to Andhra and Tamil Nadu.

This is not a mere law and order problem. Violence, extortion, armed struggle and adventurism are the obvious outward manifestations of a long-festering and deep-seated socio-economic malaise rooted in feudal relations, ruthless exploitation in disregard of the law, bondage and violent caste oppression congealed in the established order. The victims are dalits and tribals and the lower strata among the Other Backward Classes. These elements have suffered erosion of forest rights and land alienation at the hands of upwardly mobile politicians and corrupt bureaucrats with a contractor-criminal nexus. The warning signs have long been there; but far from any display of political will, there has been an unholy conspiracy of silence.

The criminalisation of lumpen educated unemployed elements along with growing agrarian unrest has in the words of one keen observer "resulted in the development of crime as a mode of surplus appropriation without any link with production … But the most insidious outcome is the crisis in governance, which manifests itself in the ruling elite appropriating (misappropriating) development funds while long-standing productive infrastructure like canal systems languish, and there are no new investments in infrastructure". (Sharma, Alakh N. 2005)

In some states like Karnataka and Madhya Pradesh the process of updating and computerisation of land records has been initiated. This has to be the first step in ensuring a semblance of order and accountability. It is on that basis that meaningful agrarian reforms can be completed. This is not to be achieved through ceilings, after their wholesale evasion through *benami* (fraudulent) transfers, but by enforcing security of tenure for the actual cultivator, indemnity for usurious debts, fair rents, homestead plots, approach roads and assurance of credit and inputs.

The grant of homestead plots to the landless (an accepted policy), with the right to seek marginal enlargement of the area through purchase of contiguous strips at discounted prices, could be a new prong of meaningful land distribution and agrarian reform. Kerala's experience shows how productive such garden plots can be for self- consumption and market gardening, with special gains in regard to nutrition and gender equity. (Hanstad, Brown and Prosterman, 2002). A special drive on some such lines is indicated in Bihar, Eastern U.P. and perhaps even Assam to impart fresh rural dynamism into the GBM region.

The question of employment is critical. The absence of work is compelling tens of thousands to migrate out of Bihar and Eastern U.P. to greener pastures. However, the labour intensity of agriculture could rise substantially with enhanced productivity and the development of farm capital assets and rural infrastructure through such activities as desilting canals and tanks, repairing embankments, land levelling, constructing drains and approach roads and so forth. Indeed, a pilot scheme for the repair and renovation of water bodies directly related to agriculture was approved by the Central government in 2005 with an outlay of Rs 30 crores. A rise in agricultural production would also create related job opportunities in the service and processing sectors. Yet, in the longer term, it will be necessary to move people from the land to off-farm pursuits.

This remains among the major challenges that the GBM basin has to overcome.

U.P. WATER SECTOR RESTRUCTURING PROGRAMME

Some years ago, the U.P. Irrigation Department commenced work on renovating and rehabilitating the almost 150 year-old Ganges Canal. This task has been more or less completed. Typical of the kind of remodelling and modernisation of the irrigation hardware and software now required for good, sustainable integrated water management, is the $ 150 m 15 year Uttar Pradesh Water Sector Restructuring Project (UPWSRP) launched in 2002 with World Bank assistance. The project encompasses 10 of UP's 70 districts in the (Central and) Eastern part of the state covering 300,000 ha in the 3.6 m ha Gomti-Ghaghra doab within the Sharda Sahayak-Saryu command, with 65-70 per cent of irrigation coming from private tubewells.

Western Uttar Pradesh, with moderate rainfall, regulated water supplies and a long tradition of state-run canal irrigation was, with Punjab and Haryana, among the pioneers of the green revolution. This was always the more progressive and prosperous part of the state under peasant proprietorship (after zamindari abolition), in contrast with the more feudal permanently settled areas of Eastern UP. However, the green revolution gradually diffused into this region too, with tubewell irrigation and a growing water market providing the impetus to small farmers to adopt the new farm technology. This was to lead to diversification into animal husbandry and other non-farm and service activities and the development of rural growth centres.

A depleting groundwater table and soil fatigue from a continuous wheat-cane crop cycle were symptoms of non-sustainability in Western UP, subsequently matched by the growth of *usar* lands and sodicity in the poorly drained Eastern districts. Increasingly manifest too was the baneful effect of a huge, centralising irrigation bureaucracy of the kind Wittfogel warned in "Oriental Despotism" as inherent in "hydraulic" as opposed to "hydrological" civilisations. With old-time construction-oriented engineers leading the system without adequate social science inputs, the emphasis was and remained on hardware at the cost of an increasingly relevant approach towards providing service, participatory systems and cost recovery as critical elements of integrated water resource management (IWRM). Population increase and double and triple cropping accentuated the problem. Weak, short-lived coalition governments in turn baulked at raising water and power tariffs with an eye on their vote banks. Good economics, it seemed, did not make for good politics. Despite its parlous finances, UP spends Rs 800-900 crores per annum on farm subsidies in the form of unsustainable water and electricity tariffs.

This is the situation that the UPWSRP seeks to reform through demonstrating what can be done in a Phase-I pilot project, 2002-07, in the command of two branch canals covering 300,000 ha. (World Bank. New Delhi, November 1, 2001). The objective is to proceed holistically towards institutional reform, downsizing the irrigation bureaucracy through a voluntary retirement scheme, retraining those who remain and introducing multi-disciplinary staffing patterns. Mindsets must change. Also envisaged is encouragement to participatory management though water user associations (WUAs), setting realistic tariffs and undertaking infrastructure modernisation and rehabilitation to attain sustainability. WUAs, working under sub-basin management and development boards for individual canal branches are to receive volumetric supplies, which they will retail, recovering the cost on the basis of metered billing, while ensuring sound operations, distributive equity, timely maintenance, rainwater harvesting and drainage through a local level IWRM approach.

Uttar Pradesh has appointed an Interim Water Tariff Commissioner to advise on the establishment of an independent State Water Tariff Regulatory Commission to set sustainable water charges without political interference. Over and beyond that is envisaged the establishment of a Ghaghra-Gomti Basin Development and Management Entity to refine and implement environmentally and socially sustainable water resource development and management plans for the Basin. This could truly be the county's first ever River Basin Authority.

There have been teething troubles and delays as political and bureaucratic cultures are resistant to change. Parting with power and empowering others is not easy. Transition from a top-down system to a participatory, user-led regime entails a major paradigm shift. Three changes of government in as many years and frequent transfers of officials down the line have retarded progress and allowed feudal and criminal mafias to intimidate and coerce functionaries and hold up contracts. Yet, there has been commitment to the project concept across party lines as the very lack of sustainability of the existing system has brought home realisation that there must be reform. Nor is the World Bank's funding something that a cash-strapped economy will want to jeopardise.

Phase-I has a commitment of Rs 800 crore bank funding over 2002-07 to commence institutional reform, revise tariffs, downsize the irrigation bureaucracy and train and reorient cadres to adapt to the new regime. The next phases will be devoted to consolidating and deepening these reforms and mainstreaming them across the Sharda-Saryu command and, finally, throughout the entire state. With the slippages that have taken place, Phase-I, clearly the most difficult stage, may now run to 2008-09, especially as the state is to have general elections in 2007.

Paradigm Shift in Irrigation and Diversified Agriculture

There has been another major transformation bearing on the irrigation regime. Until the Fifth Plan, state-run canals provided the primary thrust for growth in irrigation. Since then, private tubewells have come to the forefront. Water markets have allowed small and marginal farmers to drill their own tubewells and trade in water or to access market-driven water supplies from their neighbours. The huge pool of groundwater still available in Eastern U.P., therefore, more than ever dictates the need for conjunctive use of surface and ground water with good vertical and horizontal drainage to prevent waterlogging and salinity. Private tubewells are farmer-led and not dependent on the irrigation bureaucracy (or public investment) though much recharge comes from state-owned canal systems.

The shift in balance from state-run canal systems to private tubewells has, however, led to other concerns. Electricity shortages and unreliable power supply have enhanced dependence on diesel pumps. These entail higher pumping costs (especially with long-duration pumping for watering sugarcane and wheat, with a corresponding fall in the water table in western U.P.), a rising draft on foreign exchange for oil imports and rising greenhouse gas emissions.

These factors have lent urgency to the rural electrification programme. The Rajiv Gandhi Mission for Rural Electrification has set a target to electrify within three years the remaining 40,000 "dark" villages out of UP's 100,000 villages.

In the background of fears of climate change, the endeavour is now to maximise returns on every drop of water rather than on each unit of land or to achieve "more crop per drop". This places water conservation at the forefront. Given the emerging realities of the next green revolution, economics has hopefully begun to move politics along the reform path.

By 2005 there were only around 70 WUAs in place in the UPWSRP command. These participatory irrigation bodies are competing with watershed management associations and panchayati raj institutions for grassroots supremacy as has happened in other states. Other issues such as farm subsidies and minimum support prices for particular crops (the cane-wheat, paddy-wheat, oilseeds-pulse cycles in different regions for example) have also to be tackled.

UPWSRP will also need to dovetail with other state programmes. Crop diversification with the spread of private tubewells has found a nice fit with the pilot U.P. Diversified Agricultural Support Programme of 1994, also assisted by the World Bank. This has demonstrated the viability and economics of diversification into vegetable and horticultural crops, livestock farming and organic farming, which have in turn encouraged and been stimulated by contract farming and the establishment of cold chains to preserve perishable commodities. A second phase was launched in 2003 to spread this production and marketing technology to other districts and encourage the processing industry.

Kitchen gardening has become popular in some places under the crop diversification programme and has been linked with the drive to improve nutritional standards. All these developments, and the off-farm activity and employment it has spawned, has given rise to the growth of agro-business centres. These are steadily multiplying and have the potential of becoming rural growth poles in a urbanising countryside, and check dams against wholesale migration of some of the best rural talent to the cities.

When Uttaranchal was hived off as a separate state some years ago, U.P. lost most of its reserved forest in the Himalaya. The State Forestry Department has, therefore, perforce had to turn to social forestry and agro-forestry to create carbon sinks with funding from the Global Environmental Fund.

With the growth in population and division of holdings, 88 per cent of U.P. farms are under two hectares and fall in the category of small and marginal holdings. Fortunately, consolidation has been an on-going process in the state, undertaken in a ten-year cycle district by district. U.P. has shown leadership from the start in implementing this wise policy. Simultaneously, land records are being computerised and the process should be completed by 2007. This should offer the farmer great comfort.

The diffusion of technology has been shown to be neutral to size of holding and has impacted on income and employment levels of small and marginal farmers and generated off-farm employment opportunities. Altogether, it has been a force for poverty alleviation. (Sharma, Rita and Thomas T. Poleman. 1995).

None will dispute that all methods of water conservation, non-structural as well as structural, need to be employed across the whole range, from micro and mini to large and mega. Each has its place and none is mutually exclusive. Thus rainwater/rooftop harvesting is good practice to catch the raindrop where it falls. So are groundwater, recharge, watershed management, tanks and *bandhs* and larger storages. The notion that small is solely, universally and eternally beautiful is as fallacious as the reverse assertion that large works obviate lesser efforts. While bandhs can store water and have even revived streams, as the Tarun Bharat Sangh has shown on the River Arvari, near Alwar in Rajasthan, there is evidence that such efforts, including rainwater harvesting, though fully deserving of every encouragement, have their own limitations. Capture of rainfall at any one point can impact on aquifers and stream flows elsewhere. Likewise, excessive groundwater pumping has a measurable and well-documented impact on both aquifers and stream flows.

An integrated watershed development programme has been under way since 1990 through a participatory approach. It has been operationalised in 100 districts in 14 states including several in the GBM. By the turn of the century, 27.5 m ha of the 107 m ha of degraded lands had been treated and plans made to cover the rest within the next 20 years. Additionally there are two on-going Central soil and water conservation programmes for soil conservation in catchments of river valley projects and another for integrated watershed management in the catchments of flood prone rivers. Both programmes are to cover 96 m ha (Planning Commission, September 2001). All this indicates appropriate concerns; but social and water conservation measures will have to be sustained and built into all development programmes if they are to have a permanent impact.

The reckless mining of groundwater and even fossil water underlines the urgency of reviewing the legal framework. Who owns water? At present the Indian Easement Act prevails and vests the landowner with water beneath his property irrespective of depth. This is no longer tenable. If minerals belong to the state, why should not water below a certain depth, say 100 m, more or less, also not belong to the state or to the community, maybe a watershed community, if that can be defined. Given such a law, water rights could be regulated with regard to spacing and pumping so that water rights are clearly established and cannot be (mis)appropriated by the wealthy and powerful. A similar problem exists with regard to water rights on small streams.

Coping with Floods

Floods remain a problem. Embankments will no longer serve as they take up more and more land and tend to build up riverbeds. Pressure of population has forced the landless and livestock farmers to encroach not merely on the flood plain but on sand banks or char lands or even the riverbed itself. Flood losses in terms of lives, livestock and loss of crop and infrastructure have, therefore, been mounting despite rising expenditures on flood proofing. Afforestation, watershed management and keeping the land under vegetative cover are all necessary and such programmes are being pursued. There is still a long way to go.

Flood forecasting and warning systems and other non-structural measures are being steadily expanded and upgraded, nationally and across borders. But at the end of the day, engineering solutions cannot be entirely disregarded. Large storages with flood cushions and smaller detention reservoirs can play a significant role in moderating peak flows and facilitating flood routing. The latest National Flood Commission (2005) has reiterated this view. It has additionally recommended a Rs 50,000 crore revolving fund with the Water Resource Minister for urgent flood control schemes and would have this amount raised from a one to two per cent flood cess on all new infrastructure located in flood prone states.

The Ganga Flood Commission has from time to time led discussions with the Nepalese authorities on flash floods from small trans-boundary rivers that become raging torrents during the monsoon. The mechanism of an Indo-Nepal Standing Special Committee on Inundation Projects (SCIP), first set up in 1985, has been strengthened. However, relations with Nepal and political conditions in that country of late have inhibited progress with regard to the investigation and construction of a series of flood detention reservoirs within the Kingdom to protect the Nepalese terai, North Bihar and Eastern U.P., from the annual visitations they suffer.

Nevertheless, preparation of a joint Indo-Nepalese detailed project report on the Kosi High Dam-cum-Kurule-Kamla Diversion Project is under way. This is planned to provide a substantial flood cushion (apart from irrigation, energy, navigation and augmentation benefits). It would in effect at long last complete the third and last stage of the Kosi flood defence strategy that was initiated in the 1950s and 1960s, with the construction of the Kosi barrage and embankments in the two countries constituting the first two stages. The Kosi High Dam will moderate floods in Nepal, north Bihar, West Bengal and even Bangladesh. It is therefore a project of regional importance that, hopefully, will now move towards completion without undue delay.

Flood planning in the Northeast was initially entrusted to the Brahmaputra Board, which completed master plans for the main stem of the Brahmapuntra, its major tributaries and the Barak and eight Tripura rivers in the 1980s. A number of multipurpose dams and drainage schemes were projected, with flood moderation as the main focus. The centrepiece of its proposals was three projects: the Dihang and Subansiri dams in Arunachal in the Brahmaputra Valley and the Tipaimukh dam on the Barak in Manipur. All three entailed large storages, and presaged very considerable multipurpose benefits, flood moderation being foremost among them. However, inter-state controversies intervened. Arunachal objected to the submergence of some of its most promising new townships (Along, Daparijo, Tamen and Yingkiong), and was not prepared to accept the displacement and forest loss that the Dihang and Subansiri mega dams entailed. Manipur and, initially Mizoram, were in turn opposed to the Tipaimukh project on similar grounds.

Sub-Optimal Flood Cushioning in New Cascades

All three projects were subsequently reviewed and revived, but were transferred to the National Hydroelectric Power Corporation (NHPC) and North Eastern Electricity and Power Corporation (NEEPCO), respectively. Agreement was reached between the Centre, Arunachal and Assam that the Dihang and Subansiri projects would be reworked as cascades in order to mitigate submergence and displacement. As a result, what emerged is three and four run-of-the-river-cum-storage cascades instead of two single terminal mega dams. However, the problem is that these cascades offer large energy benefits but inadequate flood or conservation storage that Assam and India require for optimising flood moderation and (future) augmentation benefits, respectively.

The figures tell their own story. The Brahmaputra Board's original single mega Dihang dam provided for 47,000 m cu m of gross storage (with a 8500 m cu m dedicated flood cushion) as against 25,680 m cu m and 10,139 m cu m of storage, respectively (without any dedicated flood cushion), in the alternative three and four dam cascade configurations as suggested by NHPC. By far the largest single storage component of the four dam alternative, however, would still entail submergence of Yingkiong town (the Arunachal chief minister's constituency) as well as a biosphere reserve and part of the Tuting monastery.

The Subansiri cascade seeks to replace the single high dam earlier proposed at Gerukamukh with a gross storage of 14,000 m cu m (and a dedicated flood cushion of 2500 m cu m) with a three dam cascade that would store 4808 m cu m (with a dedicated flood cushion of 494 m cu m). The installed hydro capacity of 5600 MW would, however, be larger than in the case of the single dam (4800 MW).

The Lower Subansiri dam was cleared for construction but the Supreme Court intervened with an order on a writ petition in April 2004 making this conditional on NHPC abandoning all further projects in the Subansiri valley, including the proposed middle and upper cascade segments, on environmental considerations. Meanwhile, the Water Resources Ministry has also stepped in to withhold consent for the terminal dam in the Dihang cascade unless flood storage is optimised as part of an integrated multipurpose project.

Issues are delicately poised. But there no doubt that to forego optimal flood cushioning in the Brahmaputra and Barak basins would be to condemn Assam to suffer permanent and cruel annual flooding. Assam is the largest state in the Northeast and the geo-strategic pivot on which the other dormitory states depend for regional coherence and connectivity with the Indian heartland through the Siliguri corridor. So if Assam remains depressed, the Northeast cannot truly prosper. This is not to say that valid human, environmental and political considerations can or should be ignored but to argue for reconsideration on the basis of an alternative calculus of longer term regional and national costs and benefits, with suitable trade-offs and more imaginative parameters of resettlement and compensation.

Arunachal can perhaps be brought around to make a compromise if both Assam and the Centre make the effort. Some more submergence that would give larger storage and adequate flood moderation may be acceptable if Arunachal–or any similar upper riparian in other regions–is assisted to develop coping mechanisms for humane and culturally viable R&R.

Localised R&R through Area Development

A large dam in a remote region is not to be seen as a single project. Its very investigation and construction comprehends multiple preliminary and ancillary activity in building roads, townships and critical infrastructure that itself creates connectivity, market linkages and a basis for superior land use and crop planning, income and employment generation and opportunities for tourism. In short, it encourages urbanisation, industrialisation and skill formation all of which, properly fostered, could make for intra-regional balance through area development.

Connectivity, which is a precondition for dam construction, could also be the basis for better administration, social development and, together with area development, become an instrument for poverty alleviation and the provision of basic services. There are earmarked budgetary resources for all of these, not least under the Northeast's Central Non-Lapsable Fund. Therefore, given a gestation period of five to eight years before a dam is completed and displacement takes place, there is no reason why area development cannot provide for in situ resettlement and rehabilitation of displaced persons above the shoreline of the newly formed reservoir.

This would obviate R&R for project-affected families on the land (or otherwise) in distant locations in the command area where they would be separated from their cultural environment and kinship groups and resented by host populations. But those who wish to migrate or seek new job opportunities further afield, could find an exciting new frontier in special economic zones created to develop a variety of processing and energy intensive industries that offer economies of scale and attractive investment opportunities.

Such an approach would call for modification of the draft National Rehabilitation and Resettlement Policy that has been under consideration for the past many years. Despite much public debate and consequent amendments, the new policy has yet to be put into effect. Unfortunately the latest draft still harks back to the discredited land-for-land formula. This is made absolute in the case of tribal displaced persons while non-tribal PAFs losing agricultural land are given first right to resettlement in the command of an irrigation project. (Rural Development Ministry, 2004). The alternative of in situ R&R through area development of the catchment offers a far better alterative, with land for land remaining one possible option when and where land is readily available.

In many run of river projects displacement is quite small and land for land has not been an issue. Teesta-V in Sikkim, for instance, will displace 46 families. NHPC's R&R package for each family includes 0.02 ha homestead plots, Rs 5,000 by way of land development charges, a house construction grant of Rs 1 lakh, a variable disturbance allowance of Rs 7,000-10,000, a transportation allowance of Rs 10,000, a fertiliser and seed grant of Rs 5000, water supply, provision of land for and construction of common facilities like a school, primary health centre, panchayat *ghar* and two shopping complexes, land for an approach road and drainage system, a subsistence allowance until one family member gets permanent employment, preference for jobs with project, access to the project school, technical training with scholarships, and a special grant of Rs 10,000 to scheduled caste, scheduled tribe and OBC project-affected families.

The draft National Tribal Policy also advocates land for land for tribal PAFs with a minimum two-hectare R&R allotment. This again is mistaken policy if imposed as a rigid criterion rather than an option where feasible. This draft policy too merits reconsideration. (Tribal Affairs Ministry, 2004).

Creating Trusteeship Zones

Under the current national hydropower policy, states hosting hydro projects are entitled to receive 12 per cent free power from each project as a form of royalty for use of what is assumed will be a depleting natural resource site, given reservoir siltation over time. Some of this power will undoubtedly be used for domestic and municipal lighting, water supply and sanitation and some limited industrial purposes, but energy demand is likely to be limited, at least initially, and experience shows that a good deal of the "surplus" power is exported through the national grid. As more hydropower stations are commissioned, the pool of free "royalty" power will rise by leaps and bounds. Rather than sell this raw power, the host state could well utilise it to promote income and employment generating activities, benefiting from both the value addition and multiplier effect. In Arunachal's case, such "royalties" are likely to exceed the state's annual revenue of around Rs 1,000 crores by many times. This kind of income is not to be scorned.

Arunachal can also be assured of some land, especially flat land, in compensation for the area dispossessed by submergence or acqusition, on which one or more fine new townships and vibrant growth centres can be constructed if any goes under the reservoir. But where is such land to come from?

The carving out of Arunachal, Meghalaya, Mizoram and Nagaland from Assam left strips along the new borders in dispute. This stems from the fact that the British drew an Inner Line along the foothills to protect the Assam plains and tea gardens from marauding hill men. The lands beyond were designated Frontier Tracts and, later, "excluded areas", and very lightly administered by Delhi through the Governor of Assam.

Subsequently, certain forests beyond the Inner Line were transferred to Assam for better management as reserved forests. Some of these forest lines were subsequently redrawn leaving behind several notional forest "boundaries" demarcating the transferred areas. This did not matter as long as the entire region remained part of Assam. It was only when the new states came into being one by one post–Independence on the basis of ethnic identities that what was earlier no more than a simple administrative distinction translated into a political difference. There has since been tension and intermittent clashes along these border strips which have become bones of contention. The area in dispute between Assam and Arunachal, for instance, is approximately 700 sq km. These border disputes have affected peace and development, become a refuge for dubious elements and criminal gangs and inhibited cooperation by keeping alive mistrust.

What might now therefore be considered is that some part or all of these areas be declared "Trusteeship zones" by mutual agreement for a 30 or 50 year period on a case by case basis, with the two contending states in question and the Centre as partners. These zones could then be developed as infrastructure estates and industrial parks with railway yards, road transport depots, airports, warehouses, cold storages and townships with schools, hospitals, technical training centres, shopping areas, banking and other facilities and recreational centres. Those displaced by dams could, if they so desired, be resettled here and employed in any one of the many newly created job opportunities. Given the availability of cheap and plentiful power, especially secondary power, water and SEZ infrastructure these could also be well suited to attract energy-intensive industries, with convenient transport connections by road, rail and a revivified Brahmaputra-Barak inland waterway.

Electricity is not merely a raw material to be exported but could become a basis for value addition (agro-processing, for example), employment, new investments and capacity building. It is not enough to aim at local self-sufficiency in power generation but necessary to maximise natural resources returns with sustainability. Bhutan, more modestly endowed than Arunchal, offers a striking example of the unfolding of a nation building and development vision with hydro-energy as the prime driver.

Bigger reservoirs could in some cases even be used by small passenger-cum-cargo aqua-planes, linking such water bodies with the Brahmaputra and Barak. Regulated releases through turbines would augment lean season flows and improve river drafts for inland navigation and inter-modal transportation. These are not small benefits and one should not expect decision makers in Arunachal and the other hill states, or Assam, to be unaware of the potential gains. Upwardly mobile youth would surely hold them accountable were they to forego such inviting opportunities for a new deal.

Arunachal and Assam should also both know that each could be a long time loser in declining cooperative relations with the other. Each needs the other: Assam for flood moderation (the absence of which costs it dearly) and cheap energy; and Arunachal for the connectivity and markets that Assam provides. The Centre too has a role to play in underwriting some of the collateral costs as regional gains will also undoubtedly yield large national benefits.

Hydro Initiative Must Optimise Overall Benefit

According to the 16th Electric Power Survey, the Central Electricity Authority estimates that the country must enhance generation capacity from 113,500 MW (2004) to 202, 453 MW by 2012 and 273,734 MW by 2017. This will need to include 94,104 MW of hydroelectric power if the desired hydro-thermal mix of 40:60 is to be attained and peaking shortages are to be reduced, if not contained. It has also been felt increasingly important to encourage hydrocarbon substitutes and place reliance on clean, renewable fuels while imparting greater flexibility and stability to the grid.

A 1987 CEA reassessment placed the nation's hydropower potential at 84,000 MW at 60 per cent load factor from 845 schemes. Additional pump-storage sites were also identified. Thereafter the CEA went through a careful ranking process based on pre-feasibility studies. This narrowed the field to 162 projects with a total installed capacity of just over 50,000 MW. These are now candidates for the 50,000 MW Hydro Initiative announced in 2003 and have been farmed out to a number of agencies for preparation of detailed project reports.

A region-wise break up of the Hydro Initiative allocates 32,107 MW to the NE, including 25,690 MW to Arunachal, 1870 MW to Mizoram, 1680 MW to Sikkim, 1490 to Meghalaya, 970 MW to Nagaland and 407 MW to Manipur (excluding Tipaimukh). Institutional changes have been announced to strengthen the planning and implementation mechanisms for this purpose. As far as the rest of the GBM is concerned, 6374 MW of the 50,000 MW Initiative target is to be met by Uttranchal and 3750 MW by Himachal.

Emphasis is being placed on basin-wise development. Thus the NHPC is developing the Teesta-V (510 MW), in Sikkim, which should be complete by early 2007, just about the time Teesta-III (132 MW) in West Bengal goes on stream. The corporation is meanwhile awaiting clearance for Teesta-IV (160 MW) in West Bengal and is investigating several other potential sites on the Teesta in Sikkim.

The contracting public sector and corporate power companies working on the Hydro Initiative appear to have aimed at energy maximisation, relegating water benefits. Energy is clearly favoured as a profit maximiser as opposed to water, which has traditionally been regarded as a social rather than as an economic good. However, with the Northeast accounting for some 30 per cent of the national river run-off, it is disconcerting to see a design trend favouring energy maximisation through run-of-the-river projects without looking sufficiently at the water storage and flood cushion components in order to secure an optimal project mix in each case in the interest of the overall national benefit.

Run-of-the-river hydro projects entail minimal submergence and displacement and do not impose the collateral environmental R&R costs that storage dams have to bear. They are also much cheaper to build, with a far shorter gestation period. There is therefore much to commend them. But they do not store water, a very precious commodity, or contribute to flood mitigation, irrigation, water supply or navigation, all of which confer large benefits on millions. Storage sites are also a scarce natural resource and if not used or pre-empted by other developments entail a national loss in terms of foregone potential benefits.

National and regional social accounting, therefore, cannot entirely disregard natural resource optimisation. Any nation or people that does so will be unmindful of longer-term benefits and the larger common good. Large dams of course have their immediate and long-term costs, which must be kept in mind. But certain impacts can be mitigated and it is possible to take decisions that ensure a positive social and economic cost-benefit outcome over time and space, matched against the equivalent cost and benefit of doing nothing or doing things differently and the opportunity cost of delay.

There is yet another factor that merits consideration. This is climate change. The effects of global warming are evident in warmer days, shorter winters, aberrant rains, glacier retreat and the melting of the Tibetan permafrost and polar ice caps. Glacier retreat and alpine cloudbursts are aggravating erosion and causing debris dams to form in the folds of the Himalaya. Debris-lake outbursts have been experienced in Arunachal. In Himachal too, the Perechu, a tributary of the Sutlej was blocked by a debris dam in Tibet that then gave way both in 2004 and 2005, causing a sharp rise in flows resulting in panic evacuation of stretches along the Sutlej Valley and leaving a trail of damage in its wake. The pattern and magnitude of climate change and its effect on river flow regimes remains uncertain. This by itself is cause for greater insurance. Storage dams are one means of redistributing rainfall over space and time.

Everything said, there is clearly a strong case for both a regional and national review of an exclusively energy-maximising water resource development strategy in favour of a more optimal approach that also takes account of water storage and flood factors. The danger of postponing such a review could be that some of the best storage sites could be pre-empted by sub-optimal development. The tools are there. The Indian Space Research Organisation (ISRO) has the capability to create virtual 3-D imagery on the basis of which optimality can be established by computer modelling and simulation studies under various assumptions and hypotheses.

Environmental Impacts and Sustainability

The concept of sustainable development can be traced to the first World Environment Conference in Stockholm in 1972 following which India legislated to conserve forests and protect the environment. Environmental clearances were mandated and lending agencies insisted that certain guidelines be followed. Since then all project clearances are based on environmental impact assessments (EIA), conforming to specified checklists. There is also a requirement for public hearings to ensure stakeholders and project affected persons are duly consulted.

The spread of irrigation and forest conservation has left its imprint nationally and in the GBM region. With the passage of the Forest Conservation Act, 1980, and the National Forest Policy, 1988, the aim of forest policy has shifted from production and revenue to conservation, afforestation and community participation through joint forest management. The latest *State of Forest Report*, 2001, issued by the Forest Survey of India, shows national forest cover having increased in the preceding two years from 19.49 per cent of India's total land area to 20.55 per cent, or an increase of approximately 3.5 m ha. A National Forestry Action Programme is now under way. Water resource projects have been instrumental in expanding forest cover as they are enjoined to and in fact do plant many more trees by far than they destroy. Irrigated tree farming and canal side and roadside plantations have also seen rapid growth.

One negative consequence, however, has been the spread or resurgence of malaria and other water borne vectors to irrigated areas or wherever there is stagnant water (around wells, pumps and domestic water coolers). Malaria surveillance has degenerated and new vectors have sprung up that are resistant to anti-malarial drugs and sprays. A whole new approach and a renewed drive is, therefore, necessary to control what could be a rising menace in both rural and urban areas.

The possible environmental impacts of hydro-power projects have been listed to include, submergence, displacement, loss of forests, habitats and cultural heritage, rim instability and reservoir siltation, impediments to fish runs, infringement of riparian rights and adverse effects on downstream users, estuaries and the coastal ecology, ground water, water quality and health. Also mandated are an environment management plan (EMP), a catchment area treatment plan, schemes for compensatory afforestation, restoration of construction sites, seismic and other dam safety studies and, most important, an adequate resettlement and rehabilitation (R&R) package. Public hearings in this regard should involve state authorities, NGOs, environmental interest groups, local communities, public leaders, elected representatives and so forth. Early in 2005, NEEPCO faced popular ire at a public hearing convened for the 110 MW Dikrong Project in Arunachal's Papumpare district. Another hearing had to be scheduled as objection was taken to the fact that the EIA report was not available to the affected community in their own language.

These are wise cautions, but can be pushed too far from failure to comprehend direct and indirect costs and benefits over time and space. There is a cost for doing nothing and, sometimes, immediate pain may need to be suffered for the future environmental and social health of the community and the nation. Some years ago, the Supreme Court imposed a complete ban on all forest felling except by or through state forest corporations. It gave this ruling in response to excessive and illicit logging for saw mills and veneer plants making plywood in the Northeast. The order caused widespread hardship and had ultimately to be modified.

Subansiri Judgement

In the midst of these dilemmas has come a Supreme Court judgement that further complicates the issue. Some years ago, the Ministry of Environment and Forests accorded conditional clearance to the NHPC to divert 4,000 ha of forest land (3,183 ha in Arunachal and 816 ha in Assam) as part of the Lower Subansiri Project (LSP), subject to the outcome of a Public Interest Litigation (PIL) writ of 1995 pending before the Supreme Court. The LSP at Gerukamukh, the terminal dam with 2,000 MWs of installed capacity in the NHPC's reworked Subansiri cascade, is estimated to displace 24 families from two villages and submerge 3436 ha of land, including 42 ha in a rocky outcrop of the Tale Valley wildlife sanctuary, which the Supreme Court was approached to condone.

In its verdict handed down on April 19, 2004, the Court ruled that the Tale Valley submergence area shall legally remain part of the sanctuary. The reserved forest forming part of the LSP catchment is also to be declared a protected national park, the exact area to be left for determination by the state government in consultation with experts. It is estimated that some 5,000 persons reside in 14 villages within the perimeter of the proposed new national park. Their relocation and resettlement has been charged to the NHPC, as has the complete funding of a 10-year management plan for the new national park, including the reforestation of degraded sites within it. Finally, the court ordered "there shall be no construction of (any) dam upstream of the Subansiri river in future", noting that the "Parties are agreed" that the LSP may proceed subject to these conditions.

The order that no dam shall be constructed upstream of LSP is sweeping and calls for review. The ruling could set a false precedent and benchmark for other hydro projects. It has already acted as a dampener on the NHPC with regard to the Dihang cascade. Further, in view of forest submergence under the LSP, the NHPC has already had to deposit a sum of Rs 453 crores with Arunachal and Assam towards compensatory afforestation in addition to an amount of Rs 8.71 crores for catchment area treatment. With such a heavy burden loaded on it upfront, NHPC or any other developer will understandably put a premium on high profitability in order to remain in the black. The cost of power would also be that much more. Can therefore some way be found of reordering such costs and ensuring a more optimal project mix in the Subansiri and other basins?

Quite obviously Assam and Arunachal must come to terms if storages are to be built in the Himalayan catchment of the Brahmaputra. About 65 per cent of Arunachal is under forest and around 82 per cent under tree cover. Furthermore, about 10,000 square kilometres, or an eighth of its total area, fall under designated national parks or wildlife sanctuaries and there are proposals to triple such protected areas. So wildlife and biosphere protection is not being neglected by any means. It is therefore unlikely that the Supreme Court will stand in the way of dam construction in the upper catchment of the Subansiri if the concerned parties come forward with an agreed formulation to resolve their differences. It is here that the trusteeshsip zone idea offers what could be a happy solution. Arunachal and, indeed, the other Northeast states have a stake in mitigating the Assam floods, which disrupt communication with the rest of the country, thereby raising prices, dislocating trade and retarding development. The North Council and Centre should accordingly be willing to share the burden of flood mitigation, especially as the railways and national highways would be spared recurring losses.

As far as forest losses are concerned, compensatory afforestation and the creation of gene banks in bio-diversity parks or biosphere reserves are known mechanisms that could be invoked under appropriate supervision and within a given framework.

The Supreme Court's conditional clearance of the LSP imposes extremely onerous, even sweeping conditions. It merits consideration whether protection of the part may inadvertently be at the cost of the whole. Forests are obviously important and it can be nobody's case that they should be wilfully destroyed. But this has to be set against the public interest and the larger common good in implementing any otherwise well-conceived project whose long term multiplier effects may engender far greater environmental benefits and human welfare than the corresponding loss entailed in the short run, much of which may be partly or even fully compensated through the mandated R&R and Environment Management Plan (EMP) mechanisms. This is a general principle that would apply not merely to LSP and in Arunachal but to all projects anywhere in India. Any blanket ban on further projects upstream of LSP would require the most rigorous substantiation on specific grounds. The issues at stake here are prima facie economic and social rather than judicial.

Issues in Cost Burden Sharing

The multipurpose Tipaimukh project (1,500 MW) on the Barak has also been reworked, by NEEPCO, not with regard to its basic features, which remain unchanged, but in terms of ancillary packages for R&R, road alignment, flood cushioning and security. The Fulertal barrage and irrigation canals have been taken to Phase II. The Project will, however, confer considerable navigation benefits both above and below the dam in Assam, Manipur (along the Barak, Irang and Makhru rivers) and Mizoram (along the Tuvai river), opening up hitherto inaccessible areas.

The Project received Stage-I forest and environment clearance in May 2002 and a revised DPR was approved by the Central Electricity Authority for a cost of Rs 5163 crores (at 2002 prices) in July 2003. A "letter of comfort" for funding from the Power Finance Corporation was received in July 2004 following which the Corporation has sought Rs 157 crores to carry forward Stage-II activities.

Unresolved issues pertain to who should bear the Rs 280 crore cost for raising and maintaining four Central security battalions against the depredations of various insurgent groups; Rs 280 crores for the quantum of flood cushioning sought by the Ministry of Water Resources; and Rs 105 crores for the realignment of the National Highway from Silchar to Imphal and the construction of three new bridges along it over the Irang, Makhru and Upper Barak rivers, which will be submerged. NEEPCO being a power company feels that it should be relieved of some or all of these burdens, as it must operate on commercial principles.

Some of these costs are a legitimate charge on the Central government, which should be prepared to do some pump priming to get the Northeast moving. Tipaimukh could be transforming and is obviously a key project for the southern tier of the region.

Decommissioning Gumti Dam

Not all projects are sustainable or better than the alternatives that present themselves. Nothing is static and circumstances change. This is well demonstrated in the case of the now de-rated 10 MW Gumti hydro project in south Tripura that was commissioned in 1976. That was a time when the state was starved of power and lacked the considerable gas resources subsequently discovered as a thermal energy base.

Tripura, once a tribal majority state, had even before Partition begun to attract Bengali settlers along the western plains and was thereafter swamped by refugees and illicit immigrants from East Pakistan and, later, Bangladesh. This tilted the demographic balance to create a Bengali majority. The resultant cultural and political trauma was a major factor in triggering the tribal discontents that sparked what led to multiple insurgencies in the state. Construction of the Gumti dam at Dumbar aggravated the situation, widening the ethnic divide. Some 8000 to 10,000 tribal families were displaced by the reservoir as it filled the 46 sq km fertile Raima bowl. Many of those displaced received little or no compensation as they were coparceners or could not show title to the land. This compelled them to settle in the surrounding hills where they felled the forests to resume slash-and-burn jhum farming. Accelerated erosion in consequence resulted in higher-than-calculated siltation of the Gumti reservoir and a corresponding reduction of power output over time.

Gas was discovered in Tripura thereafter and gas turbines (Agartala, 84 MW; Rohia-I, 48 MW) now more than supply the state's energy needs. Further gas turbines programmed, Rohia-II and III (42 MW) and a second large Central gas turbine of 750 MW, whose foundation stone was laid in October 2005, will leave Tripura with a considerable exportable energy surplus. In the circumstances it has been suggested that the Gumti hydel plant, now possibly fully amortised, can be shut down with advantage. While there will be some loss of peaking power (which an uprated Gumti project might provide under a proposal that has been mooted), the ethno-ecological benefits could be greater. If the 46,000 ha reservoir bed, enriched with silt-laden deposits, is returned to cultivation, the 27,000 or more landless tribal families in the state and those previously displaced by the Gumti dam could be resettled in the Raima valley. Production from here could help wipe out Tripura's grain deficit, constitute a major step in ecological restoration and be seen as a gracious act of ethnic reconciliation between the tribal people and the in-migrant Bengali settlers. It could be a turning point in race relations and quite possibly end the on-going insurgencies. (Bhaumik, Subir. 2002).

The decommissioning of the Gumti dam could be an act of statesmanship and confidence building not only in Tripura but for all of the Northeast. The message would go forth that the authorities are determined to uphold sustainability and the public good.

Such an act would be consistent with the draft National Environment Policy 2004 which has been published to elicit public opinion. This sets out broad objectives and principles, such as that the "polluter pays", proposed strategies and actions and process related reforms. It deals specifically with forests and wildlife, biodiversity, the management of surface and ground water, wetlands and mountain eco-systems, climate change, and environmental standards and building partnerships. (Environment and Forest Ministry, GOI. November 2004).

Institutional Restructuring in the Northeast

The Government of India's concern for the promotion of peace and development in the troubled Northeast and led it to undertaker some institutional restructuring.

A Department for Development of the Northeast Region (DONER) was established some years ago under a Union Cabinet Minister. More recently the North Eastern Council, located in Shillong, has been reconstituted as an empowered regional planning authority. It is chaired by the DONER Minister and has three Members, one of whom is a Member of the Planning Commission with territorial responsibility for the region. Simultaneously efforts are under way to remodel the now-moribund Brahmaputra Board as a North East Water Resources Authority (NEWRA) organically linked to the NEC. It is proposed to empower NEWRA to grant environmental and financial clearances up to a given limit. This restructuring, if brought into effect, should facilitate the planning and expeditious implementation of water resource projects in the Northeast.

NEWRA will not interfere with ongoing projects, as its mandate is prospective. But it has been mooted that should any state in the region take up a new scheme, NEWRA may be enabled to enter into an MOU with it for a 50:50 cost and benefit sharing partnership, without prejudice to the 12 per cent royalty payable to the host state in respect of hydro-electric projects. Arunachal is disinclined to go along with this proposition and would prefer to develop its hydro-projects on its own with private participation. Apart from fending off pressures for undertaking particular schemes, it fears that NEWRA could become yet another regulatory and supervisory layer that delays project sanctions and execution. On the other hand, there are limits to the funds that any of the Northeastern states is going to be able to raise or leverage on its own. The matter, therefore, calls for discussion and it should be possible to persuade Arunachal that its fears are unfounded and that partnership with NEWRA could greatly strengthen its hands and enable it to use its hydro-electric potential to accelerate development.

River Action Plans

With urbanisation, industrialisation and the chemicalisation of agriculture and vector control, the pollution of rivers and groundwater is assuming increasing urgency. The Ganga Action Plan was a first effort in this direction. It was a valuable learning experience in dealing with a truly gigantic problem. Phase-I aimed to improve water quality in the Ganga by intercepting and diverting for treatment 873 million litres per day (MLD) of municipal sewage in 25 towns, constructing sanitary latrines and electric crematoria. A sewage treatment capacity of 865 MLD had been created by March 2000 at a cost of Rs 452 crores when Phase-I was closed.

Water quality is being monitored from 27 stations from Uttranchal to West Bengal and some improvement has indeed been registered. Phase-II is now under way and has been extended to cover the Yamuna, Gomti and Damodar. This now forms part of a larger River Action Plan (RAP) for pollution abatement works in 157 towns covering 31 rivers in 18 states. RAP is being implemented by a National River Conservation Directorate at a sanctioned cost of Rs 4492 crore.

The Yamuna Action Plan covers 21 towns. A treatment capacity of 738 MLD has been created with Japanese assistance and a YAP-II is currently under implementation for pollution abatement in Delhi, nine towns in Uttar Pradesh and eight towns in Haryana. Industrial effluents are the major problems and fish have been a major casualty. Lack of headwaters has become a major problem here as in many other rivers as water is diverted and stream flows are inadequate for regeneration. The criticality of leaving untouched a minimum quantum of ecological flows in rivers is becoming apparent and the Supreme Court has intervened on occasions to warn polluting industries to install treatment plants or face penalties, even closure, for fouling stream flows. Public awareness has grown and civic authorities too are now more vigilant about river and groundwater pollution.

Tehri Dam Leads Upper Ganga Development

The Phase-I Tehri Dam and 1000 MW component is virtually complete after years of controversy and misguided efforts to stall it at every stage. The last diversion tunnel was blocked and the reservoir started filling after September 2005. The first turbine is ready for commissioning. All legal issues have been resolved and PAFs resettled, including those who were holding out in Old Tehri Town that has now gone under water. Work is in progress on the Phase-II Koteshwar re-regulating dam (400 MW) and final clearance for the Phase-III Pumped Storage Scheme (1,000 MW) is awaited. The overall cost of the project is estimated at Rs 6,700 crores, of which Rs 1,000 crores will have gone towards R&R. The Tehri project will firm up irrigation in 604,000 ha and newly irrigate 270,000 ha in Central U.P. Once the reservoir fills, it will supply 300 cusecs of drinking water per day to Delhi and 200 cusecs per day for a number of towns and villagers in U.P.

The Tehri Hydro Development Corporation (THDC) has been entrusted with constructing the 440 MW run of river Vishugad Pipalkoti project (440 MW) near Joshimath by the pilgrim route to Badrinath, while Jaiprakash Power Ventures Ltd is engaged in the Vishnuprayag Project on the Alaknanda, which should be commissioned before the end of 2006. Several other projects in Uttranchal are also likely to be allotted to THDC under the 50,000 MW Hydro Initiative for which the relevant MOUs are under negotiation.

The Maneri Bhali and Srinagar schemes on the upper Ganga are ongoing and the National Hydro Power Corporation is working on the 280 MW Dhauliganga project that is scheduled to be commissioned in 2006 or 2007. The NHPC has also negotiated a MOU with the Uttranchal Government to take up a three-stage Kotli Bhel cascade on the Alaknanda-Ganga just above and below Devprayag, with a combined capacity of 850 MW. It is also preparing a revised DPR for the Lakhwar Vyasi project (420 MW) in the Yamuna basin.

Nepal Emergency Stalls Decision-Making

Turning to the international sector, the Mahakali and Ganges Treaties were landmark events in South Asian water relations. They not merely broke a longstanding impasse in each case but laid down guiding principles to chart the way forward. Unfortunately, the promise inherent in them is yet to be harvested, with bilateral relations having deteriorated in each case.

In Nepal, the Maoist insurgency, itself a part product of lagged development, unemployment, regional disparities and failing governance, imposed an involuntary moratorium on development. The King took over the reigns of administration and finally declared an emergency in February 2005. This polarised the nation as never before and invited international disapproval. The crisis had been building over some years and the climate of indecision and mistrust engendered could not but impact on the water resource sector, breeding a sense of xenophobia in negotiating further steps in furtherance of the opportunities for water resource cooperation opened up by the Mahakali Treaty with India. Beyond a point, delay amounts to denial and this was a poor option for Nepal to adopt, perhaps not consciously but by default. This is not a tenable situation and it is for India as much as for the international community to help rectify and assist Nepal to return to normalcy through peaceful dialogue leading to the restoration of multiparty democracy. The powerful economic stimulus provided by purposeful water resource development would address the economic emergency confronting Nepal, reverse the downward spiral in internal relations within the Kingdom and trigger a multiplier that engenders employment and income generation, regional equity and national reconciliation.

The Mahakali Treaty foundered on an underlying misperception in Nepal that equated its stipulated half share in any jointly constructed storage on this border river with "ownership" of its natural trans-boundary flows. The principles of equity and equal entitlement to water use along the common Indo-Nepal Mahakali boundary was somehow seen as translating into an equality of shares in the waters of the river per se. The fact that Uttar Pradesh had long back developed water uses on the natural flows of the Mahakali after it leaves Nepal and enters India as the Sharda river, without prejudice to any Nepalese rights, appeared incomprehensible. This remains a sticking point in relation to the "sankalp prasthava" or so-called "strictures" passed by the Nepalese Parliament at the time of ratification of the Mahakali Treaty. It is an issue that needs to be amicably resolved and laid to rest. Article 5 of the Treaty provides that the "water requirement of Nepal shall be given prime consideration in the utilisation of the waters of the Mahakali River". This must be honoured in letter and spirit in implementing the Treaty and there is no reason to suppose that past grievances in this regard will not be removed in the future.

Nepal represents a paradox of poverty amidst plenty, much as India's Northeast and large parts of the GBM region. The Kingdom's population of 23 m is expected to increase to 36 m by 2027.The current population distribution is skewed, with the western and far-west zones being the least peopled and least developed. These regions and the mid-hills have tended to empty into the more populous central and eastern zones and the sub-montane terai tract, with India absorbing the overspill. Agriculture supports almost 80 per cent of the population and accounts for 41 per cent of GDP. However, only 2.64 m ha or 18 per cent of the country's land area is cultivated. Of this, less than half the irrigable area of 1.76 m ha is actually irrigated. The very heavy dependence on non-commercial energy has contributed to degradation of the environment, erosion and loss of agricultural productivity, giving another avoidable twist to a vicious cycle.

Kathmandu's Cautious Water Vision 2027

Nepal's water vision is detailed in its Water Resources Strategy of January 2002. It describes Nepalese aspirations, "viewed in the context of the difficulties and opportunities that currently confront the country's water sector, and provide a strategy that will make water-induced prosperity a reality rather than just a mirage".

The national goal is to ensure that living conditions are significantly improved in a sustainable manner. The goal is broken down into three phases: to meet basic needs and build institutional capacity in the short term (five years); provide "substantial benefits" in the medium term (15 years); and to "maximise" benefits from water resources over the long term (25 years). Cost-effective hydro development and regional cooperation are among the mechanisms to be employed. The external factor is given importance. It is argued that "in the context of agricultural demand and supply and prices in South Asia, intensification of agricultural production is both essential and profitable". It is expected that the Indian power market will continue to grow and power exports will be commercially viable.

The Strategy paper declares that the people of Nepal will decide on the potential trade-off between water resource development and environmental impacts. It calls for a "compatible regional climate for water sharing", leading to international recognition of "the (fundamental) right of a nation to an equitable share in its own water resources". It sets a target of irrigating 90 per cent of all irrigable land by 2027, with 60 per cent efficiency.

By 2027, 60 per cent of all households will have access to electricity and Nepal will be exporting substantial amounts of power. It expects 150 MW power exchange with India by 2007 (as against 50 MW in 2002), 400 MW by 2012 and 15,000 MW out of an installed capacity of 22,000 MW by 2027. This sensibly presumes encouragement of energy intensive industries and power based transportation systems to reap the gains of value-addition and employment. This pattern of growth is premised on dependable electricity supplies at attractive prices in contrast with high unit costs of generation hitherto. Indeed, a World Bank report on Nepal's proposed Power Sector Development Strategy (March 2001) rated Nepal's power tariff in 1999 as among the highest in Asia with the cost per MW of installed capacity ranging between $ 2-3 per MW as against about $ 1 per MW in India. The recently commissioned 144 MW Kali Gandaki project for instance costs NL $ 450 m.

Among reasons adduced for such high costs are the extensive employment of international contractors and consultants, failure to exploit economies of scale, high dependence on run of the river projects, heavy transmission and distribution losses and management problems. Two private joint ventures, Bhote Kosi (36 MW) and Khimti (60 MW) have come on stream. But the Nepal Electricity Authority is having problems with the power purchase agreements relating to mandated purchases and dollar-determined pricing, similar to what India experienced with the earlier aborted Dabhol power contract with Enron in Maharashtra.

Electricity exports to India are rendered possible by the Indo-Nepal Power Trade Agreement (February 1996), which Nepal has yet to ratify. The Strategy paper curiously states that the agreement will in fact only be "amended or ratified" by 2007. Further, "riparian issues between neighbouring nations (read India), including inundation problems along the Indo-Nepal border, are likewise planned to be resolved by 2017" when "a workable regional cooperation mechanism" will hopefully be established! The approach seems sadly lacking in a sense of urgency.

The financial outlays to implement the Water Strategy by 2027 in the irrigation, hydropower, water supply and sanitation, fisheries and other sectors is estimated at $ 13 billion, excluding investments in hydro-power exports and mega projects like Pancheshwar. A quarter of the outlay is expected to come through private investment, the bulk of this in the power sector.

Under the Mahakali Agreement, costs are to be borne by the parties in proportion to the benefits accruing to them. Thus the net power benefit shall be assessed on the basis of "savings in costs to beneficiaries as compared with the relevant alternatives available". Nepal at first asserted that the replacement cost would be that of an equivalent thermal or nuclear power station. India countered this by pointing out that comparable hydro projects are under construction in the Indian Himalaya in Uttranchal, Himachal and the Northeast and that these are relevant alternatives.

Changing Market Conditions in India

There have been several major developments affecting the Indian power market since the Mahakali Treaty was signed. In the first place, power reforms have set in motion a process of unbundling monopoly state electricity boards. Power generation and trading have been thrown open to private, including foreign, investment and to joint ventures. The various regional electricity grids are being interlinked to facilitate large volume interchange across the country through extra-high voltage transmission lines. The interchange capacity exceeds 8000 MW and is expected to reach 30,000 MW by 2012, with HVDC (high voltage direct current) and 765 KV systems along national transmission corridors.

With the enactment of the Electricity Act, 2003, and statutory Central and State electricity regulatory authorities in place, charged with quantitative, qualitative and tariff regulation, the stage has been set for market driven competition. The adoption of a system of unscheduled interchange (UI) in a regime of Availability Based Tariffs (ABT) puts a premium on economy and efficiency with reliability. This emphasises customer sovereignty, permits market choice and rewards performance. In the circumstances all players, internal as well as international, will have to be competitive if they are to get a share in the rapidly growing India energy market. ATB recognises the value of hydroelectricity, more especially for peaking power, which commands a better price.

The Mahakali project reached a dead end around 2001 when the Rupaligad re-regulating dam site favoured by HMG proved technically infeasible. The Nepalese side steadfastly declined to permit investigation of the alternative Poornagiri site that was preferred by India for its larger pondage and power output though, undoubtedly, with higher displacement as well. A prolonged impasse was broken in 2004 with India agreeing to consider a site a couple of kilometres downstream of Rupaligad for the re-regulating dam. This may offer slightly larger pondage but for a lower peaking output of 5600 MW in two phases in place of the earlier planned 6480 MW. Nepal appears agreeable to this modification and, if an MOU is signed, investigations can proceed and work commence on Phase I of the reworked Mahakali Project. The phasing will also better enable India to absorb the quantity of peaking power generated as a number of Indian power projects are also moving forward in the Himalayan region under the 50,000 MW Hydro Initiative.

The NHPC is interested in an Indo-Nepal joint venture to generate 300 MW on a run of river drop in the upper Karnali bend. The Nepal Electricity Authority seeks 49 per cent equity and once it comes up with the matching funds the project can move forward. The Snowy River Electricity Corporation of Australia holds a license from HMG to proceed with the 750 MW West Seti project. The bulk of the power generated is to be exported to India but the initial asking price by SMEC was prohibitive. This has subsequently been revised downwards and if Nepal ratifies the Power Trade Agreement a deal could be struck. A third project that HMG would like India to take up is Burhi Gandaki (600 MW).WAPCOS, an Indian consultancy firm, has prepared a project report. However, decision-making on all these projects has been inhibited by the continuing political crisis in Nepal. Unless this shows some signs of resolution, it is unlikely that any progress will be registered.

Meanwhile, the two sides reached an understanding in 2004 to establish joint field offices in respect of the Kosi High Dam-cum-Kurule-Kamla Diversion Multipurpose project. This mega-project could augment lean season flows in the Lower Ganga and provide flood moderation and improved navigation. Bangladesh had earlier expressed interest in the project and formally indicated that it would like to participate, bearing its due share of the costs in proportion to the benefits received. This interest should be nursed and Bangladesh brought into the loop as a partner at an appropriate stage.

Hydro Development Driver in Bhutan

Contrast this with Bhutan. Indo-Bhutan cooperation has been a model that has benefited both countries and propelled Bhutan on to a faster but sustainable growth trajectory. The Tala project (1020 MW) will come on stream late in 2006. WAPCOS is preparing a DPR on the 870 MW Punatsangchu project and India will then decide whether it is prepared to finance it ($ 813 m) as it has earlier projects. The Royal Government is also keen that India underwrite the 360 MW Mangdechu project ($ 349 m). The cost of all these project appears to be under Rs 4 crore per MW of installed capacity. .

Much of Bhutan's power is being exported to India at a tariff that has risen from an initial 27 P per unit to Rs 2 at present. Even this may appear an unduly low price for Bhutan but is not really so in view of the fact that India's project financing has so far been on a 60 per cent grant and 40 per cent soft loan basis, with generous grace periods. Moreover, guaranteed year-round power import has meant that eastern India hydro stations have had to back down during the monsoons when the dams are spilling water, entailing a Rs 40 crore annual subsidy by the Ministry of External Affairs to compensate their loss.

A large part of Bhutan's revenue comes from hydropower, which has become and is likely to remain the main driver of its development, export growth and goal of enhancing "Gross National Happiness". (Royal Government of Bhutan, Ministry of Planning, 1997). The country exported 1564 m u of power to India in 1995.This is expected to touch 6400 mu by 2006 and could grow exponentially thereafter. A DPR for the twin dam Sunkosh multipurpose project (4060 MW) was prepared in 1997 and envisaged a 141 km canal that might transfer water to the Teesta and Mahananda in India. This has been put in cold storage for the moment on account of environmental concerns as the canal traverses a national park and slices through some tea gardens. A southward realignment of the canal to sanitise the route would entail losing head and subsequent pumping to transfer water through the Siliguri neck, an expensive proposition.

Dhaka Fails to Convert Ganges Treaty to Advantage

India's water relations with Bangladesh, like those with Nepal, have been affected by an adverse turn in the general political climate of relationships on matters pertaining to border demarcation and management, trade and transit, the continuing influx of in-migrants from Bangladesh, sanctuaries for Indian insurgent groups and the rise of Islamic radicalism in that country. Bangladesh has its own list of grievances against India as well, some of them water-related.

The Ganges Treaty of 1996 was seen as a major milestone but progress thereafter has been disappointing. The treaty came under harsh attack in Bangladesh in the very first lean season on both technical and allegedly substantive grounds but the fact that Dhaka did not call for a two-year or five-year review as provided for was indication enough that the rhetoric unleashed was excessive. The real tragedy, unfortunately never publicly addressed, is that even until now Bangladesh has been unable to use more than a fraction of its share of lean season supplies for the benefit of the southwest (Khulna) region whose alleged devastation on account of Farakka diversions was at the core of Bangladesh's grievance. A $ 50 m Dutch assisted Gorai Resuscitation Project to make a capital dredging cut through the 30 km long and five m high hump at the offtake of the Gorai deltaic spill from the Ganges was abandoned in 2000 with a change in regime. The Bangladesh government had from the start preferred a Ganges Barrage at Pangsha to pond the Ganges and force its backflow over the Gorai hump to water the southwest region. The donors differed and insisted on the Gorai Resuscitation Programme as the better alternative. They have subsequently been chary of supporting the Ganges Barrage, which is seen as having a high opportunity cost. India has, however, offered technical assistance as a fist step, but has heard nothing further.

The Gorai hump is the outcome of a secular morphological shift of the Ganga eastwards, resulting in the successive closure of deltaic spills moving west to east over the past two hundred years or more. The first spill channel to close was the Bhagirathi-Hooghly, taking off from Farakka, which marks the apex of the great Gangetic deltaic fan. Hence the Farakka Barrage, commissioned in 1975, to rescue Calcutta Port which is situated on this dying river. The Gorai outfall had begun to choke well before that date. Official East Pakistan records showed that, depending on the hydrological cycle, the Gorai would cease drawing water at a certain point during the recession of the Ganga flood, any time after November-December. The by-passing of the Gorai outfall gradually led increasing silt deposits to form a massive Gorai hump that now effectively seals off the river in the low season.

Both sides have commissioned ambitious irrigation projects, but sharing its lean flows has become another bone of contention. The earlier flow data has been jettisoned as unreliable and a new series is now being jointly compiled on a more scientific basis. An interim sharing formula has eluded the two sides as the earlier formula is not acceptable. At the Track-II level, it has been proposed that both countries should consider running the two barrages and canals as a single integrated system, which would probably be a more efficient way of handling the distress until augmentation is possible, and even thereafter.

Nor has any progress been made as yet with regard to sharing the Brahmaputra, Barak and other smaller rivers. In fact, Bangladesh has expressed concern over the proposed Tipaimukh project on the Barak (Meghna) with emotional apprehensions regarding both flood and drought impacts on its territory. Both sides need to sit together and exchange information. In doing so they would probably find considerable coincidence of interest and mutual benefit in cooperation.

India is the upper riparian in the case of all of Bangladesh's rivers barring some of those originating in the Chittagong Hill Tracts. Virtually all the high ground is in India and the rivers fan out in broad, lazy, braided channels as soon as they debouch on the totally flat Bangladesh plain. It would therefore be easier and cheaper for India to regulate these rivers. This being so, it would make sense for the two countries to join hands in working out mutually beneficia projects, which could be jointly funded and managed. Canals taking off from the Fulertal barrage on the Barak near Silchar and, say, a Jogighopa barrage on the Brahmaputra could run into Bangladesh. Apart from irrigating tracts in that country, such canals could augment the Teesta-Mahananda and many of the smaller North Bengal and Tripura streams that would otherwise be subject to distress sharing between the two countries. Inland navigation could be extended and inter-modal transport connectivity established to provide a large enough hinterland to justify a major regional deep-water port around Chittagong. All of this would fit into the South Asian Free Trade Association (SAFTA) framework and vision of a South Asian Community.

Demonising Inter-Linking Rivers

Tragically, India's Inter-Linking of Rivers (ILR) proposal in 2002 was drummed up into a major controversy in Bangladesh. This was wholly avoidable had India simply shared the concept and its plan of action with Bangladesh and Nepal and had the others not jumped to extreme conclusions without seeking clarification. The language of discourse officially used in India in advocating ILR was misplaced. It was unhappily named for a start. Inter-linking of rivers sounds crude and is a methodology at best and not an objective. A far better and more accurate title would have been A Programme for National Water Security with Regional Equity. This would have made the approach inclusive, not exclusive, combining all means from micro to mega.

ILR is not a "project" but a concept. It is not driven by any Supreme Court directive to complete it within 10 years at a cost of Rs 56,00,000 crores. Obiter dicta was misconstrued as rulings. A Task Force was set up to examine, distil and then carefully work out sustainable projects from the menu prepared by the National Water Development Agency over the past 20 years. This aimed at transferring waters from surplus to deficit basins on the basis of water balance studies projected up to 2025. Of the 30 links that appeared feasible for inter-basin transfer, 16 were Himalayan components and 14 peninsular. Since it was apparent that the Himalayan links entailed international agreements, examination of these was at the very start put off to a later stage, though the NWDA concept as a whole was given due publicity along with notional calculations of overall benefit in terms of irrigation, power, flood moderation and so forth.

The 14 Himalayan links conceptualised by the NWDA, but not pursued at any stage by the Task Force, are Kosi-Mechi, Kosi-Ghaghra, Gandak-Ganga, Ghaghra-Yamuna, Sharda-Yamuna, Yamuna-Rajasthan, Chunar-Sone Barrage, Sone Dam–Southern Tributaries of the Ganga, Brahmaputra-Ganga (Manas-Sunkosh-Teesta-Ganga),Brahmaputra-Ganga (Jogigopha-Teesta-Farakka), Farakka-Sunderbans, Ganga (Farakka)-Damodar- Subernarekha, Subernarekha-Mahanadi. In any event, each case, only flood flows are to be tapped.

As an upper riparian, Nepal would not be affected unless it agrees to the construction of any dam(s) on its territory. In that case the project(s) would be governed by the Mahakali or other agreed principles. As far as Bangladesh is concerned, India is bound by the 1996 Treaty to make every effort to maintain lean season flows in the Ganges and, indeed, to endeavour to augment supplies. ILR aims to store monsoon flows and not to divert lean season supplies. It is therefore in every sense dedicated solely to augmentation. So there can be no reason to fear that it will dry up the rivers flowing into Bangladesh. In point of fact, what the NWDA contemplated was a more modest version of storages Bangladesh itself favoured in Nepal when proposals were exchanged with India for augmentation of lean season Ganga flows between 1978 and 1982. .

The hysteria whipped up in Bangladesh even after Indian explanations were offered, even if belatedly, was quite extraordinary. At an officially sponsored international conference on trans-boundary rivers and the impact of ILR, held in Dhaka in December 2004, a Minister spoke of millions having to migrate from northwest Bangladesh, which, he said, was in danger of desertification, while more than one delegate inveighed against Farakka. However, a paper presented by a former British water consultant who had worked in Bangladesh for many years, asked if Bangladesh could not benefit from ILR. In the course of preparation of the Bangladesh National Water Plan in 2003, he had suggested a Mawa-Paksi-Farakka complex of barrages, the first on the Padma (below the confluence of the Brahmaputra/Jamuna with the Ganges) and the second on the Ganges near Hardinge Bridge. His calculations showed that the Mawa pond would stretch back to the Paksi Barrage along a very gentle gradient and that these Brahmaputra waters could then be pumped 10 m into the Paksi pond and, thereafter, lifted another eight metres to the Farakka pond, involving a total lift of 18 m. In his view, augmentation from Brahmaputra storages in India could be split 50:50 with Bangladesh, the Indian share being transferred to Farakka through the Mawa-Paksi lift. He believes such a transfer would be environmentally benign and a lower-cost alternative than any hitherto proposed Indian option for inter-basin transfer. (Brichieri-Colombi, December 2004).

This is one of many alternatives that could be considered, with transfers being effected along different alignments. The benefits would be mutual. In fact, ILR could provide opportunity to revisit regional cooperation in the Eastern Himalaya with Nepal, Bhutan and Bangladesh. The first step would need to be confidence building through a meeting of minds. Each country is in the process of firming up long term water strategy plans. None knows what the other is doing. Each has been talking at rather than with one another. Were the four water resource ministers to meet, narrate their problems and talk about what they are endeavouring to do to overcome them, they would probably discover an enormous amount of congruence. Each could do more with less if they cooperated rather than decided on doing it alone.

A single basin-planning unit for the vast expanse and immense population of the GBM – many times the size of the Mekong, Nile and other basins–might be premature. But cooperation on individual projects could forge a number of interlocking linkages and mechanisms, which could be reviewed at annual ministerial meetings for a start. These institutional links could embrace power grids, joint ventures in dam construction, cross-boundary irrigation canals, a regional flood forecasting and warning network, data exchange, and the creation of inland navigation and inter-modal transport corridors.

Calcutta's IWT Future in lieu of Faded Ocean Glory

Demand management is an important means of conserving water. There is a high opportunity cost for water and it is time that India looked at the economics of flushing the Hooghly to keep alive the fiction that Calcutta (other than its Haldia docks) is a viable ocean port. Cargo handling for the twin Calcutta and Haldia Docks that come under the Calcutta Port Trust, touched a record high of 46.16m t in 2004-05. On an average about 80 per cent of the total cargo moves through Haldia. In the past few years, ship calls to Calcutta have been approximately half those to Haldia. Smaller vessels can visit Calcutta only at high tide, and have to be lightened and topped up because of restrictions on account of drafts, bends and dock gate sizes. Calcutta is ideally suited to be a great inland navigation and coastal-carrier port, a role it has studiously neglected. On the other hand, its pretensions to be a mother port is a millstone around Haldia and has long discouraged port expansion further out to sea that would provide capability for berthing even larger vessels that now use Colombo and Singapore as hubs by default.

The government is committed to a Maritime Development Programme (earlier conceived of as an ambitious garland port development programme christened Sagarmala). This aims to upgrade minor and intermediate ports and build new ones to handle India's fast growing ocean trade. In the circumstances, it seems unwise to permit Calcutta docks forever to try and keep up with the Joneses. The port is choking the city and sitting on prime land, which could be more imaginatively used than become a cover to subsidise Calcutta's growing irrelevance to ocean trade. Instead, a string of barge ports from Haldia to Farakka could come up around a Calcutta IWT hub to move 100 m t of traffic along the Ganga-Brahmaputra-Barak waterway, open up the Bengal countryside and decongest metropolitan Calcutta. If Calcutta were to see such an overdue metamorphosis, it would require maybe no more than 15,000 cusecs of flushing against the 35,000-40,000 cusecs being sent down from Farakka in the leanest April-May period. The more than 20,000 cusec saving in water could be used for irrigation in West Bengal, augmentation for Bangladesh (in a new cooperative relationship that could bring enormous gains to India and the Northeast in particular), and yet leave something for transfer further south or west. There must also be a viable plan to check the Ganga eroding its banks below Farakka.

Such a plan of action calls for invigorating the Inland Waterways Authority of India and the Central India Water Transport Corporation. More vigorous inland water movements to and through Bangladesh could provide stimulus to developing trade and transit between the two countries. Opening the sector to private enterprise is overdue. With containerisation, inter-modal transport should come into its own with roll-on and roll-off combinations. The creation of industrial parks along specially designated waterfront zones would also generate traffic and take the pressure off trunk rail and road routes.

The government has fortunately started thinking on these lines. The 2006 Budget announced steps to locate a deep draft ocean port in West Bengal. National initiatives include empowering IWAI to raise tax free bonds to raise finances and to enable it to enter into commercial joint ventures with a 40 per cent cap on build-operate-transfer projects. A full tax exemption to investors for five years, enhanced depreciation for vessels, a vessel-building subsidy and customs rebates on imports are among the other incentives offered. The newly established Inland Water Development Council will hopefully empower this sector and matters might look up if the government accords IWT the same priority as the national highways programme in matters of investment and project execution. A separate IWT development fund is also proposed and the capacity ceiling of 1,000 tonnes for barges is to be removed.

Things are moving under the gathering impetus of the Inland Water Transport Policy of 2001 which has given a fillip to hydrographic surveys and related development of the fairways, barge construction, infrastructure such as permanent jetties, floating jetties and cranes, a floating dry dock, acquisition of dredgers, extension of night navigation, and the establishment of a National Inland Navigation Institute at Patna. The State IWT Departments are being strengthened too.

A moribund Central Inland Water Transport Corporation (CIWTC) is in the process of being wound up and its 100 or so serviceable vessels are in the process of being leased out to private parties. Private operators are coming to recognise the potential of IWT. This is exemplified in a Rs 10 crore investment made by a private barge company in the construction of a dedicated loading terminal on the Lower Ganga to ship fly ash from West Bengal thermal stations to Bangladesh where there is a growing demand for this material for cement manufacture. As much as 600,000 tonnes of fly ash was shipped to Bangladesh in 2004-05 and the market is expanding.

The IWT Policy envisages the inter-linking of inland waterways and ports with coastal shipping. This approach needs to be integrated with the proposed National Maritime Policy.

According to the IWT Policy document, the potential movement by the country's waterways is estimated at 50 billion tonne-kms as against the one billion tonne-kms actually moved through inland waters at present. It further estimates that every shift of one billion tonne-kms of traffic to inland waterways will reduce fuel costs by about Rs 25 crores.

It may be worth exploring whether a waterways development organisation could be set up under the auspices of the Indian Navy to give impetus to the IWT programme. This could be on the lines of the Border Roads Organisation and geared to service the eastern and northeastern region.

Water Markets and Basin Boards

Pricing offers a powerful instrument for demand management in the water sector. Though India has shied away from the concept, there is evidence of vigorous water markets in the private shallow tubewell sector. Water markets could work as well for bulk consumers or even states as much as for individuals or single entities. The ILR exercise was mistaken in failing to consider this option in the initial stages of federal bargaining with regard to water rights and determining true surplus and deficit regions/users. Instead, the debate was politicised with upper riparians claiming that they had no immediate or longer-term surplus while lower riparians exaggerated their needs and current deficits. If a sensible pricing framework were evolved, with due safeguards for weaker sections/entities, non-commercial sectors and so forth, the resultant equations could be very different. "Surplus" entities might be inclined to re-examine their water usage and needs if they could make an attractive water sale that could be utilised for beneficial purposes in other sectors. Hoarding water, like hoarding gold, is useless – at least beyond a point—as a hedge against future adversity. Marginal cost principles apply.

Could the same principle be applied in "marketing" surplus waters in the GBM over and above basic national requirements? One could make due allowance for the superior political and economic buying/bargaining power of a big player like India. Similarly, socially important but less profitable sectors like rural water supply and sanitation could be protected against highly profitable commercial uses such as hydro-energy.

The other problem that the ILR exercise showed up was the disconnect between political/administrative boundaries and river basins. In order to find a way around the Cauvery impasse, a group of well-respected citizens got farmers, economists and water experts from Tamil Nadu and Karanataka to discuss the issues in contention and see it they could come up with agreed answers. The venture was useful in promoting understanding though not otherwise conclusive. On a smaller scale, the Tarun Bharat Sangh has set up a river parliament in the regenerated Arvari river valley in Rajasthan to take decisions on conservation and utilisation of this resource. River boards, essentially river basin authorities, are prescribed under the Constitution but have never been established. The one exception was the Damodar Valley Authority, modelled on the TVA. But this was soon scuttled by West Bengal, the principal beneficiary, while Bihar tired of making investments the benefits of which largely passed on to Bengal.

It would be useful to see if cross-border river valley authorities could be set up as a means of harmonising national and basin interests. Something like the Mahakali Commission could possibly transmute into such an authority if properly structured. Likewise, would a Lower GBM and Sunderbans Authority (or Forum for a start), with civil society representation be politically viable? In both cases, the first requirement would be cordial diplomatic relations. Given a cooperative framework, much is possible, perhaps incrementally.

International Initiatives and Climate Change

Three other elements of the international dimension are noteworthy. The Central Water Commission has at the instance of the Yangon Government submitted a detailed project report on the 1200 MW Tamanthi dam as part of a Chindwin cascade in Myanmar. Once finally approved, it is envisaged that this could be developed as a "mutual interest" project, with Tamanthi power surplus to Myanmar's requirements being evacuated to Phek in eastern Nagaland to feed into the Northeastern Grid. Such a link could mark a first step towards developing a valuable South Asian-ASEAN grid connection.

Railway International Technical and Engineering Services (RITES) has submitted a project report for creating an inland waterway down the Kaladan/ Kolodyne (Chimmtuipui) river in southern Mizoram to the port of Sitwe (Akyab) on Myanmar's Rakhine (Arakan) coast. A parallel road is contemplated to facilitate inter-modal carriage. This has been submitted to the Myanmarese authorities and discussions are in progress regarding construction and cost sharing.

Thirdly, there was considerable excitement and concern in 2003 when reports appeared that the Chinese were planning to build a dam on the great U-Bend of the Brahmaputra in Tibet and divert the waters north to the Gobi desert. The reports were specious and ill-informed, not least about the geography of Inner Asia. No such project is under way and an official Chinese spokesman denied that any such dam or power station was planned but said that some hydropower plants had been constructed on the tributaries of the Tsang-po, as the Brahmaputra is known in Tibet. However, should China plan any project on the U-Bend, it would need to take the interests of the lower riparians fully into consideration. In any event 70 per cent of the discharge of the Siang/Dihang is generated south of the Himalayan divide. .

Meanwhile, China has resumed sending hydrological data on the Dihang/Tsang-po to India, which was suspended around 1962. Discharge data on the Subansiri has also been sought, together with alerts on the formation of debris or glacial dams across trans-boundary streams in the High Himalaya. A debris-dam outburst in Tibet caused havoc in Arunachal some years ago while a similar blockage on the Perechu, a tributary of the Sutlej in Tibet, gave India, and Himachal Pradesh in particular, some anxious moments in 2004. Since the occurrence of debris/glacial dams tend to be located in remote, inaccessible and unpopulated areas, satellite surveillance could be employed to monitor events and issue timely warnings. Thereafter, steps would need to be taken to dislodge or puncture these obstructions before they build up large, unstable lakes and attain destructive proportions. Close collaboration could help avert untoward debris dam bursts that have played havoc in the past.

Glaciers are shrinking worldwide and the Himalayan glaciers are no exception. The Himalayan snow and ice cap constitute a vast water reservoir whose health, like that of the Tibetan Plateau permafrost region, is of critical concern to South Asia in as much as these waters drain southwards. This is a manifestation of global warming, even if only over a short 50-year cycle as some believe, and on first reading could augment stream flows over the next few decades until the snow-ice cap steadily shrivels and almost disappears. The other manifestation of climate change could be heavier precipitation. Either way, more Himalayan storage is indicated to conserve these flows, and not to plan for the future would be imprudent.

Perfervid environmentalists who tirelessly inveigh against greenhouse gas (GHG) emissions are prone to apply brakes to their logic when it comes to building dams, both to store possibly rising flows as well as to generate clean, renewable hydro-power. There are admitted environmental losses in dam construction, though some or much of these can generally be compensated. But the benefits are large and normally far outweigh the gains over time and space. Hence the institution of clean development mechanisms and carbon trading to give credit for the creation of carbon sinks and avoidance of GHG releases by substituting hydro for more toxic fuels like coal.

India had a per capita electricity consumption of 474 KWH in 2000 (as against 1019 KWH in China, 2749 KWH in Malaysia and 12,406 KWH in the U.S.). Using this as a base, it is estimated by CEA that India's carbon dioxide emissions totalled 0.5 and 1.1 per metric tons per capita in 1980 and 1999, respectively, as against 1.5 and 2.3 for China, 2.0 and 5.4 for Malaysia and 20.4 and 19.7 for the United States in those same years. There is a global need to reduce GHG emissions and to halt and then reverse global warming. Hydropower could be a powerful instrument in that cause and Bhutan, Nepal and India could all look on carbon trading as a mechanism for leveraging funds to develop their hydro potential on the basis of rigorous norms.

The Kyoto Protocol on reducing global GHG emissions has finally been ratified by the United States. India too must play its role in what has to be a cooperative global alliance.

The UN Convention on the Non-Navigational Uses of International Watercourses has, however, failed to muster the minimum majority for ratification. The Convention was to come into force 90 days after 35 countries had signed it. But to date only 18 signatures have been appended, none from among the GBM countries.

Technological and Management Factors

As in most other fields, water resource engineering, from macro to micro, has seen revolutionary change. Satellite imagery and airborne laser photography with sub-metre capability have become powerful aides to 3-D terrain and vegetative mapping and modelling. Geological, hydrological, snow and ice, flood, erosion, forest, dam-site, catchment and command area mapping is simple and submergence areas and environmental losses can be measured. Canal alignments can be studied and crop-soil profiles prepared. It is possible to develop thematic maps on land use and soil types to make land-irrigability assessments and design suitable cropping patterns and canal networks. Waterlogging and salinity can be monitored.

Computer simulated models enable rapid cost-benefit analyses so that alternatives can be considered and their pros and cons weighed without long delays. Some ground-truthing is of course required, but this is necessary even otherwise. The Indian Space Research Organisation (ISRO) now has proven and versatile capability to map, analyse and monitor much of the data that is required for good project design, optimisation studies and integrated water resource management.

Similar advances have been made in structural design, materials, the manufacture of specialised machinery and equipment and so forth. All these help reduce costs, ensure better quality and enhance dam safety. This not to say that error or failure is impossible, but it does provide real assurance that confidence levels in technical and socio-economic judgements are likely to be higher than before.

The exercises undertaken by the ILR Task Force also shows that far more sophisticated socio-economic analysis is possible than previously. New financial instruments are also available for funding large and complex projects. The Government has also put in place specialised institutions to cater to specific needs. The Power Grid Corporation, the Power Trading Corporation, the Power Finance Corporation, and so forth have the mandate, skills and leverage to ensure comfort and viability. But the legal framework pertaining to water still remains weak in India and is a matter that invites early attention.

GBM Fruit There for Plucking

There is a whole new challenge and opportunity ahead. Water is life and will forever remain a key element in human progress, especially in the earlier stages of development where its availability and management is closely related to poverty alleviation. Integrated Water Resource Management is central to sustainable development and, in the case of trans-boundary waters, demands regional cooperation. This is ever so true of the GBM region, which is yet to emerge out of the poverty trap despite being so richly endowed by nature.

International support would be forthcoming for bold development initiatives and regional cooperation. After walking away from the water sector for well over a decade following the criticism it took on the Sardar Sarovar Project (on mistaken premises) and other large dams, the World Bank has reconsidered its mission and come out with a new water policy. Its latest Water Resources Sector Strategy recognises that it cannot alleviate poverty if it does not help developing nations to build on their natural endowments, including water resources. "To be a more effective partner, the World Bank will re-engage with high-reward-high-risk hydraulic infrastructure, using a more effective business model" and upholding strict social and environmental standards. (World Bank, 2004).

The bank's Uttar Pradesh Water Sector Restructuring Project and its current engagement in a Study on Natural Resources, Water and the Environment Nexus for Development and Growth in Northeast India testify to this renewed interest. So funding will not be lacking for worthwhile projects relating to modernisation and integrated management of water resource programmes across the GBM region. Private investment too will be forthcoming. Memoranda of Agreement were signed by the Arunachal Government in February 2006 with five private Independent Power Producers to develop 4,600 MW in a cascade of run-of-the-river and storage dams on the Dihang (investigated by NHPC under the Hydro Initiative) in eight years from financial closure on attractive financial terms. It is for the individual states and actors to show the will and imagination to proceed forward and harvest the rich fruit that awaits plucking. Regional cooperation remains of pivotal importance. And India's role in this endeavour will be critical.

Glossary

Bandh – an earthen dam or embankment.
Beel – ox-bow lake.
Bhoodan – Vinoba Bhave's land-gift movement.
Boro – winter crop in Bengal.
Chak – block commanded by the smallest irrigation outlet. Also Kulaba.
Chipko – forest protection movement in Garhwal.
Command area – irrigable area within an irrigation system as opposed to the area actually irrigated.
Dead storage – that part of a reservoir reserved to absorb sedimentation and not available for operational use.
Diara – exposed floodways and riverbed, often cultivated after flood recession.
Firm power – assured year-round output of a hydel plant.
Gross irrigated area – total area irrigated with multiple cropping.
Jalkar – water body.
Jalkar mahal – a waterbody estate.
Jheel, haor, tal, chaur – lake or depression.
Jhum – shifting cultivation. Tseri in Bhutan; podu in parts of India.
Kharif – monsoon crop.
Kul – irrigation channel in the hills.
Live storage – total reservoir storage less dead storage.
Load factor – Planned operating level of a hydel plant as a ratio of installed capacity.
Panchayat – a (village) council.
Panidari – a zamindari holding (fishing) rights over a waterbody.
Pumped storage – cyclical refilling of a hydel reservoir during off-peak hours by reverse turbines energized by unutilized base load generation.
Rabi – winter crop.
Recharge – refilling of aquifer by seepage or infiltration from rainfall.
Secondary power – energy generated over the firm power output in hydel systems when the reservoir is full as during the monsoon.

Usar	–	saline affected lands. Also reh.
Warabandi	–	rotational system for allocating irrigation supplies; katil in northwest India; osrabandi in UP; tatil and satta systems in Bihar; and shejapali and phad systems in Maharashtra.
Zamindar	–	a revenue-paying landlord-rentier. Intermediary between tiller and the state.

References

Abbas, B.M., Chairman. Bangladesh Water and Power Development Authority. Foreword to "Water Resources Development and Flood Control in Bangladesh". Dhaka, 1971.

Abbas, B.M. The Ganges Water Disputc, University Press Ltd., Dhaka, 1982.

Abbas, B.M. Agreement on the Ganges Regional Symposium on Water Resources Policy in Agro-Socio-Economic Development. Dhaka, August 1985.

Abbie, Leslie, Harrison, James Q and Wall, John W. Economic Return to Investment in Irrigation in India. World Bank Staff Working Paper No. 536. Washington, 1982.

Aboriginal Water Rights. International Rivers and Lakes No. 9. UN Department of Technical Cooperation for Development, New York. November 1987.

Adams, R.D. The Haicheng, China, Earthquake of 4 February, 1975: The First Successfully Predicted Major Earthquake. Bulletin of the New Zealand National Society for Earthquake Engineering, Vol. 9 No. 1, Wellington, March 1976.

Advisory Board on Energy. Towards a Perspective on Energy Demand and Supply in India in 2004-05. Government of India. New Delhi. May 1985.

Advisory Board on Energy. The Energy Scene. December 1986.

Agarwal, Anil. Human-Nature Interactions in a Third World Country. The Fifth World Conservation Lecture, World Worldlife Fund,U.K. from "The Environmentalist", Vol. 6, No. 3, 1986.

Agarwal, Anil et al. the Wrath of Nature, The Impact of Environmental Destruction on Floods and Droughts. Centre for Science and Environment, New Delhi, April 1987.

Agarwal, P.P., Kumar, Devendra, and Singh, Prasidh. Environmental Aspect of Tehri Dam Project. Proceedings of the International Seminar on Environmental Impact Assessment of Water Resources Projects. W.R.D.T.C., University of Roorkee, December 1985.

Agarwala, V.P. and Tyagi, Pramod, Rangelands of India, Extent and Management. Society for the Promotion of Wasteland Development, New Delhi, November 1988.

Agricultural Productivity in Eastern India, Committee on Agricultural Productivity in Eastern India. Reserve Bank of India, Bombay, 1984.

Agriculture Department, India. Manual on Irrigation Water Management, New Delhi, 1975.

Agriculture Department, India. Annual Report, '1987-88, New Delhi, 1988.

Agriculture Ministry Bangladesh. Agriculture in Bangladesh, Dhaka, 1981.

Ahmad, Razia S. Financing the Rural Poor- Obstacles and Realities. University Press Ltd., Dhaka, 1983.

Ahmad, S.U., Prakash, Suraj and Sharma C.P. Investigations of Multi-purpose and Hydroelectric Projects – Necessity and Needs. Seminar on 25 years of Multi-purpose and Hydro-electric Development of the Yamuna and Ganga Valleys. U.P. Irrigation Department, Lucknow. May 1986.

Ailleret, Jean Claude. Navigation on International Inland Waterways. The Framework of Laws and Regulations. Planning and Development of Inland Waterways. ESCAP Inland Waterways Development Series No. 1. Bangkok 1979.

Alagh, Y.K. Planning and Management of Water Resources. Inaugural Address at First National War Convention, New Delhi. November 1987.

Ali, Salim. The Himalaya in Indian Omithology. From Himalaya, Aspects of Change. Ed J.S. Lall. Oxford University Press, New Delhi, 1981.

Amazon Pact. Inter-American Affairs – Foreign Broadcasting Information Services. San Paulo, Brazil. July 6, 1978.

Anderson J.G., Bodin, P., Brunne, J.N., Prince, J., Singh, S.K., Quass R, and Onate, M. Strong Ground Motion from the Michoscan, Mexico, Earthquake. Science Vol. 233, September 5, 1986.

Amon. Background Paper, Aravalli 2001 A.D. Conference organized by Ubeshwar Vikas Mandal, Udaipur, January 1987.

Anwar, Jamal. Geology of Coastal Area of Bangladesh and Recommendations for Resource Development and Management. National Workshop on Bangladesh Coastal Area Resource Development and Management, Dhaka, October 1988.

Applegate, G.B. and Glimour, D.A. Operational Experiences in Forest Management in the Hills of Nepal. ICIMOD Occasional Paper No. 6, Kathmandu. January 1987.

Appu, P.S. Tenancy Reform in India. Planning Commission, New Delhi, June 1975.

Archaeological Survey of India. Archaeological Remains, Monuments and Museums. New Delhi. 1964.

Arlosoroff, Saul. Water Resources Development and Management in Israel. Kidma, Israel's Journal of Development No. 10, Vol 3 No. 2. Tel Aviv 1977.

Arokiaswamy, N.S.S. Electric Lift Irrigation – Its Viability and Success. Aquaworld, New Delhi. November 1986.

ARTEP-ILO. Labour Absorption in Indian Agriculture – Some Explanatory Investigations by Bardhan, P.K., Vaidhyanathan, Alagh, A., Y.K. Bhalla G.S. and Bhaduri A. Bangkok. November 1978.

ARTEP-ILO. Employment Expansion in Indian Agriculture. Proceedings of a National Seminar held in Bangalore. Bangkok. February 1979.

Arya, Anand S., Gupta, Satyendra P., Lavania, B.V. and Kumar, Ashwini. Report on Dharamsala, Himachal Pradesh Earthquake, April 26, 1986. Department of Earthquake Engineering, University of Roorkee, July 1986.

Asaduzzaman, M. Coastal Area Development, Environmental Changes and Their Social-Economic Implications for Bangladesh. A Study carried out for ESCAP, Bangkok, February 1987.

Associated Press. Making a Desert Bloom with Man-Made River. Indian Express. New Delhi. September 15, 1988.

Bahadur, Jagdish. Some Environmental Problems for Development of Himalayan Water Resources. Proceedings of the International Seminar on Environment Impact Assessment of Water Resource Projects. Roorkee University, December 1985.

Bali, J.S., et al. Agricultural Finance Corporation, India. Evaluation Study of Social Conservation in the River Valley Projects of Matatila, Nizamsagar and Ukai. Bombay. 1988.

Bangladesh Agricultural Development Corporation (BADC). Agriculture in Bangladesh, Dhaka. 1981.

Bangladesh Water Development Board (BWDB). Water Resources Development in Bangladesh. Dhaka, 1979.

Bansal, R.C., and Grewal, S.C. Annual Progress Report. Studies on Sedimentation of Sukhna Lake. Central Soil and Water Conservation Research and Training Institute, Chandigarh. 1986.

Barcelona Convention and Statute. April 20, 1921. Text from Legislation Branch, FAO, Rome.

Barns, Margarita. The Indian Press. George Allen and Unwin. 1940.

Barooah, Nirode K. David Scott in North-East India, 1802-31. Munshiram Manohar Lal, New Delhi. March 1970.

Bhaumik, Subir. Tripura: Decommissioning of Gumti Hydel Crucial for Conflict Resolution. Sent to author and published in the Statesman and other journals, 2002.

Bhattacharya, S. Regional Economy, Chapter III – Regional Economy 2. Eastern India. Cambridge Economic History of India, c. 1757 – c. 1970 Volume II. Orient Longman Hyderabad 1982.

Bhumbla, D.R., and Khare, Arvind. Estimate of Wastelands in India. Society for the Promotion of Wastelands Development, New Delhi. 1986.

Bhutan, Royal Government, "Bhutan 2017: A Vision for Peace, Prosperity and Happiness". Thimphu. November 1998.

Bihar Planning Department. Seventh Five Year Plan, 1985-90 (Draft), Patna.

Bilgrami, K.S. and Data Munshi, J.S. Ecology of River Ganges – Impact of Human Activities and Conservation of Aquatic Biota (Patna to Farakka). Final Technical Report (May 1982 – April 1985) under MAB Research Project. Department of Botany, Bhagalpur University, Bhagalpur, April 1985.

Biotechnology Department, Government of India. Annual Report 1987-88. New Delhi. 1988.

Bos, Robert. Executive Summary of Workshop on Irrigation and Vector-Borne Disease Transmission. Joint WHO/FAO/UNEP Panel of Experts on Environmental Management for Vector Control. International Irrigation Management Institute, Digana Village, via Kandy, Sri Lanka. December 1986.

Botanical Surveyof India. Studies on the Vegetation of Tehri Dam and Some Rare Plants in the Garhwal Himalaya, Howrah, July 1982.

Bottrall, Anthony F. Comparative Study of the Management and Organisation of Irrigation Projects. World Bank Staff Working Paper No. 458. Washington, May 1981.

Boyce, James K. Impase in Bengal: Agricultural Growth in Bangladesh and West Bengal, 1949-1980. Oxford University Press, 1987.

Brahmaputra Board. Master Planof the Brahmaputra Basin, Part I Main Stem, part II Barak Basin. Brookes, Warren. T. The Global Warming Panic. Forbes, December 25, 1989.

Brichieri-Colombi, J.S.A., "Could Bangladesh Benefit from the River-Linking Project? Regional Cooperation on Transboundary Rivers: Impact on the Indian River-Linking Project". Published by BAPA, BEN, BEA et al. Editors: M. Feroze Ahmed, Qazi Kholiquzzaman Ahmad, Md Khalequzzaman. Dhaka, December 2004.

Brown, Lester R. and Postel, Sandra. Thresholds of Changes. State of the World, 1987. A Worldwatch Institute Report. Prentice Hall (P) Ltd., New Delhi, 1987.

Canadian Government. Canada-U.S. Cooperation in the Field of Trans-Boundary Waters. Economic Commission for Europe. Committee on Water Problems' Seminar on Cooperation in the Field of Transboundary Waters. Dusseldorf. October 15, 1984.

Cano, Guillenno J. The "Del Plata" Basin, Summary Chronicle of its Development Process and Related Conflicts. Proceedings of a Workshop on the Management of International River Basin Conflicts. Edited by Ivan Vlachos. Laxenburg. September 1986.

Caponera, Dante A. The Roleof customary International Water Law. Regional Sympoisum on Water Resources Policy in Agro-Socio-Economic Development, Dhaka. August 1985.

Carson, Brian. Erosion and Sedimentation Processes in the Nepalese Himalaya. ICIMOD Occasional Paper No. 1. Kathmandu, August 1985.

Central Board for the Prevention and Control of Water Pollution (CPCB). Yamuna Sub-Basin (Part I of The Ganga Basin Sub-Basin Study of Water Pollution), April 1977 – December, 1978. New Delhi, 1980-81.

Central Board for the Prevention and Control of Water Pollution (CPCB). Comprehensive Pollution Survey and Studies of Ganga River Basin in West Bengal. Assessment and Development Studyof River Basin Series. 1982-83.

Central Board for the Prevention and Control of Water Pollution (CPCB). Ganga Basin, Part II, New Delhi, 1984.

Central Bureau of Statistics, Population Census Nepal, 1981. Kathmandu, 1984.

Central Electricity Authority (CEA), India. National Power Plan, A Long Term Development Profile – Generation Expansion Programme, 1985-200, New Delhi, June 1987.

Central Groundwater Board, India (CGWB). Groundwater Development in India. Ministry of Water Resources, New Delhi, 1986.

Central Institute of Fisheries Education. Fish Based Mixed Farming in Waterlogged Areas. Bombay, 1986.

Central Water Commission (India), (CWC). Agreements on Development of Inter-State and International Rivers, New Delhi,1 979.

Central Water Commission (India), (CWC). (Niten Desai) Committee to Review Existing Criteria for Working Out Benefit-Cost ratios for Irrigation Projects, New Delhi. February 1983.

Central Water Commission (India), (CWC). Improvement of River and Flood Forecasting Systems in India – Pilot Project. Yamuna Basin up to Delhi. Ministry of Water Resources, New Delhi, 1986.

Central Water Commission (India), (CWC). Water Resources of India, New Delhi, April 1988.

Centre for Science and Environment. Chapter on Health in The State of India's Environment, 1984-85 – The Second Citizen's Report, New Delhi, 1985.

Chambers, Robert. Farmers Above the Outlet, Irrigators and Canal Management in South Asia. Journal of Indian Water Resources Society, Vol. 6 No. 3 and 4, July and October 1986.

Chandra, Umesh and Kumar, Rajesh. Problem in Forest Clearance and Right of Way for Transmission Lines, "Urja", New Delhi. Vol. XXII No. 4, October 1987.

Chaphekar, S.B., and Mhatre G.N. Human Impact on Ganga River Ecosystem. Concept Publishing Company, New Delhi. 1986.

Chari, V.V. Text of Statement of Secretaries' level talks at Islamabad. Issued by the Press Information Bureau, Government of India, February 24, 1970.

Chaudhry, Praveen K. Agrarian Unrest in Bihar – A case study of Purnea District, 1960-84. Economic and Political Weekly, Bombay, January 2-9, 1988.

Chaudhry, M., and Siddiqui, M.H. Towards a National Water Plan in Bangladesh. Regional Symposium on Water Resources Policy in Agro-Socio-Economic Development, Dhaka, August, 1985.

Chokkalingam, G. Land Revenue: Resource or Burden/ Financial Express, New Delhi, April 20, 1988.

Chopra, Kanchan, Kadekodi, Gopal and Murty M.N. Economic Evaluation of People's Participation in the Management of Forest Resources. Institute for Economic Growth, Delhi, 1988.

Choudhury, A.K.M. Kamaluddin. Land Use in Bangladesh. Regional Symposium on Water Resources Policy in Agro-Socio-Economic Development, Dhaka, August 1985.

Chowdhry, K.R., Subba Rao, D.V., Krishnamurthy G. and Narendranath G. Srisailam. The shadow Grows Longer. Lokayan's Second Report, Lokayan Bulletin, Vol 3, Nos. 4/5, New Delhi. October 1985.

Chowdhury, Kamla. Afforestation Only with Popular Help. Times of India, New Dehi. June 7 & 8, 1988.

Chowdhury, Mahiuddin. Inland Water Transport of Bangladesh. An Analysis and Evaluation. Journal of the National oceanographic and Maritime Institute (NAOMI) Vol 3, No. 1. Dhaka, June 9186.

Chugh, K.L. Bhadrachalam Paperboards Ltd. Greening Through Plantations. Paper presented at Assocham's Workshop on the Greening and Cleaning of India – An Industry Initiative. New Delhi, August 1988.

Columbia River Basin Treaty between the U.S.A. and Canada with Annexes. Treaties and Other International Acts Series 5638. Department of State, Washington.

Committee on Land Reforms, Report of Chairman, Prof. Raj Krishna. Department of Agriculture, New Delhi, 1978.

Committee on Power Report, Ministry of Energy, new Delhi, September 1980.

Comptroller and Auditor General of India, Report No. 2of 1990. Union Government, Ministry of Environment and Forests: Ganga Action Plan (for the year ended March 31, 1989). New Delhi, May 1990.

Consulting Engineering Services (India) Pvt. Ltd., (CES). All-India Transport System Study (Inland Waterways) for the Planning Commission. Vol I Draft Main Report, Volume II – Annexures and Tables. New Delhi, March 1987.

Crow, Ben. The Politics and Technology of Sharing the Ganga. Ph. D. thesis for the University of Edinburgh. 1980.

Crow, Ben and Lindquist, Alan. Development of the Rivers Ganges and Brahmaputra: The Difficulty of Negotiating a New Line. Mimeographed. October 31, 1989.

Crow, Ben and Lindquist, Alan. Development of the River Ganges and Brahmaputra: The Difficulty of Negotiating a New Line. Development Policy and Practice Research Group. The Open University, Faculty of Technology, Milton Keyes, U.K., February 1990.

Dalai Lama. My Land and My People – Memoirs of His Holiness. Asia Publishing House. Bombay, 1962.

Damodar Valley Corporation (DVC). Harnessing a Great River Valley. DVC, Calcutta, December 1986.

Dani, Anis A., and Campbell, J. Gabriel. Sustaining Upland Resources – People's Participation in Watershed Management. ICIMOD Occasional Paper No.3. Kathmandu, July 1986.

Dantwala, M.L. Prices and Cropping Pattern. Economic and Political Weekly, Bombay. VOl. XXI, No. 16, April 19, 1986.

Das, D.C. Soil Moisture Storage and Land Use Variations for Flood Risk Cushioning. Paper presented at the International Conference on Flood Disasters, New Delhi. December 1981.

Das, D.C., et al. Status of Hydrologic and Sediment Monitoring. Data Compilation and Analysis for Selected Watersheds of River Valley and Flood Prone River Catchments. Department of Agriculture, Soil and Water Conservation Division, New Delhi. 1985.

Das, P., Kapoor D. and Mahanta P.C. Genetic Improvement of Fish Stock and Resource Conservation, NBFGR Bulletin No. 1 (Allahabad) September 1986.

Dayal, Maheshwar. Strategies for Development of Appropriate Rural Technologies and Their Extension. Appropriate Rural Technologies Seminar. Lucknow, April 16, 1984.

Dayal Maheshwar. Development and Energy. 17th Bhagvantham Birthday Commemoration Lecture. Osmania University, Hyderabad, October 14, 1986.

Department of Non-Conventional Energy, India (DNCE). Annual Report, 1987-88, New Delhi.

Department of Non-Conventional Energy, India (DNCE). Energy – 2001. Perspective Plan for Non-Conventional Energy Sources, New Delhi, February 1987.

Department of Science & Technology, India (DST). Earth and Atmosphere Division. Deep Sea Fans of the Ganga Basin. National Consultation, New Delhi. October 1984.

Department of Science & Technology, India (DST). All-India Coordinated Project on the Study of Seismicity and Seismotectonics in the Himalayan Region. Workshop held on December 3-5, 1984 at Wadia Institute of Himalayan Geology, Dehra Dun. New Delhi, 1984.Department of Science & Technology, India (DST). Committee of Experts Report: Five to Ten Year Profile of Seismological Studies in India, New Delhi, June 1987.

Dhagamwar, Vasudha. Rehabilitation, Policy Required and Institutional Changes. Multiple Action Research Group, New Delhi. Paper presented at Workshop on Development, Displacement and Rehabilitation. Indian Social Institute, New Delhi. April 8, 1988.

Dhanju, M.S. Space Applications Centre. Studies of Himalayan Snow Cover Area from Satellites. Ahmedabad. August 1983.

Dhawan, B.D. Output Impact According to Main Irrigation Sources – Empirical Evidence from Four Selected States. Institute of Economic Growth, Delhi. December 1985.

Dhawan, B.D. Management of Groundwater Resources – Direct versus Indirect Regulatory Mechanisms. Economic and Political Weekly, Bombay. September 5-12, 1987.

Dixit, Kanak Mani. Highlanders on the Move – A Quest for Survival. "Himal", Lalitpur, Nepal. Vol. I, No. 1, July 1988.

Durant, Will. The Story of Civilisation. Volume I. Our Oriental Heritage. Columbia University Press. New York, 1958.

Dutt, Romesh. The Economic History of India, London. 1901. Volume I Under Early British Rule in India 1757-1837. Volume II. In the Victorian Age, 1837-1900. Publications Division, Ministry of Information and Broadcasting, New Delhi. 1960.

Dwivedi, S.N. Culture of Marine Prawns and Fishers at Sultanpur, Haryana. Central Institute of Fisheries Education, ICAR, Bombay, 1984.

Eckholm, Eric. Losing Ground. Worldwatch Institute/UNEP, Washington, 1976.

Egyptian Ministry of Irrigation. Planing the Development and Utilisation of International Rivers – The Nile. Experiences in the Development and Management of International River and Lake Basins. Proceedings of the U.N. Inter-regional Meeting of International River Organisations. Dakar, May 1981. United Nations Natural Resources/Water Series No. 10, New York, 1983.

Elding, Bo. Guinea Worm Eradication – An Integrated Approach. Proceedings of ICMR/WHO Electric Power Development Company of Japan. Draft Terms of Reference of Pre-Feasibility Study for Himalaya Hydro-Power Development Project, Tokyo. 1988.

Electricity Department, Nepal. Hydro-Power Potential of Nepal, Kathmandu, 1971.

English, Richard. Himalayan State Formation and the Impact of British Rule in the 19th century. Mountain Resources & Development. Vol. 5 No. 1, 1985.

Environment Folio, Vol. II, No. 3. 1986.

Environment & Forests Ministry, India. Guidelines for Environmental Impact Assessment of River Valley Projects, New Delhi. January 1985.

Environment & Forests Ministry, India. Action Plan for the Prevention of Pollution of the Ganga Delhi, July 1985.

Environment & Forests Ministry, India. Guidelines for Diversion of Forest Lands for Non-Forest Purpose under the Forest Conservation Act, 1980, July 1986.

Environment & Forests Ministry, India. Environmental Guidelines for Thermal Power Plants. 1987.

Environment & Forests Ministry, India. National Forest Policy, December 1988.

Environment & Forests Ministry, India. Biosphere Reserves in India, June 1989.

Environment and Forests Ministry, Government of India. National Environment Policy. Delhi. October 2004.F

Environmental Service Group, World Widllife Fund-India. Ghotge, Sanjeev, Namra, Shyma Bahadur., Das, Utpala. Sponsored by NORAD, Royal Norwegian Embassy, New Delhi. October 1986.

ESCAP, Committee on Natural Resources. Environmental Issues of Water Resources Development in the ESCAP Region. 13th Session. Note for Item 5,Bangkok, October 1986.

Expert Committee on Rise in Costs of Irrigation and Multipurpose Projects, 1973.

Famine Commission Report, Part II. Government of India. 1880.

Films and Publications Department, Bangladesh. Country-wide Canal Digging Programme, Revolution First Phase, Dhaka, September 1980.

Finance Commission, Government of India. Sixth (1973). Seventh (1978) and Eighth (1984) Reports. New Delhi.

Finance Ministry, Government of Nepal. White Paper on Economic Situation in Nepal. Kathmandu, May 25, 1990.

Fodder and Grasses Committee Report. National Wastelands Development Board, New Delhi 1987.

Forest Survey of India. The State of forest Report, 1987, Dehra Dun, July 1988.

Forest Survey of India, State of Forest Report, 1989. Dehra Dun, 1990.

Forests and Soil Conservation Ministry, Nepal. Master Plan for the Forestry Sector, Nepal, Kathmandu, May 1988.

Framji, K.K. A Project to Save Calcutta Port. Bhagirath Vol. IX. New Delhi, July 1962.

Framji, K.K. The Farakka Barrage – The Fulfilment of a Dream. Farakka Barrage Project Sourvenir, May 1975.

Friedkin, J.F. International Water Treaties, United States and Mexico. Regional Sympoisum on Water Resources Policy in Agro-Socio-Economic Development, Dhaka. August4, 1985.

Fuller, Kathryn S. Debt-for-Nature Swaps – A New Conservation Too. Economic Impact, No. 65, U.S. Information Agency, Washington. October-December 1988.

Gandak Project Agreement between India and Nepal. December 4, 1959.

Gandhi Peace Foundation. Recommendations of the National Workshop on the Integrated Development of the Ganga-Brahmaputra-Barak Basin. New Delhi, December 15-17, 1978.

Ganga Action Plan. An Action Plan for Prevention of Polution of River Ganga at Varanasi and Conservation of the River Front. Project Manager GAP, Varanasi. 1988.

Ganga Action Plan. Development Works at Kanpur. Project Manager GAP, Kanpur, 1988.

Ganga Flood Control Commission. Proceedings of the Seminar on Morphology of the Ganga River. New Delhi, November 1996.

Gaur, Vinod K. Earthquake Risk to Tehri Dam. National Geophysical Research Institute, Hyderabad, October 1984.

Gee, E.P. Journal of the Bombay Natural History Society. Vol. 50, No. 3, Bombay, 1951.

George, M.J. Shrimp Resources in the Seas Around the Asian Countries with special reference to India. Fisheries Research Cell, Programme for Community Organisation. Trivandrum July 1988.

Ghosh, A.K. A Breath of Life Beneath the Waves. "The Telegraph" special anniversary supplement on the Ganga. Calcutta. July 7, 1986.

Gleick, Peter H. Climate Changes and International Politics: Problems Facing Developing Countries. From "Ambio" – A Journal of the Human Environment, XVIII, 6, 1989 and reproduced in Tisglow, Tata Energy Research Institute, New Delhi, April 1990.

Goldsmith, E and Hilyard, N. The Social and Environmental Effects of Large Dams. Published by the Wadebridge Ecological Centre, Camelford, Cornwall, U.K. 1984.

Golubev, Genady N. and Biswas Asit K. Inter-regional Water Transfers, Projects and Problems. Reprinted from Water Supply and Managemnt. Vol. 2, No. 2, International Institute for Applied Systems Analysis, Laxenburg, Austria, RR-79-1, June 1979.

Goswami, Delep. A Handbook on Pollution Control by Industries and Government Bodies with Supreme Court Decisions. Emcom Business Review, New Delhi. 1988.

Griffith, Percival J. A History of the Joint Steamer Companies.

Gubin, Igor. Feeling the Seismic Pulse of the Planet. An Interview in "Science", No. 17, Moscow. May 4, 1987.

Guha, Amalendu. Cambridge Economic Hitoryof India, Volume I, c. 1200 – c. 1756. Appendix. The Medieval Economy of Assam. Orient Longman, Hyderabad, 1982.

Guha, S.K. and Sen Sharma S.B. Farakka. A Gordian Knot (1978). In Farakka – A Gordian Knot, problems on Sharing Ganga Waters. Edited by Sunil Sen Sharma, Ishika, Calcutta. April 1986.

Gulati, N.D. Development of Inter-State Rivers, Law and Practice in India. Allied Publishers, New Delhi, 1972.

Guller, Peter. Regional Development Policy in Swiss Mountain Areas. Report for the Directorate of Development Cooperation and Humanitarian Aid in Berne, Zurich. 1986.

Gupta, Harsh K. Seismicity in the Vicinity of Dams and Problem of Reservoir-Induced Earthquakes. Environment Impacts of Water Resource Development in Himalaya, Geo-Physical Aspects Journal of the Geological Society of India, 1984.

Gupta, Y.P. Pesticides in Agriculture. Financial express, New Delhi, February 2, 1989.

Gurung, Harka. The Himalaya-Perspective of Change. Occasional Paper No. 5. New Era, Kathmandu. May 1982.

Gyawali, Dipak. Water in Nepal. East-West Environment and Policy Institute. Occasional Paper No. 8. East-West Centre, Hawaii 1989.

Habermehl, M.A. The Great Artesian Basin, Australia. BMR Journal of Australian Geology and Geophysics, May, 1980.

Habib, Irfan. An Atlas of the Mughal Empire. Oxford University Press, 1982.

Habib, Irfan. Cambridge Economic History of India, Volume I, c. 1200 – c. 1756. Chapter II Agrarian Economy. Orient Longman, Hyderabad, 1982.

Hagen, Toni. Nepal – The Kingdom of the Himalayas. Kummerly & Frey, Berne. 1961.

Hakluyt, Richard. Principal Navigations. London, 1599. Cited in R.C. Prasad's "Early Travellers in India", Motilal Banarsidass, Delhi, 1965.

Hall, Warren A. Principles of Conjunctive Use in Water Resources Planning and Management. Colorado State University. Paper presented at Seminar on Conjunctive Use or Surface and Ground Water Resources organized by CGWB and UNDP, New Delhi. February 1986.

Hamilton, Lawrence S. Towards Clarifying the Appropriate Mandate in Forestry for Watershed Rehabilitation and Management. Guide 14. Rome, 1986.

Hamilton, Lawrence S. What are the Impacts of Himalayan Deforestation on the Ganges-Brahmaputra Lowlands and Delta? Assumptions and Facts. Mountain Research and Development Vol. 7, No. 3, 1987.

Han, Boacheng. Three Gorges Project, Is It Feasible; and Benefits of the Three Gorges Project. Beijing Review Nos. 29 and 30, July 21 & 28, 1986.

Hanks, Thomas C. The National Earthquake Hazards Reduction Programme – Scientific Status, U.S. Geological Survey Bulletin 1659.

Hanstad, Tim. Jennifer Brown, Roy Prosterman. Larger Homestead Plots as Land Reform"? Economic and Political Weekly, Bombay, July 20 2002.

Harrer, Heinrich. Seven Years in Tibet. Rupert Hart Davis. London, 1953.

Haskoning (Royal Dutch Consulting Engineers and Architects) and CES, New Delhi. Navigation on the Narmada River from Hoshangabad to the Sea. Feasibility Study Phase I – Methods to Pass Four Major Dams. Ministry of Shipping and Transport, New Delhi, April 1985.

Haton, R.D. The Law of International Water Resource Systems. National Symposium on Integrated River Basin Development, Dhaka, December 1981.

Himachal Government. Agricultural Research and Development in Himachal Pradesh. Simla September 1986.

Home Ministry, Government of India. Research and Policy Division. Nature of Current Agrarian Tensions, New Delhi, August 1969.

Hossain, Liaquat. Water Resources Planning for Regional Development of Bangladesh. Bangladesh University of Engineering and Technology, Dhaka, July 1974.

Hossain, Mosharaff, Aminul Islam, A.T.M. and Saha, Sant Kumar. Floods in Bangladesh-Recurrent Disaster and People's Survival. Universities Research Centre, Dhaka, August 1987.

His, Chango-hao, and Kao, Yuan-mei. Tibet Leaps Forward. Foreign Languages Press, Peking. 1977.

Hukku, B.M., Srivastava, K.N. and Gupta, S.K. Post-Earthquake Surveys. Proceedings of National Meet on Earthquake Mechanism and Mitigation. Department of Science and Technology, New Delhi, August 1986.

Hume, A.O. Agriculture Reform in India. 1879.

Indo-Bangladesh Joint Rivers Commission Statue. JRC Annual Report, 1972-73. New Delhi and Dhaka, 1973.

Indo-Bangladesh Joint Rivers Commission. Updated Proposals and Comments of Bangladesh and India on Augmentation of the Dry Season Flows of the Ganges, Dhaka, May 1985.

Indus Waters Treaty. Government of India, New Delhi, 1960.

Indian Agricultural Research Institute (IARI), Water Technology Centre. Water Requirements an Irrigation Management of Crops in India. New Delhi,1977.

Indian Agricultural Research Institute (IARI) Water Technology Centre. Resources Analysis and Plan for Efficient Water Management – A case study of the Mahi right bank canal command area, Gujarat, new Delhi 1983.

Indian Agricultural Research Institute (IARI). Water Technology Centre. Resource Analysis for Integrated Development – Sultanpur District, U.P., New Delhi 1986.

Indian Council for Agricultural Research (ICAR) Complex for the NE Hill Region. Soil Erosion Hazards in North Eastern Hill Region. Shillong, 1981.

Indian Council for Agricultural Research (ICAR) Complex for the NE Hill Region. Shifting Cultivation in North East India. Shillong, 1983.

Indian Express (UNI). "Country heading for good monsoon", and The Times of India, "Success story of monsoon forecasting", by Surinder Sur, New Delhi, May 25 and June 2,1 990.

India Council for Medical Research (ICMR) Bulletin. Bio-Environmental Control of Industrial Malaria, Vol. 17, No. 7. New Delhi, July 1987.

Industrial Toxicology Research Centre. Ganga Action Plan, Progress Report, February 1987 – June 1987. Lucknow, 1988.

Information Director, Nepal, Kathmandu, November 1978.

Inland Water Transport (IWT) Working Group Report for the 7th Five Year Plan, India. 1985-90. Annexure IV. 1 – Narmada Water Transport Project, Pre-feasibility Study. Planning Commission, New Delhi, 1985. Annexure IV. 2 – Study of the Reactivation of DVC Canal for Navigation. New Delhi.

International Irrigation Management Institute (IIMI). Annual Report 1986. Digana Village, via Kandy, Sri Lanka.

International Law Commission (ILC) Reports. International Rivers and Lakes. Department of Technical Cooperation for Development. Newsletter. No. 8. United Nations, New York. May 1987.

International Union for the Conservation of Nature, U.N. Environment Programme and World Wildlife Fund. World Conservation Strategy. Geneva, 1980.

Irrigation Commission Report. Ministry of Irrigation and Power. New Delhi, 1972.

Irrigation Ministry (India). National Perspective for Water Resources Development. New Delhi, August 1980.

Irrigation and Water Resource Ministers Conference (India). Recommendations. New Delhi. July 21, 1986.

Ishikawa, Shigeru. Labour Absorption in Asian Agriculture. Asian Regional Programme for Employment Promotion, ILO, Bangkok, June 1978.

Itaipu Binacional, Itaipu, Preservation of the Environment, Brazil. 1980.

Ives, Jack D. Glacial Lake Outburst Floods and Risk Engineering in the Himalaya. ICIMOD Occasional Paper No. 5, Kathmandu, November 1986.

Iyer, Ramaswamy. For a National Water Policy. A Compendium of Issues. Unpublished. New Delhi 1987.

Jain, S.N. Jacob, Alice and Jain, Subhash C. Inter-State Water Disputes in India. Suggestions for Reform in Law. Indian Law Institute, New Delhi. N.M. Tripathi, Bombay, 1971.

Jain, S.N. Legal Aspects of Groundwater Management. Journal of the Indian Law Institute, New Delhi. Vol 23, 2, 1981.

Jannuzi, F. Tomasson and Peach, James T. The Agrarian Structure of Bangladesh. Sangam Books, New Delhi, 1982.

Jhingran, A.G. The Himalaya, Aspects of Change, Ed J.S. Lall, India International Centre, New Delhi. Oxford University Press, 1981.

Jhingran, A.G. The Fish Genetic Resources of India, NBFGR, Allahabad, 1984.

Jhingran, A.G. and Ghosh K.K. The Fisheries of the Ganga River System in the Context of Indian Aquaculture. "Aquaculture", Elsevier Scientific Publishing Company, Amsterdam. No. 14, 1978.

Jodha, N.S. Common Property Resources and Rural Poor in Dry Regions of India. Economic and Political Weekly, Bombay, July 5, 1986.

Jodha, N.S. Potential Strategies for Adapting to Greenhouse Warming. Perspectives from the Developing World, ICIMOD, Kathmandu, 1988.

Jones, Paul H. Water Resources Development in the Ganges Basin. P.H. Jones Hydrogeology, Inc. Baton Route, Louisiana, USA, October 1983.

Jones, Paul H. Geology and Ground Water Resources of the South Asia Region. From World Bank Proceedings of the Groundwater Seminar and Technical Session. Washington, May 1986.

Jones, Paul H and Hofmann, Walter. Water Resources Investigation Programme for Upper Gangetic Plain, India. Water Resource Division, U.S. Geological Survey, Washington, May 1967.

Jones, P.H. Hydrogeology Inc, Baton Rouge, Louisiana, USA. Geology and Groundwater Resources of Bangladesh. Prepared for the World Bank, November 1985.

Jones, P.H. Deep Aquifer Exploration Project – Upper Gangetic Plain, India. Prepared for the World Bank, January 1986.

Jones, P.H. Deep Aquifer Exploration Project in the Ganges and Bengal Basins in India. Prepared for the World Bank, June 1987.

Joshi, P.C. Problems of Land Reforms in the Second Stage. Institute for Economic Growth, Delhi, August 1978.

Joshi, S.C. Forestry Handbook of Bhutan. International Book Distributors, Dehra Dun. 1986.

Kautilya. Arthasastra. Translated by R. Shamasastry, 5th edition. Mysore. 1956.

Kaye, Lincoln, Resources and Rights, Rivalries Hamper Into-Bangladesh Water Sharing. Far Eastern Economic Review, Hong Kong, February 2, 1989.

Keshavamurth. G.S. Role of South India Viscose in Greening India. Assocham Worksho, New Delhi, August 1988.

Kesinger, Tom G. Regional Economy (1757-1857) I-North India. Camrbdige Economic History of India. Volume II c. 1757 – c. 1970. Orient Longman, Hyderabad 1984.

Khan, Abbas Ali. Economic Considerations and Alternatives in Water Policy Formulation in Bangladesh. Regional Symposium on Water Resources Policy in Agro-Socio-Economic Development, Dhaka, August 1985.

Khan,Amjad Hossain and Khan, Akbar Ali. Surface Water Strategy, Policies and Laws in Bangladesh. Regional Symposium on Water Resources Policy in Agro-Socio-Economic Development. Dhaka, August 1985.

Khan, Hamidur Rahman. Water Resource Development in Bangladesh. Problems and Prospects. Regional Symposium on Water Resources Policy in Agro-Socio-Economic Development, Dhaka, August 1985.

Khan, Khafi. "Muntakhabu-I Lubub" in Elliot and Dowson's History of India as told by its Own Historians. Sushil Gupta (India) Ltd., Calcutta 1877.

Khan, Tauhidul Anwar. Water Resources Situation in Bangladesh. Regional Symposium on Water Resources Policy in Agro-Socio-Economic Development, Dhaka, August 1985.

Khattri, K.N. Prediction and Monitoring of Earthquakes. Proceedings of National Meet on Earthquake Mechanism and Mitigation, DST, New Delhi, August 1986.

Khattri, K.N. Chander R, Gaur V.K. and Sarkar I. New Seismological Constraints on the Tectonics of the Garhwal Himalaya. Paper prepared for presentation at the IUGG General Assembly, Vancouver, August 1987.

Khoshoo T.N. Environmental Priorities in India and Sustainable Development. Presidential Address at 73rd Session of the Indian Science Congress. Indian Science Congress Association, Delhi. January 1986.

Khoshoo T.N. and Ahmad K.J. Air Pollution and Plants. Published by the Indian Science Congress Association, Calcutta. 1981.

Khurshida Begum. Tension Over the Farakka Barrage. A Techno-Political Tangle in South Asia. K.P. Bagchi and Co., Calcutta, 1988.

King Mahendra Trust for Nature Conservation 34d Annual Report, 1986-87, Kathmandu, 1988.

Kingdom-Ward, F. Notes on the Assam Earthquake. 'Nature', London, Vo. 167. Jan 27, 1951.

Kosi Project Agreement between the Government of India and the Government of Nepal. April 25, 1954.

Kosi Agreement. Revised. December 19, 1966.

Krishna, Jai. Seismic Environment for Brahmaputra Valley projects. Appendix VI-B, Master Plan of Brahmaputra Basin, Part I. Brahmaputra Board, Ministry of Water Resources, New Delhi. 1986.

Krishna, Raj. River Basins and International Law. Working Paper No. 1. Prepared for the World Bank, Washington, 1979.

Krishna, Sumi. Developing India's Wastelands. Centre for Science and Environment, New Delhi. 1986.

Kumar, Devendra. Environmental Aspect of Tehri Dam Project. Their Dam Circle IV, Rishikesh. 1988.

Kumar, L.V. Environment and Water Resources, Arid Zones, WAPCOS, New Delhi, 1988.

Lal B.B. A 2000-Year Old Feat of Hydraulic Engineering in India (with K.N. Dikshit). "Archaeology", New York. January/February 1985.

Lal, J.B. India's Forests. Myth and Reality, Natraj, Dehra Dun. 1988.

Land Acquisition and Rehabilitation Directorate, Sinha B.K. and Asthana, Shivraj. Rehabilitation Plan for Displaced and Affected Families, Koel Karo Hydro-Electric Project. Government of Bihar, Ranchi, October 1986.

Land Resources Mapping Project. Draft Land Utilisation Report, Kathmandu 1985.

Li, Rongxia, Large Water Diversion Project Under Way. Beijing Review, June 29 – July 3, 1988.

McCaffrey, Stephen C. Special Rapporteur. Third Report on the Law of the Non-Navigational Uses of International Watercourses. International Law Commission, 39th Session. U.N. General Assembly, New York, A/c N. 4/406, March 30, 1987.

MacNeill, Jim. World Commission on Environment and Development. Perspectives of Environmental Mangement, Edited by T.N. Khoshoo, Oxford and IBH Publishing Co, New Delhi. 1987.

Madhya Pradesh Government. Revised Action Plan of Compensatory Afforestation for Narmada Sagar and Sardar Sarovar, Bhopal. December 1986.

Madhya Pradesh Rehabilitation of Displaced Persons Act. Government of Madhya Pradesh, Bhopal, 1985.

Madras Group. Indian Agriculture at the Turn of the Century. PPST Bulletin, Vol. 2 No. 2, Madras. November 1982.

Mahanta, P.C. and Lahon B. Beel Fisheries in Assam – A Source for Conservation and Stock Improvement of Carps. Proceedings of Symposium on Conservation and Management of Fish Genetic Resources of India. NBFGR, Allahbad, April 1986.

Mahat, T.B.G., Griffin D.M. and Shephard, K.R. Human Impact on Some Forests of the Middle Hills of Nepal, Parts 1 to 5: Mountain Research and Development. Vol. 6, Nos. 3 and 4, 1986; Vol. 7 Nos. 1 and 2, 1987; and Vol. 8, No. 1, 1988.

Malaria Research Centre, ICMR. Integrated Vector Control of Malaria – Science and Technology project on Integrated Vector Control of Malaria, Filaria and Other Vector Borne Diseases. Half-Yearly Progress Report, January-June, 1988, New Delhi.

Malhotra, S.P. The Warabandi System and Its Infrastructure. Central Board of Irrigation and Power Publication No. 157. New Delhi, April 1982.

Mani, Anna. Climate of the Himalaya. From Himalaya, Aspects of Change. Ed. J.S. Lall, Oxford University Press, New Delhi, 1981.

Mann, H.S. Introduction to "Desertification and its Control". Indian Council of Agricultural Research, New Delhi. August 1977.

Martins, Paul J. Determining Human Carrying Capacity: A Case Study in the Central Himalaya. Thesis submitted for Degree of Master of Science in Forestry. University of Toronto, Canada, 1987.

Master Plan Organisation and Harza Engineering. National Water Plan Project-Third Interim Report, Dhaka, December 1984.

Master Plan Organisation. National Water Plan, 1985-2005. Ministry of Irrigation, Water Development and Flood Control in cooperation with the UNDP and World Bank, Dhaka. December 1986.

Mathrani, K.P. The Case of the Eastern Rivers. Extracts from speech delivered at Indo-Pakistan (Secretaries') meet ng. New Delhi, July 1969. From Farakka – A Gordian Knot – Problems on Sharing Ganga Waters. Published by Sunil Sen Sharma, Ishika, Calcutta, April 1986.

Mehr-Homji, V.M. Trends in Rainfall in Relation to Forest Cover. In "Deforestation, Drought and Desertification", INTACH, New Delhi, 1989.

Mekong Committee for the Coordination and Investigations of the Lower Mekong Basin. Ish and the Mekong Project, ESCAP, Bangkok, September 1972.

Mekong Committee for the Coordination and Investigations of the Lower Mekong Project. Archaeology and the Mekong Project. Committee for the Coordination of Investigations of the Lower Mekong Basin, Bangkok. March 1973.

Mekong Interim Committee, 1982. Perspectives for Mekong Development. Revised Indicative Plan (1987) for the Development of Land, Water and Related Resources of the Lower Mekong Basin. Bangkok. April 1988.

Miah, M. Maniruzzaman. Professor, Dhaka University. Floods in Bangladesh. A case for Regional Cooperation. Presented at ICSAC Seminar, New Delhi, February 1989.

Mintzer, Irving. A Warming World, Challenges for Policy Analysis. "Economic Impact", No. 65, U.S. Information Agency, Washington. October-December 1988.

Molnar, peter. The Distribution of Intensity Associated with the 1905 Kangra Earthquake and Bounds on the Extent of the Rupture Zone. Journal of the Geological Society of India. Vol 29. February 1987.

Mondal, A.K. and Jhingran, A.G. Impact on Frogleg Culture on Agriculture and Public Health, Central Inland Capture Fisheries Research Institute, Barrackpore, 1986.

Mookerjea, D. My Reminiscences of Farakka, Souvenir. Farakka Barrage Project, May 1975.

Morris, Morris D. The Growth of Large-Scale Industry to 1947. Cambridge Economic History of India. Volume II c. 1757 – c.1970. Orient Longman. Hyderabad, 1986.

Mukherjee N. The Port of Calcutta – A Short History. Published by the Commissioners for the Port of Calcutta, 1968.

Mukherji, Partha N. Naxalbari Movement and the Peasant Revolt in North Bengal. Centre for the Study of Social Systems, Jawaharlal Nehru University, New Delhi. 1978.

Murty, Y.K. Safety of Dams and Reservoirs. Journal of Institute of Engineers, India. Vol. 28, No. 8-9, Bulletin, 1978.

Nadkarni, M.V. and Pasha, Syed Ajmal and Prabhakar, L.S. Political Economy of Forest Use and Management in the Context of Integration of a Forest Region into the Larger Economy. Institute for Social and Economic Change, Bangalore. September 1987.

Nag, B.S. and Kathpalia, G.N. Water Resources of India Paper presented at the Second World Congress on Water Resources, New Delhi. December 1975.

Nair, C.T.S. Crisisin Forest Resources Management. From India's Environment, Crises and Responses. Edited by Bandpadhyay J., Jayal N.D., Schoetti, U and Singh, Chhatrapati. Natraj Publishers, Dehra Dun, 1985.

Narain, Jagdish. Irrigation and Water Management in India, Education and Training Needs. Sixth IHD Endowment Lecture, Anna University, Madras December 12, 1985.

Narayanamurthy, S.G. Study of Methods for Improving Canal Regulation in Northwest India. World Bank, New Delhi, December 1985.

Narmada Water Disputes Tribunal Report. Vols. I and II. Government of India, New Delhi, 1978.

Natarajan, A.V. Overview of Central Inland Fisheries Research Institute's Contribution to Research, Training and Transfer of Technology in Fresh and Brackish-water Aquaculture and Management of Natural Fisheries. In Souvenir Volume for 4th Advisory Committee Meeting of NACA (FAO/UNDP Project). Bhubaneshwar, December 3-6, 1984.

National Bureau of Fish Genetic Resources (NBFGR). Allahabad, Annual Report, 1985.

National Commission on Agriculture, India (NCA). Ministry of Agriculture, New Delhi, 1976.

NCA Part II – Policy and Strategy.

NCA Part III – Demand and Supply.

NCA Part V – Resource Development – Irrigation

NCA Part VI – Crop Production, Sericulture and Apiculture

NCA Part VII – Animal Husbandry

NCA Part VIII – Fisheries

NCA Part IX – Forestry

NCA Part XV – Agrarian Reforms

National Commission on Urbanisation, Government of India. Vols. I and II, Ministry of Housing and Urban Development, New Delhi, August 1988.

National Council of Applied Economic Research. Pre-Investment Appraisal of the Development of Inland Water Transport Services on the Ganga between Allahabad and Calcutta. New Delhi, July 1976.

National Council of Power Utilities. Need for Accelerated Hydro-Power Development in India. New Delhi, February 1986.

National Egg Coordination Committee. Indian Poultry in the 21st Century, Pune, 1987.

National Environmental Engineering Research Institute. River Ganga – An Overview of Environmental Research (citing Kuldeep Kumar et al). Nagpur, 1987.

National Federation of Fishermen's Cooperatives Ltd. Leasing System of Inland Water. Study Report. New Delhi, January 1988.

National Geophysical Research Institute. Annual Report 1986-87. Hyderabad 1987.

National Land Use and Conservation Board (NLUCB). Report of the Committee of Experts on Draft Outline of National Land Use Policy, New Delhi, 1988.

National Planning Commission, Nepal. The Seventh Plan, 1985-90, Kathmandu. June 1985.

National Remote Sensing Agency (NRSA). Mapping of Forest Cover in India from Satellite Imagery, 1972-75 and 1980-82. Department of Space, Hyderabad December 1983.

National Transport Policy Committee Report. Planning Commission, New Delhi, May 1980.

National Wasteland Development Board (NWDB). National Land Use and Wastelands Development Council, New Delhi, February 1986.

National Wasteland Development Board (NWDB). Afforestation and People's Involvement. A Study of China's Experience. New Delhi. May 1987.

National Water Development Agency. Annual Report. 1984-85. Ministry of Water Resources. New Delhi, January 1986.

National Water Development Agency. Proposals for Large Scale Inter-Basin Water Transfer. New Delhi, 1988.

Nelson, Gerald C. Agricultural Price Policy in Nepal. Asian Development Bank Economic Staff Paper N. 35, Manila, March 1987.

Nepal, Royal Government,. "Water Resources Strategy". Water and Energy Commission Secretariat. Kathmandu, January 2002.

Netherlands-Norway Study by Institute of Social Studies Advisory Service. The Hague, and Chr. Michelsen Institute, Bergen. The Country Boats of Bangladesh, Social and Economic Development and Decision-Making in Inland Water Transport. Draft Report, BITWA, Dhaka, February 1984.

Newsweek. Buying Debt, Saving Nature – The Third World Gets a Ransom for its Forests. August 31, 1987.

Nickum, James E. Irrigation Management in China – a Review of the Literature. World Bank Staff Working Paper No. 5445. Washington, 1982.

Nicolson, Nigel. The Himalayas. The World's Wild Places/Time-Life Books. Amsterdam, 1975.

Nishat, Ainun and Chowdhury, Shahjahan Kabir. Water Quality Problems and Needs for Integrated Control in Bangladesh. Regional Symposium on Water Resources Policyi n Agro-Socio-Economic Development. Dhaka. August 1985.

North Eastern Council, India. Report of the Working Group on Development of the North Eastern Region during the 7th Five Year Plan, Shillong, March 1985.

Padhye, M.G. Environment vs Water Resources Development. Times of India, New Delhi, January 28, 1987.

Pakistan Government, Ministry of Information and Broadcasting. Islamabad. Facts about Pakistan – Glaciers.

Pandeya, S.C. Jiwaji University Gwalior, Presidential Address at the 3rd International Rangeland Congress, New Delhi, November 1988.

Pant, Niranjan. Some Aspects of Irrigation Administration (A Case Study of the Kosi Project). Naya Prakash, Calcutta, 1980.

Pant S.D. The Social Economy of the Himalaya. George Allen & Unwin Ltd., London 1935.

Paranjpe, Vijay. Evaluating the Tehri Dam. INTACH, New Delhi. June 1988.

Patkar, Medha. Development or Destruction – Case of Sardar Sarovar Project. Presented at Workshop on Justification for Large Dams in India. India International Centre, new Delhi, December 26, 1987.

Pereira, H. Charles. The Management of Tropical Watersheds. Published in Strategies, Approaches and Systems in Integrated Watershed Management. FAO Conservation Guide, Rome, 1986.

Planning Commission, Bangladesh. Third Five Year Plan, 1985-90. Dhaka, December 1985.

Planning Commission, India. University and Eco-Development, New Delhi, March 1982.

Planning Commission, India. Report of the Task Force on Framework Action Plan for Foodgrain Production, New Delhi, March 1988.

Planning Commission, India. Transport Planning Framework, Policy Issues and Perspective. New Delhi, April 1988.

Planning Commission. Economic Development of Assam: Report of the Committee on Clause 7 of the Assam Accord. New Delhi, April 1990.

Planning Commission. Approach to the Eighth Five Year Plan, 1990-95: Towards Social Transformation, New Delhi, May 1990.

Planning Commission. Employment, Past Trends and Prospects for 1990s, New Delhi, May 1990.

Planning Commission, Government of India. Report of the Working Group on Watershed Development and Rainfed Farming and Natural Resource Management for the 10th Five-Year Plan. Delhi. September 2001.

Postel, Sandra and Heise Lori. Reforesting the Earth. "Economic Impact", No. 65, US Information Agency, Washington, October-December, 1988.

Power, Water and Flood Control Ministry, Government of Bangladesh. Proposal for Augmentation of the Dry Season Flow of the Ganges, Dhaka, March 1978.

Pramanik, S.K. and Mukherjee S.M. The Assam Earthquake of 1950. A Compilation of Papers on the Assam Earthquake of August 15, 1950. Publication No. 1of the Central Board of Geophysics, Government of India, Calcutta, 1953.

Prasad, Pradhan H. Reactionary Role of Usurer's Capital in Rural India. Economic and Political Weekly, Bombay, Special Number. August 1974.

Prasad, Pradhan H. Towards a Theory of Transformation of Semi-Feudal Agriculture. Economic and Political Weekly, Bombay. August 1, 1987.

Prembhai. Labour Bank. A People's Plan for Poverty Alleviation. (Unpublished note given to author). Banwasi Seva Ashram, Govindpur, via Turra, Mirzapur District U.P. 1986.

Public Accounts Committee (1975-76). Fifth Lok Sabha. 196th Report: Farakka Barrage Project. Lok Sabha Secretariat, New Delhi. January 1976.

Public Undertakings Committee. 7th Report on Central Inland Water Transport Corporation, 1977-78. Lok Sabha, New Delhi.

Punjab SEB Expert (Johl) Committee. Level and Structure of Electricity Tariff for Agricultural Consumers in Punjab, Patiala, May 1984.

Radcliffe Awards. Reports of the Bengal (and Punjab) Boundary Commission(s) Government of India, New Delhi, 1955.

Rahman, Atiur, Grameen Bank Evaluation Project. Working Papers 2 and 3; Impact of GB Intervention on the Rural Power Structure; and Consciousness-Raising Efforts of GB, Bangladesh Institute of Development Studies, Dhaka, July 1986.

Rai, Usha. Times of India, "Ganga Project Ambitious, Expert", New Delhi, December 28, 1987.

Raina, B.N. Hukku, B.M. and Chalapati Rao, R.V. Geological Survey of India. Lucknow. Geological Features of the Himalayan Region with Special Reference to their Impact on Environmental Appreciation and Environmental Management. Proceedings of the National Seminar on Development and Environment in the Himalayas Region. DST, New Delhi, April 1978.

Rajagopalan, P.K. and Das, P.K. Filariasis Control by Integrated Vector Management. Proceedings of ICMR/WHO Workshop to review research results of Community participation for Disease Vector Control. Malaria Research Centre, New Delhi, February 3-9, 1986.

Rajagopal, P.R. Social Change and Violence – The Indian Experience. Uppal Publishing House. New Delhi, 1987.

Ramachandra Rao, M.B.A. Compilation of Papers on the Assam Earthquake of August 15, 1950. Publication No. 1of the Central Board of Geophysics, Government of India, Calcutta, 1953.

Ramakrishna, P.S. The Science Behind Bush Fallow Agriculture System(Jhum). Proceedings of the Indian Academy of Sciences (Plant Sciences). Vol. 93, July 1984.

Ramalingaswami V. Health Dimensions of Developmental Activities. Second Vikram Sarabhai Memorial Lecture, September 12, 1980. Reproduced in Voluntary Action, New Delhi, January 1981.

Ramamoorthi, A.S. Snowmelt Runoff Studies Using Remote Sensing Data. 1983. National Remote Sensing Agency, Hyderabad.

Ramamoorthi, A.S. Forecasting Snowmelt Runoff of Himalayan Rivers using NOAA AVHRR Imageries. 1956.

Ramamurthy, M.K. Environment as a Public Interest Cause. The Case of the Doon Valley. From India's Environment, Crises and Responses. Edited by J. Bandopadhyay, N.D. Jayal, U. Schoettli and Chhatrapati Singh, Natraj Publishers, Dehra Dun, 1985.

Raman, C.R.V., Venkataraman S., and Krishnamurthy, V. Dew over India and its Contribution to Winter-Crop Water Balance. Agricultural Meteorology, 11. 1973.

Randhawa, M.S. History of Agriculture in India, Volumes I-IV. Indian Council of Agricultural Research, New Delhi, 1980-1986.

Rangachari, R and Mathur P.C. (CWC). Analysis of Flood Control Schemes on the River Yamuna using Computer-Based Mathematical Models. Proceedings of the Seminar on the Morphology of the Ganga River. Ganga Flood Control Commission and Central Board of Irrigation and Power, New Delhi, November 1986.

Ramaswami, K. Ganga Waters. Whose Needs Are Greater? External Publicity Division, Ministry of External Affairs, New Delhi, 1969.

Range Management Society of India. National Rangeland Symposium, Proceedings and Recommendations. Jhansi, November 1987.

Rao, C.G.Hanumantha, Ray, Susanta K. and Subbarao K. Unstable Agriculture and Droughts. Vikas Publishing House, New Delhi. 1988.

Rao, C. Sitapathi, et al. Administrative Staff College of India. River Valley Projects – A Study in Machkund Sileru in Andhra Pradesh and Orissa, Pochampad in Maharashtra. Hyderabad, July, 1987.

Rashtriya Barh Ayog (National Flood Commission) – Vols. I & II. Irrigation Department, New Delhi, March 1980.

Rastogi, B.K. Risk of Reservoir-Induced Seismicity and Necessary Investigations. Seminar on Engineering Geophysics, Perspectives and Prospects. Indian Geophysical Union, Hyderabad. December 1984.

Rau, M.A. Western Himalayan Flora. From Himalaya, Aspects of Change. Ed. J.S. Lall. Oxford University Press, New Delhi, 1981.

Ravi and Beas (Eradi) Water Tribunal Report. Government of India, New Delhi, 1987.

Raychaudhuri, Tapan. Chapter XI, Inland Trade. Cambridge Economic History of India. Volumel c. 1200 – c. 1750. Orient Longman, Hyderabad, 1984.

Regmi, M.C. Land Tenure and Taxation in Nepal. Ratna Pustak Bhandar, Kathmandu, 1978.

Rennell, James. Account of the Ganges and Burrampooter Rivers. London.1781.

Repetto, Robert. Skimming the Water – Rent-seeking and the Performance of Public Irrigation Systems. Research Report 4, World Resources Institute, Washingtonecember 1986.

Revelle, Roger and Herman T. Some Possibilities for International Development of the Ganges-Brahmaputra River Basins. Research Report, Harvard University Centre for Population Studies, Cambridge, Mass. USA 1972.

Revelle Roger and Lakshminarayana V. The Ganges Water Machine. Science, Vo. 188, May 9, 1975.

Review Committee on Rights and Concessions in Forest Areas, Report of Ministry of Environment and Forests, New Delhi, 1981.

Ribeiro, Edgar F. Improved Sanitation and Environmental Health Conditions, An Evaluation of [illegible]bh International's Low-Cost Sanitation Project in Bihar, Patna 1985.

[illegible]. Dillon. Some Considerations on the State of the Present Climate and Environment in India – An Essay in Decline and Fall. Perspectives in Environmental Management. Edited by T.N. Khoshoo, Oxford and IBH Publishing Co., New Delhi. 1986.

Rogers, Peter., Lydon, Peter and Seckler, David. Eastern Waters Study, Strategies to Manage Flood and Drought in the Ganges-Brahmaputra Basin. Prepared for USAID by the Irrigation Support Project for Asia and the Near East, Washington, April 1989.

Roy, L.B. Alternative to Farakka. Hindustan Times, New Delhi. October 2, 1974.

Roy, Pranab. Fisheries with Ecology of the Sunderbans. From "Voice of the Storm", National Fishermen's Forum, Cochin, April 1988.

Rural Development Department, Government of India. Annual Reports 1986-87 and 1987-88, New Delhi.

Rural Development Department, Government of India. National Technology Mission on Drinking Water, New Delhi. January 1988

Rural Development Ministry, Government of India. National Policy on Resettlement and Rehabilitation for Project Affected Families. Delhi, February 2004.

Sagar, R.K. Comparative Economics of Inland Water Transport. A Case Study of the Ulhas River-Thana Creek Waterways (Bombay). Planning Development of Inland Waterways. Proceedings of a Seminar held at Calcutta. ESCAP Inland Waterways Development Series No. 1, Bangkok, September 1979.

Sahni, K.C. Botanical Panorama of the Eastern Himalaya. From Himalaya, Aspects of Change, Ed. J.S. Lall. Oxford University Press, New Delhi, 1981.

Sain, Kanwar. Reminiscences of an Engineer. Young Indian Publications, New Delhi1 978.

Samarasinghe, M.U.L.P. The Present Malaria Situation in Sri Lanka with Particular Reference to Areas Where Irrigation has been Introduced Recently. Proceedings of the Workshop on Irrigation and Vector Borne Disease Transmission, IIMI, Digana Village, Sri Lanka, December 1986.

Sancton, Thomas A. Time Magazine. Planet of the Year, Hands Across the Sea. January 2, 1989.

Santhanam Committee Report, Home Ministry, New Delhi, 1964.

Saxena, N.C. Participatory Planning for Wasteland Development. Council for Social Development, New Delhi, 1988.

Schwebel, Stephen M. Special Rapporteur, Third Report on the Non-Navigational Uses of International Watercourses. International Law Commission 34th Session. United Nations General Assembly, New York. A/c. No. 4/348, December 1981.

Sehgal, K.L. Vanishing Genetic Resources of Commercially Important Endemic Fish of Uplands of India and Their Possible Conservation. Proceedings of Symposium on Conservation and Management of Fish Genetic Resources of India. NBFGR, Allahabad, April 1986.

Sethi, Nitin. "Truth is More Slippery". Down to Earth, Delhi, May 15, 2005.

Sen, Bhowani. Evolution of Agrarian Relations in India. People's Publishing House, New Delhi, 1962.

Shah, P.P. Chief Engineer, Hydro-Power Potentiality of Nepal. Department of Electricity, Ministry of Water and Power, Kathmandu, 1971.

Shahjahan, M. Regional Cooperation for Flood Control. Paper for Indian Council for South Asian Cooperation. Seminar on Regional Cooperation for the Protection of the Environment in South Asia. New Delhi, February 1989.

Shankar, Kripa. Land Transfers in Uttar Pradesh. Economic and Political Weekly, Bombay, July 23, 1988.

Sharma, Alakh. N., "Agrarian Relations and Socio-Economic Change in Bihar". Economic and Political Weekly, Bombay, March 5, 2005.

Sharma, C.K. Water and Energy Resources of the Himalayan Block. Published by Sangeetha Sharma, 23/282 Bishalnagar, Kathmandu, 1983.

Sharma, Kulshekhar et al.S tudyon the Land Tenure System of Nepal. Integrated Development Systems, Kathmandu, May 1986.

Sharma, Suresh. Development and Diminishing Livelihood, Report on the Singrauli Loyayan-Lokhit Samiti Workshop at Bina, Madhya Pradesh. Lokayan Bulletin, New Delhi. Vol. 3:4/5, October 1985.

Sharma, V.P. The Green Revolution in India and Ecological Succession of Malaria Vectors. Joint WHO, FAO, UNEP Panel of Experts on Environmental Management for Vector Control. Seventh Annual Meeting, Rome, September 7-11, 1987.

Sharma, V.P., Sharma R.P., and Gautam A.S.Bio-Environmental Control of Malaria in Nadiad, Kheda District, Gujarat. Indian Journal of Malariology, Vol. 23, December 1986.

Shawkat Ali, A.M.M. Groundwater Policies, Options and Laws in Bangladesh. Regional Symposium on Water Resources Policy in Agro-Socio-Economic Development Dhaka, August 1985.

Shibusawa, A.H. World Bank. Cooperation in Water Resources Development in South Asia with particular reference to the Ganges-Brahmaputra Basins and the Deep Artesian Aquifers of the Area. Address at the 13th Session of the Committee on Natural Resources, ESCAP Bangkok, October 14-20, 1986.

Shrivastava, M.B., Shrivastava, Minakshi and Lal. C.B. Grazing Lands, Causes of Their Deterioration and Improvement in India. Indian Journal of Range Management, Vol. 9, Jhansi, 1988.

Singh, Chhatrapati. On Survival, Forestry and Law, Lokayan Bulletin, No. 5, Delhi, March 1987.

Singh, Gurdip. Climatic Changes in the Indian Desert. From Desertification and its Control, ICAR, New Delhi. August 1977.

Singh, Kavaljit. Woes of the Oustees of Pong Dam. Lokayan Bulletin, Delhi, Vol. V:3, 1988.

Singh, Nandita. Plants for Abatement of Air Pollution by Thermal Power Plants. Northern India Patrika, Lucknow, June 5, 1986.

Singh, Panjab, Indian Rangelands, Status and Improvement. Plenary address at the Third International Rangeland Congress, New Delhi, November 1988.

Singhal, M.K. Challenges in Irrigation Managmeent in U.P. WALMI, Okhla, March 1984.

Singhal, M.K. High Technology in Irrigation Management. WALMI, Okhla, December 1986.

Sinha, Basawan. Assesment and Valuation of Natural Systems and Environmental Consequences of Water Resources Development. Proceedings of International Seminar on Environmental Impact Assessment of Water Resources projects. University of Roorkee, December 1985.

Sharma, Rita and Thomas T. Poleman., "The New Economics of India's Green Revolution: Income and Employment.Diffusion in Uttar Pradesh". Vikas Publishing House Pvt Ltd. Delhi, 1995.

Sinha, Shekhar Kumar, and Jayesh Talati. "Impact of System of Rice Intensification (SRI) on Rice Yields: Results of a New Sample Study in Purulia District, India". IWMI-Tata Water Policy Program, Anand, Gujarat. February 2005.

Sinha, S.K., Rao N.H. and Swaminathan M.S. Food Security in the Changing Global Climate. Presented at World Conference on the Changing Atmosphere. Toronto, June 1988.

Small, Leslie E., Adriano, Marietta S. and Martin Edward D. Regional Study on Irrigation Service Fees. Report submitted to the ADB by IIMI, Sri Lanka, January 1986.

Sneider, Daniel. Japan's $ 500 Billion Plan for Reversing World Depression. Executive Intelligence Review, New York. February 23, 1982.

"South", China's Great Divide. London. July 1988.

Srivastava, H.N. Forecasting Earthquakes. National Book Trust, New Delhi. 1983.

Stokes, Eric. Cambridge Economic History of India, Volume II. C.1757-c.1970. Chapter II-Agrarian Relations – I, Northern & Central India, Orient Longman, Hyderabad 1982.

Subbarao, S.K. The Anopheles Culicifacies Complex and Control of Malaria. Parasitology Today, Vo. 4 No. 3 Elsevier Publications, Cambridge. 1988.

Sulabh International. Eradication of Scavenging – Need for a National Technology Mission. New Delhi, July 1988.

Swaminathan, M.S. Development of the Silent Valley Reserve Forest, Kerala, A Report. Department of Agriculture, New Delhi, 1979.

Swaminathan, M.S. New Strategies in Agriculture-Taking Technology's Help. The Hindu, New Delhi, July 14, 1988.

Tangri, A.K. and Sharma, R.P. A Study of Changing Drainage Patterns and Their Tectonic Implications in Parts of North Indian Using Remote Sensing Techniques. Remote Sensing Applications Centre, Lucknow.

Task Force on Agrarian Relations. Planning Commission. India. Two Decades of Land Reform. New Delhi, 1973.

Task Force on Migration, Nepal. Internal and International Migration in Nepal. National Commission on Population, Government of Nepal. August 1983.

Tata Energy Research Institute. International Conference on Global Warming and Climate Change – Perspectives from Developing Countries Recommendations. New Delhi, February 1989.

Tehri Dam Organisation. Scheme for Treatment of Catchment Area of Ganga Valley. U.P. Irrigation Department, Dehra Dun, August 1986.

Tejwani, K.G. Water Management in the Indian Himalaya. Paper presented at ICIMOD Workshop on Watershed Management in the Hindu Kush-Himalaya Region at Chengdu, China. ICIMOD, Kathmandu, October, 1985.

Thomas, William L. Man's Role in Changing the Face of the Earth, University of Chicago Press, 1956.

Thompson, M. and Warburton M. Uncertainty on a Himalayan Scale. Mountain Research and Development, 1985.

Thorner, Daniel. The Agrarian Project in India, Allied, Bombay, 1981.

Thukral, Enakshi Ganguly. Dams, For Whose Development? Multiple Action Research Group, New Delhi, April 1988.

Tribal Affairs Ministry, Government of India. National Policy on Tribals. Delhi January 2004.

United Nations. Yearbook of the International Law Commission, Vol. II, Part Two. Documents of the 26th Session of the Commission prepared by the Secretariat. New York, 1974.

United Nations. Treaties Concerning the Utilisation of International Watercourses for Other Purposes Than Navigation. Natural Resource/Water Series No. 13, New York. 1984.

UN/UNDP, Hydrological Conditions of Bangladesh. 1982.

UNDP. Bangladesh Flood Policy Study. Final Report. Bangladesh Ministry of Planning. Dhaka. May 1989.

UNICEF. A Review of the Situation of Children in Bhutan/Nepal/Bangladesh. SAARC Conference on South Asian Children New Delhi. October 27-29, 1986.

UN Technical Assistance Programme, Water and Power Development in East Pakistan. Report of a Mission led by J.A. Krug, June 1957.

Uphoff, Norman, Meinzen-Dick, Ruth and St. Julian, Nancy. Improving Policies and Programmes for Farmer Organisation and Participation in Irrigation Water Management. Cornell University, Ithaca, NY 14853, U.S.A., December 1985.

Uppal , H.L. Study of Himalayan River Systems and Their Origin. Presented at Ganga-Brahmaputra-Barak Workshop. Gandhi Peace Foundation, New Delhi, December 1978.

U.P. Irrigation Commission Report. Government of Uttar Pradesh, Lucknow, December 1984.

Uttar Pradesh Irrigation Department, Performance Budget, 1984-85, Lucknow.

Uttar Pradesh Irrigation Department. Development of Irrigation – Perspective Plan, 2020 A.D., Lucknow, April 1985.

Valdiya, K.S. Environmental Aspects of Tehri Dam Project. Tehri Dam Circle IV, Rishikesh. 1988.

Varma, S.C. Human Resettlement in Lower Narmada Basin. Narmada Valley Development Authority, Government of Madhya Pradesh, Bhopal, July 1985.

Varshney, R.S. Concrete Dams (2nd Edition). Oxford and IBH Publishing Co. Pvt. Ltd., New Delhi. 1988.

Vasudev, N.N. Transport Requirement by 2000 A.D. and the Role of IWT. National Workshop on Inland Waterways, IWAI, New Delhi, August 1988.

Verghese, B.G. Kosi: A People's Project. A Journey Through India. The Times of India Press, Bombay, May 1959.

Verghese, B.G. Gift of the Greater Ganga, An Approach to the Integrated Development of the Ganga-Brahmaputra Basin. 8th Coromandel Lecture, December 1977. Published by Coromandel Fertilisers Ltd., New Delhi, 1978.

Verghese .G. Postscript on Kosi Kranti. Voluntary Action, AVARD's Monthly Journal, New Delhi, November, 1981.

Verghese B.G. A Water Revolution in Gonda. Voluntary Action AVARD's Monthly Journal, New Delhi, November 1981.

Verghese B.G. Not by Cusecs Alone. Indian Express, New Delhi, March 17, 1987.

Verma, P.C. Surplus Labour in Agriculture: Negative Aspects of Economic Development in India. Paper presented at National Seminar on Four Decades of Economic Development in India. Patna College, February 22, 1988.

Visaria, Leela and Pravin. Population (1757-1947). Cambridge Economic History of India, Vol 2 c. 1757 – c. 1970. Orient Longman, Hyderabad, 1982.

Voelcker, J.A. Report on the Improvement of Indian Agriculture, 1891.

Vohra B.B. A Charter for the Land, Soil Conservation Digest, Dehra Dun. Vol. 2, No. 2, October 1974.

Vohra, B.B. The Greening of India: Land and Water – Towards a Policy for Life-Support Systems. INTACH Environment Series 1 and 2 New Delhi, 1985.

Vohra B.B. Issues in Water Management, New Delhi. INTACH January 1987.

Vohra, C.P. Himalayan Glaciers. From Himalaya, Aspects of Change. Ed. J.S. Lall, Oxford University Press, New Delhi, 1981.

Wade, Robert. The Systems of Administrative and Political Corruption – Canal Irrigation in South India. The Journal of Development Studies Vol. 18 No. 3, London, April 1982.

Wadhwa, D.C. Guaranteeing Title to Land, A Preliminary Study. Planning Commission, New Delhi, 1989.

Wadia Institute of Himalayan Geology, Souvenir, Dehra Dun, October 183.

Wadia Institute of Himalayan Geology. Detailed Report of Geological and Tectonic Studies (1982-86) under the All-India Cordinated Project n Seismicity and Seismotectonics of the Himalayan Region. Dehra Dun. 1986.

Walker, Tony. Water Shortage the Modern Way. A Yemeni city is draining its ancient underground lake too fast. Financial Times, London, April 7, 1988.

WALMI. Seminar proceedings. Significance of CAD Programme for Better Water Management, Patna, August 1987.

Water and Energy Commission, Nepal. Five Energy Workshops, Kathmandu, November 1985.

Water Resources Ministry, India. National Water Policy. New Delhi, September 1987.

Water Resources Ministry, India. National Workshop on CAD Programme. Strategies for Improving Performance, New Delhi, February 1988.

Water Resources Ministry, Nepal. Water-Key to Nepal's Development, Kathmandu, 1981.

Water Resources Ministry, Nepal. International Collaboration in the Development of Nepal's Water Resources. Prepared fro the 12th Congress of the World Energy Conference in New Delhi. Kathmandu, September 1983.

Water Resources Ministry. Performance Budget for 1990-91. New Delhi, May 1990.

Water Resources Ministry, Nepal. Water Resource Development in Nepal. Kathmandu. March 1985.

Wesson, Robert L and Wallace, Robert E. Predicting the Next Great Earthquake in California. Scientific American Vol. 252 No. 2, February 1985.

West Bengal Department of Environment. Management of Hazardous Chemicals and Plant Safety in Some Selected Industries in West Bengal, Calcutta, January 1987.

Western Kosi Canal in Nepal. Agreement on the Renovation and Extension of the Chandra Canal, Pumped Canal and Distribution System. April 7, 1978.

Whitcombe, Elizabeth. Agrarian Conditions in Northern India. Vol. 1, The United Provinces under British Rule, 1960-1900. University of California Press and Thomson Press (India) Ltd. 1971.

Whitcombe, Elizabeth. Cambridge Economic History of India, Volume II. C. 1757 – c. 1970. Chapter VII, Irrigation. Orient Longman, Hyderabad, 1982.

Wimco-Nabard. Agro-Forestry Project for Poplar Plantations. Assocham Workshop, New Delhi. August 1988.

Wittfogel, Karl A. The Hydraulic Civilisation. From Man's Role in Changing the Face of the Earth. Edited by William L. Thomas Jr. University of Chicago Press, 1956.

Working Group on Energy Policy, Report. Planning Commission, New Delhi, 1979.

Works and Housing Ministry. National Master Plan-India for International Drinking Water Supply and Sanitation Decade, 1981-1990. New Delhi, July 1983.

World Bank. Bangladesh – Recent Economic Developments and Selected Development Issues. Washington, March 1982.

World Bank. Upper Ganga Irrigation Modernisation Project. Staff Appraisal Report No. 4992-IN. April 1984.

World Bank. Recent Irrigation Management Experience – A Review of Selected Programmes and Their Implications for the Proposed National Water Management Project, New Delhi, October 1984.

World Bank. Nepal Deep Aquifer Project. April 1985.

World Bank. Irrigation Division Nepal – Deep Aquifer Exploration Project – Technical Supplement, Washington. April 1985.

World Bank. Operational Manual Statement. Washington, April 1985.

World Bank. Country Study China. Agriculture in the Year 2000, Washington, 1985.

World Bank. Country Study China. The Transport Sector. Washington 1985.

World Bank. Proceedings of the Ground Water Seminar and Technical Session. Washington. May, 1986.

World Bank. Lending Conditionality: A Review of Cost Recovery in Irrigation Projects. Washington, June 1986.

World Bank. Dam Safety and the Environment. Technical Paper No. 115. Edited by Moigne, Guy Le., Barghouti, Shawki, and Plusquiellec, Herve. Washington, February 1990.

World Bank, Nepal: "Proposed Power Sector Development Strategy". Energy Sector Unit, South Asia Regional Office, March 19, 2001.

— Uttar Pradesh Water Sector Reconstucturing Project (Project Appraisal). Rural Development Sector Unit. South Asia Regional Office. November 16, 2001

— Water Resources Sector Strategy. Washington, 2004.

World Commission on Environment and Development. Our Common Future United Nations. Oxford University Press, New York, 1987.

World Development Report (World Bank) 1988. Oxford University Press Washington. June 1988.

World Resources Institute, World Bank and UNDP. Tropical Forests. A Call for Action. Report on an International Task Force, New York, October 1985.

Wyatt-Smith, J. The Agricultural System in the Hills of Nepal. Agricultural Project Services Centre. Occasional Paper No. 1, Kathmandu, 1982.

Xinhua. New Life for Tibetan Fishermen. Lhasa. July 10, 1989.

Yadava, Y.S., Goswami M., Kar D., and Choudhury, M. On the Conservation of Hilsa Illisha (Hamilton) in the Water Bodies of Assam. Proceedings of the Symposium on Conservation and Management of Fish Genetic Resources of India. NBFGR, Allahabad, April 1986.

Yanhua, Liu, Agriculture-Population Interaction in Lhasa District, Tibet (Preliminary Analysis). Mountain Farming System Division, ICIMOD, Kathmandu, August 1988.

Zaheer, M. Measures of Land Reform – Consolidation of Holdings in India. Behavioural sciences and Community Development. Vol. 9, September 1975.

Zaman, M.Q. Crisis in Chittagong Hill Tract, Ethnicity and Integration Economic and Political Weekly, Bombay, Vol. XVII, No. 3. January 16, 1982.

Zollinger, F. Analysis of River Problems and Strategy for Flood Control in the Nepalese Terai, Government of Nepal with FAO and UNDP, 1977.

Additional References

Administrative Staff College. Socio-Economic Evaluation of THDC Resettlement and Rehabilitation. Hyderabad, December 1992.

Bangladesh Government. Ministry of Water Resources. International Seminar on Water Resources Management and Development – with Particular Reference to the Ganga River. Dhaka, March 1998.

Bangladesh Government. Options for Development in the Ganga Dependent Areas of Bangladesh. Historical Perspective. March 1998.

Bangladesh Government. The Ganges Water Sharing Treaty and the Resulting Opportunities, March 1998.

Heard, Daniel. Address to the International Commission for Irrigation and Drainage. Varna, Bulgaria, May 18, 1994.

Brahmaputra Board, Ministry of Water Resources, Guwahati, 1997.

Calcutta Port Trust. "Port of Calcutta: 125 Years, 1870-1995". Commemorative Volume. Ed. Dr. Satyesh Chakraborty. Calcutta, October 1995.

Central Electricity Authority, Government of India. Fourth National Power Plan. Delhi, March 1997.

Char, N.V.V. Augmentation of Water Resources in the Ganga Basin. Paper prepared for Eastern Himalayan Rivers three-country study. Centre for Policy Research, 1997.

Char N.V.V. Integrated Water Resources Development of GBM River Systems. International Dimensions. As above.

Committee on Pricing of Irrigation Water (Vaidyanathan Committee) Planning Commission, Delhi. September 1992.

"Economist, The". Environmental Scares: Plenty of Gloom. London, December 20, 1997.

Esterbrook, Greg. "A Moment on Earth: The Coming Age of Environmental Optimism". Penguin. United States, 1996.

Expert (Hanumantha Rao) Committee Report on the "Environmental and Rehabilitation Aspects of the Tehri Hydro-Electric Project". Ministry of Power, New Delhi, October, 1997.

Expert Group Report on "Seismic Safety of Tehri Dam", Ministry of Power, New Delhi, February 1998.

FAP-4 Southwest Area Water Resources Management Project. GOBD Ministry of Irrigation, Water Development and Flood Control; Flood Plan Coordination Organisation; UNDP; Asian Development Bank. Sri Wiliam Halcrow & Partners Ltd. In association with the Danish Hydraulic Institute, Engineering & Planning Consultants Ltd. And Sthapati Sangshad Ltd. Dhaka, August 1993.

Flood Management for the 9th Five Year Plan, 1997-2002. Working Group Report. Central Commission, Ministry of Water Resources, Delhi, June 1996.

Gaur, Vinod K. "Earthquake Hazards and Large Dams in the Himalaya". INTACH, Delhi, December 1993.

Hasan, Z. et al. Theme Paper for Water Resources Day on River Basin Management; Issues and Options. Indian Water Resources Society, Delhi, March 21, 1997.

International Commission for Irrigation and Drainage. International Seminar on Evolution of a Scientific System of Flood Forecasting and Warning in the GBM River Basins. Dhaka, December 5-6, 1997.

IUCN-World Bank. "Large Dam: Learning From the Past, Looking at the Future", Workshop Proceedings. Gland, Switzerland. April 11-12, 1997.

Iyer, Ramaswamy R and Rangachari R. "Indo-Bangladesh talks on "The Ganga Waters Issue" in "Harnessing the Eastern Himalayan Rivers. Regional Cooperation in South Asia" edited by B.G. Verghese and Ramaswamy R. Iyer. Konark Publishers Pvt. Ltd., Delhi 1993.

Jha, Dr. Hari Bansh; Mahakali Treaty: Implications for Development. See Chapters entitled "Benefits to Nepal" by Pashupati Shumsher Rana (Water Resources Minister) and "A Vision for the 21st Century" by Dr. Prakash Chandra Lohani (Foreign Minister). Foundation for Economic and Social Change, Lalitpur, 1996.

Khattri K.N. "Perceptions of Seismic Hazard for the Tehri Dam". Bhagirathi ki Pukar, Vol. 6, No. 2, INTACH, Delhi, February 1996.

Major and Medium Irrigation Programme for the 9th Five Year Plan, 1997-2002. Working Group Report. Central Water Commission, Ministry of Water Resources. Delhi 1996.

McCully, Patrick. "Silenced Rivers: The Ecology and Politics of Large Dams". Zed Books, London, 1996.

Mohile, A.D. "Brahmaputra. Issues in Development", Paper presented at the Ganges Forum Seminar sponsored by IWRA and the UN University, Calcutta, March 18-20, 1998.

Mukherjee, Somnath "Water Resource Development and the Environment in Bhutan" Paper presented at the Ganges Forum Seminar sponsored by IWRA and the UN University Calcutta, March 18-20, 1998

National Institute of Public Finance and Policy Report of the International Seminar on Water as a Social and Economic Good. Delhi, December 11-12, 1997

Planning Commission. "Transforming the Northeast: Tackling Backlogs in Basic Minimum Services and Infrastructural Needs". Report of a High Level Commission to the Prime Minister chaired by S.P. Shukla, Delhi, March 1997.

Planning Commission, Ninth Five Year Plan, 1997-2002. Draft Volumes I and II. Delhi. March 1998.

Prakasam, K.P. "Greenhouse Gases or a Greener Planet?" Encounter, Delhi, January/February 1998.

Rahman, Khalilur. "Treaty on Sharing Ganges Waters at Farakka ... and the Ganges Barrage Multipurpose Project in Bangladesh". Paper presented at Eastern Himalayan Rivers Conference sponsored by the Global Infrastructure Fund Research Foundation of Japan, Kathmandu. February, 1998.

Rangachari, R and M.L. Baweja. "Flood Problem of GBM Basin Countries". Paper presented at the Eastern Himalayan Rivers, Three-Country Study Seminar. Centre for Policy Research, Delhi, November 1997.

Sambamurti, M.K. The Eastern Power/Energy Grid. Prepared for Centre for Policy Research Eastern Himalayan Rivers Study, Phase II, Delhi, November 1997.

"Scientific American", "Peaceful Nuclear Explosions: Chinese interest in this technology may scuttle a test-ban Treaty". Washington June 1996.

Sivaramakrishnan, K.C. and Dalwani. "Water Quality Monitoring and Management in the GBM Region". Paper presented at the Eastern Himalayan Rivers Conference. Centre for Policy Research, Delhi, November 1997.

United Nations. Report of the Sixth Committee convening as the Working Group of the Whole. General Assembly, New York, April 11, 1997.

United Nations. Draft Articles on the Law and on the Non-Navigational Uses of International Watercourses and Resolution on Confined Transboundary Groundwater (with Commentary). New York, 1996.

United Nations. Report of the Sixth Committee Working Group of the General Assembly on the Convention on the Law of the Non-Navigational Uses of International Watercourses, April 11, 1997.

United Nations. "Comprehensive Assessment of the Freshwater Resources of the World", June 1997.

United Nations. International Rivers and Lakes, Newsletter No. 26, December 1996.

Verghese B.G. "Winning the Future: From Bhakra to Narmada, Tehri, Rajasthan Canal". Konark Publishers, Delhi, 1994.

Index

D

E

H

I

J

K

Y

Z